Latinas
in the
United States

A Historical Encyclopedia

VOLUME 3

Quesada through Zúñiga
Index

Edited by
Vicki L. Ruiz
and Virginia Sánchez Korrol

INDIANA UNIVERSITY PRESS
Bloomington and Indianapolis

Publication of this book is made possible in part with the assistance of a Challenge Grant from the National Endowment for the Humanities, a federal agency that supports research, education, and public programming in the humanities. Any views, findings, conclusions, or recommendations expressed in this publication do not necessarily reflect those of the National Endowment for the Humanities.

This book is a publication of

Indiana University Press
601 North Morton Street
Bloomington, IN 47404-3797 USA

http://iupress.indiana.edu

Telephone orders   800-842-6796
Fax orders   812-855-7931
Orders by e-mail   iuporder@indiana.edu

The paper used in this publication meets the minimum requirements of American National Standard for Information Sciences—Permanence of Paper for Printed Library Materials, ANSI Z39.48–1984.

Manufactured in the United States of America

Library of Congress Cataloging-in-Publication Data

Latinas in the United States : a historical encyclopedia / edited by Vicki L. Ruíz and Virginia Sánchez Korrol.
    p. cm.
    Includes bibliographical references and index.
    ISBN 0-253-34680-0 (set : alk. paper)—ISBN 0-253-34681-9 (vol. 1 : alk. paper)—
ISBN 0-253-34683-5 (vol. 2 : alk. paper)—ISBN 0-253-34684-3 (vol. 3 : alk. paper) 1.
Hispanic American women—Biography—Encyclopedias. I. Ruíz, Vicki. II. Sánchez
Korrol, Virginia.
    E184.S75L35 2006
    920.72089'68073—dc22   2005034986

1 2 3 4 5 11 10 09 08 07 06

Contents

Volume 1

Preface	xv
Acknowledgments	xix
Introduction: A Historical and Regional Overview of Latinas in the United States	1
Latinas in the Southwest	1
Latinas in the Northeast	7
Latinas in the Midwest	14
Latinas in the Southeast	18
Latinas in the Pacific Northwest	24

Abarca, Apolonia "Polly" Muñoz	29
Acosta, Lucy	30
Acosta Vice, Celia M.	31
Aging	33
Agostini del Río, Amelia	35
Alatorre, Soledad "Chole"	35
Albelo, Carmen	36
Alfau Galván de Solalinde, Jesusa	37
Allende, Isabel	38
Alonzo, Ventura	38
Altars	40
Alvarez, Aida	41
Alvarez, Cecilia Concepción	42
Alvarez, Delia	43
Alvarez, Julia	44
Alvarez, Linda	44
Alvarez v. Lemon Grove School District	45
Americanization Programs	46
Antonetty, Evelina López	48
Antonio Maceo Brigade	49
Anzaldúa, Gloria	51
Apodaca, Felicitas	52
Aprenda y Superese	54
Aragón, Jesusita	54
Arballo, María Feliciana	55

Arguello, María de la Concepción (Sister María Dominica)	56
Arías, Anna María	57
Arizona Orphan Abduction	58
Armiño, Franca de	59
Arocho, Juanita	60
Arroyo, Carmen E.	61
Arroyo, Martina	62
Artists	63
Asociación Nacional México-Americana (ANMA)	67
ASPIRA	68
ASPIRA v. New York City Board of Education	69
Avila, María Elena	69
Avila, Modesta	70
Aztlán	71
Babín, María Teresa	74
Baca, Judith Francesca	74
Baca Barragán, Polly	75
Baez, Joan Chandos	76
Barceló, María Gertrudis ("La Tules")	78
Barnard, Juana Josefina Cavasos	79
Barraza, Santa Contreras	80
Barrera, Plácida Peña	81
Belpré, Pura	83
Bencomo, Julieta Saucedo	84
Bernal, Martha	85
Bernasconi, Socorro Hernández	86
Betances Jaeger, Clotilde	87
Betanzos, Amalia V.	88
Bilingual Education	88
Black Legend	90
Blake, María DeCastro	91
Borrero Pierra, Juana	93
Boyar, Monica	94
Bozak, Carmen Contreras	95

Contents

Bracero Program	96
Braga, Sonia	99
Briones, María Juana	99
Burciaga, Mirna Ramos	100
Caballero, Diana	103
Cabeza de Baca, Fabiola	104
Cabrera, Angelina "Angie"	105
Cabrera, Lydia	106
Calderón, Rose Marie	107
California Missions	108
California Sanitary Canning Company Strike	110
Callejo, Adelfa Botello	111
Callis de Fages, Eulalia Francesca y Josepha	112
Calvillo, Ana María del Carmen	113
Canales, Laura	114
Canales, Nohelia de los Angeles	115
Canino, María Josefa	116
Cannery and Agricultural Workers Industrial Union (CAWIU)	117
Cántico de la Mujer Latina	118
Capetillo, Luisa	119
Carbonell, Anna	119
Cardona, Alice	120
Carr, Vikki	121
Carrillo de Fitch, Josefa	122
Casal, Lourdes	123
Casals, Rosemary	124
Casanova de Villaverde, Emilia	125
Casita Maria, New York	126
Castillo, Ana	128
Castillo, Guadalupe	129
Castro, Rosie	130
Castro, Victoria M. "Vickie"	131
Ceja, Amelia Moran	132
Central American Immigrant Women	134
Centro de Acción Social Autónomo (CASA)	137
Centro Hispano Católico	139
Centro Mater	139
Cepeda-Leonardo, Margarita	140
Cervantes, Lorna Dee	140
Chabram, Angie González	142
Chacón, Soledad Chávez	143
"Charo" (María Rosario Pilar Martínez Molina Baeza)	144
Chávez, Denise	144
Chávez, Helen	146
Chávez, Linda	147
Chávez Ravine, Los Angeles	148
Chávez-Thompson, Linda	149
Chicana Caucus/National Women's Political Caucus	150
Chicana Rights Project	151
Chicano Movement	151
Chicanos Por La Causa (CPLC)	155
Cigar Workers	156
Cinema Images, Contemporary	159
Círculo Cultural Isabel la Católica	161
Cisneros, Sandra	161
Clínica de la Beneficencia Mexicana	162
Collazo, Rosa Cortéz	163
Colón, Miriam	164
Colón, Rufa Concepción Fernández ("Concha")	166
Comisión Femenil Mexicana Nacional (CFMN)	167
Communist Party	168
Communities Organized for Public Service (COPS)	169
Community Service Organization (CSO)	170
Congreso del Pueblo	172
Córdova, Lina	173
Corridos	175
Cossio y Cisneros, Evangelina	176
Cotera, Martha	177
Crawford, Mercedes Margarita Martínez	178
Cruz, Celia	179
Cuban and Puerto Rican Revolutionary Party	181
Cuban Independence Women's Clubs	182
Cuban Women's Club	183
Cuban-Spanish-American War	184
Cuero, Delfina	185
Davis, Grace Montañez	187
De Acosta, Aida	188
De Acosta, Mercedes	189
De Aragón, Uva	190
De Arteaga, Genoveva	191
De Avila, Dolores C.	192
De Burgos, Julia	193
De la Cruz, Jessie López	194
De la Cruz, Sor Juana Inés	196
De la Garza, Beatríz	197
De León, Patricia de la Garza	198
Del Castillo, Adelaida Rebecca	199
Del Prado, Pura	200
Del Río, Dolores	201

Del Valle, Carmen 202

Delgado, Jane L. 203

Demography 204

Deportations during the Great Depression 209

DiMartino, Rita 211

Dimas, Beatrice Escadero 212

Domestic Violence 214

Domestic Workers 216

Dominican American National
Roundtable (DANR) 217

Dueto Carmen y Laura 218

Durazo, María Elena 219

Echaveste, María 221

Education 222

El Congreso de Pueblos de Hablan Española 226

El Monte Berry Strike 226

El Movimiento Estudiantil Chicano de Aztlán
(MEChA) 227

El Paso Laundry Strike 228

El Rescate 229

Entrepreneurs 229

Environment and the Border 232

Escajeda, Josefina 236

Escalona, Beatríz ("La Chata Noloesca") 236

Escobar, Carmen Bernal 237

Espaillat, Rhina P. 238

Espinosa-Mora, Deborah 239

Esquivel, Gregoria 240

Esquivel, Yolanda Almaraz 241

Estefan, Gloria 242

Esteves, Sandra María 243

Family 245

Farah Strike 249

Farmworkers 250

Feminism 253

Fernández, Beatrice "Gigi" 255

Fernández, Mary Joe 255

Fernández, Rosita 256

Ferré Aguayo, Sor Isolina 257

Fierro, Josefina 259

Figueroa, Belén 260

Figueroa Mercado, Loida 261

Flores, Diana 263

Flores, Francisca 264

Florez, Encarnación Villarreal Escobedo 265

Folk Healing Traditions 266

Fontañez, Jovita 270

Fornés, María Irene 270

Friendly House, Phoenix 271

Fuerza Unida 272

Gallegos, Carmen Cornejo 274

Ganados del Valle 274

Gangs 276

García, Cristina 278

García, Eva Carrillo de 280

García, Providencia "Provi" 280

García Cortese, Aimee 282

García-Aguilera, Carolina 283

Garcíaz, María 284

Garment Industry 285

Giant 286

Gómez Carbonell, María 288

Gómez-Potter, Socorro 289

Gonzáles, Elvira Rodríguez de 290

González, Laura 290

González, Matiana 292

González Mireles, Jovita 292

Govea, Jessica 294

Grau, María Leopoldina "Pola" 295

Great Depression and Mexican
American Women 297

Guerra, Fermina 300

Guerrero, Rosa 300

Guerrero, Victoria Partida 302

Guillen Herrera, Rosalinda 303

Gutiérrez, Luz Bazán 305

Guzmán, Madre María Dominga 306

Volume 2

Hamlin, Rosalie Méndez 308

Hayworth, Rita 309

Head Start 310

Health: Current Issues and Trends 311

Henríquez Ureña, Camila 315

Hernández, Antonia 317

Hernández, Ester 318

Hernández, María Latigo 319

Hernández, Olivia 320

Hernández, Victoria 322

Herrada, Elena 323

Herrera, Carolina 324

Herrera, María Cristina 325

Hijas de Cuauhtémoc 326

Hinojosa, Tish 327

Contents

Hispanic Mother-Daughter Program (HMDP)	328
Houchen Settlement, El Paso	329
Huerta, Cecilia Olivarez	331
Huerta, Dolores	332
Hull-House, Chicago	333
Idar Juárez, Jovita	336
Immigration of Latinas to the United States	337
Immigration Reform and Control Act (IRCA)	341
Intermarriage, Contemporary	342
Intermarriage, Historical	344
International Ladies Garment Workers' Union (ILGWU)	348
Jaramillo, Cleofas Martínez	351
Jiménez, María de los Angeles	352
Journalism and Print Media	353
Jurado, Katy	358
Kimbell, Sylvia Rodríguez	359
Kissinger, Beatrice Amado	360
La Llorona	362
"La Lupe" (Guadalupe Victoria Yoli Raymond)	363
La Malinche (Malinalli Tenepal)	364
La Mujer Obrera	366
La Raza Unida Party	367
Labor Unions	368
Lares, Michelle Yvette "Shelly"	372
Las Hermanas	373
Latina U.S. Treasurers	374
Latinas in the U.S. Congress	375
League of United Latin American Citizens (LULAC)	378
Lebrón, Dolores "Lolita"	380
Ledesma, Josephine	381
Lee Tapia, Consuelo	382
Legal Issues	383
León, Ruth Esther Soto ("La Hermana León")	384
León, Tania	385
Lesbians	386
"Letter from Chapultepec"	388
Liberation Theology	389
Líderes Campesinas	390
Literature	392
Lobo, Rebecca Rose	396
Lomas Garza, Carmen	397
Lone Star	397
López, Lillian	401
López, María I.	402
López, Nancy Marie	403
López, Rosie	403
López, Yolanda	404
López Córdova, Gloria	406
Lorenzana, Apolinaria	407
Los Angeles Garment Workers' Strike	408
Lozano, Alicia Guadalupe Elizondo	410
Lozano, Emma	411
Lozano, Mónica Cecilia	412
Lucas, María Elena	413
Machuca, Ester	415
Madrid, Patricia A.	415
Madrigal v. Quilligan	416
Maldonado, Amelia Margarita	419
Maquiladoras	420
Mariachi	421
Mariachi Estrella de Topeka	422
Marianismo and Machismo	423
Marshall, Guadalupe	424
Martí de Cid, Dolores	425
Martínez, Agueda Salazar	426
Martínez, Anita N.	426
Martínez, Demetria	428
Martínez, Elizabeth Sutherland "Betita"	429
Martínez, Frances Aldama	430
Martínez, Vilma S.	431
Martínez Santaella, Inocencia	433
McBride, Teresa N.	433
Mederos y Cabañas de González, Elena Inés	434
Media Stereotypes	436
Medicine	438
Medina, Esther	440
Meléndez, Concha	441
Meléndez, Sara	442
Méndez, Consuelo Herrera	443
Méndez, Olga A.	444
Méndez v. Westminster	445
Mendieta, Ana	447
Mendoza, Lydia	448
Mendoza, María Estella Altamirano	448
Mendoza v. Tucson School District No. 1	450
Mercado, Victoria "Vicky"	451
Mesa-Bains, Amalia	452
Mestizaje	453
Mexican American Legal Defense and Educational Fund (MALDEF)	457

Mexican American Women's National Association (MANA) 458

Mexican Mothers' Club, University of Chicago Settlement House 459

Mexican Revolution 460

Mexican Revolution, Border Women in 464

Mexican Schools 466

Migration and Labor 468

Military Service 473

Miller, Esther 475

Mining Communities 476

Miranda, Carmen 478

Mistral, Gabriela (Lucila Godoy Alcayaga) 479

Mohr, Nicholasa 480

Mojica-Hammer, Ruth 481

Molina, Gloria 482

Montemayor, Alice Dickerson 483

Montes-Donnelly, Elba Iris 484

Montez, María (María Africa Gracia Vidal) 485

Mora, Magdalena 487

Mora, Patricia "Pat" 488

Moraga, Cherríe 488

Moraga, Gloria Flores 489

Morales, Iris 491

Morales-Horowitz, Nilda M. 492

Moreno, Luisa 492

Moreno, Rita (Rosa Dolores Alverio) 494

Morillo, Irma 496

Mothers of East Los Angeles (MELA) 497

Movie Stars 497

Mugarrieta, Elvira Virginia (Babe Bean; Jack Bee Garland) 502

Mujeres in Action, Sunset Park, Brooklyn 503

Mujeres Latinas en Acción (MLEA) 505

Mujeres por la Raza 506

Mujerista Theology 507

Munguía, Carolina Malpica de 508

Muñoz, María del Carmen 509

National Association for Chicana and Chicano Studies (NACCS) 510

National Association of Puerto Rican/Hispanic Social Workers (NAPRHSW) 511

National Chicana Conference 512

National Conference of Puerto Rican Women (NACOPRW) 513

National Council of La Raza (NCLR) 514

National Hispanic Feminist Conference 515

National Puerto Rican Forum 516

Naturalization 517

Navarro, M. Susana 519

Nerio, Trinidad 520

New Economics for Women (NEW) 521

New York City Mission Society (NYCMS) 522

Nieto, Sonia 523

Nieto Gómez, Anna 524

Norte, Marisela 525

Novello, Antonia Coello 526

Nuestra Señora de la Divina Providencia 528

Núñez, Ana Rosa 529

Nuns, Colonial 530

Nuns, Contemporary 531

Obejas, Achy 533

Ochoa, Ellen 534

O'Donnell, Sylvia Colorado 535

Olivares, Olga Ballesteros 535

Olivarez, Graciela 537

Olivera, Mercedes 538

Ontiveros, Manuela 540

Operation Pedro Pan 541

Orozco, Aurora Estrada 543

Ortega, Carlota Ayala 544

Ortiz Cofer, Judith 545

Ortiz y Pino de Kleven, María Concepción "Concha" 546

O'Shea, María Elena 547

Otero-Smart, Ingrid 548

Otero-Warren, Adelina 549

Pachucas 552

Palacio-Grottola, Sonia 555

Pantoja, Antonia 557

Parsons, Lucia González 558

Patiño Río, Dolores 559

Pauwels Pfeiffer, Linda Lorena 561

Payán, Ilka Tanya 562

Pedroso, Paulina 563

Peña de Bordas, (Ana) Virginia de 563

Peñaranda, Ana Marcial 564

Pentecostal Church 565

Perales, Nina 569

Pérez, Eulalia 570

Pérez, Graciela 571

Pérez v. Sharp 573

Phelps Dodge Strike 573

Phillips, Carmen Romero 574

Pilsen Neighbors Community Council 575

Contents

Pinedo, Encarnación 576

Politics, Electoral 577

Politics, Party 579

Popular Religiosity 581

Prida, Dolores 582

Propositions 187 and 209 583

Puerto Rican Association for Community Affairs (PRACA) 584

Puerto Rican Radical Politics in New York 585

Puerto Rican Women Political Prisoners 587

Puerto Ricans in Hawaii 591

Volume 3

Quesada, Alicia Otilia 596

Quesada, Dora Ocampo 597

Quinceañera 598

Quintanilla Pérez, Selena 600

Quintero, Luisa 601

Race and Color Consciousness 603

Ramírez, Emilia Schunior 607

Ramírez, Sara Estela 608

Ramírez, Tina 609

Ramírez de Arellano, Diana 609

Rangel, Irma 611

Rape 611

Reid, Marita 613

Reid, Victoria Comicrabit 614

Religion 615

Reyes, Guadalupe 622

Rico, Angelina Moreno 623

Rincón de Gautier, Felisa 624

Rivera, Aurelia "Yeya" 625

Rivera, Chita 626

Rivera, Graciela 627

Rivera, Roxana 629

Rivera Martínez, Domitila 630

Robles Díaz, Inés 631

Rodríguez, Hermelinda Morales 632

Rodríguez, "Isabel" Hernández 633

Rodríguez, Josefa "Chepita" 634

Rodríguez, Patricia 634

Rodríguez, Sofía 636

Rodríguez Cabral, María Cristina 637

Rodríguez de Tió, Lola 637

Rodríguez McLean, Verneda 639

Rodríguez Remeneski, Shirley 640

Rodríguez-Trias, Helen 641

Romero Cash, Marie 643

Rosado Rousseau, Leoncia ("Mamá Léo") 644

Ros-Lehtinen, Ileana 645

Roybal-Allard, Lucille 646

Ruiz, Bernarda 647

Ruiz, Irene Hernández 649

Ruiz de Burton, María Amparo 650

Sada, María G. "Chata" 652

Salsa 652

Salt of the Earth 656

San Antonio, Ana Gloria 657

San Antonio Pecan Shellers' Strike 658

San Joaquin Valley Cotton Strike 659

San Juan, Olga 662

Sánchez, Loretta 662

Sánchez, María Clemencia 663

Sánchez, María E. 664

Sánchez Cruz, Rebecca 666

Sánchez Garfunkel, Aura Luz 667

Santería 669

Santiago, Petra 670

Saralegui, Cristina 672

Saucedo, María del Jesús 673

Schechter, Esperanza Acosta Mendoza "Hope" 674

Scientists 675

Sena, Elvira 679

Sepúlveda, Emma 680

Sexuality 681

Silva, Chelo 682

Silva de Cintrón, Josefina "Pepiña" 682

"Sister Carmelita" (Carmela Zapata Bonilla Marrero) 683

Slavery 684

Sloss-Vento, Adela 686

Smeltertown, El Paso 687

Smith, Plácida Elvira García 689

Soldaderas 690

Solis, Hilda L. 691

Sosa-Riddell, Adaljiza 692

Soto Feliciano, Carmen Lillian "Lily" 694

Souchet, Clementina 695

Southwest Voter Registration Education Project (SVREP) 696

Spanish Borderlands 697

Colonial Law 700

Comadrazgo 703

Early Settlement Life in the Borderlands 704
Encomienda 708
Women in California 709
Women in New Mexico 710
Women in St. Augustine 714
Women in Texas 716
Women's Wills 719
Spiritism 720
Spiritism in New York City 721
Sterilization 723
Street Vending 725
Student Movements 727
Substitute Auxiliary Teachers (SATs) 728
Swilling, Trinidad Escalante 730
Tabaqueros' Unions 732
Talamante, Olga 733
Tarango, Yolanda 734
Telenovelas 735
Television 736
Tempe Normal School 740
Ten Years' War 742
Tenayuca, Emma 743
Tex-Son Strike 745
Theater 746
Padua Hills Theater 748
Playwrights 748
Puerto Rican Traveling Theater (PRTT) 751
Teatro Campesino 752
Villalongín Dramatic Company 753
Toraño-Pantín, María Elena 754
Torres, Alva 756
Torres, Ida Inés 757
Torres, Lourdes 758
Torres, Patsy (Patricia Donita) 759
Tovar, Lupita 760
Toypurina 761
Trambley, Estela Portillo 762
Treaty of Guadalupe Hidalgo 762
Treaty of Paris 766
Treviño-Sauceda, Mily 766
Tufiño, Nitza 767
Ulibarrí Sánchez, Louise 769
United Cannery, Agricultural, Packing, and Allied Workers of America (UCAPAWA/FTA) 770

United Farm Workers of America (UFW) 772
Women in the United Farm Workers (UFW) 773
U.S.-Mexican War 776
Urquides, María Luisa Legarra 779
Urrea, Teresa 780
Valdez, Patssi 782
Vallejo, Epifania de Guadalupe 783
Vallejo de Leese, María Paula Rosalía 784
Vanguardia Puertorriqueña 785
Varela, Beatriz 786
Varela, María 787
Vásquez, Anna 788
Vásquez, Enriqueta Longeaux y 789
Velázquez, Loreta Janeta 790
Velázquez, Nydia M. 791
Vélez, Lupe 793
Vélez de Vando, Emelí 793
Vélez-Mitchell, Anita 795
Vicioso Sánchez, Sherezada "Chiqui" 797
Vidal, Irma 798
Vidaurri, Rita 799
Villarreal, Andrea and Teresa 800
Viramontes, Helena María 800
Virgen de Guadalupe 801
Virgen de la Caridad del Cobre 803
Voting Rights Act 804
Watsonville Strike 805
Welch, Raquel 806
West Side Story 807
Wilcox, Mary Rose Garrido 808
Wolf, Esther Valladolid 809
World War II 810
Ybarra, Eva 815
Young Lords 815
Zamora, Bernice B. Ortiz 818
Zárate, Rosa Marta 819
Zúñiga, Alejandra Rojas 820

List of Biographical Entries 823
List of Organizations 829
Selected Readings in Latina History 831
Notes on Contributors 835
Index 851

Latinas
in the
United States

QUESADA, ALICIA OTILIA (1923–   )

Born in 1923, Alicia Otilia Quesada descends from a pioneer Mexican Arizona family that founded the town of Wickenburg in 1863. Her maternal grandfather, Teodoro Ocampo, and maternal great-grandfather, Ramón Valencia, voted in 1894 to create the Wickenburg School District No. 9. The youngest daughter of Francisca Ocampo and José F. Quesada, a professional vaquero from La Paz, Baja California Sur, who worked at the Ocampo-Valencia ranch, Alicia grew up with one central task—to attend school. Her literate, bilingual parents espoused education and secured transportation—horses and cars—from the ranch to the town to ensure that their children maintained near-perfect attendance.

Quesada was the 1941 high-school salutatorian and enrolled in Lamson Business College in Phoenix, fifty-eight miles southeast, where her sister Josephine already worked and lived with family friends. With shorthand, stenography, and bookkeeping skills, Alicia Quesada advanced immediately to a work-study job as an insurance company stenographer. In the spring of 1943 she temporarily withdrew from college to accept a full-time position for $5 a day as a stenographer for the Arizona House of Representatives, Sixteenth Legislature. She was assigned to Representatives Talmadge McGowan and Frank Robles, and her shorthand and typing speeds often landed her on the house floor to transcribe the public debates. When the session ended, she returned to college, but soon attorney Z. Simpson Cox recruited her as a legal secretary. In 1945 Cox opened a new firm with his father-in-law, retired Arizona Supreme Court justice Alfred Lockwood, and his daughter, Lorna E. Lockwood, who became the first woman appointed to the Arizona Supreme Court in 1961. Quesada joined the new firm and stayed until 1946, when she returned to Wickenburg to care for her ailing mother.

During World War II Quesada participated in social organizations, most notably the Flamingo Club, a social circle of young, single, and employed Mexican American women. A founding member, Quesada helped form the club after the Phoenix chapter of the United Service Organization (USO) denied her participation because its "quota was filled for persons of Spanish origin." With twenty-six members, the Flamingo Club hosted regular activities, including "church functions," picnics, parties for returning GIs, and even a formal ball at the Westward Ho Hotel.

After her mother's recovery Quesada returned to Phoenix in 1947, only to encounter similar discriminatory attitudes in employment. Private secretarial agencies declined "hiring Mexicans and Indians." Instead, she returned to public service, garnering another stenography post at the Arizona legislature. She continued in state employment, working for the Arizona Industrial Commission and Arizona State University (ASU). From 1952 to 1954 she worked with Nicholas "Nick" Dragon, the regional director of the Congress of Industrial Organizations. She often translated for Dragon, who did not know Spanish, when he met with Mexican and Latin American labor leaders.

A modern "working woman," Quesada sat for a civil service examination and secured an appointment at the Social Security Administration (SSA), where she worked for thirty years, from 1954 to her retirement in 1984. Hired as a clerk typist, she advanced through the administrative ranks to lead secretary. In 1967 Quesada earned national recognition when she won the SSA's Commissioner's Citation for "consistently being a superior and a dedicated public servant." From 1952 to 1974 she traveled annually throughout Mexico with her friend Mavis Green. She credits those adventures with fortifying her cultural identity.

Prevented from political participation during her civil service career, Quesada has dedicated her retirement to public advocacy. In 1987 she joined her sister Dora in a preservationist campaign and lawsuit to save Phoenix's South Mountain Park and South Phoenix's Chicano and Native American communities from gentrification and commercialization. When the lawsuit generated referenda, Quesada became a "precinct challenger" for the Democratic Party. She provided financial support to political campaigns and to the Guadalupe Organization, which resulted in the incorporation of the Yaqui Indian and Mexican immigrant community of Guadalupe, Arizona.

Quesada passionately promotes the historical preservation and recuperation of Arizona's Mexican American heritage. A former board member of Wickenburg's Desert Caballeros Western Museum, she helped integrate Mexican Americans, their contributions, and their life experiences into permanent exhibits. Quesada family photos, anecdotes, and artifacts, including her mother's *limpiaplatos*, tea towels made from flour sacks and fabric remnants, as well as her father's self-styled horsehair lariats, comprise the ranching exhibits. In 2003 she joined the committee to save Wickenburg's original Little Red School House, which opened in 1905 on land donated by Mexican American citizens, and where her mother and, later, she and her siblings attended school. Quesada oversees the Ocampo Family Papers, the largest collection of Mexican and Mexican American documents in Arizona, which is housed at ASU's Chicano Research Collection. With her brother Eugene she also manages the endowed José F. Quesada and Francisca Ocampo Research Scholarship, an annual competition that underwrites Chicana/o studies at ASU.

See also Education

SOURCES: Ocampo Family Papers. Chicano Research Collection, Department of Archives and Manuscripts, Arizona State University, Tempe; Quesada, Alicia Otilia. 2004. Interview by Laura K. Muñoz, February 16; ———. "Incidents in the Life of Alicia Otilia Quesada." Ocampo Family Papers. Chicano Research Collection, Department of Archives and Manuscripts, Arizona State University Libraries, Tempe.

Laura K. Muñoz

Dora Quesada in San Antonio, 1945. Courtesy of the Ocampo Family Collection, Chicano Research Collection, Department of Archives and Manuscripts, Arizona State University, Tempe.

QUESADA, DORA OCAMPO (1921–1998)

A quintessential politician, Dora Ocampo Quesada embraced many roles in her lifetime—nurse, teacher, political activist, and philanthropist. A native of Wickenburg, Arizona, and descendant of the Ocampos, a pioneer family that helped establish the town in 1863, Quesada devoted her life to preserving Arizona's Hispanic heritage and to organizing for social justice issues affecting the state's Mexican American communities. In 1989 she and her siblings endowed a research scholarship for the Department of Chicana and Chicano Studies at Arizona State University (ASU) in honor of her parents, José Franco and Francisca Ocampo Quesada. The family visionary, she was instrumental in donating her family manuscripts and photographs to ASU's Chicano Research Collection. The Ocampo Family Papers are the largest collection of Mexican and Mexican American historical documents in the state.

In her early adult life Quesada trained as a nurse at St. Joseph's Hospital School of Nursing in Phoenix and later graduated with the first bachelor of science degree in nursing issued by Arizona State University in 1951. Stationed at the White Sands Proving Ground nuclear first aid station in Alamogordo, New Mexico, and at the San Antonio Air Command Hospital, Kelly Air Force Base, she served as a second lieutenant in the U.S. Army Air Corps Nurses Squad during World War II. Honorably discharged in 1946, she returned to Phoenix and continued her civilian career at several metropolitan hospitals, where she worked in tubercular, surgical, and obstetrics wards. In 1953 local newspapers featured a photo of Quesada, then the nurse in charge of the newborn nursery at Mesa's Southside District Hospital, holding in her palms a baby girl born two months premature.

From 1958 to 1980 Quesada changed careers and

taught in the Phoenix and Tempe schools, most notably at the Veda B. Frank Elementary School in Guadalupe, a Pasqua Yaqui Indian and Mexican American community on the eastern edge of Phoenix's South Mountain Park. Students recall her passion for promoting cultural awareness and pride in achievement despite large enrollments, up to forty-five children per class, and the legacy of racial inequity she encountered in those schools. She garnered funding for extracurricular music and literary programs, sponsoring el Folklórico Estudiantil de Guadalupe and producing *Poems and Stories to Suit Each Kid's Mood* (1968), a collection written by her sixth-grade class.

Teaching spurred Quesada's political activism. Along with her sister Alicia and brother Eugene, she joined the Guadalupe Organization, a community group that incorporated the square-mile town and sued the Tempe Elementary School District No. 3 (TESD) for its failure to provide bilingual, bicultural education for their children. A union representative of the American Federation of Teachers, AFL-CIO, Local 3312, Quesada often accompanied teachers in school-district grievances involving racial discrimination, wage disputes, and free-speech issues. In the 1970s she contributed to a U.S. Commission on Civil Rights report on desegregation in Tempe, served on the Mexican-American Educational Advisory Committee to the TESD, and chaired the Minority Elementary School Teachers Association, which promoted educational equality for minority and non-English-speaking youth. She also was a delegate candidate to the Arizona state Democratic Party convention in 1972.

In retirement Quesada's activism increased. As a citizen plaintiff in the Arizona Supreme Court case *Hamilton v. Superior Court* (1987), she lobbied against the commercial development of Phoenix's South Mountain Park, the largest city park in the United States and sacred land of the Pasqua Yaqui. A longtime resident of South Phoenix, she and her siblings owned a home near the mountain's eastern base and challenged the city's right to develop the preserve without voter approval. The case resulted in a city charter amendment halting land trades after 1989. Despite the political heat, including threats to her home, Quesada continued as a preservationist, representing South Phoenix as a mayoral appointee to the City of Phoenix Parks and Recreation Citizens' Advisory Committee.

Days before her death the Arizona Women's Hall of Fame honored Quesada in a special exhibit on notable Arizona women. She served on the board of trustees for the Phoenix Museum of History and the Desert Caballeros Western Museum in Wickenburg. She maintained memberships in the Society of Hispanic Historical Ancestral Research, the Arizona Historical Society, the First Families of Arizona, American Legion Post 41

in Phoenix, and St. Anthony's Catholic Church in Wickenburg.

See also Education; Military Service

SOURCES: Leach, Anita Mabante. 1999. "Portal to the Past Website: A Link to Latino Heritage in Arizona." *The Arizona Republic*, November 21, EV8; "Obituaries." 1998. *The Arizona Republic*, September 24, D8; Ocampo Family Papers. Chicano Research Collection, Department of Archives and Manuscripts, Arizona State University, Tempe; "Park Preservationists Won't Quit Golf Course Taking Shape." 1987. *The Phoenix Gazette*, November 13, B1.

Laura K. Muñoz

QUINCEAÑERA

The quinceañera is a traditional Latin American coming-of-age ritual celebrated upon the fifteenth birthday (*quince años*) of Latina girls. The term can be used to indicate the celebration or to refer to the young woman herself. It is a rite of passage symbolizing the life cycle from childhood to adulthood. Traditionally in Latin American cultures it has served as a public announcement of the girl's journey into womanhood, indicating that she is prepared to handle adult responsibilities such as public service to the poor, marriage, and motherhood. Girls were not allowed to wear makeup, go out alone, or date before their fifteenth birthday. Only after this particular birthday could men ask her father (or guardian) for permission to escort her to public outings and ask for her hand in marriage.

Some anthropologists have stated that there is no conclusive evidence that the quinceañera is linked to an ancient indigenous tradition from Central America, but rather argue that it is an adaptation from the European coming-of-age ritual that was celebrated upon the girl's eighteenth birthday. Others claim that its foundation is rooted in the Aztec custom of sending daughters from a noble family to schools called *calmecac* that prepared them for a life of religious service as a priestess or for marriage, while daughters from a working-class family went to a school called *telpochalli*, which prepared them for marriage. The particular life decision was to be made at the age of fifteen since the population had a life expectancy of thirty years. When the Spaniards conquered the Americas, all religions except Roman Catholicism were forbidden. It is believed that the Aztec and Roman Catholic traditions merged over time and evolved into the celebration of the quinceañera.

The quinceañera can be as expensive, time-consuming, and extravagant as a wedding; there are families that begin saving and planning for the quinceañera upon the birth of the baby girl, as can be found among Mexican Americans in the Southwest.

The quinceañera is celebrated with a special Catholic mass (or a Protestant church ceremony), although it is not rooted in church traditions.

At the church the parents walk the honoree down the aisle. Her *corte de honor* (court of honor) goes before her and consists of fourteen couples, aside from the birthday girl and her *chambelán de honor* (escort of honor); each couple represents one year of her life. The young men are known as *chambelanes* or *caballeros* (lords or gentlemen), and the young women are called *damas* (ladies). All present are dressed in formal attire. Although the color of the dress has traditionally been a pastel shade for honorees in Mexico, Central America, Cuba, and Puerto Rico, because white is reserved for the wedding day, the color of the dress varies. Nowadays many quinceañeras do wear white, particularly in the United States, Puerto Rico, and some areas in Mexico. The damas traditionally wear pastel-colored dresses, but this has also changed over time, with the exception that white is not worn by the damas.

In a tradition that stems from the biblical and pre-Second Vatican Council requirement of women wearing a covering over their heads, the quinceañera bears a crown of flowers on her head (either natural or dipped in wax) or a tiara/diadem made of glass or embedded with rhinestones. She carries a prayer book and rosary beads, as well as a bouquet of flowers in her hands. In the Mexican community the flowers are given to honor the Virgen de Guadalupe (the Virgin of Guadalupe), and the entire ceremony is performed in devotion to her. The honoree is also given jewelry and a gold medal that is religious in nature, usually bearing the image of the Virgen de Guadalupe. In some ceremonies the celebrant is given a doll, which she either

hands down to her younger sister as a symbolic gesture of leaving childhood things behind or receives as the last doll she will ever receive. Another interpretation for this is that it is symbolic of the new role of motherhood that she will be facing as a woman.

In most celebrations the quinceañera also wears flat shoes that are exchanged for shoes with heels to symbolize that she has entered womanhood. This usually occurs during the fiesta that follows the religious ceremony, which is celebrated with foods favored in that culture, live music, and dancing. The quinceañera's first dance partner of the evening is her father, and they dance to a song titled "Linda Quinceañera" or a song with a slow tempo that has sentimental value and is appropriate for the occasion.

The quinceañera celebration differs from one Latin American culture to the next; the U.S. Latina celebrations are distinct from those in Latin America as well, and some Latino/a cultures do not celebrate it at all. Much is known about the Mexican quinceañera because it is a very strong tradition there, perhaps because of its roots in the Aztec religion. In Cuba the quinceañera is celebrated with a fiesta, but not with a mass, because of the political fallout of the Cuban Revolution of 1959. The fiesta's centerpiece is the elaborately choreographed dances accompanied by the honoree stepping out of a huge clamshell. In El Salvador the celebration is known as *mi fiesta rosa* (my pink party). Some U.S. Latinas have opted to celebrate their quinceañera upon their sixteenth birthday, as is traditional among non-Latina U.S. American girls who celebrate their sweet sixteen, but in the traditional spirit and style of a quinceañera.

Latino/a families celebrate the quinceañera as a

The sweet sixteen party is an American adaptation of the Latin American celebration of a young woman's fifteenth birthday. Courtesy of the Justo A. Martí Photograph Collection. Centro Archives, Centro de Estudios Puertorriqueños, Hunter College, CUNY.

means of showering the birthday girl with attention and affection and to express pride in who she is and the promise of who she is to become. It also serves to reinforce cultural traditions in a new homeland so that she is firmly rooted in her identity, which will in turn enable her to bloom in her new roles and responsibilities as a woman.

SOURCES: Cantú, Norma E. 2002. "Chicana Life-Cycle Rituals." In *Chicana Traditions: Continuity and Change*, ed. Norma E. Cantú and Olga Nájera-Ramírez. Urbana: University of Illinois Press; Castro, Rafaela G. 2001. *Chicano Folklore: A Guide to the Folktales, Traditions, Rituals, and Religious Practices of Mexican-Americans.* Oxford: Oxford University Press; Davalos, Karen Mary. 1996. "La Quinceañera: Making Gender and Ethnic Identities." *Frontiers* 16, nos. 2/3:101–127; King, Elizabeth. 1998. *Quinceañera: Celebrating Fifteen.* New York: Dutton Children's Books.

María Pérez y González

QUINTANILLA PÉREZ, SELENA (1971–1995)

Selena Quintanilla Pérez (stage name "Selena") was born in Lake Jackson, Texas, on April 16, 1971, to Abraham Quintanilla and Marcella Pérez. Although Selena followed in the footsteps of a generation of Tejana (Texas Mexican) women solo singers such as Lydia Mendoza, Chelo Silva, Laura Canales, and Patsy Torres and Tejana duets such as Carmen y Laura, las Hermanas Cantú, las Hermanas Gongora, and numerous others, she made significant strides in transforming the sound of Tejano music and Tejano popular culture in general.

Selena began singing at the age of eight when her father Abraham discovered her strong vocal capabilities. Abraham was the major musical influence in the family, having been a member of the doo-wop band los Dinos as a young man. Selena's father quickly engaged the rest of Selena's older siblings: her brother A. B. became lead guitarist and producer of most of her music, and her sister Suzette became the only Tejana drummer within the contemporary surge in Tejano music. Originally the group was country-and-western influenced and went by the name of Southern Pearl.

Selena gained her earliest musical experience by singing in the family Tex-Mex restaurant business, Papagallo's. She made one of her first live television appearances on *The Johnny Canales Show* in Corpus Christi, Texas. In 1994 *Hispanic* Magazine estimated her worth at $5 million. Nonetheless, Selena continued to make her home in the working-class district of Molina in Corpus Christi, living next door to her parents.

Selena's influences included country-and-western, English-language pop, old-school, and especially African American music, including R&B, funk, and disco. Among the influential artists in Selena's young life were Donna Summer, Cool and the Gang, and Janet Jackson. Although most of the media attention paid to Selena had to do with her beauty, sexuality, and youthful impact on the Tejano music scene, Selena y los Dinos musically transformed the Texas Mexican music scene. With their rendition of songs such as "La carcacha," "Bibi bidi bom bom," and "Techno cumbia," Tejano cumbias would never be the same. In Selena's songs young Tejanas/Latinas found a cultural site for articulating movement along with sound, and for the gendered particularities of expressing love and pain, as well as sexuality and passion.

Among Selena's biggest accomplishments was the success she attained within the Tejano music industry itself. Not only did she break open the space for young women of her generation to follow in her footsteps, but she took Tejano music to locations it had never been before. Although Tejano groups such as la Mafia and Mazz had established fans of the music in Central America, northern Mexico, and Mexico City, Selena y los Dinos translocated the unique cultural production of Tejano music to Puerto Rico, Central America, and throughout Mexico. At the time of her death Selena y los Dinos had scheduled tours for Chile, Brazil, and Venezuela. To her credit, Selena, unlike any other Tejano music artist, both transformed and translocated what had originally been a regionally based musical sound.

Selena y los Dinos began its recording career in the mid- to late 1980s with Tejano record labels GP, Cara, Manny, and Freddie Records. Its albums included *Alpha* (1986), *Dulce amor* (1988), *Preciosa* (1988), *Selena y los Dinos* (1990), *Ven conmigo* (1991), *Entre a mi mundo* (1992), *Selena Live* (1993), *Amor prohibido* (1994), and *Dreaming of You* (released posthumously in 1995). In 1987 Selena won the Tejano Music Award for Female Entertainer of the Year, the first of many Tejano Music Awards in the years to come. After her performance at the Tejano Music Awards in 1989, a steady flow of Tejano music artists began to sign with EMI Latin Records. With its release of *Ven conmigo* in 1991, Selena y los Dinos established its dominance in the music industry and never relinquished its top position. With the 1992 release of *Entre a mi mundo*, Selena became the first Tejana to sell more than 300,000 albums. Selena's significance in contemporary U.S. popular music was recognized in 1994 when she won the Grammy for Best Mexican-American Album for *Selena Live*.

Moreover, Selena's creative talents were vast, particularly in the area of material aesthetic production. Selena worked diligently at her talents in clothing design, usually designing and sewing her own costumes. A number of drawings and sketches indicate an early goal to develop a clothing line of her own. Selena originally named the clothing line Moon (the translation of the Greek name Selena). In 1992 her dream became reality when she started her own clothing line. That resulted in the opening of the first Selena Etc. Boutique-Salon in Corpus Christi, Texas, which was followed by a boutique in San Antonio. That same year she married the lead guitarist of her band, Chris Pérez.

Selena's tragic death on March 31, 1995, at the hands of fan-club manager Yolanda Saldívar became one of the most significant historical markers in the public memory of Latinas/os in the United States during the last several decades of the twentieth century. The magnitude of media coverage of the death of this contemporary Mexican American music artist was unprecedented. The *New York Times* reported the event in a front-page story, and there was brief coverage on nationwide news programs such as *Dateline NBC, People* magazine ran a commemorative issue on her life that sold out in a matter of hours. In fact, it was this mostly Latina/o consumer response to the *People* magazine commemorative issue that spawned the creation of *People en Español.* Musicians also honored her life in music. Familia RMM, a group of Caribbean artists including Celia Cruz, Manny Manuel, Yolanda Duke, and Tito Nieves, produced the CD *Recordando a Selena,* a collection of some of Selena's most popular songs reproduced as salsa and merengue tunes. The all-female Mariachi Reyna de Los Angeles also included in its CD *Solo Tuya* a song tribute titled "Homenaje a Selena." In the years following her death Selena has been remembered through music television tributes by *Johnny Canales, VH-1,* and *El Show de Cristina.* Her life has been captured in the Hollywood production *Selena* and in the Broadway musical *Siempre Selena.* Chicana filmmaker Lourdes Portillo produced and directed the video documentary *Corpus: A Home Movie for Selena.* Today Corpus Christi, Texas, still entertains a steady flow of fans who visit her grave site, her statue by the ocean, the Selena Boutique, and the museum established in her honor at Q Productions, the family recording studios.

SOURCES: Calderón, Robert. 2000. "All over the Map: La Onda Tejana and the Making of Selena." In *Chicano Renaissance: Contemporary Cultural Trends,* ed. Daniel R. Maciel, Isidro D. Ortiz, and Maria Herrera-Sobek. Tucson: University of Arizona Press; Coronado, Raul, Jr. 2001. "Selena's Good Buy: Texas Mexicans, History y Selena Meet Transnational Capitalism." *Aztlán* 26, no. 1:59–100; Paredez, Deborah. 2002. "Remembering Selena, Remembering Latinidad." *Theatre Journal* 54, no. 1 (March): 63–84; Patoski, Joe Nick. 1996. *Selena: Como la flor.* Boston: Little, Brown; Vargas, Deborah R. 2002. "Bidi Bidi Bom Bom: Selena and Tejano Music in the Making of Tejas." In *Latino/a Popular Culture,* ed. Michell Habell-Pallán and Mary Romero. New York: New York University Press; _____. 2002. "Cruzando Frontejas: Remapping Se-

lena's Tejano Music Crossover." In *Chicana Traditions: Continuity and Change,* ed. Norma Cantú and Olga Naajera-Ramírez. Urbana: University of Illinois Press.

Deborah Vargas

QUINTERO, LUISA (1903–1987)

More than a decade after Luisa Quintero's death, reporters at the *El Diario/La Prensa* newspaper still met devoted readers of her "Marginalia" column who remembered her impassioned writings and her active involvement in New York City politics. The daughter of Engracia Serrano and Miguel Salgado, Luisa Amparo Salgado was born in the rural town of Toa Baja, Puerto Rico. In a 1952 Mother's Day article for the weekly *Ecos de Nueva York,* the journalist included a rare reference to her childhood years: "It is piercing, the yearning for those long-gone days when, with our sister Pepita, we were led by the hand by that beautiful, young, almost childish, happy mother, who was loved by all and indulgently cared for by our father, many years older than her. Then, the agonizing memory of losing her at the hands of a treacherous heart malady, in the prime of her youth; and remembering that it was our name—Luisa Amparo—the last that her lips pronounced on that never-forgotten Palm Sunday, there in our Toa-Baja."

After completing studies at a Gregg School in San Juan, Quintero worked for Cafeteros de Puerto Rico, a coffee growers' cooperative, and was a secretary for poet Luis Llorens Torres in 1926. In December 1928, two months after arriving in New York aboard the steamship *Carabobo,* she was hired by the newspaper *La Prensa,* where she initially worked in the advertising department and wrote for a lifestyle section under the pseudonym Beatriz Sandoval. During subsequent decades she continued working intermittently for *La Prensa* while writing and editing at other publications, such as the *United Nations Spanish Bulletin,* and kept working for *La Prensa* after it merged with its rival newspaper, *El Diario,* in 1963. She was also employed as an assistant publicist by Columbia Pictures.

Quintero was one of the founders of New York's Puerto Rican Day Parade and helped establish ASPIRA, the Puerto Rican Forum, and other community organizations. But she is perhaps best remembered for "Marginalia," a daily column that covered wide-ranging themes, including listings of community events, Puerto Rican history, religion and culture, and, above all, politics.

In her newspaper column Quintero kept a keen eye on the city's leaders, reminding them of their obligations toward the growing Puerto Rican population. "We keep waiting, Mr. Beame," was Quintero's message when Mayor Abraham Beame was making the first ap-

Luisa Quintero's impassioned writing made her an important journalist for the Spanish-language newspaper *El Diario/La Prensa*. Courtesy of the Justo A. Martí Photograph Collection. Centro Archives, Centro de Estudios Puertorriqueños, Hunter College, CUNY.

pointments of his administration. When it appeared that Terence Cardinal Cooke would not continue his predecessor's tradition of participating in the Fiesta de San Juan Bautista, "Marginalia" readers were asked to send protest telegrams to the cardinal. Quintero is credited also with a leading role in the campaign to revoke the death sentence against Salvador Agrón, convicted in the famous Capeman murder case.

Many rising Puerto Rican politicians who later became prominent personalities were championed by Quintero in her writings. Probably none received more favorable treatment in her influential column than Herman Badillo, whom the "Marginalia" creator promoted to the point of asking readers to send monetary contributions to his mayoral campaign fund.

In addition to writing about politicians, Quintero sometimes worked for them, participating, for instance, in the senatorial campaign of Robert F. Kennedy, who was said to have felt great affection for her. A founding member of the New York committee of the Partido Independentista Puertorriqueño, Quintero often wrote in favor of causes related to Puerto Rican independence.

Some of the articles written by Quintero and her colleagues hint at a difficult personal life. She married fellow journalist José A. "Babby" Quintero in June 1930. The couple divorced three decades later. Upon his death in 1968, Luisa Quintero wrote, "We cannot say that our union was serene and quiet as that of many couples. We had happiness, pain, laughter and tears, enthusiasm and dedication to the good of the community and to the effort of creating honest and constructive journalism." From her first marriage with Pedro Echeandía of San Sebastián, Puerto Rico, she had one son, Luis Alberto Echeandía Salgado.

In 1972 more than 300 people, including many of the city's political leaders, attended a dinner in honor of Luisa Quintero at Lincoln Center. A few years later Quintero suffered a stroke and stopped writing. She died at St. Luke's Hospital in August 1987. In an essay about Puerto Rican newspapers published in that year, sociologist Joseph Fitzpatrick wrote, "For a generation Luisa Quintero's influence was outstanding. No one has emerged to take her place."

See also Journalism and Print Media

SOURCES: Atanay, Reginaldo. 1987. "Muere la periodista Luisa Quintero." *El Diario/La Prensa,* August 19; Fitzpatrick, Joseph. 1987. "The Puerto Rican Press." In *The Ethnic Press in the United States: A Historical Analysis and Handbook,* ed. Sally M. Miller. Westport, CT: Greenwood Press.

María Vega

R

RACE AND COLOR CONSCIOUSNESS

Among Latinas and Latinos in the United States, race and color consciousness are historical fictions that profoundly influence the concrete material opportunities and outcomes persons of dark skin color enjoy. Since the beginning of the twentieth century biologists and anthropologists worldwide have repudiated the concept of race as patently false. It lives on, nevertheless, having taken distinct meanings and forms over the course of time. Skin color, the most commonly recognized aspect of race, is the result of physical adaptation to environment, devolved genetically from one generation to the next. In the Hispanic world race as a concept was first used to explain the putative inferiority of the peoples Spaniards encountered in Africa and the Americas.

The word *race* entered European languages at the beginning of the sixteenth century in tandem with voyages of discovery and encounter to Africa, Asia, and the Americas. European residents in agrarian societies during the Middle Ages had a clear understanding of the role of breeding and heredity in livestock production, and from such understandings they borrowed the concept of race to explain outward physical differences in human appearance, particularly that based on physical color. No one has yet established the exact etymology of the word *race*. Cambridge anthropologist J. C. Trevor maintains that *race* derives from the Latin *ratio*, originally a word used in the classification of animals into "species," "kind," and "nature." The Spanish word *raza*, the Italian *razza*, the French *race*, and the Portuguese *raça* also came from the Latin *ratio*.

Skin color as a physical assessment of a person's social worth is unique and yet quite modern in human history as a form of differentiation and discrimination. Scholars of earlier periods in world history are in general accord that while well-known antipathies and stereotypes, due mainly to religious differences, deeply structured how peoples interacted with each other, no real textual evidence has yet been found in Greek, Roman, or Jewish sources showing low esteem for peoples with dark skin and high esteem for lighter complexions.

The particular evolution of the concept of race in Latin America results from the conquest and colonization of America's Indians and the importation of black African slaves. By the time Christopher Columbus sailed westward seeking a shorter route to India, the dark-skinned peoples of Africa were widely known to Europeans. Beginning with the Crusades and then with the Moorish occupation of the Iberian Peninsula from 711 to 1492, Spain's Christian kings waged vicious war against the infidel followers of Mohammed, who were marked by their physical color. While religious difference marked the Moors as infidels, it was color that distinguished the black slaves bought and sold by African kings and European merchants. For the native populations of the Americas who became known to the Spaniards as Indians, a similar notion of religious difference was the principal basis upon which the conquerors racialized the conquered.

The Spaniards relied on a number of metaphors to describe the difference between conquerors and conquered, namely, that they were *cristianos* (Christians) and the Indians *paganos* (pagans), that they were *gente de razón* (people of reason regarding the precepts of the Christian faith), and the Indians were *gente sin razón* (people lacking such reason), and that they were *cristianos viejos* (old Christians) and long protectors of the faith, while the Indians were *cristianos nuevos* (new Christians), recent converts who were flaccid in their faith. These "us-them" distinctions were thoroughly imbued with notions of race. The Spaniards were Christians, rational and "civilized" men who by force of arms had won titles, honors, tribute, and lands, and were known by their fair skin, their fine clothing, and their refined demeanor and comportment. The vanquished Indians were heathens, irrational, lacking intelligence, mere children before the conquistadores and their laws, and easily recognized by their crude behavior, their physical features, and particularly their dark skin.

Race and Color Consciousness

In medieval Spain families of nobility and wealth guarded their heredity with great care, maintaining their *limpieza de sangre,* their blood purity, by avoiding mixture with Jew, Moors, and others deemed infamous and vile. In Spanish America men of honor similarly protected their bloodlines against pollution by Indians, half-breeds, and persons of despicable birth, closely monitored the behavior of their daughters, prohibited marriage to racial inferiors, and tolerated cohabitation, but profoundly stigmatized the racially mixed progeny of such unions.

The conquering soldiers who accompanied Spanish expeditions to the Americas were largely single men between the ages of seventeen and thirty-five. By European rights of conquest these men could lay claim to the spoils of the land. Because the Indians resisted and did not immediately submit, the soldiers waged wars of blood and fire, unmercifully unleashing horses, guns, and dogs against them. Rapes and acts of sexual violence accompanied every military campaign. Indeed, the conquest of America was a sexual conquest of Indian women further compounded through the sexual exploitation of female slaves. The biological legacy of such conquests was the mixed-race children begotten of acts of violence and domination.

To curtail the high levels of sexual violence against indigenous women, the Catholic clergy urged soldiers to take Indian brides. Some did. The majority preferred non-marital liaisons with Indian women through concubinage and cohabitation, especially with domestic servants and female African slaves. Casual encounters, promiscuity, and rapes, as well as stable unions, greatly expanded the number of persons of mixed racial ancestry during the seventeenth and eighteenth centuries.

From roughly 1500 to the early 1700s the Spanish Crown tolerated unions between Indian women and Spanish men in the Americas as a necessary evil it hoped would stabilize colonial society, improve trade and tributary relations with the Indians, cement military alliances, and promote the extension of missionary work. But prejudice against these mixed unions and particularly against the children of mixed racial ancestry was always present and intensified in the late eighteenth century when French-inspired Enlightenment ideas about social hierarchies diffused from Spain into the colonies.

In colonial society children of mixed racial ancestry were despised as vibrant symbols of defilement and were often treated as outcasts by Spaniards, Indians, and Africans alike. Most were born or presumed to have been born of sinful relationships and illicit liaisons between Spanish men and Indian or African women. Simply put, these children were bastards of il-legitimate birth and were so regarded in custom and law. In 1542 the Spanish legal theorist Juan de Solórzano Pereira noted about mestizo and mulatto children that "generally they are born in adultery and other ugly and illicit unions, because there are few Spaniards of honor who marry Indians or Negroes. This defect of their birth makes them infamous to which are added the stain of different color and other vices." For Solórzano, racial mixing was synonymous with illegitimacy and infamy.

From 1500 to roughly 1700 the *castas* (mixed-blood populations) in Spanish America seem to have been easily amalgamated, albeit marginally, either into their mothers' communities or into Spanish colonial society. *Mestizaje* or miscegenation nevertheless became the norm between the dominant Spaniards and Indians and Africans, both slave and free, resulting in high levels of illegitimacy, particularly throughout the eighteenth century. The children born of interracial unions and liaisons were carefully classified and ranked hierarchically according to the degree of putative mixing between the races through elaborate legal color categories and codes, known generically as the Régimen de Castas. A Spaniard and an Amerindian mother engendered a mestizo. A Spaniard and a black woman begot a mulatto. A mestizo and a Spanish woman produced a *castizo*. A Spaniard and a mulatto woman produced a *morisco*. A Spaniard and a *morisco* woman produced an *albino*, and so on. Precise legal color categories existed for most known combinations among Spaniards, Amerindians, and Africans, and these distinctions were imagined as rooted in blood and visually manifested in phenotype and color. The racial stereotypes that were deemed to be created through different degrees of racial mixing among Spaniards, Indians, and Africans can still be seen in the *casta* paintings from colonial Mexico and Peru, which depict the ideal physical types created through miscegenation.

Rising levels of illegitimacy in the 1700s throughout Spanish America were met with heightened racial prejudice against persons of mixed ancestry. In the eighteenth century "pure" Spaniards forcefully articulated elaborate explanations of their own superiority and, conversely, of the inferiority of *castas*. To guarantee that such notions were enforced through law, whenever a person stood before a civil or ecclesiastical court, his or her *calidad,* literally, his or her "quality" or social standing, was one of the first facts that entered the written record. A person's *calidad* usually began with age, sex, and place of residence, followed by the race and birth status, whether legitimate or illegitimate. The type and extent of punishment one could possibly receive was based on this information. Spaniards could not be given vile forms of punishment.

Indians, by virtue of their childishness and irrationality, could not be held accountable for certain acts, particularly heresy. Persons of mixed racial ancestry were held accountable, punished, differentially taxed, and prohibited from ostentatious displays of pomp and wealth.

Because of the high levels of illegitimacy created through racial mixing or miscegenation during the eighteenth century, physical color distinctions in the population rapidly began to blur, allowing individuals to pass as members of higher or lower castes, depending on what was most in their favor. As the population of Spanish America numerically increased in the eighteenth century, people began to move about more freely. Prestige hierarchies based on color became much more difficult to maintain and even more difficult to enforce. The Spanish Crown during the reign of King Charles III (1759–1788) reinforced legal color distinctions, demanded their mention in all legal proceedings, and promulgated a number of laws that strengthened the power of parents over their children, particularly in the selection of marriage partners. The state reasoned that if parents controlled the selection of marital partners for their children, social hierarchies and the racial integrity of elite families would be maintained. Had the Crown not been strapped for cash and resorted to the selling of titles and the whitening of stained lineages, the laws might have worked.

By the early 1800s the biological mixing that had taken place in Spanish America was so extensive that legal color codes were impossible to enforce, to say nothing of visually recognizing distinct physical types or races, except perhaps at the "pure" extremes. As one Spanish American province after another declared its independence from Spain between 1810 and 1821, legal color categories were abolished. Color consciousness remained, incorporating distinct, often class meanings that varied significantly according to regional histories and demography.

The particular racial understandings and color consciousness that exist today in each of the Latin American republics, former colonies of Spain, can largely be explained through the historic demographic mix among Indians, Europeans, and Africans during the colonial period. Latin America is generally thought of as composed of three racial regions: Afro-Latin America, mestizo America, and Euro-Latin America. Each region incorporates an understanding of race as a hierarchical continuum of color in which the lighter one's skin, the higher one's status, the darker the skin, the lower.

Afro-Latin America largely comprises the Caribbean islands and northeastern Brazil, where the indigenous population at the time of conquest was quickly deci-mated through violence, disease, and Spanish labor demands. African slaves were imported in large numbers to these areas precisely to provide the needed labor for plantation agriculture.

Mexico, Guatemala, and the Andean republics are thought of as constituting mestizo America. At the time of the Spanish conquest immense indigenous populations existed in the Andean highlands, central Mexico, and Guatemala. While disease and exploitation equally ravaged the native populations gathered here, enough of them survived to meet the labor needs of Spanish settlers. African slaves were also imported into these areas, but in much smaller numbers and in more specifically restricted ecological zones. These were the low-lying coastal areas of Mexico, Colombia, Venezuela, Peru, and Ecuador, where plantation agriculture prospered, but where the indigenous population was either too limited numerically or too poorly suited physically for the rigors of toil in hot humid climes. In these countries the African population blended into the whole and was particularly erased with the rise of nationalist ideologies in the twentieth century that glorified the disappearance of the original races of the conquest and the birth of a new hybrid mestizo race that united the nation.

Finally, Argentina, Uruguay, southern Chile, and southern Brazil are often classified as Euro-Latin America. These places neither had dense indigenous populations at the moment of colonization nor developed coastal plantation economies that required African slaves in large numbers. These countries were largely populated during the nineteenth century through European immigration and for that reason largely think of themselves as racially white.

The racial system that evolved in Latin America is quite distinct from the one that developed in the United States. In those parts of Latin America that have been characterized here as mestizo and Afro-Latin, racial categories and color consciousness have long been measured along a continuum through gradations that recognize hybridity and fluidity. Indeed, in the twentieth century some Latin American countries such as Mexico and Ecuador celebrated their mixed mestizo character and the simultaneous disappearance of "pure" races. This polychromatic system contrasts sharply with the hegemonic monochromatic racial order of the United States, which sharply differentiates only two races, black and white. In the United States any taint of black racial ancestry automatically made a person black, but the converse was not possible. Although in Latin America the mestizo emerged in the twentieth century as a positive symbol of amalgamation into which all persons could fit, immigrants in the United States who did not easily fit the black/white dichotomy were progressively placed into a new category of nonwhite that developed in the nineteenth century to categorize ambiguous racial classification of Asian and Latin American immigrants.

Race lives on in contemporary times as a significant divide among U.S. Latinos for a number of complicated reasons. Their ancestors came as colonizers to areas that eventually became parts of the United States, were themselves colonized by the United States starting in 1836, and, particularly in the twentieth century, became active agents in the global labor flows that brought millions of Latin American immigrants to the United States.

The scholarly literature on the racialization of Latinos in the United States is divided into two discrete traditions. The first addresses Spanish colonial ideas and practices as they developed out of conquered societies. The second treats Latinos as a population incorporated into the United States through conquest and annexation, beginning with the Texas Revolution of 1836 and continuing with the U.S.-Mexican War of 1848 and the Spanish-American War of 1898. Nineteenth-century U.S. territorial expansion into Mexican territory was premised on racist assumptions embedded in the doctrine of Manifest Destiny. Historians R. Reginald Horsman (1981) and Frederick Merk (1963) make clear that American state nationalism was deeply anti-Spanish and anti-Catholic, was anchored in a republican ideology that disparaged feudal and monarchical forms of government, and was wedded to an evolutionary science that deemed it the duty of superior races to eradicate inferior mongrel ones such as the Mexican. Sentiments akin to these are easy to access in such best-selling travel and adventure narratives as James O. Pattie's *The Personal Narrative of James O. Pattie* (1831), Josiah Gregg's *Commerce of the Prairies* (1844), and Richard Henry Dana's *Two Years before the Mast* (1840). Studies show that Americans depicted Mexicans as a breed of cruel and cowardly mongrels, indolent, ignorant, and superstitious and given to cheating, thieving, gambling, drinking, cursing, and dancing. The duty of the United States was to rescue such "greasers" from themselves. Indeed, this became a justification for war against Mexico in 1846 and the search for territory to expand American slavery.

Mexicans residing in the United States after territorial acquisition lost their lands and power and were residentially segregated, politically disenfranchised, and racialized as nonwhite. Although Anglos viewed Mexicans as a unitary and inferior conquered race, Mexicans saw themselves as complexly stratified by color, class, and generation and constantly emphasized these distinctions in their self-representations.

How a system of racial domination that thought of the color line as rigidly divided into black and white reconciled a Latino population that saw gradations and shades of color is the intriguing story told by Tomás Almaguer in his *Racial Fault Lines: The Historical Origins of White Supremacy in California* (1994). He shows how Mexicans occupied an intermediate space in the American racial order, the bottom of which was occupied by Indians, Asians, and blacks. By virtue of Spanish origin, Mexicans could legitimately claim a European genealogy, a Latin-derived language, belief in a Christian god, and thus Caucasian and white status. Neil Foley (1998) points out that while Mexicans may have been considered legally white, in practice they were treated as nonwhites. The term "Mexican" in popular usage from 1870 to the 1950s was persistently deemed a nonwhite racial status. This point was clearly underscored in 1930 when the U.S. census listed Mexicans as a separate race. The politics of racial categories used by the U.S. census over time to describe Latinos is an excellent entry point into the emergence of the "nonwhite" as an inferior and stigmatized racial group between blacks and whites.

Because Latinos were first annexed into the United States and ever since have continued to arrive as immigrant laborers and political refugees, their polychromatic understanding of race suffers in the United States. While gradations of color and hybridity are celebrated in Latin American national cultures, in the United States the hegemony of the black/white binary forces Latinos to identify with American taxonomies of race and to discriminate against persons of their own ancestry with darker skin.

In the contemporary United States skin color carries significant weight in social outcomes among Latinos of ethnic Mexican and Caribbean origins. Sociologists Edward Telles and Edward Murguía (1990) tested the widely reported observation that darker-skinned Chicanos were economically disadvantaged in the United States. Using the 1979 Chicano National Sample drawn from the Southwest, they asked whether those individuals rated as light skinned by interviewers had higher average earnings than those who were darker. Since the light-skinned group was too small for sound statistical comparisons, it was merged with a group judged to be of medium skin color, and a comparison was then made with the darkest group. The researchers found that there was a strong tendency for the lighter group to earn more than the darker one, and they argued that this could not be explained in terms of educational differences, for the two groups had similar levels of education. Carlos Arce, Edward Murguía, and W. Parker Frisbie (1987) similarly concluded that phenotype—defined in this study as dark skin and Indian facial features—correlated rather closely with socioeconomic status among Chicanos, a result Clara E. Rodríguez (1990,

1991) also found among U.S. Puerto Ricans with dark skin and "African" features.

Richard Zweigenhaft and G. William Domhoff (1998) tested a similar hypothesis about the relationship between color and class among Latinos by using two samples composed mainly of elites. The first consisted of photographs of Latino directors of Fortune 500 companies. The second sample was photos of the 188 individuals identified by *Hispanic Business* as the "top influential" Latinos in 1993 and 1994. Two independent panels of reviewers concluded that the Fortune 500 Latino directors were overwhelmingly "white" or "Anglo." About 50 percent of the influential Latinos were deemed "white," but the rest were readily identified as "Hispanic."

Social scientists also found that the Latino experience of residential segregation in the United States significantly increased as one's skin color darkened from apparent mixed race or black ancestry. Nancy Denton and Douglas Massey (1989) found the effects of race on housing discrimination to be most pronounced among Puerto Ricans of this origin. The biological fiction of race lives on, having first been used to discriminate against the conquered residents of Latin America and Africa in the sixteenth century, later to justify the conquest of such putative inferiors as the mongrel Mexicans in the nineteenth century, and to limit the opportunities persons of dark skin color enjoy in the Americas to this day.

See also Mestizaje

SOURCES: Almaguer, Tomás. 1994. *Racial Fault Lines: The Historical Origins of White Supremacy in California.* Berkeley: University of California Press; Arce, Carlos, Edward Murguía, and W. Parker Frisbie, 1987. "Phenotype and Life Chances among Chicanos." *Hispanic Journal of Behavioral Sciences.* 9: 19–32; Denton, Nancy A., and Douglas C. Massey, 1989. "Racial Identity among Caribbean Hispanics: The Effects of Double Minority Status on Residential Segregation." *American Sociological Review* 54: 790–808; Foley, Neil. 1997. *The White Scourge: Mexicans, Blacks, and Poor Whites in Texas Cotton Culture.* Berkeley: University of California Press; Gutiérrez, Ramón A. 1989. "Aztlán, Montezuma, and New Mexico The Political Uses of American Indian Mythology." In *Aztlán: Essays on the Chicano Homeland,* ed. Rodolfo Anaya and Francisco Lomelí. Albuquerque: University of New Mexico Press; ———. 1991. *When Jesus Came, the Corn Mothers Went Away: Marriage, Sexuality, and Power in New Mexico, 1500–1846.* Stanford: Stanford University Press; Horsman, Reginald. 1981. *Race and Manifest Destiny.* Cambridge: Harvard University Press; Meléndez, Edwin, Clara E. Rodríguez, and Janis Barry Figueroa, eds. 1991. *Hispanics in the Work Force.* New York: Plenum Press; Merk, Frederick. 1963. *Manifest Destiny and Mission in American History.* New York: Knoph; Rodríguez, Clara E. 1990. *Puerto Ricans: Immigrants and Migrants, A Historical Perspective.* Washington, DC: Portfolio Project; Solaún, Maurico, and Sidney Kronus. 1973. *Discrimination without Violence: Miscegnation and Racial Conflict in Latin America.* New York: Wiley; Telles, Edward E., and Edward Munguía. 1990. "Phenotype, Discrimination, and Income Differences Among Mexican Americans." *Social Science Quarterly* 71:682–696; Zweigenhaft, Richard, and G. William Domhoff. 1998. *Diversity in the Power Elite.* New Haven: Yale University Press.

Ramón A. Gutiérrez

RAMÍREZ, EMILIA SCHUNIOR (1902–1960)

Born in Sam Fordyce, Texas, in 1902, Emilia Schunior Ramírez was one of the few Mexican American women professors before the 1970s. Her parents were George J. Schunior and Angela (Vela) Schunior. She grew up in Mission and Edinburg, Texas, and graduated from Edinburg High School in 1919. She studied at Southwest Texas State Teachers College in San Marcos and at the University of Texas at Austin and obtained her B.A. at the College of Arts and Industries in Kingsville. At Southwest she was referred to as "Schuniorita." Her college education was a rarity for Mexican Americans during the early decades of the twentieth century. In 1921, at the age of nineteen, she married Rafael R. Ramírez, and the couple had three children.

As a married teacher with children, she was an anomaly for her times. She taught in schools in Roma, Rio Grande City, Edinburg, La Joya, and Pharr, all southern Texas communities, and she served as a principal in Rio Grande City and Roma. In Roma she was offered the position of superintendent but declined. Ramírez obtained her master's degree in education at the University of Texas in 1950. She attended summer school while her son Alfonso pursued his undergraduate degree at the same university. Her thesis was a study of more than 1,000 children in Rio Grande communities, but had the unfortunate title "Wetback Children in South Texas." Her mentor was the legendary education professor George I. Sánchez, a pioneer in bilingual education. In 1952 she became an assistant professor of Spanish at Pan American College (now the University of Texas, Pan American) in Edinburg.

In 1954 she was asked to contribute a chapter to a history of Hidalgo County. She wrote the chapter, but the book was never published. In 1971 her son Alfonso published the work, *Ranch Life in Hidalgo County after 1850,* a rare account of Mexican-origin women in the late nineteenth century based on interviews with twelve women and three men. She discussed early settlers, folk beliefs, festivities, holidays, and the landscape.

Active politically, she ran for the position of school superintendent of Starr County in 1950, but ironically lost to her cousin's husband. She was a member of the Pan American Round Table, the Texas State Teachers

Association, and the National Education Association. In 1960 she represented the Round Table at a meeting of the Inter-American Alliance in Guatemala City. She died of pancreatic cancer in 1960 at the age of fifty-eight. A dormitory at the University of Texas, Pan American, campus bears the name of this early Tejana historian and college professor.

See also Education

SOURCES: Orozco, Cynthia E. 1996. "Emilia W. Schunior Ramírez." In *New Handbook of Texas* 5:423–424. Austin: Texas State Historical Association; Ramírez, Emilia Schunior. 1971. *Ranch Life in Hidalgo County after 1850.* Edinburg, TX: New Santander.

Cynthia E. Orozco

RAMÍREZ, SARA ESTELA (1881–1910)

Praised as la Musa Tejana by fellow writer and friend Jovita Idar, Sara Estela Ramírez was born in the Mexican state of Coahuila in 1881. Although she lost her mother as a young child, the notable activist, poet, and prolific writer managed to finish her public education in Monterrey, Nuevo León, and to attain a graduate degree in teaching from the Ateneo Fuentes in Saltillo, Mexico. In 1898, fifty years after the signing of the Treaty of Guadalupe Hidalgo, at the age of seventeen, Sara Estela Ramírez relocated to Laredo, Texas, where she took a position as a Spanish teacher at the Seminario Laredo and acted as well as a key political supporter of the Partido Liberal Mexicano (PLM) that arose in opposition to Porfirio Díaz's regime in Mexico.

From Laredo, young and strong-willed, Ramírez offered her oratory, writing skills, and political support to the PLM and volunteered her home as the Texas headquarters for the party during a time in which political agitators were harassed and arrested. Working to advance the cause of the Mexican Revolution through economic and political means and social writings that boosted Mexican heritage and addressed the needs of the Tejano community in Laredo, Ramírez printed essays, speeches, and poems in the local Spanish-language papers *El Demócrata Fronterizo* and *La Crónica* and also published her writings in two feminist newspapers, *Aurora* and *Justicia y Libertad.*

Twenty-one of her poems and essays discussing philosophy, political views, and women's rights, published between January 8, 1908, and April 9, 1910, have survived. *Diamantes negros, A Juárez,* and *Huye* are some of her most popular works. In April 9, 1910, Ramírez published *Surge surge,* a poem directed "a las mujeres" and emphasizing female power and assertion. "Tu la reina del mundo. . . . Una mujer que lo verdaderamente es, es mas que diosa y que reina" (You are the queen of the world. . . . A woman who is truly a woman is more than a goddess or a queen). "Solo la acción es vida; sentir que se vive, es la mas hermosa sensación" (Only action is life; to feel like you are alive, that is the most beautiful of sensations). Aside from poetry, Ramírez wrote a play titled *Noema* and published various speeches written on behalf of the Sociedad de Obreros of Laredo.

Sara Estela Ramírez's involvement in the Tejano community introduced a feminist perspective to the revolution through her political leadership and community activism. Ramírez allied herself with other women in the resistance movement, including Dolores Jiménez y Muro, Juana Belén Gutiérrez de Mendoza, and Elisa Acuña. Most of the essays written by Ramírez expressed her open support for the working classes and stressed *mutualismo* as a guiding principle in all social relations. In a speech titled *Alocución,* given on April 17, 1909, Ramírez addressed an organization of workers by identifying herself as a "ferviente admiradora del mutualismo" (a fervent admirer of *mutualismo*), emphasizing that "para llamar hermano al obrero solo me basta tener corazón" (to call the worker my brother I need only have a heart). *Mutualismo,* argued Ramírez, represented nothing less than a noble mission of charity.

Upon her premature death at the age of twenty-nine friends and supporters bade her farewell, lamenting, "Ha fallecido la mujer Mejicana mas ilustrada de Texas" (The most illustrious woman of Texas has passed). Eulogized in the local newspaper *La Crónica,* Ramírez was also remembered as "la mas noble, mas sentimental y primera de las poetisas de la region" (the most noble, most sentimental, and the first among the female poets of the region). Her literary career spans the short but fruitful period lasting from 1898 to 1910. Ramírez's lasting contributions through inspiring literary works serve as testimony that Mexican women intellectuals of her time actively joined the revolutionary movement to overthrow Porfirio Díaz, acted politically to support Laredo's local labor-unionizing efforts among Hispanics, and contested sexual, racial, and gender expectations of the time.

See also Feminism; Journalism and Print Media; Literature

SOURCES: Acosta, Teresa Palomo, and Ruthe Winegarten. 2003. *Las Tejanas: 300 Years of History.* Austin: University of Texas Press; Hernández Tovar, Inés. 1984. *"Sara Estela Ramírez: The Early Twentieth Century Texas-Mexican Poet."* Ph.D. diss., University of Houston; Mora, Magdalena, and Adelaida R. Del Castillo, eds. 1980. *Mexican Women in the United States.* Los Angeles: Chicano Studies Research Center, University of California; Zamora, Emilio, Jr. 1980. "Sara Estela Ramírez: Una rosa roja en el movimiento." In *Mexican Women in the United States,* ed. Magdalena Mora and Adelaida R. Del Castillo. Los Angeles: Chicano Studies Research Center, University of California.

Soledad Vidal

RAMÍREZ, TINA (1925–)

Tina Ramírez is the founding director of the most renowned Hispanic dance company in the United States, New York City's el Ballet Hispánico. The daughter of María Sestero, a Puerto Rican housewife with aspirations of becoming an actress, and José "Gaonita" Ramírez, a Mexican bullfighter, Tina was born in Caracas, Venezuela, where her father was appearing in the bullring. Tina was still a child when her parents separated, and she, her siblings, and her mother returned to Puerto Rico, where María Sestero was able to find work at the board of elections. When Tina was six years old, the family relocated to New York City. She was raised in an Italian neighborhood of East Harlem on the corner of 114th Street and Second Avenue. They lived with her grandmother, who had been a teacher in Puerto Rico. Her mother worked as a dishwasher and later a waitress in Child's Restaurant. They later moved to the neighborhood called Fort Apache in the Bronx.

Tina Ramírez started learning to dance when a doctor recommended that her sickly younger sister take dance lessons to become stronger. Ramírez accompanied her, and by the time she was twelve, she was begging her mother to let her become a dancer. By age thirteen she was entertaining on Sundays at the Spanish mutual-aid societies in New York. She also began performing in actress Marita Reid's *tertulia* and variety shows at the Spanish clubs by age fourteen, quite often lining up two engagements for Sundays, making $2 to $5 per performance. At times Ramírez toured with the Spanish variety acts as far west as Ohio. In her teens she began taking ballet lessons, as well as learning Spanish folk dances and flamenco with Spanish dancer Lola Bravo. She also began performing at nightclubs and on the road, making $25 a show at each of three different hotels in the Catskill Mountains' Borscht Circuit. This was during World War II, when no entertainers from Europe were available. By the age of fifteen she joined Spaniard Federico Rey's Rhythms of Spain company and toured the United States, Canada, and Cuba. At seventeen she went to Spain to study ballet and Spanish classical dance for two years. During this time she studied flamenco with la Quica and the Príncipe Gitano troupe and even performed a one-woman show at the Ateneo in Madrid.

Tina Ramírez returned to the United States in 1963, worried about losing her U.S. citizenship, and again took up performing on the nightclub circuit. She and her sister performed with Xavier Cugat for two years and were later signed by MCA Music Company to perform at supper clubs all over the United States. After that Tina Ramírez signed with General Artists and performed in two Hollywood films, *Casa Cugat* and *No Men Allowed*. On her return to New York City she studied modern dance with Anna Sokalow and began performing in musical comedies on Broadway, including *Hello, Dolly!* (1964).

In 1963 the retiring Lola Bravo requested that Ramírez take over her studio. After a trial year Ramírez had found her greatest calling, and the Tina Ramírez Dance School became a wonderful success. During the War on Poverty of President Lyndon B. Johnson she was successful in obtaining funding from the government to implement her Operation High Hopes, a program in dance instruction for inner-city poor children. From 8 A.M. to 3 P.M., she taught dance to some 130 students in the public schools and then promptly at 4 P.M. returned to her studio to teach her regular paying customers. She was on the way to learning how to raise funds and how to bring dance into the lives of inner-city children. In 1970 she was awarded a grant for $20,000 from the New York State Council on the Arts to start a dance company for young people aged twelve to fifteen. By the end of the year Ballet Hispánico was born. It first concentrated on the dance culture of her own backgrounds: Puerto Rican, Spanish, Mexican, and Venezuelan. As her company evolved, she wanted to present more than "roots" and also concentrated on presenting how Hispanics actually looked and dressed and acted in the United States "so that we are seen on a higher plane, as we really are, not just one type, not just stereotypes."

During the last thirty years el Ballet Hispánico has grown to national prominence, performing at elite venues, as well as in ethnic centers, throughout the United States. It has toured Europe and Latin America and represented the United States at the international exposition in Seville, Spain (1992). Among the graduates of el Ballet Hispánico are such Hollywood actors as Michael De Lorenzo and Rachel and Nancy Ticotín. The graduates also include scores of professional dancers and dance teachers who are making careers far and wide. Among Tina Ramírez's and el Ballet Hispánico's many awards are the Hispanic Heritage Award (1999), the Governor's Art Award (1987), and the Mayor's Award of Honor for Arts and Culture (1983).

See also Theater

SOURCES: Breslauer, Jan. 1995. "Ballet Hispánico: On the Move in So Many Ways." *Los Angeles Times*, March 30; Gladstone, Valerie. 1999. "A Culture That Sells Itself." *New York Times*, November 21; Kisselgoff, Anna. 1998. "A Simpatico Connection for Two Genres." *New York Times*, December 3.

Nicolás Kanellos

RAMÍREZ DE ARELLANO, DIANA (1919–1997)

Diana Ramírez de Arellano was the author of numerous books of poetry and literary criticism and became a poet laureate of Puerto Rico. She had a long and distinguished academic career and was a professor of Spanish at City College of the City University of New York and at Rutgers University. She was the president and founder of the Ateneo Puertorriqueño de Nueva York and a leading force in the literary and intellectual circles of Puerto Ricans and Latin Americans in New York.

Born in New York in 1919, Ramírez de Arellano was raised in Ponce, Puerto Rico. Her parents, Enrique Ramírez de Arellano Brau and María Teresa Rechani, were prominent members of Puerto Rico's social and intellectual elite. Her grandfather, Salvador Brau, was one of the first and most important Puerto Rican historians. Ramírez de Arellano completed her elementary and secondary schooling in Ponce and in 1941 graduated from the University of Puerto Rico with a degree in pedagogy. She worked as a high-school teacher in the town of Manatí and in 1944 traveled to New York for graduate studies. In 1946 she received a master's degree in pedagogy from Teachers College, Columbia University. From 1946 through 1951 Ramírez de Arellano taught at Women's College at the University of North Carolina and at Douglass College at Rutgers University. In 1951 she enrolled in the University of Madrid, Spain, to complete her doctoral studies. She graduated in 1952. Her doctoral thesis, titled "Genealogical Comedy in the Works of Lope de Vega and a Critical Edition of Los Ramírez de Arellano," was later published as *Los Ramírez de Arellano de Lope de Vega* and explored her own family roots. After defending her thesis she returned to the faculty at Douglass College, but moved on from there to City College, CUNY, in 1958 to teach language and literature where she remained until her retirement.

Most of Ramírez de Arellano's published works were books of poetry. Among them are *Yo soy Ariel* (1947), *Albatros sobre el alma* (1955), *Angeles de ceniza* (1958), *Un vuelo casi humano* (1960), *Privilegio* (1965), *Del señalado oficio de la muerte* (1974), *Arbol en vísperas* (1987), and *Adelfazar* (1995). In literary criticism she published several books, including *Caminos de la creación poética de Pedro Salinas* (1956), *Poesía contemporánea en lengua española* (1961), and *El himno deseado* (1979). Ramírez de Arellano was also a frequent contributor to literary publications throughout Latin America and Spain and to Puerto Rico's *El Mundo* and *Alma Latina*.

One of her most important contributions, apart from her books, was the creation of the Ateneo Puertorriqueño de Nueva York, which she founded in 1963 "to bridge the gap of silence and loneliness of the Puerto Rican artist and scholar in New York." She served as the Ateneo's first president and turned it into a space for nourishing the intellectual and cultural life of Puerto Ricans in New York. Ramírez de Arellano was a member of diverse organizations such as the Modern Language Association and the American Association of Teachers of Spanish and Portuguese, which gave her emeritus status in 1983.

Among the many awards she received are the Medalla de Oro del Ateneo de Puerto Rico (the Gold Medal of the Ateneo of Puerto Rico) (1958), Medalla de Plata del Ministerios de Educación por Poesía de Bolivia (Silver Medal for Poetry of the Ministry of Education of Bolivia), and the Medal of Honor of the Ateneo Puertorriqueño de Nueva York. La Sociedad de Autores Puertorriqueños de San Juan, Puerto Rico (the Society of Puerto Rican Authors) gave her a special tribute in 1966.

Diana Ramírez de Arellano died on April 30, 1997, in New York City. She made significant contributions to

Writer Diana Ramírez de Arellano, founding president of the Ateneo Puertorriqueño de Nueva York. Courtesy of the Diana Ramírez Arellano Paps. Centro Archives, Centro de Estudios Puertorriqueños, Hunter College, CUNY.

the cultural and literary life of Puerto Ricans and other Latinos in New York and left an important body of published works. Her collected papers at the Library and Archives of the Center for Puerto Rican Studies at Hunter College, City University of New York, reveal her work as a poet and literary critic and safeguard the history of the Ateneo Puertorriqueño de Nueva York.

See also Literature

SOURCE: Ramírez de Arellano, Diana. 1919–1997. Papers. Centro Archives, Centro de Estudios Puertorriqueños, Hunter College, CUNY.

Ismael García, Nélida Pérez, and Pedro Juan Hernández

RANGEL, IRMA (1931–2003)

Irma Rangel was a pioneer legislator from Texas. The first Mexican American woman to serve in the Texas legislature, Representative Rangel was instrumental in the advancement of education in the state of Texas in the last quarter of the twentieth century. Irma Rangel was born in the small southern Texas city of Kingsville on May 15, 1931. This was for Mexican Americans in Texas, and almost everywhere else, a time of harsh, Jim Crow–style segregation. Forced to go out into the fields of neighboring Robstown to pick cotton as a young girl, she never lost sight of her community or its struggles. Rangel graduated from Texas A&I University (now Texas A&M University, Kingsville) in 1952, when, in her own words, "you could count the Hispanic students on two hands." She became a schoolteacher and principal for schools in southern Texas, California, and Venezuela. Rangel eventually changed careers, graduating in 1969 with a law degree from St. Mary's University School of Law in San Antonio.

Rangel's life was a string of firsts. For the next two years she was one of the first female Hispanic law clerks for federal district judge Adrian Spears of San Antonio. From 1971 to 1973, as assistant district attorney for Nueces County, she became one of the first Hispanic women in the state to hold this office. A successful practicing attorney, Irma Rangel ran for and was elected to the Texas House of Representatives in 1976, representing the Kingsville district, thus becoming the first Latina ever to serve in the state legislature, where she remained for twenty-six years until her death on March 18, 2003.

Irma Rangel was responsible for the first meaningful positive action taken by the state of Texas immediately following the disastrous *Hopwood* decision from the federal judiciary that banned the state from using affirmative action both in the higher-education admissions process and for scholarships. In 1997 Rangel, as chairperson of the House Committee on Higher Education, argued in favor of the Top 10 Percent Law that guaran-

teed state university admission for all students graduating in the top 10 percent of all Texas high schools. Although then governor George W. Bush eventually claimed credit for this legislation, it was actually the brainchild of Rangel. It was through her personal leadership and effort that the Texas legislature passed this partial blunting of the negative, exclusionary effects of *Hopwood.*

In addition to education, Rangel also championed the rights and opportunities of mothers with dependent children, better highways and roads, and efforts against malnutrition. Rangel was widely recognized and accumulated many honors and awards: Legislator of the Year by the Mexican American Bar Association in 1997, Latina Lawyer of the Year by the Hispanic National Bar Association in 1998, the García Public Service Award from the Mexican American Legal Defense and Educational Fund (MALDEF) in 1993, and induction into the Texas Women's Hall of Fame in 1994.

Recalling Rangel, state senator Gonzalo Barrientos of Austin said, "She had to be smart, she had to be articulate and she had to be tough. And she was all of those." Senator Leticia Van de Putte of San Antonio remembered, "She had a terrific way of making us all her children. She had a special feeling about the women who served in this body. Party labels made no difference." Shortly after her death public officials of both parties named a new pharmacy school, the Irma Rangel School of Pharmacy, at Texas A&M University, Kingsville, after her.

See also Politics, Electoral

SOURCES: Harmon, Dave. 2003. "Irma Rangel, 1931–2003: The First Mexican-American Woman Elected to the Texas House of Representatives Died Early This Morning." *Austin American Statesman,* March 18; Javelina Alumni Association. 2001. "Representative Rangel Named Distinguished Alumnus for 2001." *Tusk,* Summer. www.tamuk.edu/javalumni/tusk/2001/summer/rangel.shtml (accessed May 25, 2003); Leo, Myra. 2003. "It Was Always about the Students." *Texas Observer,* April 11; Meighan, Ty. 2003. "Lawmakers Share Their Memories of Irma Rangel: Kingsville Representative Is Remembered as a Teacher Whose Guidance Spanned Party Lines." *Corpus Christi Caller Times,* April 1; Orozco, Cynthia E. 2003. "Mexican-American Women." In *The Handbook of Texas Online.* www.tsha.utexas.edu/handbook/online/articles/view/MM/pwmly.html (accessed May 25, 2003).

Carlos Kevin Blanton

RAPE

Rape is commonly defined in state penal codes as a forceful sexual act perpetrated on a person without that person's consent that involves penetration of the anus or vagina by any object or penetration of any body orifice by a phallus. Non-Hispanic American women experienced a rate of rape or sexual assault of 1.4 for every 1,000 women in the population. For Hispanic women, the rate was 1.5. Moreover, since rape is a largely underreported crime, it is very likely that the actual figures are even higher.

Rape can happen to any woman at any time. According to federal crime figures, for 1998 and 2000 there are no significant differences in rates of reported victimization in terms of region (urban, suburban, or rural), although there are slightly more rapes reported in urban areas and in the Midwest. Significant differences were found in terms of marital status, with the majority of reported rapes occurring among single (3.1 per 1,000) or divorced or separated women (2.6 per 1,000). Significant differences were found in age; the majority of the victims were under twenty-five years of age. Specifically, 3.5 per 1,000 women were twelve to fifteen years of age, 5 per 1,000 were between sixteen to nineteen years old, 4.6 per 1,000 were twenty to twenty-four years of age, and only 1.7 per 1,000 were twenty-five to thirty-four years old.

Federal figures suggest that young, urban, poor, and unmarried women are more likely to be the targets of rape than married, more affluent, and older women. The majority of reported rapes occurred among women whose household income was less than $35,000, and the largest proportion (3.2 per 1,000) occurred among women whose household income was less than $7,500 per year. There are no data specifying the demographics of Latina rape victims.

Sexual crimes against women have been committed by men from the beginning of recorded history, notably during times of war and conquest and as retaliation against opposing tribes, armies, and nations. Rapes are crimes of violence rooted in patriarchal notions of women as booty, male possessions, or dehumanized objects. In inner cities gang rapes are common as rites of passage. The rape of women who are affiliated with or relatives of men in opposing gangs is sanctioned behavior. Feminists argue that as long as women are perceived as second-class citizens, property, or devalued human beings, rape will continue to occur.

Many women who are raped do not report the crime. A primary reason for not reporting is the treatment of the rape victim by the police and the judicial system. Often women are not believed. There must be physical evidence that a rape occurred. Many rapists use condoms to eliminate physical evidence. Some rapes are not accompanied by physical violence, and this reduces the credibility of the event. Once a woman reports a rape, a medical examination must follow in order to collect forensic evidence. The investigation of rape is generally carried out by male police officers. After a woman has suffered the trauma of rape, she

may be terrified to speak to another man, particularly one who will ask intimate questions concerning the assault and begin to inquire into her own sexual history. Police departments have increasingly incorporated more sensitive interview techniques. Some departments include women officers who interview victims. Nevertheless, women often feel that they are not believed, particularly when they are asked questions that cast blame, including why they were in the place, situation, or location where the assault occurred. Invariably they will be asked if they know the perpetrator. If a woman does, a question as to whether the rape was in fact consensual sex often follows. If the perpetrator is found and apprehended and prosecution occurs, the woman's sexual history is brought into the case, whereas the male's past history of sexual crimes often is not included because it could prejudice the jury. Cases where accused rapists were acquitted because the focus became the victim's attire at the time of the assault, past sexual history, or use of alcohol serve to deter reporting and further traumatize women.

A number of cultural factors may deter Latinas from reporting. Traditional Latino cultures reify virginity and fidelity. These views are influenced by the dichotomization of women into virgins and whores, rooted in the colonial experience of the American continent and the prevalence of Christianity among Latinos. It is generally believed that a Latina's worth is tied to her morality and purity. Parents are expected to protect their daughters from men's sexuality to ensure virginity at marriage. While many Latinas are sexually active from a young age, the cultural ideal remains strong. Therefore, the sexual assault of a daughter has multiple implications. She may no longer be perceived as pure and therefore deserving of a good marriage. The honor of the father has been sullied, and great shame has been brought on the family. Often the father's shame and pain become the focus of the family's attention, not the woman's victimization. Her own trauma and the psychological sequelae of the assault may be overlooked. Families may not want to report the assault because they are worried about "el que dirán" (what people will think). Thus Latinas may not report rapes to protect the father from shame. If the woman is married, the same dynamics may operate. She is expected to protect both her husband and her father from the shame of the crime.

An additional barrier to reporting is the fact that men of the same ethnic or racial background as the victim commit most rapes. Thus a Latina who reports a rape by a Latino is in fact "turning a brother in" to the authorities. In urban communities where police relations with the residents often are poor, women may be reluctant or discouraged from turning a man in to the police. Thus a combination of cultural and sociopolitical factors may play a role in deterring reporting.

Rape is an act of violence that assaults a woman's sense of self physically, psychologically, and spiritually. She may suffer physical injuries and run the risk of contracting a sexually transmitted disease (STD), including HIV infection. STDs can have long-term consequences if they are untreated, including infertility. A woman may become pregnant as a result of a rape. If she terminates the pregnancy, she will have to face the social, emotional, and familial consequences of an abortion. If she keeps the child, she will have a lifelong reminder of her victimization.

While most women are aware of the dangers they face as they negotiate their life simply because they are women, rape is a confirmation of a woman's vulnerability and lack of safety. Consequently, rape victims often experience tremendous fear and a number of psychological symptoms best described by the diagnosis of post-traumatic stress disorder. If the rape occurred in the home, the sense of violation is twofold. The victim's intimate space, once considered safe, has been violated, as has her body. Hypervigilance, anxiety, panic, and gastrointestinal distress are among the most common sequelae. Furthermore, fear and distrust of men increase. Women who have been raped often experience problems with intimacy and decreased sexual desire.

Among the most powerful healing methods to recover from rape are training programs that teach women self-defense. Among these, Worth Defending focuses on connecting women with their sense of agency and efficacy. The experience of feeling safe and of being able to protect oneself against sexual violence can facilitate women's efforts to recover from rape experiences. In order to heal and to reclaim her sexuality, her agency and her faith, a rape survivor needs to not blame herself and to understand rape as a product of misogyny and racism.

See also Domestic Violence; *Marianismo* and *Machismo*

SOURCES: Bandura, Albert. 1997. *Self-Efficacy: The Exercise of Control.* New York: W. H. Freeman; Brownmiller, Susan. 1975. *Against Our Will: Men, Women, and Rape.* New York: Simon and Schuster; Bureau of Justice Statistics. 2000. *Sourcebook of Criminal Justice Statistics, 1998.* Washington, DC: U.S. Department of Justice, Office of Justice Programs; Flores-Ortiz, Yvette. 1997. "The Broken Covenant: Incest in Latino Families." *Voces: A Journal of Chicana Studies* no. 2, 1:48–70; Wilde, Susan. 2002. Worth Defending (program description). www.wildelife.com/worth/ (accessed June 28, 2005).

Yvette G. Flores-Ortiz

REID, MARITA (?–1980s)

From the 1920s to the 1950s Marita Reid was the most renowned *primera dama* (leading lady) of the Hispanic stage in New York, as well as a distinguished director. Born in Gibraltar to a Spanish mother and an English father, Marita Reid grew up bilingual and initiated her life on the stage at age seven. Her early experience was derived from performing on tours in extreme southern Spain. In the early 1920s she made her debut in Spanish dramatic companies at the National and Belmont theaters of New York City. After 1922 she acted in the companies of Pilar Arcos, Narcisín, and others in a variety of genres, from serious drama to zarzuela (Spanish-style operettas). Sometime later she followed the example of many outstanding women of the stage who became entrepreneurs, as well as artists, and formed her own company. The Compañía Marita Reid performed steadily on a circuit of mutual-aid societies, such as the Calpe Americano and the Casa Galicia, as well as at the Ateneo Hispano, a cultural and intellectual center in Manhattan.

When the depression and World War II sharply curtailed the opportunities for live performances in theaters, Reid was one of the persons most responsible for keeping Spanish-language drama alive by producing works at numerous halls and mutual-aid societies, as well as at conventional theater houses. Because of her perfect English and biculturalism, Reid was able to cross over to American, English-language mainstream theater. Her career extended to Broadway and to Hollywood, including live television drama in the *Armstrong Circle Theatre*, the *U.S. Steel Hour*, and *Studio One.*

During the course of her career Reid wrote four plays, all of which have remained unpublished: *Patio gibraltareño* (A Gibraltar Patio), *Luna de mayo* (May Moon), *Sor Piedad* (Sister Piety), and *El corazón del hombre es nuestro corazón* (A Man's Heart Is Our Heart). These ran the gamut from comedic farce to serious drama, but Reid herself was very modest about her playwriting skills.

In addition to being a leader in the Latino artistic community, Reid was a staunch activist in support of the Spanish Republic. She produced, directed, and acted in numerous antifascist plays, most of which were fund-raising efforts for the Republican army. The performances were usually followed by rallies and speeches of the diverse ethnic elements in the Latino community of New York. The broadside for one such performance in 1934 openly proclaimed the producers' and audience's political sentiments: "La lucha entre el capital y el trabajo, entre el facismo y la libertad ha tomado los caracteres más trágicos en el suelo español. Los valientes campesinos españoles agobiados por el trabajo, se revelan pidiendo justicia" (The strug-

Marita Reid on the right in *Doña Diabla* at the Teatro Hispano in New York. Courtesy of Arte Público Press.

gle between capital and labor, between fascism and freedom has assumed its most tragic character on Spanish soil. The valiant Spanish campesinos, overcome with work, are shown begging for justice). Reid's commitment to the cause lasted throughout her life. In 1957, on the occasion of the twenty-sixth anniversary of the Republic (in exile), Marita Reid was paid homage at a special performance of one of the plays that she had made famous in New York: the Alvarez Quintero brothers' *Lo que hablan las mujeres* (What Women Talk About). Unfortunately, the evening was marred by supporters of dictator Francisco Franco who barged in and attempted to disrupt the affair. The police had to be called to the scene. Marita Reid died in New York without much notice sometime during the 1980s.

See also Theater

SOURCES: Kanellos, Nicolás. 1984. *Hispanic Theatre in the United States.* Houston: Arte Público Press; ———. 1990. *A History of Hispanic Theatre in the United States: Origins to 1940.* Austin: University of Texas Press.

Nicolás Kanellos

REID, VICTORIA COMICRABIT (1808–1868)

Born around the year 1808 in a *ranchería,* an Indian village, near the Mission San Gabriel, Victoria Comicrabit came from an elite Native American family and underwent the full cycle of Spanish evangelizing and civilizing practices. The *ranchería's* proximity to the San Gabriel Mission ensured that its inhabitants were forced into daily religious rituals and agricultural cycles dictated by the Catholic fathers. Following the prescribed doctrine for female *neófitos,* baptized Indians, Victoria was allowed to live with her parents until the age of six or seven and then was removed to the *mon-*

jería (nunnery) of the mission. There she was schooled in the principles of Christianity and was taught reading, writing, and fundamental Hispanic household skills such as cooking, sewing, washing, and gardening. At the mission she received special attention from Eulalia Pérez, the mission's *llavera,* or key keeper, who chose her as one of her assistants.

Upon reaching sexual menarche, Comicrabit was encouraged by the fathers to marry a fellow neophyte, Pablo María of the neighboring Ytucubit *ranchería.* Marriage, however, did not remove Victoria or Pablo from service to the mission, and she continued to assist Pérez after her marriage. In 1823, at the age of fifteen, she gave birth to her first child, Felipe. Three more children, José Dolores, María Ygnacia, and Carlitos, followed. As thoroughly Hispanicized neophytes, and with Pérez's assistance, Victoria and Pablo María received their entitled *parajes,* plots of land, the Rancho Santa Anita, and la Huerta del Cuati, from the San Gabriel fathers. After Pablo María's death in 1835, Victoria married Hugo Reid, a Scottish merchant. Reid benefited from the marriage because Victoria's land turned Reid into a ranchero.

Genuine affection did exist between Victoria and Hugo, who adopted all four of her children. In turn, Reid's European surname gave Victoria and her children access and fuller integration into the elite Californio class. Moreover, Victoria was an active partner in the maintenance and supervision of the two ranchos. Indeed, because of Hugo Reid's chronic stomach pains, Victoria's previous supervisory skills were highly useful, if not essential, in overseeing and managing the couple's properties. Her marriage to an obviously white man deepened the patina of Victoria's Hispanicization, but neither she nor her children could completely forget their racial origins. Victoria's "Indianness" caused people to remark on the uniqueness of this union. The most intimate and personal account of Victoria and her racial dichotomy came from Laura Evertson King, who was a young child of perhaps eight or nine when she first met Victoria. King noted that everyone called Victoria *Doña,* with the privileges and respect such a name should invoke; yet, simultaneously, King could not completely erase Victoria's Indian origins.

Lamentably, during the 1840s the Reids faced a steady economic decline that heightened a growing estrangement between them. All of Hugo Reid's business ventures failed, forcing him to sell both the Huerta de Cuati and Rancho Santa Anita. By the 1850s all the advantages and privileges of being married to Victoria crumbled. Before the onslaught of American hegemony Spanish Mexican society excused and accommodated the union of a white man and a neophyte woman. In the emerging and transforming world of Euro-American dominance interethnic alliances were reluctantly a fact of life but hardly acceptable to Euro-American racist, prejudiced mind-sets. Although Spanish Mexican neighbors accepted and supported the Reids' marriage, with new American neighbors the history and social forces that supported such unions were swept aside, and interest in this exceptional union diminished. However, in an ironic twist the story of Victoria and Hugo Reid became immortalized in one of the most important nineteenth-century novels, *Ramona.*

First published in 1886, *Ramona* was Helen Hunt Jackson's attempt to write the *Uncle Tom's Cabin* of California mission Indians. Set in early-nineteenth-century California, the novel's plot involved the ill-fated love between a half-Indian, half-Scottish Indian woman, Ramona, and a full-blooded Indian, Allesandro. Helen Hunt Jackson researched in California and, learning of Victoria and Hugo's marriage, incorporated them into her novel. Victoria was never named in the novel, but it was her historical reality that allowed Ramona to be born in fiction. On December 23, 1868, Victoria Reid the former *señora,* died like many other California Native Americans, ignored and destitute.

See also Spanish Borderlands

SOURCES: Casas, María Raquel. "Victoria Reid and the Politics of Identity." In *Latina Legacies: Identity Biography, and Community,* ed. Vicki L. Ruiz and Virginia Sánchez Korrol. New York: Oxford University Press. Dakin. Susana Bryant. 1939. *Scotch Paisano: Hugo Reid's Life in California, 1832–1852.* Berkeley: University of California Press; Davis, William Heath. 1929. *Seventy-five Years in California, 1831–1906.* San Francisco: John Howell; Jackson, Helen Hunt. 1912. *Ramona.* New York: Grosset and Dunlap; King, Laura Evertson. 1898. "Hugo Reid and His Indian Wife." *Historical Society of Southern California and Pioneer Register* (Los Angeles), 111–113; Mathes, Valerie Sherer. 1990. *Helen Hunt Jackson and Her Indian Reform Legacy.* Austin: University of Texas Press.

María Raquel Casas

RELIGION

Latinas have traditionally assumed a central role in the maintenance and transference of religious beliefs and practices for their families and their communities. Although many Latinas participate in patriarchal religions that attempt a male monopoly over the sacred, Latinas carry on with their own understandings of the sacred and have often carved autonomous spaces for women within these religions. Other Latinas engage in religions such as Santería, in which women maintain equal leadership status with men (although they are forbidden to achieve the position of *babalawo* or to be deviners), *curanderismo,* in which "el don" or the gift of healing enables women to transcend gender constructions, or indigenous spiritual paths that are traditionally egalitarian. Although many Protestant denominations ordain women as ministers, obstacles remain as they strive for full acceptance as religious leaders. Catholic Latinas remain excluded from ordination, but many serve as volunteer lay ministers or as professional associate pastors.

The legacy of Latinas shaping religion can be traced to women who acted as priestesses, spiritual intermediaries, and healers throughout indigenous pre-Hispanic societies. Christian missionaries demonized native women because their high degree of involvement in spiritual practices threatened the missionaries' own male authority. Native women dominated the private sphere of the home, where missionaries feared to enter. Domestic rituals performed by women kept daily life and the cosmic order in balance, spiritual practices that the friars could not control.

The female legacy continued in colonial Latin America through women religious writers and theologians in Spanish Catholic convents, such as the renowned Sor Juana Inés de la Cruz. *Curanderas* (healers) provided holistic healing outside of institutional power structures, and *rezadoras* (prayer leaders) of rural communities served where male clergy were virtually absent. Independence movements from Spanish rule beginning in the nineteenth century throughout Latin America often meant a rupture in state-church relations that resulted in a decreased visibility of priests and an increased dependence on women's religious authority within familial spaces.

Latina religious authority exercised outside and within institutional structures continued during the various migrations of Latino populations in the nineteenth and twentieth centuries. After the signing of the Treaty of Guadalupe Hidalgo in 1848 the Irish- and

German-dominated U.S. Roman Catholic Church found itself unprepared to minister to its new Spanish-speaking members, Mexican Catholics. In impoverished barrios and rural towns women carried on the traditional role of teaching religious doctrine in the home and conducting familial and communal rituals. The home altar, as a domestic sacred site, increased in importance. Daily recitations of the rosary became a primary way to pass on the mysteries of Catholicism. Devotions to Our Lady of Guadalupe and the multiple manifestations of Mary, the mother of Jesus, ensured the centrality of female divine powers. *Rezadoras* assisted the dying in their final prayers and reconciliation with loved ones. These women also helped grieving families by leading the prayers at the *velorio* (wake) and at the *novenario,* the nine consecutive days of prayer following a death. *Parteras* (midwives) took on not only the responsibility of assisting a laboring woman, but also that of baptizing newborn children because of high infant mortality and the absence of clergy.

Curanderas, women with specialized and exceptional healing powers, such as Teresa Urrea, healed those who were physically and spiritually ill. Urrea's powers reached beyond political and geographic borders when she lived in exile in the United States after being accused by the Mexican government of inciting rebellion among the Mayo people of Sonora, Mexico. Other less famous *curanderas* have played a crucial role in the well-being of barrio residents. The holistic knowledge of *curanderismo* offers Latino communities access to ancient and natural medicinal knowledge.

Religious options widened for Latinos/as through U.S. imperialism in 1898 in Puerto Rico and Cuba. The military and economic power of the United States also represented the power of Protestantism. Anti-Catholic sentiments in the United States flourished at the turn of the twentieth century, and many Latinos converted to Protestant traditions as a way to better their socioeconomic prospects. Others converted out of desire to read the Bible, a practice not encouraged for lay Catholics, and to have greater institutionalized leadership opportunities. Women played a crucial role in a family's decision to convert.

Conversion to Protestant Christianity was not done uncritically. Toward the end of the 1920s the Congreso Evangélico Hispanoamericano del Norte de América Latina came together in protest over the process of Americanization inherent in Protestant missionary work in Latin America. Organized in Havana, Cuba, in 1929, the congress marked a rupture of Latin American Protestantism with imperialist elements. It raised issues about the development of a Latin American identity in the Protestant missionary movement in Mexico, Colombia, Venezuela, Central America, Cuba,

and Puerto Rico. For the first time a congress of this nature was organized and led by Latin American leaders. Among the list of leaders involved in this movement were two women, Lidia Huber and Edith M. Rivera.

Also during the 1920s the theological journal *La Nueva Democracia* was published and distributed throughout Latin America and the Caribbean. Latino Catholic and Protestant intellectuals contributed to this journal in an effort to join the celebrated Chilean poet Gabriela Mistral in the cause to "exile ignorance and misery, despotism and civil corruption, imperialism and international oppression." Among the contributors were women such as Amanda Labarca, Margarita Robles, Esthercita Wellman, and Helena Arizmendi.

As indigenous Latino/a leaders rethought the faith from the perspective of their national identity and interests, they separated the religion from the cultural wardrobe in which it originally had been dressed. All over Latin America both Catholic and Protestant sectors of the church responded to military interventions by the United States. This included the church in the diaspora, composed of individuals who had immigrated to cities in the United States. A fluid leadership among Protestants in the Caribbean, Latin America, and the United States ensured that a politicized ethnic consciousness shaped distinctive Latino Christianities.

New Protestant churches developed in the United States as the population became more Latin American. The leadership of the churches included women in positions such as treasurers, trustees, religious educators, and community workers. As faith communities acquired buildings for worship and conducted significant outreach in their communities, female leadership and labor supported the development of new churches.

It was the understanding of the people in the congregations that in many cases the pastor's wife was also a pastor who served as the right hand of the pastor in his work. An entry in the history of the Hispanic Baptist churches reads: "Mr. Herminio Quiroga's wife Mercedes, once their children were grown, returned to school and obtained a B.S. degree at Hunter College. She was at the time, a devoted helpmate of her husband and a leader of every activity in the church. Second Spanish Church owes a great debt of gratitude to Mercedes Quiroga."

Other women leaders in their own right included Eva Torres Frey, who came from the San Juan Baptist Church in Puerto Rico during the 1930s and devoted herself to the work of the Second Baptist Church in New York City. When the pastor of the church resigned in 1953, she became the president of the board of trustees. For the first time a congregation named a woman to take complete charge of its affairs and keep it very much alive and prospering. As a trustee, she handled the church finances during the construction of a new church building. Torres Frey also served on the board of the Baptist Society and the Southern New York Baptist Women Association. In these positions she represented the interests of the Hispanic community and led the way in bridging the two communities. She steered her congregation in community outreach and provided significant opportunities for collaborative undertakings for her working-class community. Her death on June 23, 1971, left a void among the American Baptist Hispanic Churches.

Mexico also experienced an attraction toward Protestantism when reformers in the nineteenth century modeled new governments on U.S. republican democracy and white settlers brought their Protestant faiths with them into northern Mexico. Pentecostalism blossomed at the Azusa Street revival in Los Angeles, California, in 1906 and attracted many Mexicans and Puerto Ricans as the spiritual fervor spread.

After World War II the massive migration of Puerto Rican Catholics to the United States and the migration of Mexican Americans to cities challenged the Catholic Church to broaden its understanding of Catholicism. Catholic parishes were forced to rely on the expertise of lay Spanish-speaking Latinas to minister to the needs of rapidly growing Latino Catholic communities. As members of volunteer organizations, such as Las Guadalupanas and Ladies of the Sacred Heart, or catechists (lay teachers of religious education), Latinas served their communities despite their subordinate status in the hierarchy of the institutional church. As Ana María Díaz-Stevens points out, these women became indispensable leaders within parish communities. Their duties included visiting the sick in hospitals

and homes, counseling families, gathering clothing and food for the poor, conducting prayer meetings at church and at homes, organizing choirs, and conducting fund-raising activities. Ironically, reliance on the volunteer assistance of women has influenced the practice of Catholicism despite institutional limitations on the authority of women. For example, popular religious practices, such as public dramas of biblical stories, continue to thrive among Latino Catholic communities. Although popular religious rituals involve men and women, women continue to play a primary role in the maintenance of religious traditions. Public processions honoring Mary or patron saints often include a young female portraying the sacred personage accompanied by numerous devotees, both male and female.

The mass exodus of primarily Catholic Cubans to the United States beginning in 1960 challenged the Catholic Church to serve another Spanish-speaking population. An increased religiosity among exiled Cubans resulted in institutional support for a Catholic educational system in southern Florida, staffed by exiled Cuban nuns and priests. The public shrine in Miami dedicated in 1973 to Cuba's patroness, Our Lady of Charity, attracts hundreds of thousands of pilgrims annually, the majority of whom are women of Cuban descent. The Madonna in her various Latina manifestations maintains the significance of the female in Latino Catholic popular religiosity. Sociologist Ana María Díaz-Stevens calls women's dedication to maintaining and molding religious traditions "the matriarchal core" of Latino religious practice.

The rapid growth of Latino populations in the United States continues to challenge Catholic parishes and Protestant congregations, both mainline and non-

Latino family during a Roman Catholic baptism. Courtesy of the Justo A. Martí Photograph Collection. Centro Archives, Centro de Estudios Puertorriqueños, Hunter College, CUNY.

denominational, to minister in culturally relevant ways. Institutional support for leadership that values the contributions of Latinas appears to be the only way to adequately meet ministerial needs.

At the heart of Latina pastoral ministry is agency. To have agency is to see oneself in one's own eyes and to act in ways congruent with who one believes oneself to be in the world rather than to internalize and act out of the narrative constructed by others about oneself. In the church this takes the form of a "call." It is the understanding of the church that the Holy Spirit empowers one for ministry through the distribution of spiritual gifts to be used for carrying out different ministries. Prayer and a process of discernment put one in touch with one's gifts and release them for ministry. This understanding has become revolutionary for women in the Latina Protestant church. A woman will dare to obey what she understands to be the call of the Holy Spirit and go against the authority of others in the church. This has been the way that women have entered the pastoral ministry even when the denominational bodies they belonged to did not affirm their call.

One such woman, Leoncia Rosado Rousseau, or Mamá Léo, was like a mother to those to whom she ministered. Born in Toa Alta, Puerto Rico, in 1912, Mamá Léo responded to a call to become a missionary and evangelist at the age of twenty. She moved to New York City in 1935, where she visited the sick and became involved in the general ministry of the congregation. She also preached on street corners. When her husband was drafted into the army, she officially took on what had been his pastoral duties at the Damascus Christian Church. The empowerment of the Holy Spirit in her life led her to pioneering work with substance abusers, an ecclesial taboo at the time. Her compassion led her to see the potential of people and to believe that the power of God could make the difference in a person's life. She established a grassroots program that provided rehabilitation for gang members, addicts, alcoholics, and ex-convicts. Her program preceded better-known programs such as Teen Challenge or secular-based programs such as Odyssey House. Like most pioneering work, this caused much controversy, but Mamá Léo's strength and resolve to carry out this ministry enabled her to underwrite it with church funds. The program expanded into the five boroughs of the city. Many persons who came through the program later became ministers themselves, and some established similar work in other cities.

Another strong pastoral leader was the Reverend Aimee García Cortese, born in New York in 1929. She grew up in the South Bronx and became a "missionary evangelist" for the Assemblies of God. This position, although reserved for women gifted in ministry, does not identify them as ordained ministers, yet they

Popular representation of the spirit protector of the home used by Afro-Cuban believers of Santería. Photograph by and courtesy of Carlos A. Cruz.

preach and perform difficult outreach work with some of the poorest people in the city. García Cortese eventually became the first female chaplain to serve in the New York State Department of Corrections. She also founded the Crossroads Tabernacle Church in the Bronx. This church provides a variety of programs for youths, support programs for women, men, and families, and a rehabilitation program for substance abusers.

Like these two, other women have become innovative pastors in their communities. Ana María Falcón García is the highest-educated pastor in the Iglesias de Dios Pentecostal. She pastors the largest church of her denomination in Willimantic, Connecticut. Julie Ramírez of the Assemblies of God pastors one of the largest Hispanic churches in Hartford, Connecticut, with a facility that encompasses half a city block. Both of these women were sent to these churches after their male counterparts failed to bring to fruition the work in these congregations. Even with no funds for their work, these women overcame impossibilities and turned around these ministries, converting them into

Religious procession, circa 1930. Courtesy of the Pura Belpré Papers. Centro Archives, Centro de Estudios Puertorriqueños, Hunter College, CUNY.

organizations that have made a tremendous impact in their communities.

Other women have worked outside the support of their denominations because of the institution's unwillingness to recognize their calling or support the vision of their work. One such woman, Esmeralda Collazo, started el Movimiento del Dios Vivo (the Movement of the Living God). Her ministry in Framingham, Massachusetts, involves outreach to children and single mothers, including an after-school program called Mejores Días/Better Days.

Among Catholics numerous Latinas have also contributed enormously to ministry programs despite their lack of ordination. Sister Yolanda Tarango cofounded and directs Visitation House, a residence for homeless and battered women in San Antonio, Texas. Sister Alicia Salcido served for many years as codirector of Mission San Alfonso among impoverished Mexican neighborhoods, where she developed small base communities, a housing and food cooperative, and a medical dispensary. Small base communities offer Christians the space to dialogue and link their social injustices with their religious faith, followed by critical action.

Sister Margarita Castañeda has for many years lived out her commitment "to walk with the people of God whose faith does not depend on the institution" by organizing small base communities in Texas. Rosa Marta Zárate led the San Bernardino Diocese in California in the development of base communities during the 1970s and 1980s. Her work so threatened the hierarchy of the church that she sued the diocese for wrongful termination. Zárate continues to offer pastoral care to immigrant communities in southern California and to indigenous communities in southern Mexico. Sister Sylvia Sedillo of New Mexico directed the Women's

Spiritual Center in Santa Fe, an interfaith and multicultural retreat center where, she says, "women of all paths can explore their spirituality together—outside the confines of traditional religious institutions." Consuelo Covarrubias also coordinated small base communities for the Hispanic Ministry Office in the Diocese of Gary, Indiana, and ministered at Sacred Heart Parish

To commemorate her first communion, Marina Briones poses for a portrait with her beaming *madrina* (godmother). Courtesy of Vicki L. Ruiz.

in Michigan City. All of these women understand themselves as agents of change with a commitment to social justice reflected in how they use the relative degree of power they hold within the Roman Catholic Church. For them, as for Latina Protestants, pastoral ministry inevitably intertwines with social justice issues.

In the last twenty years Latinas have entered the ranks of Protestant denominational leadership. Irma Violeta Cruz served as the director of Hispanic Educational Ministries for the American Baptist Churches. The Reverend Liliana Da Valle presently serves as an area minister for the American Baptist Churches of Massachusetts. The Reverend Minerva Carcaño has risen through the ranks of the United Methodist Church and stands a very good chance of becoming a bishop. In Puerto Rico the Reverend Yamina Apolinaris served until 1998 as the first executive minister of the American Baptist Churches of Puerto Rico. In addition, the Protestant denominational leadership includes the Reverend Felicita La Salle Vega in the Council of Damascus Christian Churches. The first woman to assume leadership since Mamá Léo, La Salle Vega has been vice president and serves as president.

In 2001 the Evangelical Lutheran Church in America elected Margarita Martínez the first Puerto Rican Latina bishop in the Caribbean Synod. The Reverend Blanca Ortiz, a Guatemalan woman who was ordained as a licensed evangelist of the Church of God International, is the first woman to assume the position of district overseer in Queens, New York. Marta Cabrera, a Dominican, was the first woman to become the youth director of the Northeast Territory of the Church of God International.

Catholic Latinas have also risen to leadership positions within the church, although their positions tend to be regional rather than national. The first Latina to achieve national leadership was the late Encarnación Padilla de Armas. Her career included working in the first national Catholic program for the Spanish speaking, training New York diocesan priests in language and culture, challenging the hierarchy on its responsibilities to Puerto Ricans, helping develop the National Secretariat for the Spanish Speaking, and organizing the First National Hispanic Encuentro in 1972. Many other Latinas have accompanied the efforts of Padilla de Armas. Sister María Jesús de Ybarra directs the Office of Hispanic Ministry for the Yakima Diocese in Washington State. Olga Villa Parra directed the Midwest Hispanic Ministry Office during the 1970s with a focus on immigrant rights, farmworkers, and the urban poor. Sister Consuelo Tovar served as national chairperson of the Third Encuentro, a 1985 convening of bishops and laity regarding Hispanic ministry in the U.S. Catholic Church. Sister María Iglesias directs RENEW, a national organization that focuses on revi-

A home altar to the *oricha* Eleguá, the messenger of the gods and controller of the roads of the world. Photograph by and courtesy of Carlos A. Cruz.

talizing parish communities. In 1992 Sister Anita de Luna assumed the presidency of the Leadership Conference of Women Religious, the national organization of Catholic nuns.

Many of the outreach grassroots ministries that women have initiated have become nonprofit organizations. The Reverand Elizabeth Ríos, a certified minister of the Assemblies of God, was chief administrative officer of the Latino Action Pastoral Center in New York City. She spearheaded a program called the Center for Emerging Female Leadership (CEFL). The program seeks to empower women in ministry by training them to create nonprofit organizations. This gives the women freedom to exercise their unique leadership styles without being hindered by the patriarchal structures of their denominations and churches.

The Reverend Olga Torres directs Angels Unaware, the only U.S. Hispanic agency in the state of New York that serves special-needs children. Alexie Torres Fleming developed Youth Ministries for Peace and Justice, a program that supports young people who seek to be involved in their communities around issues of peace and justice for the poor. Brixeida Marquez is the founder of the Free Forever Prison Ministries program in Bridgeport, Connecticut. Because she had been a successful businesswoman, she did not need assistance from the CEFL. Her program reaches out to incarcerated persons in the state of Connecticut. It also includes a facility that provides care for ex-convicts with AIDS. She works with a board and an extensive group of volunteers.

Many Latinas within patriarchal traditions challenge the gender constructions that limit women and carve spaces for themselves in parallel organizations or networks. Las Hermanas, a national organization of Latina Catholic feminists founded in 1971, exemplifies the efforts of Catholic Latinas to transform their church, but also to create spiritual community beyond the confines of the institution. Meeting biennially at national conferences, members create the space to conduct women-centered rituals, express a Latina theology and spirituality, and provide a forum to discuss and strategize about issues affecting their daily lives.

Latina theologians Ada María Isasi-Díaz and Yolanda Tarango have stated that a four-part methodology often informs the structure of these gatherings. The interrelated parts include telling participants' stories, analyzing, strategizing, and liturgizing. Participants engage in a process of self-reflection that gives importance to their experiences, reveals shared experiences, and leads to the recognition that the personal is political and communal. Analysis requires a deeper inquiry beyond the obvious into the forces of oppression in order to make the connections between its different manifestations. Liturgizing enables Latinas to design their own rituals that negate the sense of unworthiness or absence often experienced in patriarchal rituals. Strategizing seeks to find ways to change oppressive situations by transforming a domineering use of power into an enabling and creative use of power.

At the 1989 Las Hermanas national conference in San Antonio, Texas, the issue of power held primary attention. Defining power as enablement, creativity, and the ability to act rather than dominate set the framework for the participants to examine their own concepts of power, how they use their power in their daily lives, and what social forces, including religion, attempt to keep women powerless. Using the women's own experiences as a starting point validated grassroots Latinas who are usually ignored in the institutional church. Recognition of power coming from within the individual, existing between companions in the struggle for liberation, and emerging from the desire to make a difference in one's life gave the women a deep sense of their own personal power. Conference participant Teresa Barajas describes the impact that redefining power had on her life: "I saw in many of us that the word [power] awakened a fear because we have always associated it with oppression, violence and absolute control that many of us have experienced since we were little. We learned that power is something very good in us if we know how to use it. . . . We also saw that we often use our power without even knowing it." Amid the stories of abusive power due to the actions of priests, bosses, fathers, husbands, children, and the government, the women also shared experiences of resistance, struggle, and liberation. Discussing power and the limitations of prescribed gender roles imbued the women with the knowledge that they were not alone in the struggle for self-determination. As one participant remarked, "Together we have the ability to plan and act—therefore WE HAVE POWER."

Solidarity among Latinas, relative autonomy from the institutional church, and a striving for justice in all aspects of life characterize the spirituality of these Latinas. As member Yolanda Tarango states, they understand the struggle for spiritual and social equality to be a struggle Latinas "must embrace and learn to love in order to survive in the present and envision life with dignity in the future." Their understandings provided the seedbed for *mujerista* theology, a feminist Latina theology first articulated by Ada María Isasi-Díaz and Yolanda Tarango in *Hispanic Women: Prophetic Voice in the Church.*

Other Latina theologians emerged in the late 1980s and 1990s. Their writings contribute to the growing body of work that articulates a Latina feminist theological discourse. These theologians include María Pilar Aquino, Jeanette Rodríguez, Daisy Machado, Ana María Pineda, Gloria Loya, Nancy Pineda, Michelle González, Anita de Luna, Loida Martell-Otero, and Joanne Rodríguez. Recent annual gatherings of Latina theologians, sponsored by the Hispanic Theological Initiative under the direction of Zaida Maldonado-Pérez, ensure a safe space to discuss gender politics within the production and praxis of Latino/a theology.

Latinas who decide to struggle for reform within patriarchal religions understand that if religions were to denounce sexism, it would be a significant moment in the process of the liberation of women. Many do not leave patriarchal religions because they have a strong sense of ownership of their tradition. As Tess Browne of las Hermanas states, "If the boys want me to leave, they are going to have to carry me out, because it is not their church!"

Least studied have been Chicanas and Latinas who (re)turn to the spiritual legacy of their indigenous ancestors. Small circles of native-identified women support this evolving consciousness that is nurtured through ancestral spiritual practices such as the *temascal* (sweat lodge), ritual dances, naming ceremonies, puberty rites, and social justice activism. Women such as Patricia Parra, Linda Vallejo, Rita Marmelejo, and Sybil Vanegas maintain the sweat lodge tradition in southern California and facilitate ceremonies for female prisoners. Others such as Yolanda Broyles-González and Patricia Rodríguez are involved in land rights issues and the preservation of sacred sites and burial remains. La Red Xicana Indígena, a network of native-identified Chicanas, organizes "to heal and rebuild our identities as women in resistance of the continued colonization and oppression of our people and Mother Earth." Chicana writers and artists, including Cherríe Moraga, Gloria Anzaldúa, Naomi Quiñonez, Santa Barraza, Yreina Cervantez, and Celia Rodríguez are in the forefront of expressing through word and image a Xicana/Indígena spirituality.

Santería priestesses communing with divinities, *cu-*

randeras healing the sick, Catholic nuns challenging racism and sexism, Latinas doing theology, laywomen teaching religious doctrine, temple keepers cleaning and beautifying sanctuaries, Protestant ministers preaching and organizing, urban sweat lodge keepers, sun dancers, and ritual planners all replicate the great diversity of Latina religiosity. The commitment of Latinas to shaping their religious traditions reflects their vitality and determination to supplant patriarchal interpretations of the sacred.

See also Pentecostal Church; Popular Religiosity

SOURCES: Anzaldúa, Gloria. 1987. *Borderlands/La frontera: The New Mestiza.* San Francisco: Spinsters/Aunt Lute; Aquino, María Pilar, Daisy Machado, and Jeanette Rodríguez, eds. 2002. *A Reader in Latina Feminist Theology.* Austin: University of Texas Press; Conde-Frazier, Elizabeth. 1997. "Hispanic Protestant Spirituality." In *Teología en conjunto: A Collaborative Hispanic Protestant Theology,* ed. José David Rodríguez and Loida I. Martell-Otero. Louisville: Westminster John Knox Press; Díaz-Stevens, Ana María. 1994. "Latinas in the Church." In *Hispanic Catholic Culture in the U.S.: Issues and Concerns,* ed. Jay P. Dolan and Allan Figueroa Deck. Notre Dame, IN: University of Notre Dame Press; González, Baez Camargo. 1930. *Hacia la revolución religiosa en Hispanoamérica.* Mexico: Casa Unida de Publicaciones; Isasi-Díaz, Ada María, and Yolanda Tarango. 1988. *Hispanic Women: Prophetic Voice in the Church: Toward a Hispanic Women's Liberation Theology.* San Francisco: Harper and Row; Medina, Lara. 1998. "Los espírtus siguen hablando: Chicana Spiritualities." In *Living Chicana Theory,* ed. Carla Trujillo. Berkeley, CA: Third World Press; Sánchez Korrol, Virginia. 1988. "In Search of Unconventional Women: Histories of Puerto Rican Women in Religious Vocation before Mid-century." *Oral History Review* 16, no. 2 (Fall): 47–63; Silva Gotay, Samuel. 1997. *Protestantismo y política en Puerto Rico, 1898–1930.* San Juan, Puerto Rico: Editorial de la Universidad de Puerto Rico; Soto Fontanez, Santiago. 1982. *Misión a la puerta/Mission at the Door.* Santo Domingo, Dominican Republic: Editora Educativa Dominicana.

Lara Medina and Elizabeth Conde-Frazier

REYES, GUADALUPE (1918–2000)

Born in the farmlands of Oklahoma in 1918, Guadalupe Alcalá was the oldest of four daughters in a family of migrant farm laborers. At the age of three Lupe lost her mother and, along with her father, became the primary caregiver for her younger sisters. When she was twenty, her family left the fields of Oklahoma in search of greater opportunities in Chicago. Two years later Lupe met and married Andrés Reyes, a steelworker in one of the city's mills. Together Lupe and Andrés had eleven children. The couple began raising their family in the South Side community of Hyde Park until urban renewal forced them to move fifteen years later.

The family settled in the Pilsen community, a growing Mexican immigrant port-of-entry neighborhood.

Reyes became one of the earliest and most noted Latina activists in Chicago. Her activism began in 1951 when she received the devastating news that her son, Bobby, only nine months old, had contracted spinal meningitis. Her son became severely disabled, and doctors told Reyes that he would never walk or talk. Determined to help her son, however, Reyes developed her own physical therapy for him at home and taught him how to walk and talk. Her struggle with a disabled child became more difficult when she searched for educational services in her community. After years of searching for a school for her son, she decided to start her own school. She placed a small advertisement in the local newspaper and soon had a group of parents with disabled children meeting in a church basement. Together with these parents Reyes organized and founded the Esperanza School to serve children with disabilities in 1969.

When her son reached adulthood and could no longer attend Esperanza, Reyes focused on services for adults with disabilities. Knocking door-to-door in search of other families who could benefit from services for the disabled, she founded El Valor Corporation in 1973, an agency that provides employment and life-skills training for adults with disabilities. Reyes did not limit her activism, however, to her son's disability. During this time she became involved in the Mexican community of Pilsen, in particular through the Pilsen Neighbors Community Council. She helped lead the fight for a new high school in the community and was instrumental in establishing the Fiesta del Sol community festival in 1972 to commemorate the new school, Benito Juárez High School. She helped with various other community campaigns, including bringing a library and field house to the neighborhood, establishing a Latina/o senior citizens' group, and advocating for health care for the elderly in local community clinics.

Reyes maintained her tenacity for community work even during the most difficult times of her life. She cared for her ailing father until he died in 1968. Reyes then lost her husband to cancer in 1970. Her disabled son, Bobby, for whom she had advocated over the years, passed away in 1983. Yet her commitment to community activism did not waver. Fifteen years after her son's death she explained, "Bobby was my inspiration. But just because he has passed on doesn't mean that other people don't need help."

In 1991, while still active with El Valor and various other community projects, Reyes accepted an appointment to the Chicago Transit Authority board, where she served until she passed away. She advocated repairing public transit services for low-income African American and Latina/o neighborhoods and supported the expansion of El Valor's facilities to include services for families and children such as Head Start and parenting programs. Thirty years later the agency has grown into a community organization that serves 1,500 families a day and has several sites throughout the city.

Guadalupe Reyes was an extraordinary woman remembered fondly in Chicago's Mexican community as a persistent and dedicated activist. She instilled a commitment to activism in her children, many of whom continue to be involved in Pilsen's community organizations.

SOURCES: Johnson, Geoffrey. 1997. "Guadalupe Reyes: Founder, Esperanza and El Valor." *Chicago* (January): 45, 47; Reyes, Jaime J. 2001. "Guadalupe Reyes: Una vida al servicio de la comunidad." *La Raza News,* January 14–20, 6.

Lilia Fernández

RICO, ANGELINA MORENO (1898–1984)

Born in Mexico City, Mexico, Angelina Moreno Rico formed part of the first wave of Mexican migration to the Midwest. The Mexican Revolution of 1910 left many Mexicans landless, and jobs were scarce. At the same time, propelled by a labor shortage during World War I and debilitating union strikes, U.S. industrial companies sent contractors to recruit Mexican workers. Between 1916 and 1926 Mexican laborers flooded into midwestern railroads, stockyards, and steel mills. Angelina Rico's husband, José T. Rico, left Mexico City in 1926. Three months later his wife and sons George, Angelo, and Manuel joined him in Chicago.

The Mexican presence in Illinois grew in three identifiable enclaves: South Chicago, Back of the Yards, and the Near West Side. Adjustment, however, was not easy. Immigrants faced employment exploitation, substandard housing, poor health, discrimination, and hostility from established European immigrants who resented incorporating Mexican newcomers into the workforce. Often used as strikebreakers, rather than achieving prosperity, Mexican workers found themselves in economic limbo.

The Ricos settled in the Near West Side, where José Rico worked primarily as a mechanic. Within their first year they lost their youngest son, Manuel, to rheumatic fever. In 1929 they welcomed another son, also named Manuel, and two years later a daughter, Elena. With two years of university studies behind her, Angelina, together with José, enrolled in night classes at Crane High School. Besides learning English, they completed elementary, high-school, and several college courses. Despite poverty and other hardships, Angelina Rico made sure that all the children attained a strong musical foundation, including violin, piano, and voice.

After the onset of the depression, the U.S. government implemented repatriation policies and deported thousands of Mexicans, both undocumented residents and legal citizens. These actions fueled disparaging stereotypes and fostered fear and shame. As the Ricos became more involved in the community, Angelina noticed that many Mexican youths were passing as Italians and refused to learn Spanish. Under Angelina's leadership the Ricos began singing Christmas *posadas* and other traditional Mexican songs as a way of promoting Mexican culture. Additionally, performances were accompanied by a display of Angelina's Mexican artifacts. The family sang in various Chicago churches during the Christmas season, as well as at Firman House, a Presbyterian-affiliated settlement house on the Near West Side.

During the 1940s the Ricos sought other venues to improve sociocultural conditions. They joined the Mexican Civic Committee, which dealt with issues such as high infant mortality, lack of educational opportunities, rising delinquency, poor housing, and substandard health conditions. José joined the board of directors of the Mexican Civic Committee and took charge of the city's first Mexican Boy Scout troop in 1944, and Angelina served as president of the Mothers' Club.

Still, the family remained committed to presenting folkloric Mexican music and dance to Chicago audiences. In 1946 the Ricos began to perform in the Museum of Science and Industry's Christmas around the World program, which showcased songs from ethnic Chicago's native Christmas celebrations. The Ricos presented a three-part rendition of the *posadas.* The first featured Mary and Joseph's *peregrinación* (pilgrimage) through Bethlehem, ending with the couple's lodging in a stable. The second began after the birth of Jesus and featured hymns dedicated to the newborn Messiah. The third was "La Fiesta," a celebration complete with the breaking of a piñata and Mexican folkloric dances like *el jarabe tapatio* and *la bamba.* The Ricos created the show from the ground up. Without proper sheet music, Angelina sang and her eldest son George wrote the accompanying music. Angelina, a professional seamstress, and other women made all the clothing and accessories, detailing them according to the songs' regional/folkloric characteristics. The Ricos' performances quickly became a favorite; they soon gave five hour-long performances in one day. These activities continued for twenty-five years.

With Angelina's encouragement, George Rico created the Chicago Fiesta Guild, a Mexican folkloric dance group, in 1949. It involved the entire Rico family and Mexican youths from the Chicago area. Its members not only took pride in the wealth of their heritage, but were encouraged to learn Spanish. By the 1950s those who had survived the depression and repatriation were already more adapted to an American lifestyle. The Chicago Fiesta Guild provided a way to

Musician and folklorist Angelina Moreno Rico and her family. Courtesy of Elena Rico.

maintain ties to Mexican culture. Angelina valued their performances for their educational components. She thought it important to challenge prevailing stereotypes and show the "gringos" that "Mexicans did more than sleep under the sombrero." For more than twenty years the Chicago Fiesta Guild performed year-round and regularly participated in pan-American parades, civic celebrations, Mexican Independence Day, settlement houses, including Hull-House, and local events.

Despite various illnesses and nineteen operations, Angelina's energy did not wane. She extended her love of music to everyone around her and through personal sacrifice and dedication taught Mexicans to be committed to their community. Her children became involved professionally in music: Elena became a soprano with the Chicago Symphony Chorus, and George established several symphonic orchestras and organizes an annual performance of Handel's *Messiah*. A teacher since 1949, he has helped develop performers renowned throughout the world. After a lifetime of promoting Mexican values and culture, Angelina Moreno Rico died on June 23, 1984, at the age of eighty-five.

SOURCES: Espinoza, Martha. 2001. "Rico, Angelina Moreno." In *Women Building Chicago, 1790–1990: A Biographical Dictionary*, ed. Rima Lunin Schultz and Adele Hast. Bloomington: Indiana University Press; Rico, Angelina Moreno. Oral history interviews with Martha Espinoza. Hull-House Papers, Special Collections, University Library, University of Illinois at Chicago.

Martha Espinoza

RINCÓN DE GAUTIER, FELISA (1897–1994)

Felisa Rincón, or "Doña Fela," as she was affectionately known throughout most of her political career, was born in the northeastern Puerto Rican town of Ceiba in 1897. Her parents were an attorney, Enrique Rincón Plumey, and a schoolteacher, Rita Marrero. The family moved to San Juan when she was ten. When she was eleven, her mother died, which forced Rincón, the eldest, to abandon her studies to take care of her seven siblings. She was later sent to live with relatives in the town of San Lorenzo. At an early age Rincón became a prolific and accomplished seamstress. Her tailoring and fashion skills later played a role in her life in New York City and in San Juan.

In the 1930s she migrated to New York to improve her financial situation. She returned to San Juan a few years later and opened a clothing store there called Felisa Style Shop. In 1940 she married Jenaro A. Gautier, a well-connected lawyer who, at the time, worked in the Attorney General's Office.

Rincón came from a family with deep political roots. She was active, as a member of the Liberal Party, in the campaign that gave women the right to vote in 1932. During these years she met Luis Muñoz Marín and supported his political ambitions. Rincón was among the founding members of the Popular Democratic Party when Muñoz and others abandoned the Liberal Party. In 1940 she was appointed by party leader Muñoz to be the president of the San Juan Committee of the Popular Democratic Party, a position she held until 1970. In 1946 she was selected to replace Roberto Sánchez Vilella as mayor of San Juan. Sánchez had won in 1944 but had resigned to take another position within the party. Rincón had been nominated for mayor earlier, in 1944, but she declined when faced with opposition from both her husband and her father. Rincón served continuously as mayor from 1946 until 1968, when she retired from public office. During her tenure the city grew from about 180,000 to 500,000 residents.

Rincón was a very popular mayor. She called her political philosophy "benevolent maternalism" and focused on populist issues such as street cleaning, hy-

Former mayor of San Juan, Felisa Rincón de Gautier, at left, supports Mario Procaccino for mayor of New York City. Courtesy of the Justo A. Martí Photograph Collection. Centro Archives, Centro de Estudios Puertorriqueños, Hunter College, CUNY.

giene, restoring the historic section of San Juan, and expanding services to children and to the poor. In Puerto Rico's political folklore Rincón will always be remembered as the mayor who in 1955 had cargo planes carry ice from the United States for thousands of spectators gathered in a city park waiting for Rincón to keep her promise to bring "snow" to the children of San Juan. She also practiced a politics of "open access," stressing the need for direct contact between San Juan residents and herself. Every Wednesday Rincón held extensive "open-house" hours in city hall to receive people who wanted to convey their concerns and problems directly to the mayor. Rincón was a relentless ally of Governor Muñoz and a devout defender of commonwealth status. She was also extremely active in mainland Democratic Party politics, participating in nominating conventions and in numerous committees pertaining to urban affairs. Since her days as mayor she had been a delegate to Democratic Party nominating conventions. In 1992, the last convention she attended at age ninety-five, she achieved the distinction of being the oldest delegate at the convention. Rincón died in San Juan in 1994.

See also Politics, Electoral

SOURCES: García-Ramis, Magali. 1995. *Dona Felisa Rincón de Gautier: Mayor of San Juan.* Morristown, NJ: Modern Curriculum Press; Gerber, Irving. 1979. *Felisa Rincón: Woman of the Americas.* New York: Book Lab; Gruber, Ruth. 1972. *Felisa Rincón de Gautier, the Mayor of San Juan.* New York: Thomas Y. Crowell; Walzer, Robert P. 1994. "Doña Felisa Rincón Dies at Age 97." *San Juan Star,* September 17, 10.

Félix V. Matos Rodríguez

RIVERA, AURELIA "YEYA" (1909–)

Aurelia Rivera, born on August 26, 1909, in Cayey, Puerto Rico, and raised in Caguas, migrated to New York City in 1941. Known as "Yeya" to her friends and family, she is one of the many unheralded matriarchs of the pioneer, pre–World War II wave of Puerto Rican migration to New York City. Tenacious, natural leaders, these women frequently provided a broad range of options and accommodations for relatives who migrated after them. Along with others of her generation, she exemplifies the toughness of the pioneer Puerto Rican migrants.

Despite her personal hardships and the poverty of her homeland, Yeya Rivera refused to accept the limitations imposed by her environment, whether in Puerto Rico or in New York City. At the age of six, when her mother died, Rivera and her two sisters were separated, and each of the siblings thereafter received a different religious upbringing. The eldest lived with Baptists, the youngest was raised Catholic, and Yeya Rivera went to live with her father, who ran a Spiritist *centro.* Rivera overcame the effects of poor living conditions, coupled with malnutrition that had increased the incidence and mortality of a deadly tuberculosis epidemic that took her sister and several of her in-laws.

Rivera married as a teenager and had two sons, the youngest of whom was raised by her remaining sister, Mary, and her husband, a childless but financially stable couple. After Yeya Rivera's husband left the family in the late 1920s, she worked in a tobacco factory

Aurelia Rivera, aunt of former Congressman Hermán Badillo, at her second marriage. Courtesy of David A. Badillo.

curing leaf tobacco. She was one of some 2,500 female and 1,000 male tobacco workers in Caguas who earned an average per capita wage of $183 in the winter of 1928–1929. Fortunately for Rivera, she had completed three years of high school, surpassing most of her contemporaries. She learned to speak a little English, which helped her land a job with the Puerto Rican Emergency Relief Agency ("la PRERA"), a territorial New Deal government agency, where she worked in the countryside distributing goods to impoverished families.

The next phase of her life began at the age of thirty-one. Without a husband and with two young boys to feed, her son José Luis and her nephew Hermán, Badillo whom she had raised since his parents died of tuberculosis, Rivera embarked for New York City and settled in El Barrio (Spanish Harlem). As a migrant she became adept at family fund-raising and cementing family networks. She liked El Barrio for its familiar sights and sounds. She soon discovered the vast open market under the train tracks on Park Avenue, spanning several blocks around 116th Street, "where were Cubans, Dominicans, *de todo*." Due to unforeseen economic hardships and complicated family jealousies, Rivera felt pressured to place her nephew, Hermán, in the care of relatives in southern California for a few years. When circumstances improved for her in New York City, she again cared for him.

Drawing on the political savvy she had gained in Puerto Rico as an activist for the Unionist Party, as well as her gregariousness and neighborhood contacts, she met many of the Puerto Rican political figures in El Barrio. It was Rivera who introduced Hermán Badillo to a local Democratic club leader and jewelry store owner, Tony Méndez, who helped launch his political career in East Harlem. A graduate of City College and Brooklyn Law School, Rivera's nephew rose to serve four terms in the Congress of the United States, the first Puerto Rican to do so. His impressive career also included the Bronx Borough presidency and chairmanship of the Board of Trustees of the City University of New York.

In the late 1950s Rivera remarried and moved to southern California, where she lived for another fifteen years. After returning briefly to Puerto Rico she relocated to central Florida, a place that reminded her of southern California. In her later years she returned to New York and spent several years at a senior center in the Melrose section of the Bronx.

Rivera's legacy was not merely that of a catalyst for inexorable developments; she clearly played a vital role in her family's survival, taking decisive steps at crucial junctures. Despite omnipresent poverty, she retained aspirations for advancement and mobility for herself and for her family: "I always believed in progressing, getting ahead, going forward" ("yo me movía"). In her nineties she retains the tenacity and resourcefulness that made her a family matriarch, an important legacy that involved raising a son and her sister's son and building a successful life in the United States. Her famous nephew summed up her role, and that of other matriarchs of the migration, pragmatically and concisely: "She had to scrap, she always worked, and she took care of us."

SOURCES: Badillo, David A. 2005. "Titi Yeya's Memories: A Matriarch of the Puerto Rican Migration." In *Race and Ethnicity in New York City*, ed. J. Krase and Ray Hutchinson. Wisconsin: University of Wisconsin Press; Chenault, Lawrence R. 1938. *The Puerto Rican Migrant in New York City.* New York: Columbia University Press; Sánchez Korrol, Virginia. 1994. *From Colonia to Community: The History of Puerto Ricans in New York City.* 2nd ed. Berkeley: University of California Press.

David Badillo

RIVERA, CHITA (1933–   )

Dolores Conchita Figueroa del Rivero better known as the actress, singer, and dancer Chita Rivera, was born on January 23, 1933 in Washington, D.C., the third child of Pedro Julio Figueroa and Katherine del Rivero. From childhood Rivera loved to perform and was fortunate to be enrolled in singing, piano, and ballet lessons. Her brother organized shows in the basement of their home, and Rivera was the major performer. She was encouraged to pursue a career as a dancer because of her talent in this area. At the age of seventeen Rivera auditioned for a scholarship to George Balanchine's

School of American Ballet in New York City and was accepted.

Rivera had just completed her high-school education at Taft High School in the Bronx when she accompanied a friend to Manhattan for an audition for a road company of the Broadway musical *Call Me Madam* and won the role herself. Within a year she was back in New York as a featured dancer in *Guys and Dolls*. Within six years Rivera had played roles in *Can-Can*, *The Imogene Coca Show* on national television, the Off-Broadway *Shoestring Review*, and *Seventh Heaven* on Broadway and a major role in *Mr. Wonderful*. In addition to critically acclaimed theatrical exposure, numerous appearances on popular network television shows positioned Rivera for what became the first truly major role in her career—that of Anita in *West Side Story*.

The musical ran for 732 performances, and the role of Anita on stage became synonymous with Chita Rivera. She was nominated for her first Tony but did not win the award. During this time Rivera married Anthony Mordente, a dancer in the show. After the birth of their daughter, Lisa Angela Mordente, who became an actress herself, the couple resumed their parts in the London production of the show.

In 1959 a second big hit featured Rivera in a costarring role, that of Rosie Grant in *Bye Bye Birdie* with Dick Van Dyke. She received a second Tony nomination for *Birdie* and a third nomination for her next role as Anyanka the gypsy princess in *Bajour*. Not one to rest on her accomplishments, Rivera developed a cabaret act with the collaboration of lyricist Fred Ebb and composer John Kander that she took on the road throughout the United States and Canada. But within a short time her first love, the stage, beckoned her back to Broadway in the late 1960s, where she performed in *The Threepenny Opera, Flower Drum Song,* and *Sweet Charity*. On tour once again in the early 1970s, Rivera's performances included *Jacques Brel Is Alive and Well and Living in Paris, Born Yesterday, The Rose Tattoo,* and *Kiss Me Kate*. By now Rivera had developed into a superb actress who could portray either serious or comedic roles, as well as sing or dance. In 1975 Rivera opened as Velma Kelly in the extraordinary Broadway production of *Chicago*. She received a fourth Tony nomination, but the award was not forthcoming. This happened again with the poorly received sequel to *Bye Bye Birdie, Bring Back Birdie,* but with the musical *The Rink*, created especially for Rivera by Ebb and Kander, her riveting performance was finally recognized by the judges, and she garnered the Tony as outstanding actress in a musical.

Accolades and awards surround Rivera in recognition of her great contributions and accomplishments on the American stage. Few other actresses are gifted with the talent to perform so well in so many venues.

After her induction into the Television Academy Hall of Fame, Rivera suffered severe injuries in a car accident that required her to overcome compound fractures at the age of fifty-three. By 1992, however, Rivera was back on Broadway in the smash hit *Kiss of the Spider Woman*. Almost sixty, Rivera played a series of sensual, beautiful, and complex characters from movie musicals that required her to act, sing, dance, and emote. This role garnered Rivera a second Tony.

Now in her seventies, at an age when one contemplates retirement or perhaps slowing down the responsibilities of daily life, Rivera continues to make history. She was honored by the Kennedy Center in 2002. The effervescent and versatile Rivera has also conquered Broadway once more. In 2003 she appeared opposite Antonio Banderas and a bevy of younger female performers in the award-winning musical revival of *Nine*, acting, singing, and dancing as the definitive queen of the stage that she is.

See also West Side Story

SOURCES: Maldonado, Adál Alberto. 1989. "Chita Rivera." In *Portraits of the Puerto Rican Experience*, ed. Luis Reyes Rivera and Julia Rodríguez. New York: IPRUS Institute; Joseph C. and L. Mpho Mabunda, eds. 1996. *Dictionary of Hispanic Biography*. New York: Gale Research.

Virginia Sánchez Korrol

RIVERA, GRACIELA (1921–)

A spirited description appears in a published profile of Graciela Rivera's debut in the role of Lucia in *Lucia di Lammermoor* at the Metropolitan Opera House in 1952. "The audience of opera buffs swelled with those unexpected fans who had come to hear the first Puerto Rican ever to sing at the Met. Cries of, '*Que viva Puerto Rico libre,*' punctuated the applause of seven curtain calls elicited by Rivera's unprecedented performance." Rivera's recollection of the event: "It was unbelievable."

Rivera, who was not all that interested in opera when she was young, was born on April 17, 1921, in the southern coastal city of Ponce, Puerto Rico, and raised in Santurce, a short distance from the capital, San Juan. Rivera concedes that her high-school music teacher almost forced her to attend a performance of *The Pirates of Penzance*. She had expected to become an English teacher, a professional choice in keeping with her fondness for English-language songs, but exposure to *Pirates* completely changed her life. From that point on Rivera became immersed in music, joined the chorus, and appeared in numerous operatic performances at Central High School. After graduation Rivera toured the island performing in concert. A chance meeting with a young sailor, Joseph Zumcheck,

Opera singer Graciela Rivera. Courtesy of the Justo A. Martí Photograph Collection. Centro Archives, Centro de Estudios Puertorriqueños, Hunter College, CUNY.

was fortuitous for several reasons. An avid fan of Rivera's, he helped raise funds to pay for her admission to New York's prestigious Juilliard School of Music and eventually became her husband and manager. In addition to voice, Rivera studied harmony, music theory, piano, counterpoint, and composition. She graduated from Juilliard in 1943.

Two years later Rivera launched her musical career by interpreting the role of Adele in *Rosalinda,* a Broadway version of Johann Strauss's *Die Fledermaus.* She reprised her role in several of the opera houses in France and Germany, but Rivera's operatic debut actually took place in the late 1940s when she sang the role of Rosina in Rossini's *The Barber of Seville* at the New Orleans Opera. Rivera's distinguished career as a coloratura soprano soared with critically acclaimed performances throughout the United States and abroad. She sang at the New York City Opera and the San Carlo Opera and with the Havana Philharmonic. In 1952 Rivera opened as Lucia in her historic debut at the prestigious New York Metropolitan Opera, realizing the dream of an operatic career at the age of thirty-one.

The press hailed Rivera, comparing the enormously accomplished soprano to the legendary Lily Pons. Considered among the best on the American stage, Rivera solidified a stellar reputation by giving concerts at Avery Fisher Hall, Alice Tully Hall, Madison Square Garden, and Radio City Music Hall. The weekly WHOM radio program *Graciela Rivera Sings,* a semiclassical and popular music offering, was on the air for five consecutive years. In addition, Rivera appeared on national television, NBC, CBS, and WOR. During a fifty-year career in classical music and performance Rivera has interacted with great conductors and singers: Oliviero de Fabritiis, Francesco Molinari Pradelli, Antal Dorati, Robert Merrill, Giuseppe di Stefano, and Giacomo Lauri-Volpi.

By 1972 Rivera's personal and family life limited extensive traveling, and she accepted an assistant professorship in music at the City University of New York. Through specialized courses on the history of Puerto Rican music, the Puerto Rican chorus, and music theory, Rivera introduced new generations to Boricua heritage and the classics. She became artistic director and president of the Puerto Rico Opera Company of Hostos College and premiered *Nela.* Composed by Manuel B. González, *Nela* is based on the novel *Marianela* by Benito Pérez Galdós and is the first Puerto Rican opera ever presented in the United States. Rivera's accomplishments have been recognized by countless organizations, universities, and professional music associations throughout the years with awards, citations, proclamations, and other testimonials to her contributions and advancement of classical music and performance. Catholic University in Ponce in 1993 and Lehman College in New York City in 1996 honored her with honorary doctorates.

SOURCES: Maldonado, Adál Alberto. 1989. "Graciela Rivera." In *Portraits of the Puerto Rican Experience,* ed. Luis Reyes Rivera and Julia Rodríguez. New York: IPRUS Institute; Fundación Nacional para la Cultural Popular, San Juan, Puerto Rico. Toro, Clarissa Santiago. 2004. "Graciela Rivera." www.prpop.org/biografias/g_bios/graciela_rivera.shtml (accessed July 23, 2005).

Virginia Sánchez Korrol

RIVERA, ROXANA (1977–2003)

Roxana Rivera was born in Monterey Park, California, in 1977 to Mexican immigrants Victor Manuel Rivera, a U.S. Postal Service worker, and María Eugenia Baeza, a Los Angeles County Clerk's Office employee. The oldest of three offspring, she grew up in Lynwood, an area near South Central Los Angeles, with her sisters, Brenda Rivera Lázaro and Ruby Rivera. Roxana Rivera demonstrated an inclination for writing during her early school years when a story she authored about her family won first place in a local writing competition.

Her interest in writing continued throughout her childhood, and she emerged as a star pupil. However, when she reached adolescence, Rivera's dedication to writing began to wane. As her writing faltered, her academic standing also suffered. Her desire to communicate persisted, but it was manifested through graffiti spray cans that her mother discovered lodged under Rivera's bed. Concerned over her daughter's questionable activities, Rivera's mother persuaded her brother-in-law, Daniel Villarreal, to talk to the girl. A well-known local screenwriter and actor who appeared in the films *Stand and Deliver* (1988) and *American Me* (1992), Villarreal appealed to Rivera's creative energies and handed her several books for inspiration. One was Sandra Cisneros's *The House on Mango Street* (1984). As Rivera later recalled, this event was a turning point because it introduced her to Chicana writers who shared her experiences and had found constructive ways of expressing themselves.

Rivera graduated from Downey High School in 1995 and immediately enrolled at Long Beach City College. In 1999 she transferred to California State University, Long Beach (CSULB), and three years later earned a baccalaureate degree in women's studies and English, with an emphasis in creative writing. During those years Rivera regularly appeared on the list of high achievers and became committed to various cultural and feminist causes. On campus she used her writing skills as a venue to address political issues. She helped organize Movimiento Estudiantil de Teatro y Arte (META), a student theater group whose performances included an act that Rivera cowrote in support of the California Faculty Association's efforts to challenge unfair labor practices for lecturers. An active volunteer at the Women's Resource Center, Rivera cofounded Sirens between the Lines, a poetry-reading series that featured the writing of women of color.

Rivera's endeavors were infused with social activism. In 2001 and 2002 she tutored English classes at David Starr Jordan and Woodrow Wilson high schools in the Long Beach area under the Pre-collegiate Academic Development Program and developed lesson plans that included Chicana/o and Latina/o culture

Poet and student activist Roxana Rivera is on the right. Courtesy of Thanya Mercado.

and literature. In April 2002 Rivera and three other students completed a yearlong independent study project on the role of media in shaping identity in young women of color. Their findings were presented at the National Association of Ethnic Studies (NAES) in Vancouver, British Columbia.

The feminist themes that Rivera pursued in the classroom also made their way into her writing. As her work developed, her poetry increasingly explored women's experiences and issues such as the spiritual connections between women and their families, and female friendships. She began to write what she referred to as her "dirty girl" poems, works that possessed a sensual lyricism and addressed bold, intimate topics. In 2003 she was awarded a Long Beach Festival of Authors Literary Women's Scholarship.

After graduation Rivera worked closely with award-winning novelist and poet Rigoberto González, who provided professional and critical guidance. She enrolled in the master of fine arts program for creative writing at Southern Illinois University in Carbondale (SIUC). Attracted by the program's reputation, its *Crab Orchard Literary Magazine,* and a fellow poet mentor, Allison Joseph, Rivera held a PROMPT (Proactive Recruitment of Multicultural Professors and Teachers), fellowship and taught English. She continued community outreach in university-sponsored projects and participated in poetry readings. Rivera was scheduled to read her work at the Association of Writers and Writing Programs (AWP) conference in Chicago in March 2004. Sadly, in the prime of her youth, Roxana Rivera was killed in a car crash on November 21, 2003. In recognition of her feminist contributions and creative talent, the Department of Women's Studies at SIUC created the Roxana Rivera Memorial Poetry Contest. Various commemorative projects in process will honor Rivera's passion for writing and addressing women's issues.

SOURCES: Peach, Brian. 2003. "Rivera SIUC Graduate Student Killed in Car Crash." *Southern Illinoisian* (Carbondale, Illinois), November 22; Rios, Jennifer. 2003. "Third Annual Poetry Night Takes Place as Part of Hispanic Heritage Month." *Daily Egyptian* (Southern Illinois University student newspaper), September 25; Youngman, Rochelle. 2003. "Gifted Writer, Former Student Remembered." *49er* (California State University, Long Beach student paper), December 15.

Maythee Rojas

RIVERA MARTÍNEZ, DOMITILA (1898–1979)

Domitila Rivera was born in Chimalhuacán, Mexico, to Bernardino and Jesusita Villanueva Rivera. In 1906 Jesusita converted to the Church of Jesus Christ of Latter-Day Saints (LDS) and encouraged her daughters to investigate the precepts of this faith. One of the primary assertions of Mormon devotion is that Mormons are duty-bound to return to the service of God the descendants of people known as "Lamanites." In the modern world their successors are the mestizos of the Americas. Until these progeny are converted, the millennial kingdom will not begin. Thus Mexicanos have a key role to play in bringing people to eternal salvation. For the rest of her life Domitila Rivera served as a missionary, church officer, and religious leader who worked tirelessly to spread her faith among Spanish-speaking people.

Although she was warned that friends and neighbors would ostracize individuals who left the Catholic Church, Domitila Rivera and her sisters Agustina and Dolores converted. The fear of being snubbed and ridiculed was not their only concern. The family was also in constant fear of reprisals from both Mexican national troops and Zapatistas. Amid the chaos Bernardino struggled to raise the amount necessary to send his daughters to safety. Through great sacrifice they raised the necessary funds, and the sisters reached Salt Lake City by 1919. Shortly thereafter a church official approached the Riveras and asked if they would be willing to work as missionaries to *su gente* (their people), many of whom were working for the Utah-Idaho Sugar Company (UISC) in the town of Garland.

During the 1910s Utah's sugar-beet industry grew dramatically, and because of the economic expansion of World War I local labor was in short supply. The UISC recruited about 2,000 workers, mostly Mexicanos, to work in its fields. Between 1919 and 1921 Domitila and her sisters traveled to Garland to spread their faith among *betabeleros* (beet pickers). By early 1921 such efforts had borne fruit, and about 100 persons were attending Spanish-language services in Salt Lake City. The LDS Church officially recognized the group, naming it the Local Mexican Mission. In 1923 church leaders renamed the mission the Rama Mexicana. This entity served a myriad of functions for Mexican Mormons in Salt Lake City's west side. It was a spiritual home, a gathering place, and a haven for social activities and networking. The Rivera sisters all met their future husbands at Rama events. Domitila met her husband, Castulo Delgado Martínez, and the couple married on October 3, 1923. They had six children, five of whom lived to adulthood. He died in Salt Lake City in April 1972.

Within the Rama, Domitila, Agustina, and Dolores held leadership positions in entities such as the Sociedad de Socorro (Relief Society). This association helped sick or injured members, raised money for the needy, and quilted blankets and other goods for distribution to the poor. During the Great Depression the Rama's Relief Society provided assistance to the indigent and destitute. Among the Mexican Mormons ethnic ties caused most to overlook denominational differences. As Domitila's niece, Ruth Torres, stated in a 1996 interview, "We saw good (and need) in all of our people, both Catholics and Mormons."

Between 1923 and 1961 the Rivera sisters were presidents of the Sociedad de Socorro for a total of seventeen years. Domitila directed the organization from August 1942 through July 1943. Each of the sisters also served the group as counselor, teacher, and secretary. In addition to working for the Sociedad, Domitila and her siblings increased awareness and appreciation of Mexican culture and folklore among Mormons. From 1925 through the late 1950s the sisters, often with children and spouses in tow, visited congregations throughout the West and helding "Mexican-style" dinners, stage plays, and traditional dances. These events helped the Rama raise money for a permanent building and increased awareness of the need to convert the descendants of the Lamanites. In sum, the families of the three Rivera sisters formed the core of the Rama between the 1920s and 1960. Domitila, Agustina, and Dolores's husbands, children, nieces, and nephews sustained the Rama and worked tirelessly to expand the LDS Church's ministry among the growing number of Spanish-speaking people in Utah. She died in 1979.

Several authors have written about the role of *mujeres Católicas*, but not much attention has been paid to the activities of women in other churches. The story of Domitila Rivera and her sisters shows that Latinas of other denominations have also worked to benefit the spiritual and social lives of their families and communities.

See also Religion

SOURCES: Iber, Jorge. 1998. "El Diablo nos esta llevando: Utah Hispanics during the Great Depression, 1930–1940." *Utah Historical Quarterly* 66 (Spring): 159–177; _____. 2000. *Hispanics in the Mormon Zion, 1912–1999.* College Station: Texas A&M University Press; Ulibarri, Richard O. 1989. "Utah's Unassimilated Minorities." In *Utah's History*, ed. Richard D. Poll, 629–650. Logan: Utah State University Press.

Jorge Iber

ROBLES DÍAZ, INÉS (1933–)

Community activist Inés Robles Díaz was born in 1933 in Barrio Nuevo, Naranjito, Puerto Rico. Her father, Emiliano Izcoa, was a landowner, farmer, and tobacco grower. Her mother, María Magdalena Díaz Cruz, was a homemaker. They lived on the family land in rural Puerto Rico. At the age of six Inés was sent to live with relatives in a less rural area of Naranjito in order to attend better schools. She believes that this early separation from her family made her independent from an early age.

In 1950 Robles Díaz attended the University of Puerto Rico in Río Piedras, where she studied teaching for three and a half years. After her one-year teaching practicum she taught for two years in Naranjito. She subsequently took and passed the government social work exam and became a welfare investigator for the government of Puerto Rico. In this role she became aware of the extent of poverty in Puerto Rico and zealously assisted Puertorriqueños in applying for benefits to which they were entitled. Annoyed by investigators who felt that they were gatekeepers of government money rather than helpers of the poor, she reminisces that "this job made me realize that what I wanted to do were things that involved helping people."

Robles Díaz married Emilio Robles Hernández in 1956, and they moved to Bridgeport, Connecticut. Sensing that only factory jobs were available to newly arrived Puerto Ricans, they moved to New York and in 1958 settled in Brownsville, Brooklyn. Within a year Inés and Emilio opened a combination travel agency and insurance brokerage in Brownsville. Emilio also prepared tax returns. They owned the business—which was moved to East New York, Brooklyn, in 1964—until 1999.

Robles Díaz's interest in helping the poor and disenfranchised continued in Brooklyn. Horrified by complaints from East Brooklyn residents about their apartments, she heard tales of falling ceilings, lack of heat, and roach infestations that property owners ignored. While helping her husband in the travel agency, she processed English-language housing forms and welfare applications and called upon agencies to advocate for neighborhood residents. Inés remembers Emilio's annoyance when he came to the travel agency in the middle of the day and found it closed, a crowd of clients gathered outside. Expected to mind the business, Inés often left to assist those in urgent need of welfare assistance.

Robles Díaz's commitment to improving the living conditions of Puerto Ricans in New York led to her interest in voter registration and community activism. She felt strongly that if one lived in a community, one had to be interested in it and become involved in school meetings and political affairs. Puerto Ricans were shy and fearful of taking the English-language exam needed to register to vote; many were cynical about the value of politics in helping them. Convincing Puerto Ricans of their electoral duties, she "took them by the hand" to the polling sites and tutored them on passing the test.

Denouncing increasing racial and ethnic segregation in Brownsville schools, Robles Díaz advocated for the creation of Educational Park, an integrated junior-high-school and high-school complex in Brooklyn that would draw students from white, African American, and Latino neighborhoods. The board of education did not implement the ambitious program, largely because of the objections of white parents.

Community volunteer Inés Robles Díaz. Courtesy of Sally Robles.

With community agency funds available from President Lyndon Johnson's War on Poverty programs, Inés and Emilio Robles helped start a variety of organizations. In 1967 they formed Acción Cívica Hispana, with Emilio as president. The organization existed from 1966 to 1970 and created youth sports and recreational programs. It supplied Spanish-speaking interpreters, processed English-language applications, advocated for Hispanics denied full welfare benefits, provided remedial tutoring for children, assisted with health care and school problems, and collected toys for children.

Inés Robles became the secretary of the Puerto Rican Organizations of Brownsville and East New York (PROBE) and the Brownsville Community Council, organizations that assisted East Brooklyn residents with a variety of social service concerns. For two years she directed Brownsville Community Council's Action Center No. 4, a multiservice agency that assisted residents with an assortment of problems, including social services, housing, and health care. Along with Evelyn Aberson, Robles incorporated the East Brooklyn Mental Health Project in 1967 and received funding to establish a mental health clinic in East New York.

Robles recalls that these organizations were male dominated, and "women had to be pushy, even with their husbands. They didn't think we could do things." Partly out of the feeling that women were not respected, Inés Robles, along with Felicia Arroyo, Ramonita García, and Marcelina Díaz, proposed the formation of a group, subsequently funded in 1967, called the Ladies Committee for Puerto Rican Culture. The organization sought to infuse Puerto Ricans in East Brooklyn with a sense of pride about their cultural heritage. The founders felt that New York Puerto Ricans quickly lost their cultural connections, and that the mainland-born generation did not speak Spanish. In a state of "cultural limbo," youths were not accepted as Americans and faced considerable discrimination. By preserving and transmitting Puerto Rican culture in Brooklyn, the organization would help increase self-esteem among Puerto Ricans. In 1967 the Ladies Committee successfully advocated for an elementary school in Brownsville named after Puerto Rican abolitionist Dr. Ramón Emeterio Betances. The curriculum included African, African American, and Puerto Rican culture. In addition, the committee had every public library in Brooklyn order books by Puerto Rican authors. The Ladies Committee for Puerto Rican Culture still exists in Brooklyn and provides residents with free GED and English-language classes.

Robles feared that her own children would internalize the low academic expectations held by many schoolteachers and administrators about Puerto Ricans. She consequently instilled the expectation that each would attain a college degree. Concerned also that her children would be victims of discrimination in school, she would say, "You don't have to like them [the teachers] but you have to respect them." She spoke about the possibility that teachers would judge them intellectually inferior because of their bilingual-bicultural Puerto Rican background. Academic excellence, she reasoned, was the way to establish that one was not only equal but often intellectually superior to one's classmates. Robles transmitted a sense of Puerto Rican pride by exalting the language, food, music, holidays, and people of Puerto Rico. Sundays were "Puerto Rican Culture Day," when only traditional foods were served. She made being Puerto Rican seem like a special entrée into a cohesive, warm, and festive community that nurtured its own. Until the children were in their late teens, there were yearly visits to the rural town of Anones, Naranjito, where Robles had spent much of her youth.

Robles's children are Daniel Emilio Robles, Edna Inés Robles-Brutus, Carol Ann Robles-Roman, Sally María Robles-Rodríguez, Melisa Marie Robles, and Frances Teresa Robles. She also has six grandchildren. Inés and Emilio Robles retired in 1999.

SOURCES: *Brownsville Counselor.* 1967. "Puerto Rican Culture Group." July 28; Pritchett, W. E. 2002. *Brownsville, Brooklyn: Blacks, Jews, and the Changing Face of the Ghetto.* Chicago: University of Chicago Press.

Sally Robles

RODRÍGUEZ, HERMELINDA MORALES (1903–?)

Born in Sabinas Hidalgo, Nuevo León, Mexico, Hermelinda Morales Rodríguez, a Mexican immigrant, became perhaps the most prominent Mexican woman business owner in Texas during the first half of the twentieth century. Her parents were Anastacio Morales and Flora de los Santos. It remains unclear when she arrived in the United States. She married Guadalupe Rodríguez Jr., who with his father established the Rodríguez and Son Bottling Company in 1918 in San Antonio, Texas. Five years later their root beer business was flourishing, and they moved the factory to larger facilities. When her husband died in 1929, Hermelinda Rodríguez joined her father-in-law in business. She proved an excellent businesswoman and by 1933 had bought out her father-in-law and assumed control of the company as its president and chief executive officer.

As the business grew, she brought in her brothers Armando and Melchor to assist with the operations. Reflecting the shift in the family business, they changed the name of Rodríguez and Son Bottling to Dragon Bottling Company in 1934, and the company began to manufacture new soft drinks. Five years later Dragon Bottling was one of the most prominent Mexican-owned businesses in the state. Using state-of-the-art equipment, the company produced twelve different flavors of soft drinks at the rate of 120 cases per hour. Buying the latest trucks, Dragon Bottling distributed its soft drinks within a 160-mile radius of San Antonio. Unlike most business owners of her day, Rodríguez ran a company with regional reach, not a "mom-and-pop" store catering to local neighbors, but like many Mexican American businesses, the company sponsored local sports teams, including a championship baseball team.

Hermelinda Morales Rodríguez is one of a few women listed in the *Primer Anuario de los Habitantes Hispano-Americanos* (First Yearbook of the Latin American Population of Texas), a Latino who's who of Texas published in 1939. According to the *Anuario,* she was an unusual entrepreneur, given her involvement in manufacturing and in selling products not specifically geared to women (e.g., cosmetics). In 1942 she expanded her operations, and the result was the Dragon, Hernández, and Rodríguez Bottling Companies. However, by 1962 her companies had ceased to exist, a typical pattern affecting small bottling firms across the United States as soft-drink manufacture and sales became consolidated within a handful of national corporations.

See also Entrepreneurs

SOURCES: Garcia, Richard A. 1991. *Rise of the Mexican American Middle Class, San Antonio, 1919–1941.* College Station: Texas A&M University Press; Orozco, Cynthia E. 1996. "Hermelinda Morales Rodríguez." In *New Handbook of Texas* 4. Austin: Texas State Historical Association.

Cynthia E. Orozco

RODRÍGUEZ, "ISABEL" HERNÁNDEZ (1950–)

Born in Ciudad Juárez, Chihuahua, Mexico, Isabel Hernández Rodríguez immigrated with her mother and eight brothers to the United States at the age of seven and settled in public housing in the Boyle Heights area of Los Angeles, California. After briefly attending public school she attended parochial grammar and then high school. In 1968 she entered Pitzer College as a freshman, but later transferred to the University of California, Los Angeles. In 1982 she received a J.D. from the People's College of Law in Los Angeles. Rodríguez's formal postsecondary schooling went hand in hand with an education in community and political activism through involvement in the Chicano movement. She married Carlos A. Chávez in 1972; the union dissolved in 1996. She has one daughter, Marisela.

Influenced by what is commonly referred to as the Chicano movement of the late 1960s and throughout the 1970s, Rodríguez actively participated in various organizations. She began with the student-based United Mexican American Students (UMAS) and later joined more politically radical organizations, the Committee to Free Los Tres and el Centro de Acción Social Autónomo (CASA). Her membership in these two organizations reflects the change in her political thought. Although she identified as a Chicana during her involvement with UMAS, Rodríguez later came to identify herself as a Mexicana, which she felt more accurately reflected her experiences as an immigrant and her beliefs in a transnational Mexican working class not bounded by borders between the United States and Mexico.

As a member of CASA, she became editor of the organization's newspaper, *Sin Fronteras,* served on the governing body of the organization, the Political Commission, and directed study groups. During the Chicano movement Rodríguez viewed feminism as a "narrow" ideology. However, she still worked within CASA to promote what were deemed "women's issues." Therefore, she states, "we talked about male supremacy and how to combat it. . . . I dealt with it more on a personal level . . . than on an organizational level." Yet within its Marxist-Leninist stance the organization did address gender through its political activities, such as sponsoring women's conferences, promoting film series on women, and devoting special issues of its newspaper to women's struggles. In the end, however, the organization never succeeded in incorporating these issues into its overall political vision.

CASA ceased to exist as an organization in 1978 because of infighting, lack of finances, member disillusionment, and the stress of constant surveillance by the Federal Bureau of Investigation. In addition, historian Ernesto Chávez argues that CASA's attempt to merge cultural nationalism with Marxism-Leninism brought forth a fundamental contradiction in philosophy that also played a major role in CASA's demise. After CASA's downfall Rodríguez, like most of the members of the now-defunct organization, continued to work in the political arena by organizing around undocumented workers' rights and other injustices borne by ethnic and racial people of color.

Today Rodríguez continues to involve herself in political issues affecting primarily the Mexican American and Mexican immigrant communities in Los Angeles. She practices civil rights, criminal defense, workers' compensation, and personal injury law, is a founding member and vice president of the Latina Lawyers Bar Association in Los Angeles and a member of the American Bar Association and the Mexican American Bar Association, founded the Workers' Compensation

Committee and sat on the Board of Trustees of the Mexican American Bar Association, and sits on the Board of Directors of Proyecto Pastoral, a faith-based community empowerment organization in the public housing projects of Boyle Heights.

Rodríguez's experiences as an immigrant, student, activist, and professional reflect the diversity within one Latina life experience. Yet while Rodríguez's experiences may be unique, her life parallels the lives of the many women active not only in CASA, but the Chicano movement as a whole. During the *movimiento* these women who dedicated their lives to work for social change were rarely recognized for the work they did, yet remained active because they wholeheartedly believed in their cause. Like Rodríguez, most of these women continue to work for social change through professional and community efforts.

See also Centro de Acción Social Autónomo (CASA)

SOURCES: Centro de Acción Social Autónomo. Papers. M0325, Department of Special Collections, Stanford University Libraries, Stanford, CA; Chávez, Ernesto. 2000. "Imagining the Mexican Immigrant Worker: (Inter)Nationalism, Identity, and Insurgency in the Chicano Movement in Los Angeles." *Aztlán* 25 (Spring): 109–135; Chávez, Marisela R. 2000. " 'We lived and breathed and worked the movement': The Contradictions and Rewards of Chicana/Mexicana Activism in el Centro de Acción Social Autónomo–Hermandad General de Trabajadores (CASA-HGT), Los Angeles, 1975–1978." In *Las obreras: Chicana Politics of Work and Family*, ed. Vicki L. Ruiz, 83–105. Los Angeles: UCLA Chicano Studies Research Center Publications.

Marisela R. Chávez

RODRÍGUEZ, JOSEFA "CHEPITA" (?–1863)

Though practically no details exist of Chepita, or Chipita, Rodríguez's early life, the date of her death on November 13, 1863, is very much in the Texas public record. Apparently Chepita came from Mexico as a youth during the 1820s or the 1830s to escape the political turmoil in her homeland, but her mother died soon after the family arrived in Texas, and her father perished in the Texas war for independence of 1836. She grew up without receiving the benefits of an education and never learned to speak the English language.

For most of her life Chepita Rodríguez lived in San Patricio County. There she supported herself by using her old shack, located on the Aransas River where Highway 77 intersects it today, as a resting place. Among those who stopped at Chepita's Inn was John Savage, who in September 1863 was making his way south after having sold a horse herd in San Antonio. Some time after the fateful evening of Savage's

stopover at Chepita's, a ranch family discovered the horse trader's body on the Aransas River. His murderer had apparently used an ax to accomplish the deed and then wrapped the body in gunnysacks. The sheriff soon arrested the old woman, as well as a neighbor named Juan Silvera, whom the sheriff believed had helped dispose of the body.

The case against Rodríguez began on October 5, 1863. Little primary evidence exists on the trial proceedings. From what may be pieced together, the sheriff testified that Savage had been killed on the night of his stay at Chepita's Inn, that blood had been found near the spot where the traveler had slept, and that $600.00 in gold, still in his saddlebags, had surfaced downriver from Chepita's Inn.

Other than to explain that the blood on her porch came from a chicken she had killed for a meal, Rodríguez remained silent. It is possible that Juan Silvera became a witness against her so that he could get a lighter sentence.

Folklorists and historians have speculated that Rodríguez said nothing for a variety of reasons, among them that she sought to protect a son, the actual perpetrator. This reasoning holds that Rodríguez had many years before given birth out of wedlock, that the baby's father had taken the infant from his mother, and that the grown child appeared on the night in question and killed Savage.

The jury found Rodríguez guilty, but it recommended mercy, given her advanced age. But the judge ruled that Rodríguez be put to death on November 13, 1863. On that date Rodríguez was hanged from a tree, her body was laid in a coffin and loaded on the same cart that had taken her to the place of execution, and she was buried immediately without ceremony.

Chepita Rodríguez's execution for years concerned many people in southern Texas, and a groundswell for gaining a pardon for her accelerated during the later 1970s. In 1984 Senator Carlos Truán of District 20 initiated efforts to get the Texas legislature to clear her name. On June 13, 1985, the legislature adopted a resolution absolving her of the crime.

SOURCES: Guthrie, Keith. 1990. *The Legend of Chipita: The Only Woman Hanged in Texas.* Austin: Eakin Press; Smylie, Vernon. 1970. *A Noose for Chipita.* Corpus Christi: Texas News Syndicate Press.

Arnoldo De León

RODRÍGUEZ, PATRICIA (1922–1968)

An energetic nonconformist, Patricia Rodríguez was a community activist and union organizer during the 1950s and early 1960s in New York City. Born in Puerto Rico on August 25, 1922, in the small southern coastal

Patricia Rodríguez giving toys to the children on el Día de los Reyes, circa 1965. Courtesy of Milga Morales.

town of Guayanilla, she was the founder of several community organizations in New York, including the Gowanus Youth and Parents Civic Association in downtown Brooklyn, the Puerto Rican Women's Sewing Organization, and various hometown organizations, such as the Sons of Guayanilla. An activist in the development of the Hospital Workers Union, the current Local 1199, Rodríguez rejected stereotyped notions of Latina female roles through her organizing and participation in demonstrations, boycotts, pickets, and strikes for better wages and working conditions for all people.

Following a mostly unsuccessful venture in a takeout food business, or *fonda,* as it is called in Puerto Rico, Rodríguez left the island in 1947 and came to the United States with her husband, Crecensio. While they sought employment, the couple counted on friends and family members already established in the city for food and lodging. Longing for a career in nursing, the community activist, union organizer, and mother of five struggled with severe asthma, an illness she contended with for most of her life.

The daughter of Jose Rodríguez and Inocencia Maldonado, Rodríguez valued the familial traditions she had experienced as a child. After two years in New York City she reunited the family in Brooklyn. Grandparents, uncles, and children all lived in a small apartment on Walton Avenue in the Bronx and shared a kitchen with three other families. Rodríguez's first job was making artificial flowers in a factory. She also worked as a presser in an industrial laundry, Star Overalls, in Williamsburg, near the Greenpoint section of Brooklyn. Her daughter, Gladys, recalls the difficulty her asthmatic mother had breathing in that steam-bath environment.

Tending to and providing for her family were paramount. Nonetheless, Rodríguez used her home as a neighborhood base, always available to its residents. Most had recently migrated from Puerto Rico and were not fluent in English. She helped them obtain information on welfare, health, other social services, and educational opportunities. In the early 1950s most of her time was dedicated to organizing within the hometown organizations, particularly the group representing Guayanilla. These hometown groups were organizations in the United States that promoted the social and cultural traditions of Puerto Rico, emphasizing the contributions of their native sons and daughters. Rodríguez was involved as well in the Puerto Rican Day Parade, the Council of Brooklyn Organizations, and la Fiesta Folklórica Puertorriqueña. Rare was the moment that was not dedicated to family or to community.

Despite her limited formal instruction, Rodríguez attained a sixth-grade education in Puerto Rico. Her dream of becoming a nurse was partially realized in the late 1950s when she became a nurse's aide in Brooklyn's Long Island College Hospital. However, the dream was short lived. The hospital administration at the time refused to accept responsibility for the existence of dangerous working conditions. It was because of these conditions that Rodríguez sustained a serious head injury while carrying out hospital duties. Her experience with bureaucracy and the insensitivities of the hospital administration led her to examine the strategies she would employ to fight institutional injustice. She joined the union movement and, with her children in tow, became a fixture on the picket line in front of those city hospitals that refused to recognize the unionization of their workers.

Rodríguez admired the activist Antonia Denis. Denis, considered an elder statesperson in the community, was one of the original Puerto Rican pioneer women in Brooklyn's downtown area. Together they established Casa Puerto Rico, a culturally focused neighborhood oasis located on the corner of Hoyt and Bergen streets. From this office Rodríguez and many of those who followed her leadership supported and actively worked on local campaigns for mayors John Lindsay and Abraham Beame and Congressman Fred Richmond. In addition, she traveled to Washington, D.C., in support of the bilingual voting ballot and visited the Capitol in support of Salvador Agrón, a Puerto Rican youth dubbed the "Capeman" by the media. Agrón faced death in the electric chair, but the community felt that he had been judged unfairly and had been sentenced in an atmosphere of racism and nativism. The community's mobilization on his behalf resulted in a stay of execution.

In 1965 Rodríguez founded the Organization of Puerto Rican Notaries. Because she was able to witness legal statements and documents, her home was constantly filled with neighbors who needed documents witnessed but were afraid to go to lawyers who might overcharge them. Rodríguez was known to charge only the requisite fifty cents and also provided her neighbors with information and resources.

The civil rights movement of the 1960s and the federal War on Poverty initiatives provided opportunities for local community members to work in neighborhood projects such as consumer awareness and jobs orientation for young people. Rodríguez's home served as a lunch distribution center for neighborhood children. Her involvement in the development of the Puerto Rican Community Development Project (PRCDP), a major initiative of the War on Poverty in New York City, was a conflictive one. She criticized spending War on Poverty program funds to support salaries of noncommunity members with academic credentials but little knowledge of local community issues.

In August 1968 Rodríguez's previously undiagnosed breast cancer caused her to be hospitalized. Almost immediately after a mastectomy she left the hospital to join a picket line in front of New York's city hall protesting the deaths of thousands of young men and women in Vietnam. Rodríguez was buried in a Brooklyn cemetery on Christmas Eve of that year. At her funeral hundreds of community leaders and residents, as well as her five adult children, reflected on the contributions of this Puerto Rican woman with few material assets but with fervor for justice and an unquenchable desire to serve.

See also Labor Unions

SOURCES: Alvarez, Gladys. 2001. Interview by Milga Morales, April 3; Ribes Tovar, Frederico. 1968. *El Libro Puertorriqueño,* vol. 1. New York: Editorial El Libro Puertorriqueño; Rodríguez, Crecensio. 2001. Interview by Milga Morales, June 4.

Milga Morales

RODRÍGUEZ, SOFÍA (1922?–)

Born in San Antonio, Texas, Sofía Rodríguez was the third youngest of thirteen children; the first five had died before she was born. Rodríguez attended James Bowie Elementary School, but as the youngest she had the responsibility of helping her pregnant sister. Rodríguez recalls, "I had to stay there [Fort Worth, Texas] two to three months. Once she was able to get around, they would send me back home. So I went over there about three times during childbirth." While she was in Fort Worth with her sister, she attended school for a short while. Her sisters married as teenagers, but Sofía Rodríguez decided that since her parents allowed her to make her own choices, she would finish high school. She earned a high school diploma and shortly thereafter began working in the defense industry during World War II, where she remained for eighteen months. Obligated to do her part for the war effort, Rodríguez believed that had she not completed high school, she would not have had the ability to pass the job's aptitude test. It was while she was living in San Francisco that she began her life in the music industry by singing at local taverns.

Rodríguez sang in Chicago for a short time, headlining as "Linda the Cuban Bombshell." She lost her voice and could not continue with the show or its tour. Returning to San Antonio, she discovered that she had a hand for business and opened the Frisco bar on Ruiz Street. In 1954 she moved to Corpus Christi and opened a lounge. "When I started in '55 I had a little corner and I started with a little band they called 'Los Cachitos.' . . . I converted it into Sofie's Lounge in 1955." She also promoted bands and brought *orquestas* from Mexico, booking them on two- and three-week tours from the South Texas Valley to Houston. She recalls having to take care of business when on the road with a band, having to "take care of the gate, the promotion, the tickets, and everything."

Rodríguez had a reputation for running a strict business, not letting anyone get by for free and collecting a cover charge for the wives and girlfriends of band members. She believed, "If they're not in the band, then they pay." Her hard-nosed business tactics gave her the pull to become active in politics, and she offered her establishment as a meeting place for Democratic supporters. She also served as the first Mexican American woman president of the Coastal Bend Beer Retailers, and during her tenure it lobbied to extend bar hours until 2 A.M. and have liquor served over the bar.

Rodríguez married twice, had a son and a daughter, and raised a granddaughter as her own. She believes that her business sense gave her children a better life than she could have otherwise afforded. Retiring in 1995 because bands charged more than a local bar could handle, she explained that making ends meet was not worth the hassle anymore. "It's not like a grocery store; you have to go get groceries because you have to eat. You don't have to go to a nightclub."

See also Entrepreneurs

SOURCE: Rodríguez, Sofía. 2001. Oral history interview by Mary Ann Villarreal, March 28.

Mary Ann Villarreal

RODRÍGUEZ CABRAL, MARÍA CRISTINA (1959–)

Cristina Rodríguez Cabral is an Afro-Uruguayan writer who is presently completing a Ph.D. at the University of Missouri, Columbia, and specializes in Afro-Hispanic literature. She received a master's degree in English from Indiana University of Pennsylvania. In Uruguay she held degrees in nursing and undergraduate studies from the Universidad de la República Oriental de Uruguay.

Rodríguez Cabral began to write at the age of twelve but did not become serious about it until the publication of her first book in prose, *Bahía, mágica bahía* (Bay, Magic Bay), in 1986, for which she won first prize in Cuba's Casa de las Americas literary contest. Although the author has written nine books of poetry, only one, *Desde mi trenchera* (From My Trench), has been published. Others include *Pájaros sueltos* (Loose Birds), *Entre giros y mutaciones* (Between Turns and Changes), *La mujer del espejo y yo* (The Woman in the Mirror and I), and the recent *Memoria y resistencia* (Memory and Resistance), which was written in the United States.

Rodríguez Cabral's poetry and prose reflect a great sensitivity, tenderness, nostalgia, strong passion, and support for freedom and identity. Alberto Britos Serrat has compared the literary work of Cristina Rodríguez Cabral to that of Nicolás Guillén and José Martí in that she expresses a cosmic vision similar to that expressed by these poets in their work. In her work there is a call to unity, understanding, and mutual respect without

the destructiveness of discrimination. Her poetry and prose also reflect a woman-centered, or "womanist" concept similar to that of the African American writer Alice Walker. Rodríguez Cabral believes in "the empowerment of women but without the total exclusion of men."

Rodríguez Cabral is a member of the interim secretariat of the Intercontinental Union of Writers, which consists of representatives from several continents, including America, Europe, and Asia. Her poetry has appeared in journals such as the *Afro-Hispanic Review* and *PALARA*. In the United States she continues to be involved in literary and cultural events such as the Afro-Hispanic Research conferences at the University of Missouri, Columbia, and the Yari Yari Black Women's Conference in New York.

As a female Afro-Hispanic writer in the United States, Cristina Rodríguez Cabral has contributed to making the black experience and culture in Latin America more accessible and visible. Her works are incorporated into anthologies on Afro-Hispanic writings currently in use in college literature courses in women's and minority studies. Rodríguez Cabral's literary work has also had the effect of extending the confines of what is generally considered African American literature and what is considered Latin American literature. She expresses both an Afrocentric and a Hispanic perspective when she states, "In the United States, I feel more Afro-Latina, or rather a minority among other minorities. . . . I defined myself as a Black woman, a broader concept than that of an Afro-Uruguayan." She takes her role in the American and the international community seriously and believes that it is her responsibility "to share her experiences and vision in order to elevate the consciousness of others."

See also Literature

SOURCES: Adams, Clementina R., ed. 1998. *Common Threads: Afro-Hispanic Women's Literature.* Miami: Ediciones Universal; Britos Serrat, Alberto, ed. 1990. *Antología de poetas negros uruguayos.* Montevideo, Uruguay: Ediciones Mundo Afro; DeCosta-Willis, Miriam, ed. 2003. *Daughters of the Diaspora: Afra-Hispanic Writers.* Kingston, Jamaica: Ian Randle; Rodríguez Cabral, María Cristina. 1983. *The Role of Women in Caribbean Prose Fiction.* Ann Arbor, MI: University Microfilms International; ———. 1990. *Bahía, mágica bahía: Antología de poetas negros uruguayos.* Montevideo: Ediciones Mundo Afro; ———. 1993. *Desde mi trinchera.* Montevideo: Ediciones Mundo Afro; ———. 2003. Interview by Wendy McBurney-Coombs, University of Missouri, Columbia, August.

Wendy McBurney-Coombs

RODRÍGUEZ DE TIÓ, LOLA (1843–1924)

Essayist, poet, and political activist Dolores Rodríguez y Ponce de León was born in San German, Puerto Rico,

Poet and supporter of Puerto Rican independence Lola Rodríguez de Tió. Courtesy of Proyecto de Digitalización de la Colección del Periódico El Mundo, Universidad de Puerto Rico, Río Piedras.

in 1843. Her parents were Sebastián Rodríguez de Astudillo and Carmen Ponce de León. Her father was a distinguished lawyer and law professor and one of the founding members of the Puerto Rican Bar Association. Rodríguez de Tió was educated by private tutors and had access to her father's extensive library as a young girl. In 1863, at the age of twenty she married Bonocio Tió Segarra, a respected journalist and poet, also from San German. In their household they held numerous intellectual, political, and literary *tertulias* (gatherings). These get-togethers, usually frequented by abolitionists and by opponents of continued Spanish colonialism, caught the attention of Spanish officials.

Rodríguez de Tió was known for her support of independence for Puerto Rico. She considered Spanish colonialism and slavery decadent. Her connections with some of the leaders of the failed 1868 Lares uprising made her the source of constant surveillance. In 1877 Rodríguez de Tió was exiled to Venezuela by Spanish colonial authorities. During her years in Venezuela she befriended the Puerto Rican intellectual Eugenio María de Hostos and served as maid of honor in his wedding to Belinda de Ayala. Rodríguez de Tió returned to Puerto Rico in 1880 to continue her activism on behalf of Puerto Rican independence, only to be exiled again by Governor Segundo de la Portilla in 1889. She, her husband, and their children went to Cuba, where they quickly joined the revolutionary ranks. Their political activities also enraged Spanish

officials in Cuba, and in 1892 the couple was forced to leave Havana for New York City. In New York Rodríguez de Tió joined a sizable Spanish, Cuban, and Puerto Rican community. She continued her literary and political work in New York and was particularly active in several organizations, such as Club Político Ruis Rivera, which advocated for the independence of both Cuba and Puerto Rico from Spain. In New York she collaborated with political and literary figures such as José Martí, Pachín Marín, Román Baldorioty de Castro, Sotero Figueroa, Luis Muñoz Rivera, and Rubén Darío, among others.

Rodríguez de Tió returned to Cuba after the Cuban-Spanish-American War of 1898. Later, after a twenty-three-year absence, she visited Puerto Rico in 1915. Her return to the island was a very welcoming one that included impressive tributes at the Ateneo Puertorriqueño and the University of Puerto Rico. After some time in Puerto Rico Rodríguez de Tió returned to Havana, where she continued to write. She was a well-known figure outside the Caribbean. In 1924, for example, she engaged in an extensive European tour, with poetry recitals in Madrid and Paris.

Although Rodríguez de Tió is remembered as a romantic poet, she was valued more by her nineteenth-century contemporaries for her recitals than for her poetry. She was an accomplished performer and enjoyed reciting poetry in bohemian gatherings. She wrote several volumes of poetry, including *Mis cantares* (1876), *Claros y nieblas* (1885), and perhaps her most famous, *Mi libro de Cuba* (1893). A collection of her poetry titled *Poesias* was published posthumously in 1960. Her writings reflected her love for Puerto Rico and her concerns about the subordinate role of women in society. At an 1884 inauguration of a new school for young women, for example, Rodríguez de Tió lectured on the importance of educating women. Rodríguez de Tió and her husband collaborated as editors of numerous literary journals, many of them short lived, including *La Almojabana,* launched in 1881. She was also an essayist and a prolific letter writer. Rodríguez de Tió was credited with writing the lyrics of "La Boriqueña," which was initially conceived as a nationalist inspirational song. "La Boriqueña" later became Puerto Rico's national anthem. Rodríguez de Tió died in Havana in 1924 at the age of eighty-one.

See also Cuban-Spanish-American War; Feminism; Journalism and Print Media

SOURCES: Acosta-Belén, Edna. 2005. "Lola Rodríguez de Tió and the Puerto Rican Struggle for Freedom." In *Latina Legacies: Identity, Community, and Biography*, eds. Vicki L. Ruiz and Virginia Sánchez Korrol. New York: Oxford University Press; Cadilla de Martínez, María. 1936. *Semblanza de un caracter (Apuntes biográficos de Lola Rodríguez de Tió).* San Juan: n.p.; Rivera de Alvarez, Josefina. 1974. "Rodríguez de Tió,

Lola." In *Diccionario de literatura puertorriqueña,* 2:1384–1388. San Juan: Instituto de Cultura Puertorriqueña.

Félix V. Matos Rodríguez

RODRÍGUEZ McLEAN, VERNEDA (1918–1982)

Verneda Rodríguez McLean was born on January 11, 1918, in Chicago, Illinois. To honor all aspects of their daughter's heritage, Ann and John Rodríguez named her Verneda Gunda Rodríguez. Ann, named Onika Kirstina Rasmussen Hansen at birth, had been born in Denmark, and her father Juan Francisco Rodríguez de Jardín, had emigrated from British Guyana. Verneda was the name of a Native American princess, Gunda a Danish name. Verneda listed 445 East Ninety-first Place on Chicago's South Side as home in her pilot-training classbook. The family, which eventually included five children, two of whom died before the age of five, lived in a South Chicago *colonia* that, in 1948, extended from Eighty-fourth Street to Ninety-second Street east of Commercial Avenue. Most wage earners in this part of town worked in the steel mills or for the railroad, but Verneda's father found work at the Cook County Hospital before moving on to the Welfare Department of the city of Chicago; her mother worked for the wife of the governor of Illinois after emigrating to the United States. The couple decided that their children would speak English exclusively.

After high school Verneda Rodríguez attended a teachers college in Chicago before leaving for Sweetwater, Texas, and army pilot training. She graduated along with seventy-one other women in class 44-W-6 on August 4, 1944, and became one of the now-legendary Women Airforce Service Pilots (WASP). Classmate Joan Lemley remembers "Roddy" as a good friend, a "beautiful, sweet person" with blonde hair and a fair complexion who was fond of poetry, especially that of A. A. Milne, author of the Winnie the Pooh stories. Indeed, under her photograph in the 44-6 classbook is the inscription "James Morrison Weatherby George Dupre," the first line of Milne's "Disobedience." Persuaded by a friend to leave Chicago and strike out for Texas, Rodríguez had been influenced by the Katharine Hepburn movie *Christopher Strong* (1933), in which Hepburn played a record-setting woman pilot, and the great women pilots of the 1930s, such as Amelia Earhart, Florence "Pancho" Barnes, and Jacqueline "Jackie" Cochran.

After pilot training Rodríguez reported for duty at Moore Field in Mission, Texas. The women pilots at the field flew tow target missions for the men who were taking gunnery training at the field, one of the most dangerous jobs any person could hold in the Army Air Forces Training Command. It was not unusual for a WASP's plane to be shot up during a tow target mission as she trailed a target on a line behind her for novice pilots to shoot at. The women also ferried aircraft from factories to airfields and flew administrative missions.

Verneda Rodríguez, standing in the middle, graduated from army pilot training at Avenger Field in Sweetwater, Texas, on August 4, 1944. Courtesy of U.S. Air Force, No. 1330 N-1.

When the war neared its end and an increasing number of male pilots returned stateside, the army terminated the WASP program in December 1944 and released the women back to civilian life without any of the veterans' benefits provided to other servicemen and servicewomen.

After leaving the WASP Rodriguez returned to Chicago and worked for the weather service, then moved to Langley Air Force Base, Virginia, as an aircraft accident analyst. At Langley she married Edward Ridley McLean, who had flown B-25 bombers in World War II and went on to complete a career in the air force. The couple traveled the world, including stops in Tokyo and Manila, West Point, and the Air Force Academy. While living in the Far East, Rodríguez took up and became skilled in Oriental brush painting, and later, when the McLeans lived in Virginia Beach, Virginia, she, along with some friends, opened a gift store called the Late Possum that featured artworks. In the early 1960s she co-owned a coffeehouse, the Place, that featured folk music.

Edward McLean served two tours of duty in the Pentagon at the end of his career, and the McLeans settled in Annandale, Virginia. While living in the national capital area, Rodríguez taught brush painting and held one-person shows throughout the state. In the mid- and late 1970s she was also active in the successful fight to gain veterans' rights for the WASP, correcting what many had felt to be a long-standing inequity. In this contest Rodriguez was joined by her daughter MaryLynn, then a college student. It is believed that Rodríguez, who died on March 19, 1982, was the first member of the WASP to be buried with full military honors in Arlington National Cemetery, a right she earned in the skies over Texas.

During World War II women performed many jobs that had traditionally been done by men. New opportunities in aviation and aerospace industries provided work for tens of thousands of women, and many served with the armed forces. By definition, the members of the Women Airforce Service Pilots were exceptional. From among some 25,000 applicants, the army accepted 1,830, and 1,074 actually completed the training. Because they had to prove themselves in a "man's world," recruitment standards were high, and many members of the WASP were among the most capable pilots in the nation. In what many considered at that time the ultimate "machismo" occupation, Verneda Rodríguez McLean earned a place among the American aviation heroes of World War II. Helen (Kelly) Drake, who grew up in Sweetwater during World War II, remembered the WASP as role models, noting that "These 'high class' women held a powerful fascination for me. . . . They were tan; lithe; bold in appearance, speech, and behavior. . . . They will always be golden eagles who soar through my memories of other times and other places."

See also Military Service; World War II

SOURCES: Drake, Helen (Kelly). "Memories of Other Times and Other Places." *WASP World Wide.* http://wasp-wwii.org/wasp/memories.htm. Howell Granger, Byrd. 1991. *On Final Approach.* Scottsdale, AZ: Falconer Publishing; Paz, Frank X. 1948. *Mexican-Americans in Chicago: A General Survey.* Chicago: Council of Social Agencies; Verges, Marianne. 1991. *On Silver Wings.* New York: Ballantine Books.

Bruce Ashcroft

RODRÍGUEZ REMENESKI, SHIRLEY (1939?–)

A lifetime of achievement and service marks the roads traveled by Shirley Rodríguez Remeneski. Born in New York City shortly before the United States entered World War II, Shirley was the youngest of Armando Rodríguez's and Providencia O'Neill's three daughters. Her parents came to New York City from San German, Puerto Rico, in the 1920s, fleeing the oppressive economic hardships of an island described as the poorhouse of the Americas by Eleanor Roosevelt. The end of the war and the introduction of inexpensive air flights to New York City triggered a massive migration of Puerto Ricans looking for a better life. Young Shirley served as guide, interpreter, advisor, and social worker for the newly arrived members of her extended family who spoke no English and were ill prepared to meet the challenges of the city. The frustrations, discrimination, and ignorance she encountered fueled her anger as she dealt at a young age with a system that was indifferent to the suffering of its newest residents. A strong sense of service imbued in her by her parents and the importance of helping others served to shape her future path.

Her parents worked in low-paying jobs. Armando found employment in a New York hotel kitchen, while Providencia worked in a pocketbook factory. Her grandmother, Elvira O'Neill, came to the city to care for the children and played a significant role in raising young Shirley. A strong-willed woman who stressed independence and a woman's right to form the future, she bestowed on her youngest granddaughter a virtual road map that instilled in her confidence and a strong work ethic. Shirley Rodríguez was educated in New York City's public schools. The system provided little motivation for academic advancement to young children of "foreign-language parents." Rodríguez graduated from school, became a clerical worker, married, and had children, as was expected of a young woman of her generation. During the turbulent 1960s she found herself immersed in the social upheavals of the period. Events that were often generated by anger about American involvement in Vietnam and the social injustice that marginalized Latinos, especially Puerto Ricans, in New York consumed her interests. A meeting in the South Bronx to push the candidacy of a young Puerto Rican–born attorney, Herman Badillo, who was running for Bronx borough president, triggered her desire to change a system of exclusion affecting Hispanics. The campaign gave Rodríguez Remeneski a creative outlet for her need to serve. Her experience and sensitivity learned from a childhood of helping people deal with unresponsive landlords, government officials, and society in general made her invaluable to the young candidate's campaign efforts. The 1965 election results declared Badillo a winner and, equally as important, signaled a major turning point for Puerto Ricans in New York City politics.

In 1966 Rodríguez Remeneski began a career in public service by establishing and directing the first social services unit in the office of the newly elected Bronx borough president. Many young Hispanics were encouraged to enter public service because of her initiatives. Upon his election to Congress in 1971, Badillo invited her to run his New York office. Her many responsibilities included drafting federal legislation that resulted in the Bilingual Education Act and amending the Voting Rights Act.

In 1978 she was appointed assistant deputy mayor to Mayor Ed Koch and worked on concerns that affected inner-city residents. Lack of affirmative action programs, limited community development plans, employment, education and health services were the major areas of concern. Rodríguez Remeneski's main role was the creation of several programs aimed at helping mainstream the city's poor and marginalized populations. She served as legislative coordinator for the South Bronx Development Organization, working with the nationally known urban developer Edward Logue, and she lobbied successfully for funding and legislative support for new and refurbished inner-city residential units with low interest rates.

In 1981 she became a district administrator for the New York State Department of Labor. Five years later Governor Mario Cuomo invited Rodríguez Remeneski to head his newly created Office for Hispanic Affairs. Under her leadership the office became a focal center for cultural and educational advocacy and provided information for the governor and other officials serving Hispanics throughout the state. She initiated programs for government collaboration with officials in Puerto Rico and created highly regarded mentorship programs.

Founder and president of the 100 Hispanic Women's organization, Rodríguez Remeneski provides leadership committed to advocating and promoting the em-

powerment of Latina women. She has received numerous awards for her good works. In 1990 the Puerto Rican Day Parade in New York City was dedicated to her. In 1997 Governor George Pataki presented her with the New York State Leadership Award, and the Puerto Rican Bar Association gave her its Excellence in Government Award, to cite just a few.

Rodríguez Remeneski is currently a senior vice president with the New York State Empire Development Corporation. Her key responsibility is to ensure the continued economic growth of all New Yorkers. In many ways Shirley Rodríguez Remeneski continues to form the future, a mandate handed down to her from her grandmother.

See also Politics, Party

SOURCES: Maldonado, Adál Alberto. 1984. "Shirley Rodríguez Remeneski." In *Portraits of the Puerto Rican Experience,* ed. Louis Reyes Rivera and Julio Rodríguez, 139–140. New York: IPRUS Institute; Rodríguez Remeneski, Shirley. 2002. Résumé. Biography Profile. August 8.

Edward Mercado

RODRÍGUEZ-TRIAS, HELEN (1929–2001)

Dr. Helen Rodríguez-Trias was born in Puerto Rico on the eve of the Great Depression in 1929 and came to New York in 1939. The struggles faced by the women in her family inspired her early politicization. Her mother was a schoolteacher who struggled to teach in Spanish, but could not get a license to teach once she was in New York City. She encouraged Rodríguez-Trias to return to Puerto Rico to study. Rodríguez-Trias returned to Puerto Rico in 1948, studied at the University of Puerto Rico, and became a student activist in support of Puerto Rican independence. She joined a 6,000-student strike protesting the university's decision to ban Pedro Albizu Campos's appearance. Her political involvements created tensions with her brother, who was paying for her education, and Rodríguez-Trias moved back to New York City, where she married and had three children. While she continued her political involvement in the United States, joining her husband in unionizing Puerto Rican steelworkers in Lorain, Ohio, she felt isolated, and seven years later she returned to Puerto Rico to study medicine. Seven years after that, with another child and another husband, she graduated with honors in 1960.

In 1963, making the most of her residency and specialty in pediatric medicine, she founded the first clinic for newborns in Puerto Rico. The infant mortality rate at the hospital decreased 50 percent within the following three years. During her medical training Rodríguez-Trias began healing the most vulnerable

Rodríguez-Trias, Helen

Puerto Ricans at a time when physicians were only beginning to acknowledge the correlation of health problems and the island's economic, social, and political context. She was particularly influenced by the unequal access poor and wealthy women had to safe (albeit illegal) abortions. Increasingly Rodríguez-Trias viewed Puerto Rico as a laboratory for developing birth-control technology and considered health and politics inextricably linked phenomena.

Rodríguez-Trias's return to New York, her involvement in the women's health movement, and her leadership of the Pediatric Department at Lincoln Hospital became turning points in her life. At Lincoln she served a Puerto Rican community of the South Bronx that had one of the lowest-income populations in the United States at the time. Thus her work grew beyond providing better health care to participating in patients' struggle for greater political power. She led community campaigns against lead paint, collaborated with the Young Lords on issues of health care delivery to the Bronx community, lobbied to give all workers a voice in administrative and patient care issues, and struggled to raise awareness of cultural issues in the Puerto Rican community among health care workers at the hospital.

Rodríguez-Trias used a political approach to promote broader change within the medical profession at various levels. She was a founding member of the Women's and Hispanic Caucus of the American Public Health Association. In 1993 she became the first Latina elected president of the American Public Health Association, and in 1994 she was named chair of the American Public Health Association's Standing Committee on Women's Rights. She taught medicine at the Sophie Davis Center for Biomedical Sciences at City College of New York and was an associate professor of pediatrics at Albert Einstein College of Medicine, Yeshiva University, and later at the College of Physicians and Surgeons of Columbia and Fordham universities. She was also assistant professor of pediatrics at the University of Puerto Rico School of Medicine and the University of Medicine and Dentistry of New Jersey.

Within the health care system Rodríguez-Trias worked at St. Luke's–Roosevelt Hospital Center in Manhattan from 1974 through 1985, first as director of primary care and then as director of the Children and Youth Project. In 1985 she directed the Pediatric Primary Care Program at Newark Beth Israel Medical Center in New Jersey, and three years later she became the medical director of the New York State Department of Health's AIDS Institute. In her work at the AIDS Institute and with the New York Women in AIDS Task Force, Rodríguez-Trias not only developed programs for women with HIV and HIV-affected families, but also played an important role in making New York a national model for quality assurance in HIV care.

In addition to her work within medical communities, Rodríguez-Trias served on various executive and advisory committees and organizations, including the IOM (Institute of Medicine) Committee on Unintended Pregnancy, the National Women's Health Network (1988–1996), the Boston Women's Health Book Collective, the Center for the Advancement of Health Scholars, the Health Disparities National Advisory Committee, the Community Anti-drug Coalitions of America (CADCA), the Reproductive Health Technologies Project, the Society of Physicians for Reproductive Choice and Health, Education, Training, and Research Associates (ETR), and the Opening Doors and Fight Back Drug Abuse Prevention Project. She was a member of the Women's Health Council of the California State Office of Women's Health and the Policy Committee of the Latino Coalition for a Healthy California.

At the federal level, in 1970 Rodríguez-Trias was a founding member of the Committee to End Sterilization Abuse (CESA). Nine years later, in 1979, she testified before the Department of Health, Education, and Welfare for federal sterilization guidelines. As a founding member of the Committee for Abortion Rights and against Sterilization Abuse (CARASA), she helped draft the guidelines that require information provided in a language a woman can understand, written consent for sterilization, and a waiting period between consent and the sterilization procedure.

Rodríguez-Trias carried her work on reproductive rights and HIV/AIDS from New York to the West Coast and, indeed, to the rest of the world. In the late 1980s after moving to California, Rodríguez-Trias made numerous trips to Cuba and contributed her skills toward its universal, community-based health care system. In 1996 she helped found the Pacific Institute for Women's Health, a Los Angeles–based nonprofit research and advocacy group dedicated to improving women's health and well-being worldwide. She consulted with the International Health Programs' Public Health Institute on improving family planning and health care in South and Central America. Her latest work involved developing sustainable public health programs and identifying and enlisting local, rural Indian leaders to carry out reproductive health programs in El Salvador, Guatemala, and Mexico.

In January 2001 she received the Presidential Citizen's Medal for her work on behalf of women, children, people with HIV and AIDS, and the poor. During that event, continuing a legacy of political advocacy, Rodríguez-Trias's granddaughter gave President Clinton a handwritten letter asking him to stop the bombing of Vieques. Helen Rodríguez-Trias died on December 27, 2001, from lung cancer. The National Women's Health Network named its leadership development program after Dr. Helen Rodríguez-Trias.

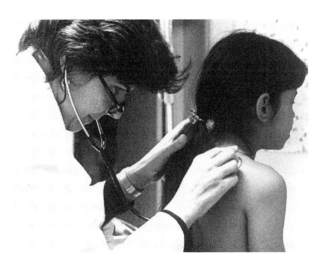

Dr. Helen Rodríguez-Trias received the 2001 Presidential Citizen's Medal for her work on behalf of women, children, and people with HIV and AIDS. Courtesy of the Helen Rodríguez-Trias Papers. Centro Archives, Centro de Estudios Puertorriqueños, Hunter College, CUNY.

See also Sterilization

SOURCES: *Changing the Face of Medicine.* "Physicians Biography: Dr. Helen Rodríguez-Trias." www.nlm.nih.gov/changingthefaceofmedicine/physicians/biography_273.html (accessed July 12, 2004); McNamara, Mary. 2001. "Obituaries: Helen Rodríguez-Trias, 72; Health Care Advocate for Women, Youth." *Puerto Rico Herald*, December 29. www.puertoricoherald.org/issues/2002/vol6n02/ObitHRodri-en.shtml (accessed July 12, 2004); National Women's Health Network: A Voice for Women, a Network for Change. 2004. "The Helen Rodríguez-Trias Women's Health Leadership Program." July 12. www.womenshealthnetwork.org/helen.htm (accessed July 12, 2004); Vázquez, Blanca. 1988. "Mi Gente Interview: Dr. Helen Rodríguez-Trias." *CENTRO: Journal of the Centro de Estudios Puertorriqueños* (Hunter College, CUNY) 2, no. 4 (Fall): 56;

Wilcox, Joyce. 2002. "The Face Of Women's Health: Helen Rodríguez-Trias." *American Journal of Public Health* 92, no. 4 (April): 566–569.

Nicole Trujillo-Pagán

ROMERO CASH, MARIE (1942–)

Marie Romero Cash, a native of Santa Fe, is a multifaceted award-winning artist. Many members of her family are also artists, including her late parents, Emilio and Senaida Romero, both of whom were masters of tinwork. In 1959 she graduated from Santa Fe High School, and in 1997 she received her college degree in cross-cultural studies from Lesley College in Cambridge, Massachusetts. Immersed in the creativity of the Romero family throughout her life, Romero Cash began to pursue her individual artistic career in the 1970s. At that time she received a National Endowment for the Arts grant to apprentice and learn the art of tinwork from her parents. By the mid-1970s she had begun her career as a *santera* (female maker of saints).

Attention, acclamation, and awards quickly followed. Many of these honors have been presented at the Spanish Market held every July on the Santa Fe Plaza. In 1992 she received the Master's Award for Lifetime Achievement from the Spanish Colonial Arts Society. Her many accolades also include awards for originality and expressive design, first-place awards, and poster awards.

Romero Cash creates *bultos* (three-dimensional religious sculptures), *retablos* (two-dimensional religious paintings usually on wooden boards), and other works from wood, gesso, tempera, and varnish. In keeping with the Romero family legacy, she often incorporates

Acclaimed New Mexican folk artist Marie Romero Cash. Courtesy of Marie Romero Cash.

handmade tin accents as well. When she is not creating artwork that meets the criteria of the Spanish Market's guidelines of what is "traditional" and "New Mexican," Romero Cash finds artistic inspiration by creating other pieces, such as carved and painted figures of Frida Kahlo, Diego Rivera, the Statue of Liberty, animals, Noah's ark, and nursery rhymes. She also incorporates women's themes and issues, both religious and secular, and other religious subject matter. Among her favorite topics are biblical and religious women, including various Marian representations, as well as female saints such as Santa Librada (a crucified female saint).

Romero Cash's works are held in the collections of numerous public museums and private individuals, as well as in churches and chapels both in New Mexico and around the country. The major collections are in the Museum of International Folk Art and the Museum of Spanish Colonial Art in Santa Fe, the Maxwell Museum of Anthropology in Albuquerque, the Taylor Museum of Colorado Springs Fine Arts Center, and Heard Museum in Phoenix. Her stations of the cross are located at St. Francis Cathedral in Santa Fe. During her prolific artistic career Romero Cash has also contributed significant scholarship in the field of New Mexican and Latino art by authoring three books: *Built of Earth and Song: A Guidebook to Northern New Mexico's Village Churches* (1992), *Living Shrines: Home Altars of New Mexico*, with photographs by Siegfried Halus (1998), and *Santos: Enduring Images of Northern New Mexico Village Churches* (1999).

In order to achieve all that she has, Marie Romero Cash has often had to struggle and go against the norm in an area of art that was dominated by male *santeros*. In addition to her important historical research, Romero Cash often consults on conservation issues and related projects. She unselfishly shares her knowledge and lectures on a wide variety of Hispano culture- and arts-related topics, and her artistic peers and the local community members consider her an expert on New Mexican religious art.

See also Artists

SOURCES: Pierce, Donna, and Marta Weigle, eds. 1996. *Spanish New Mexico: The Spanish Colonial Arts Society Collections.* Santa Fe: Museum of New Mexico Press; Rebolledo, Tey Diana, ed. 1992. *Nuestras mujeres: Hispanas of New Mexico, Their Images and Their Lives, 1582–1992.* Albuquerque: El Norte Publications; Romero Cash, Marie. 1998. *Living Shrines: Home Altars of New Mexico.* With photographs by Siegfried Halus. Santa Fe: Museum of New Mexico Press; ———. 1999. *Santos: Enduring Images of Northern New Mexico Village Churches.* Boulder: University of Colorado Press.

Tey Marianna Nunn

ROSADO ROUSSEAU, LEONCIA ("MAMÁ LÉO") (1912–   )

The Reverend Leoncia Rosado Rousseau, endearingly called Mamá Léo, was the second of five children born in Toa Alta, Puerto Rico, to Gumersinda Santiago and Manuel Rivera. She states that her life is an example of God's saving grace from the time when she was a little girl thrown accidentally from a truck to the time when a hurricane tore her house apart, but she and her family were able to take refuge in a makeshift house she claims God assembled from the pieces of houses torn apart by the same hurricane, and to the time of her grave illness when Jesus Christ appeared to her and she was healed both physically and spiritually.

She became part of the Disciples of Christ denomination and in 1932, at the age of twenty, upon having another vision in which, she states, God called her to preach and to the ministry, she became a missionary and an evangelist. She immigrated from Puerto Rico to New York City in 1935. She felt that her calling was to bring the "good news" of God's love to the lost and needy of New York City. She eventually became a cofounder, along with her husband, Willie Rosado, who served as the founding pastor, of the Bronx based Pentecostal denomination Concilio de Iglesias Cristianas Damasco (Council of Damascus Christian Churches) in 1940. When her husband was drafted during World War II, the church called her to be its pastor until his return. Although it is not certain, this bold move probably made her the first Latina Pentecostal pastor in New York City. With her authority as pastor, she began to engage in activities that addressed the dire living conditions of the numerous newly arrived Puerto Rican immigrants. Although she believed, as did other Puerto Rican and Spanish-speaking Pentecostals, that the spiritual needs of people are of primary importance, she insisted that the material and physical needs of people must be addressed because these also have an impact on spiritual well-being. She thought that the mission of a church should include being an agent of positive change in society.

In 1957 Rosado opened a drug and alcohol rehabilitation program called Cruzada de Jovenes Cristianos de la Iglesia Cristiana de Damasco (Damascus Christian Youth Crusade) in the church and eventually in a separate building where more addicts could receive physical and spiritual liberation from "the strongholds of the devil." Her work with the addicts, mostly young men, became that of a mother figure, and it was among these young people that she became known as Mamá Léo. Her ministry has served as a catalyst for many other such centers, organizations, and large churches throughout the United States and Puerto Rico that have been founded by people transformed from a life of drugs and "gang-banging" to a life of service and community building as a result of her intervention. Following the death of her husband due to illness, one of the young men, Cedric Rousseau, who had experienced transformation under Rosado's ministry several years earlier, became her husband in 1967.

The Concilio de Iglesias Cristianas Damasco has eight churches on the East Coast of the United States, with an average of 100 members each, thirty-nine churches and missions in Ecuador, fourteen in Mexico, and nineteen in the Caribbean and elsewhere. The denomination also founded a school and an orphanage. Although Mamá Léo was a co-founder and a very strong figure in shaping the direction of the denomination, it has had a majority of male leadership subsequent to her tenure. In 2000 Reverend Felicita La Salle Vega, then vice president elect, became president of the denomination because of the unexpected demise of the incumbent. She has been an exemplary leader within the denomination, serving fervently in various capacities, but the more recent conservative slant of the denomination has tended to shy away from female leadership. However, Reverend La Salle Vega became president-elect in the summer of 2001 and is expected to be successful in the August 2005 election. Once again the legacy of Mamá Léo will see a woman as head of its denomination.

Mamá Léo continued to preach, teach, and minister throughout the world, well into her nineties. Until then, she continued her roles as founding pastor of the Jamaica Christian Church in Queens, New York City and founding executive director of the Asociación Ministerial de Mujeres Cristianas (Ministerial Association of Christian Women), established in 1986, which trains, equips, educates, and empowers women from various Christian denominations who are called to ministerial leadership. She is assisted in this endeavor by Reverends Elizabeth Gómez and Edith Alomar, women who have served the community through their ministries of outreach to victims of domestic violence, sexual abuse, homelessness, and drug addiction. Reverend Rosado Rousseau celebrated her ninety-third birthday in 2005, and although she is a bit frail, when she was invited to preach, her crystal-blue eyes reflected her clarity of mind and her petite body straightened out as she delivered impassioned sermons full of experience and conviction that matched her fiery red hair. She continues to be revered in evangelical circles for her pioneering spirit, her skills as a "princess of the pulpit," and her bold and challenging statements of reproach to those who attempt to curtail what the spirit of God is doing among women and through interdenominational efforts. In 2005 Reverand Rosado

Rousseau entered a nursing home. She suffers from Alzheimer's disease.

See also Pentecostal Church; Religion

SOURCES: Pérez y González, María E. 2001. "Latinas in the Barrio." In *New York Glory: Religions in the City,* ed. Tony Carnes and Anna Karpathakis. New York: New York University Press; Sánchez Korrol, Virginia. 1988. "In Search of Unconventional Women: Histories of Puerto Rican Women in Religious Vocations before Mid-century." *Oral History Review* 16, no. 2 (Fall): 47–63.

María Pérez y González

ROS-LEHTINEN, ILEANA (1952–)

Congresswoman Ileana Ros-Lehtinen was born in Havana, Cuba, on July 15, 1952. Shortly after the 1959 revolution led by Fidel Castro, seven-year-old Ileana and her parents, Amanda Adato Ros and Enrique Emilio Ros, immigrated to the United States. Like many other Cuban refugees, the family settled in Miami, Florida. After earning an A.A. degree from Miami-Dade Community College in 1972, Ros-Lehtinen graduated from Florida International University with a bachelor's degree in English in 1975. She then founded Eastern Academy, a private elementary school where she was a teacher and principal for ten years.

In 1982 she was elected to the Florida House of Representatives. During her service in the state legislature (1983–1986) she met and eventually married attorney and lawmaker Dexter Lehtinen. They had two daughters, Patricia and Amanda. Ros-Lehtinen served as a state representative until 1986. In that year she was elected a state senator and served in that capacity from 1986 until 1989. She resigned from the state senate to campaign in the special election held to fill the vacancy in the U.S. House of Representatives left by the sudden death of Claude Pepper, who had held the seat for twenty-six years.

The race was an especially bitter one that divided voters along ethnic lines. But with the strong support of President George H. Bush, his son Jeb Bush, and the Spanish-language radio stations, Ros-Lehtinen won 95 percent of the Cuban American votes and 53 percent of the total vote. Her victory on August 29, 1989, made her the first Cuban American woman to be elected to Congress. When the seat came up for election the following year, she won 60 percent of the district's votes.

As a member of the House of Representative, Ros-Lehtinen has focused on a number of issues: affordable child care, education, including prepaid college tuition programs, senior citizen concerns, environmental efforts to clean up the Miami River, and foreign policy, especially in Latin America and the Caribbean. These interests have led to her participation on committees such as

Congresswoman Ileana Ros-Lehtinen. Courtesy of Ileana Ros-Lehtinen.

sponsorship of the Breast and Cervical Cancer Treatment Act (H.R. 1070).

In the 109th Congress, Ros-Lehtinen's many committee assignments include the International Relations Committee, the Committee on Government Reform, and the Budget Committee. On the International Relations Committee, she is the chair of the House Subcommittee on the Middle East and Central Asia, the first Latina to chair a congressional subcommittee.

See also Latinas in the U.S. Congress; Politics, Electoral

SOURCES: Fernandez, Mayra. 1994. *Ileana Ros-Lehtinen, Lawmaker.* Columbus, OH: Modern Curriculum Press; Novas, Himilce. 1995. *The Hispanic 100.* New York: Carol Publishing Group; U.S. House of Representatives. "Congresswoman Ileana Ros-Lehtinen." www.house.gov/ros-lehtinen/welcome.html (June 28, 2005).

Bárbara C. Cruz

the International Relations Committee, the Government Reform Committee, the Foreign Affairs Committee, the Subcommittee on Human Rights and International Organizations, the Subcommittee on Employment and Housing, and the Speaker's Task Force for a Drug Free America. When she chaired the Subcommittee on International Economic Policy and Trade, she became the first Latina to chair a congressional subcommittee.

As a Republican, Ros-Lehtinen differs significantly from the political views of other Latinos in Congress. While she is liberal on some issues such as child care, the elderly, the English-only movement, and immigration, Ros-Lehtinen's most controversial stances center on her blanket condemnation of Fidel Castro's regime in her native Cuba. She has argued against lifting the U.S. economic embargo imposed on the island nation, believing that economic trade would only support Communist rule. She was instrumental in the passage of the Cuban Democracy Act of 1992 and the Cuban Liberty and Democratic Solidarity Act of 1996, popularly known as the Helms-Burton Law. The latter, intended as a catalyst to the collapse of the Castro regime in Cuba by prohibiting foreign investment, has been widely regarded as a failure. Instead, the economic embargo has been used by Fidel Castro as a political rationale for the nation's economic troubles.

Nonetheless, Ros-Lehtinen has enjoyed significant political support in southern Florida. In 1999, in honor of the congresswoman, six southern Florida cities declared March 19 Ileana Ros-Lehtinen Day. That same year Ros-Lehtinen received an award from the National Breast Cancer Coalition for her leadership and

ROYBAL-ALLARD, LUCILLE (1941–)

In 1992 California native Lucille Roybal-Allard made history. She became the first Mexican American woman to be elected to the U.S. Congress. Congresswoman Roybal-Allard was born and raised in Boyle Heights, California, the eldest daughter of Lucille and retired congressman Edward R. Roybal.

Born into a political family (her father served in Congress for thirty years), Roybal-Allard had served three terms in the California State Assembly before being elected to the U.S. House of Representatives. She lists her earliest career as a public relations and fundraising executive. Her Los Angeles district (the Thirty-third California District) includes downtown Los Angeles, East Los Angeles, and eight southeast cities of Los Angeles County. It is a diverse urban/suburban area with a largely Hispanic hardworking and upwardly mobile constituency. Roybal-Allard represents part of her father's old district, which was divided by redistricting.

In Congress Roybal-Allard distinguished herself as a consensus builder and hardworking champion of working families and won important leadership positions. In 1999 she became the first Latina to be appointed to the powerful House Appropriations Committee, sometimes called the "purse strings" of the federal government. Before that, in the 105th Congress (1997–1999) she was elected chair of the twenty-nine-member California Democratic congressional delegation, the first woman and first member to assume that position through election rather than seniority. In the 106th Congress (1999–2001) she became the first woman elected to chair the influential Congressional Hispanic Caucus, composed of eighteen members of

Congresswoman Lucille Roybal-Allard. Courtesy of Lucille Roybal-Allard.

Congress from throughout the United States and its territories.

During nearly ten years in the nation's second-highest deliberative body, Roybal-Allard's legislative priorities have included improving school safety, modernizing and upgrading public schools, increasing the minimum wage, addressing the high Hispanic school dropout rates, saving Social Security, and stimulating economic growth. As chair of the Congressional Hispanic Caucus, she focused on education, economic development, the 2000 census, and health care.

Roybal-Allard serves on two influential subcommittees of the Appropriations Committee: the Subcommittee on Commerce, Justice, State, and the Judiciary and the Subcommittee on Energy and Water Development. These subcommittees oversee funding issues affecting small business, international trade, the census, national security, law enforcement, the Department of Energy, and several independent agencies of the U.S. government.

During the 107th Congress Roybal-Allard sponsored legislation to prevent underage drinking, protect children employed in agriculture, create a tax credit to help low-income working families buy homes, protect consumers from unreasonable practices by credit card

companies, and provide grants to clean up lead-based paint hazards, particularly in schools and day-care centers in low-income areas, as well as other bills to improve the quality of life for her constituents and families throughout the nation. She has spoken out forcefully on the issue of teen pregnancy, citing the country's highest rate among comparable nations and the particularly high rate among Hispanic teens.

On September 12, 2001, the day after the attacks on the World Trade Center and the Pentagon, Roybal-Allard took the floor of the U.S. House of Representatives to console the victims and families directly impacted. "Our hearts and prayers go out to the families and loved ones of the victims, and I assure them that we as a nation will not rest until the enemies responsible for this attack upon our country—and indeed, democracies everywhere—have been brought to justice." She coordinated with local officials to provide information and assistance in the wake of this tragedy.

In the 109th Congress, 1st session, Roybal-Allard is the first Latina to serve on the House Appropriations Committee and, as part of her duties, she serves on the Homeland Security Subcommittee as well as on the subcommittees for Labor, Health, and Human Services, and Education.

Roybal-Allard is married to Edward T. Allard III and is the mother of two adult children, Lisa Marie and Ricardo Olivarez. She is a 1965 graduate of California State University at Los Angeles.

See also Latinas in the U.S. Congress; Politics, Electoral

SOURCES: Machamer, Gene. 1996. *Hispanic American Profiles.* New York: One World, Ballantine Books; Tardiff, Joseph C., and L. Mpho Mabunda, eds. 1996. *Dictionary of Hispanic Biography.* New York: Gale Research; Telgen, Diane, and Jim Kamp, eds. 1993. *Notable Hispanic American Women.* Detroit, MI: Gale Research; U.S. House of Representatives. "Congresswoman Roybal-Allard." www.house.gov/roybal-allard/ (accessed July 18, 2005).

Bettie Baca

RUIZ, BERNARDA (1802–1880)

Nineteenth-century champion of civil rights Bernarda Ruiz was born and raised in a small adobe in the Santa Barbara Presidio. She was the daughter of María Ygnacia Lugo and Sergeant José Pedro Ruiz. Through intermarriage of families at that time, Bernarda was related to many of California's most prominent Mexican citizens. In 1817, fifteen-year-old Bernarda married José de Jesús Teodoro Rodríguez, a presidio soldier. In time they became the grantees of the Conejo Ranch and the parents of eight children. Sergeant Ruiz died when the children were young. Bernarda's four sons later operated a pony express mail service between Santa Barbara and Mexico City.

Late in December 1846, during the U.S. war with Mexico, Colonel John C. Frémont arrived in Santa Barbara with a 400-man California battalion, headed toward Los Angeles to battle with the Mexican National Army. Frémont and the California battalion needed to spend a few days in Santa Barbara to recuperate from a torrential storm they had encountered on the journey. Nearly 100 horses had been lost on the trek. Upon arrival Frémont and his men took possession of several dozen horses belonging to the Ruiz family. Rumors had spread throughout Mexican California that Colonel Frémont and Commodore Robert Stockton might impose harsh punishments on the defeated Mexicans because it appeared that the war was coming to an end. The Californios were concerned that their property would be seized and that they might be incarcerated, or worse.

While Frémont was delayed in Santa Barbara, Ruiz made arrangements to speak with him. This alone was quite a feat for a woman living in a patriarchal frontier community. Her purpose in seeing Frémont was to use her influence for peace. She persuaded Frémont that it would be to his advantage to win the Mexican Californians over to his side, rather than making them enemies by inflicting harsh sanctions. Ruiz advised Frémont that a generous peace that respected property rights would be to his advantage and political gain. She outlined plans to enable contending forces to be brought together on just and friendly terms. She suggested that residents should receive the same equal rights and protection granted to American citizens. Frémont was impressed by her sincerity, her sound reasoning, and the name-dropping that she did of her family and contacts in California.

Bernarda Ruiz and Don Jesús Pico, a cousin of the former governor of Mexican California, made arrangements for a special meeting between the colonel and the Mexican authorities. They traveled with Colonel Frémont to the San Fernando Mission to meet with General Andrés Pico and representatives of the Mexican regiment. At that time General Pico was reluctant to meet with the American military commanders and representatives of the United States. He was upset about rumors that were spreading among the Californios that Commodore Stockton and General Stephan Kearny were planning to impose stiff sanctions on the Mexicano residents because the battles were coming to an end. Ruiz alone went to General Pico's encampment to tell him about the peace agreement she and Frémont had discussed two weeks earlier in Santa Barbara. On January 13, 1847, Colonel Frémont and General Andrés Pico, along with six oth-

Bernarda Ruiz was influential in drafting the Treaty of Cahuenga 1847. Courtesy of Jeff Paul.

ers, signed the Articles of Capitulation at the Campo de Cahuenga near Los Angeles. That agreement became known as the Treaty of Cahuenga. The document, in English and Spanish, included seven articles. It ended the Mexican War in California, defined the terms of the settlement, and promised full civil and property rights to residents in the territory while it was occupied by the United States. It also granted persons the right to leave the territory. Bernarda Ruiz was present when the representatives of the two nations signed the document. Frémont acknowledged in his memoirs that the Treaty of Cahuenga actually started with the conversation with Bernarda Ruiz in Santa Barbara.

Bernarda Ruiz was a community leader, an early champion for property and civil rights for Mexicanos and women, and an activist for peace. The agreements she articulated with Colonel Frémont that ended the Mexican War in California served as a model for the Treaty of Guadalupe Hidalgo.

See also Treaty of Guadalupe Hidalgo

SOURCES: Rasmussen, Cecilia. 2002. "Los Angeles—L.A. Then and Now: Woman Helped Bring a Peaceful End to Mexican-American War." *Los Angeles Times*, May 5, B-4; Tomkins, Walker A. 1967. *Old Spanish Santa Barbara: From Cabrillo to Frémont.* Santa Barbara, CA: McNally and Loftin.

Jeff Paul

RUIZ, IRENE HERNÁNDEZ (1920–)

Born in San Antonio in 1920, Irene Hernández Ruiz enjoyed a comfortable childhood because of the success of her restaurateur father, Antonio "Tony" Dorado Hernández, and the business sense of her boarding-school-educated mother, María de la Luz Vela Benavides. The second of six surviving daughters, Ruiz attended private Catholic schools until she entered Brackenridge High School, from which she graduated in 1939, and San Antonio College (SAC). While her Mexicano father ran the downtown Liverpool Café, her Tejana mother managed rental properties, a beauty salon, and a household where her daughters spent hours studying languages and practicing for piano recitals.

In December 1941 the attack on Pearl Harbor significantly changed Ruiz's life. A judge who frequented her father's café asked if his daughters would consider working for the Office of Censorship. With knowledge of English, Spanish, and Portuguese, Ruiz immediately volunteered. From January 1942 to August 1945 she worked full-time as a translator and phone monitor, listening to cross-border telephone calls between the United States and Latin America.

After the end of World War II Ruiz resumed her studies at Our Lady of the Lake University, earning a teaching certificate in 1948. A year before graduation Ruiz assumed her first teaching post at a nearby country school in Bigfoot, Texas. Every Sunday evening she commuted with colleagues to Bigfoot, resided at the teacherage during the week, and drove home on Friday. After graduation Ruiz accepted a job at Grulla, Texas, in Starr County. A year later she returned to San Antonio, where she taught at the Edgewood and San Antonio independent school districts. In 1956 she married teacher Francisco H. Ruiz (d. 1998), and the couple had three sons: A. Duane, F. Brent, and R. Bret.

Sharing a love of languages, the couple pursued higher education together, attending summer language institutes for teachers at Texas Tech University in Lubbock and the University of Kansas (KU) in Lawrence. Later Irene Ruiz attended a third institute at Vanderbilt University. However, in 1963 KU Spanish professor Agnes Brady recruited the couple to Lawrence and then to Kansas City, where she helped them gain employment. Ruiz taught Spanish in the secondary schools, while her husband oversaw the school district's language programs. In the summer of 1969 she began library studies at Emporia State University and also taught evening courses as an adjunct English professor at Penn Valley Community College from 1971 to 1976.

When Kansas City schools were wrestling with integration in the 1970s, the district transferred Ruiz to Lincoln High School, a formerly segregated African American high school, and later to the new Martin Luther King Junior High School, where she continued to teach for four years until she accepted a librarianship at the Kansas City Main Library. Encouraged to pursue her interests in preserving Mexican American community history, Ruiz organized an oral history project of early West Side settlers who had lost family photographs and documents in the infamous flood of 1951, the largest in twentieth-century Kansas history. Ruiz conducted fifty-nine interviews, including six in Spanish, essentially recovering a community history "on tape."

In tandem with historical recovery efforts, Ruiz also transformed the storefront West Branch into a bilingual collection that better served community needs. Attending meetings at churches and the Guadalupe Center, a Catholic women's settlement house whose papers constitute part of the Hispanic collection, she invited Mexican American residents to join the library. Eventually residents recognized Ruiz as a steady beacon and solicited her assistance with translations for job applications and finally with queries about the library's Spanish selections. When voters passed a tax levy in 1996 to build a permanent home for the branch, Ruiz finally agreed to retire.

In 2000 West Side community leaders successfully lobbied the library board to rename the West Branch after Ruiz for her accomplishments as an educator and librarian. For two decades the popular West Branch librarian had augmented the district's Spanish-language materials collection to serve the growing Latino, mostly Mexican American, population in Kansas City's West Side barrio. In 2001 Kansas City residents reopened the West Branch in a new 4,000-square-foot building now called the Irene H. Ruiz Biblioteca de Las Americas. The Ruiz Branch features bibliographic and audiovisual resources related to Latina/o culture in Spanish and English, as well as bilingual staff members who offer dual-language programming. The Main Library's Special Collections also contain the Kansas City Latino Heritage Collection, which comprises original documents, including organizational archives and the fifty-nine oral histories that Ruiz conducted from 1977 to 1982.

In retirement Ruiz continues her educational activism as a "storytime" reader at the Ruiz Branch. Various Kansas City organizations, including Azteca, MANA (Mexican American Women's National Association), and the Women's Foundation of Greater Kansas City, have honored her achievements. Ruiz is a past president of the Alpha Chapter of Alpha Delta Kappa, an international honorary sorority for women educators. Her own oral history is part of the History Speaks Project: Visions and Voices of Kansas City's Past in the

Western Historical Manuscript Collection at the University of Missouri, Kansas City.

See also Education

SOURCES: Kansas City Latino Heritage Collection. Kansas City Public Library, Kansas City, MO. www.kclibrary. org/sc/db/ethnic/latino/resources.htm#Resources (accessed July 18, 2005), Ruiz, Irene Hernández. 2002. Interview by Gene T. Chávez, June 7. The History Speaks Project: Visions and Voices of Kansas City's Past (KC400). Western Historical Manuscript Collection, Kansas City, University Archives, University of Missouri, Kansas City; _____. 2004. Interview by Laura K. Muñoz, February 9.

Laura K. Muñoz

RUIZ DE BURTON, MARÍA AMPARO (1832–1895)

Probably the first U.S. Latina to publish her work in English, María Amparo Ruiz, the daughter of Jesús Maitorena and Isabel Ruiz de Maitorena, was born in Loreto, Baja California, in 1832. Her grandfather, José Manuel Ruiz Carrillo, served as a northern Baja frontier soldier and officer and in 1822 retired to Loreto, then the capital of Baja. Shortly after his arrival Don José Manuel was named governor of Baja California (1822–1825), a post he held until the newly established Mexican republic appointed a *jefe político* for the Californias. This connection with the cash-poor but socially privileged Ruiz family perhaps explains María Amparo Ruiz's use of the Ruiz surname throughout her life.

The future California writer grew up in La Paz, Baja California, a small village but by then the new capital, where she was schooled in Spanish and French. María Amparo Ruiz was fourteen years old when the United States invaded Mexico in 1846. A year later U.S. troops, under the command of Lieutenant Colonel Henry Stanton Burton, an army officer trained at West Point, took over Baja California. The war in Baja saw both resistance and accommodation on the part of the Mexicans. In 1848, after the signing of the Treaty of Guadalupe Hidalgo, which reduced the Mexican territory by half, but left Baja under Mexican control, U.S. troops departed, along with a number of Baja residents who decided to cast their lot with the invaders. Sixteen-year-old María Amparo, her mother, her sister, and her brother-in-law were among this group. A year later the Catholic María Amparo Ruiz married Captain Henry S. Burton, a Protestant, to the consternation of the Catholic Californios.

Her marriage to an army officer provided her with the opportunity to learn English, socialize with prominent army officers and their wives in Monterey and the Bay Area, live for a period in San Diego, where he was later stationed, and travel to the East Coast at the outbreak of the Civil War. Before they went east in 1859, she and Burton had purchased Rancho Jamul, a former Pío Pico rancho in the San Diego area. The mother of two children, Nellie and Harry, Ruiz de Burton lived in various eastern seaboard cities and spent a good deal of time in Washington, D.C., where she met President Abraham Lincoln and his wife and made contact with the Mexican consulate and the leading men of Mexico as well. Indeed, she became a personal friend of First Lady Mary Todd Lincoln. Her sojourn in Washington gave her the opportunity to observe firsthand the federal government and culture, especially during the Civil War, and afforded her a unique critical distance from which to view and critique the transformations taking place in the United States.

Ruiz de Burton spent the rest of her life in the United States, living on the East Coast until 1870 and, after the death of her husband, relocating to California, where she fought to retain ownership of Rancho Jamul. After extensive litigation title was confirmed, but the land was ultimately lost to creditors and lawyers. The period between 1848 and 1900 witnessed U.S. imperial expansion, modernization, war, monopoly capitalism, graft, antilabor legislation, and speculative investment, all developments that ground the life and writing of Ruiz de Burton. All of her experiences became grist for her pen.

While living in San Diego in the early 1850s, she wrote, produced, and later published (1876) a five-act comedy based on *Don Quixote.* In 1872 she published her first novel, *Who Would Have Thought It?*, a bitingly satirical text set during the period of the Civil War that reveals the hypocrisy of some abolitionists, as well as the outright privateering and opportunism of the emerging capitalist class, the "robber barons" of the so-called Gilded Age. This novel may be the first English-language publication written by a Latina. Her second novel, *The Squatter and the Don* (1885), stands out as the first published narrative—written in English—to give the perspective of the conquered Mexican population that, despite being promised full rights of citizenship after the U.S.-Mexican War, was already by 1870 a subordinated and disenfranchised minority. She was a voluminous correspondent, and there exist more than 200 of her letters to and from a wide range of people. These letters reveal her complex, multifaceted personality and the diverse issues with which she engaged throughout her life. Writing from a Latina identity, she articulated the bitter resentment of Californios who endured the onslaught of Anglo-American domination in the period after 1848, and she early on warned against the dangers of an expanding United States. In the end Ruiz de Burton lost most of her property and businesses and died in straitened circumstances; at her death in 1895, however, she was still involved in litigation regarding her claims to property in Baja California.

Ruiz de Burton's novels, articles, and letters provide insights into her own complicated life as well. Her dual identification and nationality, her sense of displacement, her contradictory accommodations to and disidentification with the United States, her sense of a "Latin" race that goes beyond national identity and citizenship, and her strong sense of herself as a woman challenged by gender constraints are all traits that make Ruiz de Burton a very complex and modern Latina subject, worthy of critical study.

See also Literature

SOURCES: Ruiz de Burton, María Amparo. 1995. *Who Would Have Thought It?* Ed. Rosaura Sánchez and Beatrice Pita. Houston: Arte Público Press (orig. pub. Philadelphia: J. B. Lippincott, 1872); _____. 1997. *The Squatter and the Don.* 2nd edition [C. Loyal, pseud.]. Ed. Rosaura Sánchez and Beatrice Pita. Houston: Arte Público Press (orig. pub. San Francisco: S. Carson and Co., 1885); _____. 2001. *Conflicts of Interest: Letters of María Amparo Ruiz de Burton.* Ed. Rosaura Sánchez and Beatrice Pita. Houston: Arte Público Press; Sánchez, Rosaura, and Beatrice Pita. 2005. "María Amparo Ruiz de Burton and the Power of Her Pen." In *Latina Legacies*, ed. Vicki L. Ruiz and Virginia Sánchez Korrol. New York: Oxford University Press.

Beatrice Pita

SADA, MARÍA G. "CHATA" (1884–1973)

María "Chata" Sada was born in Iraxuato, Guanajuato, Mexico. She and her husband Juan operated a trading post, restaurant, and general store in the Big Bend area of Texas during the 1920s and 1930s, when the area was still relatively remote. Chata's Place provided a sense of community life for Big Bend because it served as the social hub where weddings, birthday celebrations, and other festivities were held. It even doubled as a Catholic church on occasion.

María married Juan Sada in 1901, and they crossed the border at Boaquillas, becoming one of two families to settle in the area. Like Spanish-speaking settlers of the eighteenth and nineteenth centuries, they made their own adobe home. However, unlike their predecessors, the Sadas did not rely on a horse and buggy, but on a newfangled automobile. María Sada took charge of Chata's Place because her husband operated a silver mine in Coahuila. She learned English in order to serve hunters, geologists, engineers, and naturalists who ventured into Big Bend. For those who needed lodging in this isolated area, she provided hot meals and spare rooms. She also kept beer cold in a kerosene-powered refrigerator, even during Prohibition. María Sada also served as an informal bank, cashing checks for customers.

She and Juan Sada adopted six children and served as godparents for others. María Sada developed a reputation as a midwife, pharmacist, judge, teacher, and gardener. She also raised livestock and, given the rugged terrain with mountain lions and rattlesnakes, was handy with a rifle. A 1955 *Dallas Morning News* article described her as a friendly, affectionate hostess who also had a certain regal bearing. When Juan Sada died in 1936, María closed the trading post and moved to Del Rio, Texas, to live with a son. She died in 1973. María Sada was a successful businesswoman who provided services to travelers and created community in a remote region of Texas.

See also Entrepreneurs

SOURCES: Orozco, Cynthia E. 1996. "Maria Sada." In *New Handbook of Texas* 5. Austin: Texas State Historical Association; Smithers, W. D. 1976. *Chronicle of the Big Bend.* Austin, TX: Madrona Press.

Cynthia E. Orozco

SALSA

In Latin America popular music has traditionally been conceived through the bodies and the voices of women. Women have been major icons of romantic ballads, boleros, and folkloric music in various national traditions. From bolero interpreters such as the Argentinian Libertad Lamarque, the Puerto Rican Ruth Fernández, and the Mexican Toña la Negra to the folkloric compositions and performances of the Chilean Violeta Parra, the Peruvian Chabuca Granda, and the Argentinian Mercedes Sosa and to all-women bands such as Grupo Anacaona in Cuba and others in Cali, Colombia, in the 1980s, women have been important agents of popular music, as well as serving as inspiration for the greatest male songwriters.

In contrast to this very rich female musical tradition, women in salsa music have been historically excluded as interpreters and instrumentalists. As a musical industry that emerged in New York City among second-generation Puerto Rican musicians, salsa music developed all-male networks of musical training and jamming sessions that kept women from participating in its popular, oral transmission. Major musicians such as Willie Colón, Héctor Lavoe, Ray Barretto, and others transmitted a symbolic gendering through the music, its lyrics, its instrumentation, and album designs, which reaffirmed the male voice, subjectivity, and stage presence and the historical narratives about the music itself. Sexist attitudes that perceived women as unfit to play certain instruments and the cultural mores that kept women at home and away from the clubs and the public spaces of musical performance also added to the exclusion of women.

It is surprising that, given the rich history of women in Latin American popular music, particularly in countries such as Cuba, Puerto Rico, and Mexico, from

Salsa singer Merceditas Váldez in New York, circa 1950. Courtesy of the Justo A. Martí Photograph Collection. Centro Archives, Centro de Estudios Puertorriqueños, Hunter College, CUNY.

which U.S. Latino communities have emerged, only a few female names have been associated with salsa music in the United States since the late 1960s. While the name of Cuban exile singer Celia Cruz easily comes to mind when one speaks of salsa, the popular music of the urban Caribbean and of its diaspora, historical revisions and recoveries by cultural critics and feminist scholars have foregrounded the ways in which other women have played important roles in its development. Likewise, since the 1990s there has been a growing number of younger *salseras,* or female salsa composers, interpreters, and instrumentalists, who are changing the masculine discourse of the music and who will continue to appropriate this style in order to express and perform, through their bodies, their songs, and their voices, their experiences and perspectives as Latinas in the United States.

During the second half of the 1960s the early period of salsa music was characterized by a strong, brassy, urban sound that distinguished New York salsa music from more traditional Cuban forms, such as the *son,*

the *guaguancó,* and the *guaracha.* However, the particular sound of salsa—what César Miguel Rondón calls "war-like, *aguerrida*"—was, ironically, articulated in its early stages by a woman, La Lupe. La Lupe, whose real name was Guadalupe Victoria Yoli Raymond, was born in Santiago, Cuba, and, after achieving national popularity for her transgressive performances in local clubs in Havana, came to the United States in 1962. She became known for her collaborations with Tito Puente, as a major interpreter of Tite Curet Alonso's compositions "Puro teatro" and "La gran tirana," and, of course, for her performative excesses on stage, dramatic interpretations, and provocative gestures of voice and body. La Lupe, historians believe, helped reinforce the warlike, masculine sound of early salsa music in New York.

Despite this central role in salsa music, La Lupe's career never developed. Rather, her agency was undermined by male producers, other musicians, and the media. Her personal experiences and drug abuse seemingly led to a perception that she was unprofessional, unruly, and, from a masculine perspective, not really a singer, but more of a performer. Since the music industry rejected her presence and agency, she fought back partly through her own songs, "Dueña del cantar" and "Yo soy como soy," in which she denounced male musicians who had negatively affected her career and in which she reaffirmed her artistic rights and authorship regarding salsa music. After her death in 1992 La Lupe was memorialized in multiple ways. Through drama and biographical movie projects, the redigitalization of her classics and recovery of her songs by singers like Yolanda Duke and La India, and the reprisal of her artistic style by Cuban American performance artist Carmelita Tropicana. La Lupe's posthumous fame and popularity have elevated her music to classic standards, revealing the singular talent of this great Cuban singer in exile. This talent was partly recognized during her lifetime, but was mostly shadowed by controversy and abjection.

The inverse of the musical career of La Lupe is embodied by Celia Cruz, also a Cuban exile, who arrived in the United States in 1961 after a long and successful singing career with la Sonora Matancera. If La Lupe erotized herself on stage and embodied the *puta* image, the sexual and sensual woman, Celia Cruz constructed a public persona as *la gran dama de la música cubana* (the great dame of Cuban music). She was known as the Queen of Salsa, la guarachera de Oriente, and so on, and her fame crossed national borders, hemispheres, generations, and racial and socioeconomic barriers. Musically speaking, Celia Cruz brought the Cuban forms and genres back into salsa music. Throughout the 1970s, 1980s, and 1990s she continued to entertain Latino/a audiences in the

United States and cross-cultural audiences internationally with her talent for *sonear* (the ability to improvise call and response in the musical genre elision) and for improvisation, and with a magnificent alto voice that projected itself with volume and power, just as it had when she was a young girl in Cuba. Cruz began singing in radio shows and winning radio contests and soon became the lead singer for la Sonora Matancera, Cuba's most important entertainment band and musical ambassador during the 1950s to the rest of Latin America. In this role Celia Cruz became a Cuban icon and, after her exile, an important public voice of the exile community in the United States and of antisocialist Cuba.

Celia Cruz sang with major salsa musicians such as Tito Puente, Johnny Pacheco, Willie Colón, and Rubén Blades and later with El Canario, La India, and Albita. Although during the 1970s she interpreted boogaloos, *nueva onda* music from Latin America, and Cuban *guarachas,* rumbas, and *guaguancós*, she also performed religious Afro-Cuban chants, Mexican classics and rancheras, and Puerto Rican music, among other Latin American classics. The diversity and impressive gamut of her repertoires, the flexibility of her range, and the cross-cultural, transnational, and pan-Latino elements of her shows and concerts established her legendary status in a musical career that lasted for more than sixty years.

At a concert in Chicago in August 2000, Celia Cruz publicly recognized that Albita, her younger Cuban counterpart in the United States, had a wonderful talent for musical improvisation. This comment signals a major shift in the agency and presence of women as *salseras.* During the early 1980s Celia Cruz had stated in an interview that the lack of women in salsa music had to do with the fear or resistance of women to improvise and *sonear.* Twenty years later the emergence of younger salsa singers, such as Albita, La India, Brenda K. Starr, Corrine, Lisette Meléndez, Yolanda Duke, Helena Santiago, Jaci Velázques, and others, as well as the burgeoning of all-women salsa bands in Cali, Colombia, attests to major shifts in the role of women in music that have been informed by the increasing power of women in public spaces, and to their growing presence as composers and trained instrumentalists. Youth, young women as potential consumers, and the emergence of particular audiences and fans are also factors that have guaranteed a good level of successful sales figures for these women singers. One cannot forget the impact of the late Mexican American singer Selena (Selena Quintanilla Pérez), whose untimely death cut short a promising career both in Tex-Mex music and in Anglo pop. The age factor of the U.S. Latino population has also informed the centrality of young singers as representatives of the culture.

Thus a new generation of *salseras* during the 1990s has given salsa a more feminine voice and face. Among them, La India, born Linda Caballero in the Bronx, New York, has stood out for her talented improvisatory skills, feminist lyrics, and powerful stage presence. Her music illustrates a new, generational taste that fuses salsa structures, rhythms, and arrangements with other urban musical forms with which younger Latinos/as have identified: hip-hop, R&B, pop, gospel, jazz, dance, and house music. Her musical development began when she sang freestyle house and dance music in local New York clubs. These forms clearly continue to inform her salsa style, arrangements, and interpretations. Like her generational peer Marc Anthony, La India's shift into salsa and into singing in Spanish has been incorrectly labeled as "crossover" when in fact this change is the inverse, from English into Spanish. La India's incursion into salsa, and particularly into *salsa romántica*, was influenced by contemporary male musicians, such as Eddie Palmieri and her then husband and producer, Little Louie Vega. Moreover, like La Lupe before her, and like other contemporaries, including Yolanda Duke, La India's development in salsa music was also overtly mediated by the major male figures of the industry. Her first album, titled *Llegó la India via Eddie Palmieri* (1992), is a testament to Palmieri's "discovery" of her singing talents. The title song, "Llegó la India," and "Mi primera rumba" describe La India's own awareness of her debut as a salsa singer.

La India's struggle for an increasing autonomy is evident in the progression of her musical career and is symbolically articulated in the sequence of her CDs. La India dedicated the CD *Dicen que soy* (1994) to Celia Cruz and *Sola* (1999) to La Lupe. These dedications to women singers have served to resituate La India within a history of women *salseras*, rather than as the musical discovery or product of her *salsero* male counterparts. She has also expressed this feminist stance in the song "La voz de la experiencia" (in *Sobre el fuego*, 1997), which she composed as an homage to Celia Cruz and performed as a duet with the Cuban singer and role model. The song is not only a public relations tool for RMM Records that highlights its two major female *salseras*, but also a complex text that, musically and in its lyrics and performance, attests to the influences of both singers, as well as to the meanings that salsa music has had for both Cuban and Puerto Rican listeners. The fact that La India's most recent recording is titled *Sola* suggests that reaching a certain level of autonomy in her musical career and performances has been an important goal for this Puerto Rican *salsera*.

La India's feminist lyrics in *salsa romántica* have had a significant impact on female audiences and listeners.

Some of her most popular cuts—such as "Ese hombre," "Dicen que soy," and "Me cansé de ser la otra"—are overt expressions against patriarchy and against the double standards of male-female relationships. While critics have dismissed *salsa romántica* as a trend created by the industry to appease and neutralize the cultural politics of the music of the 1970s—what is now being called *salsa dura*—it is also true that La India's contributions to *salsa romántica* offer her listeners strong, feminist denouncements of male behavior in heterosexual relationships.

Cuban singer Albita, who crossed the U.S.-Mexico border in the early 1990s, has become a well-known *salsera* in the United States. While her reputation and fame in Cuba were based on her talented interpretations of Cuban folkloric music, such as the *guajiras*, in the United States her musical selections have included more salsa arrangements, jazz-infused cuts, and more traditional Cuban music. Her first CD, *No se parece a nada* (1995), suggests androgynous and homoerotic discourses on love and sexuality, a perspective that has been historically silenced in the music industry. Other women *salseras* whose work contributed to the emergence of a Latino/a new salsa in the 1990s are Brenda K. Starr, Corrine, Lisette Meléndez, Helena Santiago, and Yolanda Duke. Together these voices continue to fuse salsa rhythms with other popular dance forms, such as dance, house, R&B, merengue, reggae, and vallenatos. They are singing in Spanish and in English and combining both, linguistic choices that reflect the fluid, interlingual practices of second- and third-generation U.S. Latinos/as. Born in East Harlem, Lisette Meléndez has improvised in both English and Spanish and has interpreted *salsa romántica* under Sir George Productions in a duet with Frankie Negrón, thus foregrounding the dialogic perspectives of both men and women as they negotiate love relationships. Corrine, whose CD *Un poco más* (1999) was produced under Ralph Mercado, mixes hip-hop and salsa in rewritings of pop classics, such as Madonna's "La isla bonita." Her collaboration with, and the arrangement of, Wyclef Jean offer listeners a hybrid, remix freestyle salsa version of Madonna's tropical representation of Latino/a culture, one that reclaims the song by using Spanish and English and infusing it with the rhythms and musical language of the Latino/a youth communities themselves.

Generational identities are also evoked in Corinne's version of the classic Cuban bolero "Lágrimas negras," which is now interpreted as a remix of hip-hop, salsa, and rap. In fact, Corinne's *soneo* (call and response improvisation to the music) brings in the woman's voice, which in this version resists going back to the man, a perspective absent in the traditional boleros of the 1940s and 1950s. Brenda K. Starr has also made signif-

icant contributions to the new salsa with her 1998 recording *No lo voy a olvidar*, in which she sings "I Still Believe" in a salsa version. This is meaningful because, again, it reclaims a pop song made famous by Mariah Carey, but originally interpreted by Starr herself. Of half-Jewish, half-Puerto Rican heritage, Brenda K. Starr, born Brenda Kaplan, began by singing pop in English and is now gaining popularity as a major female interpreter of *salsa romántica* in Spanish. She has received numerous national awards as a salsa interpreter, and her career continues to be very promising within the industry. The younger Helena Santiago, who debuted on stage at Cleveland's Rock and Roll Hall of Fame on October 11, 1997, has a CD titled *Yo vine a cantar* and also fuses salsa, merengue, and house music in her work.

Given the systematic exclusion of women that characterized the salsa music industry from its beginnings, the emergence of numerous younger *salseras* since the 1990s is definitely cause for celebration. The presence and contributions of these singers and composers are providing much-needed feminist and female perspectives to the ongoing dialogues and gender politics behind salsa lyrics. Yet the absence of women and Latina producers within the larger music industry reveals that the decision-making power is still in the hands of men. The struggles for autonomy and freedom that have been evident in the musical careers of Celia Cruz, La Lupe, and La India reflect the ongoing struggles that Latinas continue to face in their personal and professional realms and in society in general. Thus it is important to continue to document and trace the contributions of early figures such as La Lupe, to pay homage to the many years of music making of Celia Cruz, and to patronize the musical products of the younger generation of *salseras* such as La India, whose talents and feminist voices will provide models for the newer generations of Latinos and Latinas in the United States.

SOURCES: Aparicio, Frances R. 1998. *Listening to Salsa: Gender, Latin Popular Music, and Puerto Rican Cultures.* Hanover, NH: Wesleyan University Press and University Press of New England; Duany, Jorge. 1998. " 'Lo tengo dominao': El boom de las merengueras en Puerto Rico." In *Diálogo* (Revista de la Universidad de Puerto Rico), October, 28–29; Puleo, Augusto C. 1997. "Una verdadera crónica del Norte: Una noche con la India." In *Everynight Life: Culture and Dance in Latin/o America*, ed. Celeste Fraser Delgado and José Esteban Muñoz. Durham, NC: Duke University Press; Rondón, César Miguel. 1980. *El libro de la salsa: Crónica de la música del Caribe urbano.* Caracas, Venezuela: Editorial Arte; Waxer, Lise A. 1998. "Cali Pachanguero: A Social History of Salsa in a Colombian City." Ph.D. diss., University of Ilinois at Urbana-Champaign.

Frances R. Aparicio

SALT OF THE EARTH

Released in 1954, *Salt of the Earth* holds the distinction of being the only film ever banned in the United States. Blacklisted and branded as Communist by conservative politicians and the Hollywood studio system, a small group of filmmakers set out to document a recent strike by Mexican American miners in Silver City, New Mexico. Filmed right after the strike was settled and shot on location, the movie documented a substantial union victory against the powerful Empire Zinc Corporation. Miners, their wives, and their children, people who had actually walked the picket line, played important roles in the film. Clint and Virginia Jencks, the principal union organizers, also collaborated with the production company.

The Empire Zinc Company, a subsidiary of the largest zinc company in the United States, owned a company town and mines in Grant County, New Mexico. In 1950 the miners, members of Local 890 of the International Union of Mine, Mill, and Smelter Workers (Mine-Mill), voted to strike for an end to the dual wage structure and for better working conditions. A series of injunctions barred the male workers from the picket line. In their place stood their wives and sisters—women from the Ladies Auxiliary Local 209. Both Virginia and Clint Jencks encouraged women's leadership and participation. From October 1950 until January 1952 women held the line while men assumed traditional domestic and child-rearing responsibilities, learning what it was like to run a household without indoor plumbing or hot water. Although the women were harassed and arrested by local law enforcement, they refused to budge. Mariana Ramírez remembered, "We had knitting needles. We had safety pins. We had chili peppers." In the words of historian Vicki L. Ruiz, "The movie documents the changes in consciousness about women's place within mining families as a result of the temporary role reversals." Indeed, this new consciousness was reflected in the settlement that was reached in 1952. With women at the bargaining table, the settlement included both higher wages and hot water.

What attracted the blacklisted Hollywood filmmakers, Herbert Biberman, Paul Jerrico, Michael Wilson, and Adrian Scott, to this saga of Mexican American women on the picket line was the larger story of vast racial, class, and gender inequalities in the cold war United States. The film also stressed a feminist perspective on social problems, gender, and class issues. It documented a union victory that was rare during the cold war era and a victory by an alleged radical union.

But the film never found its way into U.S. cinema distribution because it was blocked by the conservative Projectionists' Union, the House Committee on Un-American Activities (HUAC), the U.S. Central Intel-

Picketing and knitting during the Empire Zinc mining strike, 1951. This strike was the basis for the film *Salt of the Earth*. Courtesy of the Los Mineros Photograph Collection and the Clint Jencks Papers, Chicano Research Collection, Department of Archives and Manuscripts, Arizona State University, Tempe.

ligence Agency, and even business tycoon Howard Hughes on the grounds that it was pure Communist propaganda. The Immigration and Naturalization Service arrested the lead actress, Rosaura Revueltas, shortly before the film crew wrapped up the final scenes, and she was later deported. During the late 1960s and early 1970s both feminists and Chicano activists rediscovered *Salt of the Earth* when it finally received the circulation and acclaim that it had been denied almost two decades earlier. As Ruiz notes, "*Salt of the Earth* remains emblematic of a long history of labor activism among Mexican women in the United States."

Children on the line, Empire Zinc mining strike, 1951. Courtesy of the Los Mineros Photograph Collection and the Clint Jencks Papers, Chicano Research Collection, Arizona State University Libraries, Tempe.

Elvira Molano, cochair of the union negotiating committee during the Empire Zinc mining strike, 1951. Courtesy of the Los Mineros Photograph Collection and the Clint Jencks Papers, Chicano Research Collection, Department of Archives and Manuscripts, Arizona State University, Tempe.

SOURCES: Lorence, James J. 1999. *The Suppression of* Salt of the Earth: *How Hollywood, Big Labor, and Politicians Blacklisted a Movie in Cold War America.* Albuquerque: University of New Mexico Press; Ruiz, Vicki L. 1998. *From out of the Shadows: Mexican Women in Twentieth-Century America.* New York: Oxford University Press; Wilson, Michael. 1978. *Salt of the Earth.* Screenplay with commentary by Deborah Silverton Rosenfelt. Old Westbury, NY: Feminist Press; Wilson, Michael, Herbert Biberman, and Paul Jarrico. 1954. *Salt of the Earth.* U.S. Independent Production Company and International Union of Mine, Mill, and Smelter Workers. U.S.A. black and white. 94 minutes.

Ronald L. Mize and Vicki L. Ruiz

SAN ANTONIO, ANA GLORIA (1915–   )

Ana Gloria Cabañas Villanueva de San Antonio was born on the edges of the Vivi River in Utuado, Puerto Rico, to parents who were descendants of Catalans on the paternal side and Canary Islanders on the maternal side. In the 1940s, after her parents passed away and she herself became a widow with a young child, Susanne, she decided to come to the United States, where she found life very difficult, as did other migrants during that decade. She studied domestic science at the University of Puerto Rico in Río Piedras and later obtained a baccalaureate degree in social work from St. Francis College in Brooklyn, New York. She also pursued graduate studies in romance languages and political science at Hunter College, City University of New York.

Despite her academic education, she found herself obligated to work in factories until she was able to obtain a position in the Department of Welfare in New York City, where she worked for five years. During this period she met and wed her lifelong partner and mate, Félix San Antonio. He died in 1988. This union resulted in a second daughter, Ana. In 1959 the family went to Cuba, where she was appointed chief of the Department of Special Cases for the Ministry of Social Services in Havana. Returning to New York, she applied and was accepted for a position in the Department of Social Services of the Commonwealth of Puerto Rico in New York City, where she assisted migrant Puerto Ricans with urban adjustment problems, employment, health, education, and identity documentation. She left

Ana Gloria San Antonio, second row in the middle, with other members of the Orden de la Estrella de Oriente. Courtesy of the Juanita Arocho Papers. Centro Archives, Centro de Estudios Puertorriqueños, Hunter College, CUNY.

this position to accept a position with the city of New York as director of area services in Manhattan Valley, the Lower East Side, and East Harlem. She gained recognition by knocking on doors of people in need in order to help resolve their social and economic problems. Always shying away from political favors and patronage, she advanced solely on the basis of her hard work and the civil service exams. Her last position before she retired was that of director of the Office of Evaluation and Compliance with the Housing and Development Administration of the city of New York.

A lifelong community activist, Ana Gloria San Antonio was connected to many organizations. She served on the Board of Directors of the John F. Kennedy Library for Minorities and the Board of Directors of the Lower East Side Neighborhood Association and chaired the Northeast Narcotics Association Committee. She was secretary of the Círculo de Escritores y Poetas Iberoamericanos (CEPI), vice president of the Asociación Puertorriqueña de Escritores (APE), and cofounder of the Eslabón Cultural Hispanoamericano (ECHA). She held membership in the League of Women Voters, la Unión de Mujeres Americanas (UMA), and the Puerto Rican Hall of Fame. In 1981 she was elected president of the Hispanic Day Parade and went on to found the Immigrants Day Parade. Together with her husband, Félix, a Mason and grand master of the Gran Logia de Lengua Española in New York City, and her sister, Rosario Cabañas de Aguiar, she founded the Spanish Chapter of the Order of the Eastern Star in New York City, where she has remained active.

SOURCES: Arocho, Juana Papers. Centro Archives, Centro de Estudios Puertorriqueños, Hunter College, CUNY; San Antonio, Ana Gloria Cabañas Papers. Eastern Star Archives, Gran Logia Masonic Lodge, New York.

Susanne Cabañas

SAN ANTONIO PECAN SHELLERS' STRIKE

During the 1930s Texas controlled about 40 percent of the nation's pecan production. San Antonio stood at the center of this industry. Julius Seligmann, owner of the Southern Pecan Shelling Company, initiated a contracting system that proved exploitative. It was common to find 100 pickers sitting around a long table in a space of only twenty-five feet by forty feet, working under poor illumination. Because there was no ventilation, the brown dust from the pecans hung heavy in the air, and many drew a connection between the polluted air and the high rate of tuberculosis among pecan-shelling families. Sanitary facilities in a typical sweatshop consisted of one toilet for workers of both sexes. Workers received pitiful wages in this female-dominated industry. The average annual family income of shellers was $251. An individual might make a weekly salary of $2.73.

On January 31, 1938, the Southern Pecan Shelling Company's contractors announced a pay cut from six to seven cents per pound to five to six cents per pound. Wages for pecan crackers were cut from fifty cents to forty cents per 100 pounds. A spontaneous walkout in-

Mexican women pecan shellers, San Antonio, Texas. Courtesy of the Library of Congress, America from the Great Depression to World War II: Photographs from the FSA-OW1, 1935–1945 (Digital ID: fsa 8b1319).

volving between 6,000 and 10,000 strikers ensued. The strikers were represented by the International Pecan Shellers Union No. 172, which was affiliated with the United Cannery, Agricultural, Packing, and Allied Workers of America (UCAPAWA), a Congress of Industrial Organizations (CIO) union that had granted the pecan shellers a temporary charter. UCAPAWA had also encouraged cooperation with other groups representing agricultural workers. One such group was the San Antonio chapter of the Workers' Alliance of America, a national organization to protect the rights of the unemployed. Emma Tenayuca, the popular director of the local Workers' Alliance, emerged as the pecan shellers' strike leader. Tenayuca, married to Homer Brooks, a onetime Communist Party gubernatorial candidate in Texas, was well known in San Antonio for her fiery speeches demanding justice for workers, leadership in sit-downs at city hall, and public battles against the Work Projects Administration in response to workers' pay cuts.

The pecan shellers' strike lasted three months. One thousand picketers were arrested. Tear gas was used several times, the police and fire departments were drafted for "riot duty," and both Mayor C. K. Quin and Police Chief Owen W. Kilday refused to acknowledge the strike. Kilday, in particular, used the local media to ridicule Tenayuca and the strikers. The gross mistreatment of the strikers attracted national attention, and Texas governor James V. Allred ordered the Industrial Commission of Texas to investigate violations of civil liberties. Commission hearings determined that Kilday's police department had overstepped its authority.

Violations of civil liberties by the police occurred in an environment marked by strong anti-Communist and antiunionist sentiment. City officials, as well as representatives from the National Catholic Welfare Council, attacked the strike, characterizing it as Communist inspired and, therefore, illegitimate. Tenayuca became an easy target because of her Communist Party affiliation. Soon UCAPAWA made it clear that in order to maintain its support, Emma Tenayuca had to step down as strike leader. UCAPAWA's decision fell in line with the CIO's, and more generally the leftist position on Communists within its ranks during the 1930s. Union leaders were willing, and often eager, to receive assistance from Communists as long as they kept their political and ideological identities hidden. By 1938 Emma Tenayuca's reputation as an outspoken Communist made her not only the target of reactionaries, but also a potential liability for the Left, which hoped to achieve revolutionary changes in American society by attempting to mainstream its radical programs. Removing Tenayuca from a visible leadership role seemed the safer route for the union.

UCAPAWA president Donald Henderson took charge of the strike, with advice from CIO leader Luisa Moreno. Henderson, Moreno, and George Lambert, the UCAPAWA representative in San Antonio, negotiated the strike settlement. In 1938 the CIO secured the initial wage of seven to eight cents per pound of pecans for shellers, which increased when Congress passed the Fair Labor Standards Act that same year. This act established a minimum wage of twenty-five cents an hour for pecan shellers. The settlement came after the governor persuaded Seligmann to negotiate and the union to arbitrate. Soon, however, the pecan-shelling industry turned to mechanization, and as many as 10,000 pecan shellers lost their jobs. The significance of the pecan shellers' strike is not the short-lived pay increase but the political galvanization of workers and a community.

See also Labor Unions; United Cannery, Agricultural, Packing, and Allied Workers of America

SOURCES: Menefee, Selden, and Orin C. Cassmore. 1940. *The Pecan Shellers of San Antonio.* Washington, DC: Government Printing Office; *San Antonio Light.* 1938. "Pecan Plant Workers Strike." January 31; Tenayuca, Emma. 1986. "Interview with Emilio Zamora with the Participation of Oralia Cortez." San Antonio, TX, June. Emma Tenayuca MSS 420, Box 11, Folder 5, the Woman's Collection, Texas Woman's University, Denton; _____. 1987. Interview with Gerry Poyo, February 21. Institute of Texan Cultures Oral History Program, University of Texas at San Antonio; *Texas Observer: A Journal of Free Voices.* 1983. "Living History: Emma Tenayuca Tells Her Story." October 28; Turner, Allan. 1986. "A Night That Changed San Antonio." *Houston Chronicle*, December 14.

Gabriela González

SAN JOAQUIN VALLEY COTTON STRIKE

In October 1933 more than 18,000 cotton workers went on strike in California's agricultural heartland, the San Joaquin Valley. Seventy-five percent were Mexicans. The strike in California's most valuable crop lasted more than a month, eventually covered the 200-mile cotton belt of California, and was marked by violent confrontations and the death of several strikers.

By the fall of 1933 the economic depression had reached its nadir. New Deal programs seemed to promise government support for union organizing. The toothless section 7a of the National Recovery Act, which supported workers' right to organize and bargain collectively, excluded farmworkers, yet they interpreted the act as proof that President Franklin Roosevelt wanted them to organize. By 1933 growers had slashed farmworkers' wages. Between April and December 1933 more than 50,000 workers launched thirty-two strikes in agriculture, creating in effect a

Family scene from a strikers' camp in Corcoran, California, during the 1933 San Joaquin cotton strike. Courtesy of the Bancroft Library, University of California, Berkeley.

general strike in California agriculture. Workers spread the strikes as they migrated from the southern tip of the state north into El Monte's berry fields, across the Tehachapi Mountains into the San Joaquin Valley, and, in October, to the valley's 200-mile-long cotton belt.

When cotton growers cut wages, workers walked out of the fields. Growers evicted strikers and their families from the labor camps. With no place to go, strikers formed camps on the outskirts of several towns in the San Joaquin Valley. The largest was near Corcoran, California, where 3,500 Mexican workers formed the Corcoran camp. Lines of workers' cars and tents on the dusty lot formed makeshift streets that were named after revolutionary heroes and towns. Veterans of the Mexican Revolution organized an armed sentry system. Women set up a camp kitchen. In the center of the camp the Cannery and Agricultural Workers Industrial Union (CAWIU) hung out a handwritten sign next to a table that served as a makeshift meeting place. Another sign above it proclaimed, in Spanish, workers' 100 percent support for the National Recovery Act.

To understand Mexicanas' participation, it is necessary to reexamine assumptions about Mexican women. The rough conditions in rural Mexico had forced Mexicanas to work hard and deal with hardship, hunger, and violence. When men began to migrate to find work or, later, join an army of the Mexican Revolution, women took over the men's work. During the revolution women faced roving bands of troops and the threat of rape, starvation, and death. Women migrated, usually with men but, as Vicki Ruiz points out, sometimes with only their children or other women. Some worked in factories or sold food in the growing cities of

Mexico. In the United States some took in boarders and cooked for workers; others established food services or ran cantinas. Single women found jobs outside the home. Married women often stayed home to care for children, yet desertion, poverty, and widowhood forced women to find work. Women learned the tricks of survival and made strategic decisions for their family's welfare. This could include relations with men. Some left one man for another to improve the situation for themselves or their children. Younger women in the strike were savoring the greater freedom of the Jazz Age. Some cut their hair and wore makeup, donned short dresses, and wanted a more companionate marriage.

Mexicanas were not new to the idea of struggle and had a long tradition of fighting for the good of their communities and families. Women in Mexico City had rioted for just and fair corn prices since the colonial era. Women in Mexican factories had organized strikes. During the Mexican Revolution of 1910–1920 some traveled with male soldiers as *soldaderas*, who foraged for food, cooked, and nursed soldiers. Others smuggled guns and ammunition, spied, took up guns and fought as soldiers, worked as strategists, and served as officers.

These Mexicanas also knew firsthand the hard work of farm labor. Those who picked cotton knew the backbreaking weight of the 100-pound bags of cotton that they carried along mile-long rows of cotton. They watched the effects of the low pay and abysmal conditions on their families. In the isolated labor camps housing was a car, a tarp thrown over a branch, or, at best, a wood-frame house that lacked running water, sanitation, or insulation against cold valley nights. Far from the markets in town, women were forced to buy inferior food at inflated prices at the company store or during the depression scrounged for food. They hauled water and cooked on makeshift stoves fashioned over open fires or empty oil barrels. They nursed their family members who contracted diseases caused by these conditions, such as tuberculosis or valley fever. They wept when their children died of illness or were killed in field accidents, such as the child smothered by cotton piled high in a wagon.

These wretched conditions galvanized women to organize and in effect politicized their informal social networks. Mexicanas became the core of the strike that enabled workers to survive. They established a de facto child-care system and set up a camp kitchen. Dolores Galvan, a local cantina owner, helped distribute federally supplied food. Women organized and walked on picket lines and harassed and ultimately confronted strikebreakers who remained in the fields.

Some women participated in the CAWIU. At least two bilingual "girls" (their ages are unclear) were on the Corcoran camp's central committee and acted as interpreters. A number attended nightly strike meetings. Yet the union made few attempts to include women or address their specific concerns, and Mexicanas were not part of the leadership structure of the small union. Understandably, while many women remembered women leaders and how women fed their families and confronted strikebreakers, they remembered nothing of the union.

Focusing only on the union is misleading. The strikes' success depended in large part on the informal networks Mexicanos developed among themselves, networks that stretched from home communities in Mexico to their counterparts in the United States and to the cotton ranches, networks among Mexicanos who had been in earlier strikes, and those of anarchists and Communists who organized the strike as part of a broader desire for social change. These networks and experiences were the glue, the connecting link, among Mexican strikers and the base for the union. One of the most important was the network of women.

Women met and organized together. Women in rebozos and long braids, younger women with makeup and flapper dresses, and young girls all joined on the picket lines, calling on people to support the strike. Women appealed to strikebreakers working in the fields as Mexicanos, as paisanos, as neighbors or compadres to join the strike. Women who spotted a strikebreaker they had fed at the strikers' camp threatened to poison him if he showed up again.

As the strike wore on, Mexicanas in Corcoran, reasoning that men would be more likely to be arrested or beaten, organized brigades of women to enter the fields and confront strikebreakers. According to Belén Flores, the women appealed to strikebreakers as fellow "Mexicanos" and "poor people" to walk out. They cursed strikebreakers who remained, chastising them as national traitors, comparable to those who "sold the head of Pancho Villa." When supplications did not work, some women went after the strikebreakers with lead pipes and knives. They ripped the cotton sacks and pummeled strikebreakers with the pipes. The male strikebreakers retaliated, and at least one woman was badly beaten. Belén Flores remembered the women as strong, but the male strikebreakers as whiny cowards. When the strikebreakers pleaded that they were simply poor and wanted enough money to go home, Belén Flores remembered that the women responded in one voice, "Yes, we also have to eat and also have a family. But we are not sellouts."

After weeks of striking and the killing of several strikers, the U.S., Mexican, and California governments arbitrated a compromise to end the conflict. Wages increased to seventy-five cents for 100 pounds of cotton. Workers carried the momentum of this strike into a November strike by 1,500 cotton workers in Arizona and the January 1934 strike by 5,000 Mexicans in the Imperial Valley. But the union was not recognized, farmworkers were never covered by national legislation, and the ambivalent victories of the strike were not carried over into long-lasting changes for farmworkers.

Yet the legacy of these strikes remained an important memory. Fifty years later strikers remembered the women who "could fight like a man," the woman who seized the pistols of a highway patrolman, and another who threw the keys of a police car into the bushes. They remembered the Mexicanas arrested throughout the strike. Women's participation in the cotton strike was not an anomaly. Hundreds of similar confrontations, in which women actively organized and fought for the community, continued to pepper the history of Mexicanas. Women's actions in this strike emphasize the need to reassess lingering myths of a cultural or church-induced passivity of Mexican women and recognize the diversity of conditions, culture, and experience that helped shape their participation in this strike.

See also Labor Unions

SOURCES: Ruiz, Vicki L. 1998. *From out of the Shadows: Mexican Women in Twentieth-Century America*. New York: Oxford University Press; Weber, Devra. 1994. *Dark Sweat, White Gold: California Farm Workers, Cotton, and the New Deal*. Berkeley: University of California Press; _____. 1994. *"Raiz Fuerte*: Oral History and Mexicana Farmworkers." In *Unequal Sisters: A Multicultural Reader in U.S. Women's History*, 2nd ed., ed. Vicki L. Ruiz and Elhan Carol Du Bois, 395–404. New York: Routledge.

Devra A. Weber

SAN JUAN, OLGA (1927–)

Recognized as a versatile musical entertainer, Olga San Juan, also known as the Puerto Rican Pepper Pot, was born in Brooklyn, New York, of Puerto Rican parents on March 16, 1927. She married fellow actor Edmond O'Brien in 1948, and the marriage produced a daughter, María O'Brien, also an actress. The couple divorced in 1976, and Edmond O'Brien died in 1985 from Alzheimer's disease.

San Juan began her career on Broadway, where she won a Donaldson Award, precursor to the Tony Award, for *Paint Your Wagon.* In 1942 she landed a contract with Paramount Pictures when she was only fifteen. Originally a singer, San Juan was featured in musicals as competition to the "Brazilian Bombshell," Carmen Miranda, and appeared in supporting roles with many stars of her generation, including Fred Astaire, Bing Crosby, and Dorothy Lamour. San Juan offered one of the most memorable performances in Irving Berlin's *Blue Skies,* dancing to "Heat Wave" with Fred Astaire. She also skillfully played comic roles in films such as *The Beautiful Blonde from Bashful Bend* (1949), with Betty Grable and Cesar Romero.

As was the case for many Latina stars who began their careers in the 1940s, San Juan's roles often consisted of ethnic dancer-singers, destined to be the female (blonde) star's best friend and confidante, in B

Left to right, Alan Young, actor, Olga San Juan, actor and singer, and TSgt Bill Stewart, USA AFRS producer, circa 1950s. Courtesy of Armed Forces Radio and Television Services.

movies, comedies, and musicals. She played the attractive sidekick to the established star with wit, irony, and discipline, delivering reflective commentary, as when she played Conchita, a Mexican passing as an Indian born in Guatemala, who had trouble staying in her place: "I ain't pure." Not unlike other Latina actresses who achieved greater visibility during this period, most notably Rita Moreno, San Juan provided comic relief through her "spicy" accented lines and hip movements, despite being light skinned and American born and raised. While she was largely cast for her Latin sensuality, San Juan's characters were never considered competition for the main star, and, of course, she rarely got close to the leading man.

From the vantage point of the contemporary Latino demographic explosion and pop culture visibility, San Juan's pioneering work set an important precedent for other performers who later excelled in music, dance, and acting on the screen and the stage. Simultaneously, the limitations imposed on her career by the studios can only allow one to imagine how her talent could have developed under more conducive circumstances.

See also Movie Stars

SOURCES: *Olga San Juan.* Filmography. *Rotten Tomatoes.* 1998–2005. IGN Entertainment, Inc. Rotten Tomatoes.com/p/olga_san_juan; *Olga San Juan.* 2005. The New York Times on the Web. July 18; All Media Guide, LLC. http//movies2.nyt.com/gst/movies/filmography.html?p_id=62873; Rivera, Miluka. 1999. "Leyendas puertorriqueñas en Hollywood." *El Mundo* (December 16): e–8; Vannerman, Alan. 2004. *Blue Skies. Bright Lights Film Journal.* (November) issue 46. www.brightlightsfilm.com/46/blueskies.htm.

Frances Negrón-Muntaner

SÁNCHEZ, LORETTA (1960–)

Born in Anaheim, California, Loretta Sánchez is one of seven children of Mexican immigrant parents. Her father, Ignacio Sánchez, worked in a Los Angeles steel foundry. As a child growing up in a working-class neighborhood, she attended a Head Start program and may hold the distinction of being the first Head Start graduate ever elected to the Congress of the United States.

When her family moved to Orange County, Sánchez learned early lessons about racism against Mexican Americans. "The neighbors on both sides of us put their homes up for sale because we were Hispanic." Her father counteracted this experience with useful advice: "Never let them tell you, you are a dumb Mexican."

Her first love was business, and she attended Chapman College in Orange County, where she earned a degree in economics. At American University in Washington, D.C., she earned an M.B.A. in finance. Sánchez became a financial analyst and also president of the National Society of Hispanic MBAs. She took an active interest in local community issues and in 1990 successfully fought state officials to have a freeway sound barrier built in her Anaheim neighborhood. Putting her financial skills to work, she raised funds for several community agencies, particularly those that brought educational opportunity to disadvantaged Latino students. In 1992 she changed her political party affiliation from Republican to Democratic because "I saw that what was driving the Republican Party was a very extreme agenda to the right—it wasn't inclusive."

She ran for Anaheim City Council, in 1994 finishing sixth in a field of sixteen. Her hyphenated married name appeared on the ballot as Sánchez-Brixley. In Sánchez's historic run for Congress in 1996, she dropped Brixley and worked hard for the support of women and Latino voters. Although her two opponents in the Democratic primary (both white men) outspent her by more than three to one, Sánchez won a close victory and went on to face ultraconservative Republican congressman Robert Dornan in the general election. As in the primary, political observers gave Sánchez little chance to unseat incumbent Dornan, a nationally known figure who was then running for president. Sánchez enlisted her six siblings to walk door-to-door, while her mother spoke on her behalf at local senior centers. Orange County Latino activists enthusiastically supported her, and many newly naturalized citizens registered to vote just so they could cast ballots for Sánchez.

Counted ballots in the final tally showed Sánchez to be the winner of the Forty-sixth District of California by 984 votes. Sánchez instantly became a national figure because she had unseated one of the most conservative members of Congress, and in the process she became the only Democratic member of Congress from Orange County, a traditional Republican stronghold. Dornan immediately contested the bitter election, alleging that Sánchez had won because large numbers of non-citizen Latinos had voted for her. After a year-long investigation the House of Representatives upheld the results of the election. Sánchez quickly earned a reputation as something of a maverick. An avid seamstress, she made her own gown to Bill Clinton's inaugural ball on her grandmother's sewing machine. Loretta Sánchez embraced education reform as one of the issues closest to her heart and became a member of the Blue Dog Coalition, a group of moderate and conservative Democrats.

Women's labor, pro-choice, and gay and lesbian groups contributed heavily to Sánchez's 1998 reelection campaign, in which Dornan once again opposed her candidacy. In this election Sánchez won by more than 14,000 votes. "Adios, Bob Dornan," she proclaimed on election night.

In November 2002 Sánchez was elected for the newly created Forty-seventh District. Her sister Linda Sánchez was elected to represent the Thirty-ninth Congressional District. They are the first pair of sisters to serve in the U.S. Congress.

In the 109th Congress, 1st session, Sánchez is the ranking female member on the House Armed Services Committee. She is also the second ranking member of the Committee on Homeland Security.

See also Latinas in the U.S. Congress; Politics, Electoral

SOURCES: Fiore, Faye. 1998. "Decision 98: Sánchez Beats Dornan." *Los Angeles Times*, November 4, A3; Hernández, Greg. 1996. "Voter Turnout is Crucial for Sánchez." *Los Angeles Times*, April 14, B1; Romney, Lee. "Dornan Gets Surprise Challenger." *Los Angeles Times*, March 28, B1; U.S. House of Representatives. "Congresswoman Loretta Sánchez." www.lorettasanchez.house.gov (accessed July 23, 2005); Zoreya, Gregg. 1997. "The Freshman." *Los Angeles Times Magazine*, July 13, 8.

Virginia Espino

SÁNCHEZ, MARÍA CLEMENCIA (1926–1989)

Dubbed "la madrina" (the godmother) of the Latino and Puerto Rican community in Hartford, Connecticut, María C. Sánchez arrived in the city in 1953 and established herself as a neighborhood activist. From her strategically located candy store, María's News Stand, on Albany Avenue, she knew everyone in the Spanish-speaking barrio. She advised politicians, discussed business, monitored grassroots social services, and lobbied in educational affairs. Before long she was serving on the city's board of education and was elected to the Connecticut General Assembly.

Born in 1926 in the lush green mountains of Comerio, Puerto Rico, to poor, illiterate farmworkers who struggled to make ends meet, Sánchez was a twin and one of six children. Neither of her parents attended school, but Sánchez aspired to become educated. Severe poverty, compounded by the depression, forced her to leave school to care for younger siblings while her parents alternated employment between the fields and the factories. At the age of twenty-seven she decided to end years of child care and left Comerio in search of better opportunities. Along with thousands of other Puerto Ricans leaving the island, Sánchez became a statistic in what was called the Great Migration. She chose Hartford as her destination because she had an aunt who lived there.

Sánchez's first job was in the tobacco fields of Connecticut, and since she possessed natural leadership abilities, she soon became a crew leader. Shortly thereafter she found work in New Britain, Connecticut, in a meatpacking factory. At some point in those early years she met and married a family friend, but the relationship turned abusive and resulted in a miscarriage that robbed her of ever mothering her own children. She turned to the Sacred Heart of Jesus, the Roman Catholic church on Ely Street, for solace and discovered the first opportunities to engage in group organization and mobilization. Sánchez believed strongly in the power of organization. She founded the Society of Jesus, Daughters of Mary, Women of Our Lady of Providence, Legion of Mary, and Girl Scout Troop 107. But if the church offered her a chance to bring groups together, it unwittingly gave her a taste of organizing for empowerment.

Sánchez, with an angry cohort of parishioners, confronted the church hierarchy on the issue of appointing a Spanish-speaking priest to offer mass in Spanish at the main altar and not in the church's basement, as was the case in other churches. Predominantly a German church, Sacred Heart was headed by Father Joseph Otto. A petition to remove him was circulated, and the Chancery appointed Father Andrew Cooney, a Spanish-speaking priest familiar with the Hartford Puerto Rican community.

Sánchez's candy store, bought with savings accumulated over time, was at the crossroads of the community, a center for political activity and an attraction for schoolchildren who often stopped by at lunchtime and after school. Sánchez ran the establishment like a neighborhood hub, and politicians frequented the store to learn the issues of the community. Involved in voter registration drives and mediating between elected officials and the people they represented but barely understood, Sánchez was soon involved in politics. In 1966 she was treasurer of the Puerto Rican Democratic Club of Hartford and a member of the Latin American Action Project. She sat on the Hartford Democratic Committee and served for sixteen years on the Hartford Board of Education.

In keeping with her commitment to empower the Latino and Puerto Rican community through organization, Sánchez helped found dozens of associations. Among them are the Puerto Rican Parade Committee, la Casa de Puerto Rico, the Society of Legal Services, the Spanish American Merchants Association, the Puerto Rican Businessmen's Association, the Puerto Rican Coronation Ball, and the Puerto Rican state parade. Profiled in an interview printed in the *Hartford Courant*, Sánchez remarked, "I don't like publicity. I don't like newspapers. I don't do things because I get paid or because I have been promised positions or titles. I do things because I like them. I work

for a goal. I work so someone can benefit from what I accomplish."

Despite her many accomplishments, life was not always smooth sailing for Sánchez. In 1977 she was charged with fraud when state police claimed that she failed to deliver $12,193 to the state gaming commission. She was ultimately cleared of the charges, but the issue was embarrassing and damaged her reputation. Nonetheless, she was reelected to the Hartford Board of Education for a fifth term. A strong proponent of bilingual education, she was instrumental in developing the Ann Street Bilingual School in 1972, the first two-way bilingual school in the city.

In 1988 she challenged the incumbent for a seat in the Connecticut House of Representatives and won. However, the victory was short lived. On November 25, 1989, Sánchez, a diabetic, succumbed to poor health and died at the age of sixty-three. To commemorate her life and achievements, a school, the María C. Sánchez Elementary School on Babcock Street, was dedicated in her honor in 1991.

See also Bilingual Education; Politics, Electoral

SOURCES: Glasser, Ruth. 1992. *Aqui me quedo: Puerto Ricans in Connecticut.* Hartford: Connecticut Humanities Council; *Hartford Courant.* 1981. "An Institution Called Sanchez: Politician, Role Model, Refuge." January 15; Ubinas, Helen. "The Life and Times of Maria Clemencia Colon Sanchez: Hartford's Puerto Rican Community's Matriarch, 1926–1989." Paper, Trinity College, Hartford, CT.

Virginia Sánchez Korrol

SÁNCHEZ, MARÍA E. (1927–1999)

María E. Sánchez's accomplishments as a pioneer in bilingual education, supervisor of auxiliary teachers in the New York City public schools, university professor, and advocate for the fledgling field of Puerto Rican studies craft an impressive legacy. Credited as a mentor with launching the careers of hundreds of students and faculty, Sánchez did not believe in receiving accolades and praise and, when complimented, often commented, "Don't thank me; go do this for someone else." Enormously proud of former students or colleagues lauded for their contributions to academia and the Puerto Rican and Latino communities, Sánchez believed in empowering others to widen, organize, and strengthen communal circles for further advancement.

The youngest of farmer Julio Rodríguez and Modesta Rivera's three daughters, Sánchez was born in the picturesque southeastern mountains of Cayey, Puerto Rico, on February 25, 1927. At a time when women married early, she aspired to become a teacher and honed adolescent pedagogical skills by teaching catechism at the local Catholic church. Awarded a full scholarship, she was one of only four girls in her high-school graduating class to enroll at the University of Puerto Rico, Río Piedras campus. During her second year of college she accepted a position teaching elementary school in Cayey, a unique opportunity for education majors when hordes of male teachers left the classrooms of Puerto Rico to serve in World War II. She received her normal diploma from the University of Puerto Rico in 1945, and in 1952 she completed the bachelor of arts degree, graduating magna cum laude.

Sánchez married José Miguel Sánchez on July 1, 1953, and the couple left for New York City, which became their permanent home. After the births of three daughters, Evelyn, Annabelle, and Madeleine, Sánchez returned to work. During these years the dramatic expansion of the Puerto Rican community in New York City meant that hundreds of newly arrived Spanish-speaking children were coming into the school system and overwhelming instructional resources. Teachers were desperately needed to meet the needs of these children, and with a handful of mostly Puerto Rican professionals, María Sánchez became an educational pioneer in a newly created position, the substitute auxiliary teacher (SAT). Employed to help the monolingual classroom teacher deal with Spanish-speaking youngsters, the SATs connected the schools with the community through reciprocity, rapport, and a bilingual communication network. Essentially these teachers were the precursors to the field of bilingual-bicultural education.

Sánchez helped create the Society of Puerto Rican Auxiliary Teachers (SPRAT), the Puerto Rican Educators Association (PREA), and the Hispanic chapter of the United Federation of Teachers. These educational and quasi-political groups produced a cadre of leaders, instructional materials for bilingual education, and

María E. Sánchez. Courtesy of Virginia Sánchez Korrol.

classroom methodology; they also lobbied for formal recognition and licensure of the bilingual teacher.

In 1972, after some fourteen years of experience as a teacher and supervisor, María Sánchez was recruited by Brooklyn College of the City University of New York to establish a bilingual education program for future teachers. Appointed to the Department of Puerto Rican Studies, a newly created academic unit of the college, Professor Sánchez worked with Sonia Nieto and colleagues in the School of Education, Carmen Dinos and Margarita Mir de Cid, to establish the undergraduate and graduate program in bilingual-bicultural education. But in 1974 the department lost its chairperson, and Sánchez was unanimously chosen by students and faculty as the successor, but not by the college administration. When the president autocratically appointed a professor from Puerto Rico, Dr. Elba Lugo, as the new chairperson, students and faculty mounted a two-year organized protest with massive press coverage that resulted in the arrests of forty students and four faculty members and the takeover of the offices of the vice president and registrar and seriously disrupted campus affairs. During the two years under siege Lugo was never allowed to set foot in the department, while María Sánchez enacted all the duties of chairperson without portfolio.

The president capitulated and named Sánchez chairperson. Under her guidance the department stabilized and grew into a significant unit of the college. It boasted an expanded interdisciplinary curriculum that included the Puerto Rican experience within a hemispheric perspective, a strong bilingual program that prepared many of the teachers of the city's schools, inclusion in the college's core curriculum, and graduate offerings for master's degree programs in bilingual education, school supervision, and guidance and counseling. In 1981, after a tumultuous fiscal period that curtailed expansion in the City University's Ethnic Studies departments and programs, Sánchez spearheaded the rebirth of the field in the first conference on Puerto Rican Studies. Celebrating the department's tenth anniversary, scholars from Puerto Rico, Chicano Studies, Mexican American Studies, and Cuban Studies deliberated the interconnections and implications for future research in their areas of expertise. In the process this conference laid the seeds for comparative Latino Studies.

A firm believer in process, Sánchez excelled in organizing groups for empowerment and enrichment. She created the Student Union for Bilingual Education, the Graduate Association for Bilingual Education, the Latino Faculty and Staff Association, and the Puerto Rican Students Alumni Association.

On her retirement in 1990, Brooklyn College named her professor emerita. An endowment was established in her name for the Center for Latino Studies, an adjunct to the department. Attended by all of her fellow chairpersons, faculty, alumni, and students, Sánchez's retirement celebration was a testimony to the many contributions she had made to the college and the community. At the podium the dynamic, green-eyed redhead addressed the audience by recalling that there was a life before Brooklyn College and that there would be a life afterward as well. After nine years of retirement, surrounded by a growing family, friends, and her beautiful garden in Staten Island, María Sánchez succumbed to cancer. She died on December 23, 1999.

See also Bilingual Education; Education

SOURCES: Malaspina, Anne. "María E. Sánchez (1927–   )." In *Notable Hispanic American Women*, ed. Joseph M. Palmisano. Detroit: Gale Research; Sánchez, María E., and Anthony M. Stevens-Arroyo. 1987. *Toward a Renaissance of Puerto Rican Studies: Ethnic and Area Studies in University Education.* Princeton, NJ: Atlantic Research and Publications.

Virginia Sánchez Korrol

SÁNCHEZ CRUZ, REBECCA (1936–2003)

A social worker responsible for the first bilingual drinking driver program in New York State, Rebecca Sánchez Cruz was born in New York's Spanish Harlem on September 21, 1936, the fourth of five children. Her father, Fernando Sánchez, came from Aguada, Puerto Rico, and moved to the United States in 1917 at the age of twenty-one. He worked for the Pennsylvania Railroad for forty years until his retirement. Her mother, Venera Cruz, came to New York City from Maricao, Puerto Rico, in her late teens shortly after her mother died. Rebecca's parents met and married in the United States. She and her siblings were raised speaking Spanish, but quickly learned to speak English in the public schools and as they negotiated life in the city's tenements. When Rebecca was four years old, the family moved to the South Bronx, which offered better housing and was quickly becoming an important Puerto Rican enclave.

A lively and talented girl, Sánchez Cruz once put together a play by gathering neighborhood children, teaching them their lines, making costumes, and performing at the local high school. Developing creative talents early in life, she painted with oils and acrylics and crafted an artistic technique using layered colored linoleum and then carving out images revealing beautiful pictures. She proudly displayed her artwork in street exhibits in the Bronx and Manhattan.

But Sánchez Cruz was also strong-willed, intelligent, and very daring. She ignored boundaries, which

often worried her parents. Passing as sixteen, she worked at the age of fourteen sorting buttons on a factory assembly line and quickly learned that earning money would enable her to pursue her dreams. She attended Jane Addams High School and midway through her course of study unconventionally arranged to take night classes to complete requirements for the diploma. In many ways Sánchez Cruz was ahead of her time. Growing up in the 1940s and 1950s, she had always been an independent and modern thinker. At the age of twenty-three she briefly followed convention by marrying and starting a family, but could never quite keep up with the customs of the period that dictated women's roles and behavior. As a single parent, she wanted more out of life. It was this sense of rebellion against conformity that led her to become very passionate about her work and the people she served.

In 1970 Sánchez Cruz was employed by the Hospital for Joint Diseases as a social service coordinator. In 1975 Prospect Hospital Medical Foundation in the South Bronx hired her to implement the bilingual drinking driver program and to direct the community resident programs in alcoholism. Highly noted and respected for this work, she also designed the detoxification program for the Spanish-speaking and African American populations, serving more than 7,000 people. She provided counseling for both the patients and their families and often acted as a liaison between outside public and private agencies on their behalf. Because she was a recovered alcoholic herself, her intrigue with alcoholism and desire to learn everything she could about the disease, including the damage it caused within the family, drove her to strive to change the lives of those she counseled.

In this quest Sánchez Cruz completed coursework at Hunter College's School of General Studies in New York City, Rutgers University in New Jersey for alcoholism studies, and John Jay College of Criminal Justice and earned a master's in social work, specializing in a Hispanic social work program for alcohol abuse and alcoholism, at the State University of New York at Stony Brook in Long Island. The daunting task of commuting to school, working, and raising three daughters alone never slowed her momentum. She continued her training and became a certified social worker and a certified alcoholism counselor. In an effort to reach more people, she also studied client-counselor relationships, alcoholism and domestic violence, victim and perpetrator, incest and sexual trauma in alcohol and substance abuse settings, and alcoholism treatment with gay and lesbian clients.

Throughout the course of her career Sánchez Cruz often appeared in the media on programs such as *The Puerto Rican New Yorker, Life Styles with Beverly Sills,*

Social worker Rebecca Sánchez Cruz. Courtesy of Celest Smith.

Rafael Piñera, and *The New York Journal* with Herman Badillo. She remained committed to the Latino community, embracing her Puerto Rican culture and heritage. She felt a close bond to individuals in need and used whatever means were available to her in order to help them through their addictions and struggles. In her later years she became a psychiatric social worker and worked for the Suffolk County Department of Health Services, Alcoholism and Substance Abuse Division, on Long Island. At a time when bilingual health professionals were scarce, she strategically placed herself in situations where her bilingual abilities could be used to serve the Spanish-speaking population. She was instrumental in writing proposals that benefited Latinos and their communities, and she advocated on their behalf on statewide and federal committees.

For her achievements and contributions Sánchez Cruz was lauded by the Hispanic Association of Health Services Executives and Robert Abrams, former president of the borough of the Bronx. She received the Bronx Council on Alcoholism's Leadership, Commitment, and Consistent Dedication award and Channel 47's Meritorious Service to the Community award on three occasions. Nonetheless, her greatest personal achievement, according to Sánchez Cruz herself, was starting her own private practice. It gave her the op-portunity to implement her own ideas for helping and motivating her clients to improve their lives and achieve their goals. She endured hardships and sacrificed having a "charmed life" to achieve her dreams and become a mentor to her Latino community. Suffering from diabetes and heart disease during the final years of her life, Sánchez Cruz died in 2003.

SOURCES: Sánchez Cruz, Rebecca. Personal papers and journal. Celest Smith Private Collection. Clovis, California. 1978. "Hospital Based Drinking Driving Program Established in the South Bronx." 1978. *Journal of American Hospital Association.* (September) 1;52 (17): 28–30.

Celest Smith

SÁNCHEZ GARFUNKEL, AURA LUZ (1941–)

Boston activist and writer Aura Luz Sánchez Garfunkel was born in the South Bronx on September 20, 1941, to Elisa Santiago Rodríguez and Antonio Sánchez Feliciano, Puerto Ricans who came to New York in the mid-1920s. By the time their youngest daughter, Aura Luz, was born, they had moved to the South Bronx.

A meld of her Taino and Hispanic ancestry, Sánchez Garfunkel stood out against the blue-eyed blond students, mostly of Irish descent, at St. Anselm's Elementary School in the Bronx. The daily transition from the warmth and succor of her home, filled with the savory aroma of *sofrito* (Puerto Rican sauce) frying for the evening meal, to the alien environment of school, narrow-minded students, and strict, intolerant nuns roused in her young mind questions of identity and belonging. It was the age-old battle that ensued between old- and new-world traditions that shaped and complicated her understanding of identity, a theme that permeated her life. Early feelings of alienation, reinforced throughout her later years, contributed to her sensitivity to issues of marginalization and discrimination. The plight of the poor also nagged at her. When she was a little girl, her dreams of becoming an astronaut or ballerina dimmed in the face of her growing concerns about discrimination and poverty, conditions that surrounded her.

The Sánchez family lived in the South Bronx until 1952 and moved to Brooklyn to escape the increase in drug use and crime in their neighborhood when Sánchez Garfunkel was twelve. Making multiethnic friends in Brooklyn was easy for her. "It [the neighborhood] was diverse ethnically and homogeneous economically. We were all working-class poor." Despite her strong desires to "hang out" with her friends, she somehow found the time to do her schoolwork and maintain a high-enough average to get into Brooklyn

College. Although she recalls strong ties with her friends, "As the metamorphosis from adolescents to young adults took place, our indivisibility began to fracture, at first by the duality of our dreams. Mine were of getaways from the griminess of gray concrete lives, theirs of wedding aisles leading to tiled kitchens and umbrella strollers."

Her "getaway" began with the long train ride from South Brooklyn to Flatbush, where she attended Brooklyn College. Here she studied sociology and anthropology and met her first husband, Jim Monahan. They married after graduation and moved to Cambridge, Massachusetts, where Monahan attended Harvard Law School and Sánchez began working for a new antipoverty agency called ABCD, an exciting multiservice agency established in response to America's War on Poverty. Three years later they went to live in Lima, Peru, where Sánchez worked as a research assistant for an anthropological institute. After a year in Peru, the couple returned to Washington, D.C., and had a child named Dylan. They divorced shortly after Dylan's birth. A single mother, Sánchez returned to Boston.

Determined to "make a difference" in the lives of poor people and minorities, especially Latinos, Sánchez received an M.A. from the Harvard Graduate School of Education. She worked as an organizer in the then-transitional district of the South End, where displacement and gentrification were rapidly altering the neighborhood. She also worked for a Boston University research project, assessing the success of Head Start programs aimed at integrating disabled children into their classes. In 1970 she married Frank Garfunkel, a professor at Boston University and a disability rights advocate. They traveled abroad, settling in Israel for a year. On their return to the United States the couple made their home in Winthrop, Massachusetts, a blue-collar, mostly white suburb contiguous to Boston. Aura Sánchez Garfunkel worked as a consultant to the Massachusetts State Department of Education evaluating the impact of future desegregation plans on bilingual education classes. Subsequently the couple had two children, Seth and Anelisa.

During the ugly Boston desegregation years Sánchez Garfunkel fought to have a metropolitan busing program brought into her Winthrop community that would allow black and Latino children to access Winthrop schools. Although noble, the efforts failed. Her frustration and disappointment influenced her decision to go to law school. As a lawyer, she reasoned, she would have greater clout to pursue her dreams of justice. She attended Northeastern University Law School and graduated in 1980. After graduation she joined Greater Boston Legal Services. She advocated for hundreds of poor and mostly Spanish-speaking

Attorney and author Aura Luz Sánchez Garfunkel. Courtesy of Anelisa Garfunkel.

clients and defended immigrants, welfare recipients, tenants, and children with special needs. She fought for the rights of homeless people before the term had even been coined. She became an associate director with greater say in the organization's agenda.

Eventually she left to become an assistant to the receiver for the city of Chelsea, the only city in the Commonwealth of Massachusetts ever to be placed in a legislatively created receivership. There she again responded to the demands of a mostly disenfranchised minority community and established a Department of Health and Human Services for the municipality. She stayed in this position for seven years and developed a large and effective municipal response to the enormous needs of the poor and minority population of Chelsea. She created a community schools program and a health outreach "promotoras" program. She expanded a refugee assistance program, integrated the senior center by ensuring that Latino elders were not excluded from participation, assisted in community efforts to establish a culturally sensitive battered women's program, and helped establish a bilingual mediation program within the police department to address the many conflicts that often ended up on police blotters. All were efforts to alleviate the economic and social scourges of poverty and to ensure dignity for the residents of Chelsea. In great measure her contributions to city government culminated with Chelsea's selection as an All-American City in 1998. After her husband's death she took her concerns for the have-nots of the world overseas. Named the country director of the U.S. Peace Corps program in Micronesia, she served for two years overseeing volunteers who were working to improve public health, environmental protection, youth services, and school libraries.

Sánchez Garfunkel's communitarian dedication was not limited to her work. She was a performance artist, and her published essays and poetry focused primarily on Puerto Rican life in the New York of her childhood. She became a member of Streetfeet, a women's multicultural performing group. Through her writing she was able to reflect on the perennial question that had intrigued her from the start: just how did she fit into the intricate tapestry of America? "I learned to love my Puerto Rican roots even as I came to understand that I was very much east-coast American with an Irish-Catholic elementary schooling and a baccalaureate from a predominantly Jewish city college. I came to appreciate my Taino cheekbones, my Spanish name, and the Caribbean emotions that flowed through my veins."

SOURCES: Sánchez Garfunkel, Aura Luz. 2002. Oral interview by Anelisa Garfunkel, January; The Streetfeet Women. 1998. *Laughing in the Kitchen.* Boston: Talking Stone Press.

Anelisa Garfunkel

SANTERÍA

Santera, *iyalocha*, and *mamalocha* are terms used to designate a priestess of the Afro-Cuban religion called Santería, also known as Regla de Ocha or Regla Lucumí. The best known of Afro-Cuban religions, which also include Regla de Palo, Mayombe, and the Abakua Secret Society, Santería has a large and very visible following. Santería is essentially the religion of the Yoruba-speaking people of southwestern Nigeria who were brought to Cuba as slaves. In Cuba the Yoruba religion underwent dogmatic and functional changes while adapting to the new milieu. It assimilated other African beliefs and practices and borrowed from Spanish Catholicism and European Spiritualism.

The Yoruba religion brought to Cuba by enslaved Africans eventually gained a following among the people of non-Yoruba ancestry. Its social, supportive, and magical aspects were exalted, while others lost importance. Some individuals afflicted by disease sought the assistance of *santeros*. Others were attracted to this religion by its rich mythology, engaging ritual music and dances, accessibility of the divinities, and well-structured oracles that placed at their disposal magical means of controlling situations and solving problems and conflicts.

In the 1950s Santería was known in many parts of Cuba, but primarily in and around the city of Havana and in the provinces of Matanzas and Las Villas. In the last forty years it has gained importance and followers throughout Cuba. This trend is due, in part, to the government's persecution of the more institutionalized religions and its policy of enhancing the African roots of Cuban culture. However, the major reason for its widespread appeal lies in people's need to rely on magical practices to assume mastery of situations beyond their control, prevalent among people who live under a paternalistic and oppressive regime.

Santería has also become quite visible in certain parts of the United States, as well as in other countries where Cuban exiles have settled. Followers include Latin Americans who reside in strong Spanish-speaking communities in the United States and in their own countries of origin. In addition, Santería has also gained a following among many non-Latin Americans, predominantly in areas of the United States such as Miami, New Jersey, New York, Chicago, and California. Santería offers its followers a complex dogma, rich mythology and religious paraphernalia, highly structured rituals, rich and engaging ritual music and dances, and a viable road to priesthood and leadership.

The Yoruba religion's pantheon is presided over by Olodumare, the Supreme Being, who possesses the sublime qualities of creator gods in institutionalized religions. Olodumare, also known as Olorun and Olofin, is eternal, omnipresent, just, merciful, and all-knowing. He is all-powerful, but distant and nonresponsive to the basic needs of humans. He distributes his supernatural power or *ashé* among his children, the *oricha/santos*, and virtually leaves them in charge of mankind. Among the Yoruba of Nigeria, more than 2,000 *orichas* were worshipped in the past. In Cuba only the cult of the most important generic and creation gods, known throughout Nigeria, was established.

The *oricha/santo* is basically a Yoruba divinity who, after being associated with a Catholic saint, incorporated some of its attributes and characteristics, as well as those of non-Yoruba African gods with whom there was an association or identification. Some of the *oricha/santos* are the personification of the forces of nature, such as Changó/St. Barbara (thunder), Agayú/St. Christopher (volcanoes), Oyá/Virgin of Candlemas (tornadoes), Ochún/Virgin of Charity (the river), and Yemayá/Virgin of Regla (the sea). Others are patrons of human activities, such as Oricha Okó/St. Isidro Labrador, patron of farmers, and Ogún/St. Peter, patron of soldiers and of people such as mechanics and surgeons who use metal tools. Orunla/St. Francis is the god of wisdom and the oracles, and Babalú Ayé/St. Lazarus is the god of epidemics, while Obatalá/Virgin of Mercy is the god of peace and justice. Eleguá/the Holy Child of Atocha is the messenger of the gods and controls the roads of the world.

The *orichas* share with humans their emotions, virtues, and vices, are susceptible to human approaches, and can be unconditional allies when they are adequately propitiated with offerings of food, sacrifices of animals, and other things of their liking. However, when they are angered by what they perceive as neglect or disrespect, they can become unmerciful enemies. Even though the *oricha/santos* are the brokers of Olodumare's power or *ashé*, in most instances they act with great independence and seem to be primarily motivated by their quasi-human personality. Some *orichas* also own or control parts of the human body. For example, Yemayá owns the intestines, Oblatá, the head, and Ochún, the genitals. In this context, if the *oricha* is enraged with a person, it can afflict those parts of the body and make them sick. Conversely, when a person is afflicted by disease, the *oricha*, if appropriately propitiated, can effectively heal him or her.

Most believers are content with caring for their *oricha* by offering it sacrifices and attending to the rituals celebrated in its honor. However, there are other persons who, either because they are called to the priesthood or at the request of their *oricha*, must go through the ceremony of *asiento*, which means that they are initiated into the priesthood of the *oricha* that claims their head. Others decide to be initiated because of poor health, since it is believed that if a person is initiated, the *oricha* will be more prone to help that person recover his or her health. Then there are those who are eager to be initiated because they feel insecure and want to engage supernatural help to cope with their existential difficulties.

Santería's priests perform as officiators in worship ceremonies, as medicine men, and as soothsayers. Priesthood is open to both women and men except the priesthood of Orunla or Babalawe, which is only open to males. The Orunla priest has the highest authority within Santería. However, seniority of the practitioner despite gender is a respected norm.

More than half of Santería practitioners are women priests, which has given them a high profile of leadership within the Santería religion and social recognition in the community. Women have achieved a prominent place in Santería. In Miami Olympia Alfaro, who died on January 18, 2001, was a much respected *santera* and a renowned *akpuona*, a lead singer in drum festivals. Juanita Baró, who was the lead dancer in the Ballet Folklorico de Cuba in the 1970s, is also much respected. Nery Torres is a renowned dancer of ritual music who leads an ensemble of dancers and musicians of sacred music. Carmen Rodríguez Plá is also very well known. She is the mother of Ernesto Pichardo, the *santero* who won the case in the U.S. Supreme Court that legalized the use of animal sacrifices in Santería.

Women have also achieved academic preeminence through undertaking research and ethnographic accounts on the subject of Santería. Lydia Cabrera, now deceased, authored books that are recognized as classics in the field. Isabel Castellanos and Mercedes Cros Sandoval, still active, have achieved international recognition for their research and publications about Santería And the Afro-Cuban heritage in Cuban culture.

See also Folk Healing Traditions; Religion

SOURCES: Cabrera, Lydia. 1954. *El monte.* Havana: Ediciones Chichereku; _____. 1957. *Anago: Vocabulario Lucumí.* Havana: Ediciones Chichereku; Castellanos, Isabel, and Jorge Castellanos. 1994. *Cultura afrocubana.* 4 Vols. Miami: Ediciones Universal; Cros Sandoval, Mercedes. 1975. *La religión afrocubana.* Madrid: Editorial Playor; _____. 1977. "Afrocuban Concepts of Disease and Its Treatment in Miami." *Journal of Operational Psychiatry* 8 no. 2: 52–63; _____. 1979. "Santeria as Mental Health Care System." *Social Science and Medicine* 13 B, no. 2 (April): 137–151; _____. 1983. "Santeria." *Journal of the Florida Medical Association* 70, no. 8: (August) 620–628; _____. 1994. "Afro-Cuban Religion in Perspective." In *Enigmatic Powers: Syncretism with African and Indigenous Peoples' Religions among Latinos*, ed. Anthony M. Stevens-Arroyo and Andrés I. Pérez y Mena, 81–98. New York: Bildner Center for Western Hemisphere Studies.

Mercedes Cros Sandoval

SANTIAGO, PETRA (1911–1994)

For more than forty years Petra Santiago was an activist and well-known community organizer in the Lower East Side of Manhattan (Loisaida). Renowned journalist Luisa Quintero of *El diario/La Prensa* referred to her as the "first woman mayor of the Lower East Side" (October 21, 1963). Santiago mobilized people for community participation, founded key grassroots organizations such as the United Organization of Suffolk Street, and was also deeply committed to working with youth, particularly in promoting recreational programs such as Little League Baseball teams. Pulitzer Prize–winning journalist Harrison E. Salisbury recognized her work as a youth worker in his book *The Shook-Up Generation.*

Born in Humacao, Puerto Rico, on May 31, 1911, Petra Santiago was the daughter of Arturo Figueroa Miranda and Brígida Hernández. Santiago spent her early youth in her native town, where her father organized for the Socialist Party founded by Santiago Iglesias Pantín and represented the party in the assembly. From an early age Petra Santiago participated in her father's political activities, accompanying him to meetings and working on campaigns. She attended Ponce de León High School and in 1930 matriculated at the Río Piedras campus of the University of Puerto Rico, where she completed an associate's degree in teaching.

Graduating from the university in 1933, she traveled to New York, where she stayed for six months. Returning to Puerto Rico, Santiago found employment with a New Deal agency, the Puerto Rican Reconstruction Administration (PRRA), and was soon assigned to work in the countryside distributing food to needy families. She also worked as an enumerator for a census of the area Candelaria Arriba in Humacao, carried out by the PRRA in 1935. Her final job with the PRRA was as a social worker in the urban center of Humacao. When her employment with the PRRA ended, Santiago took over the running of her father's grocery store.

In December 1938, after separating from her first husband, Santiago returned to New York on the steamship *San Jacinto*. She arrived on New Year's Day and went to live with a cousin on East 114th Street and Fifth Avenue. Her first job was in a factory that manufactured handbags. On June 14, 1941, she married Manuel Santiago, and they moved to 65 East 102nd Street, between Park and Madison Avenues in East Harlem. Santiago stopped working outside the home after her first child, Emanuel, was born in 1942. Her second child, Arturo, was born in 1943. In 1945 she traveled to Puerto Rico with her children aboard the SS *George Washington* to care for her ailing father. She stayed for ten months and wanted to remain there, but her husband insisted upon her return to New York. Upon her arrival the family settled in Lower Manhattan on Norfolk Street.

Santiago's interest in community work began as a result of her participation in parents' meetings at her children's school, where she served as an interpreter for Latino parents who did not speak English. Soon she was active in political campaigns and in organizing the Latino community in her neighborhood. She was a founder and secretary of the Council of Puerto Rican and Hispanic Organizations of the Lower East Side (1961–1963), the first major Latino organization in that area. Its objective was to improve conditions for Latinos in housing, education, employment, medical care, and recreation. Worry over her young boys and other children led Santiago to form baseball leagues for youths between the ages of fourteen and seventeen. She helped organize the Independent Juvenile Baseball League, which she directed (1950–1962), and the Nativity Mission Center Baseball Team (1945–1963).

Volunteer work played an important role in Santiago's life. From 1959 to 1963 she volunteered for the Lower East Side Neighborhood Association. From 1962 to 1967 she worked as a social worker for Mobilization for Youth, a federally funded agency dedicated to the prevention and elimination of youth gangs. The agency provided training and classes in various areas, including sewing, typing, and photography, and sponsored trips and voter registration programs. As part of her work Santiago organized a group called Mobilization for Mothers. Among the key organizations she helped establish was the United Organization of Suffolk Street (1967–1976), which provided day care, English-language classes, and other social services. Active in tenants' rights, she worked for the Coalition for Decent Housing that she helped create. Throughout her life she remained involved in electoral politics and was a member of the New Jíbaro Democratic Club, of which her son Arturo Santiago was cofounder. He was a Democratic district leader in Lower Manhattan and ran for state assembly.

Santiago was on the board of directors of numerous organizations, including the United Child Day Care Council (1968–1975), where she served as treasurer.

Petra Santiago. Courtesy of the Petra Santiago Papers Collection. Centro Archives, Centro de Estudios Puertorriqueños, Hunter College, CUNY.

She was a member of the steering committee of a group that founded the Community Corporation of the Lower East Side, was named to the Anti-poverty Council, and was elected to Community Board Number 3.

For her many contributions, she received numerous awards and tributes. She was honored with the Lena Award for her service to the Lower East Side community (1963, 1964), by the Department of Parks (1965), by Mobilization for Youth (1967), and by Mayor Edward I. Koch in 1989 at an event recognizing the "pioneros," the first Puerto Rican migrants.

Petra Santiago was a dynamic leader who remained active in the affairs of the community of the Lower East Side until she was eighty years old. She died on January 13, 1994, after a brief illness. Her collected papers at the Library and Archives of the Center for Puerto Rican Studies at Hunter College, City University of New York, offer insight into the development of the Puerto Rican community of Lower Manhattan and document the history of numerous organizations.

SOURCES: Salisbury, Harrison E. *The Shook-Up Generation.* New York: Harper Brothers; Santiago, Petra. 1935–1995. Papers. Centro Archives, Centro de Estudios Puertorriqueños, Hunter College, CUNY.

Ismael García, Nélida Pérez, and Pedro Juan Hernández

SARALEGUI, CRISTINA (1949–   )

Cristina Saralegui was born in Havana, Cuba, to the scion of a family that owned a journalism empire. Her grandfather, Francisco Saralegui, was the co-owner of the best-known and most widely circulated Cuban magazines in the 1950s, *Vanidades, Bohemia*, and *Carteles.* He had a great influence on Cristina.

In 1960, when she was only eleven years old, Saralegui left Cuba with her family and settled in Miami. She studied journalism and communications at the University of Miami while doing an internship with *Vanidades*, the number one women's magazine in Latin America. Later she worked at three of the most successful Latin magazines published in the United States. In 1979 she was appointed executive director of *Cosmopolitan en Español*, a very popular magazine with a wide readership throughout Latin America and the United States. After a successful performance as director of this magazine, she was offered the opportunity to host a daily Spanish television show. She accepted the challenge and the risks of this change into a new medium at the height of her professional success in print journalism. She embarked on an experiment that resulted in the incredible success of *El Show de Cristina,* named after her. It was produced by Univision, the first national television channel in the Spanish language. The program was seen throughout the United States, Latin America, and Europe on a network of 1,161 channels affiliated with Univision. Saralegui was more than the host of her successful talk show; she was also the executive producer who made all the decisions concerning the content of the programs, the guests, and other matters. *El Show de Cristina*, during twelve years in production and more than 3,000 programs, was awarded ten Emmys and was recognized as the Spanish talk show with the largest worldwide audience, more than 100,000,000 viewers. Spontaneous, daring, and iconoclastic, Saralegui broke all taboos. Her program was not only informative but also entertaining, and themes and situations that no Hispanic personality, much less a woman, had dared to discuss were openly addressed by this classy popular entertainer.

Saralegui is also the editor of the monthly magazine *Cristina*, published in association with Editorial Televisa, the most important editorial company for Spanish magazines. In addition, she has a daily radio program called *Cristina Opina*, broadcast by Radio Única, the first and only radio network that broadcasts in Spanish twenty-four hours a day in the United States. The American Broadcasting Company International Network distributes *Cristina Opina* in Latin America.

Since October 1998 Saralegui's bilingual website on the Internet, Sitio Web de Cristina, has offered visitors information concerning Saralegui's projects and her business enterprises, C.S.E. More than 90 million visitors have accessed this site. She founded, in addition to her corporate enterprises, the Up with Life or Arriba la Vida Foundation for AIDS research.

In 1998 Saralegui completed her autobiography, *Cristina! Confidencias de una rubia.* An adventure in self-determination, humor, and common sense, Cristina Saralegui emerges as a complex but well-balanced personality. A rare combination of the traditional and the modern woman, she is pragmatic, energetic, and self-confident. She is willing to take challenges and necessary risks, but at the same time she is a woman who greatly favors and flavors family life and values.

Saralegui, despite her modernity, is very proud of her ancestry, appreciative of her husband's support and protectiveness, and disciplined when it comes to her children. These qualities, her intelligence, and her love of life may be the secret of her success. Her advice to professional women is worth thirty credits in psychology and thirty hours of marriage counseling: "She [the professional woman] must be very careful with the person she chooses to share her life, since it has to be somebody who will feel proud of her success, someone who will consider her success as their success. The woman that chooses a man with an inferiority complex, is going to have in her home a guy sabotaging her."

See also Television

SOURCES: Doria, Luz Maria. 2001. "Una jefa que no se parece a nada." *Cristina* (Miami: Editorial Televisa), November; Hernandez, Rubén. 1998. "Cristina Saralegui." *Holá* (Madrid), January; Saralegui, Cristina. 1998. *Cristina! Confidencias de una rubia.* New York: Warner Books.

Mercedes Cros Sandoval

SAUCEDO, MARÍA DEL JESÚS (1954–1981)

In 1959 Chicana activist María Saucedo immigrated to Chicago from Monterrey, Mexico, along with her mother and two sisters. They reunited with her father, Juan Saucedo, who had arrived four years earlier. The family settled in Pilsen, a low-income neighborhood in the Near West Side of Chicago, a regular port of entry for eastern Europeans since the turn of the century, but which was becoming increasingly Mexican. Despite holding permanent residency, the Saucedos, like most immigrants, faced language problems, low-wage employment, inadequate health care, and harsh stigmatization and discrimination, among other difficulties. In 1962 Saucedo's mother, María Reynosa, began a lifelong commitment to fight for the rights of the oppressed. Spurred on by her mother's activism, Saucedo was attending and organizing strikes, rallies, and solidarity marches in Pilsen by the time she reached high school.

Saucedo's activism gained momentum at Northeastern Illinois University (NEIU). When she enrolled in 1973, the school had a negligible Latino student population, the majority of whom were Puerto Rican. She joined the Chicano Caucus, a committee within the school's only Latino organization, the Union for Puerto Rican Students (UPRS). Tension mounted between the two groups because of Saucedo's efforts to emphasize Chicano issues and the UPRS's position that two Latino groups would be competing for the same resources. Saucedo and three other members broke away in 1974 and founded the Chicano Student Union (CSU). The author of the CSU's constitution, Saucedo also published a newsletter, *Contra la Pared* (Against the Wall). She immediately began to push for increased recruitment of Latino students, hiring Chicano faculty, and providing courses in Chicano studies, particularly history and bilingual education. Through the CSU Saucedo initiated the Noche de Familia, an annual event that encouraged interaction between students, parents, and NEIU faculty. With the intermingling of the community and the institution, the Latino student population began to increase steadily. Today NEIU is a major Hispanic-serving institution. In 1975 Saucedo graduated with honors in early childhood education.

Firm supporters of the Chicano movement, Saucedo and Reynosa endorsed the work of César Chávez and the United Farm Workers (UFW) union. By the late 1960s Chicago was responding to the militant ethos fueled by the southwestern Chicano movement that strove to redress the racism and economic deprivation hindering Latinos through grassroots organizations and community-driven services. Saucedo and other young activists recognized the obstacles confronting minorities in education, employment, health, and legal institutions as structural and systemic problems that required fundamental reform both in Chicago and in the broader governmental structure. Organizations such as el Centro de la Causa, Mujeres Latinas en Acción, and Casa Aztlán originated in Pilsen in the early 1970s. Saucedo was involved with Mujeres Latinas during its inception; however, at odds with the organization's strictly feminist agenda, she left. After 1975 she focused her efforts on Casa Aztlán, which became the headquarters of the Chicano movement in Chicago.

Saucedo joined Compañia Trucha, a street theater group that performed political satire. Often used in protests, their skits largely aimed to educate the masses about their rights. Their dramatizations tackled important working-class issues, including educational reform, the quality of medical services, and ruthless harassment by Immigration and Naturalization Service officers. As part of the theater's leadership, Saucedo and her childhood friend María Gamboa urged Trucha to distance itself from the prevalent virgin/whore stereotype and portray women's influential roles within the home, culture, society, and the *movimiento*. Although Saucedo and Gamboa were not feminists, they advocated for a unified struggle that addressed the community's holistic needs, accomplishments, and struggles. During protests and other travels with Trucha, Saucedo sang *corridos* and wrote poetry in support of the cause. Politically identifying as a socialist, Saucedo maintained a global perspective and fought for the rights of all oppressed people. During this time Saucedo married Filberto "Cookie" Martínez, another Trucha actor and fellow activist. They had one son, Albizu Emiliano.

Saucedo's lifework was rooted in education. She was involved in efforts to build the Benito Juárez High School, which helped alleviate some of the overcrowding in Pilsen schools. When she graduated from NEIU, she took a teaching position at Kosziusko Elementary School. She later taught at Pickard School, where she was terminated for refusing to ask students to present a green card. To improve the quality of education and support bilingual education, Saucedo cofounded the Mexican Teachers Organization (MTO).

Saucedo died on November 12, 1981, when her apartment building caught fire. Blocked access to the fire escapes, combined with the fire department's tardiness and inadequately prepared firemen, forced the residents to jump from the building. Saucedo's husband and son both suffered severe injuries, but Saucedo, who was eight months pregnant, died upon impact. A crowd of approximately 300 gathered for her wake and marched through Pilsen carrying a banner that read, "Maria Saucedo: Revolutionary, Teacher, Mother." Many read her poetry. In 1986 Harrison High School was renamed the María Saucedo Scholastic Academy.

See also Education

SOURCES: Espinoza, Martha. 2001. "Saucedo, Maria del Jesus." In *Women Building Chicago, 1790–1990: A Biographical Dictionary,* ed. Rima Lunin Schultz and Adele Hast. Bloomington: Indiana University Press; Rosales, F. Arturo. 1996. *Chicano! The History of the Mexican American Civil Rights Movement.* Houston: Arte Público Press: University of Houston.

Martha Espinoza

SCHECHTER, ESPERANZA ACOSTA MENDOZA "HOPE" (1921–   )

The daughter of Mexican immigrants, labor activist Esperanza (Hope) Acosta was born to Celso Acosta and his wife, María de Jesús Salas, on July 10, 1921, in the copper-mining town of Miami, Arizona. The family soon moved to southern California. The eldest of twelve surviving children, Hope learned responsibility early. Her father deserted the family when she was just a toddler. Hope's Spanish-speaking mother worked long hours, first as a domestic and then rearing a growing family with her second husband, Edviquez Martínez. "I had to speak for my mother," Hope remembers, and "I learned to take charge."

Despite missing school frequently to care for her pregnant mother and new siblings, Schechter earned strong marks in school. In the eighth grade, when students chose either an academic or vocational track of study, she elected academics. A racist guidance counselor, looking at her brown skin, changed the selection to vocational. Schechter explains that, bored with cosmetology courses, she "lost interest and coasted." By the eleventh grade she had dropped out of high school.

As a teenager, Schechter went to work in the Los Angeles garment industry in 1938 and later on a wartime assembly line for Lockheed Aircraft Company. Returning to the garment industry after the war, she became disturbed by the existing labor conditions and joined the International Ladies Garment Workers' Union (ILGWU). "The union was the turning point; it exposed me to a different world academically and politically," she recollects.

From her union sisters and brothers Schechter learned social theories that explained exploitative labor conditions and strategies to change them. In 1946 she began working as an "in-shop" organizer for the ILGWU. She would secure a job in a garment factory, befriend the Mexican women workers, explain in Spanish about the union, and sign up new members. When enough workers had joined the union to require an election for the right to collective bargaining, Schechter would quit the job and move to another factory to repeat the organizing process. After two years she was so successful and well known by the factory owners that she could no longer continue as an in-shop organizer.

ILGWU union official Sigmund Arywitz "insisted" (her emphasis) that Schechter enroll in union-sponsored leadership training classes. In 1948 she successfully completed the Harvard University Trade Union Fellows Program, a three-month intensive curriculum cosponsored with labor organizations. That same year the union hired her as an organizer and business agent in the sportswear division. She had been married to Horace Mendoza since 1940; the couple divorced in 1950.

With her union education and labor activism, Schechter had a solid base from which to work for political and social change in the community. In 1949, when Edward Roybal campaigned to become the first Mexican American member of the Los Angeles City Council, she worked for his election and helped found the Community Service Organization (CSO). She served as chair of the CSO Labor Relations Committee, where she supervised educational, strike support, fund-raising, and lobbying activities.

Schechter describes herself as "playing a dual-role as an activist in the Mexican American community, and as a part of the labor movement." After passage of the McCarran-Walter Immigration Act in 1952 she served simultaneously on the CSO Immigration Committee and as the immigration liaison for Congressman Chet Holifield's district office. Her political activities continued to expand. She served many times as a delegate to national Democratic Party conventions and under the Johnson administration was appointed to both the National Advisory Council of the Peace Corps and the founding Advisory Council of Project Head Start in Los Angeles.

Somehow, in the midst of all her political activity, Schechter found time to return to school. In 1957 she

Labor leader Hope Mendoza Schechter and Dr. John Dunlop, Harvard professor emeritus and former U.S. secretary of labor, at the fiftieth anniversary of the Harvard Trade Union Fellows Program. Courtesy of Hope Mendoza Schechter.

graduated as class valedictorian from Hollywood High Adult Evening School. She also learned court reporting and, from 1960 to 1986, ran her own successful deposition intake firm. She found her life partner in Harvey Schechter, a community activist whose forty-one-year career on the professional staff of the Anti-defamation League of B'nai B'rith culminated with the position of western states director. They have been married since March 20, 1955. Of their shared interests and commitments, Schechter explains: "We're both so active in the community. We both understand the problems of two people who are activists. . . . It works out beautifully, because we both understand each other very well in that sense." The Schechter family also includes Hope's nephew Bruce, whom they have raised since he was five years old.

After retiring Schechter resumed her education to fulfill an important personal goal. In 1995 she earned a baccalaureate degree in history from California State University, Northridge, graduating magna cum laude. When one has been in politics, she explains, one learns to be "like a racehorse: the gun goes off, and the horse goes!" Hope Mendoza Schechter's life shows just how far one intelligent and determined woman can go to overcome racism and poverty and improve opportunities for Mexican Americans in her community.

See also Community Service Organization (CSO); International Ladies Garment Workers' Union (ILGWU); Labor Unions

SOURCES: Rose, Margaret. 1994. "Gender and Civic Activism in the Mexican American Barrios in California: The Community Service Organization, 1947–1962." In *Not June Cleaver: Women and Gender in Postwar America, 1945–1960*, ed. Joanne Meyerowitz, 177–200. Philadelphia: Temple University Press; Schechter, Hope Mendoza. 1977–1978. "Activist in the Labor Movement, the Democratic Party, and the Mexican American Community." Oral history by Malca Chall. Women and Politics Oral History Project, Regional Oral History Office, Bancroft Library, University of California, Berkeley.

Nancy Page Fernández

SCIENTISTS

Although women have always been involved in scientific pursuits, historically they were not welcomed or encouraged in these activities. The sciences were considered fiercely protected male bastions, and the prevailing view was that the abstract laws of nature could be fully understood only by men. Documented contributions and scientific biographies are virtually all androcentric. For years it was argued that women did not contribute significantly to science because they were deemed to be inferior or were intellectually incapable (the notion was that only men were capable of scientific thinking and experimentation). These interpretations were, at least in part, due to the conception of what constituted "real" science. What counts as science? How does one "do" science? What are the boundaries of science? Clearly, depending on how scientific endeavors are defined and circumscribed, entire groups of people and their activities can be excluded.

Women were also barred from attending institutions of higher education until the twentieth century. Popular notions deemed the education of girls a waste of time and money and held that too much schooling could actually harm women's reproductive health.

For Latinas, the barriers to higher education have been even greater. Before the 1960s higher education was not even an option for most Latinas. Once they entered postsecondary educational institutions, Latinas faced a number of cumulative obstacles, including few role models and mentors, inadequate academic counseling, financial hardships, and lack of supportive collegial relationships. Women, in general, tend to leave the "scientific career pipeline" during senior high school and college; Hispanics drop out much earlier.

For Latinas, the situation has been particularly challenging because racism converging with sexism enabled systematic discrimination and exclusion from scientific fields. In a study of the intersection of immigration and gender among scientists and engineers, researchers found a series of disadvantages that negatively impacted immigrant women scientists. Many of the disadvantages have a direct bearing on Latinas, for example, migrating primarily for the career advance-

Research physician Dr. Irma Vidal. Courtesy of Jorge Sastre Vidal.

ment of their spouses, having varying levels of English proficiency, and having family responsibilities that may conflict with their careers. Marriage tends to impede women's scientific careers but to have either a neutral or positive effect on men's professions. Researchers note that female Ph.D. scientists and engineers are less likely than men to be married and that women earned 79 percent as much as their male counterparts.

The American Association for the Advancement of Science's 1998 report on the status of minorities in graduate programs revealed mixed trends. The number of Latina/o students who earned bachelor's degrees in the sciences and engineering had increased by more than 50 percent. A National Science Foundation Study also revealed that the number and proportion of women and minorities earning science and engineering degrees continues to increase yearly. The report also noted that the percentage of Latina/o students taking basic and advanced mathematics courses doubled and that the "gender gap" in mathematics achievement on the National Assessment of Educational Progress is disappearing. Clearly the reduction in ethnic and gender discrimination has led to heartening gains.

Yet despite the encouraging news, women, minorities, and Latinas in particular remain underrepresented in the sciences and engineering. The number of Latino students enrolled in science and engineering Ph.D. programs has declined by more than 18 percent. Some explanations have been offered for Latinas' relatively low representation in graduate science programs. While more minority graduates may choose to enter the workforce rather than attend graduate school,

other factors are more likely to be at fault: decreasing financial support, a politically hostile climate for affirmative action, and an inhospitable environment for minority students on many college campuses. The National Science Foundation reports that of all employed doctoral scientists and engineers, Latinas make up only 5 percent, yet Latinas earn 41 percent of science and engineering degrees awarded to Hispanics.

In righting the record, one must also go beyond the formally recognized scientific fields and venues. For example, since women have historically been health care providers, primary agriculturalists, and workers in food preparation and nutrition, it is evident that women have had scientific interests, developed agricultural knowledge, practiced medicine, and observed chemical reactions in foods. *Curanderismo*, with its attendant knowledge and usage of the medicinal properties of plants, is one obvious example. Also, since gynecology, obstetrics, midwifery, and pediatrics were usually the "natural" domain of women, Latinas no doubt contributed to science not only as medical practitioners, but also as innovators of new techniques, practices, and discoveries. Increasingly the value placed on science and technology by patriarchal societies has begun to acknowledge the importance of the scientific work of women as well. Historian Londa Schiebinger, who has written about the history of women in science, notes: "The legal barriers to progress have been removed. . . . So what we're left with are the things that aren't very well perceived. And these are things that can be hard to talk about, not only because they're unquantifiable, but because they also evoke a lot of hostility when you mention them to men."

Before the twentieth century Latina contributions and inventions—and women's in general—were not recognized in formal ways and were often preempted by their male counterparts or supervisors. For example, Lady Ana de Osorio, the countess of Chinchón, Peru, introduced the curative powers of quinine to the European medical establishment in the seventeenth century. Quinine was known for a while as *pulvis comitessa* (the countess's powder), but the name was soon anglicized, and her contribution was lost to history. The existing record of Latina scientists and Latinas' contributions to science almost certainly represents only a fraction of the work in which they engaged.

One of the few recorded lives was that of Ynés Mexia (1870–1938), a Mexican American botanist who conducted pioneering research into the medicinal properties of plants. On her many trips through North and South America Mexia collected, described, classified, and photographed more than 150,000 plant specimens. A self-proclaimed "nature lover and a bit of an adventuress," she is credited with discovering one new plant genus and more than 500 new species.

While the contributions and achievements of Latina scientists have historically been marginalized, in recent years there have been some high-profile accomplishments in the sciences and engineering. Obstacles notwithstanding, Latinas have contributed to scientific knowledge in a number of ways. Latina scientists in biology, geology, chemistry, physics, and space exploration have been recognized for their breakthrough, pioneering work.

Many contemporary Latina scientists credit their mothers, grandmothers, and aunts as the catalyst and support for their own careers. Plant biologist María Elena Zavala (1950–), for example, grew up in La Verne, California, next door to her *curandera* (medicine woman) great-grandmother. In her great-grandmother's vast herbal garden Zavala developed an intense interest and understanding about plants and their properties and uses. She earned her bachelor's degree in 1972 from Pomona College, her master's degree from the University of California at Berkeley in 1975, and her doctorate in botany from the University of California at Berkeley in 1978. Her interest in plant root systems is leading to advances in cold-hardy crops that can be planted much earlier by farmers.

Another plant biologist, Elma González (1942–), grew up in Hebbronville, Texas. Although her father was sometimes employed as a ranch hand, more often than not, González and her family were migrant farmworkers. Although she was not able to attend school or learn English until she was nine years old, she nonetheless graduated at the top of her high-school class. After earning degrees in biology and chemistry she was awarded a Ph.D. in cellular biology at Rutgers University in 1972. Her research into the role of enzymes and proteins in plant cells furthers knowledge in the structure of human cells.

Elvia Niebla (1945–) has used her expertise as a soil scientist to inform and advise the U.S. Environmental Protection Agency (EPA) and policy makers about industrial sludge, global change, and other environmental issues. Her knowledge of soils (Niebla was awarded a Ph.D. in soil chemistry in 1979) has also been critical in the preservation of adobe structures in the American Southwest. In addition to winning the EPA Bronze Medal, she was also honored by the Federal Executive Association as Manager of the Year for creating a system that increased minority representation at the federal level.

France Anne Córdova (1947–) is by training an astrophysicist who was the youngest person ever to hold the post of chief scientist at NASA. After earning her doctorate in physics from the California Institute of Technology in 1979, she worked at the Los Alamos National Laboratory in New Mexico and was one of the first astrophysicists to assess the radiation emitted by white dwarf stars. In 1996 she left NASA to serve as vice chancellor for research at the University of California at Santa Barbara to support research in all academic areas. She proved a gifted administrator, and in 2002 France Córdova became Chancellor of the University of California, Riverside, the first Latina to head a University of California, campus.

Adriana Ocampo (1955–) is a planetary geologist who has conducted research on Earth, as well as on Mars and Jupiter. She was the first to recognize that a ring of sinkholes in the Yucatán peninsula is related to the Chicxulub impact 65 million years ago that caused the extinction of more than 50 percent of Earth's species, including the dinosaurs. She has also been the science coordinator on the exploratory missions of the spacecrafts *Galileo* and the *Mars Observer*. Ocampo's tireless support of science education for the general public, as well as mentoring programs for girls and young women, has earned her awards and recognition from a number of professional societies.

Lydia Villa-Komaroff (1947–), who was born and raised in Santa Fe, New Mexico, became the third Mexican American woman in the United States to receive a doctorate in cell biology in 1975. Despite having her career choices questioned by some relatives and college counselors, she completed her dissertation on the polio virus at MIT, where women made up only one-third of her small graduate class. As a molecular biologist, Villa-Komaroff specializes in neurology. Her work has led to advanced understanding of how naturally occurring chemicals promote brain cell growth. Her work at Harvard Medical School was instrumental in the development of insulin that has been produced in bacteria.

Another molecular biologist, Leticia Márquez-Magaña (1963–), serves her community as a role model for women and minority students while indulging her lifelong fascination with science. After earning her Ph.D. in biochemistry from the University of California, Berkeley, in 1991, she joined the faculty of the biology department at San Francisco State University. There Márquez-Magaña teaches science using innovative methods such as case-based teaching, and actively motivates students of color to prepare for professional careers in the biological sciences.

Aida Casiano-Colón (1958–) used her Ph.D. in microbiology to diagnose the causative infectious agents of diseases and thus inform physicians about the most effective course of treatment. As a child growing up in Puerto Rico, Casiano-Colón exhibited interests in two career paths, biology and theater, and she has been able to practice both. In addition to family responsibilities, Casiano-Colón has pursued her love of acting by maintaining a part-time theater career. She starred in the feminist comedy *Rosa de dos aromas* in Rochester, New York, which was performed in both English and Spanish.

Evelyn M. Rodríguez (1957–) credits her mother's unwavering encouragement as a source of inspiration in pursuing and earning an M.D. from Harvard Medical School. In addition to being a pediatrician, Rodríguez is a physician epidemiologist whose specialty includes perinatal epidemiology and HIV/AIDS. Her work resulted in important public education programs warning mothers of hard-drug use as a risk factor in HIV transmission.

Marian Lucy Rivas (19??–) has applied her expertise in computer science to the field of medical genetics. Her work has led to breakthroughs in human genetic mapping, genetic counseling, and computer applications of clinical genetics. A native of New York City, after Rivas earned her M.S. and Ph.D. in medical genetics from Indiana University, she completed a two-year fellowship in medical genetics at Johns Hopkins. Rivas is a professor in the Department of Pediatrics at the University of Tennessee at Memphis, where she also serves as course director of medical genetics.

Latinas such as Margarita Colmenares (1957–) are noteworthy for infiltrating the traditionally male bastion of engineering. Colmenares has been the president of the Society of Hispanic Professional Engineers, was selected to participate in the White House Fellowship Program (the first Hispanic engineer to do so), and was appointed director of corporate liaison by Secretary of Education Richard Riley in 1994. In these last two posts Colmenares worked to improve math and science education in U.S. schools and involve businesses in improving education.

Luz J. Martínez-Miranda (1956–) combines her training in physics with her expertise in engineering to conduct research in liquid crystals. She served as an exemplary role model by teaching and directing experiments in the Materials and Nuclear Engineering Department of the University of Maryland. Additionally, she cultivated her interest and talent in music by earning a bachelor's degree in music from the Conservatory of Music of Puerto Rico.

Victoria Aguilera (19??–) is another noteworthy engineer who emigrated to the United States from Mexico when she was eight years old, smuggled in the back seat of an American couple's car. After she was reunited with her parents in California, adjustment to a new life and language proved to be difficult. Language barriers led to Aguilera's placement in remedial classes, but as soon as she mastered English, teachers learned that she was an able student with a special talent for mathematics. After college training in mechanical engineering she was soon hired by Walt Disney Imagineering to design rides and attractions at Disney theme parks. For her pioneering work Aguilera was featured in the PBS program "BreakThrough: The Changing Face of Science in America."

Theresa Maldonado (1958–), currently a university professor, received her Ph.D. in electrical engineering in 1990 from Georgia Institute of Technology despite being one of only two or three women in classes that typically numbered eighty. Among several areas of expertise, she is noted for her work in electro-optics, fiber optics, and electromagnetics. In 1991 Maldonado was named the National Science Foundation Presidential Young Investigator. Her excellence in teaching and scholarship has earned her several awards for teaching excellence from the University of Texas at Arlington College of Engineering, where she has been a professor in the Electrical Engineering Department.

When Argelia Velez-Rodríguez (1936–) was a child in Cuba, her teachers realized she had a special talent for mathematics after she won a competition about fractions in the third grade. When she obtained her doctorate in mathematics in 1960 from the University of Havana, she was the first black woman to have earned that distinction. She left Cuba soon after the Cuban Revolution of 1959 and settled in the United States, where she taught at several secondary schools and later at the historically black Bishop College in Dallas, Texas. She is currently the program manager of the Minority Institutions Science Improvement Program in Washington, D.C., which provides grants to improve science education at predominantly minority institutions and to increase the number of underrepresented ethnic minorities, particularly minority women, in science and engineering careers.

Increasingly, because many Latinas find the college campus to be an inhospitable environment, the private sector is becoming an important source of employment for Latina scientists. Diana García-Prichard (1949–) used her Ph.D. in chemical physics as a research scientist with the Eastman Kodak Company. She has worked with the National Science Foundation and the National Committee on Science and Technology and was a member of the science and technology cluster of the Clinton-Gore transition team.

A number of suggestions have been offered to increase the representation of Latinas in science and engineering. Mentorship, role models, a reevaluation of recruitment and retention policies, financial support for graduate study, and student support groups have all been identified as promising practices to encourage Latinas in advanced studies.

SOURCES: American Association for the Advancement of Science (AAAS). 1998. *Losing Ground: Science and Engineering Graduate Education of Black and Hispanic Americans.* Washington, DC: AAAS; Angier, Natalie. 1992. "Women Swell Ranks of

Science but Remain Invisible at the Top." *Applied Optics* 31, no. 3 (January 20): 302; Bernstein, Leonard, Alan Winkler, and Linda Zierdt-Warshaw. 1998. *Latino Women of Science.* Saddle Brook, NJ: Peoples Publishing Group; Goyette, Kimberly, and Yu Xie. 1999. "The Intersection of Immigration and Gender." *Social Science Quarterly* 80 (June): 395–409; Harding, Sandra. 1991. *Whose Science? Whose Knowledge?* Ithaca, NY: Cornell University Press; National Science Foundation 1998. *Women, Minorities, and Persons with Disabilities in Science and Engineering.* Arlington, VA: NSF; Oakes, Jeannie. 1990. *Lost Talent: The Underparticipation of Women, Minorities, and Disabled Persons in Science.* Santa Monica, CA: Rand Corporation; Schiebinger, Londa. 1989. *The Mind Has No Sex: Women in the Origins of Modern Science.* Cambridge: Harvard University Press; St. John, Jetty. 1996. *Hispanic Scientists.* Mankato, MN: Capstone Press.

Bárbara C. Cruz

SENA, ELVIRA (1925–   )

Elvira Trujillo Sena grew up on her family's ranch in Las Cruces, New Mexico, the second oldest of seven children, four boys and three girls. Her father, Alberto Trujillo, supported the family by ranching and delivering mail, while her mother was a housewife. Her mother, Lucianita Trujillo, was often very ill, so, as the oldest girl, Elvira became a "second mother" to her younger siblings. When it was time for her to enter the training school at New Mexico Highlands University in Las Vegas, World War II was under way, and tough times had gotten tougher.

Sena's family was lucky because they had cows and pigs on their farm that they used for meat, as well as vegetables from their garden they harvested and canned. Her father also received stamps for gasoline because of his job carrying the mail. According to Trujillo Sena, "It was so difficult to buy things; it was very hard for a lot of people. We didn't go through too much trouble. My father was a very, very good supporter." Her roles in the family ranged from taking care of her siblings to helping her mother with canning. The whole time she was growing up, her family had no electricity or running water. "It was hard, very hard," she said. "I guess maybe that's why there wasn't so much trouble because everyone was so busy."

Even though times were difficult, her father still managed to put Sena and her older brother through the private training school in Las Vegas. "I wanted to work to help pay because it was a big family but he wouldn't let me work," she said. "My father would go out and sell a cow or something and give me whatever I needed for school. Just the essentials, nothing extra. It was very hard, but we pulled through." Education was very important to Sena, and in the war she saw an opportunity for more. She wanted to enlist in military service, because she wanted to go into nursing and thought that would be a way to pay for her schooling.

Even so, her mother did not like the idea. "She said military is not for women; I did not see it that way, but she did and she said, 'No, that's not for you.' I just wanted an education."

After a blind date in December 1944, plans for her education were put on hold. Elvira was paired with Luis Sena, who had just returned from overseas, and her cousin was set up with his brother. Luis Sena had served in New Guinea, earning many medals, including a Purple Heart. Elvira Sena recalled that they spent a long time talking, and he was "respectable and very nice to me." Not long after that first meeting Luis Sena proposed, and they were married in January 1945.

"It was just a few weeks," Elvira Sena said. "I have not regretted any bit of it. I have five children, and they are all healthy." Her husband wanted her to finish school, but her father insisted that she go with her husband because she made the choice to get married. "I missed my parents very much and my brothers and sisters," she said. "I had never been away from home for that long of time, but we did it and we are still married."

Even though she left school to go with her husband, her dreams of finishing her education and becoming a nurse were not completely shattered. Elvira Sena finished high school after she had her first child; she began college courses but never completed the degree. In 1952 Sena began working for New Mexico State Hospital (now Las Vegas Medical Center) and retired from that job in 1998. She eventually became a licensed practical nurse (LPN), although she never went

Luis and Elvira Sena, 1945. Courtesy of the U.S. Latino and Latina World War II Oral History Project, University of Texas, Austin.

to school to become one. She challenged the board and passed the state board tests. She still works part-time at a doctor's office.

See also World War II

SOURCES: Mokry, Allison. "Blind Date Put Education Plans on Hold." *Narratives: Stories of U.S. Latinos and Latinas and World War II* (U.S. Latino and Latina WWII Oral History Project, University of Texas at Austin) 4, no. 1 (Spring): 53; Sena, Elvira. 2002. Interview by Adriana Lujan, Santa Fe Vet Center, Santa Fe, NM, November 3.

Allison Mokry

SEPÚLVEDA, EMMA (1950–   )

Noted educator, poet, and literary critic Emma Sepúlveda was born in Mendoza, Argentina, and moved to Chile at the age of seven. Sepúlveda left Chile in 1973 as a result of Augusto Pinochet's military coup. A university student at the time, she opted for political exile four months shy of earning her university degree in history. She settled in Reno, Nevada, and in 1978 she completed baccalaureate and master's degrees in Spanish at the University of Nevada. She received a Ph.D. from the University of California, Davis, in 1987. That year she joined the faculty of the Department of Foreign Languages and Literatures at the University of Nevada, Reno, where she became a tenured professor in Spanish.

A true Renaissance woman, Sepúlveda, the writer, is also an award-winning photographer and a political activist. She published two books of poetry, *Tiempo cómplice del tiempo* (1989) and *Death to Silence/Muerte al silencio* (1997). Divided into three sections, the latter explores the central themes of death, life, exile, and social and political denouncement. The overarching theme of the volume, silence, is also a primary concern in many of Sepúlveda's works. The poetics of silence are explored in *Los límites del lenguaje: Un acercamiento a la poética del silencio* (1990), in which, for instance, the silence of death is described, and in which she also cherishes silence as the ideal space for communication between intimates. The final section of *Death to Silence* deals with a form of silence that must be broken by revealing the pain, the suffering, and the loss of victims, both the dead and the living, of the Chilean dictatorship. This commitment to articulating the suppressed voices of the Pinochet regime also has led Sepúlveda to record the testimonies of the *arpilleristas* (women textile artists) that form the volume *We, Chile: Testimonies of the Chilean Arpilleristas* (1996), adding to the "silent social art" of the *arpilleras*.

This sense of social obligation, evident in giving a voice to the voiceless, drove Sepúlveda to run in 1994 for the Nevada Senate as the Democratic Party candi-

Writer, poet, and educator Emma Sepúlveda. Courtesy of Emma Sepúlveda.

date. One of the first Latinas to do so, Sepúlveda offers an account of her experience in *From Border Crossings to Campaign Trail* (1998).

Sepúlveda's critical and creative work benefited from collaboration with another Chilean American writer, Marjorie Agosín. They met as teenagers in Chile, and their friendship has often been channeled into joint projects. These efforts have taken a variety of forms: literary criticism in *Otro modo de ser: Poesía hispánica de mujeres* (1994); *Silencio que se deja oír* (1982), with poems by Agosín and photographs by Sepúlveda (then Nolan); *Generous Journeys/Travesías generosas* (1992), Agosín's poetry illustrated by Sepúlveda's images; and *Amigas* (2001), a chronicle of their relationship, as the subtitle states, in *Letters of Friendship and Exile*. Sepúlveda also edited a collection of critical articles on the work of her lifelong friend, *Las ciudades del cuerpo: Aproximaciones a la obra de Marjorie Agosín* (2003).

In 1993 Sepúlveda won a Peabody Award and was nominated for an Emmy for her role as a consultant in the documentary *Threads of Hope*. On the national level Sepúlveda has held an appointment to the U.S. Hispanic Task Force since 1994, advising the Senate on Hispanic issues. Locally she founded Latinos for Political Education and is president of Nevada Hispanic Services. On more than one occasion she has been recognized by the state of Nevada for her distinguished service to the Hispanic community, and she received the Thornton Peace Award in 1994 from the University of Nevada, Reno, for her work with women's groups in Chile. She has won numerous awards for her poetry and her photography; most notably she was the recipient of the first Woman of the Year Award for literature in 1997 from the GEMS International Television Network. Emma Sepúlveda is married to attorney John Mulligan, and they have a son, Jonathon.

See also Literature

SOURCES: Fahey, Kay. 1996. "Sepúlveda." *Silver and Blue*, January/February, 14–17; Sepúlveda, Emma. 1998. *From Border Crossings to Campaign Trail: Chronicle of a Latina in Politics.* Falls Church, VA: Azul Editions; Sepúlveda, Emma, ed. 1996. *We, Chile: Personal Testimonies of the Chilean Arpilleristas.* Trans. Bridget Morgan. Falls Church, VA: Azul Editions; Sepúlveda, Emma, and Marjorie Agosín. 2001. *Amigas: Letters of Friendship and Exile.* Trans. Bridget Morgan. Austin: University of Texas Press.

Benjamin Torres

SEXUALITY

Recent research on sexuality has contributed to a more nuanced understanding of the complexity of Latina identities, yet traces of traditional notions of an ideal Latina sexuality can still be seen. These notions draw on traditional gender norms to venerate sexual prowess and sexual dominance for men and passivity, subversion of sexual pleasure, and "purity" for women. In this traditional ideal of Latina sexuality, virginity stands as the embodiment of purity for women and remains central to a woman's reputation, as well as the reputation of her family. Only after marriage does the ideal of womanhood prescribe that a woman be sexually open, but then only in order to suit her husband's sexual needs. Such notions can be traced back to Spanish colonization and the centrality of notions of honor.

In Spanish colonies honor held at least two roles. On the one hand, honor was determined by the social status one was born into. For instance, one's perceived "race," occupation, ancestry, nativity, or religion might determine one's honor status. On the other hand, honor lay at the heart of Spanish colonial society's moral system. Thus what was deemed right and good was also honorable and could be attained, and lost, through one's public conduct. In Spanish colonial society honor was primarily a male attribute. It could also belong collectively to a family and could be secured by men, who were perceived to be the primary guardians of their own or their family's honor. In Spanish colonial society the feminine counterpart to masculine honor was *vergüenza,* or shame. Thus shame and honor shaped acceptable patterns of behavior for men and women. According to the honor discourse of Spanish colonial society, honor could be acquired by the male members of the family and maintained by women's conduct, but women could only impinge upon the family's honor. If a woman lost the honor of the family, for instance, by losing her virginity before marriage, it was left to the male to restore that honor (for instance, her brother or father might go to the courts to demand that the partner marry his daughter or sister).

While such notions of gendered sexuality persist, they are fluid, varying according to a particular historical context and specific and intersecting ideas about class and race. The traditional trope of gender roles remains constantly negotiated by Latinas in the United States in their varied social contexts. Challenges to traditional ideals of Latina sexuality come from a broad spectrum of women who resist conventional roles through daily expressions of nontraditional identities and for some political mobilization. The most significant period of mobilization occurred with the emergence of Latina feminism in the second half of the twentieth century. For instance, the writings of Chicana lesbian feminist Gloria Anzaldúa helped highlight subjectivities that are formed through interrelations of sexuality, race, class, and gender.

In the 1960s and 1970s Latinas in the United States brought attention to the problem of coerced sterilization, the most extreme and aggressive effort to police Latina sexuality. Under the influence of the eugenics movement, some physicians, social reformers, welfare workers, and county hospital workers advocated the sterilization of poor women as a means of controlling what they perceived to be a "population problem." Poor women of color, in particular, were targeted as "unfit" mothers and coerced into sterilization operations. Because of racism and stereotypical beliefs about Latina women, as well as limited government oversight of hospital procedures, large numbers of women were sterilized without their consent. Several highly publicized court trials, such as the case of *Madrigal v. Quilligan* in 1978, brought long-overdue attention to an epidemic of forced sterilizations in public hospitals of Mexican, Native American, African American, and Puerto Rican women in the 1970s.

See also Feminism; Lesbians; *Madrigal v. Quilligan; Marianismo* and Machismo; Sterilization

SOURCES: Anzaldúa, Gloria. 1987. *Borderlands/La frontera: The New Mestiza.* San Francisco: Spinsters/Aunt Lute; Gutiérrez, Ramón. 1991. *When Jesus Came, the Corn Mothers Went Away: Marriage, Sexuality, and Power in New Mexico, 1500–1846.* Stanford, CA: Stanford University Press; Lancaster, Roger N., and Micaela di Leonardo, eds. 1997. *The Gender/Sexuality Reader: Culture, History, Political Economy.*

New York: Routledge; Moraga, Cherríe, and Gloria Anzaldúa, eds. 1981. *This Bridge Called My Back: Writings by Radical Women of Color*. Watertown, MA: Persephone Press.

Julie Cohen

SILVA, CHELO (1922–1988)

The oldest daughter in a family of seven children, Chelo Silva was born in 1922 in Brownsville, Texas. She began singing as a teenager at school and church and made her debut during Brownsville's Charro Days, accompanied by Orquesta Tipica Mexicana's leader Vincent Crixell. By her late teens she was singing regularly with the local Tito Crixell Orchestra. In 1939, when her career was gaining momentum locally, she was invited to sing on a radio program hosted by the then-unknown poet and composer Américo Paredes. They married in the early 1940s, had a son, Américo Paredes Jr., and divorced shortly thereafter. After a few idle years Silva was singing radio jingles and performing at the Continental Club in Corpus Christi. She married Leopoldo Pérez Morales in 1953 and gave birth to two daughters, René and Garnette, and another son, Leslie. This marriage also ended in divorce.

In 1952 she was signed by Discos Falcón in McAllen, Texas, and recorded more than seventy titles with it. In 1955 she signed with Columbia Records and began her long list of hits, including "Imploracíon," "Está sellado," "Sabes de qué tengo ganas," "Inolvidable," "Amor aventurero," and "Soy bohemia." Silva was considered the premier female interpreter of boleros and recorded the majority of her music with the accompaniment of los Dandys or los Principales. Eventually Silva became known as la Reina de los Boleros for her ability to interpret songs and to make them her own through stylized vocals and bent notes. During the late 1950s she was probably the best-selling female recording artist on either side of the border. However, she acquired a reputation for partying, and by the late 1970s her voice became affected by poor health. Nevertheless, she continued to perform and entertain crowds. When she walked on stage and began to sing, her fans would go wild.

Like many early *cantantes*, she did not receive her share of royalties, even though she was one of the best-selling international artists during her peak in the 1970s. Money did not inflame her desire to sing. Rather, she sang for the love of her singing and the response she received from her fans. She was known for her easygoing nature, and whenever anyone requested a song, even if she was not performing that night, she would oblige and sing for the whole crowd. At one of her last public performances at San Antonio's Rosedale Park in 1983, though not feeling well, Silva carried on with an outstanding performance. In her opening words she told her audience, "A KCOR, no tengo palabras con que, que feliz me han hecho este día de hoy. . . . les voy a decir una cosa . . . me puse un poco enferma. Y yo dije, yo creo que aquí en San Antonio voy a quedar yo, como dice mi canción. . . . Esto nunca se me olvidará" (I do not have the words for KCOR, how happy they have made me today. . . . I am going to tell you something . . . I got a little sick. And I said, I think I am going to stay here in San Antonio, like my song says. . . . This I will never forget). She died in 1988.

SOURCES: Burr, Ramiro. 1999. *The Billboard Guide to Tejano and Regional Mexican Music*. New York: Billboard Books; Silva, Chelo. *Chelo Silva: La reina tejana del bolero*. Tejano Roots. Arhoolie Records. Vargas, Deborah Rose Ramos. 2003. "Las tracaleras: Texas-Mexican Women, Music, and Place." Ph.D. diss., University of California, Santa Cruz; Villarreal, Mary Ann. 2003. "*Cantantes y Cantineras*: Mexican American Communities and the Mapping of Public Space." Ph.D. diss., Arizona State University.

Mary Ann Villarreal

SILVA DE CINTRÓN, JOSEFINA "PEPIÑA" (1885–1986)

The cultural life of New York's Puerto Rican community during the 1930s and 1940s was considerably enriched by the contributions of Josefina ("Pepiña") Silva de Cintrón. She was born in Caguas, Puerto Rico, in 1885 and lived for more than a century; her long life was dedicated to many civic and cultural pursuits. She was a graduate of the select group of women who attended the University of Puerto Rico's Normal School and were trained as teachers. This was one of the few opportunities for Puerto Rican women of her generation to receive a higher education.

Before leaving Puerto Rico and moving to New York in 1927, Silva was involved in the island's suffragist movement. Along with several other educated women from the middle and upper classes, she collaborated in the publication of the Puerto Rican feminist journal *La Mujer en el Siglo XX* (Women in the Twentieth Century). She also was a member of the Asociación Puertorriqueña de Mujeres Sufragistas (Puerto Rican Association of Women Suffragists). Through the efforts of this and other women's organizations voting rights were secured for educated women in 1929 and universal women's suffrage in 1935.

In New York Silva married Felipe Cintrón, a minister and head of the Hispanic Episcopal Mission. She founded and edited the *Revista de Artes y Letras* (1933–1945), a publication that for more than a decade promoted the work of Hispanic writers and artists to an international audience, since the journal circulated in the United States, Puerto Rico, and other Spanish-speaking countries. Aimed mostly at an educated reading public, the journal provided substantial evidence of the cultural vitality among Puerto Ricans and other Latinos in the New York communities by including creative literature, as well as information on theater, cinema, and musical activities by prominent Spanish-speaking performers. It also promoted a panethnic sense of *hispanismo* (Hispanicism) in the U.S. metropolis.

See also Journalism and Print Media

SOURCES: *Revista de Artes y Letras.* 1933–1945. New York; Sánchez Korrol, Virginia. 1994. *From Colonia to Community: The History of Puerto Ricans in New York City.* 2nd ed. Berkeley: University of California Press.

Edna Acosta-Belén

"SISTER CARMELITA" (CARMELA ZAPATA BONILLA MARRERO) (1905–2003)

Sister Carmelita was born in Cabo Rojo, Puerto Rico, where her father owned farmland and boats and was an associate in the Pepe Campos Maritime Company, a business enterprise in the Spanish-speaking Caribbean islands. When her mother died in 1918, she went to live with family members in Mayagüez, seldom seeing her father and experiencing want for the first time. During her formative years in the Immaculate Conception Catholic School, where she was taught English, she saw ads encouraging young women to join the catechists in Indiana, which sparked her interest in helping the poverty-stricken children of Puerto Rico. When Carmelita was in the eighth grade, she volunteered to teach the third-grade boys' class when the teacher fell ill. Father Thomas Agustin, a Vincentian priest, heard of her interest in the convent and encouraged her to join. She left Puerto Rico a year later in 1923 by ship with a second-class ticket in hand to join the Order of the Trinitarian Sisters, becoming the first Puerto Rican to serve in that religious community.

She was a novice for two years in the southern part of the United States, before serving at the Gold Street center in Brooklyn, New York. Sister Carmelita actively engaged in providing community services to hundreds of neighborhood children from mostly Irish, Polish, Lithuanian, and Italian backgrounds, with a few Puerto Rican, Chinese, and Pilipino newcomers to the neighborhood. Responsible for many, Sister Carmelita particularly felt called to serve the poor immigrants from Puerto Rico. She remembered that she served primarily as a social worker for the children and their families. At that time there was no welfare, people were easily dispossessed from their homes, and there was a high unemployment rate. She became acquainted with the police, who were predominantly Irish Catholic at the

time, politicians, although she tended to stay away from the Democratic Club on Adams Street because of rumored Mafia connections and frequent shootouts, bankers, the staff and administrators at Cumberland Hospital, "boliteros" (illegal numbers runners and gamblers), who among the Spanish-speaking people had access to a lot of money, and the powers at borough hall with the sole purpose of serving her clientele in the best possible way. She was actively involved in many organizations and was a founder of Casita Maria, a community settlement house established in 1934 in Spanish Harlem to serve as translators and advocates for the Spanish-speaking community's educational and social service needs. She remained in the United States until 1940, when she returned to Puerto Rico.

Every weekend for six years Sister Carmelita taught religion in the prison system in Río Piedras, Puerto Rico, to the male inmates. She was in Puerto Rico during the 1960s when Dr. Pedro Albizu Campos (Don Pedro), the foremost Nationalist/independence leader of the twentieth century, was imprisoned. She recalls the times when she would encourage Don Pedro to eat to keep up his strength, despite the fact that he was fasting as a means of protest against U.S. colonialism in Puerto Rico. She considered herself a Democrat, which meant that she tended to lean toward the commonwealth political platform of the Popular Democratic Party because "we lose the island if it goes to the Nationalists. Being a state wouldn't be good because we would lose a lot of things." She was referring to the possibilities that independence would bring socialism to Puerto Rico and that statehood would mean that the Puerto Rican culture and the Spanish language would be replaced by the dominant culture of the United States and the English language.

In 1967 she returned to New York to work at St. Joseph's Roman Catholic Church on Pacific Street in Brooklyn. When she reflected on the changes she had seen in the city since she first arrived in the early 1920s, Sister Carmelita lamented the ways Puerto Ricans viewed themselves. When she first arrived, Puerto Ricans were very proud of being Puerto Rican; there were no Puerto Rican gangs; out of all the groups she worked with, Puerto Ricans were the only ones with no one in jail; and the attitude of the community was one of great reverence and appreciation when she visited their homes to talk about "the things of God and religion." She firmly believed that what changed all of that for the Puerto Rican community was the amount of freedom they received in New York and welfare, both of which led the new generations to be apathetic and lose respect for authority. What she did not lament was loss of the assumption that every Spanish-speaking person was Puerto Rican. Early on, Puerto Ricans re-

Sister Carmelita, circa 1994. Courtesy of Missionary Servants of the Most Blessed Trinity Archives.

ceived blame incessantly whenever a Latino/a would do something. It was also unknown that, unlike other immigrant groups, Puerto Ricans had been U.S. citizens since the 1917 Jones Act. According to Sister Carmelita, distinction among Latino/a groups was a positive change.

Her educational background included obtaining a bachelor of arts degree from the University of Puerto Rico at Río Piedras and a master's degree from Santa María in Ponce in the area of social work. Sister Carmelita continued ministering in New York and New Jersey. In November 1991 she moved into the motherhouse of the Blessed Trinity Mother Missionary Cenacle in Philadelphia, Pennsylvania, where she was assigned to the ministry of prayer. She remained a member of the Trinitarian Sisters until her death on August 21, 2003. Sister Carmelita is widely recognized for her spirit of dedication, perseverance, and love of the work God had called her to in spite of having to wear "este traje feo" (this ugly dress). Her sense of humor helped move her forward. Her legacy is the labor of love that brought about change in the lives of thousands from diverse linguistic and cultural backgrounds.

See also Nuns, Contemporary; Religion

SOURCES: Ahern, Sister Teresa, archivist of the Blessed Trinity Mother Missionary Cenacle, Philadelphia, PA. 2004. Phone interview by María Pérez y González, August 26; Pérez y González, María E. 2000. *Puerto Ricans in the United States*. Westport, CT: Greenwood Press; Sánchez Korrol, Virginia. 1988. "In Search of Unconventional Women: Histories of Puerto Rican Women in Religious Vocations before Mid-century." *Oral History Review* 16, no. 2 (Fall): 47–63; Zapata Bonilla Marrero, Sister Carmela. 1977. Interview February 19. Centro Archives, Centro de Estudios, Puertorriqueños, Hunter College, CUNY.

María Pérez y González

SLAVERY

Slavery in Latin America was a system of forced labor that pressed large numbers of Native Americans and Africans into service to undertake domestic household chores, agricultural production, mineral extraction, and industrial manufacturing. African slaves accompanied the initial voyages of Spanish discovery to the Americas. When Christopher Columbus spotted land in the Bahamas in 1492, slavery was already a widely known and practiced institution in Europe, Africa, and the Americas. African slavery took root in Spanish America in the early 1500s as an indispensable part of the colonization process. It grew slowly in the sixteenth century and reached its greatest numeric extent during the second half of the eighteenth and first half of the nineteenth century. Slavery was finally eclipsed in the hemisphere between the 1820s and 1860s, replaced by more efficient and less costly forms of free wage labor.

Among the many privileges Spain's king granted Christopher Columbus and his compatriots as conquering lords was the right to exploit Indian labor under a number of institutional forms equated with slavery. At the time of the conquest the most dominant way to accomplish this was through the allocation of entire Indian communities to specific Spanish conquistadores as *encomiendas*. *Encomenderos*, the Spanish holders of *encomiendas*, were entrusted with the protection of their Indian charges in return for indigenous tribute and labor. Rotational labor levies known generically as *repartimientos* and more locally as *mita* in Peru and as *cuatequil* in Mexico were next in importance. For centuries before the Spanish conquest, natives, particularly in Mexico and Peru, had had to supply labor to state authorities for public works. *Repartimiento* drafts were likened to these older traditional forms of servile labor. Finally, throughout the Americas, an indigenous trade in captives and prisoners of war existed. Colonialism accelerated this market in two ways. First, the Indians began selling captives to Europeans for guns, ammunition, liquor, and manufactured products. Known in Spanish as *rescates*, this commerce only led to higher levels of indigenous warfare aimed at obtaining human chattel with which to barter for coveted European goods. Under the doctrine of "just war" the Spanish themselves also staged raids into enemy territory to capture Indian slaves. Spanish law maintained that those who resisted conversion to Christianity and the call for allegiance to Spain's monarch could be killed or enslaved. Indian enslavement was thus rationalized as justified because of native heathenism, resistance to Spanish authority, and, in some cases, the putative practice of cannibalism.

By the early 1500s it became crystal clear that Indian slavery simply would not work as an extensive institution in Spanish America. The island of Hispaniola, which today comprises the countries of Haiti and the Dominican Republic, is a good case in point. In 1492 Hispaniola boasted a native Taino population of some 400,000. By 1508 this group had dwindled to 60,000, by 1519 only 3,000 remained, and by 1540 they had all but disappeared. By the end of the sixteenth century the indigenous population of the entire Caribbean had met a similar fate; it was virtually wiped out. The same thing happened to Brazil's Indians in the seventeenth century.

To curtail the level of Indian depopulation, the Spanish Crown instituted the New Laws of 1542, which curtailed the extent of the *encomienda* system and constrained the levels of the *repartimiento*'s use. Spanish colonists intensely resisted the New Laws, and it was not until 1720 that the *encomienda* was finally abolished. Nevertheless, the legal enslavement of Indians and their exploitation through *encomiendas, repartimientos,* and *rescates* was allowed to flourish into the nineteenth century in peripheral areas of the empire, like the Amazon, Chile, Colombia, and what is now the American Southwest. Spanish authorities rationalized that without slavery as a human spoil of war and conquest, few colonists would brave the settlement of marginal areas of Spanish control where "wild" Indians deterred settlement.

As the supply of Indian slaves disappeared in the Caribbean and on the continent's coastal lowlands, the European colonizers turned to Africa for labor, on which they had depended only sparingly because of its prohibitive cost since 1441. By 1550 all this had changed. Europeans by then had developed a taste for cigars, coffee, chocolates, and sweets, making the cultivation of tobacco, coffee, cacao, and sugar on lowland plantations in the Americas much more profitable and the cost of importing African slaves much more feasible. African slaves became the principal labor sources throughout the Caribbean, as well as those tropical and semitropical coastal lowland areas of the Americas where the aboriginal population was sparse, nomadic, and completely unaccustomed to intense field labor or traditional labor drafts.

In the highlands of Mexico and in the Andes where formerly the Aztecs and Incas had ruled, the Spanish conquistadores found dense settled indigenous populations. Although the number of Indians declined precipitously here too because of the violence of the conquest and its aftermath, the sheer density of indigenous peoples guaranteed that they were not wiped out. These peoples had long been accustomed to state-extracted labor drafts devoted to agricultural, architectural, and mineral production before the conquest. Such systems of peasant labor were kept intact by the Spanish, organized, as they had always been, around kinship and residential affiliations and administered by native bureaucracies and indigenous lords. African slavery did not become a major institution in highland areas of dense Indian population because forced labor levies (*encomienda, repartimiento*) accomplished the same end.

Between 1502 and 1867 more than 10 million African slaves were imported into the Americas. Roughly 4 million went to Brazil, 1.7 million to what is now Haiti, 1.7 million to the Spanish American colonies, 1.7 million to the British West Indies, 600,000 to the United States, and 500,000 to the Dutch colonies of Guyana and Surinam.

Sociologist Orlando Patterson maintains that three essential features have characterized the slave condition. First, slavery rather universally has been culturally explained as a substitute for violent death in warfare. Imagined as a benevolent act of ransom, slavery nevertheless rendered the individual socially dead. Second, as socially dead individuals who had social personalities only through their masters, slaves were humans who had been alienated from their natal group, ripped from the fundamental fabric of kinship based on ties to family, ancestors, and blood relations. Finally, because slaves were pressed into slavery through a violent act of domination and lacked the most rudimentary kinship ties to a community, the slave condition was one of dishonor. These three characteristics were what made slaves highly coveted as laborers. They could be moved around easily at the will of their master at slight cost because their lives were not enmeshed in the ties of reciprocal obligation that were common among even the lowest free persons of Indian descent.

The massive importation of African slaves into the Americas owes its origins to the development of large-scale plantation agriculture devoted to the cultivation of tobacco, which became the area's first major commercial crop. In time indigo became a major plantation crop because of its importance as a European textile dye. Finally came sugar, which became the most lucrative and extensive crop in the Americas. The techniques, capital, tools, and African slaves that ultimately transformed the islands of the Caribbean—British, French, and Spanish—into major sugar-producing areas were drawn largely from the experiences and resources amassed by Dutch planters and merchants through the Dutch West Indies Company in Brazil in the early 1600s. From there the Dutch introduced modern sugar-milling and production techniques in Barbados, Martinique, and Guadalupe in the 1640s and rapidly transformed these islands. By 1680 British Barbados had some 350 sugar estates, worked by 37,000 black slaves; similar levels of labor and production were eventually found on Martinique, Guadalupe, and the western half of the island of Santo Domingo, which the French claimed as Saint Domingue in the 1650s.

Most of the plantations that evolved on the Caribbean islands during the seventeenth century were in the 200-acre range, worked by 100 or so slaves. This acreage and number of slaves climbed significantly in the eighteenth century. By 1750, for example, about two-thirds of all plantations in the Caribbean were more than 1,000 acres in size, and some reached much greater expanse, each worked at times by as many as 15,000 slaves. Blacks dominated the population ten to one, and well over 80 percent of them worked in the rural cultivation of sugar. By the middle of the eighteenth century sugar was the single crop most extensively cultivated by African and African American slave labor.

Before the Industrial Revolution plantation slavery was the most productive form of labor available. All the major tasks involved in planting, cultivation, and harvesting were undertaken without regard to the sex of the worker. Only age mattered, with the old tending to infants and to livestock and the young working at weeding and other minor chores until they were old enough to join field gangs. Slaves were constantly supervised and frequently disciplined with whips and other forms of corporal punishment. Plantations were highly productive units, making use of 80 percent of all slave labor available and of the entire age spectrum of the slave population.

African and African American slavery ended in the Americas largely because the institution was increasingly seen as immoral, illegitimate, and economically anachronistic by many of the leading European thinkers of the Enlightenment. In the late 1740s, for example, in his book *The Spirit of Laws*, Montesquieu questioned the legitimacy of slavery. In *The Wealth of Nations* (1776) Adam Smith concluded that free labor was simply more competitive than slavery. Beginning first with the Quaker clergy and then influential political theorists, the abolitionist movement gained more proponents in the last quarter of the eighteenth century. Then countries like Portugal, England, and France enacted legislation that abolished slavery on the Continent. By the time of the American Revolution in 1776 some states less dependent on slaves, like Vermont (1777), Pennsylvania (1780), Massachusetts (1780), and Rhode Island and Connecticut (1784) enacted gradual abolition laws that began by freeing newborns. The French Revolution of 1789 accelerated the pace of abolition. The Revolution's egalitarian ideals clashed with the reality of slavery and eventually led to the emancipation of slaves in Guadeloupe and Saint Domingue in February 1794.

The end of the slave trade was mainly championed by the English Society for the Abolition of the Slave Trade. By 1820 it had largely managed to stop the transport of African slaves to the Americas, though not without some intense resistance from the Spanish and Portuguese traders. Finally, in the 1860s, through effective blockades by the United States and England, the slave trade to Cuba and Puerto Rico was ended.

The end of the slave trade did not automatically mean the emancipation of all slaves. Emancipation was more gradual, beginning first with the passage of "free womb" (children born to slave mothers would be free) laws in 1821 in such newly independent Spanish American republics as Ecuador, Venezuela, and Colombia, which guaranteed that slavery would persist into the 1850s. Other countries, like Chile in 1823 and Mexico in 1832, completely emancipated their slaves. Cuba and Brazil were slavery's last bastions, finally abolishing it in 1883 and 1888, respectively.

See also Race and Color Consciousness

SOURCES: Bowser, Frederick P. 1974. *The African Slave in Colonial Peru, 1524–1650.* Stanford, CA: Stanford University Press; Boxer, Charles. 1957. *The Dutch in Brazil, 1624–1654.* New York: Oxford University Press; Davis, David Brion. 1976. *The Problem of Slavery in the Age of Revolution, 1770–1823.* Ithaca, NY: Cornell University Press; Klein, Herbert S. 1967. *Slavery in the Americas: A Comparative Study of Cuba and Virginia.* Chicago: University of Chicago Press; Knight, Franklin. 1970. *Slave Society in Cuba during the Nineteenth Century.* Madison: University of Wisconsin Press; Palmer, Colin. 1976. *Slaves of the White God: Blacks in Mexico, 1570–1650.* Cambridge, MA: Harvard University Press; Patterson, Orlando. 1982. *Slavery and Social Death: A Comparative Study.* Cambridge, MA: Harvard University Press; Price, Richard. 1973. *Maroon Societies: Rebel Slave Communities in the Americas.* New York: Anchor Press; Scarano, Francisco A. 1984. *Sugar and Slavery in Puerto Rico: The Plantation Economy in Ponce, 1800–1850.* Madison: University of Wisconsin Press; Schwartz, Stuart B. 1985. *Sugar Plantations in the Formation of a Brazilian Society: Bahia, 1550–1835.* Cambridge, MA: Harvard University Press.

Ramón A. Gutiérrez

SLOSS-VENTO, ADELA (1901–1998)

Adela Sloss-Vento was born to Anselma Garza and David Sloss in 1901. Her mother was a midwife and a *curandera* with a reputation as a self-made woman. Adela graduated from Pharr–San Juan–Alamo High in 1927 and quickly became a young community activist. As a secretary to the mayor of her hometown of San Juan, Texas, she worked to get rid of the red-light district located in the Mexican side of town. She also worked to end corruption in the mayor's office. In 1931 she organized a benefit to raise funds for a school desegregation case litigated by the League of United

Latin American Citizens (LULAC). Although the case was unsuccessful, *Salvatierra v. Del Rio Independent School District* was the first class-action lawsuit against the segregation of Mexican schoolchildren in Texas. While LULAC argued that Mexicans were "white" and thus did not merit segregation, the judge disagreed, remarking on the "decided peculiarities" of Tejano children. In 1932 Vento wrote an essay highlighting the significance of LULAC, even though the organization did not permit women as full members until 1933. That year she founded a Ladies LULAC Council in Alice, Texas.

Like her contemporary Alicia Dickerson Montemayor, she was a vocal feminist who condemned machismo. She wrote "Why There Exists No True Happiness in Many Latino Homes," a stinging critique of women's subordination in the home. In her late thirties she married Pedro Vento, a man who encouraged and supported her political activism. The couple had two children, and she frequently brought her children with her to political functions and community meetings.

An aspiring writer, she penned newspaper articles in both English- and Spanish-language newspapers from the 1920s through the 1980s. In 1943 her article "The Problem of Many Texas Towns" condemned "hatred against people of Mexican descent." In addition to her writing, community work, and family life, she worked as a prison matron beginning in 1949.

She held strong political opinions. She refused to support Lloyd Bentsen as state representative. She wrote letters to President Eisenhower condemning the Bracero Program and was critical of the exploitation of farmworkers. During the cold war she expressed strong anti-Communist views. Twenty years later she was a strong supporter of the Chicano Movement and bilingualism. She gave J. Luz Saenz money for his civil rights activism and wrote a tribute to him.

At the age of seventy-five, she wrote a tribute to lawyer and LULAC founder Alonso S. Perales. This book, *Alonso S. Perales: His Struggle for the Rights of Mexican Americans,* is a gold mine for Chicano scholars. Perales's widow acknowledged Vento's decades of civil rights work: "Mrs. Vento has been a collaborator since she was young. She's a brave woman and decided very early on to get to work. She too recognized that our community pleaded to bring forth justice." Unlike many community organizers who never saved any of their documents, Adela Vento scrupulously preserved her correspondence, articles, and ephemera. In 1968 she was the only women to receive a Pioneer Award at the Fifth Annual Statewide LULAC Founders' Pioneers and Awards Banquet in San Antonio. Adela Sloss-Vento died at the age of ninety-seven in 1998. Her son, Dr. Arnoldo Carlos Vento, a professor of Spanish and Chicano literature, has written several novels, referring to her in *La Cueva de Naltzatlán* and *En el nombre del Padre y del Hijo.*

See also League of United Latin American Citizens (LULAC)

SOURCES: Sloss-Vento, Adela. 1978. *Alonso S. Perales: His Struggle for the Rights of Mexican Americans*. San Antonio: Artes Gráficas; _____. 1934. "Por que en muchos hogares latinos no existe verdadera felicidad." *LULAC News*, March, 31–32; _____. 1978. "To Speak English and Spanish Means We Are Better Prepared to Know Our Culture." *La Verdad*, June 23.

Cynthia E. Orozco

SMELTERTOWN, EL PASO

With the arrival of the railroad and firms such as the Kansas City Consolidated Smelting and Refining Company, El Paso, Texas, emerged as an important center for mining and smelting activity in the U.S. Southwest in the late nineteenth century. Purchased and incorporated by the American Smelting and Refining Company (ASARCO) in 1899, the smelter processed lead, copper, and other ores transported by rail to El Paso from mines throughout the Southwest and northern Mexico and became the largest employer of ethnic Mexicans in El Paso by the turn of the twentieth century. The smelter's need for a large labor pool, coupled with the social, economic, and political upheaval caused by the Mexican Revolution (1910–1920), precipitated the migration of thousands of Mexicans to El Paso. From the plant's inception workers and their families began to establish homes around the smelter, giving birth to a dynamic and vibrant community called Smeltertown, or la Esmelda, as its predominantly ethnic Mexican inhabitants called it. Other industries established operations in the area, including a brick plant, a cement plant, and a quarry, that provided additional employment opportunities for Smeltertown's residents. With an estimated population of 5,000 residents at its height in the 1920s and 1930s, Smeltertown was one of the largest residential and occupational centers for Mexicans in El Paso.

Located on the banks of the Rio Grande approximately three miles northwest of downtown El Paso, Smeltertown was divided into two major sections. Upper Smeltertown, or El Alto, sat on plant property on a bluff overlooking the river. Mexicans resided in company-owned tenements in the Mexican section, while the predominantly Anglo managerial staff and their families lived in homes in what was called Smelter Terrace. Lower Smeltertown, or El Bajo, was situated below the plant, between the County Road (now Paisano Drive or U.S. Highway 85) and the river. Residents of El Bajo rented small parcels of land from private individuals, upon which they built adobe and wood-frame homes. El Bajo was further divided into smaller neighborhoods with which residents identified.

Smeltertown was more than a labor camp or a company town; it was a virtual city within a city. Although the residents did not own the property upon which their community was built, they claimed ownership of their community in a variety of ways. They built permanent homes and beautified them with gardens and other personal touches, established a significant Mexican-owned business district with restaurants, small grocery stores, barber shops, taverns, and bakeries, formed athletic leagues, musical groups, and community organizations like the Smelter Community Center Association (1936), and organized dances, bazaars, and other social and cultural activities through the schools, the local YMCA chapter, and the Catholic parish. After World War II they renamed the streets after local young men who had died in service in the U.S. armed forces.

From the beginning women played a vital role in the formation of community in Smeltertown. For the most part, Smeltertown was a community of families—nuclear and extended, male and female headed. According to the 1920 census, women constituted more than half the population of Smeltertown. These women contributed directly to the industrial economy of the community. Although the workforces of the neighboring industries were exclusively male, the industrial character of the work at the various plants created important employment opportunities for women. The 1920 census reveals that many Smeltertown women worked as maids and laundresses for private families and in the smelter hospital, as seamstresses, and as merchants, store clerks, and street vendors, and some women rented rooms to workers in the neighboring plants. In addition, women participated in the economic life of Smeltertown in ways not captured by the census. Several women ran informal "restaurants" for workers out of their homes, sold homemade items like cheeses, and worked as midwives in the community. Some women who had been educated in Mexico ran small preschools out of their homes known as *escuelas particulares*. For a small tuition the women taught children how to read and write in Spanish, prepared them for religious sacraments, and introduced them to enough English for their entry into the El Paso County school system. According to ASARCO employee records, between 1942 and 1946 a very small but significant number of women found their way into the smelter to fill labor shortages caused by the war.

In the early part of the twentieth century immigrant women were often the targets of Americanization efforts. In Smeltertown the establishment of the Smelter Vocational School in 1923 provided a means by which to create not only a self-replenishing, better-trained male workforce for the smelter, but also a more Americanized family for workers. A joint venture between the county of El Paso and ASARCO, the Smelter Vocational School offered courses for both men and women in an effort to transform perceived "idleness" into "industry." While male students took courses in industrial topics, women learned skills such as dressmaking and homemaking. Students also took classes in subjects such as mathematics, English, science, citizenship, and personal hygiene. In addition, the school sponsored evening courses and workshops for mothers on topics including food for children, millinery, and food preservation, advertised to the community through the Catholic parish. Despite the negative connotations of the Americanization efforts, the students of the Smelter Vocational School used the lessons and skills learned at the school to help create a sense of identity and to help foster their sense of community. Some women earned vocational teaching credentials and returned to teach at the school. In addition, women became actively involved in social and community service activities—teaching sewing and homemaking courses, assisting the distribution of milk and food to the community, becoming involved with depression-era aid organizations, and participating in organizations like the Smelter Community Center Association, a group dedicated to the welfare of the community.

Women also played an active role in the social and cultural life of the community through the various activities of the San José del Río (later San José de Cristo Rey) Catholic parish. Through their work in a number of devotional societies, women were at the center of the social and religious life of the predominantly Catholic community. They organized bazaars and sold homemade food and other homemade items to help raise money for church improvements and other expenses; they lent their voices to los Trovadores, a choir sponsored by the church that gained citywide acclaim; and in the 1930s they and their fellow parishioners labored to erect the monument of Cristo Rey (Christ the King) in the neighboring hills. Women carried sand and other materials in their aprons and in pails to the top of the hill, where a forty-three-foot sandstone sculpture of Christ with outreached arms now stands. Adopted as a diocesan and international project in 1937 and dedicated on October 17, 1940, Mt. Cristo Rey is one of the most prominent features on the El Paso skyline.

By the 1970s Smeltertown was home to roughly 100 families and was no longer the bustling community it had once been. Many families relocated in the postwar period when they were able to buy houses in other parts of the city. Others were forced to move because of plant expansion and when the county widened what is now Paisano Drive into a four-lane highway. Smeltertown's demise came in the early 1970s. After an air-pollution suit was filed against ASARCO, health and environmental officials discovered dangerously high levels of lead and other contaminants in the ground and in the homes of Smeltertown residents. More alarmingly, they discovered that a number of children in the area had high lead concentrations in their bloodstreams. Response to the environmental and health hazards was mixed. While residents complied with testing and medical treatment, many long-time residents of Smeltertown also fought relocation and attempted to preserve the community that had been their home for generations. After two years of litigation, testing, medical treatment, and public debates, the company and city officials decided to demolish Smeltertown and ordered the remaining residents to move by January 1, 1973. Although the physical structures of the community are long gone, Smeltertown residents continue to celebrate their community through annual Smeltertown reunions, a testimony to their enduring sense of community.

See also Environment and the Border

SOURCES: García, Mario. 1981. *Desert Immigrants: The Mexicans of El Paso, 1880–1920*. New Haven, CT: Yale University Press; Perales, Monica. 2003. "Smeltertown: A Biography of a Mexican American Community, 1880–1972." Ph.D. diss., Stanford University; Romero, Mary. 1984. "The Death of Smeltertown: A Case Study of Lead Poisoning in a Chicano Community." In *The Chicano Struggle: Analyses of Past and Present Efforts*, ed. Theresa Cordova and Juan R. Garcia, 26–41. Binghamton, NY: Bilingual Press.

Monica Perales

SMITH, PLÁCIDA ELVIRA GARCÍA (1896–1981)

Born on August 7, 1896, Plácida García hailed from the elite Hispanic gentry that had migrated from New Mexico to southern Colorado. She became a career educator whose commitment to education came from her father, a vocal political advocate for public schools. She attended elementary school in Conejos, Colorado, and then continued her education at Loretto Academy, graduating as class valedictorian in 1915. She received her certification to teach second grade that year and accepted a teaching position in Antonito, Colorado.

García taught there for the next three years until 1918, when she became principal of Conejos Grade School. In 1921 she left that position to serve as the deputy county treasurer of Conejos County. In 1924 she left Conejos for the University of Utah, where she had a teaching fellowship and earned a bachelor's degree with a major in Spanish language and a minor in soci-

ology in 1927. In 1928, after briefly undertaking graduate work in sociology at the University of California, Berkeley, she and her husband, Reginald G. Smith, moved to Phoenix, where he took a position at the *Arizona Republic*. He died in 1938 of a heart attack, leaving her with a young son, Reginald García Smith.

Even before her husband's untimely death García Smith worked outside the home, an unusual occurrence among financially secure, middle-class American women and especially among Latinas. In Phoenix García Smith initially worked as a substitute teacher at Phoenix Elementary School and at Phoenix Union High School. By 1931, however, she had moved away from the sphere of public education to begin a second career as the director of Friendly House, a community center for immigrants seeking to learn English, gain citizenship, and develop job skills. As director of Friendly House from 1931 to 1963, García Smith continued to be an educator, but of adults instead of children, as well as a community builder and promoter of Americanization.

Within her first five years at Friendly House García Smith organized Phoenix's first Spanish-American Boy Scout troop, established the Mexican Dance Project, and with New Deal funds started the Mexican Orquesta and organized the Southside Improvement Club. Between 1929 and 1934 more than 500,000 Mexicans in the United States, an estimated one-third of the population, were deported or repatriated to Mexico, even though the majority of those affected were U.S.-born children. In a controversial move García Smith and Friendly House supported the repatriation effort and facilitated the relocation of hundreds of Mexican residents of Phoenix. During the summers of 1937 and 1939 she attended the University of Denver, taking classes at the School of Social Work. During World War II García Smith was instrumental in establishing a pilot program for a well-baby clinic and a prenatal clinic in cooperation with the U.S. Public Health Department. In 1945 she served as a social worker at the Gila River Japanese Relocation Center in Chandler, Arizona, helping former Japanese American internees rebuild their lives after they were unjustly incarcerated during World War II.

During her tenure at Friendly House García Smith was quoted as stating that "[t]he best way to help people is to help them to help themselves." Many of her programs specifically targeted the practical needs of Mexican and Mexican American women and teenage girls by offering classes in housekeeping skills and English, helping them obtain citizenship, connecting women and girls with both temporary and permanent employment opportunities, and providing day care for preschool children. García Smith not only coordinated the classes, but taught several of them as well. Her favorite self-introduction when beginning classes reportedly was "My name is Plácida García Smith. A good American name; a good Mexican name."

In 1961 García Smith was named the Phoenix Advertising Club's Woman of the Year, not only for her work at Friendly House but also for her overall community involvement. She was, among other things, a charter member of the Phoenix Community Council, an organizer of the Spanish-American Minute Maids during World War II, and a member of the Phoenix Parks Board. Other honors included an award of merit from the Daughters of the American Revolution in 1953. After her death in 1981 her accomplishments were described in the *Arizona Republic* newspaper as having "helped 1,400 people to learn English and to become American citizens." She also was admitted to the Arizona Women's Hall of Fame in 1982.

See also Americanization Programs; Friendly House, Phoenix

SOURCES: Marquardt, Frederic S. 1981. "Plácida García Smith: A Life Lived through Teaching Self-Help." *Arizona Republic*, July 24, A6; Titcomb, Mary Ruth. 1984. "Americanization and Mexicans in the Southwest: A History of Phoenix's Friendly House, 1920–1983." M.A. thesis, University of Santa Barbara.

Eve Carr

SOLDADERAS

Soldaderas were women who served in Mexican armies primarily as corn grinders, cooks, foragers, nurses, and servants to soldiers from indigenous times until 1925. Mexicanas became *soldaderas* either by joining their male relatives in armies or by being kidnapped and forced to follow soldiers to cook, clean clothes, and provide other "services." They were known by many names—women warriors, *mociuaquetzque* (valiant women), *auianime* (pleasure girls), camp followers, *capitanas, coronelas,* Adelitas, Juanas, *cucarachas* (cockroaches), *viejas* (old ladies), and *galletas* (cookies).

The practice of armies using women as corn grinders can be traced back to Aztec armies. The Spaniards inherited the practice when Hernán Cortés received twenty women slaves in 1519 to cook and grind corn for maize bread, including Malinalli Tenepal, who would later become known as La Malinche. She can be considered a famous *soldadera*, a woman who rose from the ranks and became the equivalent of a *conquistadora*. Called *india molenderas*, women corn grinders accompanied most military expeditions, but often not in adequate numbers. Statistics for the numbers of women corn grinders and servants range from 20 to 30 percent of the total recruits in the armies. Official military recognition of corn grinders came during a 1700 Spanish expedition against the Mayans when "every fifteen-man squad had an Indian woman to make the *nixtamal*, grind it and make the dough into tortillas and tamales." A Spanish army officer noted the sorry condition of the "palms of the women's hands and the joints of the fingers, raw and festering from the continuous grinding."

Because so many women were in the army camps, there arose a tradition among *soldaderas* to gravitate toward the battlefields and trenches and engage in combat on a spontaneous basis. These women's actions made them "part-time" soldiers when they crossed the line from camp followers to warriors. By 1910 *soldaderas* had become a regular feature in most Mexican armies. Military officials considered them a "necessary evil" because the armies did not provide commissary corps to forage for and grind the corn or use corn mills to feed the soldiers. *Soldaderas* provided these services and in so doing decreased the number of desertions by soldiers. In 1912 the Mexican army (*los federales*) threatened to revolt when orders arrived that prohibited *soldaderas* from accompanying them. The order was rescinded, and the *soldaderas* followed their soldiers.

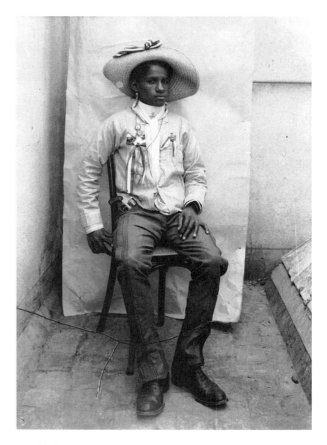

A *soldadera* during the Mexican Revolution. Photograph by Agustín Victor Casasola. Courtesy of Foteca del INAH.

During the Mexican Revolution (1910–1920) probably the most fascinating woman soldier to emerge from the ranks of the *soldaderas* was General Petra Herrera. A former corn grinder, she disguised herself as "Pedro," a male soldier, and became a heroine of several battles. She proclaimed herself *generala* and led her own army of 1,000 women. Many *soldaderas* died during the Mexican Revolution, and many soldiers' accounts lament the tragic vision of thousands of dead women on the battlefields. Not surprisingly, the most popular *corridos* were often about strong, valiant *soldaderas* such as La Adelita, La Valentina, and Juana Gallo.

The *soldaderas* were eliminated from Mexican armies in 1925. From the 1930s to the 1990s they gained notoriety in films and books about the Mexican Revolution. Their reputation became part of a national identity formation as "patriotic heroines" and at other times as "backward, wanton whores." Mexicans who migrated to the United States added additional views of the *soldaderas* as survivors. During the Chicano student movement the *soldadera* image was popular among both men and women. For men, the *soldadera* implied a woman struggling for justice alongside her man, and for women, it applied a safe space between feminist and loyalist, a strong independent revolutionary figure that did not threaten their men. Chicana feminists also embraced *soldaderas* like Petra Herrera as visionary woman warriors.

The armed rebellion by the Emiliano Zapata National Liberation Army (EZLN) in the state of Chiapas on January 1, 1894, changed the name of women fighters from *soldaderas* to Zapatistas demanding equality in the military and promotions to top leadership ranks. Infantry Major Ana María gained the attention of the world as the officer in command of the capture of San Cristobal de las Casas. Mexicanas have proven that women have always been a part of armies in a variety of roles and that a vibrant warrior spirit continues to be part of their heritage.

See also Mexican Revolution

SOURCES: Alatorre, Angeles Mendieta. 1961. *La mujer en la revolución mexicana.* Mexico City: Talleres Gráficos de la Nación; Poniatowska, Elena. 1969. *Hasta no verte Jesús mio.* Mexico City: Ediciones Era; Ruiz, Vicki L. 1998. *From out of the Shadows: Mexican Women in Twentieth-Century America.* New York: Oxford University Press; Salas, Elizabeth. 1990. *Soldaderas in the Mexican Military: Myth and History.* Austin: University of Texas Press.

Elizabeth Salas

SOLIS, HILDA L. (1957–)

In November 2000, after a tough battle against an incumbent Latino politician, Hilda Solis was elected to represent the Thirty-second Congressional District of California. California state senator Richard Alarcón of the Twentieth District endorsed Solis in her congressional race, citing her courage and dedication to issues of importance to women. As a member of Congress, she has been the first Latino to serve on the powerful House Energy and Commerce Committee, where she is the highest-ranking Democrat on the Environment and Hazardous Materials Subcommittee. This Subcommittee oversees cleanup of the nation's most polluted communities. Throughout her political career in California and in the United States Congress Solis has advocated for the issues important to working families, including the environment, health, labor, and immigration. When she was elected to the newly reapportioned Twenty-fourth Senatorial District in November 1994, Solis also made history as the first Latina elected to the California State Senate. Her successful bid for office proved that Latinas could be elected on their own initiative.

Solis was born in 1957 to a Mexican father, Raúl Solis, and a Nicaraguan mother, Juana Solis. She attended elementary school in the San Gabriel Valley, Sparks Junior High School, and La Puente High School. Her parents, Solis affirms, "view my career in a positive way. . . . they still live in the house where I was raised." Her husband Sam, a small-business owner in the San

Congresswoman Hilda L. Solis. Courtesy of the Office of Congresswoman Hilda L. Solis.

Gabriel area, is equally supportive of her endeavors. The first of seven children to attend college, she earned a baccalaureate degree at California Polytechnic, Pomona, and a master's degree at the University of Southern California. As editor in chief for the Office of Hispanic Affairs during the Carter administration, Solis also worked for the U.S. Office of Management and Budget. From 1985 to 1992 she served two terms on the Rio Hondo Community College Board of Trustees. In 1991 Solis was appointed to the Los Angeles County Insurance Commission. In 1992 she was elected to represent the Fifty-seventh Assembly District, El Monte, California.

As majority whip in the California Senate, Solis was an integral part of the senate Democratic leadership. She chaired the Senate Industrial Relations Committee, the Senate Subcommittee on Asia Trade and Commerce, and the Select Committee on Bilingual Education. She was vice-chair of the Committee on Finance, Investment, and International Trade and was a member of the Budget and Fiscal Review, Energy, Utilities, and Communications, Environmental Quality, and Health and Human Services committees. As a California state senator, Solis built a distinguished record, particularly in terms of health care and the environment. A strong advocate for battered women and senior citizens, She is associated with the passage of legislation that provided approximately one million dollars to the Department of Justice to support nursing home investigations and prosecutions in partnership with local district attorneys in the state of California.

Solis' concerns about environmental health, women, children, and farmworkers is evident in the legislation she supports. She coauthored bills to ban the use of the short hoe and to make stoop labor illegal in California. As a Senator, Solis appropriated issues other legislators feared to touch, such as crime, domestic violence, education, living wages, sweatshops, and welfare reform. In Congress she got legislation passed that prioritized ways to clean up the San Gabriel River in her community, which has been devastated by industrial pollution. The San Gabriel River Watershed Study Act, a model for the nation, was signed into law (Public Law No. 108-042).

In 2005, Congresswoman Solis is the first Latina to serve on the Energy and Commerce Committee and the ranking member of the Environmental Hazardous Materials Subcommittee. She is associated with the passage of the Military Citizenship Act that makes it easier for immigrants serving in the U.S. armed forces to become naturalized citizens. Along with Jeff Bingaman, senator from New Mexico, they have co-sponsored a congressional resolution about the 400 women murdered in Ciudad Juárez and Chihuahua

Mexico over the last decade as a way to raise greater American public awareness and, in a symbolic manner, to prod Mexican law enforcement to implement effective measures to stop the violence.

Solis is an important role model for young Latinas. In demand as a speaker, she draws upon her personal struggle as a minority woman from a working-class family to reach her goals. In 1996 California Polytechnic at Pomona, her alma mater, established the Hilda L. Solis Scholarship to honor her support of and dedication to the university. It also named a library room in her honor.

Solis has been recognized and honored for her contributions by many organizations, including the San Gabriel Valley Young Women's Christian Association (YWCA), the California State University Alumni Council, the American Diabetes Association, the Los Angeles County Board of Supervisors, Environment California, the California League of Conservation Voters, and the California Hispanic Chamber of Commerce. In addition, Solis was honored with the Profiles in Courage Award by the John F. Kennedy Library Foundation in 2000, the first woman to receive the award.

See also Latinas in the U.S. Congress; Politics, Electoral

SOURCES: Amnesty International, USA. "Take Action. Help Bring Justice to the Women of Ciudad Juárez and Chihuahua, Mexico." http://takeaction.amnestyusa.org/action (accessed July 23, 2005); Hernández, Daniel. 2003. "Military Citizenship Act Hailed." *Los Angeles Times*, December 4, B3; Pringle, Paul. "The River that LA Forgot." 2003. *Los Angeles Times*, December 23, A1; Solis, Hilda. 2001. Telephone interview with Merrihelen Ponce; U.S. House of Representatives. "Congresswoman Hilda. Solis." http://solis.house.gov/ (accessed July 23, 2005).

Merrihelen Ponce

SOSA-RIDDELL, ADALJIZA (1937–)

Notable educator and scholar Adaljiza Sosa-Riddell's philosophy of life and commitment were greatly influenced by her early experiences. A critical influence on Sosa-Riddell was her father, Luz Paz Sosa. Sosa-Riddell's parents, Luz Paz Sosa and Gregoria López, came to the United States from Mexico sometime between 1918 and 1920. Paz Sosa came first through Matamoras and worked in Texas and then in the Kansas meatpacking industry. He returned to Mexico to get Gregoria and her older sister. The family settled in New Mexico, where Paz Sosa worked on the railroad, but they separated soon afterwards. Paz Sosa left for California with friends and there joined the flow of migrant workers "pescando todo lo que había" (picking up all kinds of jobs) from southern California to San

Jose and farther. Around 1925 Gregoria came to Los Angeles, where she was reunited with Luz. Together they went to live in a shack in Colton, California, that was made of railroad siding. Ada, as those close to her called her, was born in Colton on December 12, 1937.

Though both her parents had little formal education, they were self-taught and highly literate people. They taught their children to do well in school. Politics also played an important role in the household. Sosa-Riddell's father, a revolutionary in Mexico, was arrested several times in the United States for his radical socialist activities. Sosa-Riddell called him a trade unionist.

For Sosa-Riddell, the summer was about work; the rest of the year was about school. Having a sister who studied at the University of California at Berkeley, she made up her mind that she, too, would go to Berkeley. Although she did not excel in school sufficiently to become valedictorian like her sister, she did well enough to graduate in 1955 and get accepted at the new University of California campus at Riverside. A fellow classmate, however, was going to Berkeley. He convinced Sosa-Riddell that this was her lifelong dream. She applied to the University of California at Berkeley and was accepted.

With a $200 scholarship and $200 from summer work, Sosa-Riddell set off to Berkeley to stay with her sister and attend the university. She received a B.A. in political science and later her master's degree. While she was a junior at Berkeley, she married William Riddell.

Completing their graduate studies, Ada and William returned to Colton, where she taught elementary school for seven years. It was during this time that she accomplished what she regards as her greatest life achievement: building her parents a comfortable home and providing for them emotionally and financially until their deaths.

Adaljiza Sosa-Riddell was the first Chicana to receive a Ph.D. in political science in the United States. She received her doctorate from the University of California, Riverside. In 1971 she began teaching at the University of California, Davis, and two years later she was named director of the Chicano Studies program. She was responsible for course development, faculty recruitment, budget decisions, and community outreach efforts. She created and taught courses such as Introduction to Chicano Studies, Chicanos in Contemporary Society, Women in Politics, Political Economy of Chicano Communities, and U.S./Mexican Border Relations.

Commitment to Chicanas/os and Chicana/o studies led Sosa-Riddell to become a founding member of several internationally and nationally recognized organizations, including the National Association for Chicana

Prominent Chicana feminist educator Adaljiza Sosa-Riddell, 2000. Courtesy of Adaljiza Sosa-Riddell.

and Chicano Studies (NACCS) and Mujeres Activas en Letras y Cambio Social (MALCS). The mission of both organizations is to foster the development of Chicana/o and Latina/o scholarship and nurture young scholars.

MALCS specifically is organized to confront the predominantly Eurocentric patriarchal bases of contemporary knowledge. Lobbying efforts by Sosa-Riddell and MALCS helped establish the Chicana/Latina Research Center. MALCS sponsors a yearly institute and publishes a journal titled *Voces*. During the 1990s Sosa-Riddell was general editor of *Voces*.

In addition to her scholar/activism, Sosa-Riddell has numerous publications. Among these are "Chicanas as Political Actors: Rare Literature, Complex Practice" in *National Political Science*, 1993; "The Bioethics of Reproductive Technologies: Impacts and Implications for Chicanas/Latinas" in *Chicana Critical Issues*, 1993; "Parlier California: A Case of Chicano Politics" in *Journal of Aztlán*, 1978; and "Chicanas en el Movimiento," *Journal of Aztlán*, 1974.

The recipient of numerous awards, Sosa-Riddell was Woman of the Year in Education for the Sacramento Area YWCA in 1992, Scholar of the Year for the National Association for Chicano Studies in 1989, and Scholar of the Year for the Business and Professional Women's Association in 1988.

Although Sosa-Riddell has been battling Parkinson's disease in recent years, this has not hampered her activity. She retired from the University of California at Davis, in 2004 but still mentors students, works closely with MALCS and NACCS, and continues writing and enjoying her family, and community.

See also Chicano Movement; Education

SOURCE: Telgen, Diane, and Jim Kamp, eds. 1993 *Notable Hispanic American Women*. Detroit: Gale Research.

Linda Apodaca

SOTO FELICIANO, CARMEN LILLIAN "LILY" (1933–1997)

Carmen Soto Feliciano was a lay associate in the Iglesia Luterana La Trinidad in Chicago's Humboldt Park, as well as a community organizer. She was born on November 19, 1933, in Florida, Puerto Rico, the oldest of Eulugio Feliciano and Rosa Sotomayor's three children. Along with her siblings, Julia and José Manuel, Carmen received much of her education in Puerto Rico. In 1954 she earned a normal school teaching degree from the University of Puerto Rico and taught school in Barrios Yune and Ceiba until she married Cecilio Soto in 1957 and moved to the northwest side of Chicago. Soto Feliciano viewed the move as temporary; instead, she stayed in the city for the rest of her life.

In three years, 1958–1960, the couple had three children, Evelyn, Roberto, and Pablo. Life in Chicago was not easy for the young family. Soto Feliciano was employed at the Western Electric Company for many years. Once the children were older, she added another responsibility to her busy work and home schedule by returning to evening school in a baccalaureate degree program. Eighteen years after becoming a teacher in Puerto Rico, she received a bachelor of arts degree from Chicago State University in 1974. Employed by the Chicago public school system, she became a bilingual teacher at Davis Elementary School, a position she held until 1976.

During the next ten years, 1976–1986, Soto Feliciano was employed by the Division for Mission in North America of the Lutheran Church in America as a lay associate. Her familiarity with the city and neighborhood and its institutions and diverse cultures made her an excellent choice to provide social services for la Iglesia Luterana La Trinidad. She became a community worker for the Lutheran Social Services in Illinois, particularly involved with the Humboldt Park community. In 1980 she completed a law program course for community developers and social workers at the John Marshall Law School sponsored jointly by the Cook County Legal Assistance Foundation and the law school.

Lay minister Carmen Soto Feliciano is on the right. Courtesy of Evelyn B. Soto Straw.

Soto Feliciano's broad experience served her well when she was called upon to play numerous roles. She was a community organizer, evangelist, supervisor of an outreach ministry, and a friend to all who needed her. Having lived in the Humboldt Park community for more than thirty years, she knew its residents, their problems, and how to work with the city's bureaucratic obstacles. She handled families in crisis. She provided emergency food and clothing when needed, helped secure public assistance, organized motivational and tutoring sessions, counseled families on a myriad of problems, and still had time to organize various women's groups and a Girl Scout troop. In that way she sought to cement and encourage community spirit. A brochure describing Soto Feliciano's dedication, the inspiration behind Iglesia Luterana La Trinidad, states: "Carmen even made contact with the Latin Kings, a notorious teenage gang. 'It's better to work with them, than to ignore them,' she explained. 'I know those kids and they're not bad. If you treat them as if they're somebody, they'll treat you well. When they're with me . . . they act like my kids.' "

Soto Feliciano's recognitions and awards were many. Among them was the Confessor of Christ Award in 1984 from the Lutheran School of Theology in Chicago. This award was presented to her for her "exemplary witness to Christ Jesus and the Gospel by selfless service to others." Other awards include the Distinguished Service Award for Outstanding Volunteer Support from United Way and a Certificate of Recognition for Active and Cooperative Participation in a Latin American Senior Citizen Organization in 1979. Carmen Soto Feliciano died at the age of sixty-three on January 28, 1997.

SOURCE: Soto, Evelyn. 2003. Oral history interview by Hector Carrasquillo, January 24.

Hector Carrasquillo

SOUCHET, CLEMENTINA (1932–   )

Clementina Souchet, who rose to be a governor's advisor, was born in Peñuelas, a coastal town in the southern part of Puerto Rico, in 1932. In the first chapter of her autobiography the author reminisces about life in her native town of Peñuelas. The poetic gaze of the migrant woman depicts an idyllic paradise of *flamboyanes* (a tree in Puerto Rico), chickens, and other local characteristics. She describes her life as "feliz" (happy) and herself as a delicate, fragile girl who loved to daydream. Yet there are signs of trouble in paradise when she describes the double standard characterizing Puerto Rican culture where "para el hombre habia menos restriciones y mas oportunidades" (men faced less restrictions and had more opportunities). As a woman, Souchet felt restricted by all the gender rules and codes she had to live by. She observes that she felt confused by traditional Puerto Rican gender roles. She was told to distrust all men, yet she did not know whether this also included the men in her family. She asked what the difference was between *los hombres de afuera* (the men outside) and *los hombres en la familia* (the men in the family). In doing so, she captures the predicament that women of her generation endured and the gendered double standard that has characterized Puerto Rican culture. This became more pronounced when she declared to her parents her dreams and aspirations to be an actress. One of the most insightful moments in her memoir is when she states that "during that time there was little discussion about the feminist movement but I definitely was born free."

Like other Puerto Rican women, Souchet used migration as a way to escape gender oppression and assert the female agency denied to her because of her upbringing and culture. As a young woman, she first moved to Chicago under the pretense of spending a summer vacation with male relatives who had moved to Chicago to work. Once in the city, through correspondence with her parents, she managed to negotiate a more permanent stay. To escape the restrictions placed by her family in Chicago, she married a young Puerto Rican man she met in a movie house. Though she first saw him as "mi libertador" (my liberator), eventually he became abusive. As a married woman, Souchet strategized about how to leave her husband and have control over her own actions. One of the most important moments in her life occurred when she had a back-alley abortion that nearly cost her life.

In this context her autobiography becomes a narrative that must be read as a series of boundary crossings, not as a fixed ethnic or migration story. She is part of a generation of women who with each departure, return, and migration were pushed into a movement of continuous exile and return that is fundamental to understanding the gendered dimensions of the Puerto Rican diaspora. As an immigrant narrative, her book contains some elements of the "rags-to-riches" stories that are popular in the United States, but overall it belongs to the larger choir of diasporic voices articulating the Puerto Rican experience. At another level her life story is important because it comes from the margins of the margin. Most of her life takes place in the Puerto Rican community of Chicago. Although Puerto Ricans have lived in the city of Chicago for more than half a century, autobiographical narratives are rare.

Souchet's autobiography also opens a window into the development of the Puerto Rican community of Chicago from the 1950s through the 1980s. Her story shows the many positions and roles that women played (and continue to play) in constructing community across a transnational space that involves New York, Chicago, and the island. Her involvement in communal activities began when she was selected Miss Puerto Rican Chicago in 1951, the first beauty pageant held in the early stages of community development. Today, the election of Ms. Puerto Rican Chicago has become a tradition of the Puerto Rican Parade celebration. In addition, Souchet's husband was one of the founding members of the Chicago branch of the Nationalist Puerto Rican Party, which suggests that the connections between political activists in Puerto Rico and mainland communities are much deeper than previously imagined.

Yet her political convictions placed her at the opposite end of the spectrum from her husband. As a woman who celebrated Puerto Rico's connection to the United States, she felt that her husband's activities were a threat to their family and the nation. She tried to dissuade him from these activities, but to no avail. In a desperate attempt she sought help outside her own network of family and community members. Souchet became an informant for the FBI. After the Nationalist attack in Congress by Lolita Lebrón and others, her husband was arrested and incarcerated for a short time.

Eventually Souchet divorced her husband and after a short stay in Puerto Rico returned to Chicago. Souchet's autobiography can also be read as an essay about the struggles of Puerto Rican women workers in Chicago. She describes how she dealt with sexual harassment and job discrimination at a time when women had no recourse against perpetrators. Her work experiences placed her in a range of work opportunities, breaking new ground and making history as she moved along. Souchet was nominated to become the first Latina to hold the position of aide to the lieutenant governor of Illinois, Dave O'Neal, to represent the needs of the Latino community, a position that brought her much visibility and many responsibilities. Through this position she became an important leader in Chicago Latino and Puerto Rican politics.

Carole Boyce Davies proposes that "if we see Black women's subjectivity as a migratory subjectivity existing in multiple locations, then we can see how their work, their presence traverses all of the geographic/national boundaries instituted to keep our dislocations in place." Similarly, Souchet's story also traverses national, racial, class, and gender boundaries in a way that allows her to negotiate and renegotiate them throughout the different stages of her life. Clementina Souchet belongs to a generation of women who were shaped by tradition, but were not deterred by it; through personal and collective strategies they sought to redefine what it means to be a Puerto Rican woman.

Like other women of color, Latinas have used autobiographical narratives as a way to write themselves into history. Through both fictional and nonfictional accounts Latinas have introduced people to powerful and exciting narratives of self-discovery, in the process giving voice to new politicized subjects and agents. Souchet's autobiography places her in a category of her own, a Puerto Rican migrant woman's narrative, as she gives voice to the experiences of older immigrant women, who until recently have been known only through accounts written by their daughters. The retelling of Souchet's story asserts voice and agency, which have been culturally denied to Puerto Rican women of her generation.

SOURCES: Davies, Carole Boyce. 1994. *Black Women, Writing, and Identity: Migrations of the Subject.* New York: Routledge; McCracken, Ellen. 1999. *New Latina Narrative: The Feminine Space of Postmodern Ethnicity.* Tucson: University of Arizona Press; Souchet, Clementina. 1986. *Clementina: Historia sin fin.* Mexico, D.F.: Imprenta Madero.

Maura I. Toro-Morn

SOUTHWEST VOTER REGISTRATION EDUCATION PROJECT (SVREP) (1974–   )

Founded in 1974, the Southwest Voter Registration Education Project (SVREP) is the largest and oldest orga-

nization of its kind in the United States. SVREP is a nonprofit, nonpartisan, civic education organization that was founded by William C. Velásquez. After several years of planning Velásquez opened the doors of the organization in an effort to increase the political and civic participation of Latinas/os. In 1984 SVREP opened regional offices in California and the following year chartered a partner organization (known as the Willian C. Velásquez Institute since 1997) dedicated to researching the Latina/o electorate's opinions. Since its inception SVREP has cultivated more than 50,000 Latina/o civic leaders and activists; 30,000 of them are in the Los Angeles area alone. SVREP continues to increase these numbers through its school for community organizers, the Latino Academy.

The organization's primary activities include voter registration drives and get-out-the-vote (GOTV) campaigns. In addition, SVREP sponsors publications, including a working paper series, The Mexican American Electorate. The project has also successfully litigated more than eighty-five voting rights legal suits and has conducted more than 2,300 nonpartisan voter registration and GOTV campaigns in more than 200 communities. In 1974 there were 2.4 million Latinas/os registered to vote. This number grew to 7.7 million in 2001, in no small part because of the work of thousands of grassroots activists from this project.

Antonio González heads the SVREP's current leadership. Previously González served as a SVREP organizer from 1984 to 1990 and as policy program director of the SVREP from 1991 to 1994. There are several prominent Latinas in the SVREP leadership ranks: Patricia González serves as national director of development, Sandra Pérez as the California regional director, and María Acevedo as the California Regional Staff's data processing clerk. Lydia Camarillo, who formerly served as the executive director of SVREP, made history as the first Latina chief executive officer of the Democratic National Convention Committee in 2000.

Since the 1960s, when voter participation across the country reached an all-time high of 63 percent, it has been on a steady decline. In 2000 the percentage of the voting-age population that cast ballots was only 51 percent. Among Latinas/os there are 13,158,000 voting-age citizens; however, only 45 percent reported voting in the 2000 elections. Voting rates also vary according to age and gender. For example, young people between the ages of eighteen and twenty-four are generally least likely to vote, and in recent years women have begun to vote at higher rates than men. Only 26 percent of Latinas/os between the ages of eighteen and twenty-four reported voting in the 2000 elections. Although the gender gap does not seem significantly large among Latinas/os—44 percent of Latinos reported voting in 2000, compared with 46 percent of

Latinas—Latinas who are eligible to vote outnumber eligible Latino voters by almost a million. These facts are of particular importance to Latina/o communities because there is a large proportion of Latinas/os who fall into the eighteen to twenty-four age category or will soon do so.

Latinas can no longer be underestimated as a political force in this country. Political organizations will do well to focus attention on this often ignored constituency. Therefore, the value of the work done by SVREP cannot be understated because political decisions can and will be strongly influenced by the growing Latina/o population.

See also Voting Rights Act

SOURCES: De la Garza, Rodolfo O., Martha Menchaca, and Louis DeSipio, eds. 1994. *Barrio Ballots: Latino Politics in the 1990 Elections*. Boulder, CO: Westview Press; SVREP.com: Southwest Voter Registration Education Project. http://www.svrep.org/ (accessed July 14, 2005); Yáñez-Chávez, Aníbal, ed. 1996. *Su voto es su voz: Latino Politics in California*. San Diego: Center for U.S.-Mexican Studies.

Gabriela Sandoval

SPANISH BORDERLANDS

The southern tier of states extending from California to the Carolinas constitutes the Spanish borderlands, so named because Spain explored and settled parts of this region soon after the time of Columbus. Along with the families of soldiers and settlers, Spanish conquistadores made the first permanent borderlands settlements in Florida (1565) and then in New Mexico (1598) in order to defend their colonies in the Caribbean and the rich mining districts in New Spain (Mexico). Eventually Spanish settlements emerged in today's southern Arizona and Texas and along the California coast, as well as in French Louisiana, which Spain acquired in 1763. The United States took charge of this vast area by both military conquest and purchase in the first half of the nineteenth century.

Spain incorporated much of the Indian population into its colonial communities. The rationale for doing so included religious as well as practical considerations. Spain's Roman Catholic monarchs believed that they had a religious mission to Christianize the native population and funded the work of religious orders such as the Franciscans and Dominicans. In turn, the missionaries taught Indian converts the Spanish language, inculcated Spanish cultural values, and trained them in Spanish manual arts. The practical reasons for acculturating native peoples included the need for Indian labor and the simple fact that Indians outnumbered Spaniards in most places.

The Indians had their own strongly held religious traditions and often stoutly resisted missionary efforts

and Spanish domination. The Pueblo Indians in New Mexico, where the processes of Indian resistance and accommodation are best understood, outwardly conformed to Catholic norms but continued to practice their own religion in secret. The exchange of cultural traits was a two-way affair. Spaniards and Mexicans were influenced by their Indian neighbors as they mingled, traded, and intermarried. Distinctive societies predicated on *mestizaje* emerged.

Demography also affected the social and cultural life of the Spanish borderlands. Spanish/Mexican soldiers and settlers were few in comparison with the native population, and Spanish-speaking women were scarcer still. Consequently, there were many sexual liaisons between Spanish men and Indian women. These connections included legitimate marriages, concubinage, brief affairs, and rapes. The outcome was a society that was racially and culturally mixed. This pattern began in sixteenth-century Mexico and extended into the borderlands as Spanish settlements advanced. A traveler to Texas, Juan Agustín Morfi, referred to area colonists as "a ragged crew of all colors." Indeed, historian Quintard Taylor points out that in the first census for the struggling pueblo of Los Angeles (1781), more than half the families "were of African or part African ancestry."

The experiences of women in the borderlands varied according to class, caste, and culture. Indian women were most likely to be vulnerable to sexual assaults, but in some cases Spaniards regarded "high-caste" native women as desirable marriage partners. Elite women in borderlands society (who were likely defined as "Spanish" even if their genealogy was racially mixed) lived in sequestered conditions in order to protect family honor from the stain of sexual misconduct. Poor women, especially Indians, worked in their own fields and houses or as servants and slaves for others. As Vicki L. Ruiz notes, mestizas and mulattas "over the course of three centuries . . . raised families on the frontier and worked alongside their fathers or husbands, herding cattle and tending crops."

Anglo-Americans began to move into the borderlands in the early nineteenth century when Spain's grip on the region began to loosen. In the 1820s these newcomers blended uneasily into the borderlands population. From Texas to California Anglo-American men married the daughters of Mexican families, took up the Catholic religion, and swore their allegiance to Mexico. They had many reasons for doing so. Marriages and friendships were good foundations for commercial relationships. Naturalized citizens could take advantage of Mexico's very liberal land laws, which provided free grants of thousands of acres to encourage settlement of the frontier. Nevertheless, many of these new immigrants were uneasy with Mexican government and so-

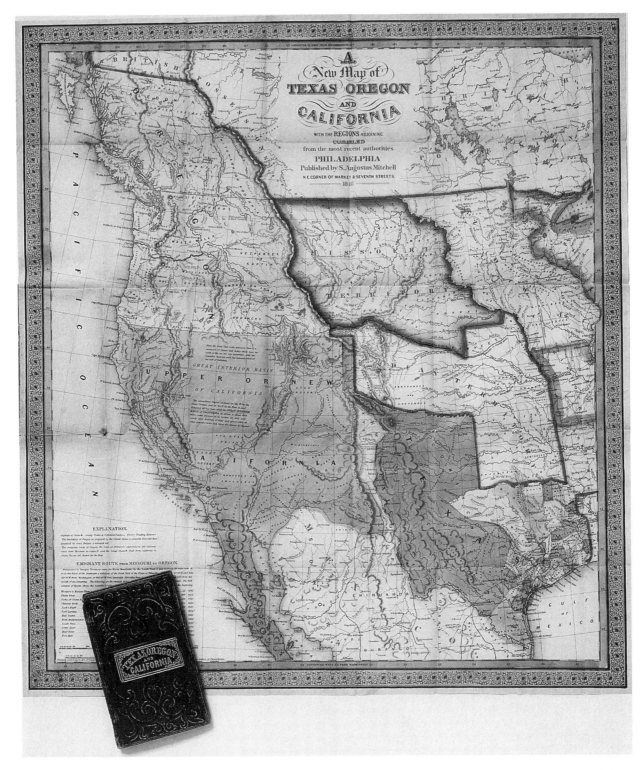

Samuel Augustus Mitchell's "A New Map of Texas, Oregon, and California: With the Regions Adjoining, 1846." Courtesy of the American West Collection, Autry National Center, Los Angeles, California, 90, 253, 289.

This photo represents the hard-scrabble pastoral life typical of New Mexico during the nineteenth century. Courtesy of the Rio Grande Historical Collections, New Mexico State University Library, Las Cruces.

ciety and clung to familiar religious and social practices. From Florida to California Anglo-Americans rebelled against and deposed Spanish and Mexican authority. With the help of these insurgents during the Mexican-American War (1846–1848) the United States completed the process by conquering Mexico and buying the Southwest.

The Spanish borderlands have captured the attention of historians for more than a century. Historians have usually concentrated on the more adventurous stories of priests, missions, soldiers, and Indian wars set in the context of Spanish, French, and British and

U.S. territorial competition. Herbert E. Bolton (1870–1953) was the most important of these early scholars. He taught at the University of Texas (1901–1909), Stanford University (1909–1911), and the University of California, Berkeley (1911–1943). Bolton wrote dozens of books and trained more than 100 Ph.D. and 300 M.A. students, including many elementary- and high-school teachers. Bolton's classic volume *The Spanish Borderlands* gave the field its name, and his interpretation dominated the field long after his death. Bolton saw the Spanish settlement in North America as a great saga that was peopled with venerable explorer-heroes like

Hispanic woman in Colorado beside her *horno* (oven), late nineteenth century. Trinidad Colorado Collection. Courtesy of the Colorado Historical Society.

Spanish Borderlands

Mission Concepción, 1900–1920. Courtesy of the Library of Congress, The Robert Runyon Photograph Collection (Reproduction no.: 04144).

Francisco Vásquez de Coronado and Juan Bautista de Anza and prominent missionaries such as Junípero Serra and Eusebio Kino. Bolton's work gained a wide popular audience for borderlands history.

The historical vision of Bolton and his students, however, was limited. They celebrated the missionaries' efforts among the Indians but ignored the negative impact of these institutions. Consequently, in recent years Indian and Mexican scholars have criticized Bolton for presenting a narrow, Hispanophilic view of the borderlands past. Also, women were far more than bit players in the stories Bolton and his students told. The histories of borderlands women generally, and especially poor women, received scant attention from historians. More recently scholars such as Ramón Gutiérrez, Antonia Castañeda, María Raquel Casas, and Vicki Ruiz have done much to correct the distorted picture that Bolton painted. Their work includes imaginative histories of Indian societies, women, and families. They consider not only the Spanish, but also the Mexican past. Anglo-American immigrants are set in the context of a long and vibrant history, rather than being presented as pioneers with a God-given license to conquer the West. Once seen as peripheral to American history, the borderlands now are central to the understanding of the multicultural American West.

SOURCES: Bolton, Herbert E. 1921. *The Spanish Borderlands: A Chronicle of Old Florida and the Southwest*. New Haven, CT: Yale University Press; Gutiérrez, Ramón A. 1991. *When Jesus Came, the Corn Mothers Went Away: Marriage, Sexuality, and Power in New Mexico, 1500–1846*. Stanford, CA: Stanford University Press; Hurtado, Alberto. 1999. *Intimate Frontiers: Sex, Gender, and Culture in Old California*. Albuquerque: University of New Mexico Press; Kessell, John L. 2002. *Spain in the Southwest: A Narrative History of Colonial New Mexico, Arizona, Texas, and California*. Norman: Univer-

sity of Oklahoma Press; Ruiz, Vicki L. 1996. "From out of the Shadows: Mexican Women in the United States." *OAH Magazine of History* (Winter): 15–18; Taylor, Quintard. 1998. *In Search of a Racial Frontier*. New York: W. W. Norton; Weber, David. 1992. *The Spanish Frontier in North America*. New Haven, CT: Yale University Press.

Albert L. Hurtado

Colonial Law

Women of Hispanic, indigenous, and African descent residing in the present-day southwestern United States lived in Spanish (1550s–1821) and Mexican (1821–1846) society whose laws were derived from Spain. Las Siete Partidas and Leyes de Toro, thirteenth- and sixteenth-century compilations of law, as well as subsequent royal decrees and canon law, defined women's legal status in marriage, the family, and society. Mexican and, earlier, Spanish legal and social norms were permeated with a patriarchal ideology that recognized men as the heads of the households to whom wives and children owed their obedience and pledge of honor. A foundation of Spanish law was the widely held tenet of paternal authority (*patria potestas*) that came from deep in the Iberian past and was embedded in Las Siete Partidas and Leyes de Toro, which located familial authority in male heads of household—fathers and husbands—on the assumption that this delegation of power assured a well-ordered family and stable society. A man had virtually complete authority over his dependents—wife, legitimate children, and any servants in the household—who, in turn, owed him their obedience in all matters. Qualifying a man's authority was his obligation to support, protect, and guide his spouse and legitimate offspring. The law and social mores also required a husband to respect a wife's person, but it conceded him the right to dole out mild punishment—the meaning of which varied with time, locale, and circumstance—to her and his other dependents as a way of guiding or teaching them. The ideal home (*casa de honor*) was a place where husband and wife, regardless of socioeconomic status or racial and cultural identity, treated each other well, supported their dependents, practiced their religion, remained faithful to one another, and otherwise set a good example for their children. Men who abandoned or neglected the livelihood of their households or engaged in excessive punishment violated not only the law but also the norms of their communities. Those same patriarchal values also placed restrictions and responsibilities on men: They had to provide food, clothing, and shelter for their families and were forbidden to use excessive force in guiding and instructing their wives, children, and household servants. Illegitimate children, or *hijos naturales*, those born out of wedlock, or *hijos espurios*, those born as a result of adultery, on the other hand, derived few, if any, benefits from *patria potestas*. Fathers were expected to support and rear them but not to provide them with any inheritance.

Mexicans inherited from Spain strong convictions about the centrality of marriage, sexuality, and the family to the survival of civilized Catholic society. These convictions seemed self-evident to Mexicans living on the northern frontier. Though most local officials lacked formal legal training, they familiarized themselves through custom handed down by previous generations with the relevant civil codes on marriage and the family. At the most elemental level stable marriages and families produced the children who would secure the future and also assure continuity in cultural and moral values. Except through death, a church-sanctioned annulment, or an ecclesiastical divorce (which allowed couples to separate but not to remarry others), marriages, preached the padres, remained indissoluble, even when one spouse was extremely cruel to the other. Regional differences sometimes occurred. In central Mexico, for example, ecclesiastical divorces were permissible in extreme cases, when one spouse was extremely cruel or had physically abused or threatened to kill the other. Additional grounds for divorce were abandonment and inadequate support that forced a spouse to commit a crime, such as prostitution. Absolute proof in the form of eyewitness accounts was necessary to substantiate the transgression. A spouse's confession was insufficient. In the colonial Southwest, for example, in California, however, these grounds were not sufficient for ecclesiastical divorces, because religious leaders agreed that even in cases of extreme cruelty limited divorce was unacceptable. The priests' reluctance to grant divorces and to break up unhappy households underscores the weight given to the family in maintaining order, reproducing the population, and developing the region, particularly on the northern frontier, where the growth of a stable society was in its early stages.

Closely regulated female sexual behavior before, during, and after marriage was key to maintaining and reproducing honorable and legitimate families, as well as children necessary in the inheritance and transfer of property. Sociosexual codes required women to maintain their sexual virtue (or honor) in and outside marriage: virginity before marriage, fidelity during marriage, and chastity in widowhood. To violate these cultural norms brought shame (*vergüenza*) to them and dishonor to the men in their homes and to their families in general. Men, in contrast, faced less severe expectations in their sexual behavior. Legally, they faced no repercussions for their sexual activity unless they committed crimes such as rape or adultery. Their role was to defend female honor and, if necessary, restore the loss of honor to their household brought about by a wife or daughter's sexual improprieties. A male had the right to place a female in seclusion, often in a convent, to protect his or the family's reputation and social standing in the community. Males thus enjoyed the benefits of a double standard of sexual propriety that reinforced their authority in marriage and the family.

Women, in particular, including wives and daughters, were expected to maintain their marital fidelity during marriage and sexual purity before marriage. Those who dishonored husbands or fathers with sexual indiscretions brought dishonor to the entire family. Honorable men, for their part, maintained their authority over the family and embodied masculinity. Threats to their authority through rape, which was viewed not only as a grave offense against a female's reputation or sexual virtue, but also as a stain on the husband's and family's honor and social standing, were remedied through the law. Hispanic law reflected this attitude, because it allowed male members of a family to kill a perpetrator who was caught in the act of rape.

Spanish-speaking women who had children out of wedlock and lived with men who were not their spouses or consorted with married men faced personal and public accusations that tarnished their and their family's honor and social standing in the community. In the Spanish era authorities sometimes publicly shamed women for leading immoral lives by shaving their heads and one eyebrow and forcing them to stand in and outside church during and after mass on Sundays. One widow who experienced this humiliation was Anastacia Zúñiga, a resident of Los Angeles, California, who had an extramarital relationship with a carpenter from Mission San Gabriel, José Antonio Ramírez, that resulted in the birth of a daughter in 1818. After she appeared in church with her head and eyebrow shaved, the governor ordered Comandante Militar José de la Guerra y Noriega, Los Angeles' *comisionado* (a military official with authority over local affairs) to remove her to the presidio of Santa Bárbara and place her in seclusion in an honorable home for six months, where she would be obligated to serve in the household and "lead a religious life as a Christian woman." Ramírez, on the other hand, faced a less severe punishment. The governor encouraged him to marry Zúñiga and, if he refused, to pay for the child's support. In the meantime, Ramírez would have to labor for one month in public works.

In contrast to Spanish-speaking women, Mexican men who had children out of wedlock or consorted with females who were not their spouses or were married faced few legal or social repercussions for their illicit sexual behavior. Unlike women who belonged to the *gente de razón* (rational people), men *de razón* benefited from a double standard of sexual mores that nearly excused them from sexual misconduct yet vilified females for it. Even when a Mexican woman openly identified a man as the father of her child, he was not publicly shamed and was allowed to retain his honor, reputation, and social standing in the community. In all likelihood, fathering an illegitimate child brought some dishonor to a man and, if he was married, to his wife and any children.

Despite patriarchal attitudes and laws that restricted women in marriage and the family, females had the legal right to acquire and use their own property. Widows and single women over the age of twenty-five could do so without interference from male family members. Married women and minor daughters, however, needed their husbands' and fathers' permission. Women's rights to land in Spanish/Mexican California derived from decrees and statutes, especially those in the Recopilación de las leyes de los reynos de las indias, a seventeenth-century compilation used to govern New Spain, and in Las Siete Partidas and Leyes de Toro, summaries that supplemented the Recopilación. During the Spanish era the monarch, as owner of all lands and natural resources in New Spain, held ultimate authority in allocating rights to such property, but the Crown frequently delegated authority to viceroys and other subordinates who, in turn, sometimes vested the power in others. Grantees, whether corporate bodies or individuals, had to fulfill stipulations for acquiring and holding on to land, beginning with an affirmation that no one else claimed the property and that it did not infringe on another's possession. A grant usually conferred on the recipient a usufruct right, not title in fee simple as in the English colonies. To obtain title, the grantee had to use and develop the land, sometimes in quite specific ways. If these requirements were met, the grantee could retain the property in perpetuity and bequeath it to family members or others. Failure to meet the requirements could result in the property being "denounced" (*denunciado*) and acquired by others.

Women, like men, had the right to acquire and retain property not only through grants but also through endowments, purchases, gifts, and inheritances. A widowed woman, for instance, inherited half of the community property (*bienes gananciales*) accumulated during a marriage, while daughters shared the remaining half of the property with other siblings. Women could also administer, protect, and invest their property, which they did in a variety of ways: initiating litigation, appearing in court and, if they so wished, acting as their own advocates, entering into contracts, forming business partnerships, administering estates,

and loaning and borrowing money and other goods. A woman's marital status, however, determined the extent of her control over property, earnings, and domestic activities. Women subject to paternal authority—married women and women under the age of twenty-five, regardless of marital status—needed their husbands' or fathers' permission to conduct business related to their holdings. Only widows and single women over the age of twenty-five had freedom from these restrictions.

Though unmarried women had the right to carry out their own *negocios* (businesses), they, as well as their married counterparts, often elected husbands and fathers or other men in the community to represent them in their property transactions. Women did so by giving men power of attorney, which allowed their representatives to conduct all of their money matters, which included the right "to claim, collect, receive, and demand of every person the amounts due," as well as "to file suits in writing, prosecuting same through all courts to final legal decision." Unlike widowed and single women over the age of twenty-five, married women who appointed an attorney needed their spouses' permission to do so. Failure to obtain it nullified the appointment and any transactions carried out. The practice of giving men power over women's affairs, however, did not diminish a woman's ability to oversee the management of her assets. Rather, the men who advocated on their behalf did so through the authority their female clients granted them. Therefore, the men were accountable to the women and were expected to carry out their dealings with honesty and integrity, though occasionally the men strayed from their obligations. Women who believed that their representatives had neglected to carry out their duties, either inadvertently or deliberately, could have local officials revoke their power and replace them with other persons.

Women's ability to carry out a wide range of business transactions, either through a representative or on their own behalf, was not limited by the inability of the majority of them to read and write or even sign their names. Illiterate women (as well as men) went to scribes or had literate family members pen their contracts, petitions, and letters. In other cases women handled their business matters in person and went before the proper authorities to articulate their needs or decisions. Nevertheless, the inability to read and write sometimes presented grave risks for women who had to rely on others who could potentially take advantage of their inability to oversee and verify written transactions.

In the colonial Southwest Hispanic law governed most aspects of women's lives, especially in marriage and the family. Legal and social codes defined the extent to which women could wield power over their property, children, and their sexuality in and outside marriage. Women who transgressed sociosexual codes of female behavior, for instance, faced serious consequences, while men who committed similar violations of sexual mores encountered few, if any, repercussions. Despite frequently oppressive cultural norms and laws, many women sought a better life for themselves and their families.

See also Marianismo and Machismo

SOURCES: Arrom, Sylvia Marina. 1985. *The Women of Mexico City, 1790–1857.* Stanford, CA: Stanford University Press; Chávez-García, Miroslava. 2004. *Negotiating Conquest: Gender and Power in California, 1770s to 1880s.* Tucson: University of Arizona Press; Gutiérrez, Ramón. 1991. *When Jesus Came, the Corn Mothers Went Away: Marriage, Sexuality, and Power in New Mexico, 1500–1846.* Stanford, CA: Stanford University Press; Lavrin, Asunción. 1989. "Introduction." In *Sexuality and Marriage in Colonial Latin America,* ed. Asunción Lavrin. Lincoln: University of Nebraska Press; Stern, Steve J. 1995. *The Secret History of Gender: Women, Men, and Power in Late Colonial Mexico.* Chapel Hill: University of North Carolina Press.

Miroslava Chávez-García

Comadrazgo

Spanish-speaking women who settled in the Spanish colonial borderlands beginning in the early sixteenth century formed women's networks based upon ties of blood, but also established fictive kinship through bonds of *comadrazgo* (comothering) that proved central to the settlement of the Spanish Mexican frontier. A close study of these complex relations reveals women's agency as both settlers and *comadres.* Women settlers participated in activities such as stock raising and cultivation; however, settler women also acted as midwives to mission Indians and served as godmothers to Indian children through bonds of *comadrazgo* formalized through the Catholic Church. Children received godparents at birth and later at the holy sacraments of confirmation, first Communion, and marriage. Bonds of *comadrazgo* enabled the rise of local and regional networks that reinforced the Spanish colonial government's goal of claiming territory, forming community, and enticing other Spanish colonials to undertake the journey to the borderlands.

Ritual kinship relations, or *comadrazgo,* extended beyond daily routines, care of the sick, celebrations of marriage, baptism, birth, and death. Bonds of *comadrazgo* brought immigrant and local families together and broadened family ties through the creation of dynamic communities that over time developed precious traditions and customs in an area that was socioeconomically isolated and subject to larger administrative control. Frontier women proved extremely resourceful in settling the borderlands through complex interactions of race, class, and geography. Yet Indian and Spanish families did not stand on equal footing. Hispanic Catholicism was intended to supplant local native religion, and racial difference between Spaniards and Indians remained a marker of separation. However, racial differentiation during the late colonial period along the northern frontiers lessened in importance as a symbol of discrimination because of the shortage of an easily exploitable native labor pool and the nature of working in the fields side by side with mestizos, Indians, blacks, and whites. Thus the practice of racial mixing between farmers, servants, soldiers, Indians, artisans, and "mixed bloods" became more prevalent along the border.

These complex networks birthed a regional history marked by tradition, obligations, duty, respect, love, and inequality. Kinship arrangements buttressed everyday life in the Spanish colonial borderlands. Although men acted as soldiers, agriculturalists, farmers, and artisans, women held their own influence rooted in these intricate female networks. Acting as midwives and as godmothers and baptizing sick or stillborn babies, they extended protection to indigenous people and in turn adopted many of the herbal remedies used in indigenous cures. However, while bonds of baptism tied Spanish settlers with indigenous women, patterns of reciprocity allowed women to care for one another as family and as neighbors under unequal arrangements, since indentured servitude was prominently practiced along the colonial frontier. Although *comadre* relations fostered ties between colonists and indigenous people, a study of fictive kinship reveals that bonds of *comadrazgo* helped extend social control over Indians and reinforced a tradition of influence emphasized and extended through female networks of social and spiritual interdependence.

Traditions of *compadrazgo* similarly extended familiar blood ties through godparenting rites formalized through Catholic ceremonies. *Compadres* would also be responsible for giving advice, financial assistance, and taking over parental duties in instances in which godchildren's parents passed away.

SOURCES: Haas, Lisbeth. 1995. *Conquests and Historical Identities in California, 1769–1936.* Berkeley: University of California Press; Hurtado, Albert L. 1988. *Indian Survival on the California Frontier.* New Haven, CT: Yale University Press; Ruiz, Vicki L., and Virginia Sánchez Korrol, eds. 2005. *Latina Legacies: Identity, Biography, and Community.* New York: Oxford University Press; Weber, David J. 1982. *The Mexican Frontier, 1821–1846: The American Southwest under Mexico.* Albuquerque: University of New Mexico Press.

Soledad Vidal

Early Settlement Life in the Borderlands

To understand the total complexity of Spanish Mexican settlement along what is now known as the Spanish borderlands, one must look beyond the physical evidence left behind, such as missions, presidios (Spanish forts), or towns, and the Spanish names of states, towns, rivers, and mountain ranges that mark the map of the United States of America. When the first Europeans set foot on North American soil, the history of these Hispanic men and women changed the human and natural geography of the region. An understanding of this phenomenon has only recently begun to be woven into the fabric of American history. Spanish attempts to establish physical control and cultural hegemony from California to Florida and for a time from Florida to New England followed similar patterns and processes. However, as the northernmost and often most remote region of the Spanish Empire, the borderlands had distinctive differences and regional identities that distinguished them from other Spanish territories. Throughout the Northern and Southern Hemispheres the Spanish encountered and negotiated with indigenous peoples, but geography and climate also flavored and influenced the resulting colonial settlements. In many ways exploration was the first and easiest phase of initial Spanish encounters; far more troublesome was the process of settlement.

The length of time and the geographic expanse of the Spanish settlement greatly influenced the success and means of Spanish colonizing practices. Contrasted with English settlement patterns, the Spanish settlement narrative is often told in overgeneralized terms of missionaries and soldiers cruelly subjugating indigenous peoples, demanding spiritual obedience and labor tribute. Spanish settlement was often seen solely as a male prerogative, in which explorers, soldiers, and friars faced the hardships of conquest and exploration without the solace and support of their womenfolk. Fortunately, recent histories are inserting women and gender perspectives into the processes and patterns of borderland settlement.

Women always accompanied Spanish conquistadores, in image if not in body. As Ramón Gutiérrez writes of New Mexico and Virginia Marie Bouvier points out for California, the female images were important symbols and useful icons in establishing the dialogue and pageantry of conquest. In New Mexico Don Juan de Oñate invaded the territory, leading soldiers who marched under a banner depicting Our Lady of the Remedies identical to the one Hernán Cortés had carried into Tenochtitlan in 1519. An Indian woman, Doña Ines, accompanied Oñate as if to mimic the role of the original La Malinche, Cortés's Indian mistress, interpreter, and invaluable cultural broker during the conquest. In the 1536 Panfilo de Narváez Florida expedition ten women did accompany the Spanish explorers but were left behind on the ship as Narváez pushed inland. Two women were among Coronado's expedition, from 1539 to 1543, across the Southeast of North America, and one woman, Ana Méndez, survived the entire ordeal. While most women followed as wives and helpmates, a few distinguished themselves through more "masculine" behavior. The most notable was Catalina de Erausco, who fled her forced convent captivity and disguised herself as a male ensign in the Spanish army. She saw service as a soldier from Panama to Peru. When her female identity was discovered, she was sent back to Spain, but rather than being punished, she became famous and notorious as the Ensign Nun.

In California the gendered and sexual nature of conquest was epitomized by the myth of the Amazons, which, according to Bouvier, formalized the policy of conquest regarding gender and race relations. Gender and race provided ideological justifications for a hierarchy of power within the changing social order.

As the final wave of colonization, the remote colonies of New Mexico, Texas, Southern Arizona, and California drew settlers mostly from the administrative province of Nueva Viscaya, the so-called heart of the North. The discovery of silver in Zacatecas, Durango, and Chihuahua soon after the Conquest of Mexico fanned out Spanish settlement in these remote regions. After 1734 Nueva Viscaya remained the keystone of the northern frontier because it would supply the model of settlement, as well as the majority of settlers to New Mexico, Texas, Arizona, and California. Settlements replicated the settlement of Nueva Viscaya and followed a general pattern of an initial *entrada*, then the establishment of mining settlements and a small number of haciendas. Agriculture and raising livestock soon developed, dominating the regional economies. Evangelizing indigenous people and increasing the settlement population were both slow processes. The establishment of various civilian settlements, *ciudades*, villas, pueblos, and *parajes*, encouraged the recruitment of a small number of settlers. Living in these varied municipalities granted settlers the rank of *vecinos* (neighbors), along with entitlement to land lots within the municipalities. Housing the largest populations, *ciudades* were the seats of civil and ecclesiastical authority. Presidios also attracted settlers but were administratively different from other civilian settlements.

Population grew steadily and included a mixed-blood group of Europeans, Indians, and Africans. During the colonial periods an estimated 150,000 to 200,000 African slaves were imported to four main areas in Mexico: Mexico City, Tlaxcala-Puebla, Michoacán, and Zacatecas. Arguments against slavery by the Catholic Church were muted by the depopulation of the Indians from disease and demand for a secure source of labor by the affluent elites. In 1646 there were 130,000 Afro-mestizos, compared with nearly 125,000 Spaniards, mostly criollos, and 1,269,607 Indians. Under Spanish law slavery was subject to manumission; therefore, free children could enter the marriage pool, assuring a triracial mixing in the areas of heavy slave importation. The development of a *casta* (caste) system to categorize and describe the emerging mestizo and mulatto population allowed Afro-mestizos a degree of social mobility from a lower class into a higher one.

Statistics show that migration within certain provinces was a fact of life. By the mid-eighteenth century the majority of inhabitants were native born and of mixed-race ancestry. As in other sites of colonization, the distinctive names used in racial identification often led to confusion. Spanish-born individuals could be called *españoles, gauchupines, criollo* (a Spaniard born in the colonies), or *peninsulares* (a Spaniard born in the peninsula of Spain), with each distinction connoting varying degrees of social status and possible prestige. An *español* born in Spain was more advantaged socially than a colonial-born *gauchupine*. After the Spaniard came the various *castas*, whose designations were crude yet often lyrical. In a series of *casta* portraits produced throughout the eighteenth century, people were categorized according to degrees of racial mixture. Three of the more interesting *casta* categories were coyote, lobo (wolf), or *no te entiendo* (I do not understand you). *Casta* designations numbered from fourteen to twenty depending on the region, and while a general hierarchy existed, with full-blooded Spaniard as the most elevated racial position and full-blooded African as the lowest, the remoteness of frontier settings mitigated how this hierarchy was enforced. Local conditions and local sensibilities distributed status and honor based on race and class; therefore, how one's community described a person's race and class varied throughout the Spanish borderlands. In the borderlands colonial conditions tended to erase the more complex and nuanced *casta* system that made sense in central Mexico, and by 1800 the majority of borderland people were officially referred to as being either *indios* or *no indios*. Another catchall phrase used for *castas* was *gente de razón*, literally people of reason, thereby excluding all Indians in the borderlands.

Another important cultural component in understanding the early settlements of the borderlands is the implementation of the Spanish honor and shame system regarding race and gender. Because Spain was a Catholic nation, the Spanish honor system was heavily steeped in the cult of the Virgin Mary, or *marianismo*, which valued female sexual chastity over male. During the Reconquista of Spain, the period when the Moorish invaders were removed from Spain, Spanish society developed a complex set of social attitudes dictating how social mobility could be achieved through definitions of honor and shame.

Embodying status and virtue, the Spanish American honor system fluctuated. Men inherently had and could achieve more in their culturally bound honor bank accounts, but women also manipulated, contributed to, and protected their personal and social honor depending on the means they had at hand. Their proper actions in maintaining their personal and public reputations allowed them to maintain or even ascend the social hierarchical ladder if they married well and remained sexually virtuous. Furthermore, honor was assigned at birth and through race, but it also influenced how Spanish subjects conducted their courtship, sexual intercourse, pregnancy, marriage, access to political office, and employment. Unlike other European women, Spanish women exercised legal privileges that included the right to own, buy, sell, inherit, and convey property in and outside marriage. Increasingly scholars are emphasizing the importance of local conditions and distributions of honor and social status in understanding the experiences of the Spanish New World. Women are often depicted as pawns in the honor system, but the fact that women protected and guarded their honor from malicious gossip either by personally confronting their defamers or especially through the legal system gives evidence of both the values and actions of women. Whether women acted through a well-placed slap to tighten a salacious tongue or through a lawsuit, and everything in between, they were highly conscious that local conditions and local communities were the final judges and arbitrators of honor, and as local actors, women were central to the play.

Communities throughout the Spanish world practiced a sexual double standard that admired men's virility and sexual conquest, yet punished a woman who brought *vergüenza*, shame, to her family's honor. Like race, social status was highly fluid in frontier communities; therefore, improper behavior by all members of the family was chastised, but women's sexuality was under far more parental control and supervision than that of male members. In the initial stages of colonization parents often chose the marriage partners of their children. The scarcities of women often led to the betrothal of girls as young as three or four to men twenty to thirty years their senior. In California the parents of María Antonia Isabela de Lugo betrothed her to Ygnacio Vicente Ferrer Vallejo on the day of her birth; he was twenty-six years old. This practice changed over time as the sex ratio became more balanced, and by the early nineteenth century it was common practice for children to select their own marriage partners. Although parents heavily guarded their female children, the countless legal cases throughout the borderlands involving the loss of virginity through seduction or consensual illicit sex and the illegitimacy rates indicate that women expressed and controlled their sexuality, but often paid a heavy social price for these actions.

Most often the decision to resettle along the frontier was made by men as husbands or fathers. If the 1776 Anza expedition is indicative of frontier settlers, then statistically women were on the average twenty-eight years old, had married in their mid-teens, were married an average of twelve years, and averaged four children. Rather than being young mothers, most of the women were in the middle of their childbearing years and traveled with their nuclear families. The scarcity of women varied over time and place. Few places were as extreme as the presidio of San Marcos de Apalachee, where in 1802 there were only three women to 168 adult males. This scarcity of women made marriage a crucial decision throughout the borderlands. In New Mexico, before 1739, the majority of men married younger women; at least 34 percent were six years or more older than their brides. But after 1770 the proportion of persons marrying someone their own age steadily increased and reached 50 percent by 1800. By 1790 women outnumbered men in New Mexico not only because of natural increase through settler marriages but also because of the number of children produced through legitimate and illegitimate unions with female Indian slaves. Illegitimacy was more common in the frontier. Twenty percent of children born in Texas in 1790 were illegitimate; in Pensacola in 1820, 25 percent were illegitimate. In New Mexico between 1693 and 1848, 82 percent of all children born to Indian slaves who were baptized were illegitimate.

As wives and mothers, frontier women faced harsh conditions. If they were soldiers' wives, they lived within the walls of the presidios. Adequate housing was a chronic problem in the presidios, and women made do in houses that averaged twenty-one by twenty-four feet. Within this small space a woman took care of her husband, their four to six children—the average family size along the borderlands—and possibly one or two servants, depending on the status of the family. If the family had not brought the necessary household items with them, the women had to survive on the provisions distributed by the military authorities. Supplies of food and clothing were very often inadequate, and the household talents and skills of the women were crucial to survival. Military concerns rather than familial concerns were a priority. Women could not leave the presidios without written permission; therefore, caring for a garden outside the presidio walls and supplementing the family diet often proved difficult. Only officers or wealthy settlers received property deeds to land outside the presidio, and only because they promised to construct a house, cultivate the land, and permanently inhabit the property. The fathers provided small plots of land but rarely property deeds for the use of the colonists who lived within or near missions, thus encouraging colonists to settle within pueblos or presidios where landownership was more likely. María Ignacia Amador, who lived near the San Gabriel Mission, earned the respect of other women because she knew how to "cook, sew, read and write, and nurse the sick—she was a good *curandera*—was employed [by the mission] in sewing and taking care of the church robes." Furthermore, "she taught some children how to read and write in her home, but she did not have a formal school." The amount of land granted to colonists ranged in size, but the average rancho was at least one square league, or 4,437 acres, but some ranchos were several square leagues and ran into the tens of thousands of acres throughout the borderlands.

The crowded presidio conditions also made disease a constant concern, as attested by the high mortality rates, both for infants and adults. More men than women died in the presidios, in some places by a ratio of two to one, which led to an unusual number of orphans, single widows, remarried widows, and widows who served as heads of families. The lack of medical personnel forced the women to provide rudimentary nursing to those in need, as well as being the midwives, *parteras,* to one another. Countless women relied on and used the various home and herbal remedies they were taught by their mothers to alleviate various illnesses and maladies. Women also relied on Native American medicinal herbal knowledge to battle the new illnesses with which they were unfamiliar, and on the knowledge and services of *curanderas,* folk healers.

If a soldier's wife survived her husband, she inherited his property and retirement pension. A few soldiers were even awarded *parajes,* small plots of land, upon retirement, and if the Indians had been adequately pacified, families could escape the overcrowded conditions of the presidio. Landownership was the most dramatic step in achieving social and economic status. The material conditions for women who were rancheras and landowners steadily improved, but even by the 1840s conditions in the borderlands remained harsh. One of the advantages to living on a rancho was more luxurious accommodation as settlers expanded from a one-bedroom house to multiroom homes. Homes were usually simple and unadorned constructions whose materials depended on the geography and native resources. For example, in the Southwest adobe bricks, sun-fired earthen bricks often one to two feet in width, were used to build a one-story structure surrounding a central courtyard or patio with small windows and doors. The thick walls provided warmth in the winter and coolness in the summer. The interiors were often devoid of furniture, and only the wealthy could afford beds, cabinets, chests, chairs, benches, mirrors, or religious paintings. Most colonists slept on the floor on mats or rolled their bedding during the daytime to provide seating for the family and visitors. Local craftsmen built the necessary home furnishings, which were often of crude but utilitarian design.

The other economic component of rancho life was the growth of livestock herds, which provided a healthier and more abundant diet. By raising either sheep or cattle, along with the necessary horses and mules, small rancheros were able to provide small inheritances to their children. In Laredo, Texas, the wills of small rancheros give an indication of these material comforts. Rather than living in adobe homes, they lived in *jacales*, houses with a roof or walls of straw, and owned several thousand head of sheep, goats, or cattle that they distributed equally to their surviving children. The distribution of household goods included furniture, clothing, and tableware; for example, in Nicolás de Campo's will, "a shotgun with its case, a sword, some silk stockings, a short undergarment, cloth trousers, a white undercoat, two large trunks with their keys, two pairs of scissors for shearing sheep, two large books and another of medium size, and two religious pictures" were left to his children. María Nicolasa Uriburu left a trunk each to her two daughters and split between them "a bed, two copper kettles, six plates, a dress of blue silk, one blouse, and her *jacale*." Wealth was highly relative along the borderlands, and any goods, regardless of condition or use, were highly prized.

Childhood for women was dictated by a close and communal family life that often extended beyond the individual households and into their communities. Family celebrations, family visits, weddings, baptisms, religious and secular holidays, dances and fiestas, horse races, cockfights, and bullfights marked the social life of these remote communities. Because of the small number of settlers, borderland communities were extremely interrelated. Extended and multigenerational families were commonplace and added to social unity. Children learned the proper social, religious, and sexual behavior from their elders, be they parents, grandparents, uncles, or aunts. Formal education for young girls was rare; instead, they were taught the household skills necessary to survive frontier conditions, such as cooking, sewing, cleaning, supervising Indian servants, maintaining household livestock, and gardening. If education was available, girls were usually taught by neighborhood women. Young women along the borderland had to pay more attention to maintaining their sexual chastity and virtue than to formal education.

The strength of family ties was tested when parents died and left orphan children. Traditionally grandparents assumed responsibility for raising orphaned children, but in the absence of grandparents, older siblings or extended relatives left few children unprotected. In the rare case when no relatives existed, neighbors or *compadres* accepted the Catholic custom of *comadrazgo* which established coparenting relationships through the rituals of baptism, first Communion, confirmation, and marriage. One of the few orphans who left a personal narrative of her life was Apolinaria Lorenzana, who arrived in California in 1800 at the age of seven. From age ten to her early teens Lorenzana was handed off from household to household, until the fathers hired her as a nurse in the San Diego Mission. Besides nursing, she also assumed supervisorial responsibilities over the Indian neophytes and servants in a variety of necessary mission duties. Apolinaria Lorenzana never married, instead becoming a *beata*, a pious and devout woman who preferred to remain single; after all, with some pride she stated how she "maintained me through the labor of my own hands." Sewing and working in the mission allowed her to escape the burdensome duties of wife and mother, a path few women chose along the frontier. Although Apolinaria Lorenzana never married, she was still an important community member. In her lifetime she estimated that she had either baptized, confirmed, or stood as *madrina* in weddings to approximately 200 persons, whether Indian or *gente de razón* (persons of reason—usually Spaniards). For this she "had the satisfaction that all young or old, rich or poor loved me, maybe for the good disposition in which I served them all as well as I could."

As stated earlier, the dangers along the frontier often left women alone and unprotected as widows, or what Deena J. González more accurately terms "women without men." Precarious frontier conditions strained marital and personal relationships to the breaking point, and in New Mexico as many as 10 percent of all women before 1848 were never legally married. At the same time an estimated 20 percent of all New Mexican women had outlived their husbands and were the heads of households. Without the economic support of a man, New Mexican women steadily and consistently remained the poorest social group within New Mexican society. If the single woman heading a household had no property or livestock, wage labor

Spanish Borderlands

was her only resource, along with forcing her children to contribute to the family economy. By 1860, 50 percent of all families headed by a woman had children working. Working as seamstresses, laundresses, or providers of other household services to richer people, as well as using familial and community resources, allowed women without men to survive the onslaught of American invasion, but they remained in greater states of poverty as American control solidified, a condition systematic throughout the borderland after 1848.

See also Marianismo and *Machismo;* Race and Color Consciousness

SOURCES: Alonzo, Armando C. 1999. *Tejano Legacy: Rancheros and Settlers in South Texas, 1734–1900.* Albuquerque: University of New Mexico Press; Bouvier, Virginia Marie. 2001. *Women and the Conquest of California, 1542–1840.* Tucson: University of Arizona Press; González, Deena J. 1999. *Refusing the Favor: The Spanish-Mexican Women of Santa Fe, 1820–1880.* New York: Oxford University Press; Gutiérrez, Ramón A. 1991. *When Jesus Came, the Corn Mothers Went Away: Marriage, Sexuality, and Power in New Mexico, 1500–1846.* Stanford, CA: Stanford University Press; Menchaca, Martha. 2001. *Recovering History, Constructing Race: The Indian, Black, and White Roots of Mexican Americans.* Austin: University of Texas Press; Monroy, Douglas. 1990. *Thrown among Strangers: The Making of Mexican Culture in Frontier California.* Berkeley: University of California Press.

María Raquel Casas

Encomienda

Encomienda was a tax imposed on the indigenous peoples as subjects of the Spanish king. It allowed the recipient, called *encomendero,* to collect that tax in the form of labor, goods, and eventually cash. The tribute collected was a reward for service to the Crown and the conquest of new territories. *Encomenderos* were obliged to "protect" their wards, Christianize them, and be ready to bear arms for the king. *Encomienda* had its roots in the territorial reconquest of the Iberian Peninsula from the Muslims who had occupied it beginning in 711. In the New World *encomienda* did not entitle the settler to land, which had to be acquired independently from the Crown, and did not give the *encomendero* juridical jurisdiction over the Indians, who remained subjects of the Crown. First used in the Antilles, by the 1520s *encomienda* was transferred to all territorial acquisitions in the continent. *Encomiendas* meant a loss of taxes for the Crown, which had no better choice for rewarding its conquistadores in the sixteenth century.

Hernán Cortés, as conqueror of Mexico, and Francisco Pizarro and his brothers, as conquerors of Peru, granted *encomienda* to their followers. When Cortés married Doña Marina (Malintzin) off to Juan de Jaramillo in 1524, he gave her the tribute of the town of Xilotepec as an *encomienda.* Tributes were also granted to Isabel and Leonor Moctezuma, who transferred them to their children after their deaths. In Yucatán Leonor de la Encarnación, a relative of Moctezuma, inherited an *encomienda* from her husband and used it as a dowry to enter the Convent of Our Lady of the Conception in Mérida. In 1583, in Peru, two of Atahualpa's daughters and a third Inca noblewoman held extensive *encomiendas* and 2,714 tributaries. In that viceroyalty four Spanish *encomenderas* held 11,390 tributaries, while thirteen others held good *encomiendas.* These facts notwithstanding, the number of women *encomenderas* was never large. Most received *encomiendas* as heirs of their husbands and had the right to transfer them to their children, irrespective of gender. If an *encomendera* widow remarried, the *encomienda* passed to her second husband, and few women succeeded in standing as sole owners. In Peru some viceroys opposed the holding of *encomiendas* by single women, arguing that through remarriage the *encomienda* could pass to unworthy men. The Peruvian viceroy the Marquis of Cañete obliged some wealthy *encomenderas* to remarry in the mid-1550s to forestall this situation. The Crown remained ambiguous about marriage policies, and while it did not revoke the right of a woman to inherit an *encomienda,* it required royal approval of the intended husband of single *encomenderas. Encomenderas* held significant power for short periods of time, but in the long term transferring entitlement to sons or husbands eroded their privileges.

Some members of the church were opposed to *encomienda* because it encouraged the exploitation of Indian labor, which was acute in the Caribbean islands. Bartolomé de Las Casas (c. 1474–1566) was the best-known opponent of *encomienda* and persuaded Charles V (1517–1556) to side with him and approve an end to *encomienda* as their holders died. Arguments over the rights of the indigenous people and those of conquistadores and settlers continued until 1542, when the Crown issued the New Laws, which abolished the enslavement of the Indians as a result of warfare and forbade new *encomiendas.* It deprived royal officers, religious orders, and ecclesiastics of *encomiendas* and reiterated the exclusive rights of the king to award them. It reduced the number of Indians entrusted to some *encomenderos,* divested those with illicit titles, and abolished the right to inherit *encomiendas* for two successive lives. The Crown expected all vacant *encomiendas* to revert to itself (escheatment) and sought to regain sovereignty over its Indian subjects.

The New Laws were not enforced in New Spain (Mexico), where the viceroy asked the king to reconsider enforcement. In Peru they induced a rebellion against the king. Charles V revoked the New Laws, but

708

a revised version was applied in 1545. The assessment of taxes by royal officials was integrated into the institution. Eventually the enjoyment for two lives was recognized. By the end of the sixteenth century the *encomienda* was a declining institution. A demographic catastrophe produced by numerous pandemics reduced the indigenous population drastically, depriving *encomenderos* of their main source of income. *Encomenderos* were only a fraction of the Spanish population that settled in the New World since not everybody could prove a key role in the conquest. *Encomiendas* were still legally held by a few in the core areas of the Spanish Empire in the seventeenth century. In peripheral areas such as Yucatán, northern Mexico, Venezuela, and Paraguay, *encomiendas* lasted through the seventeenth and even the eighteenth century.

See also Slavery

SOURCES: Himmering y Valencia, Robert. 1991. *The Encomenderos of New Spain, 1521–1555*. Austin: University of Texas Press; Martín, Luis. 1983. *Daughters of the Conquistadors: Women of the Viceroyalty of Peru*. Albuquerque: University of New Mexico Press; Simpson, Leslie Bird. 1960. *The Encomienda in New Spain*. San Francisco: John Howell; Zavala, Silvio. 1973. *La encomienda indiana*. Mexico D.F.: Editorial Porrúa.

Asunción Lavrin

Women in California

As in other Spanish settlements throughout the New World, settlement in California began in 1769 with an *entrada*, a militarized excursion in conjunction with Catholic priests to exert military and spiritual conquest and to defend New Spain's northernmost border against foreign enemies. Sixty soldiers and nineteen Franciscans constituted the initial presidio and mission settlements established in San Diego and San Francisco; however, outbreaks of violence by the Spanish soldiers, particularly sexual violence against indigenous women, hastened the need for civilian and female settlers to maintain social order. By 1773 all branches of royal authority recognized and supported the recruitment of Spanish Mexican women and families to normalize social conditions in California. The majority of colonial Spanish Mexican female settlers, *pobladoras*, arrived in California between 1774 and 1781, recruited mainly from the Sinaloa and Sonora provinces by both the church and the Crown. Spanish Mexican women in California were seen as essential settlers and helpmates in advancing the Spanish hegemonic, colonizing efforts. Women's multifaceted contributions included teaching indigenous women domestic skills such as cooking, sewing, and cleaning, supervising and disciplining the labor and spiritual lives of the natives, thereby supporting the Christianiz-

ing efforts of the friars, and finally, becoming the wives and helpmates of Spanish soldiers and settlers. An illustration of the scarcity and desirability of single women was the union of María Antonia de Lugo and Ygnacio Vallejo on September 2, 1776; he was literally present at her birth and negotiated his betrothal with her parents the same day. They married in 1791; she was fourteen, he was forty.

Living conditions in the presidio, mission, and pueblo settlements slowly improved, but colonists continuously faced sickness, Indian raids, delayed arrivals of often inadequate supplies, overcrowded housing, and inflated prices on poorly made goods. The majority of Spanish Mexican women in California were both mestizas and military wives accustomed to the harsh frontier settings, often being second- or third-generation frontier people. The Spanish frontier was expanded not by raw recruits from central urban areas, but by generations of settlers born and raised along the frontier. In terms of race, Sinaloa and Sonora developed fluid *casta* societies through the practice of assigning people into prescribed racial categories, but as Antonia I. Castañeda points out, in California "compound designations dropped off and *español*, *mestizo*, *neófito*, and *gentil* became the most frequently used terms, with some individuals moving across the spectrum from *indio*, or *mulato*, to *español*." Women's scarcity privileged them in negotiating this racial and socioeconomic "pigmentocracy," privileges they used depending on their individual means and social status.

Beyond reproduction in the settlement population, women's labor was vital to the various settlement populations and was thoroughly integrated within the labor system of both the military and mission institutions. As Antonia Castañeda points out, "Wives and daughters instructed Indian women in Hispano women's domestic work, thereby advancing the project of Hispanicizing the indigenous population." As the *llavera* (key keeper) of the San Gabriel Mission, Eulalia Pérez began her work days at daybreak, supervising the making of *pozole* (hominy soup) for breakfast, and her day did not end until she locked the neophyte girls into their sex-segregated dormitories at night. Like their menfolk, women were heavily invested in the success of conquest and made vital contributions to these hegemonic efforts. Throughout frontier settlements marriage and family were the cornerstone of successful settlement, but a few did choose to remain single. For example, Apolinaria Lorenzana, who supported herself as *llavera* in the San Diego Mission, was rewarded for her labor and diligence with two small ranch grants in 1840 and 1843.

Initially, rancho grants were awarded by the Crown to retired military personal to encourage continued settlement, but in time women were also granted land rights. These ranchos eventually became the means for the development of a Californio rancho elite that dominated social, economic, and political life. Under Spanish legal tradition women could own, sell, and buy land or property, as well as enter into binding contracts. All property brought into a marriage by either partner became communal property, and this transformed women into important economic agents. As wives and mothers, Spanish Mexican women were integral to the successful maintenance of the ranchos. The life cycle of Spanish Mexican women usually entailed being taught household skills such as cooking, sewing, cleaning, and gardening by their mothers, marrying as early as twelve or thirteen, bearing an average of six to seven children, and, if they were raised on a rancho, learning to supervise the labor of numerous Indian servants. Collectively, women were crucial to the stability, growth, and success of this remote colonial society.

SOURCES: Casas, María Raquel. 2006. *"Married to a Daughter of the Land": Interethnic Marriages in California, 1820–1880.* Reno: University of Nevada Press; Castañeda, Antonia I. 1990. "Gender, Race, and Culture: Spanish-Mexican Women in the Historiography of Frontier California." *Frontiers: A Journal of Women Studies* 11:8–20; _____. 1990. "The Political Economy of Nineteenth-Century Stereotypes of Californianas." In *Between Borders: Essays on Mexicana/Chicana History,* ed. Adelaida R. Del Castillo, 213–236. Encino, CA: Floricanto Press; _____. 2000. "Hispanas and Hispanos in a Mestizo Society." *OAH Magazine of History* (Summer): 29–33; Monroy, Douglas. 1990. *Thrown among Strangers: The Making of Mexican Culture in Frontier California.* Berkeley: University of California Press.

María Raquel Casas

Women in New Mexico (1540–1900)

Until the past few decades Spanish Mexican women's history had not been well understood nor explored. Central figures in New Mexico's history, Spanish Mexican women experienced harsh environmental and social conditions from the settlement of the first Spanish colonies in the sixteenth century through the U.S. conquest in the nineteenth century. Their survival testifies to each generation's endurance and strength.

Francisco Vásquez de Coronado's 1540 expedition into New Mexico included at least three women. Little is known about them, but they were likely the first "Spanish" women to see New Mexico. Their journey was short lived because the expedition retreated within two years after failing to locate substantial wealth. Spanish expeditions did not return to New Mexico in force until 1598, when Juan de Oñate established the first imperial settlement in New Mexico at San Gabriel del Yunque. Official records note that at least two dozen women accompanied Oñate's soldiers

"Portrait of a Girl," painting by Henri Penelon of a Sepúlveda family member, circa 1860s. Courtesy of the American West Collection, Autry National Center, Los Angeles, California. Acquisition made possible by the Ramona Chapter, Native Sons of the Golden West.

as wives and daughters. An additional unknown number of mestizo and Mexican indigenous women also accompanied the expedition as servants.

During the seventeenth century colonization developed slowly. Because of the limited number of Spanish women who accompanied expeditions into New Mexico, male colonists formed relationships with indigenous women or with black slaves. Although New Mexico's later generations frequently claimed "pure Spanish blood," racial and cultural intermixture was the historical reality. In 1631 a Franciscan priest characterized New Mexico's colonial population as "*mestizos*, mulattos, and *zambohijos* (a racial classification)." It is almost impossible, however, to document the specific racial origins of most seventeenth-century women in New Mexico. Many indigenous women joined the colonial community and were considered "Hispanicized" (*españolada*). Official records did not always note this racial and cultural mixing. Often these women and their descendants were listed as "Spanish" to contrast them with the indigenous communities.

Nonetheless, women of all racial and cultural backgrounds faced harsh conditions in Spain's expanding imperial territories. Oñate's successors became embroiled in conflicts over the division of civil and religious authority that resulted in political and military instability. Indigenous Pueblos, moreover, suffered under constraints set by Catholic priests for religious conversion and colonists' demands for labor. The ensuing tensions escalated into a massive revolt by Pueblo communities in 1680. One of the best-organized and most successful native rebellions in North America, the Great Pueblo Revolt effectively eliminated Spanish settlement in New Mexico between 1680 and 1692. Pueblos killed several hundred Spaniards, including numerous women, during the initial days of the revolt. About 2,000 colonists fled to El Paso along with their dependents and allies. After twelve years Spaniards returned to New Mexico, and the balance of authority shifted from religious leaders to civil authorities.

The number of European women arriving in New Mexico continued to be scant after 1692. Franciscan friars and government authorities kept occasional records of settlement in New Mexico, but the best demographic information derives from the census report ordered by Vicerooy Revillagigedo (Juan Vicente Giremes Pachecoy Padilla, Count of Revillagiged) in 1790. By that time the 31,000 people designated *españoles* (nonindigenous) accounted for about half of New Mexico's population. Santa Fe appeared unusual in this census because women outnumbered men (53 percent of the population versus 47). In the rest of the colonial settlements men outnumbered women, although usually by a small ratio.

Although they were almost half the population, Spanish Mexican women occupied ambiguous positions as they negotiated conflicting social and economic demands. Spain's eighteenth-century legal system did not overtly limit women's rights as severely as the English system. Women in New Mexico retained their property after marriage, conducted business in public, and filed suits in local courts. Husbands could not claim any property that a woman owned before marriage. Widows who managed their property or poor married women earning wages in public spaces were not seen as particularly unusual in New Mexico before the Mexican-American War.

Women's legally defined access to public venues did not translate into egalitarian relationships with men. New Mexico's legal and social codes limited women's rights and privileges on the assumption that women "belonged" to a family headed by a man. Ramón Gutiérrez's work remains the most widely cited study of gender and sexuality in colonial New Mexico. As Gutiérrez documented, social and legal practices in colonial New Mexico prescribed women's behaviors based on notions of honor and shame. Most Spanish colonists believed that women were more susceptible to temptations and therefore would be unable to resist men's desires. To preserve the honor of the family, men were expected to "protect" women from shame by enforcing their seclusion. Women found guilty of adultery, for example, were severely punished, while men faced few legal penalties for the same offense. Legal codes could also require women to stay in marriages regardless of abuse. The ideal woman was expected to limit her duties to her home, her family, and the Catholic Church. Some have argued that New Mexico's remoteness escalated the importance placed on this moral code.

In practice, though, only the very wealthy could afford to keep women completely secluded. New Mexico's limited economy meant that most women performed some type of labor outside their home. Harsh agricultural conditions, for instance, often required all available household members to plant and harvest. When Zebulon Pike passed through New Mexico in 1807, he noted that men, women, and children all cultivated the fields. Census records also indicate that a sizable number of women worked in paid occupations as servants, bakers, weavers, gold panners, shepherds, laundresses, stocking knitters, healers, midwives, ironers, and venders. Moreover, men in the most common occupations (soldiers, muleteers, shepherds, and hunters) frequently left their home for much of the year. During these absences women supervised households and defended the family's public rights. Many women took advantage of the frontier conditions to act independently within the legal code and to defend their own positions.

Belief in Manifest Destiny and economic expansion brought nineteenth-century Euro-Americans flooding into New Mexico in 1821. Spain's imperial policies had previously forbidden New Mexico from trading with the United States. Mexican independence ushered in an era without such restrictions. Euro-American merchants seized on the opportunity and formed the lucrative Santa Fe Trail. By the time the United States annexed Texas in 1845, New Mexico's Euro-American merchants had become vocal advocates for appropriating New Mexico as well.

In the decades before the Mexican-American War traders frequently used stories about local Mexicans' gender and sexual behavior as justification for U.S. expansion. M. M. Marmaduke's 1824 journal, for instance, asserted that the Mexican community lacked "decency." "The men and women," he complained, "will indiscriminately and freely converse together on the most indecent, gross and vulgar subjects that can possibly be conceived, without the least embarrassment or confusion." Spanish Mexican women, in particular, preoccupied the first Euro-American visitors to

New Mexico. Euro-Americans complained that local Mexican women did not conform to expected gender roles. That lack of conformity, Euro-Americans claimed, was evidence of local Mexicans' inferiority and status as "uncivilized." A Euro-American visitor asserted that Mexican women spent their lives in "one incessant round of dalliance, dancing, and devotion."

Euro-Americans also pointed to the large number of women who worked in public as troubling. Married women, under the Euro-American legal system, lost their property and were expected to avoid political or economic activities to preserve their "purity." Although similar expectations did exist in New Mexico, women commonly pursued business and commercial activities. Merchants and travelers often wrote about Mexican women's involvement with economic pursuits as the most shocking evidence of racial difference.

Doña Gertrudis "La Tules" Barceló was one of the most discussed women in nineteenth-century New Mexico. Barceló became a prominent business leader in Santa Fe by successfully capitalizing on the influx of Euro-American traders in the 1830s and 1840s. When she died in 1852, she had accumulated more than $10,000. Barceló made her fortune serving liquor and dealing cards to traveling Euro-Americans. Politicians and military leaders frequently appeared at her establishment seeking Barceló's advice. Her prominence, however, created scorn among Euro-American travelers, as well as some local Mexicans. On several occasions Barceló defended her honor in court against slanderous allegations brought by neighboring Mexican women. For many Euro-American traders, soldiers, and adventurers who traveled to New Mexico, Barceló's success and independence elicited harsh anti-Mexican stereotypes. On the eve of the Mexican-American War (1846–1848) Euro-Americans equated Barceló's success with "loose habits"

and "unbridled passions." The successful business-woman became one of Euro-Americans' favorite examples of Spanish Mexican "degeneracy."

Given this hostility toward them, Mexican women's ambivalent reaction to U.S. troops' 1846 invasion is not surprising. The Mexican governor abandoned the territory shortly before the American military arrived in Santa Fe on August 19. Mexican women and other citizens were left without military defenses as they faced a new imperial authority. According to reports from U.S. soldiers, Mexican women wailed with grief as the U.S. flag rose above the governor's palace. The majority of these women faced increasing hardship after the 1848 Treaty of Guadalupe Hidalgo finalized U.S. control over New Mexico.

Historian Deena González's pathbreaking work uncovered Mexican women's changing circumstances as New Mexico became a U.S. territory. Some of those changes appeared subtly in women's day-to-day management of business affairs. Because the U.S. legal system gave greater consideration to men's property rights, for instance, Mexican women increasingly wrote wills and conveyed property to their elder sons. Other changes appeared more dramatic. Mexican women (and the Mexican community in general) faced a steep economic decline as a result of U.S. imperialism. By 1880 the entire Spanish Mexican population had lost 90 percent of the land granted under Spain and Mexico. At the same time the number of Spanish Mexican women working for wages steadily increased. Ironically, Euro-American men had often criticized Mexican working women before the war, but U.S. economic policies resulted in almost 90 percent of Mexican women working as domestics, laundresses, or seamstresses by the end of the nineteenth century. On average, these women earned substantially less than

Traditional native dances performed by Hispanos. Fiesta, Taos, New Mexico. Courtesy of the Library of Congress, Prints and Photographs Division, FSA-OWI Collection (Digital ID: cph3b42885).

The elite Amador family on a picnic, circa 1905–1910. Courtesy of the Rio Grande Historical Collections, New Mexico State University Library, Las Cruces.

similarly employed Euro-American women. The average wage for a white domestic ranged from $1.50 to $2.00 per day, while Mexican domestics earned between 50¢ and 85¢ per day. Because of rapid inflation, many of these laborers found it difficult to maintain their families on such limited wages.

Most histories, though, have ignored Spanish Mexican women's harsh experiences with U.S. imperialism. Instead, attention has been given to intermarriage between Euro-American men and Mexican women in the early territorial period. Some have celebrated these unions as evidence of the "peaceful" incorporation of New Mexico into the United States. Yet these marriages proved much more important for the Euro-American population than for Mexicans. Indeed, while 63 percent of Euro-American men in Santa Fe married Mexican women in 1870, only 2 percent of all Mexican women married Euro-American men.

The emphasis on intermarriage points to a larger problem in the historical literature on New Mexico. Spanish Mexican women in New Mexico have been mentioned only in passing in most historical works. At best, traditional histories of New Mexico relegated women to a footnote or an occasional anecdotal reference. Likewise, the few images of Spanish Mexican women in U.S. popular culture have been highly romanticized or crudely stereotypical. Ruth Laughlin's 1948 novel *The Wind Leaves No Shadow,* for instance, portrayed historical Mexican women, like Gertrudis Barceló, as murderers, gamblers, prostitutes, and the victims of cruel Mexican men. Much remains unknown about women's lives in colonial and territorial New Mexico. Recent research has only just started to bal-

ance these inconsistencies by uncovering women's critical role in New Mexico's history.

SOURCES: González, Deena J. 1999. *Refusing the Favor: The Spanish-Mexican Women of Santa Fe, 1820–1880.* New York: Oxford University Press; Gutiérrez, Ramón A. 1991. *When Jesus Came, the Corn Mothers Went Away: Marriage, Sexuality, and Power in New Mexico, 1500–1846.* Stanford, CA: Stanford University Press; Lecompte, Janet. 1981. "The Independent Women of Hispanic New Mexico, 1821–1846." *Western Historical Quarterly* 22 (January): 17–35; Leyva, Yolanda Chávez. 1997. " 'A poor widow burdened with children': Widows and Land in Colonial New Mexico." In *Writing the Range: Race, Class, and Culture in the Women's West,* ed.

Women of the Amador family, Las Cruces, New Mexico, circa 1900. Courtesy of the Rio Grande Historical Collections, New Mexico State University Library, Las Cruces.

Spanish Borderlands

Elizabeth Jameson and Susan Armitage, 85–96. Norman: University of Oklahoma Press; Tjarks, Alicia V. 1978. "Demographic, Ethnic, and Occupational Structure of New Mexico, 1790." *Americas* 35 (July): 45–88.

Anthony Mora

Women in St. Augustine

Women of Spanish descent born in the Americas have been a critical part of the present-day United States for more than 400 years. Long before the founding of the United States, St. Augustine women helped build an American settlement that survived environmental and economic catastrophes for almost 200 years. These women served as the stalwarts of their community and were thoroughly resourceful in maintaining its everyday activities. Their active participation transformed a military outpost into a viable settlement. Maria Ximenes de Laquera, born in 1594 to María Meléndez and Juan Ximénes de Laquera, is the first known Hispanic woman born in St. Augustine, Florida. Latinas populated, stabilized, and enhanced this area's wealth before the founding of the United States. Although frequently overlooked in accounts of the historical development of the Americas, Latinas made significant contributions to early Spanish settlements.

From St. Augustine's beginnings as a Spanish colonial frontier in 1565, women's roles were paramount in creating a long-standing settlement. Two key factors help explain women's importance to St. Augustine. The first was longevity. Women outlived their spouses, married multiple times, and thus were able to accumulate wealth. Second, women owned land. In stark contrast to British society, women under Spanish law held landowning rights and thus occupied a broad array of positions within society. Women's diverse societal positions can be understood by examining how power was shared, transferred, and limited in St. Augustine. Women's unique experiences stem from the community's pivotal position as an eighteenth-century Spanish frontier colony.

At that time St. Augustine consisted of the town and three surrounding settlements. The considerable diversity of its population resulted from the inclusion of these settlements. Two were the Christian Indian villages of Nuestra Señora de la Leche and Nuestra Señora de Guadalupe de Tolomato. Blacks who fled slavery in the Carolinas populated the third, Fort Moze. Working for the Spanish in St. Augustine, they gained freedom in Florida. Together these three towns shielded St. Augustine, helped protect local Spanish interests, and enlarged St. Augustine more than would have otherwise been possible in this frontier locale.

In the 1760s St. Augustine was among the largest cities on the North American East Coast. Situated within the Spanish viceroyalty of New Spain with a good harbor, the town was well suited to act as a buffer to French and English incursions and guard New World treasure fleets. St. Augustine served the dual purpose of a military fortification, controlling the waterways surrounding Florida, and a frontier settlement, hindering the territorial gains of other European powers in the region. One objective demanded the primacy of the military, and the other the cultivation of a civilian population. Nonetheless, St. Augustine was a very low priority for the Spanish Crown.

As early as the seventeenth century Spain found itself unable to subsidize colonies like St. Augustine. Survival depended upon Spain's provision of a *situado* or subsidy—monies given to all settlements that were not self-sufficient but strategically important to the Crown. The number of soldiers in the town's total population generally determined the subsidy's amount and significantly affected the material circumstances of most inhabitants, almost half of whom were not employed by the Spanish government. The *situado*—an insufficient amount for St. Augustine—never arrived on time and required an awkward interaction with officials in Mexico City, Puebla, Vera Cruz, and Havana. Left on its own, the colony resorted to using scrip and barter in place of hard currency, which placed the majority of inhabitants in continually dire economic conditions.

The *situado*'s inadequacies directly affected St. Augustine women, since many were dependent on it for daily sustenance. Spain provided insufficient financial support for widows and orphans. Mere survival required an ongoing negotiation of the social environment.

St. Augustine had the problems of a harsh frontier environment and the attributes of a developing Spanish American community. Its location posed significant challenges to its residents. From the hurricane of 1707 that leveled most homes to severe British attacks in 1702 and 1740, St. Augustine witnessed many disasters, both natural and human created. Finally, the population boom that occurred in the 1700s, in conjunction with British-induced land contraction, presented social burdens. The population increased from 800 in 1710 to 3,000 in 1736, and hence more people depended on the *situado*.

The rigors of life in a neglected settlement impeded economic development. Survival on the frontier depended upon behavior that was treasonous to the Spanish Crown. Although Spain was at war with Great Britain, St. Augustinians traded with British American colonists to get cheaper prices and surer delivery for foodstuffs, clothing, and luxury items, practices that circumvented the Spanish trade system.

Enduring hardships, settlers continued to operate under an established social system that differentiated women's experiences along lines of race and marital status. For example, a Creole woman, born in the New World of Spanish parentage, had a very different life than an Indian woman; likewise, most married women's circumstances were better than widows' experiences. A description of various segments of the population provides glimpses into the lives of distinct groups of women.

By 1763, when the Spanish Crown ceded Florida to the British in accordance with the Treaty of Paris, St. Augustine had 3,096 inhabitants, who included 544 families and an unspecified number of household units. In 1755, 59 percent of the garrison was married, and collectively it had 520 children.

Though the average family size for Spanish Floridians in 1763 was five, for almost half the population it was below four, the smallest family size being among Catalans, Christian Indians, and free blacks, which reflected the difficulty of the immigrant experience. There were various household types within St. Augustine. Many households incorporated recent arrivals into the community. Absorption of immigrant groups from other parts of the empire caused local demographic changes.

The immense diversity of St. Augustinians was unique for a Spanish settlement of that time. Also, the integration of many Indian populations, free blacks from the Carolinas, and both Spanish and non-Spanish immigrants led to the absorption of new people. Nevertheless, St. Augustine negatively affected the surrounding Indian communities. Over time, as the general population of St. Augustine increased, the indigenous population declined by 17 percent within one year (1760). In virtually every subgroup of St. Augustine's population except Christian Indians, there was a relative lack of women, which facilitated intermarriage among the St. Augustine population.

This community's social structure incorporated numerous groups and situated individuals based on race, gender, marital status, and usefulness. Women of different racial groups and marital statuses had distinct social positions within eighteenth-century St. Augustine society. Because salaries were primarily based upon military or religious jobs, a woman's economic situation was largely dependent upon the status of her family of origin or her marital status. Many Indian women, for example, were either servants or the wives of soldiers. Although married women were better off than widows, they were still in a very different economic position from that of their husbands because they were economically dependent upon them. Gender and racial diversity existed among the majority—living at subsistence level—and the landowners. Because documentary materials about the lives of the poor are unavailable, detailed information about most of the population is absent. However, there is historical documentation of those for whom the Crown provided assistance. Approximately 10 percent of the population consisted of widows and orphans, who were some of the poorest in the community and were financially supported by the *situado*.

In stark contrast to the pittance widows and orphans received, the members of a small group of women were highly compensated for their services to the Spanish military. Eight women in the population were identified as *mujeres mercenarias,* an interestingly official female role. These women were paid by the Crown and received higher salaries than most soldiers and many military lieutenants and commandants. *Mujeres mercenarias* were women who performed sexual services for the military. The social position of these women is unknown. However, their roles as sexual objects/actors placed these women outside the standard pay scales and provided them with a more prosperous life. These women's higher economic status demonstrates how some women were privileged and others disadvantaged within the same social system. For instance, one *mujer mercenaria,* Juana Ana María Paniagua, owned a large home and slaves. Such women accounted for a small portion of the population, but their income was substantially above the St. Augustinian average.

Other women occupied a high social status through landownership. Women were 26.2 percent of all landowners; the vast majority of these women were single. By comparison, 21.2 percent of all St. Augustinians owned private land.

The percentage of women landowners is unsurprising for eighteenth-century Spanish America; however, the numbers for British America pale in comparison. Single Spanish American women were neither discouraged nor barred from owning land, and they might accumulate property through a series of widowhoods, pensions, and remarriages. This accumulation of wealth enabled some to attain fair-sized estates and independence from marriage of necessity. Despite the continual state of deprivation and war, a potential for social mobility existed for some women and men, making land acquisition more likely in St. Augustine.

The percentage of nonwhite landowners was very significant as well. In 1763, 8.3 percent of the landowning population was nonwhite, when nonwhites comprised 17 percent of the total population. Of the free black and mulatto population, 16.4 percent owned land, compared with 10 percent of the total white population.

Diversity ceased at the top of the social ladder with the homogeneous Creole elite who held a disproportionate amount of the colony's wealth. Those in the

Spanish Borderlands

elite were differentiated from the general landed population by the amount of land owned, types of homes, and ownership of slaves. Like their British American contemporaries, the elite enjoyed the finest goods and services.

The key difference between the landowners and the elite was simply a matter of opportunity. Many Creole elites had attained greater wealth through exploiting the traditional trade process to their advantage. The wealthiest were those who controlled how needed supplies were distributed. Because the majority of the population depended on elite merchants for their sustenance, these elites remained in positions of power. Although this distribution system fostered a highly inequitable social system, it provided the best supply source to the colonies at the least cost to a substantially indebted government. This trade not only rewarded elites with money, land, and status, but extended upward mobility to merchants and traders, who previously had been excluded from upper-class Spanish society.

These Creole elite consisted of a very close kinship network in which many persons were familial relations by blood or marriage. Approximately one-third of all landowners were blood related. Within this network the primary means of incorporation was marriage to a Creole woman. Several men married Creole women who owned considerable amounts of land themselves and whose families were able to assist politically and financially in their spouses' advancement; half were marriages to widows.

Overall, frontier life allowed for a less rigid social hierarchy than that of Spain and the British colonies. Landownership was available to women and free blacks, two groups prohibited from ownership rights in British America. Women's ability to own property made them more economically independent than women in many other eighteenth-century locales. However, the society was by no means egalitarian, distinctions based upon gender and race permeated social relations, and slavery was legally practiced. Despite these social inequities, the demographics and location of St. Augustine fashioned a complex and multiracial community that provided some economic opportunities for women, free blacks and mulattos, and Indians.

Women's economic stability soon became irrelevant when their entire community was completely disrupted by St. Augustine's evacuation. As a result of Great Britain's seizure of power in 1763, the majority of these women were uprooted and transported to Cuba. Thus ended a unique social experience that accentuated Latinas' role as a critical force within the first Hispanic community in what would later become the United States.

SOURCES: Landers, Jane G. 1999. "Female Conflict and its Resolution in Eighteenth Century St. Augustine." *The Americas* 54, no. 4: 557–574; Pickman, Susan L. 1980. "Life on the Spanish-American Frontier: A Study in the Social and Economic History of Mid-18th Century St. Augustine, Florida." Ph.D. diss, State University of New York at Stony Brook.

Susan L. Pickman and Dorcas R. Gilmore

Women in Texas (1716–1890)

Spanish Mexican women's participation in public life has grown throughout Texas history since the Spanish conquest in the eighteenth century. Although domestic responsibilities consumed much of their time during the era of Spanish colonization, women began to assert their rights to own property and to contribute to economic productivity. Opportunities for paid work and interethnic cooperation emerged during the first half of the nineteenth century. As Texas became integrated into the United States during the last half of the nineteenth century, women's participation in the labor force grew, and they became more involved in civic organizations.

From 1716 to 1721 Spanish women participated in two of three expeditions to found permanent colonial settlements in Texas. Women accompanied their soldier husbands who were part of an expedition to reestablish missions among the Tejas Indians. Along with missions and presidios, the colonists established ranchos and pueblos for the civilian population. The presence of families distinguished the second colonization effort and increased women's responsibilities. Among their duties were raising children, preparing food, making and washing clothes, tending gardens, and making soap.

Women and their families figured prominently among the settlers who established the town of San Antonio as well as its presidio and five missions. In 1721 several hundred colonists, including twenty-eight families, established a presidio at Los Adaes to protect eastern Texas from further French expansion beyond Natchitoches, located only eighteen miles away. In all, some 500 Spanish settlers lived in Texas by 1731.

During the colonial period the Spanish population of Texas increased steadily and spread to other settlements. The majority of early settlers came from New Spain's northeastern provinces of Coahuila, Nuevo León, and Nuevo Santander. The Spanish pioneers struggled against the isolation of settlement life, which exposed them to continued attacks from enemy Indian nations. Harsh frontier conditions contributed to high levels of infant mortality, which suppressed population growth and increased the necessity of immigration to the region. Immigrants from the Canary Islands came to San Antonio, as well as Europeans and Anglo

(North) Americans who eventually fanned out across the Spanish settlements of eastern Texas. In 1777 the diverse population of Spanish subjects reached 3,103 people, distributed among the principal settlements of San Antonio, La Bahía, and Nacogdoches. Colonial officials classified people into several racial categories, including Spaniards, mestizos, mulattoes, blacks, and Indians, but these categories functioned more as indicators of social status than as lifelong racial identities. Because the ethnic origins of most settlers were diverse, it was common for a colonist to transcend racial categories as her or his wealth increased. By the end of the colonial period this varied mix of colonists numbered only 4,500, placing Texas among the regions with the fewest Spanish subjects.

Because of the region's isolation and small Spanish population, social life in colonial Texas revolved around the family. Women and men married young (averages in San Antonio were eighteen for women and twenty-four for men), but also tended to be widowed at an early age. The majority of Spanish women were married (82 percent), and widows made up more than 10 percent of all adult women in 1784. In some communities widows outnumbered widowers, but both usually remarried within a few years because life on the frontier was difficult for single heads of household. Rudimentary housing, the scarcity of household goods, and the demanding chores of life in Texas forced wives and husbands to cooperate in their domestic responsibilities. Although women were principally responsible for domestic chores, they also assisted their husbands with ranch, farm, and craft jobs. In some cases women temporarily carried out political duties for their husbands. María Gertrudis Pérez Cassiano, for example, managed the affairs of the governor's office between 1810 and 1820 during her husband's absences. Similarly, Josefa Becerra Seguín assumed her husband's role in a dispute with San Antonio city authorities over water rights while he visited Mexico City to attend congressional sessions. Men's military or ranching duties often took them away from home and forced women to assume the double duty of maintaining the household and caring for the family's land and livestock. These characteristics of frontier society, according to some scholars, decreased the degree of female subordination and lessened the sharp sexual division of labor that existed elsewhere in New Spain.

Spanish law granted women specific legal and property rights that allowed some to maintain their independence. Women were governed by both restrictive and protective legislation. Restrictive laws prevented women from exercising control over men. According to this legislation, women could not vote, hold office, serve on local tribunals, serve as witnesses in legal transactions, or appear in court on behalf of another. Unless they obtained permission from a male-dominated court, women could not adopt children or serve as legal guardians. Protective laws, on the other hand, were designed to prevent women from becoming victims of economic or social adversity. Inheritance laws stipulated that daughters receive the same amount of property as sons and also required the courts to give a widow a portion of her spouse's estate. The law allowed adult women to own their own property and to maintain this ownership even after marriage to safeguard their economic status if their husbands died or encountered financial difficulties. Moreover, the courts did not hold wives accountable for their husbands' debts.

Spanish women actively exercised their property rights, obtaining more than sixty Spanish and Mexican land grants in Texas before 1848. One of the most successful women was Rosa María Hinojosa de Ballí, a widow who amassed a fortune in land and livestock. After receiving a Spanish land grant (1790) near the Rio Grande (part of the province of Nuevo Santander during the Spanish period), she skillfully managed her property and acquired large herds of cattle, sheep, and horses. She continued to apply for additional land grants and to purchase property, and by the time of her death in 1803 she owned more than 1 million acres, thus becoming the first "cattle queen" of Texas. Widows in San Antonio also successfully managed large livestock herds. In 1779 María Ana Curbelo and Leonor Delgado were among the top five cattle owners in San Antonio. Indeed, more than one-fifth of all civilian households in the city were women headed, and their wealth was largely dependent on land and livestock ownership. Landowning women not only managed extensive livestock and property, but also supervised considerable numbers of employees. Some owned African slaves, and most hired a variety of servants to perform the large number of domestic and ranch duties required on their estates.

Although their legal rights were limited, women used protective legislation to pursue their interests. A young woman remained under her father's control until she became an adult. Nevertheless, with her father's permission, she could sue a man over insults or inappropriate courting that might decrease her social mobility or her family's honor. Unmarried women could also initiate seduction lawsuits if their suitors broke off marriage plans after initiating sexual relations. In cases where a man broke promises to marry after his female partner became pregnant, the young woman often sued the man to obtain child support payments. Married women also used the courts to defend their interests. Women could protect their financial interests by filing lawsuits to stop their husbands from mismanaging their property or selling their property without permission. Wives also pursued legal action if husbands did not provide for their families' financial need and to protect themselves against physical abuse. Occasionally the threat of a lawsuit was enough to persuade a recalcitrant husband to mend his ways. If the abuse or neglect continued, wives could sever their marriage bonds by asking for a divorce, but would face significant odds since the Catholic Church rarely granted divorces.

After Mexico's independence from Spain in 1821 women witnessed gradual changes in their legal and occupational status. Mexican law followed the model of Spanish statutes; therefore, unlike women living in the United States, Mexican women retained ownership of their property when they married. Any property that a couple obtained while married became community property; a husband had to obtain his wife's approval before selling any property held in common. Mexican law also allowed widows and unmarried adult women to litigate and to establish business contracts independently.

Spanish Mexican women had faced limited occupational opportunities outside the established towns. Domestic service on the ranchos or in towns was one of the few paid jobs available for Indian women and mestizas. As the population increased, however, new opportunities opened in urban areas for women who worked as seamstresses, *planchadoras* (clothes pressers), launderers, and *tortilleras* (tortilla makers). Some became petty entrepreneurs in a burgeoning urban economy as small-shop owners, handicraft saleswomen, and food peddlers.

The population of Texas changed dramatically during the period of Mexican rule (1821–1836). Unable to attract additional colonists to settle in Texas, the Mexican government began a colonization program to attract Anglo-American and European settlers. Although the colonization program was a big success for U.S. citizens, it proved disastrous for Mexico because Anglo-Americans came to outnumber Mexicans two to one. When the Mexican government moved to restrict immigration, enforce laws against slavery, and impose taxes, Anglo Texans and Texas Mexicans launched a successful separatist rebellion and established the Republic of Texas in 1836. Women were active on both sides of the conflict, accompanying Mexican troops sent to suppress the rebellion and helping care for Tejano and Texan rebels at the Alamo and Goliad battles. Several of the noncombatants at the Alamo were women and children who survived the battle and subsequently received state pensions for their service. Because of increasing military and interethnic tensions during the Texas Revolution, women often acted as intermediaries between Anglo Texans and Mexicans. Francisca Alavez, for example, was known as the Angel of Goliad for intervening to save the lives of several Texas rebels from execution by Mexican troops. Patricia de la Garza de León and her family, founders of the predominantly Mexican colony of Victoria, supported the Texas rebels with smuggled weapons. Unfortunately, the Leóns had to flee to New Orleans to escape the anti-Mexican violence that swept the state after the revolution. Like many other Spanish Mexicans, the Leóns had family members killed and property confiscated by vigilantes who believed that Spanish Mexicans had supported Mexico during the armed conflict.

As ethnic tensions increased following the Texas Revolution, Spanish Mexican women assumed larger roles as intermediaries between Mexican and white Texans. The surge in the Anglo-American population created more interethnic marriages, mostly between Anglo men and Mexican women. Intermarriage was more common in areas like eastern Texas with a small population of white women, but it also occurred in central and southern Texas among Mexican families who believed that interethnic unions might protect their property and political rights. Interethnic accommodation became an important safety strategy for Mexicans after Texas gained its independence because the Texas Mexican population was suspected of disloyalty and complicity with Mexico's troops. Unruly Texans acted on their suspicions by violently attacking and dispossessing Tejanos of their property. The outbreak of war between Mexico and the United States in 1846 further inflamed ethnic tensions as Texas Mexicans' loyalty was questioned again.

It is not surprising that elite Tejano families made conscious decisions to establish interethnic alliances with Anglo Texans through intermarriage. In many wealthy Mexican families in San Antonio, including the Seguins, Navarros, and Cassianos, at least one daughter married an Anglo between 1830 and 1860. Tejano families with less status and wealth established ties with the new elite by asking Anglos to become patrons or godparents in marriages, baptisms, or confirmations. Whereas Texas Mexican families gained a measure of economic protection from an Anglo in-law or godparent, white men also benefited socially and politically from their familial ties to the Mexican population. This benefit was especially valuable in regions with a majority Mexican population, like the border communities, where some Anglo politicians won elective office because they garnered the overwhelming support of the Mexican electorate.

During the second half of the nineteenth century Spanish Mexican women in Texas entered the labor force in larger numbers. This was partly a result of an increase in population caused by the rapid growth in immigration from Mexico. The Texas Mexican population grew from some 18,500 in 1850 to approximately 165,000 by 1900. Most of the new arrivals settled in southern and western Texas, where the Mexican population remained the majority throughout the nineteenth century. As the state's economy changed from self-sufficiency to a system geared toward industry and commerce, the Texas Mexican population lost skilled jobs and became concentrated in the lowest-paid occupational fields. The resulting loss of earning power forced more Mexicans into the labor force, including single women and female heads of household. From 1850 to 1900 the number of Spanish Mexican women in the paid labor force increased forty-three-fold. The number of female-headed households also increased, from 5.2 percent in 1850 to 19.6 percent in 1900, as women swelled the ranks of domestic servants, peddlers, seamstresses, and field laborers. A few women also entered the workforce as schoolteachers, entertainers, and shopkeepers. In border cites from El Paso to Brownsville, Spanish Mexican women were prominent among the schoolteachers listed in the 1900 census.

The Spanish Mexican community became more politically involved during the last decades of the nineteenth century. While men could directly participate in electoral politics, women's participation was limited because the state barred them from voting or seeking elected office. Nevertheless, Spanish Mexican women's civic participation increased. Elite women donated money and land to establish schools, often with religious affiliations. Among others, Paula Losoya Taylor in Del Rio and Josefa Flores de Baker in Floresville gave land to establish or enlarge towns. Adina Emilia de Zavala of San Antonio became a teacher, an advocate for historic preservation, and a writer of folklore and history. Spanish Mexican women founded several mutual-aid societies (*mutualistas*) in the 1890s, such as the Sociedad Beneficencia in Corpus Christi and Laredo's Sociedad Josefa Ortiz de Domínguez. Others became members of auxiliaries of all-male *mutualistas*. Some women assumed leadership roles by serving as officers, heads of committees, and even presidents of these self-help groups. Luisa M. González became president of the Alianza Hispano-Americana, a mutual-aid society that welcomed women and men. The mutual-aid societies provided members with medical benefits, funeral expenses, and low-interest loans. Women were active in support networks that provided child care and childbirth assistance, and organized fund drives for needy residents. While many mutual-aid societies supported labor organizing, others took up diverse causes such as advocating for temperance and criticizing the subordination of women. Most important, the mutual-aid societies provided a forum for members to discuss politics and express pride in their Mexican cultural traditions.

By the end of the nineteenth century Spanish Mexican women in Texas had become increasingly involved in the public life of their community. Their participation blossomed into myriad activities, from organizing labor unions and advocating for additional educational opportunities for schoolchildren to supporting Mexican exile organizations and creating civil rights organizations. Women continued to play an integral part in community and political organizations as Mexican Americans struggled to claim their rights in the United States.

SOURCES: De León, Arnoldo. 1999. *Mexican Americans in Texas: A Brief History*. 2nd ed. Wheeling, IL: Harlan Davidson; Downs, Fane, and Nancy Baker Jones, eds. 1993. *Women and Texas History*. Austin: Texas State Historical Association; Griswold del Castillo, Richard. 1984. *La Familia: Chicano Families in the Urban Southwest, 1848 to the Present*. Notre Dame, IN: University of Notre Dame Press; Handbook of Texas Online. http://www.tsha.utexas.edu/handbook/online (accessed March 29, 2003); Orozco, Cynthia E. 1992–1993. "Beyond Machismo: La Familia and Ladies Auxiliaries: A Historiography of Mexican-Origin Women's Participation in Voluntary Associations and Politics in the United States, 1970–1990." In *Renato Rosaldo Lecture Series Mongraph* 10. Tucson: University of Arizona Mexican Studies and Research Center; Ruiz, Vicki L. 1998. *From out of the Shadows: Mexican Women in Twentieth-Century America*. New York: Oxford University Press.

Omar Valerio-Jiménez

Women's Wills

Women in the Spanish borderlands retained a degree of independence and autonomy unheard of among their counterparts on the Atlantic seaboard. Mexico, which gained its independence from Spain in 1821, based its legal system on Roman codes and not English ones. These legal codes gave women access to the judicial system, including the right to sue and be sued and the right to record their last will and testament. This power allowed women to pass on inheritances, no matter how small, and to participate in their communities in ways often denied women in the British colonies and later in the United States. As part of the legal system, women had certain civil rights; sometimes they sought redress from the courts for slanderous comments and at other times leveled more serious charges of battery, robbery, and murder. Records of the period are filled with women's names and complaints, indicating that Spanish Mexican women were neither subservient nor passive.

For example, Gertrudis Barceló or La Tules, owner of a popular Santa Fe saloon and gambling hall, often made use of the courts before and after the Treaty of Guadalupe Hidalgo in 1848. She sued her tenant, another woman, for "cohabitating with another woman." Barceló also went to court to assume full title of her home and to clarify the boundaries of her property with a proper deed, to which the judge agreed. She submitted a will leaving property to her adopted daughter, a niece, and her brother and his wife.

In their wills Spanish Mexican women revealed an inventory of their belongings with very clear instructions on inheritance. For example, Bárbara Baca bestowed her home and small plot of land on her son because "she had no daughters." She then listed in great detail all of her worldly possessions down to her five mattresses, two cast-iron skillets, and five bushels of beans. Not every woman who left a will was a widow. A wife could use a will as an instrument through which to distribute the separate property or dowry that she brought to her marriage. Often with flowery religious introductions, wills reveal much about the importance of Catholic spirituality in women's daily lives and the centrality of female kin and friend networks. These wills may be characterized as ritualized "female gift giving" in that women bequeathed possessions, such as clothing, land, household goods, and religious icons, to their sisters and to their *comadres.* In New Mexico after 1848 the orchestration of will making displayed by rich and poor alike in the probate courts and at the church or in neighborhoods can ultimately be understood as a symbolic intervention in the disorder of a new political, social, and economic order dominated by Euro-Americans. Wills could be symbols of community, resistance, and resilience.

See also Legal Issues

SOURCE: González, Deena J. 1999. *Refusing the Favor: The Spanish-Mexican Women of Santa Fe, 1820–1880.* New York: Oxford University Press.

Deena J. González

SPIRITISM

Studies of Puerto Rican Spiritism often mention female spiritists as "mediums" for the manifestation of spirits. This religious practice constitutes the center of spiritistic rituals, just as in African American religions. The majority of studies on African American religions describe the dominance of women in the so-called possession cults. The explanations offered for this female dominance are controversial, however. Religion is seen as an extension of the domestic sphere. Because the female role in Latin America and the Caribbean is

perceived as one in which women are confined to the private realm, women's activities are limited to responsibilities for family and household matters. Thus they can, by extrapolation, extend their responsibilities to the "temple" that is considered a kind of ceremonial house.

Moreover, anthropologists such as Melville Herskovits have argued that Brazilian women are more active in religion than men because they have more free time. This rather weak argument is not substantiated. In many Latin American and Caribbean societies women actually work more than men, and in the United States, as well as in some sectors of Latino and Puerto Rican society, women also work outside the familial sphere. How then does one explain the gender division in Puerto Rican Spiritism, the shift from equal participation to female domination?

Spiritists in Puerto Rico agree that women and men are equal as humans and as spirits; indeed, there is no female dominance in Spiritism. Every spirit and, therefore, every human being is assigned the same value. Membership in the spiritist groups, or *centros,* is highly diversified. They include lawyers, schoolteachers, doctors, and entrepreneurs, as well as housewives and unemployed people. Social status or gender does not seem to have an impact on Spiritism as practiced in Puerto Rico.

The situation is different, however, in studies of Spiritism in New York City. The main interest of researchers, including Michael García, among others, is the high rate of mental illness among Puerto Rican migrants, referred to as the "Puerto Rican syndrome." They describe this phenomenon as a form of paranoid schizophrenia linked to specific cultural roots. While they describe Puerto Rican Spiritism in general, the

Paraphernalia of Puerto Rican Spiritism. Photograph by and courtesy of Bettina E. Schmidt.

focus is mainly on female patients at medical centers, hospitals, or consultation offices. Only rarely has research been undertaken with a spiritistic group or center. Conclusions regarding the dominance of women in Spiritism have resulted from these limitations, even though other studies have found spiritistic communities centered on male spiritists. Because the work on Spiritism has continued to be linked to female clients in medical institutions, aspects of the religion have been reduced to a Puerto Rican female "syndrome."

Although researchers cannot support claims of female dominance in Spiritism, they reinforce the discriminatory perception of women's role in the religion. They have created the impression that only women are allowed to experience spiritistic manifestation, because it is too embarrassing for men to lose control. Even while researchers did not actually investigate women's role in Spiritism, they believed beyond any doubt that spiritistic communities were "naturally" dominated by women. The argument that women are better mediums than men is, therefore, based on the perception of Puerto Rican Spiritism as a "syndrome" or mental illness.

Nevertheless, in the late 1980s and 1990s this perspective influenced Puerto Rican Spiritism in New York City. Male believers became afraid of the negative image of the manifestations because of the association with femininity, so they withdrew step-by-step from the leading level of the communities, making space for women. Today an increasing number of women work as mediums or have founded new spiritistic communities. They dominate the ritual practice of Spiritism in New York City, although there still are many male believers. Current developments within Spiritism, especially the presence of an increasing number of female leaders, are thus clearly the result of adaptation to life in New York City. While connected to the appropriation of stereotypes, this process is sustained by social and economic factors.

Living in New York City has not improved the economic and social situation of most Puerto Ricans. Women, especially those with darker skin color, still suffer from double discrimination—as women and as blacks. In this context Spiritism has become a form of empowerment. By dominating spiritistic consultation, women are able to generate an income through private consultations and to strengthen their self-confidence by leading a spiritistic community. In New York City Spiritism has emerged as reemphasizing both women's roles and African American influences within Puerto Rican culture.

See also Folk Healing Traditions; Religion

SOURCES: García, Michael Anthony. 1979. "The Effects of Spiritualism and Santería as a Cultural Determinant in New York Puerto Rican Women as Reflected by Their Use of Projection." Ph.D. diss., Adelphi University; Schmidt, Bettina E. 2000. "Religious Concepts in the Process of Migration: Puerto Rican Female Spiritualists in the United States." In *Women and Migration: Anthropological Perspectives*, ed. Jacqueline Knörr and Barbara Meier, 119–132. New York and Frankfurt: Campus, in cooperation with St. Martin's Press; Singer, Merril, and Roberto García. 1989. "Becoming a Puerto Rican Espiritista: Life History of a Female Healer." In *Women as Healers: Cross-cultural Perspectives*, ed. Carol Shepherd McClain, 157–185. New Brunswick, NJ: Rutgers University Press.

Bettina E. Schmidt

SPIRITISM IN NEW YORK CITY

In the early decades of the twentieth century a significant number of Puerto Ricans began to migrate to New York City. Most of them identified as Catholic, but their everyday religious practices have not been documented. The founding year of the first spiritistic *centro* (center) in New York City cannot be determined with any degree of certainty because centers do not officially register or even announce their existence in the media. Most are hidden in private apartments and can be found only with the help of insider information. Although Puerto Rican Spiritism is likely to have arrived in New York City during the first decades of the migration, its presence increased significantly with the first massive wave of airborne migrants during the 1950s. Between 1940 and 1960 the number of Puerto Ricans in New York City increased heavily, and with them the presence of Puerto Rican Spiritism. At the same time in which it increased in New York, the importance of Spiritism in the island declined.

A *botánica* in Río Piedras, Puerto Rico. Photograph by and courtesy of Bettina E. Schmidt.

A typical *botánica* in New York City.
Photograph by and courtesy of
Bettina E. Schmidt.

Beginning in the 1950s, more *botánicas* existed in the New York City barrios than on the island. The *botánica,* a small store that sells religious paraphernalia and literature, often included a resident spiritist healer for consultations. Sometimes the *botánica* is even connected to a spiritistic community. Some centers emphasize the African tradition, while others combine Spiritism with Santería, an Afro-Cuban religion. Nonetheless, the purpose of each *centro* is to offer help.

A new center is usually started in a medium's apartment. Unlike the *botánicas,* these spiritistic groups do not normally advertise their existence. Their members usually belong to the same neighborhood and meet two or three times a week. The importance of the community and the development of the individual's power and well-being constitute the central aspects of Spiritism. This alternative healing is the main objective of every spiritistic group, and unlike the consultations at a *botánica*, the *centros* do not charge money for helping people. Alan Harwood noted that for many Puerto Ricans living in an alien place like New York City, the *centro* becomes an important primary group outside the family. Harwood compared the *centro* to voluntary organizations for migrants that perform many of the same functions. In the absence of a traditional sphere of social interaction (like ritual kinship, such as the *compadrazgo* system), Spiritism offers a structure for ordering the migrants' social world.

In a case study of a *centro* in Brooklyn José Figueroa describes how Spiritism constitutes an integral part of the believers' social reality. The members of this group live together in a building that had been neglected by its owner. During and after several meetings they dis-

cuss their problems, like the lack of heating caused by the landlord who ignores his obligations. Finally the members decide to clean the building spiritually and to cast a spell on the owner in order to throw his guardian spirits off balance. Later they organize a rally against the landlord, who is now spiritually unprotected and finally agrees to fulfill his obligations. The members' common belief has thus prepared the ground for joint action, namely, the creation of a tenants' association; on this level they then become aware of their common interests as a group.

During the late 1960s and the 1970s Puerto Rican Spiritism in New York began to receive scholarly attention. Medical anthropologists and psychiatrists, in particular, became aware of the alternative healing system associated with Spiritism. They labeled this phenomenon the "Puerto Rican syndrome" and began to conduct large-scale research on Spiritism among Puerto Ricans living in New York City. Its rising popularity notwithstanding, spiritism was portrayed in a negative manner. Most of the studies of the 1970s, and even some in the 1980s, overlooked the fact that Spiritism represents much more than a culturebound therapy. To describe Spiritism as a "healing-cult," as a "psychiatry of the poor," or as "Puerto Rican group therapy" in order to accommodate the religion to the "modern" Western worldview means degrading a sophisticated system of beliefs and practices. Spiritism is a part of Puerto Rican life and culture. Harwood even compares Spiritism with soul among African Americans: both concepts form the basis of ethnic identity.

SOURCES: Figueroa, José E. 1981. "The Cultural Dynamics of Puerto Rican Spiritism: Class, Nationality, and Religion in a Brooklyn Ghetto." Ph.D. diss., City University of New York;

Harwood, Alan. 1977. *Rx: Spiritist as Needed: A Study of a Puerto Rican Community Mental Health Resource*. New York: John Wiley; Sánchez, Franklyn D. 1984. "Puerto Rican Spiritualism: Survival of the Spirit." In *The Puerto Rican Struggle: Essays on Survival in the U.S.*, ed. Clara E. Rodríguez, Virginia Sánchez Korrol, and José Oscar Alers, 140–151. Maplewood, NJ: Waterfront Press.

Bettina E. Schmidt

STERILIZATION

Female sterilization is an irreversible and controversial form of fertility control that most often involves the surgical cutting or tubal ligation of a woman's fallopian tubes. Although it is considered a reproductive choice by some women, Latinas have been targeted for numerous sterilization programs by a variety of public agencies and social reformers. Under the influence of the eugenics movement, sterilization surgery was originally performed on the "undesirable" classes or categories of persons considered "unfit" to propagate. Many in the medical profession believed that one could reduce criminality, "feeblemindedness," and degeneracy—all thought to be inherited traits—by sterilization. Reducing the progeny of such individuals was believed to improve the genetic makeup of society. By the 1970s this theory had evolved into the coerced sterilization of poor and minority women.

Early eugenic sterilization focused on incarcerated and institutionalized people, particularly in the twelve states of California, Connecticut, Indiana, Iowa, Kansas, Michigan, Nevada, New Jersey, New York, North Dakota, Washington, and Wisconsin, that had enacted sterilization laws by 1913. At first only a small number were sterilized, but three decades later eugenic sterilization in the United States reached its peak when 27,869 individuals were sterilized in a single year. At the same time Puerto Rico was included in eugenic sterilization laws, passed in the United States and the island on May 13, 1937, which also authorized the formation of a Eugenics Board to help organize sterilization programs in public hospitals.

Some states curtailed eugenic sterilization programs in response to public revulsion over the Nazis' policies of forced sterilization in the 1930s, through which up to 3,500,000 people were forcibly sterilized. But in other U.S. states eugenics advocates hailed the "German program" for its liberal sterilization guidelines; American sterilization programs continued well into the 1950s. Not until the death of prominent eugenics advocates like Ezra S. Gosney in 1942 and a gradual shift in public attitudes toward the incarcerated and the mentally ill did the numbers of eugenic sterilizations decrease significantly.

By the 1950s the overall debate around sterilization evolved with the changes in the political climate after the war and a growing reproductive rights movement. American women began to fight for voluntary sterilizations that were not then readily available to them. Eugenics rhetoric gave way to neo-Malthusian notions of population control and poverty reduction. No longer holding to the hereditarian thesis, eugenics advocates found a more acceptable theory in the idea that overpopulation was the root cause of poverty. Women in poor communities became the victims of medical practitioners and judicial officials who believed that the reproductive habits of poor and minority women needed their control. These new advocates of coercive sterilization did not belong to a national movement but shared class and race prejudices similar to those of previous eugenicists.

In some cases officers of the court targeted poor Latina women for sterilization surgery in exchange for release from jail. Victoria Tapia of Santa Barbara is one of the earliest documented cases of a Latina being coerced into surgical sterilization. In 1965 Tapia was offered a reduced sentence with probation if she consented to sterilization. Her crime was defrauding the county welfare department. She consented to sterilization and was released. In 1966 Nancy Hernández was offered a suspended sentence and probation if she would submit to surgical sterilization. The judge believed that Hernández "should not have more children because of her propensity for an immoral life." She rejected these terms, appealed the ruling to a higher court, and was released without having to undergo sterilization surgery.

In 1969 the fear of a population crisis generated new government policies that opened the door for sterilization abuse by individuals who worked in publicly subsidized agencies. Federally supported family-planning services expanded to include sterilization surgery, even though abortion still remained illegal. In this same year the American College of Obstetricians and Gynecologists (ACOG) liberalized its guidelines for women seeking sterilizations by allowing the procedure regardless of their age and the number of their children. In 1970 the ACOG dropped its criteria that two doctors and a psychiatrist be consulted before sterilization surgery. Because sterilization surgery was paid for with government funds and no agency monitored abuses, Latinas and other women of color became victims of forced sterilizations.

The 1960s and 1970s were a time of widespread political protest. Latinas, including activist Chicanas and Puertorriqueñas, expressed their outrage at sterilization abuse in the media, in the courtroom, and on the streets. In a *Los Angeles Times* article Chole Alatorre from Centro de Acción Social Autónomo Hermandad General de Trabajadores (CASA), a Chicano activist group in the Southwest, called a 1973 pilot program to sterilize low-income women at "bargain" rates racist because she believed that the women signing up for the procedure did not fully understand the consequences. The Los Angeles Regional Family Planing Council had organized the program to give poor women access to a legal form of birth control. It used two Los Angeles hospitals, John Wesley Hospital in South Central Los Angeles and Glendale Adventist Hospital in Glendale. The program planned to sterilize up to four women a week with funds provided by the Department of Health, Education, and Welfare. While strict guidelines were implemented to secure protection for each patient's rights, the politics of sterilization remained linked to class and race—only poor women, most of them Latinas, were being offered this "free" service, but they were still being denied other options such as contraception and abortion.

In the 1970s some doctors in county hospitals performed sterilizations on poor Latinas after they had come to the facilities to give birth to children. Two landmark lawsuits, *Madrigal v. Quilligan* and *Andrade v. Los Angeles County*, brought to public attention the coerced sterilization of Mexican women at Los Angeles County–USC Medical Center. *Andrade v. Los Angeles County* was filed in 1974 as a civil suit seeking $6,000,000 in damages for the plaintiffs. Antonia Hernández and Richard Navarette from the Model Cities Center for Law and Justice filed *Madrigal v. Quilligan* in 1975, a class-action suit that sought punitive damages, as well as a change in federal guidelines and procedures for sterilization surgery that would protect Latinas' medical rights.

These cases revealed that when the women were under the duress of labor, sedated, and sometimes confined to the table, the doctors would perform sterilization surgery. *Madrigal v. Quilligan* named eleven women in the case, but the experience of Jovita Rivera typifies how the women were sterilized at the County Hospital. Rivera was approached by a staff doctor after receiving general anesthesia for a cesarean section. He told her that she should have her "tubes tied" because her children were a burden on the government. As a monolingual Spanish speaker, Rivera could not have understood the consent forms presented to her. Instead, she signed under coercion and fear rather than informed consent. It was never made clear to her what tying of the tubes meant, and it was only some time later that she learned of the operation's irreversibility.

Three women who shared experiences similar to that of Jovita Rivera were represented in the *Andrade v. Los Angeles County* case filed by the law firm Cruz, Diaz

and Durán. Melvina Hernández was also unaware that she had been sterilized in 1972 after the birth of her last child and wore an IUD contraceptive device until 1974. She does not recall the events that took place to lead to her sterilization surgery because of the sedation and physical exhaustion of labor. Her husband, who was waiting in a nearby room, was never consulted about the procedure. The women named in both lawsuits all regret having undergone sterilization surgery, and some believed that it was only temporary. All agreed that they would like to have the option to have more children.

Some Puerto Rican women on both the island and the mainland attached very different meanings to this form of fertility control than their Mexican and Chicana counterparts. While both groups suffered from sterilization abuse, an overwhelmingly large number of Puerto Rican women chose to become sterilized. On the island sterilization was promoted by a government eager to curtail population growth and emerged as the most popular form of fertility control after the passage of the 1939 law that legalized the teaching and practice of birth control. By 1954 one-sixth of all island Puerto Rican women of childbearing age received "la operación." Even today Puerto Rican women have one of the highest documented rates of sterilization in the world. In order to understand this phenomenon, one must examine the social and historical forces that shape and constrain Puerto Rican women's fertility options.

Race, class, and gender shape the reproductive experiences of women in the United States and Puerto Rico. Puerto Rican women, while opting for sterilization surgery, make the decision to become sterilized within the limits of their options. Because Puerto Rico is a territory of the United States, both the Puerto Rican government and U.S. population controllers expressed concern about Puerto Rico's "surplus population" and continuous population growth during the 1930s. Eugenic thinking also permeated the thinking of government officials and elite families who wanted to slow the population growth of the "undesirable" classes on the island. In 1937 birth-control legislation was passed, and as many as fifty family-planning clinics opened on the island. Sterilization, or "la operación," waxed and waned until the 1950s, reflecting the economic cycles of the island and philosophical challenges from Catholic Church officials. Although birth-control clinics opened in the early part of the twentieth century, many closed because of a lack of government funds and church support. In some cases the Catholic Church publicly condemned this permanent form of fertility control, and that prompted some women to seek it out. From their earliest experiences with sterilization, women began to speak about "la operación" to neighbors, friends, and family members. In some families both mother and daughter have undergone sterilization surgery with no regrets.

Aside from its early introduction as a form of fertility control on the island, other factors led to the popularity of sterilization among Puerto Rican women. The familiarity with sterilization surgery has had the greatest impact on predisposing them to it. The term alone, "la operación," illustrates that an unspoken cultural awareness is associated with sterilization surgery. It becomes part of the social repertoire of women's cultural and colloquial terminology. While many women choose this surgery (others were coerced into having the procedure, as were the women cited earlier), the history of the procedure on the island and in urban Latino communities throughout the United States illustrates how reproductive choice can be manipulated and has different meanings for women of different social and economic backgrounds.

SOURCES: Briggs, Laura. 1998. "Discourses of 'Forced Sterilization' in Puerto Rico: The Problem with the Speaking Subaltern." *Differences*, no. 10 (Summer): 30–66; López, Iris. 1997. "Agency and Constraint: Sterilization and Reproductive Freedom among Puerto Rican Women in New York City." In *Situated Lives: Gender and Culture in Everyday Lives*, ed. Louise Lamphere, Helena Ragone, and Patricia Zavella, 157–174. New York: Routledge; Petchesky, Rosalind Pollack. 1984. " 'Reproductive Choice' in the Contemporary United States: A Social Analysis of Female Sterilization." In *And the Poor Get Children: Radical Perspectives on Population Dynamics*, ed. Karen Michaelson, 50–88. New York: Monthly Review Press; Reilly, Phillip R. 1991. *The Surgical Solution: A History of Involuntary Sterilization in the United States*. Baltimore: Johns Hopkins University Press; Shapiro, Thomas M. 1985. *Population Control Politics: Women, Sterilization, and Reproductive Choice.* Philadelphia: Temple University Press.

Virginia Espino

STREET VENDING

The growth of informal-sector participation, such as street vending, is partially attributed to recent global economic processes. The restructuring of global labor markets changed the formal employment landscape and resulted in the rise of street vending in large urban centers. Thus street vending emerged as an alternative to low-wage underemployment in factory work. The relationship between the formal and informal economic sectors that ensures production and distribution is a fluid process in much the same way that street vendors, who participate in the production and distribution of goods, are seemingly fluid agents in both economies. Hence a street vendor might work in the garment industry in the morning and sell food on the street in the afternoon. Workers who participate in the informal economy are often led into that sector to aug-

The informal sector: This Latina makes a living as a street vendor. Photograph by and courtesy of Lorena Muñoz.

ment unsatisfactory or inadequate employment conditions. Often it is the more vulnerable populations, people of color, immigrants, and women who, lacking adequate wages and benefits, find themselves in this situation.

The state plays a role in the expansion of the informal economy through legislation. Policies at the local, state, and national levels often have contradictory mandates. In some cases these may create unregulated spaces of opportunity at the local level, which can encourage a vendor's engagement within informal production and distribution of goods.

Not unlike the experience in third-world countries, there has been a dramatic increase in street vendors, many of whom are women, in urban centers of the industrialized, developed world. The reemergence of street vendors in major urban cities shows that vending is not based on remnants of former economic models of redistribution. As economists who have studied the subject point out, it thrives in the midst of modern trade systems. However, the increase in the numbers of street vendors causes concern among retail merchants in cities across the United States, and they are looking to city officials to restrict them.

For the most part, cash wages, unregulated health and safety, and long working hours characterize informal-sector employment as an economic survival strategy. Hence much of the literature on street vending in developed countries indicates a complex relationship between low-wage labor, gender, immigration, and the informal economy. The rise of the informal sector in the United States since 1972 is often linked to the increase of the urban poor. Deindustrialization restructured the nation's labor economy in a way that accounts for the shrinking of unionized blue-collar workers, high unemployment, and gender and racial division of labor, thereby creating spaces where the informal economy can expand. Gender often organizes the economic space of informality; the rise of street vending hence creates a situation where labor and child care can share the same space. A Latina vendor explains how street trading is flexible and allows her to take care of her children while she is working. The vendor elaborates that she does not have help taking care of her children because her entire family still lives in Mexico. She takes care of them after school in the street while she is selling. She finds it challenging at times because she is constantly watching them so they will not get into trouble. Yet she describes how she could not have a regular job and take care of her children at the same time.

In the late 1980s there were an estimated 2,000 to 3,000 street vendors in Los Angeles, but by the late 1990s that number had grown to 10,000. It is estimated that approximately 90 percent of the street vendors in Los Angeles are Latino/a immigrants from Mexico and Central America. However, it is unclear what percentage of the vendors are recent arrivals from Latin America, or how many have dependent children with little or no access to affordable child care.

In the late 1980s numerous studies focusing on immigrants' participation in the informal economy shed light on the rise of the informal sector. According to Saskia Sassen, the fact that immigrants increasingly participate in the informal economy "is not the result of immigrant survival strategies but of structural patterns or transformations in the larger economy. Immigrants know how to seize the 'opportunities' contained in this combination of conditions, but they cannot be said to cause the informal economy." Nevertheless, there are common misconceptions about street vendors in media and film venues that perpetuate stereotypes of "illegal" immigrants as "illegally" fueling the informal sector.

The regulation of vending is implemented differently across the globe. In most Latin American countries vending is part of daily life. Although it is highly visible in the urban landscape, vendors often suffer acts of brutality from local law enforcement. Hence vending on the streets is often tied to local policies that enforce restrictions on street vending. For example, in Mexico City the local municipality controlled the growth of street vendors by enforcing brutal restrictive codes. Los Angeles also has a history of restrictive vending codes. In 1988 a group of Mexican and Central American street vendors in Los Angeles joined forces with professional organizers and community legal services attorneys to build a movement centered on street vendors' rights. The outcome was an organization called Asociación de Vendedores Ambulantes (AVA). AVA was created to respond to police harassment and legitimize a marginalized economic strategy that affected between 5,000 and 10,000 people.

In 1989 there were 2,700 street vendor arrests in Los Angeles. The following year there were twice as many arrests. Street vendors organized a coalition with city council officials and other nonimmigrant groups that produced limited success in affecting local policies. After a ten-year struggle the city of Los Angeles created street-vending districts where sellers with special permits could conduct their microbusinesses. The only district so far to have permits is MacArthur Park, where in 1999 fifteen permits were granted to street vendors. For most street vendors, purchasing a permit involves overcoming numerous barriers, specifically a capital investment that ranges anywhere from $500 to $2,000. This investment is particularly hard for vendors whose daily profits do not exceed the minimum wage.

A typical Latina vendor describes her attitude toward obtaining a vending permit. She explains that not only is the investment more than she can afford, but the daily profits are not always steady. In addition, profits can be scarce, and there are also losses to account for when the code enforcers remove the vendors from the streets. Furthermore, local policies do not equally enforce all vending activities. In certain neighborhoods of Los Angeles street vending policies are loosely enforced, while in more affluent areas they are highly enforced.

Nevertheless, "illegal" vending areas continue to gain strength not only within the central core of Los Angeles, but also in the San Fernando Valley and South East Los Angeles County, where Latino communities are transforming the urban landscape. Street vendor activism has been present in these communities as well. Hence, in addition to AVA, there are three other organizations in Los Angeles County that have responded to harassment and police brutality: the Los Angeles Street Vendors Association (AVALA), the San Fernando Vendors Association (SFVA), and the Huntington Park Vendors Association (HPVA). These organizations not only serve as vehicles to empower street vendors by mobilizing workers against police brutality and unfair law enforcement practices, but also give street vendors a space for economic organization, such as informal credit unions. Such organizations provide vendors with a source of pride and cultural citizenship by reinforcing the concept that street vending is an honorable way of making ends meet. As a result, street-vending associations take on the daily struggle to provide better working conditions for many Latina entrepreneurs.

See also Entrepreneurs

SOURCES: Chen, Martha Alter. 2001. "Women in the Informal Sector: A Global Picture, the Global Movement." *SAIS Review* 21, no. 1:71–82; Hamilton, Nora, and Norma S. Chinchilla. 2001. *Seeking Community in a Global City: Guatemalans and Salvadorans in Los Angeles.* Philadelphia: Temple University Press; Sassen, Saskia. 1998. *Globalization and Its Discontents: Essays on the New Mobility of People and Money.* New York: New Press; Spalter-Roth, R. M. 1998. "Vending on the Streets: City Policy, Gentrification, and Patriarchy." In *Women and the Politics of Empowerment,* ed. A. Bookman and S. Morgen, 272–294. Philadelphia: Temple University Press; Weber, Clair M. 2001. "Latino Street Vendors in Los Angeles." In *Asian and Latino Immigrants in a Restructuring Economy,* ed. Marta López-Garza and David R. Diaz, 217–240. Stanford, CA: Stanford University Press.

Lorena Muñoz

STUDENT MOVEMENTS (1960s AND 1970s)

Latino student movements emerged as part of the social ferment of the 1960s and 1970s. Mexican American and Puerto Rican students demanded access to quality education, an end to discriminatory practices, and a "relevant" and inclusive curriculum. They continued a long tradition of educational activism, because earlier generations had struggled to end segregation and had advocated for bilingual education. At high schools, colleges, and universities students now used confrontational tactics, such as walkouts, sit-ins, and demonstrations. As part of a larger movement for community control of the institutions that affected the lives of Chicanas/os and Puerto Ricans, students also participated in and shaped other movements of the era.

On college campuses Mexican American students held conferences, sit-ins, and demonstrations, formed organizations, and demanded Chicano studies departments and support services for Chicana/o students. In May 1967 students met at Loyola University in Los Angeles and formed the organization United Mexican American Students (UMAS). In 1968 the first Chicano studies program was founded at California State University, Los Angeles. Growing out of a 1969 youth conference at the University of California, Santa Barbara, el Movimiento Estudiantil Chicano de Aztlán (MEChA) emphasized that students should use their educations to benefit their communities. As more Chicano studies departments and programs were established, they linked academia and local communities through the curriculum and experiential learning.

Despite their active participation from the beginning of the movement, Sonia A. López noted in 1977, "Chicanas generally continued to fill the traditional roles assigned them within the Mexican culture and the American-Anglo society." Instead of leadership positions, Chicanas provided the "invisible labor by being the cooks, secretaries, and janitors." Some Chicanas left MEChA organizations, formed their own groups, such as Hijas de Cuauhtémoc at California State University, Long Beach, and continued to work for educational reforms. Still, López concluded, "It was their direct participation in the movement that made them aware of the Chicanas' double oppression," based on race and gender.

Puerto Rican students joined forces with African American students on the campuses of the City University of New York. On April 22, 1969, an estimated 150 to 300 students took over the south campus of City College and closed it until May 5, 1969. The Black and Puerto Rican Student Community and the Committee of Ten demanded access and "relevant" education. Admissions, they insisted, should reflect the racial composition of the high schools, and special admissions programs should better meet the needs of incoming students. They wanted a separate school of black and Puerto Rican studies and a requirement that all education majors take black and Puerto Rican history and Spanish courses. In response, the college instituted the requirements for education majors, introduced open admissions several years earlier than planned, and established a Department of Urban and Ethnic Studies, which continuing activism transformed into a separate Department of Puerto Rican Studies in 1971.

Student movements affected Lehman, Queens, Brooklyn, Hunter, and Bronx Community colleges, as well as some of the state university campuses and Livingston College of Rutgers University in New Jersey. Beginning in 1969, Puerto Rican studies departments and programs were established in most of those campuses. Puerto Rican women were involved, though the historical record is scant. At City College Iris Morales, later a member of the Young Lords, cofounded Puerto Ricans in Student Activities (PRISA) in 1968, which was key to campus activism, while Esperanza Martell organized evening students. At Lehman College in 1969 women constituted the majority of the Puerto Rican campus organization, UNICA, according to Federico Aquino-Bermudez, who later chaired the department at City College. In the fall of 1969 the Puerto Rican Student Union emerged as an intercampus organization that linked the student movements in Puerto Rico and the United States. It promoted independence for Puerto Rico, opened its office in the South Bronx to confront community issues such as housing, and organized a conference at Columbia University in September 1970 that was attended by more than 1,000 Puerto Rican and Latino student activists.

A committee demanding students' rights demonstrates at Brooklyn College, 1969. Courtesy of Center for Puerto Rican and Latino Studies, Brooklyn College, CUNY.

High-school students also protested, challenging discrimination, inferior education, and limited opportunities. In March 1968 more than 10,000 Chicano students walked out of five East Los Angeles schools after the school board ignored their petitions. They demanded an end to the tracking of Mexican American students into vocational education, termination of corporal punishment, more Mexican American teachers, bilingual education, and the revision of the curriculum to include Mexican/Chicano history and culture. There were other "blowouts" or walkouts in Denver, Phoenix, San Antonio, and Crystal City, Texas, where a 1969 walkout of more than 700 students was an impetus to the founding of a third political party, La Raza Unida.

In 1969 New York City's Black and Puerto Rican Coalition, a citywide group, demanded the removal of the police from schools and questioned the use of racist textbooks. It advocated self-defense classes, holidays in honor of Martin Luther King Jr. and Malcolm X, the hiring of more black teachers, and the establishment of student-faculty councils to address discipline and the curriculum. Protests occurred at several New York City high schools. High-school students also joined City University of New York (CUNY) students when an estimated 11,000 students protested in Albany on March 18, 1969, against budget cuts for the Search for Education, Elevation, and Knowledge (SEEK) program, which increased African American and Puerto Rican enrollments at the university. Some high school students participated in the Puerto Rican Student Union.

Student movements challenged institutional racism and boldly asserted that the histories, experiences, and cultures of Mexican Americans and Puerto Ricans were important. In the process they questioned the relationship between academia and their communities, as well as the ways in which traditional disciplines could privilege certain knowledge and present biased perspectives on others. Although the height of student movements was in the 1960s and 1970s, Latina and Latino students have continued to demand access, effective services, and an inclusive, transformative curriculum.

See also Chicano Movement

SOURCES: García, Alma M., ed. 1997. *Chicana Feminist Thought: The Basic Historical Writings.* New York: Routledge; Ruiz, Vicki L. 1998. *From out of the Shadows: Mexican Women in Twentieth-Century America.* New York: Oxford University Press; Torres, Andrés, and José E. Velázquez, eds. 1998. *The Puerto Rican Movement: Voices from the Diaspora.* Philadelphia: Temple University Press.

Carmen Teresa Whalen

SUBSTITUTE AUXILIARY TEACHERS (SATs)

From the mid-1940s to the 1960s, at the height of the Puerto Rican migration to New York City, the school system was inundated with non-English-speaking children. The situation was so pervasive that it was said that the arrival of a flight from San Juan on a Sunday meant that scores of youngsters would be registered for school on Monday morning. City teachers had not faced a cohort of non-English speakers since the large European immigrations at the turn of the century. The favored approach to instruct non-English speakers in the past had been total immersion, and methodologies like bilingual education or English as a second language were not in use. Language was not the only consideration. Puerto Rican youngsters were American citizens. Those formally schooled in the island were educated under American policies, often using English-language texts, but that did not guarantee fluency in the language or ability to negotiate mainland culture.

In 1949 a committee of the Association of Assistant Superintendents identified some 13,914 school children "for whom at least a year's time is needed before they are ready for preliminary instruction and language work . . . [and] ready for complete assimilation in the regular program." In response, the Elementary Division of the New York City Board of Education appointed ten Puerto Rican teachers under a new rubric, substitute auxiliary teacher (SAT), to assist those children and act as intermediaries between the community and the schools. Some 234 individuals worked as SATs from 1949 until 1971, when the position was redesignated bilingual teacher in school and community relations.

One hundred and fifty-five Spanish-speaking teachers available for employment in elementary and secondary schools applied for jobs between 1950 and 1957. Their applications, filed at the Office of Puerto Rico, Division of Migration, offer insights into their academic backgrounds, ages, gender, marital status, English-language proficiency, experience, and length of residency in the city. Most applicants were between the ages of thirty and thirty-five. Thirty-nine applicants were male, while 116 were female. One hundred and fifty-two held university degrees. Of these, 132 earned baccalaureates, and twenty held degrees at the master's level. Eighty-eight claimed English-language fluency, and fifty-eight listed their proficiency as moderate. Twenty-nine received university degrees from U.S. institutions. One hundred and thirty-eight were licensed teachers in Puerto Rico, and three held teaching licenses from the United States. All but eleven applicants had some classroom experience.

By the early 1960s 109 individuals were employed as SATs, and the board of education issued a license examination reclassifying SATs as auxiliary teachers. Stringent requirements for the position mandated that auxiliary teachers master coursework beyond the baccalaureate in guidance, social and educational services, and the cultural background of the Spanish-speaking children they taught. Additionally, they were obliged to bridge the gap between the schools and Spanish-speaking community parents. Through personal contact and a series of after-school and evening programs, auxiliary teachers worked hard to develop rapport and reciprocity. These aspects of the job faced obstacles because parents often worked during the day and were not available to attend school-oriented activities. Nonetheless, teachers provided parents with information about health, nutrition, housing, workers' rights, and the school system. Successful in developing leadership skills, parental groups became strong advocates for social and educational reform at board meetings, political rallies, conferences, and lectures. Some of the earliest Puerto Rican community leaders emerged from this experience.

As members of a tightly knit professional community, the teachers met often to share ideas, evaluate their experiences, and promote their commitment to legitimize bilingual education. They identified themselves as pioneers in unknown territory. SATs, and later auxiliary teachers, generated curriculum, created instructional materials, and wrote books to augment content material. Pamphlets, booklets, and articles on the history and geography of Puerto Rico complemented filmstrips like *Puerto Rico Today*, *Children of Puerto Rico*, and *The Bilingual Teacher in School and Community Relations*, and their accompanying teacher guides, which informed classroom instruction, also documented the progress made by the auxiliary teachers in the new field. They joined study groups, attended professional retreats, created innovative learning activities, and eventually formed a professional association, the Society of Puerto Rican Auxiliary Teachers (SPRAT).

A gathering of substitute auxiliary teachers, circa 1968. Courtesy of Virginia Sánchez Korrol.

SPRAT organized academic conferences to disseminate new scholarship. The group assessed the status of the profession and lobbied for recognition and permanent licensure. Until then the license for auxiliary teachers was temporary and was subject to periodic renewal. SPRAT argued for visibility and institutionalization of the position. In time SPRAT members helped create the Puerto Rican Educators Association and the Hispanic chapter of the United Federation of Teachers.

Among the SATs and auxiliary teachers, many rose to prominence in the field of education. Nilda Maldonado Koenig became director of substitute auxiliary teachers and non-English coordinator at the New York City Board of Education. María E. Sánchez became a supervisor in District 14. After becoming a licensed principal, she accepted a position at Brooklyn College to develop the bilingual education program at the graduate and undergraduate levels. She ultimately became chairperson of the Department of Puerto Rican Studies. Dolores Nazario worked with the Department of Welfare before becoming an SAT. She became supervisor and director of bilingual programs for District 4. Carmen Rodríguez and Laura Maldonado became district superintendents, and María Power and Pura Bonilla became principals in the school system. In the early 1970s the adoption of the professional license for the bilingual teacher in school and community affairs in New York City marked the culmination of a twenty-year campaign led initially by Puerto Rican SATs, community supporters, and other educators.

See also Bilingual Education

SOURCES: Sánchez Korrol, Virginia. 1996. "Towards Bilingual Education: Puerto Rican Women Educators in New York City Schools, 1947–1967." In *Puerto Rican Women and Work: Bridges in Transnational Labor,* ed. Altagracia Ortiz. Philadelphia: Temple University Press; Santiago Santiago, Isaura. 1978. *A Community's Struggle for Equal Education Opportunity: ASPIRA vs. the Board of Education.* Princeton, NJ: Office for Minority Education, Educational Testing Service.

Virginia Sánchez Korrol

SWILLING, TRINIDAD ESCALANTE (1847–1925)

Pioneer woman Trinidad Escalante Swilling was born in Hermosillo, Sonora, in 1847 to Ignatius and Petra Escalante, natives of Cádiz, Spain, and may have been the first woman to live in the early settlement of Phoenix. After her father's death the thirteen-year-old Trinidad traveled north with her mother to the small town of Tucson. At this time Anglo-American men were beginning to settle and intermingle in the long-established Mexican settlements in present-day southern Arizona. Since very few Anglo-American women lived on this western frontier (the census recorded only forty-four in the Arizona area in 1860), men often took Mexican or American Indian women as wives. One such individual was Jack Swilling of Missouri, a former Confederate soldier, who met Trinidad in Tucson. She married Jack at the age of seventeen, in 1864. An ambitious man of questionable integrity, Swilling pursued mining claims in the central and northern Arizona area. After their marriage they moved to the Prescott area, where Jack Swilling worked a mining claim with the well-known Arizona mountain man Pauline Weaver.

Moving once again to Wickenburg, Swilling obtained financial support to organize the Swilling Irrigating and Canal Company, a group that dug the first modern canal system in the Phoenix area, and established the town site of Phoenix, earning him the name the Father of Phoenix. His wife Trinidad moved to her new Phoenix homestead, called Dos Casas, in 1868, in time to witness the celebration when the men turned the first water from the Salt River into the town's main canal, the Swilling Ditch. Trinidad's home served both a private and public purpose. Early Phoenix residents held the first town election in her home, as well as masses for local Catholics, who were primarily from the Mexican American community. Father André Eschallier of Florence held services in the homes of Trinidad and the Otero family until a church was built in 1881.

Several accounts name Trinidad Swilling as the first woman to live in the Phoenix settlement. A few months after her arrival several other Anglo-American women moved with their husbands to the small farming community located north of the Salt River. Trinidad raised seven children, two of whom died early in childhood, and cared for two Apache children as well. After Jack Swilling's death in 1878 in the Yuma territorial prison, Trinidad worked as a seamstress to support herself and her children. With this money and income obtained through her ownership of Jack's ranch in Wickenburg, she was able to build a new house in Phoenix. At the age of thirty-three Trinidad married a German immigrant named Henry Schumaker, who operated a local bar. She stopped working and raised three more sons. Nine years later, in 1896, her second husband also died. Trinidad again resumed seamstress work.

She died in Phoenix in 1925 and was survived by one son, two daughters, and six grandchildren. Little is known about her life in general, but an *Arizona Republic* article published at her death called her "one of the best known pioneer figures of the Salt River Valley." She understood the significance of history and, before her death, donated to the present-day Phoenix Museum of History her mother's rosary, prayer book, and shawl, as well as a rifle owned by Jack Swilling. One of her daughters, Georgia, became a well-known "lady doctor" in Wickenburg, providing informal health care and midwife services to many residents in the late 1800s and early 1900s.

SOURCES: *Arizona Republic* 1925. "Pioneer Woman of Early Period Dies Following Illness." December 28; Shoemaker, Trinidad. 1923. "Statement of Mrs. Trinidad Shoemaker (Formerly Mrs. Jack Swilling)." Oral History transcript. March 2. Salt River Project History Services, Salt River Project Offices, Phoenix, Arizona.

Jean Reynolds

TABAQUEROS' UNIONS (1880s–1950s)

Cuban and Puerto Rican women cigar workers in the United States had one great advantage over women in most other occupations: they were highly unionized. Beginning in the 1880s and 1890s, the *tabaqueros'* (tobacco workers') unions accepted women as full members. The largest U.S.-based organization, the Cigar Makers' International Union (CMIU), initially denied women membership and then offered them a form of second-class membership. A craft union, the CMIU focused primarily on recruiting skilled white men. The *tabaqueros'* unions, however, functioned on anarcho-syndicalist principles. La Federación Libre de Trabajadores (FLT) in Puerto Rico and la Federación Cubana de Tabaqueros in southern Florida and New York City accepted workers regardless of race, sex, or skill, including women and Afro-Caribbeans.

The *tabaqueros'* unions organized workers in the different sectors of cigar production into separate *gremios*, or locals. Given the sexual division of labor in the industry, women tobacco stemmers and cigar banders generally established and worked within single-sex locals. Some women were elected to serve as officers of these *gremios* or as delegates to unionwide gatherings; all members voted on whether to go on strike and when to accept a settlement; and woman played significant roles in specific strikes. During an industry-wide strike in Ybor City, Florida, in 1901, for instance, Altagracia Martínez and Luisa Herrera, officers of the stemmers' local, led a mass march on the mayor's office to protest vigilante violence and vagrancy arrests that targeted their male co-workers. In addition, women's presence led *tabaqueros'* unions to view advances in women's rights as an important component of workers' struggles. They recognized that improvements in working women's educational, legal, and political rights would improve the status of cigar workers in general. Thus at its 1908 annual convention the FLT became the first organization in Puerto Rico to demand voting rights for women.

Although cigar making was difficult work, and many Cuban and Puerto Rican women labored at low wages in hot, humid, and dirty conditions, they did have higher and steadier wages and more opportunities for occupational advancement and collective action than did most Latinas employed in the United States in this period. They benefited from three developments that sustained the radical character of the *tabaqueros'* unions. First, the tradition of hiring *el lector*, a reader, to educate and entertain workers at the rolling benches was introduced in Caribbean factories in the mid-nineteenth century and was sustained in the United States until the early 1930s. Second, the embrace of anarcho-syndicalist or socialist principles by late-nineteenth-century union organizers in Spain, Puerto Rico, and Cuba assured that women would not be excluded from participation. Third, the battle for independence from Spanish rule in Cuba and Puerto Rico in this same period opened spaces for women's political mobilization and necessitated their employment in the exile communities that formed in the United States.

Employers were convinced that readers fueled labor agitation, but they were unable to eliminate the practice in places where highly organized Cubans and Puerto Ricans held a monopoly on cigar-making skills. Readers were paid by the workers and kept them apprised of political struggles throughout the Spanish-speaking world, introduced them to anarcho-syndicalist and socialist texts by a range of European and American writers, and enlivened their afternoons with serial readings of popular, often socialist realist, novels. Women who worked bunching tobacco leaves or rolling cigars listened to the reader alongside men.

Only in Puerto Rico, however, were women hired as readers. One FLT organizer, Luisa Capetillo, carried this tradition to Ybor City, Florida, in 1913–1914, where she became the first woman chosen as a reader by local workers. She regularly advocated women's, as well as workers', rights, and her presence sparked women's militancy. Yet even before Capetillo's arrival women in southern Florida's *tabaqueros'* unions considered themselves part of an international struggle for justice. During an industry-wide strike in Ybor City and West Tampa in 1910, for instance, Cuban and Italian women in Key West sent a manifesto to their striking sisters, calling on them to sustain the legacies of French martyr Joan of Arc, French Communard Louise Michel, and Spanish anarcho-syndicalists Teresa Claramunt, Belén Sarraga, and Soledad Gustavo.

Still, despite all the ways in which the *tabaqueros'* unions supported women's political mobilization and women's rights, they rarely accorded the two sexes truly equal status. During Ybor City's 1901 strike, for instance, union spokesmen declared themselves "the voice of virile labor," and women like Luisa Herrera only gained leadership positions after a significant number of male leaders had been deported or arrested. Similarly, in Puerto Rico, although the FLT demanded rights for women and women participated enthusiastically in strikes, marches, and protests, Luisa Capetillo was for a long time the only woman allowed into the top ranks of union leadership.

By the early 1900s, however, women stemmers began to recognize the power that inhered in their control of the first step in the cigar-making process. Several times they threatened to stop production unless their concerns were addressed. In addition, representatives of the CMIU, who tried repeatedly to organize Latin workers in southern Florida in the early 1900s, were forced to accept women (and Afro-Cubans) as full members of the union if they were to have any hope of success. Women also increased their leverage in the union as more and more entered the ranks of cigar rollers during the 1910s and 1920s. In the 1930s and 1940s they became the mainstay of cigar production and cigar workers' organizations as automation transformed the industry.

Machines infiltrated the industry only slowly in Cuba, Puerto Rico, and southern Florida because of the power of *tabaqueros'* unions. Even in early-twentieth-century Tampa and Key West, where employers refused to grant union recognition, workers' organizations were strong enough to delay installation of machines. When the combined forces of the Great Depression and the growing cigarette industry finally crushed union resistance, it was mainly Cuban, Puerto Rican, and Italian women who made the transition to machine work. By the 1950s women formed the majority of the workforce in factories that employed Spanish-speaking workers, and they slowly expanded their power in the unions as well. For example, second-generation immigrant Maria Pescador of Ybor City served as a vice president of the CMIU in the 1940s. In 1974, believing that only consolidation of the various cigar locals into one organization could sustain their power, Pescador formed and was elected president of Local 533, which affiliated with the Retail, Wholesale, and Department Store Employees Union. The new consolidated cigar union finally negotiated pension rights for cigar workers, assuring that many of the Cuban and Italian women who had made the difficult transition from hand work to machine work in southern Florida would be rewarded for their long years of service. Thus, despite the decline of the cigar industry in the United States, Puerto Rican and Cuban women sustained their commitment to collective action and workers' organization.

See also Cigar Workers; Labor Unions

SOURCES: Azize, Yamila. 1985. *La mujer en la lucha*. Río Piedras, Puerto Rico: Editorial Cultural; Hewitt, Nancy A. 1990. " 'The Voice of Virile Labor': Labor Militancy, Community Solidarity, and Gender Identity among Tampa's Latin Workers, 1880–1921." In *Work Engendered: Toward a New History of American Labor*, ed. Ava Baron. Ithaca, NY: Cornell University Press; Rodríguez Castro, María E. 1991. "Oir leer: Tabaco y cultura en Cuba y Puerto Rico." *Caribbean Studies* 24, nos. 2. 3–4: 221–239.

Nancy A. Hewitt

TALAMANTE, OLGA (1949–)

Olga Talamante was a political prisoner in Argentina from November 10, 1974, to March 1976. She was charged with subversive activities and weapons possession, and the police inflicted physical and mental torture to force her to admit guilt, without success. In the United States her parents, friends, and other activists started a movement that quickly reached national proportions, touching many levels of government, and spread abroad, which ultimately led to her release.

Talamante was born on December 3, 1949, in Mexicali, Baja California. Her parents raised four children, and Talamante was the only daughter. The family migrated to the United States when she was twelve years of age to join other farmworkers picking fruits and vegetables in the fields around Gilroy, California, where the family eventually settled.

Despite linguistic and cultural differences, Talamante excelled in school. At the end of her senior year she received the Outstanding Student Award. After high school she was one of a few Mexican students who went to college. As a high-school student, she was selected, along with other leaders, to address the local school board to demand an increase in the numbers of Chicana/o students placed in college preparatory courses, and a culturally relevant curriculum. Through a local priest she learned of the broad social injustices at home and Latin America, the plight of the farmworkers, the organizing efforts of the United Farm Workers (UFW), and the political and social issues affecting Mexico and Latin America.

In 1969 Talamante enrolled at the University of California, Santa Cruz (UCSC), majoring in Latin American studies. At UCSC she was active with el Movimiento

Estudiantil Chicano de Aztlán (MEChA), the UFW, and a migrant children's breakfast program. Talamante joined in pickets of stores, boycotts, distribution of leaflets, and marches. In 1971 Talamante traveled to Chiapas, Mexico, to study the effects of the government's grain reform program on the indigenous people. She described this event as a time when her "class awareness became more defined." In Mexico City she met an Argentine couple traveling through North and South America documenting political struggles. The three planned to travel to El Salvador, Costa Rica, Nicaragua, and Argentina to continue the documentation. However, in Nicaragua, the trio was deported for collecting information on the Sandinista movement. Talamante returned to UCSC to finish her studies and planned to join her friends in Argentina after graduation.

In 1973 Talamante arrived in Argentina with the desire of enrolling in graduate school, but the political climate forced her to abandon the plan, and instead she became embroiled in the social and political unrest of the time. Argentina held its first democratic election after eighteen years of military rule in 1973. Juan Perón was reelected president, and the Peronist party was reestablished. Talamante joined some friends who were active members of the Peronist Youth, a branch of the Peronist party, to work in a government project to organize health centers in the barrios. However, Argentina's social and economic fabric was shaken and in turmoil because of exorbitant inflation and worker unrest after Peron's death in July 1974. Armed resistance from the political right and left led his successor to declare a state of siege and suspend civil liberties. On November 10, 1974, Talamante and twelve friends were arrested for violating the National Security Act.

Talamante was detained in a prison in Azul, Argentina, and was tortured for four days with electrical prods, beaten, and psychologically abused. She later wrote, "Aside from the physical pain inflicted, one has to suffer the sadistic, denigrating repertory of those men." The physical and mental torture deepened Talamante's political commitments.

In the United States her working-class parents and friends learned of her detention and immediately created the Olga Talamante Defense Committee (OTDC). Talamante's mother, affectionately referred to as Doña Cuca, brought together the various integral workings of the committee. The defense committee began as a local campaign and quickly grew to a national level of substantial scope in human power, financial resources, and political support. The OTDC used the national media to alert the public about Talamante's arrest and the injustice. The committee organized vigils, held fund-raisers, and sent members throughout the nation to disseminate news about her imprisonment. Some members were sent to meet with ranking officials in the U.S. State Department, U.S. embassy bureaucrats in Argentina, and U.S. congressional leaders. Local and national government officials joined in to demand that the U.S. government pressure Argentina to release Talamante. For sixteen grueling months the members worked relentlessly to keep a national focus on Talamante's detention and to seek support at all government levels.

Upon her return to the United States Talamante continued to be involved in social and political causes important to her. Her arrest and the national movements that followed later brought attention to the abuse and torture inflicted by the Argentine government's "Dirty War." She joined with the American Friends Service Committee to campaign for the release of her Argentine friends who remained imprisoned and to educate the American public on the violations of human rights. In San Francisco Talamante became involved with a neighborhood health center, Head Start, the American Friends Service Committee, and continued to advocate for higher education for underrepresented youth. Olga Talamante remains one of the most recognized Latina leaders in California. Still living in the Bay Area, she serves as Executive Director of the Chicana Latina Foundation, an organization dedicated to advancing educational and professional opportunities for young women. Through workshops, conferences, scholarships, and mentoring, the Chicana Latina Foundation seeks to empower women as individuals and as a members of Latino communities. She has received a number of awards including "Heroes and Heroines of the Latino Community" awarded by KQED-TV, the San Francisco-based PBS affiliate.

SOURCES: Chicana Latina Foundation Web site. "Board of Directors: Olga Talamante." www.chicanalatina.org/directors.html#talamante (accessed July 24, 2005); Cortez, Alicia M. 1999. "The Struggle of the *Mujeres* to Liberate Olga Talamante, a Political Prisoner." M.A. thesis, San Jose State University; Del Olmo, Frank. 1975. "Christmas in an Argentine Prison." *Los Angeles Times*, December 25, sec. 1, pp. 3, 34, 36; *NACLA's Latin American and Empire Report.* 1975. "Free Olga Talamante." 9, no. 6 (September): 30.

Alicia M. Cortez

TARANGO, YOLANDA (1948–)

Yolanda Tarango was born in Texas in 1948. Her ancestors, Hispano refugees from the 1680 Pueblo Revolt, helped settle Ysleta near El Paso in 1682. Alongside the Tewa people, many refugee families remained in the area for generations. Tarango represents a fifth generation of Tejanos in this community.

Since "her first choice to become a priest was impossible," Tarango joined the Sisters of Charity of the

Incarnate Word in 1966. She credits her involvement in the church to her grandmother, who taught her that "loving God is loving and forgiving others, pure and simple. . . . She left me with an image of God as grandmother, with open arms, ready to draw me into her embrace."

Sister Tarango resides in San Antonio, where she directs the Visitation House of Ministries, a transitional housing program for homeless women and children that she cofounded in 1985. As a doctoral candidate in ministry at Austin Presbyterian Theological Seminary, Tarango also teaches religious studies at the University of the Incarnate Word. She completed a six-year term as general councilor of her international religious order, the first Latina to fill that position. She also served as national coordinator of Las Hermanas, a national organization of Latina Roman Catholics, for three consecutive terms (1985–1991).

Sister Tarango, the first twentieth-century published Chicana theologian, writes extensively on the spirituality of Latina Catholics. Her book *Hispanic Women: Prophetic Voice in the Church* (1988), coauthored with theologian Ada María Isasi-Díaz, made a significant contribution to an emerging Latina theological discourse. They were the first to synthesize the religious understandings of grassroots Latinas after several small-group retreats organized by Las Hermanas. Their work in articulating Latina experiences of the sacred has far-reaching implications. As feminist theologians, they emphasize "doing theology" as a liberating practice versus solely an intellectual exercise. For Tarango and Isasi-Díaz, the goal of a Latina feminist theology is to maintain Latino/a cultural values, but with a commitment to struggle against sexism in all its manifestations and to reach "not equality but liberation . . . [from] socio-political-economic oppression."

Tarango has since authored several articles on Latina feminist spirituality and coedited two books on Hispanic pastoral care. Her naming of Latina spirituality as "transformative struggle" offers important insights into Latinas' daily struggle to survive and prosper spiritually, culturally, and economically. For Tarango, relating to the struggle in a transformative way rather than in a passive mode or with a victim mentality is fundamental to Latina liberation. She states, "Hispanic women do not envision themselves apart from the struggle. . . . *La vida es la lucha,* implies the struggle we must embrace and learn to love in order to survive in the present and envision life with dignity in the future."

Tarango views her religious vocation as "the best tool to force changes in the structure of the Catholic Church, which . . . 'espouses white male superiority.' " Despite discrimination, her sustained commitment as a sister has led to a lifetime of activism focusing on women's issues. Her many years of experience in Latino pastoral ministry, her leadership skills, and her service on numerous advisory boards for health care systems have earned her several awards, including the Estrella Award from the Mexican American Business and Professional Women Association in 1998 and an honorary doctorate of humane letters from the University of the Incarnate Word in 1996.

See also Mujerista Theology; Nuns, Contemporary

SOURCES: Davis, Kenneth G., and Yolanda Tarango, eds. 2000. *Bridging Boundaries: The Pastoral Care of U.S. Hispanics.* Scranton, PA: University of Scranton Press; Deck, Allan Figueroa, Yolanda Tarango, and Timothy Matovina, eds. 1995. *Perspectivas: Hispanic Ministry.* Kansas City, MO: Sheed and Ward; Isasi-Díaz, Ada María, and Yolanda Tarango. 1998. *Hispanic Women: Prophetic Voice in the Church.* San Francisco: Harper and Row; Keller, Rosemary Skinner, and Rosemary Radford Ruether, eds. 1995. *In Our Own Voices: Four Centuries of American Women's Religious Writing.* San Francisco: Harper.

Lara Medina

TELENOVELAS

Telenovelas, Spanish-language television serials, are a defining feature of U.S. Latino life even though few are U.S. produced. More than 80 percent of U.S. Spanish television network broadcasting consists of telenovelas and related productions: tabloid news, game, and gossip-variety shows. In the United States they connect Hispanics of all social classes and nationalities as they adopt or maintain a Latino identity. Despite the modest amount of U.S.-produced Spanish-language programs, telenovelas figure prominently among the most popular television content. Many telenovela celebrities are well-known singers and performers, and these productions combine the Spanish-language music, television, and film industries.

Telenovelas are essentially formatted along the lines of old American daytime radio serials. This is not to say that U.S. commercial broadcasters invented serial fiction aimed at women but rather that they converted its narrative devices into an advertising system. As role models, the characters on these shows advertise the products that they use on stage and the lifestyle implied in their consumption. By the same token, the intermission frames advertisements that are often directly or indirectly connected to the story.

When multinational corporations such as Procter and Gamble, Lever Brothers, and Colgate-Palmolive exported this radio format to Latin America and Spain, they gradually infused indigenous narrative traditions into the telenovelas that today are a formidable parallel to American television soap operas. Unlike their U.S. counterparts, telenovelas normally end their stories after twelve weeks and feature a protagonist couple that presides over the community of characters. Although the story lines in these shows come to an end, the programs maintain continuity through fixed time slots and by typecasting actors bound through the studio-system type of contracts. The stories may change, but the format, schedule, and cast continue, by virtue of which the old shows attract viewers to new ones.

Telenovelas are U.S. television's greatest rival in the international market, primarily because these serial dramas are often closer to the popular dramas of most countries. With traditional values, predictable plots, and melodrama, telenovelas tend to be less foreign than most U.S. television shows in countries throughout Western Europe, the Middle East, and the Far East. The international expansion of the telenovela market during the late 1980s inspired several countries to develop their own versions of the format, sometimes as the catapult to launch a national television industry, as in the case of India. Today telenovelas and similar serial dramas that have emerged worldwide sell social development values with the same calculated efficacy with which they have purveyed detergent and lifestyles.

Latinas constitute one of the most interesting and important audiences in television history because of the circumstances in which they watch telenovelas. Telenovelas emerged from a format primarily aimed at women, for whom they retain their gendered nature, regardless of the diverse audience to which they now appeal. Second, powerful U.S. Hispanic media of international impact weaken the melting-pot type of assimilation that in the past vanquished immigrant media in the United States, especially as demographics and market forces brew vested interests in strengthening a distinct Hispanic culture. Hispanics or Latinos are the largest minority in the United States and represent a $600-billion consumer market. As voters, they may determine the fate of presidential elections. Third, telenovelas affect a new kind of acculturation and Latino identity based on maintaining strong connections with the countries of origin. Although acculturation has always been the function of immigrant media in the United States, Latino assimilation does not lead to cultural dissolution but rather to cultural affirmation.

Telenovelas are intrinsically didactic. Although they may not incorporate educational intentions, they always have educational effects that are cumulative and often liberating. Depending on the context of reception, a viewer may read a story against the grain. For example, a Latina in the United States may not identify with the traditional female behavior that a telenovela sanctions as a role model, but instead view it as a negative image inherent in the culture of her country of origin that she was fortunate to escape. On the other

hand, telenovelas are—within their predictable simplicity—complex and elastic stories that promote social change. In fact, Mexico's Televisa and Brazil's Globo devised widely used systems to educate audiences in matters of reproductive health, addiction prevention and treatment, AIDS education, eating disorders and breast cancer prevention, domestic violence, racism, and homophobia.

Much has been written about the impact of Globo's "marketing social" and Televisa's "entertainment-education" formulas on their countries of origin, as well as in those regions where they have been implemented. Though networks create programs with target audiences in mind, these shows do not lose their informative value in foreign markets. Stories call attention to social agendas that, while novel in their countries of origin, are often highly visible public policy issues in the United States. To immigrate means, more often than not, a search for progress, education, and freedom. By underscoring social progress, telenovelas fuel the aims for which Latinas come to the United States. At the same time telenovelas reinforce a cultural distinction that the host country permits and fosters.

SOURCES: Allen, Robert C. 1992. *Channels of Discourse, Reassembled: Television and Contemporary Criticism.* Chapel Hill: University of North Carolina Press; Fadul, Anamaría, ed. 1993. *Serial Fiction in TV: The Latin American Telenovelas.* São Paulo: Universidade de São Paulo, Escola de Comunicação e Artes; López-Pumarejo, Tomás. 1995. "The Stripper and the Chief of State: On Soap Operas, and the Presidency of Fernando Collor de Mello." In *The Destiny of Narrative at the End of the Millennium,* ed. Vicente Sánchez-Biosca and Rafael R. Tranche, 184–197 and 345–353 [original in English]. Valencia: Archivos de la Filmoteca; _____. 1997. *Aproximación a la telenovela.* Madrid: Cátedra; _____. 1999. "La naturaleza educativa de los seriales: Los soaps y las telenovelas" (The Educational Nature of Serial Drama: Telenovelas and Soaps). *Archivos de la Filmoteca* 31 (February): 8–31; Mazziotti, Nora. 1996. *La industria de la telenovela: La producción de ficción en América Latina.* Buenos Aires: Paidós; Quinones, Sam. 1997. "Hooked on Telenovelas." *Hemispheres* (United Airlines), November, Show Business sec., 27–29; Sherry, John L. 1997. "Prosocial Soap Operas for Development: A Review of Research and Theory." *Journal of International Communication* 4, no. 2 (December): 75–101.

Tomás López-Pumarejo

TELEVISION

If the Latino presence in television has been small, the presence of Latinas in the medium has been even smaller. From its inception television has been at the forefront of image making. Like other forms of communication, television reflects the dominant ideology of the birthplace of the industry, the United States. The medium tends to portray an idealized image of the nation: an upper-middle-class white world where, more often than not, families, businesses, and institutions are headed by white, English-speaking males. Television has ignored essential components of the social and economic makeup of the United States, virtually dismissing the racial, class, and ethnic diversity brought about by the great immigration movements in the history of this country. Furthermore, the absence of Latinos and Latinas in television creates a void in images that reflect the diversity of experiences within Latino communities themselves. Viewers are thus deprived of the elements that are essential in forging a realistic image of the U.S. Latino experience. As a result, stereotypical portrayals of Latinos in general and Latinas in particular tend to dominate.

When Latinas are portrayed, most roles position them as loose, hot-tempered women, suffering mothers, virginal girlfriends, or victims of male dominance. These images persist even though, ironically, women are generally the primary targets of the advertising that fuels the television industry. Soap operas, for example, are so named because the genre was targeted at housewives and paid for by the soap-product industry. The struggles of millions of Latinos/as, foreign born and native, are seldom represented, much less the essential role they have played in constructing the U.S. economy. In the case of Latinas, their role in the industrial and rural workforce has not been acknowledged. The experiences of women in the garment sweatshops

of Los Angeles and New York, fruit pickers in Oregon and Florida, domestic workers across the country, and second- and third-generation educated Latinas who have been steadily joining the ranks of professionals and the middle class have been overlooked by the mass media.

During the first decades of television programming African Americans, Asians, Latinos, and other people of color were practically nonexistent. Interestingly, however, one of the most noteworthy exceptions came during the early years (1949–1953) when television programs promoted a certain ethnic diversity. Because television programming originated by transplanting some of the most popular radio shows, many had ethnic story lines. Among these crossover series were *The Goldbergs*, which followed the life of a Jewish immigrant family, *I Remember Mama*, about a Norwegian family in San Francisco, and later the all-black *Amos and Andy* and *Beulah*, which starred a black maid to a white middle-class family. Interestingly, in the original radio version of *Amos and Andy* the voices of the black characters came from white actors. But by 1953 these shows were off the air, and, with the exception of the short-lived *Bernie Loves Bridget* in the early 1970s, it would take several decades for such diversity to be seen again on television.

One show that portrayed Latinos during the early years, *The Cisco Kid* (1950–1955), was modeled after the successful western film of the same name set in

The whole family watches Spanish-language programs on television. Courtesy of the Offices of the Government of Puerto Rico in the United States. Centro Archives, Centro de Estudios Puertorriqueños, Hunter College, CUNY.

Spanish California. The series included Latino Leo Carrillo as the sidekick to the protagonist, Duncan Renaldo. The two battled the bad guys, often other Latinos. Even though Latino actors played the leads, there were few Latina characters, and these were often played by non-Latina actresses. *The Cisco Kid* set the stage for the high-profile television series *El Zorro,* which portrayed Latino characters and was also set in Spanish California. As el Zorro, Guy Williams, a non-Latino actor, played the protagonist Don Diego.

In 1951 the blockbuster *I Love Lucy* (1951–1957) came on the air. It starred Desi Arnaz as bandleader Ricky Ricardo, who immigrated to the United States and was Lucy's Cuban husband. Arnaz was Lucille Ball's husband in real life when the network approached her to do the show. After producers turned down her request that her husband costar in the series, Ball and Arnaz decided to form their own company, Desilu Productions. Innovators in television production, Arnaz and Desilu pioneered the three-camera technique for situation comedy that is still in use today. He also oversaw the development of such shows as *The Untouchables* (1959–1963), *Star Trek* (1966–1969), and *Lou Grant* (1977–1982). But while Arnaz played an important role both as an actor and a producer, this did not open the doors to the medium for Latinos in general, much less for Latinas.

As a result of the protest movement against the Vietnam War, the civil rights and the feminist movements, and the Puerto Rican and Chicano mobilizations for social justice in the late 1960s and early 1970s, ethnic diversity became more visible on television. Argentine-born Linda Crystal was among the first to play a lead Latina character in a television series, Victoria Cannon, the strong-willed wife of rancher John Cannon, in the western *High Chaparral* (1967–1971). She received two Emmy Award nominations as Best Actress in a Drama Series for the role. Strong and dignified, the character was nonetheless confined to the role of a traditional wife. The character, Victoria, came from a wealthy Mexican family, and her sophisticated manners were often contrasted to the rougher manners of her white husband. Another strong-willed and dignified Latina character of that period was played by Elena Verdugo in the role of Nurse Consuelo López in *Marcus Welby, M.D.* (1969–1976). Verdugo was born in Los Angeles, a fifth-generation Californian of Spanish ancestry.

In the early 1970s there were also several sitcoms with African American leads, such as *The Jeffersons* and *Sanford and Son,* both spin-offs of *All in the Family.* However, nothing similar happened to Latinos, and no network series was built around a Latino family. During this period Latina characters appeared sporadically in popular programs, and their presence in some cases served as a stimulus for discussion of racial prejudice. An episode of *All in the Family* (1971–1983), for example, dealt with a Puerto Rican family moving into Archie Bunker's neighborhood. *Barney Miller* (1975–1982), considered one of the most multicultural shows of the time, included a Puerto Rican detective, Chano, and even a Latina detective. These characters at least served to offset the portrayal of Hispanics as the criminals often arrested by the detectives. *Chico and the Man* (1974–1978) was the first series set in a Mexican American neighborhood and told the story of a white garage owner and his Mexican American employee. The series was much criticized, however, because there were no Chicanos in the cast. Chico was played by Freddie Prinze, a Puerto Rican. Although some Chicano actors were added to the cast, no Latinas were featured prominently on the show, other than veteran character actress Alma Beltrán, who played Prinze's aunt.

In the 1980s Latinos and Latinas gained no new ground. In fact, during that period the general depoliticization of television programming led to fewer shows that dealt with racial or other social themes, and most Latinos were portrayed as criminal elements in the growing genre of police shows such as *Hill Street Blues* (1981–1987), and *Cagney and Lacey.* More often than not, Latinas were portrayed as prostitutes, drug dealer groupies, drug addicts, and petty criminals or the suffering wives or mothers of criminals. Although *Miami Vice* (1984–1989) included several Latino characters that were on the "right side of the law," such as Edward James Olmos, who played Detective Lt. Martin Castillo, and Saundra Santiago as Detective Gina Navarro, Latinos mainly played drug lords or petty criminals.

Other shows such as *The Cosby Show* (1984–1992), about a middle-class black family, occasionally included Latino characters portraying positive roles. Brazilian actress Sonia Braga, for example, was featured as a Latina doctor on one of its episodes. Evelina Fernández had a small role in the first season of *Roseanne* (1988–1997). The sitcom *I Married Dora* (1987–1988) featured Latina Elizabeth Peña in the role of a housekeeper for widower Peter Farrel and his family. When faced with deportation, a Salvadoran, Dora, marries Farrel in order to get her papers. This series stands out as one of the few to deal with a real problem facing hundreds of thousands of Latinos who came to the United States from Central America during that period. A year later the series *Trial and Error* (1988), based on Latino characters from East Los Angeles, came on the air. Both of these dramas had a short life.

A small number of Latinas have portrayed non-Latina characters. Elena Verdugo starred as the all-American Millie in the hit CBS series *Meet Millie* (1952–

1956); Lynda Carter played the lead in *Wonder Woman* (1976–1979). Ruth Britt played a native island girl on *Operation Petticoat* (1977–1979), and Catherine Bach costarred as Daisy in the comedy *The Dukes of Hazard* (1979–1985). Victoria Principal played Pamela Ewing in *Dallas* (1978–1991). A handful of other Latinas were also featured in daytime television. Argentina Brunette had a part in the long-running soap opera *General Hospital* (1963–), and Gina Gallegos, Karin Marcelo, and Carmen Zapata were in *Santa Barbara* (1984–1993).

One of the outstanding Latina actresses to make her mark in the entertainment industry is Rita Moreno. Born in Puerto Rico in 1931, she worked regularly on television throughout her productive career, which also included radio, film, and Broadway. In television she earned an Emmy Award for her portrayal of a Polish hooker on an episode of *The Rockford Files*. She also starred in the short-lived series *The Rita Moreno Show* (1976) about an aspiring actress, Googie Gómez, a role written especially for her, based on a character she portrayed in the Broadway production *The Ritz*. After winning an Oscar in 1961, Moreno chose her roles carefully, avoiding those that portrayed Latinas stereotypically. This may have contributed to her unemployment for about seven years of her career. For two seasons she starred as Violet on *9 to 5* (1982–1983) and as Burt Reynolds's estranged wife on *B. L. Stryker* (1989–1990). Moreno also appeared on the HBO series *Oz* (1997–2002) where she played nun and counselor Sister Peter Marie.

Among the few Latina leads in television series are Lauren Vélez in *New York Undercover* (1994), Moreno in *Oz* (1997), and Jessica Alba, who starred in Fox's *Dark Angel* (2001). However, most Latinas are relegated to guest or limited appearances. Alma Martínez played a police sergeant in the syndicated series *Adam 12* (1989–1990). Patricia Martínez guest-starred twice on *Magnum P.I.* (1980–1988), and Belita Moreno appeared in *Roseanne* and *Melrose Place* (1992–1999). Jacqueline Obradors guest-starred in an episode of *Parker Lewis Can't Lose* (1990–1993) and *Vanishing Son* (1995). Lupe Ontiveros had a recurring role on *Veronica's Closet* (1997–2000), and Dyana Ortelli played in the short-lived syndicated series *Marblehead Manor* (1987–1988). Victoria Racimo, Maria Richwine, and Chita Rivera also had limited appearances of this kind.

A few Latinas stand out for their work behind the cameras. Nancy de los Santos was associate producer and later producer of *Siskel and Ebert at the Movies*, a syndicated television show. Graciela Mazón and Laura J. Medina have worked on features and documentaries, as have Daisy Fuentes, Rosie Pérez, Nelly Galán, and María Pérez Brown.

In the summer of 1999 civil rights organizations denounced the lack of black, Latino, and Asian charac-

ters in projected programming. None of the thirty-four new series for the fall of 2000 had any Latino performers in lead roles. That summer, however, the cable network Showtime began airing *Resurrection Blvd.* (2000), a drama series with a Latino cast created by a Latino. The series was a real showcase of Latino talent. While the story line revolves around the main male characters, several Latinas are featured as part of the Santiago family. Prominent among them are Ruth Livier and Marisol Nichols and veteran actress Elizabeth Peña. The children's cable network Nickelodeon initiated its 2001 season with *Taina*, whose main character is a Puerto Rican teenager. The show, co-created and produced by Puerto Rican–born María Pérez-Brown, also features other Latino characters. Ada Maris and young Vaneza Leza Pitynski are the female members of the García family in the Nickelodeon series *The Brothers García* (2000–) about a Latino household in San Antonio, Texas. Latina Jamie-Lynn Sigler plays Meadow Soprano in the popular HBO series *The Sopranos*. PBS's fall 2001 season featured a new drama series, *American Family*, about a Latino family in East Los Angeles with a mostly Latino cast that included Sonia Braga, Raquel Welch, Constance Marie, Elizabeth Peña, Tamara Mello, and Jacqueline Obradors.

Despite such gains, Latinos and Latinas are not highly visible on U.S. network television programs. Researchers Greenberg and Batista Fernández sampled commercial fictional programming during the 1975–1976, 1976–1977, and 1977–1978 seasons. Of 3,549 characters with speaking roles in 255 episodes coded, there were only 53 reliably identified as Hispanic Americans, or less than 1.5 percent of all television characters. In the Public Advocates audit of sixty-three prime-time shows during the first week of the fall 1983 television season, Latinos/as played 0.5 percent, or 3 out of 496, of the significant speaking roles, and only 1 percent, or ten characters out of 866, of those who spoke one or more lines. A 2005 report prepared for the National Association of Hispanic Journalists (NAHJ), states that after ten years of monitoring the situation, minimal coverage is still given to Latinos and Latino issues on network news. Out of 548 hours of network news covered in 2004, only three hours and 25 minutes focused on Latinos. These statistics are glaring, given that Latinos/as make up 12 percent of the total U.S. population.

The national Spanish-language networks, Univision and Telemundo, are also key players in this important industry. These networks own the two U.S. Spanish-language cable channels, Galavision and Gems. Although a great part of their programming comes from Latin America, both Telemundo and Univision feature Latinas prominently in their U.S. news programs and talk shows. Cristina Saralegui, who has been called the

Oprah Winfrey of Spanish-language television, for example, established herself as a significant player in the entertainment industry. She hosts her own show, *Cristina*, for Univision and publishes her own magazine. Telemundo's *Primer Impacto* current events program is hosted by two women, Candela Ferro and Ana Patricia Candiani, both of whom began their careers in their native countries, Argentina and Mexico, respectively. A similar show on Univision, *Ocurrió Así*, is also hosted by two Latinas. Women are also present behind the camera. One of the best known of these is producer Nelly Galán. Two court television programs also feature Latina judges, and both are produced in Miami.

Most of the news programs on these networks are anchored by women, among them María Elena Salinas and María Antonietta Collins of Univision and María Elena Salazar of Telemundo, who play as important a role as their male counterparts. Telemundo's Elia Calderón stands out as one of the very few black faces among those presenting the news on these two networks. One of the most prominent journalists today, Denisse Oller, is an anchor newsperson for Univision. Recognized for her balanced, insightful reporting, Oller has garnered four Emmys for her work.

The cable news network CNN recognized the importance of the Latino population and initiated

Denisse Oller with the first Emmy Award given for a Spanish-language news program, *Noticias 41*. Courtesy of Denisse Oller.

Spanish-language news programming with the inauguration in 1997 of CNN en Español. As on its English-language counterpart, many women are featured as news broadcasters. Among these are Latinas Glenda Umaña, Patricia Janiot, and Celina Rodríguez. The CNN English-language news team that includes award-winning reporter María Hinojosa and producer Rose Arce, who has won two Emmys. NBC's *Weekend Today* news is anchored by Soledad O'Brian, winner of the Hispanic Achievement Award in Communications. They stand out among the very few Latinas on English-speaking national television.

In the twenty-first century few would dispute the importance of the Latino population. With an estimated population over 35 million, they form the largest minority community in the United States. But at the close of the twentieth century, in the midst of the so-called Latin boom in entertainment, the face of the Latina was still practically nonexistent on mainstream television.

See also Cinema Images, Contemporary; Media Stereotypes

SOURCES: Fregoso, Rosa Linda. 1993. *The Bronze Screen: Chicana and Chicano Film Culure.* Minneapolis: University of Minnesota Press; Reyes, Luis, and Peter Rubie. 1994. *Hispanics in Hollywood: An Encyclopedia of Film and Television.* New York: Garland Publishing. Subverbi, Federico, with Joseph Torres and Daniela Montalvo. 2005. "The Portrayal of Latinos and Latino Issues on Network Television News, 2004, with a Retrospect to 1995." Austin, Texas and Washington, D.C.: National Association of Hispanic Journalists.

Irene Sosa

TEMPE NORMAL SCHOOL (1885–1936)

Between 1885, when the charter to establish the institution was passed, and 1936, Tempe Normal School (TNS) graduated over sixty Mexican American teachers, roughly 2 percent of its student body. Mostly women (about a dozen were men), these Mexican American students earned two-year college diplomas and assumed teaching positions in Arizona's segregated public schools. Opening its doors in the fall of 1886 as the Territorial Normal School at Tempe and known by several names, including the present-day Arizona State University, TNS enrolled thirty-three students in its first year and awarded 3,522 teaching diplomas by 1936. The two-year curriculum, equivalent to the modern-day associate's degree, provided a general liberal arts education, combined with pedagogical methods, and qualified students to sit for the state teacher's examination they were required to pass in order to graduate and teach in Arizona public schools.

In 1925 the state of Arizona reclassified TNS as a four-year state teachers college offering a baccalaureate in education; however, the college continued to issue the two-year teaching diploma until 1936. Many of these two-year graduates later returned to the college to complete their baccalaureates. The coeds gained classroom experience by practice teaching in several laboratory schools, including Tempe's Eighth Street School, operated by the college. The Eighth Street School gained statewide notoriety as a result of a 1925 lawsuit, *Romo v. Laird,* which challenged an agreement between the Tempe Elementary School District No. 3 and TNS to operate the school as a "Mexican Training School" for "Spanish-American or Mexican-American children." While Mexican American parents won the right to send their children to Tempe's nearby "American" public school, the TNS and the district also secured the right under "separate but equal" laws to continue operating the segregated training school and its "Americanization" curriculum until its closure in 1945.

Rosa Jaime was the first Spanish-surnamed woman to appear on the TNS graduation roster in 1907. Oral histories suggest that Spanish-surnamed women may have attended as early as the 1890s. Teacher Petra Ochoa, who taught in rural Mexican schools and Indian reservation schools, is remembered as an 1897 TNS student. Anna "Ann" Manuela Miller Raut, the daughter of Tempe citizens Winchester Miller Sr. and Maria Sotelo, also graduated in 1897. Enrollment registers confirm that after 1910 Spanish-surnamed women, as well as women of mixed Anglo and Mexican heritage, regularly graduated from TNS, beginning with Eliza Loroña in 1911, Concepción Faras in 1913, and Carmela Martínez in 1915. By 1917 Mexican American women became easily recognizable on campus. From 1917 to 1920, three to four Mexican American women earned diplomas each year, including Rose Mary Faras, who taught at Pirtleville Elementary School in the outskirts of Douglas, Arizona, where her older sister Concepción served as principal. In 1921 Tempe native María Escalante graduated and took a teaching job at a Phoenix-area Mexican school; later she taught Spanish at Scottsdale High School.

Of fifty-one Spanish-surnamed women who enrolled at the Normal School between 1887 and 1936, the majority graduated after 1924. Thirty-five Spanish-surnamed women earned diplomas between 1924 and 1936. Among them was the 1928 valedictorian, María L. Urquides, a bilingual education advocate from Tucson who became a recognized regional leader of the National Education Association, the Democratic Party, and the Southwestern Viva Kennedy campaigns. From 1923 to 1934 TNS usually graduated a Mexican American man each year. Among these was the education civil rights lawyer Rafael Carlos Estrada (1923). Estrada, who taught for several years before entering the University of Arizona Law School, represented Mexican American plaintiffs in the Tolleson, Arizona, landmark school desegregation case *Gonzales v. Sheeley* (1951).

Like the Faras sisters, many of the Mexican American alumni shared common class and family backgrounds. Nearly half of the students shared surnames with at least one other classmate, and many were also siblings, cousins, or distant relatives of the same families. Urquides, for example, attended TNS with her first cousins Evangeline Romo Delesky (1926) and Genevieve Romo Urquides (1927). Other family sets of alumni include the Loroñas, Eliza (1911), Leonor (1920), and Adela (1924), and the Jerezes, Gilbert Joseph (1926), Hilda Virginia (1929), and Hortense Julia (1929). These alliances were further strengthened by marriages between students, such as Estrada and his student bride Ruby López Estrada. Students also hailed from Tempe's Mexican American community. Among these were Escalante, Estrada, the Loroñas, and alumna Ida Isabelle Celaya (1917), whose father Antonio was a businessman, a fire chief, and president of the Liga Protectora Latina, a statewide mutual-aid society. Other TNS Mexican American alumni include Helen V. Bracamonte (1924), Eugenie Flores (1926), Dionisia G. Estévez (1926), Mary J. Gómez (1927), Florence A. Hernán (1927), Isabel Morales (1927), Marfila S. Arballo (1928), Lydia E. Contreras (1928), Josephine F. Delgado (1928), Caroline L. Contreras (1928), Marion

Students at Tempe Normal School, Tempe, Arizona, circa 1908. Courtesy of the Library of Congress, Taking the Long View: Panoramic Photographs, 1851–1991 (Digital ID: cph 3c24486).

Figueroa (1931), Elene G. Mendoza (1931), Stella R. Pacheco (1931), Naomi Ruth Moran (1931), Otila Uribe Flores (1932), Angelita M. Salazar (1932), Rachel Marie Feliz (1933), Adeline P. Hurtado (1934), Inez Jones Gómez (1935), Lorraine J. Casañega (1936), and Paulita G. Sánchez (1936).

See also Education

SOURCES: Muñoz, Laura K. 1998. "Mexican Women and Tempe Normal School, 1887–1936." Paper Chicano Research Collection, Department of Archives and Manuscripts, Arizona State University, Tempe; *Register of Non-Degree Graduates, 1887–1936*. Arizona State College, Tempe.

Laura K. Muñoz

TEN YEARS' WAR (1868–1878)

The Ten Years' War in Cuba, known also as el Grito de Yara, and a planned and simultaneous uprising in Puerto Rico, el Grito de Lares, form preludes to the Cuban war with Spain, 1895, and the Cuban-Spanish-American War, 1898, that gave the United States colonial control over both islands. Although the Puerto Rican move for independence was squashed by the Spanish military within a month of the rebellion, both uprisings gave rise to the emigrations of hundreds of men and women who ultimately laid the groundwork for sustaining Latino communities, particularly in New York City and in Florida's Tampa and Key West. For the most part these exile communities continued to support Antillean independence during and after the Ten Years' War. They raised funds, promoted propaganda, and created effective organizations committed to liberation.

The underlying causes of the rebellion were many. By 1824 Spain had lost most of its colonies in the Americas and intensified its administrative and economic hold on Cuba and Puerto Rico. Spain failed to implement promised special laws for equal representation of the islands with Spanish peninsular provinces in legislative bodies. The imposition of taxes and other laws without Criollo (those individuals born in Cuba or Puerto Rico) participation, repression of opposing political views, and prohibitions on trade outraged colonial landowners. Moreover, Cubans in particular had enjoyed a brief period of liberal reorganization under the Bourbon Reforms of the late eighteenth and early nineteenth centuries that whetted their appetite for free trade and control of their own economic and political destiny.

Led by Carlos Manuel de Céspedes, an attorney, and promoted by a group of patriotic landowners, the Grito de Yara began on October 10, 1868, and signaled a period of warfare that essentially crippled Cuba's econ-

omy and devastated its agricultural production. The diverse rebel forces included landowners, professionals, merchants, freed slaves, and farmers. While atrocities abounded on both sides of the conflict, incidents such as the massacre of a handful of medical students for allegedly defacing a Spanish tombstone in 1871 and the serial execution of fifty-three individuals in international waters on board the steamship *Virginius* in 1873 fueled Cuban patriotism. Sanctioned by a constitutional assembly (1869) and led by seasoned war veterans such as Manuel de Quesada, who had fought under Benito Juárez in Mexico, the revolution suffered from a lack of supplies and the capture of many of its leaders. After the arrest of the president of the republic, Tomás Estrada Palma, peace negotiations in Zanjón in 1878 dismantled the Cuban government, and except for skirmishes by rebels who had fought under Antonio Maceo, the war came to an end. But Zanjón was more than just a place where a treaty signaled the official end to warfare; it initiated a cherished and patriotic heritage, fundamental to the creation of Cuban nationhood.

Families were torn apart and devastated by the war, which also changed traditional roles and lifestyles. Middle- and upper-class women accustomed to privileged circumstances were forced to work outside the home in department stores, as salesclerks, in factories, in restaurants, and in civil service. It was not unusual for men to bring their families to safety in the United States and return to participate in battle. As a result, émigré households were often headed by women. Women on their own also left Cuba with their children to escape the insurrection, especially when they became widows or lost relatives. This was the plight of Concha Agramonte, whose husband Ignacio Agramonte y Loynáz, principal author of the constitution, died in battle. She and her nine children immigrated to New York City, where she worked as a seamstress. Ana Merchan's father was an insurgent in the rebellion and fled with his family to Key West during the war. Fifteen charter members of the organization las Obreras de la Independencia, founded in 1892, included Adelaide de Rivero and the wives, widows, and daughters of men who fought in the Ten Years' War. This women's club and dozens of others like it contributed to the formation of the Partido Revolucionario Cubano and the war efforts of 1895 through fund-raising, bazaars, dinners, dances, and celebrations. Many organizations honored the deeds of women insurgents, such as the Club Ana Betancourt de Mora, named after a woman who advocated for women's rights in the 1860s.

Overall, the war promoted women's participation in the public sphere. Émigré communities found a myriad of ways to maintain patriotism and a sense of nation-

Cuban Revolutionary Society, Key West, Florida. Courtesy of the Library of Congress, America from the Great Depression to World War II: Photographs from the FSA-OWI, 1935–1945 (Digital ID: fsa *a09354).

hood. One such way was working with religious organizations. Protestantism, less identified with Spanish rule than Catholicism, had made inroads into Cuba in the late nineteenth century, and émigré women found that they could help the war effort in exile by engaging in missionary work. Isabel Prieto and Bonifacia Dealofeu, for example, worked with the missions in Key West. They sponsored social services, helped integrate recently arrived families into the community, taught Sunday school, and proselytized door-to-door.

Perhaps the best-known homage paid to Cuban women in exile appeared in the pages of the newspaper *Patria*. Penned by the Apostle of the Revolution, José Martí, himself exiled in New York since the end of the Ten Years' War, the article "El alma cubana" extolled the virtues of Doña Carolina Rodríguez. She served as a courier between the insurgent forces in Cuba in the 1870s. Forced to immigrate to Key West at the age of fifty-three, Doña Carolina made a life for herself working as a stemmer in a cigar factory and promoting Cuban liberation. She collected funds for needy émigré families and to aid renewed liberation efforts. In 1892 she resettled in Tampa. An integral activist in the Cuban émigré community, she helped found women's organizations, including las Obreras de Independencia. When Martí visited the exile communities in preparation for renewing the war against the Spanish, Doña Carolina accompanied him throughout the city on his mission. "La patriota," as Martí christened her, exemplified hundreds of Cuban exiled women whose patriotism spanned three decades and two wars.

SOURCES: Hewitt, Nancy A. 2001. *Southern Discomfort: Women's Activism in Tampa, Florida, 1880s–1920s.* Urbana: University of Illinois Press; Jiménez de Wagenheim, Olga.

1985. *Puerto Rico's Revolt for Independence: El Grito de Lares.* Boulder, CO: Westview Press; Pérez, Louis A., Jr. 1999. *On Becoming Cuban: Identity, Nationality, and Culture.* Chapel Hill: University of North Carolina Press.

Virginia Sánchez Korrol

TENAYUCA, EMMA (1916–1999)

Radical labor organizer Emma Tenayuca was born in San Antonio, Texas. On her mother's side (Zepeda) of the family, she was a descendant of Spanish settlers who came to Texas and settled in Los Adáes, the easternmost establishment in Spanish Texas. However, her father's pure Indian heritage had a much more significant impact on her development. In an oral interview recorded by the Institute of Texan Cultures, San Antonio, Texas, in February 1987, she discussed her background: "I didn't have a fashionable Spanish name like García or Sánchez. I carried an Indian name. And I was very, very conscious of that. It was this historical background and my grandparents' attitude which formed my ideas and actually gave me that courage later to undertake the type of work I did in San Antonio. . . . I think it was the combination of being a Texan, being a Mexican, and being more Indian than Spanish that propelled me to take action."

Growing up in the early years of the twentieth century in San Antonio, Tenayuca saw the economic disparities that prevailed in most of the city's West Side: low-paying, unskilled jobs, high infant mortality rates, and the dubious distinction of having one of the highest tuberculosis rates in the country. Tenayuca recalled her visits to La Plaza de Zacate (today Milam Plaza) with her Zepeda grandfather, described by her as a "very conscientious, very honest man, a devout Catholic, a good Democrat" who voted for "Ma" Ferguson because she stalwartly opposed the Ku Klux Klan. Her grandfather rallied the entire family to cast their vote for "Ma." The event was noteworthy to her, even though Tenayuca was only in the third grade at the time.

Zepeda was a major influence in shaping his granddaughter's political and socioeconomic views. He read English, participated in local politics, and was especially interested in labor issues and civil rights. At La Plaza de Zacate, a gathering place where many Mexicans and Tejanos met to discuss the events of the day, Tenayuca heard the radical rhetoric of Carrancistas, Maderistas, and Magonistas as they debated revolutionary developments in Mexico. Here she also learned of the economic plight of laborers expressed by socialists, anarchists, and Wobblies. When she read about the 1932–1933 strikes against the Finck Cigar Company, she joined the labor movement. Tenayuca was sixteen. She walked the picket line and joined strikers in jail. She founded the International Ladies Garment Workers' Union local in San Antonio and became a member of the Executive Committee of the Workers' Alliance in the 1930s.

The Workers' Alliance endorsed the pecan shellers' strike in January 1938. The pecan shellers had first walked out in 1934 to protest low wages. The issues—low wages and unfair labor practices—remained unresolved for four years. Laborers endured appalling working conditions: inadequate ventilation, no inside toilets, and wages that added up to perhaps $2 or $3 a week. In comparison, garment workers averaged $3 to $4 a week, while gardeners and domestic servants earned about $2 to $2.50 a week. By 1937 an economic recession resulted in more unemployment and another wage reduction. Government relief jobs were reduced. Across Texas the first to see their relief payments discontinued were Mexican American laborers.

Tenayuca's role in the strike earned her the name "la pasionara." She urged a walkout, and on Monday, January 31, 1938, between 6,000 and 10,000 workers, the majority of whom were women, walked out in protest. Police used tear gas to dispel the crowds and arrested more than 1,000 strikers on trivial charges such as obstructing the sidewalks. As strike representative for the 12,000 female pecan shellers who worked in 400 work sheds scattered throughout San Antonio's West Side, Tenayuca was arrested, but the demonstrations continued in downtown parks and in the Plaza de Zacate.

City officials, the Catholic Church, and the League of United Latin American Citizens (LULAC) condemned the strike, although the middle-class Mexican American establishment professed sympathy for the pecan shellers' appalling working conditions and meager wages. On the night of August 25th, 1939, a near riot took place at San Antonio's Municipal Auditorium. The consequences were significant. Mayor Maury Maverick, who gave Tenayuca permission to use the city auditorium for a meeting of the Texas Communist Party, paid a heavy political price. The riot cost him reelection. Tenayuca found herself ostracized, unable to find work because of her Communist leanings, and separated from her husband. The Catholic newspaper *La Voz* warned: "In the midst of this community exists a woman by the name of Emma Tenayuca who wants to spread disorder and hatred. This woman has all the appearances of a communist. . . . Don't give your names to her when she comes around to solicit them. Warn people when she comes around. Mrs. Tenayuca de Brooks is not a Mexican; she is a Russofile, [*sic*] sold out to Russia, communist. If she were a Mexican she would not be doing this type of work."

Sharyll Soto Teneyuca (the family surname's original spelling) recalled that her aunt's exploits were never openly discussed in the family. About the time of the thirtieth anniversary of the Municipal Auditorium riot of 1939, she picked up a newspaper to find a pictorial commemorative of the event. Soto Teneyuca wrote, "I read with awe that 'Emma Tenayuca was the charismatic leader of a movement that shook the city's labor force,' a 'fiery orator' who married Homer Brooks, a Communist. She had been involved in organizing and fighting for the rights of the city's poor against some of the city's most profitable industries. I read of the mass destruction done to the municipal auditorium by the angry mob who stormed it in protest of the Communist party meeting that was to be held there that night and at which she was to speak. I was both proud and impressed to finally learn the family secret about Aunt Emma." According to historian Zaragoza Vargas, "She had a magnetic personality and possessed extraordinary organizing abilities, honed by years of active struggle on behalf of San Antonio's Mexican community. Under the banners of the Unemployed Councils and the Workers' Alliance of America, she helped Mexicans organize hunger marches, protests, and demonstrations to gain relief, obtain jobs on public works projects, and fight against racial injustice and harassment by the U.S. Immigration Service."

Undeterred, Tenayuca continued her organizing efforts. There were laundry workers, cement workers, and onion pickers who needed her help. The Workers' Alliance desegregated a theater in San Antonio and petitioned for English classes at night. Tenayuca took low-paying jobs while going to school at night. Zaragoza Vargas noted that a Jewish garment manufacturer of army officer uniforms who had sympathized with her community work provided her with a job as a secretary and bookkeeper. One entry in her own journal as told by her niece revealed her predicament. She wrote: "On the other hand, I am going to have to face a barrage of criticisms, etc. from both members of my family as well as the so-called middle class element. It will be sometime before the matter of my divorce will have been forgotten. I am only a very insignificant little individual, who 50 years hence will have been completely forgotten, but my divorce makes a juicy piece of gossip right now."

Eventually, antiunion and anti-Mexican sentiment forced her to leave Texas in the late 1940s for her safety and economic well-being. She moved to San Francisco, where she graduated magna cum laude from San Francisco State College. Twenty years later she returned to San Antonio and found that she had acquired heroine status. She enrolled at Our Lady of the Lake University, where she earned a master's degree in education and taught in a San Antonio public elementary school until her retirement. She died of Alzheimer's disease on July 23, 1999, at a San Antonio nursing home.

See also San Antonio Pecan Shellers' Strike

SOURCES: Teneyuca, Sharyll Soto. 1999. "Save the Story: The Emma Tenayuca Project." In *San Antonio: La Voz de Esperanza*. San Antonio: Esperanza Center; The University of Texas, Institute of Texan Cultures at San Antonio. "If the Principles Are Gone." TENAYUCA, Emma." 1987. Oral interview by Gerald E. Poyo, February 21. www.texancultures.utsa.edu/mem ories/htms/tenayuca_trnascript.htm (accessed July 24, 2005); Vargas, Zaragosa. 1997. "Tejana Radical: Emma Tenayuca and the San Antonio Labor Movement during the Great Depression." *Pacific Historical Review* 66 (November): 553–580.

Nora E. Rios McMillan

TEX-SON STRIKE

On February 24, 1959, approximately 185 Tejanas and European American women left their posts at the Tex-Son clothing factory in San Antonio, Texas. This labor dispute was sparked by the company's decision to subcontract a considerable portion of its production to a factory in Tupelo, Mississippi. It was one of the earliest efforts by union members to fight for their jobs in the face of outsourcing operations to cheaper, nonunion locales, first in the Deep South and decades later across the border into Mexico and across the Pacific to China. In the words of the late historian Irene Ledesma, this was "a do or die battle."

The members of Local 180 of the International Ladies Garment Workers' Union (ILGWU) at Tex-Son were understandably concerned by the Tupelo factory. They now faced a shortened workweek and thus earned less money. For example, Helen Martínez, a single mother of four children, earned $9.12 per week. The union also protested management's attempt to restructure the grievance process and to eliminate the health and welfare fund. Harold Franzel, the owner of Tex-Son, refused to negotiate and hired an alleged union-busting attorney. The ILGWU organizer in charge of the strike was Sophie Gonzales, and Tex-Son was the first ILGWU labor action where Mexican American rank and file held actual leadership positions. Indeed, of the fourteen members of the negotiating committee, ten were Mexican American women, and their articulate spokesperson, Gregoria Montalbo, served as president of the Tex-Son local.

Within a week of the strike strikers and scabs engaged in a bitter confrontation. The police moved quickly to quell the disturbance. While local newspapers focused on hair pulling and swinging purses, the ILGWU paper *Justice* published graphic photographs of

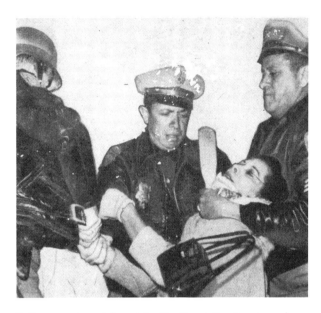

Police restrain a striker at the Tex-Son strike. Courtesy of George and Lantane Papers, Texas Labor Archives, University of Texas at Arlington.

law enforcement officers using excessive force against the women strikers. Labor unions across Texas rallied to raise funds for the Tex-Son pickets. Brewery workers, clerical employers, steelworkers, and packinghouse operatives contributed money, and in March 1959, after a union solidarity parade with more than 1,000 marchers, Franzel used the event as an opportunity to red-bait or cast "Communist" aspersions against union activists. Irene Ledesma explains that while Franzel used well-worn cold war accusations against the ILGWU (and his employees), the union itself relied on notions of domesticity and motherhood to garner support for the strike.

As in previous labor actions, Mexican American children walked the picket line. Gathering in front of local department stores, they passed out balloons to other children with the message "Don't Buy Tex-Son." They distributed bilingual pamphlets, such as one that explained the strike from a child's perspective: "My Mama sews in a factory making clothes for kids. But now she is on strike because she needs more money for my sisters and my brother and me, and her boss wouldn't let her have it."

Despite the tenacity of local strikers and their families, management refused to budge. In 1961 the national union withdrew support, and the strike ended several months later. Unemployed Tejanas willing to take jobs as scabs, the antiunion climate of San Antonio and Texas, and then the resulting diffidence of the national union marked the defeat of union militants, women who put their own jobs on the line to try to forestall outsourcing of garment production to cheaper, nonunion regions. The Tex-Son strike proved a bellwether for trends in American manufacturing and organized labor.

See also International Ladies Garment Workers' Union (ILGWU)

SOURCES: Lambert, George. George Lambert Collection. Special Collections, University Library, University of Texas, Arlington; Ledesma, Irene. 1995. "Texas Newspapers and Chicana Workers' Activism, 1919–1974." *Western Historical Quarterly* 26, no. 3 (Autumn): 309–331.

Vicki L. Ruiz

THEATER

Unlike the beginnings of the theatrical tradition in England, Spain did not prohibit women from acting, and there was no puritanical strain in Latino culture in the Americas that saw the theater as iniquitous and thus limited the development of the dramatic arts, the construction of theaters, and the enjoyment of entertainment within them. In the Spanish-speaking Americas and in Spain, theaters were called theaters, not "opera houses," respectable people could frequent them, and women had the opportunity to develop their intelligence and talent and rise to leadership in the dramatic and performing arts. Hispanic theater history is filled with reports of actresses whose beauty and artistry enchanted their audiences. These stars were held in great celebrity and commanded considerable power, not only over their audiences, but also over their managers, impresarios, and theater owners. Their power quite often extended over other men of power and rank in the general society who were smitten by these artists' charms.

During the nineteenth century the rise of melodrama brought with it hosts of interesting roles for leading ladies, roles that allowed them to display the full gamut of emotions on stage. In Spain and Spanish America numerous actresses arose who became so celebrated and sought after that their dramatic companies bore their names. The rise of vaudeville in France and its introduction into Spain and the Americas during the late nineteenth century also had the effect of further empowering women on the stage to the extent that their liberty to display previously prohibited portions of their anatomy and to sexually titillate male audiences made them the center of attention and the greatest box-office draw. By the early twentieth century many leading ladies had become the owners and directors of large dramatic and vaudeville companies, which in a very real sense were large business enterprises. Some of them even owned and operated their own theater houses.

The most famous and exemplary of these women entrepreneurs was Virginia Fábregas, whose company toured throughout Mexico and the Southwest beginning in the late nineteenth century and later went on almost yearly tours from Mexico to the Caribbean, Spain, the United States, the Philippines, and Guam. La Fábregas brought the latest in European realistic drama to the Americas and the best Spanish American playwrights to the stage, but her repertoire always carefully included only plays that presented a forum for her own virtuosity as a leading lady. Her lifelong project was to invest her earnings from her constant touring into the construction and operation of a theater and school of drama in Mexico City, which she accomplished. The Teatro Fábregas and its school are still standing and operating today in the Mexican capital.

Fábregas should also be credited for stimulating the development of theater in the southwestern United States in many ways. During the Mexican Revolution Fábregas continued touring the Southwest; however, many of her actors and technicians realized that a prosperous and successful life on stage could be had in the Mexican immigrant and exile communities here. During each tour many of her personnel dropped out of her company to remain in the United States and perform with other companies or even start their own companies. In addition, Fábregas purchased plays by promising playwrights of the Southwest and incorporated them into her repertoire to be performed throughout the Southwest and the Hispanic world. But by far her most important contribution was the quality of her stage productions and of her acting, which served as a model for all the other companies that performed during the more than forty years in which she appeared on stages of the Southwest.

Numerous other dramatic and vaudeville companies led by leading ladies followed Fábregas into the United States, such as the companies of Rosa Arriaga, María Caballé, Carmen Cassaude de León, Soledad Castillo, María Conesa, Nelly Fernández, Ligia de Golconda, Elena Landeros, María del Carmen Martínez, Angélica Méndez, Carmen du Molins, María Teresa Montoya, Marita Reid, Marita Ríos, Paquita Santigosa, and various others. Companies such as those of Camila Quiroga and Paulina Singerman were drawn from as far away as Buenos Aires. To what extent these women maintained financial and operational control of their companies is not fully known, but their leadership was never in question to their audiences and the press. All of them, in fact, served as role models and mentors for Latina actresses and performers breaking into theater in the United States.

One such actress, who in her early career in drama and vaudeville emulated the *vedette* (a star performer) Dorita Ceprano, was Beatriz Escalona. Escalona, who

An aging La Chata Noloesca in a musical review at the Teatro Hispano in New York, circa 1949. Courtesy of Arte Público Press.

became the most famous Latina comedienne under the name of La Chata Noloesca, was discovered by a traveling troupe of Cuban-Spanish actor-musicians when she was working as an usherette and box-office clerk in her native San Antonio. After divorcing her husband, the director of the company, Escalona returned to San Antonio and formed her own all-female company and began touring during the depression up to Chicago, east to Florida and Cuba, and north to New York, where ultimately she spent many years on stage performing for Latino audiences into the 1950s.

Marita Reid, an actress who debuted as a child on the stages of southern Spain, was one of the theatrical directors and impresarios most responsible for the survival of serious Spanish-language drama in New York during the depression and World War II. At the head of her companies, she not only performed on the professional circuits but also kept theater alive in the mutual-aid societies of Spaniards, Cubans, and Puerto Ricans. Reid was the first Hispanic actress to cross over into English-language drama on Broadway and into television and during the 1960s served as a mentor for such performers as Tina Ramírez, who was a member of her Spanish-language company. Ramírez went on to become the director of the most important Hispanic dance troupe and school in the United States today, el Ballet Hispánico.

Today such leading-lady company directors as Carmen Zapata of Los Angeles' Bilingual Foundation for the Arts and Miriam Colón of New York's Puerto Rican Traveling Theater are the inheritors of this tradition. Both came out of Spanish-speaking theater in New York and made the crossover to Hollywood film. Both have established and maintained companies in Latino urban centers and used them as training grounds and showcases in English and Spanish for theater arts.

SOURCES: Arrizón, Alicia. 1999. *Latina Performance: Traversing the Stage.* Bloomington: Indiana University Press; Arrizón, Alicia, and Lillian Manzor, eds. 2000. *Latinas on Stage: Practice and Theory.* Berkeley, CA: Third Woman Press; Kanel-

Carmen Zapata in the role of Queen Isabella. Courtesy of Arte Público Press.

Theater

los, Nicolás. 1990. *A History of Hispanic Theatre in the United States: Origins to 1940*. Austin: University of Texas Press.

Nicolás Kanellos

Padua Hills Theater (1931–1974)

The Padua Hills Theater in Claremont, California, featured Mexican-theme folk plays, romantic comedies, and historical dramas performed by young, local Mexican Americans. Begun as an "experiment" to save a dying community theater during the depression, the theater's troupe, the Mexican Players (or Paduanos, as the performers called themselves), became one of the most celebrated collections of Mexican American artists in southern California from 1931 to 1974. Hosting a repertoire of plays that included traditional and original songs and dialogue in Spanish, Padua Hills surprisingly drew a mostly English-speaking, white audience. After a short stint as a for-profit enterprise, proprietors Herman and Bess Garner successfully converted the theater into a nonprofit "institute" in 1936 with the expressed intent of forging "intercultural understanding" between European Americans and Mexicans.

During World War II an emphasis on women's roles increased after the U.S. military drafted theater director Charles Dickinson and many male Paduanos (male players) for service. Like industries affected by war mobilization, Padua Hills Theater grew more dependent on women workers and provided many Paduanas (female players) greater influence on the performances. For example, Hilda Ramírez-Jara took over directorial duties in Dickinson's absence. To compensate for the lack of male players, she chose plays that primarily featured women characters, including scripts about Mexican women soldiers during the Mexican Revolution (*soldaderas*) and Mexican matriarchs (*Tehuanas*) in southern Mexico. Although Dickinson directed the plays *Adelita, Noches poblanas, Juana, la Tehuana,* and *Marina* before his departure for the war in March 1943, these productions took on new importance during the mid-1940s when women dominated the ranks of the Mexican Players.

Borne of necessity, the focus and reliance on women also had the unintended consequence of empowering Paduanas, such as Hilda Ramírez-Jara, who not only directed many World War II–era plays, but also worked in the wardrobe department. When the war ended, Charles Dickinson resumed directorial duties, an act by management that reflected post-war attitudes about the temporary role of women in the workforce. Nevertheless, after her career at Padua Hills, Ramírez-Jara's stint as the theater's director provided experience that served her later as the director of the popular Ramona Pageant in Hemet, California. An-

other player, Casilda Amador Thoreson, became the lead hostess in the dining room and helped manage the theater until 1947, when she quit temporarily to marry Harold Thoreson. She recalled, "I was head of the dining room and the kitchen at one time until it was too much for me." After the untimely death of her husband Thoreson returned to the theater in 1951 to become membership chairperson and lead hostess. In 1958 Herman Garner chose her to write the *Padua Hills News Notes*, a monthly newsletter that went out to patrons and donors, announcing performance schedules and background information regarding the cast. For Ramírez-Jara, Amador Thoreson, and other Paduanas, the changes during World War II led to increased influence at Padua Hills.

SOURCE: García, Matt. 2002. *A World of Its Own: Race, Labor, and Citrus in the Making of Greater Los Angeles, 1900–1970*. Chapel Hill: University of North Carolina Press.

Matt García

Playwrights

The roots of Latinas in theater can be traced to the middle of the eighteenth century. Women have played important roles in theater ensembles as writers, directors, actresses, and, at times, owners of their own companies. The first cities in the United States to host such entertainment were those in the West Coast, such as Los Angeles and San Francisco. Later other cities in the Southwest, such as Tucson, El Paso, Laredo, and San Antonio, became important places for theater. During the 1890s cities like Tampa, Florida, hosted Spanish and Cuban theatrical companies. These were sponsored by owners of big cigar businesses who used this type of entertainment for advertising their products.

Women's participation in theater up to the first half of the twentieth century can be divided into two types: professional theater, where they performed famous works by established Spanish and Latin American writers, and a type of poor people's itinerant theater better known as *teatro de carpa*. These different companies traveled throughout the United States—the Southwest, Chicago, New York, and Florida—and Puerto Rico, Cuba, and Mexico. Middle- and working-class people had their own types of theatrical entertainment. During this time Virginia Fábregas, who owned her own company, exemplified Mexican women in professional theater geared to middle-class Spanish-speaking audiences. Originally born and raised in Mexico, Fábregas decided to relocate to Los Angeles, California. Because of its low economic maintenance and traveling cost, *teatro de carpa* was the most enduring and famous type of entertainment serving primarily working-class people.

La Sacerdotiza del Arte Celebra Esta Noche su Función de Gala.

SRA. VIRGINIA FABREGAS, distinguida Primera Actriz Mexicana, que celebra su función de beneficio y despedida en el Lyceum Hall, la noche del Martes 31 de Dicimbre.

Virginia Fábregas, distinguished Mexican actor, celebrates a benefit and farewell performance at the Lyceum Hall.
Courtesy of Arte Público Press.

A recognized woman of the *carpa* tradition was Beatriz Escalona, "La Chata Noloesca," who acted, sang, wrote, directed, and also owned her theater company. Her most famous character was a Mexican social type known as a *peladita* (a destitute, downtrodden figure), and she traveled throughout the Southwest, New York, and Cuba. There were other women like Escalona, such as Carmen Soto de Vásquez, who also owned her own theater house in Tucson, Arizona, around 1915. Yet another example in Texas is Leonor Zamarripa Mendoza (mother of the famous Tejana singer Lydia Mendoza), who was also in charge of a small traveling show composed of family members for whom she wrote, directed, and created costumes. Her contributions helped the survival of the company for the first few decades of the twentieth century.

Teatro de carpa traveled to the areas where great numbers of Mexican workers were employed in the agricultural fields, on the railroad, and in the service industries. These *teatristas* were another type of mi-

grant laborers similar to the people they entertained. Many *carpas* followed agricultural workers in particular, set up their tents on the outskirts of town, and tried to incorporate issues pertaining to the workers in that area. *Teatro de carpa* is considered one of the models on which the most famous Chicano theater ensemble, el Teatro Campesino (ETC), was based.

Most contemporary Chicana/Latina theater originates in the theater of the Chicano movement, especially in the works of el Teatro Campesino. During the 1960s and 1970s women such as Socorro Valdez, Diane Rodríguez, and Olivia Chumacero worked with ETC and made great contributions that went unrecognized. Later they went on to write, direct, and produce their own work. In 1971 various Chicano theater ensembles formed, el Teatro Nacional de Aztlán (the National Theater of Aztlán, TENAZ) as their umbrella organization. Another ensemble that belonged to this organization, el Teatro de la Esperanza (Theater of Hope), originally from Santa Barbara, California, attempted to include women's issues in most of its work. However, given the overall male-dominated environment of the period, the women involved in different *teatros* across the Southwest decided to create their own group within TENAZ and called themselves Women in Teatro (WIT). This period saw the formation of all-women theater groups in California like Teatro Raíces (Roots Theater) in San Diego and las Cucarachas (the Cockroaches) from San Francisco, led by Dorinda Moreno. This last group performed a play titled *Chicana* in 1974 in which it traced women's historical ancestors. Silviana Woods in Arizona led the ensemble called Teatro Chicano, which was one of the first affiliates of TENAZ to produce a play that dealt with issues of homosexuality.

Aside from plays, these ensembles also created a type of hybrid work called teatropoesía in which theater, poetry, and music were combined. Yvonne Yarbro-Bejarano in her study of teatropoesía in the Bay Area states that this art "exploits the beauty and power of words, a dimension often neglected in Chicano Theater, combining the compact directness and lyrical emotion of the poetic text with the physical immediacy of the three-dimensional work of theater." During the 1980s one written work included concerns pertaining to the struggles of people from El Salvador. Another famous work titled *Tongues of Fire* was based on the first Chicana/Latina anthology of feminist writings, *This Bridge Called My Back*, edited by Cherríe Moraga and Gloria Anzaldúa, as well as on the poetry of other Chicanas.

Chicanas form the largest group of women under the umbrella term "Latina," and their participation in theater has been well documented. In addition to Chicanas, there are two other major groups recognized under this category: Puerto Rican/Nuyorican and Cuban/Cuban American women. Unfortunately, the participation in theater of Latinas who can trace their roots to other Latin American countries has not been fully researched.

Some of the central themes of Latina theater include issues of gender and sexuality, class, and race. Certain writers concentrate on the exploration of subject identity (be it sexual or ethnic), family matters, and, among many other themes, the challenge of Latina stereotypes and poverty in the barrios. Works by Latinas in theater can be found in monolingual Spanish, English, or a mixture of both.

Since the 1980s there has been a small, but effective, number of theater labs that have catered specifically to the development and professionalization of the industry by Latinas and Latinos. In California José Luis Valenzuela has led the Los Angeles Theater Center's Latino Theater Lab (LTL) since 1985 and has been responsible for the production of plays like Evelina Fernández's *How Else Am I Supposed to Know I'm Still Alive* and *Luminarias*, both of which deal specifically with issues of sexuality, identity, midlife, and women's support systems. Both plays were eventually developed into films. Another lab in that same state is the Costa Mesa South Coast Repertory's Hispanic Playwrights Project, directed from 1986 to 1997 by José Cruz González. This lab produced the work of several Latinas and published an anthology titled *Latino Plays from South Coast Repertory: Hispanic Playwrights Project Anthology* (2000). A third theater lab, located in New York, is INTAR (International Arts Relations) Hispanic Playwrights-in-Residency Laboratory Group, directed from 1981 to 1992 by the recognized and established Cuban American playwright and director María Irene Fornés. The author of more than forty plays, she has contributed to the works of many recognized Latina writers in theater, among them Cherríe Moraga and Migdalia Cruz, a Puerto Rican born in the South Bronx, New York.

Among recognized Chicana playwrights is Estela Portillo Trambley, who published the first collection of Latina theater works, titled *Sor Juana and Other Plays* in 1983. Cherríe Moraga was the first to write sympathetically about issues of Chicana/Mexicana lesbian desire, as well as issues of labor exploitation among women and men in the Chicana/o and Mexican immigrant communities. Edith Villarreal, Ruby Nelda Pérez, and Denise Chávez have also written works specifically dealing with women's issues. Josefina López's *Real Women Have Curves* and Milcha Sánchez-Scott's *Roosters* have also been produced as films. In addition, both writers concentrate on themes of identity, self-image, immigrant labor exploitation, and life in the barrios.

Like Chicano theater, some Puerto Rican theater work in the United States is based on *teatro popular* or "leftist proletarian theater." One of the earliest ensembles was the Puerto Rican Traveling Theater Company, of which Miriam Colón was a founding participant. Migdalia Cruz, who resides mostly in Chicago, Illinois, is the best-recognized writer of Puerto Rican descent. Cruz has written more than thirty plays and musicals with various themes that represent life in urban settings.

There has also been a popular theater base in Cuban and Cuban American theater with origins in *teatro bufo*, but recently most of this theater has shifted to professional settings. Aside from María Irene Fornés, Dolores Prida is another Cuban American writer who has had a successful career in theater. Her best-known plays, *Coser y cantar* and *Beautiful Señoritas*, have been widely produced. Prida's work focuses on issues of Latina stereotypes and national/ethnic identity, among other topics.

As with the theatrical activities of teatropoesía of the 1980s, there has recently been a proliferation of theater work by Latinas denominated as performance art that does not necessarily fit into the strict characteristic of plays. In performance art many of the participants often present one-woman shows and incorporate multimedia materials such as slides, recorded and live music, and other types of visual art. Performance artists such as Cuban American Carmelita Tropicana (*I, Carmelita Tropicana: Performing between Cultures*), Chicana Mónica Palacios (*Latin Lesbo Comic: A Performance about Happiness, Challenges, and Tacos* and *Greetings from a Queer Señorita*), and Cuban/Puerto Rican–American Marga Gómez (*Marga Gómez Is Pretty, Witty, and Gay* and *Half Cuban/Half Lesbian*) deal specifically with lesbian issues, Latina identity, and comedy. Two additional Chicana performance artists from Los Angeles and San Antonio, respectively, are María Elena Fernández (*Confessions of a Cha-Cha Feminist*), and Laura Esparza (*I DisMember the Alamo*). Both focus on Chicana feminism and historical identity. Another important performer is María Elena Gaitán, a Chicana artist and community activist from East Los Angeles. Gaitán produced an important body of work related to the struggles of oppressed peoples. Some of her titles include *Chola con Cello: A Home Girl in the Philharmonic*, *The Adventures of Connie Chancla*, and *The Teta Show*. Her topics include issues of racial discrimination, labor exploitation, women's history, and breast cancer.

Some accomplishments have been made by women in the world of American theater as a whole. However, there continues to be a need to amplify access in all theatrical and other art spaces for the voices of Chicanas/Latinas to continue to be heard.

SOURCES: Arrizón, Alicia, and Lillian Manzor, eds. 2000. *Latinas on Stage: Practice and Theory.* Berkeley, CA: Third Woman Press; Feyder, Linda, ed. 1992. *Shattering the Myth: Plays by Hispanic Women.* Houston: Arte Público Press; Huerta, Jorge. 2000. *Chicano Drama: Performance, Society and Myth.* New York: Cambridge University Press; Kanellos, Nicolás, ed. 1989. *Mexican American Theatre: Then and Now.* Houston: Arte Público Press; Sandoval-Sánchez, Alberto, and Nancy Saporta Sternback, eds. 2000. *Puro Teatro: A Latina Anthology.* Tucson: University of Arizona Press; Yarbro-Bejarano, Yvonne. 1985. "Chicanas' Experience in Collective Theater." *Women and Performance* 2 no. 2:45–58.

Rita E. Urquijo-Ruiz

Puerto Rican Traveling Theater (PRTT) (1967–)

The Puerto Rican Traveling Theater (PRTT) is a bilingual theatrical and educational organization founded and formally incorporated in 1967. PRTT is the brainchild and labor of love of renowned actress Miriam Colón, founder and creative director of this unique enterprise, whose vision was to bring theater to those communities that could not afford to go to a live theatrical performance. She wanted more than just to provide these communities with entertainment; she wanted to use the theater as a means of communication and education. PRTT's mission statement goals are to "foster and ensure a deepening awareness of the magical, instantaneous power that the theater has as a primary force for communication among people." In particular, Colón aspired to provide a forum within which the works of Latino artists exposed young Latinos of New York to the beauty and artistry inherent in their own cultures, something visibly lacking in standard educational venues.

Over time the PRTT has grown to include a number of other complementary programs that underscore and enhance its original purpose. The Annual Summer Touring Unit is the foundation upon which PRTT was built, inspired by Colón's early theatrical experience as a member of a traveling theater company. The oldest of the theater's components, it performs plays free of charge for economically disadvantaged audiences in the New York, New Jersey, and Connecticut tristate area. Productions staged by PRTT include works by a wide range of Latino artists from a diverse cultural heritage. Playwrights, actors, directors, designers, and others from the Spanish-speaking Caribbean, Mexico, and Central and South America have been well represented in the offerings of the touring unit.

Founded to bring theater to those communities that could not afford to attend a live performance, the Puerto Rican Traveling Theater provides a means of cultural connection and education. Courtesy of the Offices of the Government of Puerto Rico in the United States. Centro Archives, Centro de Estudios Puertorriqueños, Hunter College, CUNY.

Theater

Mainstage Productions performs in PRTT's permanent 194-seat theater, housed at its West Forty-seventh Street location, and is home to an Actors' Equity Association Off-Broadway company. From its inception it has presented bilingual theatrical productions, enabling Mainstage Productions to reach a wide audience. In addition to presentations by well-known playwrights such as René Márques, Federico García Lorca, and Molière, PRTT has performed works by promising new artists, including many who have come from its very own Playwrights Unit. Moreover, numerous U.S. and world premieres have originated at PRTT's permanent theater.

The Playwrights Unit is a tuition-free writing laboratory through which aspiring playwrights from ethnically and culturally diverse origins are educated and guided in the art of writing for the theater. Its graduates represent a rich source of new dramatic material, much of which has premiered on PRTT's Mainstage. Carmen Rivera, Oscar Colón, Candido Tirado, and others are among those who have had their works premiered at the Puerto Rican Traveling Theater, as well as such venues as Repertorio Español, INTAR, Seattle Repertory Theater, the Joseph Papp Public Theater, and the Kennedy Center.

The Raul Julia Training Unit provides at-risk youth, ages fourteen to twenty-five, with tuition-free lessons in acting in English and in Spanish, singing, body movement, and improvisation. The program aims to improve literacy and encourage good reading habits, as well as train potential professionals through an after-school theater arts program that stresses knowledge and comprehension of contemporary and classical literature. Teamwork, discipline, a sense of responsibility, and sharing are important components of the program that each participant is expected to master. Among the graduates of this unit who have gained national and international recognition in various facets of the entertainment industry are Ricky Martin, Marc Anthony, and Bobby Plasencia.

In spite of its success as a theatrical venue, the organization has held fast to its founding principle of bringing theater to the people and using it as a means of communication and education. Under the nurturing leadership of Miriam Colón, an extraordinary Latina in her own right, the Puerto Rican Traveling Theater has opened avenues of opportunity for countless aspiring actors, actresses, and playwrights. It has woven itself into the fabric of the New York City theater scene and become a vibrant part of its multicultural tapestry.

SOURCE: Colón, Miriam, founder and director of the Puerto Rican Traveling Theater. 2001. Personal interview by Lillian Jiménez, Latino Educational Media Center, New York City, April.

Georgina García

Teatro Campesino

In order to understand the origin and purpose of el Teatro Campesino (the Farmworkers' Theater), one must first look at its connection with the United Farm Workers of America union (UFW) in Delano, California. Under the direction of César Chávez, Helen Chávez, and Dolores Huerta, this union was the first of its kind to fight for the farmworkers' right to organize and to earn living wages. In 1965 César Chávez invited Luis Valdez, who was a former farmworker and had theater experience, to help him create a *teatro* group in order to spread the word about the union's causes. Soon the most famous and important Chicana/o theater ensemble was born. Valdez is often credited as the mastermind of the group; however, theater critic Yolanda Broyles-González makes a strong case about the importance of offering a "non-hierarchical and non-patriarchal" definition of the ensemble in order to credit other members of it and especially the women who played an essential role.

El Teatro Campesino grounded its work on the centuries-old oral tradition of the *carpa* (popular tent show), represented best by the Mexican comedian Cantinflas. The ensemble's first actors (male and female) and audiences were the farmworkers themselves, and collectively they developed their original *actos* (skits) through improvisations. These *actos'* central themes were the farmworkers' need to unionize, their labor exploitation, their inhumane living conditions, and their struggles in general. The skits were committed to memory (not written down) and reworked according to the audience's needs and participation. Along with this oral tradition, another important element was the *rasquachi* aesthetic (making do with what they had, given their economic limitations). The costumes consisted of an occasional mask and a sign around the neck stating their characters: "esquirol/scab," "patroncito/little boss." One of the main ensemble members who imitated and at times surpassed the acting abilities of Cantinflas was Felipe Cantú, who had an amazing ability for comedy.

In 1967 the ensemble separated from the UFW and continued presenting *actos* about issues affecting the Mexican and Chicana/o communities such as the war in Vietnam and poor-quality education. It also embarked on the task of self-empowerment through the learning of indigenous cultures such as Maya and Aztec, from which it attained the idea of "In Lak'ech" (you are my other self). But in privileging the liberation of oppressed peoples the ensemble prioritized men's struggles. Male characters were more developed than the cardboard female representations. Women's issues were marginalized, and their involvement and activities within the group were not foregrounded. However, it is still essential to recognize the four most influential women in the ensemble: Olivia Chumacero, Socorro Valdez, Diane Rodríguez, and Yolanda Parra. Socorro Valdez, in addition to performing limiting female roles, became famous for her excellent portrayals of some male characters such as a pachuco called Huesos/Bones.

At the height of its fame during the 1970s, the ensemble toured throughout the United States and Europe. Unfortunately, the group dissolved in 1978, and in 1981 Luis Valdez formed a theater company called el Teatro Campesino, Inc. that should not be confused with the original ensemble. Nevertheless, el Teatro Campesino's legacy continues to be influential on the Mexican and Chicana/o communities interested in representing their struggles through the medium of theater and performance.

See also United Farm Workers of America

SOURCES: Broyles-González, Yolanda. 1994. *El Teatro Campesino: Theater in the Chicano Movement.* Austin: University of Texas Press; Huerta, Jorge A. 1982. *Chicano Theater: Themes and Forms.* Tempe, AZ: Bilingual Press/Editorial Bilingüe; Valdez, Luis M., and el Teatro Campesino. 1990. *Luis Valdez—Early Works: Actos, Bernabé, and Pensamiento Serpentino.* Houston: Arte Público Press.

Rita E. Urquijo-Ruiz

Villalongín Dramatic Company (c. 1849–1924)

The Carlos Villalongín Dramatic Company, earlier known as the Compañia Encarnación Hernández, was one of several family-based Spanish-language dramatic companies that, first as touring companies and later as resident companies, provided theatrical entertainment for Hispanic audiences in Texas during the nineteenth and early twentieth centuries. This company is notable because for a period of sixteen years, from 1888 to 1904, its director and manager was Antonia Pineda de Hernández. A native of Guadalajara, Antonia Pineda became an actress when she married Encarnación Hernández around 1849.

The Hernández-Villalongín company toured towns of northern Mexico and later southern Texas during the period from 1849 to 1924. The company originated in Guadalajara as the Compañia Encarnación Hernández around 1849. Seeking larger and possibly more receptive audiences, Hernández, the founder, moved the company north to the states of Nuevo León, Coahuila, and Tamaulipas. The cast of five to eight actors, composed of some friends but mostly family (his wife, Antonia Pineda, and his children Herlinda, Concepción, and Luis), began touring southwestern Texas and possibly other U.S. border states from about 1881. It may be that earlier performances were staged in the United

States, but the earliest known documentation, a review of a company performance, was printed in a Laredo newspaper in 1881. In 1900 the company was invited to perform at the inauguration of the San Antonio (Texas) Opera House. During these years the group maintained a home base in the town of Montemorelos, Nuevo León, until 1910.

In 1888, when Encarnación Hernández died, his widow, Antonia Pineda de Hernández, assumed management of the company. She nurtured the acting talents of her company actors and particularly encouraged her children to perform. Her daughter, Concepción Hernández, became one of the leading female actors in Spanish-language theater in northern Mexico and southern Texas.

The traveling companies with their often broad repertories gave audiences an appreciation for Spanish, European, and Mexican dramas and comedies, as well as for Spanish operettas, the zarzuelas. In many instances these companies also encouraged local playwrights in Texas by commissioning original plays. The family-centered companies—which included several generations of husbands and wives and their children, as well as brothers and sisters—appealed to Hispanic families, and their performances became social gathering places where Hispanic cultural values and traditions were reinforced.

The Hernández Company became known as the Carlos Villalongín Company after the retirement of Antonia Pineda de Hernández. Carlos Villalongín, born in Chihuahua in 1872 into a theatrical family, joined the Hernández Company when his own father's company disbanded around 1890. Eventually Carlos Villalongín married Herlinda Hernández, a daughter of Encarnación and Antonia. Carlos became a leading actor with the company and began to assist Antonia in the running of the company. When Antonia retired in 1904, he became manager. It may have been about this time that his two siblings, Mariano and Herminia, joined the company.

After 1911 the uncertainties of travel in northern Mexico during the Mexican Revolution caused the company, like many others, to remain in Texas rather than risking the hazards of travel to perform in Mexico. Henceforth the Villalongín company maintained a base of operations in San Antonio, Texas, and presented a repertory of Mexican, Spanish, and foreign plays to San Antonio and southwestern Texas audiences. The company took up temporary residence at the Teatro Aurora in San Antonio, touring only a portion of the year. The role and responsibilities of the manager, Carlos Villalongín, became more complex. The size of the company grew to fifteen employees, and his duties included those of director, business manager, and general supervisor of all activities related to staging the company's productions, according to Elizabeth Ramírez. At times the Villalongín acting group merged with other companies to perform certain plays or at certain venues.

The Hernández-Villalongín company had a repertory of about 146 plays in its stock, although not all remained active during the lifetime of the company, according to John Brokaw, who studied the archives of the company. The majority of the plays were written in Spain, with a few European examples in translation, and the rest were written by Mexican playwrights. Several original plays were apparently commissioned for the company. The actors kept their roles as long as they were members of the company, and careful preparation and continuous rehearsal gave the company a reputation for excellent acting quality, a quality that Antonia Pineda de Hernández bequeathed to her successor.

The company disbanded in 1924 when Carlos Villalongín retired from management. Several actors in the company, including Villalongín, his sister-in-law, Concepción Hernández, and his daughter, Maria Luisa Villalongín, continued to perform in local productions. But the depression and the advent of moving pictures soon replaced live theater. Spanish-language performers moved to community and church halls, where audiences were able to enjoy serious drama and comedies well into the 1950s. Carlos Villalongín died in 1936.

The archives of the Carlos Villalongín Dramatic Company are located at the Nettie Lee Benson Latin American Collection, University of Texas at Austin. They include printed plays, promptbooks, photographs, broadsides, and playbills.

SOURCES: Brokaw, John. 1983. "Mexican-American Theatre." In *Ethnic Theatre in the United States*, ed. Maxine Schwartz Seller, 335–353. Westport, CT: Greenwood Press; Kanellos, Nicolás. 1990. *A History of Hispanic Theater in the United States: Origins to 1940*. Austin: University of Texas Press; Ramírez, Elizabeth C. 1990. *Footlights across the Border: A History of Spanish-Language Professional Theatre on the Texas Stage*. New York: Peter Lang; _____. 2000. *Chicanas/Latinas in American Theatre: A History of Performance*. Bloomington: Indiana University Press.

Laura Gutiérrez-Witt

TORAÑO-PANTÍN, MARÍA ELENA (1938–)

María Elena Toraño-Pantín is a successful businesswoman and the first Cuban American to be appointed by a U.S. president to serve in a top-ranking position within the federal government. She was born in Havana, Cuba, into a middle-class family with political connections. During the late nineteenth century her grandfather Ramón Vidal held the rank of colonel in the Cuban Independence Army. Her father, Julio Díaz, was a government official tied to the Batista government before 1959.

By the end of the 1950s many of the women in her mother's side of the family, along with others of middle-class status, supported and led the Castro revolution against Batista. This support changed direction when Castro assumed control in 1959. On Mother's Day of that same year rebel soldiers entered the home of María Elena and her husband Arturo Toraño without any provocation. The soldiers seized possession of family cars and other property. Life under the Castro regime quickly became intolerable, and in 1960 María Elena and her husband fled with their son to Florida.

María Elena Toraño had lived in the United States before, as a teenager, where she attended school in New Orleans. However, her experience as a Cuban exile in the United States was much different. As she once stated, "Cuban-Americans in Florida have no limits in their need to succeed, to prove to others." Moving to Florida without any savings, Toraño took on a series of humble jobs such as bagging clothes for a dry cleaner, selling baked goods, and selling panty hose from house to house.

In 1961 her husband, along with many other anti-Castro Cubans, joined the failed attempt to oust Fidel Castro during the invasion of Bahia de Cochinos (Bay of Pigs). He was eventually captured and imprisoned in Havana for a year. During that time Toraño became the sole provider for her family while she was pregnant with their second child, who nearly died from birth complications.

When her husband was released by the Cuban government, he returned to Florida and began to work as a tobacco broker for the General Cigar Company. The Toraño family moved to different parts of the United States, where María Elena Toraño worked as an insurance clerk, social worker, child-welfare worker, and reservation agent for Eastern Airlines.

In 1968 she became an American citizen and joined the Republican Party, influenced by family and fellow Cuban Americans. However, the party's platform struck her as elitist, and she immediately switched to the Democratic Party.

A year later Toraño and her family settled in Miami, where she was promoted to the Division of Corporate Communications and responsible for developing a Spanish-speaking market for Eastern Airlines. After several years she left the airline to become director of Latin American affairs for Jackson Memorial Hospital. She also volunteered in social activities to help expand and create a new image for the Little Havana section of Miami. She soon attracted the attention of the Cuban philanthropist community including the prominent

Cuban American civic leader and insurance executive Leslie Pantín.

In 1977 a fellow Florida Democrat recommended Toraño for the position of associate director of the U.S. Community Services Administration in Washington. She became the first Cuban American appointed to a federal position by President Jimmy Carter and served until 1979.

After completing her commitment with the government, she created the National Association of Spanish Broadcasters (NASB), the first association established to represent Hispanic broadcasters in the United States and Puerto Rico. As a representative of NASB, she advocated the interests of Hispanic broadcasters to the Federal Communications Commission in the areas of funding, employment, and licensing.

In 1980 Toraño decided to open her own public relations firm. Having no money to invest, she took out a loan from the Small Business Administration and used her house as collateral. That same year she married Leslie Pantín, who for many years had been her mentor, best friend, and lover. Pantín allowed her to grow not only as a devoted wife, but also as an independent businesswoman.

Toraño became president and CEO of her public relations firm, which she named META. She selected this name because of its English translation, "goal," and because it was the acronym for Maria Elena Toraño Association. In 1984 META received government certification as a minority business, and in 1986 META's focus shifted to government contracts, especially those dealing with environmental issues. From 1988 to 1994 META was ranked the nineteenth fastest-growing Hispanic-owned company in the United States by *Lear's* magazine and in the top 500 Hispanic businesses according to *Hispanic Business Magazine*. During these years META's formulating and executing strategies produced revenues of more than $25 million with 300 employees.

In 1988 Ms Toraño was appointed by President George Bush to the U.S. Commission on Minority Business Development. In this position she was responsible for increasing the success ratio of small minority businesses and expanding business practices of existing markets.

In 1989 Leslie Pantín fell ill during a business trip and died later that year. Trying to fill the void after her husband's death, Toraño founded METEC, an asset management company. METEC managed a portfolio of almost $1 billion in nonperforming assets taken over by the Resolution Trust Corporation (RTC) and later the Federal Deposit Insurance Corporation. After the closure of RTC in 1994, METEC handled asset disposition work for the Department of Housing and Urban Development (HUD) and the U.S. Marshals, among others. She sold METEC in 1995 and continued running META.

Toraño was appointed to the U.S. Commission for Public Diplomacy in 1993 under the Clinton administration. During this period she also served as cochair of the Development Sub-committee for the Presidential Summit of the Americas, which all elected officials of each state attended. She was instrumental in providing leadership and strong support for the passage of the North American Free Trade Agreement.

While working with the federal government, she served several times (August–September 1994, February 1996) as a presidential advisor in the political crises between Cuba and the United States. She assisted in developing policies for the safe, legal, and orderly migration of political refugees from Cuba to the United States and was advisor on the Helms-Burton legislation. Because of her moderate stand on Cuban issues and her strong political position opposing severe economic sanctions against Cuba, Toraño gained many enemies from radical Cuban political circles within the United States.

Among her many achievements, Toraño created the International Health Council of South Florida. She was among the founders and executive committee members of the Hispanic Council on International Relations, the U.S. Hispanic Chamber of Commerce, and the U.S. Latin Chamber of Commerce and was chair emeritus of the National Hispanic Leadership Institute. In addition, she served on many committees, including

María Elena Toraño-Pantín with President William J. Clinton. Courtesy of María Elena Toraño-Pantín.

the Council on Foreign Relations, the University of Miami's Government Affairs and Public Policy Commission, and the Visiting Committee of the University of Miami's Graduate School of International Studies. Toraño was nominated by the U.S. Department of Transportation as Outstanding Woman of the Year 1989 and received the Governor's Award from the state of Florida in that same year.

See also Entrcpreneurs

SOURCES: Gómez, Ivonne. 1999. "Maria Elena Toraño. Determinación, intuición y riesgo." *El Nuevo Herald,* Domingo Social, October 10; Howard, Jane. 1993. "A Woman for Lear's: Maria Elena Toraño of Miami, Florida." *Lear's,* September, 100–116; Pérez-Feria, Richard. 1993. "María Elena's Renaissance." *MM,* May, 38–41; Toraño-Pantín, María. 2004. Oral interview by Carlos A. Cruz, April 28.

Carlos A. Cruz

TORRES, ALVA (1932–   )

Born in 1932, fourth-generation Tucsonan Alva Torres became a vocal community activist and historical preservationist. As urban renewal destroyed the oldest and largest barrio in the city, Torres initiated a battle over space and memory that demanded that older structures be preserved. A firm believer in the power of prayer, she convinced a small group of Mexican American women in 1967, also alarmed by the potential historical erasure of Mexican and Mexican American history, to pray and save sites in danger of destruction. These women moved to collective action and formed a historic preservationist group, the Society for the Preservation of Tucson's Plaza de la Mesilla, or La

Placita Committee. Led by Torres, the organization rallied to save a Mexican-style plaza and the small-business establishments that surrounded it from the bulldozers. Known for generations as La Placita, the structure was more than 100 years old and represented a long history of Mexican celebrations and worship in Tucson. It was also the city's cultural heart.

La Placita Committee was never a large organization; its membership remained at about twenty. But some of its members, especially Alva Torres, and the organization itself became the city's most vocal and public critics of urban renewal. They recognized the need for public sites that testified to Mexican American heritage and their involvement in the area's development. In temperatures above 100 degrees the women stood on downtown streets gathering signatures to save La Placita. Asserting their right to petition the state, they garnered support at street corners, grocery stores, and numerous gatherings during the hot summer months. The committee drew more than 100 people to its meetings and collected more than 8,000 signatures that it submitted to the mayor and council. Its actions forced city officials to leave the kiosk in the original spot where it stood in the old La Placita.

Members of La Placita Committee ultimately pushed forth the formation of, and subsequently their appointments to, the Tucson Historic Committee. Torres served on this committee for six years. The roots of the Tucson–Pima County Historical Commission, which currently remains an active and powerful voice in historical preservation matters, can be traced to the efforts of Torres and La Placita Committee. Today the kiosk stands out because it looks old and its authenticity visually marks it as different from the surrounding

Alva Torres, speaking from the kiosk at La Placita, April 2004. Photograph by Marisol Badilla. Courtesy of Lydia R. Otero.

structures. It and other sites have Arizona historical markers that mention Mexican American contributions to local history. Torres insisted that all historical markers be in both English and Spanish.

Deservingly, Torres was selected Woman of the Year by the Tucson Advertising Club in 1976. She was the first Mexican American woman to receive the award. Torres eventually became a journalist and wrote a popular weekly column in the 1980s for the local newspaper, in which she raised community concerns and issues. She also worked as director of the Legalization Amnesty program for the Catholic Community Services of Southern Arizona and served on various charities and community boards. She remains a committed activist to this day. In 2002 Torres received the YMCA's Lifetime Achievement Award for Women Who Make Tucson Better.

SOURCE: Otero, Lydia R. 2003. "Conflicting Visions: Urban Renewal, Historical Preservation and the Politics of Saving the Mexican Past." Ph.D. diss., University of Arizona.

Lydia R. Otero

TORRES, IDA INÉS (1924?–)

Labor leader, educator, and union organizer Ida Inés Torres, better known as Sister Torres among her fellow union members, describes herself as a "worker for workers." She is currently a vice president of the International Retail/Wholesale Department Store Union (RWDSU), president of Local 3, RWDSU, president of the Hispanic Labor Committee, and the treasurer of the New York City Central Labor Council. She grew up in a union family. "In my home," she says, "union was a special word." Her father, Francisco Berrocal, was a founding member of the National Maritime Union, and her stepmother, Eulogia, a needleworker, was a member of the International Ladies Garment Workers' Union.

After the death of her mother when Torres was five years of age, she and her brother spent time in foster care. One of the places where they resided was the Little Flower Institute in Wading River, Long Island. There they were forbidden to speak Spanish. "But I was a defiant child," Torres recalls. Locked up in a closet as a punishment for using Spanish, she spent the whole time singing Spanish songs in a loud voice. Some years later the family was reunited when her father, a merchant seaman, remarried.

Torres grew up in East Harlem and went to Wadleigh High School in Central Harlem. After graduating she took a job in the same factory where her stepmother worked as a sewing-machine operator. Here she began to understand the role of the union when she observed the union "chair lady" negotiate with the bosses on behalf of the workers.

Torres married young, had two children, and divorced while they were still small. Because of her circumstances she needed to work, but at that time women were supposed to stay home, and her family was set against her working. She went to work, but was made to feel guilty for not being with her children. This experience made her conscious of the special needs of women workers, and throughout her union career the rights of women workers have been a priority.

Sister Torres's first union job was as a telephone operator with Local 231 of the Federation of Architects, Engineers, Chemists, and Technicians, which merged with Local 65, a militant union that organized small shops. This became her union training ground. She notes that the first lesson she learned was that to be effective in the union, one must have the workers behind one. In 1954 she went to work as an office manager in Local 3 (RWDSU), which represented the Bloomingdale's Department Store workers. At that time the store workers were mostly women of Irish and Italian descent.

It was during a strike in Bloomingdale's in 1965 that her considerable organizing skills were recognized.

Labor leader and educator Ida Inés Torres describes herself as a "worker for workers." Courtesy of the Felipe N. Torres Papers. Centro Archives, Centro de Estudios Puertorriqueños, Hunter College, CUNY.

After the fifteen-day strike workers petitioned for Torres to become an organizer. She was appointed to the position of organizer, thus beginning a lifelong commitment of "looking out for the workers." Her responsibilities included internal organizing, negotiating contracts, and handling grievances. She also assumed a leading role in efforts to unionize nonunion shops. She was subsequently elected vice president, secretary-treasurer, and, in 1998, president of Local 3 (RWDSU) following the retirement of John F. O'Neill.

One of Torres's main concerns has been the education of workers, particularly Latino workers, for leadership positions within the union. She has dedicated her life to educating workers about their rights and training them to assume positions of power. She graduated from Empire State College and Cornell University's School of Industrial and Labor Relations. She is an instructor at Cornell University's School of Industrial and Labor Relations. She taught at the Harry Van Arsdale Center for Labor Studies. For the past twenty years she has been the workshop coordinator for the University and College Labor Educator Association's Summer Institute for Union Women. In addition, she played a key role in maintaining the Hispanic Labor Committee's job-training program for more than twenty-five years.

Ida Inés Torres has been instrumental in the founding and development of numerous women's rights and community organizations, such as the Hispanic Labor Committee, the Coalition of Labor Union Women, and the National Council of Puerto Rican Women. She has received the prestigious Susan B. Anthony Award from the National Organization for Women and the John Commerford Labor Education Award from the Labor History Association. In May 2000 she received an honorary doctorate from the Queens College Law School of the City University of New York.

Sister Torres believes that a labor leader has to be willing to do every job, no matter how menial it may seem. "Nobody washes floors better than I do!" she says with her hearty laugh. How would she sum up her career? "My career?" she objects. "I never use that word. This is my life."

See also Labor Unions

SOURCES: Torres, Ida Inés. 2001. Oral history interview by Debra Bernhardt, Ismael Garcia, and Nélida Pérez, January 22; _____. Biographical notes. Local 3, New York, RWDSU. Centro Archives, Centro de Estudios Puertorriqueños, Hunter College, CUNY.

Nélida Pérez

TORRES, LOURDES (1953–)

Lourdes Torres is a community activist from the South Bronx area of New York City. She has been active in numerous organizations, including Unión Estudiantil Pedro Albizu Campos (Pedro Albizu Campos Student Union), the National Congress for Puerto Rican Rights, and the Committee against Fort Apache. Currently she directs the Office of Development and Grants Administration at Hostos Community College, City University of New York.

Torres was born on August 2, 1953, the fifth of seven children of Clorinda Valentín and Joaquín Torres Rivera, who migrated to New York from Puerto Rico in the 1930s. Despite limited economic resources, her parents sent her to Catholic schools, believing that this would give her a more solid education. From first to eighth grade Torres attended St. Athanasius (1959–1964) and St. Thomas Aquinas (1964–1967) in the Bronx. When she started high school in the ninth grade, she received a scholarship to an all-girls school, the Academy of the Sacred Heart of Mary in Manhattan (1967–1971). In her second year she lost the scholarship and had to work in order to pay for tuition. At this point in her adolescent years she formed a club of Latina students and began to more consciously identify herself as Puerto Rican. She also participated in meetings of ASPIRA that motivated her to pursue a college education and to develop personal goals. Torres was also inspired by the Young Lords Organization, and although she was never a member, she learned from it to take pride in her Puerto Rican heritage.

In 1971 Torres entered Queens College for an undergraduate degree. It was during her college years that she became involved with the Unión Estudiantil Pedro Albizu Campos, an organization that aimed to unite Puerto Rican students through educational programs and conferences. Torres graduated in the spring of 1976 with a B.A. in education and linguistics.

In the summer of 1976 she made a first and memorable trip to Puerto Rico. Upon her return to New York she worked as a public school teacher for six months, but was dismissed because of the fiscal crisis in New York City and the lack of funds for her position. From 1977 to 1980 she taught classes on bilingual education and the Puerto Rican child in the Department of Puerto Rican Studies at Queens College. From 1977 to 1978 she completed a master's degree in bilingual education at St. John's University.

As a community activist, Lourdes Torres played a leading role in several civil rights organizations. In 1981 she became active in the Committee against Fort Apache, which was created in protest against the film *Fort Apache: The Bronx*. The film, a negative portrayal of the South Bronx community, is filled with racist overtones. Around this same period Torres joined an organizing committee for the creation of the National

Lourdes Torres. Courtesy of the Lourdes Torres Papers.
Centro Archives, Centro de Estudios Puertorriqueños,
Hunter College, CUNY.

Congress for Puerto Rican Rights, which became an important civil rights organization. She served as national secretary and as coordinator of the Puerto Rico chapter and the New York council.

During the 1980s Torres worked for various institutions. She was a curator for the Bronx Museum of the Arts (1980–1982) and a teacher trainer for the National Origins Desegregation Center (1982–1986) and for the Early Childhood Bilingual Multicultural Resource Center (1982–1986). Since 1987 she has been working at Hostos Community College of the City University of New York and has occupied the following positions: director of the Office of Community and Continuing Education and the Adult Basic Education Program (1987–1997), special assistant to the president (1987–1992), lecturer in the Department of Health and Human Services (1992–1995), and director of the Office of Development and Grants Administration.

Lourdes Torres's collected papers in the Library and Archives of the Center for Puerto Rican Studies at Hunter College, City University of New York, about language rights, educational reform, and key civil rights organizations. Torres was part of an important generation of community leaders, and her papers are a good resource for understanding the role of Puerto Rican activists in the 1980s and 1990s.

SOURCE: Torres, Lourdes. 1968–2000. Papers. Centro Archives, Centro de Estudios Puertorriqueños, Hunter College, CUNY.

Ismael García, Nélida Pérez, and Pedro Juan Hernández

TORRES, PATSY (PATRICIA DONITA) (1957–)

Patsy Torres was born in San Antonio, Texas, to Wiliado (San Antonio, Texas) and Patricia Torres (Grants Pass, Oregon) and was raised there. Unlike most other Tejana artists, Torres's parents and grandparents were college educated and thus exerted a great influence on her to pursue a college education rather than music. Torres never had singing lessons or even experience singing in a choir. Her strongest music influence was her grandfather, Dr. William Torres, who played various instruments, wrote songs, and loaned Patsy her very first instrument, a trumpet.

Attending Thomas Jefferson High School, from which she graduated in 1975, also provided a formal space to pursue music. Patsy and her sister became involved in the school band, with her sister playing the saxophone and Patsy the trumpet. In high school Patsy and her friends became well known for performing and winning many school talent shows. Yet her big break into a more formal music industry arena came while she was in college singing for a local band called Blue Harmony, for which she also began playing trumpet. When Blue Harmony was hired to sing and play at a wedding, Patsy's singing talent was noticed by a local record promoter, and she was eventually signed by Bob Grever with CBS/Sony in San Antonio.

Torres's first big record contract was with Freddie Records in 1985. Her first Tejano album with Freddie Records resulted in her first number one hit song, "Ya me voy de esta tierra," which her grandfather William had written back in 1947. Torres recalled, "My grandfather's song was a traditional mariachi but I did it in ranchera style." In 1987 Torres was awarded a Tejano Music Award for Best Female Entertainer. She has been nominated since then for numerous other Tejano Music Awards, including Single of the Year, Best Female Performance in a Video, and Album of the Year. She has also produced albums and compact discs for WEA Latina and Joey International. Her most notable contribution to Tejano music was that she was the first Tejana singer to integrate dance performance with song. Unlike earlier woman artists such as Laura Canales, Lisa López, and Elsa García, Torres took advantage of the entire stage by including dance performance and changes in costume along with song. She recalls Laura Canales giving her the nickname Chicana Madonna because of her integration of dance and performance along with music. Her physical energy and creativity on stage won her a huge following among fans of Tejano music.

Influenced by female rockers in the early 1980s such as Pat Benatar, Heart, and Chrissie Hynde, she integrated into her act the 1980s styles and aesthetics, which included headbands and spandex pants. Since this was a very popular trend of the time, she made an instant connection with the younger generation. Torres recalled, "While other girls were wearing dresses and acting more ladylike I got flack from older people who couldn't relate to what I was doing." For Tejana artists who followed, such as Selena and Shelly Lares, the model created by Torres to integrate dance, performance, and singing remains the standard. Torres's contribution to Tex-Mex was her own unique style of music that, for a woman in Tejano music, was quite original. At the end of the 1990s Torres continued to contribute to Tejano music by recording on Discos Joey International such songs as "Bien cuidada" (1996), "Bien protegida" (1997), and "Trenzas" (1999).

Torres's music has been recognized by various organizations, particularly because of her youth education project Positive Force, a music and education ensemble that tours throughout the country. In 2000 *La Prensa* awarded her the La Prensa Latina Women in Action Award for her involvement in the arts. That same year she was also inducted into the San Antonio Women's Hall of Fame. Torres's strong regional fan base, which began in the early 1980s, remains to this day. She is a local icon in her hometown, where she continues to perform and record and has been recognized as "one of the most influential San Antonians."

SOURCE: Burr, Ramiro. 1999. *The Billboard Guide to Tejano and Regional Mexican Music.* New York: Billboard Books.

Deborah Vargas

TOVAR, LUPITA (1910–   )

The oldest of nine children, film star Lupita Tovar was born in Tejuantepec, Mexico, on July 27, 1910. When she was eight years old, the National Railroad of Mexico relocated the family to Mexico City. Educated by nuns, Tovar had a very strict upbringing.

In 1928 Fox Studios sent director Robert Flaherty to Mexico to test potential starlets. Flaherty tested Tovar and about sixty other young women. Tovar took first place, and Fox Studios offered her a contract. Her father was very strict and refused until Fox allowed Tovar's maternal grandmother to act as her chaperone. Tovar signed a seven-year, $150-a-week contract.

Tovar first appeared in a Myrna Loy film, *The Black Watch* (1929), and had small parts in *The Veiled Woman* (1929) and *Joy Street* (1929). In the 1920s the studios controlled every aspect of an actor's life, including his or her appearance, publicity, and roles. Tovar learned how to walk like an actor, dress, and apply makeup. Along with English classes, she took dancing lessons from Rita Hayworth's father, Eduardo Cansino.

With the advent of sound, or "talkies," many foreign actors fell by the wayside. "Going from silent to the talkies was very difficult for everybody . . . you had to learn dialogue, which before [you did not have to], because you could say anything you wanted and then they made the titles," Tovar recalled. She feared that her career was at an end. After learning that her contract would not be renewed, she went to Universal Studios, which had a foreign film department. Here she met her future husband Paul Kohner, the head of the department. Smitten with her, Kohner gave Tovar a job and convinced the head of Universal Studios, Carl Laemmle, to produce Spanish-language films. Laemmle agreed, and Tovar starred in Universal's first such movie, *La voluntad del muerto*, the Spanish version of *The Cat Creeps* (1930). After a successful tour of Mexico with the film, Tovar returned to Hollywood to star in the Spanish-language version of *Dracula* (1931). Like *Voluntad del muerto, Dracula* was filmed at night on the same sets used in the English versions. Her other Spanish-language films included *Carne de cabaret (Ten Cents a Dance,* 1931), *Alas sobre del Chaco (Storm over the Andes,* 1935), and *El Capitán Tormenta (Captain Calamity,* 1936).

With the success of *La voluntad del muerto* and *Dracula,* Tovar was asked to star in Mexico's first talkie film, *Santa* (1931). Her costar from *La voluntad del muerto,* Antonio Moreno, a famous silent star, directed the film. The story was a remake of a 1918 film that told the story of a woman who became Mexico's most famous prostitute.

From Germany Kohner called Tovar in Hollywood, asking her to marry him. Tovar agreed and joined Kohner there, where she planned to star in German director Gustav Machaty's *Ecstasy* (1932). But Kohner forbade her to make the film, and Machaty instead chose a young, unknown actress named Hedy Lamarr. The film made Lamarr an international star.

Because of the rise of Nazism, the Kohners returned to Hollywood in 1935. Tovar made a few more films: *Blockade* (1938), *The Fighting Gringo* (1939), *South of the Border* (1939), *Green Hell* (1940), and *The Westerner* (1940). At the same time she made films in Mexico: *Mariguana* (1936), *El rosario de Amozo* (1938), *Resurrección* (1943), and *El coreo del Zar* (1943). Her last film was in 1945, *The Crime Doctor's Courage.*

Tovar retired to raise her children, Susan and Paul Jr. (Pancho) Kohner. Her daughter Susan starred in the 1959 version of *Imitation of Life,* winning a Best Supporting Actress nomination for her portrayal of Sarah Jane, the light-skinned daughter of the housekeeper, who attempts to pass for white. Paul Jr. worked as an assistant for John Huston and now is a well-established film producer.

Tovar never regretted giving up her career for her family. Her husband's talent agency thrived and kept her busy. As she said in a recent interview, "I had a very, very, very happy life. I was an actress by fate." The attention she has received in the last ten years for her work in *Dracula* and *Santa* has only made her more grateful for what she accomplished.

See also Cinema Images, Contemporary; Movie Stars

SOURCES: Ankerich, Michael G. 1998. *The Sound of Silence: Conversations with 16 Film and Stage Personalities Who Bridged the Gap between Silents and Talkies.* Jefferson, NC: McFarland; Skal, David J. 1990. *Hollywood Gothic: The Tangled Web of Dracula from Novel to Stage and Screen.* New York: W. W. Norton.

Alicia I. Rodríquez-Estrada

TOYPURINA (1761–?)

Toypurina was a Native California tribal medicine woman from the Kumi.vit tribe of southern California from the area around San Gabriel. Her tribe became known as the Gabrieleno after Spanish contact in the late eighteenth century. She is best known for her direct involvement in a planned revolt against Spanish colonial rule.

Between 1769 and 1823 Spanish Franciscan missionaries established twenty-one missions in California from San Diego to as far north as Sonoma, about twenty miles north of San Francisco. These missions, built in the homelands of various tribal nations, sought to force California Natives to become laborers for the mission, as well as convert them to the Catholic faith. They had little regard for the Native people's own indigenous religious and spiritual beliefs. The Franciscans attempted to restructure Native societies through policies of both assimilation and acculturation. In an effort to retain their tribal culture, religious practices, and beliefs, some Native people resisted the colonization efforts. Toypurina emerged as one such individual.

In October 1785 Native leaders, both traditional and so-called neophytes (the Spanish term for those newly converted to the Catholic faith), made the decision to destroy the San Gabriel Mission. The Franciscan order viewed the Native peoples as "pagan" and "heathen" and thus tried to force conversions. Various tribal leaders concluded that the new Spanish colonists, both religious and secular, were detrimental to the Native population. The leaders viewed the Spanish as paternalistic people who sought Indian land. Furthermore, as previously noted, Indians who were baptized ended up as laborers in the Spanish mission system and were viewed as culturally and socially inferior by the Spanish.

Native leaders from six nearby villages organized their planned revolt after Spanish officials told them that they could not practice traditional dances. Angered by this authoritarian decision, both traditional and mission Indians, including convert Nicolás José, planned to destroy the San Gabriel Mission, which became the symbol of suppression of local customs. The leaders requested the support of Toypurina because of her extraordinary powers as a medicine person. She was to use her divine influence to eliminate the Catholic priests, while the Native male leaders would eliminate Spanish soldiers. Toypurina appears to have joined the revolt because of her own disheartenment at the invasion of her homeland. She and other leaders wished to defend their way of life.

Unfortunately, the Spanish authorities discovered the planned revolt and punished the Native people involved in the incident. After the failed attempt military officials interrogated Toypurina and the revolt leaders to find out the extent of their plans. In 1786 Spanish officials exiled Toypurina from the San Gabriel area and sent her to another Spanish mission, San Carlos, further north. Additionally, according to trial records, she was pressured to accept Catholic baptism before banishment from her native homeland. The authorities sent two male leaders south to San Diego as prisoners. Soldiers publicly flogged the remaining Native participants to demonstrate to other Indians that troublemakers would be punished for opposing Spanish rule.

There are two significant aspects of the planned revolt of 1785. First, tribal leaders called upon the support of a Native woman in this incident. This indicates the influence of Native women at the time of early Spanish colonization. Like some men, women could also become influential medicine persons because of their medicinal knowledge, spiritual powers, personality traits, and other factors. This demonstrates one type of leadership role Native California women had both before and after European contact.

Second, the planned revolt of 1785 at San Gabriel is an example of Native resistance to the Spanish mission system that existed along coastal California from 1769 to 1821 and was finally abolished by the Mexican government in 1833. To express their extreme dislike of Spanish colonial rule, including the missions, Indians exhibited both passive and active forms of resistance. A passive form was work slowdown while performing manual labor in the missions. Active forms included running away from the missions, destroying church property, and planning revolts to eliminate the Spanish colonists. Native California women, including Toypurina, became participants in the various forms of resistance.

See also California Missions

SOURCES: Brady, Victoria, Sarah Crome, and Lyn Reese. 1984. "Resist! Survival Tactics of Indian Women." *California History* 63 (Spring): 140–145; Fogel, Daniel. 1988. *Junípero Serra,* *the Vatican and Enslavement Theology.* San Francisco: Ism Press; Milanich, Jerald T. 1999. *Laboring in the Fields of the Lord: Spanish Missions and Southeastern Indians.* Washington: Smithsonian Institute Press.

Annette L. Reed

TRAMBLEY, ESTELA PORTILLO (1936–1999)

Estela Portillo Trambley was a poet, a storyteller, and especially a playwright. The author has been considered a precursor of many Chicana writers because she was among the first Chicana to publish her writings and to produce plays.

Portillo Trambley was born in El Paso, Texas, where she spent most of her life. Along with four younger siblings, she was raised in a mixture of cultures by her Italian father and her Mexican mother. Until the age of thirteen she also spent time with her maternal grandparents, owners of a grocery store in El Paso called Amigo de los pobres (Friend of the Poor). The writer expressed a very positive attitude when speaking of the barrio and the community in which she grew up. In an interview with Juan Bruce-Novoa, the Chicana author said, "When I was a child, poverty was a common suffering for everybody around me. A common suffering is a richness in itself."

In 1947 she married Robert Trambley. The marriage produced six children. Portillo Trambley managed to combine the responsibilities of raising a family with a return to college. She received a baccalaureate and a master's degree in English from the University of Texas at El Paso. From 1957 to 1964 she taught at the high-school level and also served as chairperson of the English Department at the El Paso Technical Institute. She guest-edited the historic 1973 issue of *El Grito*, which included the first contemporary collection of works written by Chicana authors. In 1979 she worked in the Department of Special Services of the El Paso public school system.

While working as resident dramatist at El Paso Community College, Portillo Trambley produced and directed several plays. She also hosted a radio talk show, *Estela Says,* and wrote and hosted a cultural program for television, *Cumbres.* By that time she realized that she wanted to pursue a full-time writing career.

In 1971 she published her first play, *The Day of the Swallows*, for which she won the Quinto Sol Literary Prize a year later. Her play *Blacknight* was published in 1973, and in 1985 it won second place in the New York Shakespeare Festival's Hispanic American playwrights' competition.

During the 1970s Portillo Trambley's *Rain of Scorpions and Other Writings* (1975) was one of the few Chicano books available to that community. The book was well received by the Chicano audience and especially by Chicana feminists. In 1979 her play *Sun Images* was published, but she came to national attention only after the publication of *Sor Juana and Other Plays* in 1983. The collection included *Puente Negro, Autumn Gold, Blacknight,* and *Sor Juana.* At the time of *Sor Juana*'s publication the writer expressed her excitement for theater: "I have tried my hand at most genres of writing: poetry, essay, short story, novel. I have found the writing of plays the most difficult, the most exciting, and the most rewarding."

In 1986 she published *Trini*, a novel about a Tarahumara woman who crosses the border into the United States. *Trini* is a novel about struggle and achievement and thus is also a reflection of the author's own life.

Portillo Trambley was a Chicana playwright who fought for recognition and provided the first example of the new Chicana literature. After her death her husband Robert said, "Estela's insatiable thirst for knowledge and her relentless drive to change the inequitable status of womanhood shows in her books, for she writes of women who have strength in this social world."

See also Literature; Theater

SOURCES: Bruce-Novoa, Juan. 1980. *Chicano Authors: Inquiry by Interviews.* Austin: University of Texas Press; Hernández-Gutiérrez, Manuel de Jesús, and David William Foster, eds. 1997. *Literatura Chicana, 1965–1995: An Anthology in Spanish, English, and Caló.* New York: Garland Publishing; Telgen, Diane, and James Kamp, eds. 1993. *Notable Hispanic American Women.* Detroit: Gale Research; Trambley, Estela Portillo. 1986. *Trini.* Binghamton, NY: Bilingual Press.

María E. Villamil

TREATY OF GUADALUPE HIDALGO (1848)

The Treaty of Guadalupe Hidalgo was a document that ended the U.S.-Mexican War (1846–1848). It is the oldest treaty still in force between the two countries and has shaped the international and domestic history of the two countries. The North Americans viewed the forcible incorporation of almost one-half of Mexico's national territory as an event foreordained by Providence, fulfilling a Manifest Destiny to spread the benefits of American democracy to the lesser peoples of the continent. With arrogance born of superior military, economic, and industrial power, the United States virtually dictated the terms of settlement. The treaty established a pattern of inequality between the two countries, and this lopsided relationship has stalked Mexican-American relations ever since, making the resolution of mutual problems that much more difficult.

Since 1848 Indians and Chicanos have struggled to achieve some equality of political status within the United States. In this they have sought to fulfill the promises first made in the Treaty of Guadalupe Hidalgo. However, the treaty ensured that Mexico would remain an underdeveloped third-world country well into the twentieth century. Mexican historians and politicians perceive this treaty as a bitter lesson in American expansionism. The treaty has had implications for international law. Interpretations of the provisions of the treaty have been important in disputes over international boundaries, water and mineral rights, and, most important, civil and property rights for the descendants of the Mexicans in the ceded territories.

Among the many provisions of the treaty were two that were very important for Latinos and Latinas. Articles VIII and IX of the Treaty of Guadalupe Hidalgo set forth the terms by which the former Mexican citizens and their property would be incorporated politically into the United States. These provisions affected more than 100,000 Mexicans residing in the newly acquired territories, including a large number of Hispanicized, as well as nomadic, Indians in New Mexico and California. Article VIII provided that a person had one year to "elect" his or her preference for Mexican citizenship. If this were not done, it was stipulated that he or she had elected to become a U.S. citizen and would be granted citizenship by Congress at some future time. Articles VIII and IX also addressed the property rights of the conquered people. Absentee Mexican landholders would have their property "inviolably respected," and others would "be maintained and protected in the free enjoyment of their liberty and property."

In the six decades after the ratification of the treaty the deceptively clear provisions regarding citizenship and property were complicated by legislative and judicial interpretations. In the end the application of the treaty to the realities of life in the Southwest violated its spirit because many Mexicans were denied basic rights as citizens of the United States and had their lands taken from them by lawyers, bankers, speculators, and government officials. The treaty's provisions in Articles VIII and IX and the Protocol of Querétaro, which replaced Article X when it was deleted by the U.S. Senate, implied protection for private property. But in California and New Mexico this was an empty promise.

In California thousands of gold-rush migrants encroached on the Californio land grants and demanded that something be done to "liberate" the land. The result was the passage in Congress of the Land Act of 1851. This law set up a Land Commission whose members would adjudicate the validity of Mexican land grants in California. Eventually this California commission examined 813 claims and confirmed 604 of them involving approximately 9 million acres. Most Californio landholders, however, lost their lands because of the tremendous expense of litigation and legal fees. To pay for the legal defense of their lands, the Californios were forced to mortgage their ranchos. Falling cattle prices and usurious rates of interest conspired to wipe them out as a landholding class.

One of the most important court cases involving the Treaty of Guadalupe Hidalgo was that of a Californiana, Señora Dominga Domínguez, owner of Rancho las Virgenes, just east of the San Fernando Mission in California. Señora Domínguez had an ironclad title to her land, a grant from the government of Mexico dated August 28, 1835. Her ancestors had taken all the steps required to legalize this claim. For some reason she and her relatives neglected to bring their papers before the Court Land Commission within the time specified in the 1851 law. For the next thirty years a number of Mexican American and European immigrant families settled on the rancho, assuming that the land was part of the public domain, and that it had been opened for homesteading. Finally, in 1883, Brigido Botiller, a French-born Mexican citizen, headed a group of squatters to oust Señora Domínguez from her land, claiming that by the 1851 law she had no legal title to it. Domínguez then sued Botiller and the other squatters for reclamation of her land and back rents. In the 1880s both the district court and the California State Supreme Court ruled in her favor, but Botiller and the squatters appealed their case to the U.S. Supreme Court, where, in a decision issued on April 1, 1889, the court reversed the California Supreme Court decision and ruled that despite the Treaty of Guadalupe Hidalgo's guarantees, Domínguez did not have legal title.

In *Botiller et al. v. Domínguez* the Supreme Court held that the sovereign laws of the United States took precedence over international treaties. This appeared to contradict the Constitution, which (in Article VI, Section 2, and Article III, Section 2, Clause 1) gave treaties the same status as the Constitution. *Botiller et al. v. Domínguez* was an important precedent that guided the Court in its future interpretation of conflicts between treaty obligations and domestic laws. In this case the protection of private property ostensibly guaranteed by the Treaty of Guadalupe Hidalgo was essentially invalidated.

In New Mexico Territory officials were appointed who ruled on the boundaries and legitimacy of Hispano land claims. Ultimately they had to have their decisions approved by Congress, a lengthy and often politicized process. The private and communal land grants in New Mexico covered about 15 million square miles. The surveyor general was given broad powers, but a decision by the Congress took many years. By 1880, 1,000 claims had been filed by the surveyor general, but only 150 had been acted upon by the federal government. Anglo lawyers and politicians, such as Stephen Benson Elkins and Thomas Benton Catron, formed the nucleus of the Santa Fe Ring, a confederation of opportunists who used the long legal battles to acquire millions of acres of Hispano land through legislative and court manipulation.

Finally, on March 3, 1891, President Benjamin Harrison signed into law a bill to establish a Court of Private Land Claims in New Mexico. The Treaty of Guadalupe Hidalgo was specifically invoked as a guiding document. Meeting in Denver, Colorado, and Santa Fe, New Mexico, between 1891 and 1904, the New Mexico court rejected two-thirds of the claims presented before it. Ultimately only eighty-two grants received congressional confirmation. This represented only 6 percent of the total area sought by land claimants. The end result was that the U.S. government enlarged the national domain at the expense of hundreds of Hispano villages, leaving a bitter legacy that would fester through the next century.

With regard to the rights of citizenship, some, as provided in Article VIII, chose to remain Mexican citizens, either by announcing their intent before judicial officials or by returning to Mexico. No one knows their exact number, but probably they were few by comparison with the total population of the Southwest. According to the treaty, those who did not choose to remain Mexican citizens would be considered "to have elected" to become U.S. citizens. As early as 1849 the nature of the citizenship rights of these Mexicans became the subject of controversy. In California and New Mexico the delegates to the constitutional conventions wrestled with the problems of race, rights of citizenship, and the Treaty of Guadalupe Hidalgo. Mexico had granted citizenship to "civilized" Indians and to blacks, yet the Treaty of Guadalupe Hidalgo clearly stated that former Mexican citizens would be given the opportunity to become citizens of the United States. Following the biases of their age, the framers of these constitutions sought wording that would exclude blacks and Indians while including mestizos and Hispanic Mexicans.

During California's gold rush xenophobia, nativism, and racism resulted in violent confrontations between English-speaking immigrants and other residents, including Californios, who were regarded as foreigners by Anglo miners. Antonio Coronel, a native Californio resident of Los Angeles, vividly described stabbings, extortions, and lynchings as commonplace Yankee reactions to native Californios, whom they regarded as interlopers. Some Spanish-speaking natives even were issued passes, supposed proof of their new status as citizens of the United States, but this had little effect on the hordes of Yankees who crowded into the mining district.

The violations of their rights under the Treaty of Guadalupe Hidalgo were finally tested in the U.S. courts. The California Supreme Court case *People v. Naglee* (1851) confirmed that Californios had the rights of citizens, and another case twenty years later, *People v. de la Guerra* (1870), reaffirmed that view, stating that the admission of California as a state constituted the positive act that conferred citizenship on former Mexican nationals.

The biggest violation of the treaty involved various Indian tribes and groups in California and New Mexico. Under the Mexican Constitution of 1824, Indians were considered full Mexican citizens. Upon the transfer of territory to the U.S. government, however, these Mexican citizens received neither U.S. citizenship nor the protections of the treaty as specified in Article VIII. In violation of the treaty, the California Indian tribes were deprived of state or federal protections and consequently became the victims of murder, slavery, land theft, and starvation. In two decades the Indian population within the state declined by more than 100,000. In New Mexico, where the largest Hispanicized Indian population lived, the Hispanos denied them citizenship. In the territorial constitution the franchise was limited to whites only. Approximately 8,000 Pueblo Indians who had been Mexican citizens in 1848 were disenfranchised thereafter. Despite this early history of disenfranchisement, some of it voluntary on the part of the Indians, the New Mexico territorial courts later decided cases that confirmed the citizenship of the Pueblo Indians.

Other provisions of the Treaty of Guadalupe Hidalgo had international implications. In Article XI of the treaty the United States assumed responsibility for control of Indian raids originating on its national soil. This led to a series of financial claims that were eventually abrogated by the Gadsden Treaty in 1853.

Article IV of the Treaty of Guadalupe Hidalgo defined the geographic boundaries between the United States and Mexico. But the land boundary between El Paso and San Diego became a source of controversy almost immediately after the ratification of the treaty, leading to the negotiation of the Gadsden Treaty in 1853. The other portion of the boundary described by the Treaty of Guadalupe Hidalgo, the Rio Grande, also became a source of conflict between the two countries, largely because of periodic changes in the river's course caused by flooding and accretion. The most significant conflict arising from the 1848 treaty boundary involved an area of land known as the Chamizal, a 600-acre tract that eventually became part of downtown El Paso, Texas. El Chamizal had been located south of the Rio Grande and thus part of Mexico in

Disturnell's map of Mexico, published in 1847 and appended to the Treaty of Guadalupe Hidalgo to help identify the boundary. The cartographic errors in this map were the basis for a prolonged dispute that resulted in the Gadsden Treaty in 1853. Courtesy of the Bancroft Library, University of California, Berkeley.

1848, but by 1896, because of flooding and changes in the river's course, the tract became located north of the river within the territory of the United States. From 1848 to 1963 the city of El Paso, Texas, and the U.S. government exercised political jurisdiction over this section of land. After some international negotiations President John F. Kennedy in 1963 the disagreement was settled. The region became El Chamizal International Park.

For many years the Mexican government cited the Treaty of Guadalupe Hidalgo as the authority for claiming a nine-mile territorial sea boundary between the two countries. Finally, on December 26, 1969, after years of discussion between the United States and Mexico over the meaning of Article V with respect to territorial waters, both countries finally agreed to a twelve-mile limit.

The Treaty of Guadalupe Hidalgo, in Article XXI, introduced for the first time the idea of permanent arbitration of disputes in American diplomacy. This provision was one that the Mexican negotiators of 1848 had insisted upon. Many disagreements were submitted to international arbitration, and Mexico demonstrated more good faith in abiding by the results than the United States. Since 1848 Mexico and the United States have, in the spirit of Article XXI of the Treaty of Guadalupe Hidalgo, entered into arbitration, conven-

tions, and discussions to resolve mutual problems. On balance, the United States has gained more monetarily even while not fully complying with the spirit of the treaty. The Mexican government has avoided further conflicts with the United States and gained some prestige both at home and abroad by its willingness to arbitrate disputes.

The major significance of the Treaty of Guadalupe Hidalgo has been that it embodied promises that have not been kept. In 1848 the American and Mexican negotiators entered into an agreement with the understanding that the civil and property rights of the Mexican citizens who were being transferred to the United States would be respected. Today the Treaty of Guadalupe Hidalgo remains a document of great historical importance to Mexicans in the United States.

See also U.S.-Mexican War

SOURCES: Acuña, Rodolfo. 1972. *Occupied America: The Chicano's Struggle toward Liberation*. San Francisco: Canfield Press; Garber, Paul. 1959. *The Gadsden Treaty*. Gloucester, MA: Peter Smith; Griswold del Castillo, Richard. 1990. *The Treaty of Guadalupe Hidalgo: A Legacy of Conflict*. Norman: University of Oklahoma Press; Pletcher, David M. 1973. *The Diplomacy of Annexation: Texas, Oregon, and the Mexican War*. Columbia: University of Missouri Press; Rendon, Armando. 1972. *Chicano Manifesto*. New York: Macmillan.

Richard Griswold del Castillo

TREATY OF PARIS (1898)

The Spanish-American War was a relatively brief and lopsided affair that resulted in the total defeat of Spanish military forces in the Caribbean and the Pacific during the late spring and early summer of 1898. With the signing of a truce in August of that year, the Spaniards agreed to negotiate the terms of a formal peace treaty at a gathering of representatives that was held in Paris in the final months of 1898. During the deliberations, which ended in the signing of the document on December 10, 1898, the Spaniards agreed to relinquish all claims of sovereignty to Cuba, Puerto Rico, the Philippines, and Guam, also called Ladrones at that time. In return, the United States agreed to fund an exchange of prisoners and to pay the Spaniards $20 million as compensation for the loss of their colonies. The United States also agreed to permit Spanish subjects to remain on the islands and to buy, sell, or retain ownership of their properties or businesses, if they so wished. However, the treaty also stipulated that the "civil rights and political status of the native inhabitants" would "be determined" by the U.S. Congress at some future date. This provision immediately created some difficulties for Puerto Ricans, who, lacking political status, were sometimes harassed or denied entry into the United States until favorable court decisions and the granting of U.S. citizenship in 1917 put a stop to these practices.

In the years that followed the signing of the Treaty of Paris, Cuba became an independent country, but remained a de facto economic and political dependency of the United States until the end of the 1950s, when Fidel Castro and his revolutionary government established an alliance with the Soviet Union and other Soviet-bloc countries. The United States also retained the Philippines and Guam, in addition to Puerto Rico, as formal colonies or "unincorporated territories," despite a vicious war for independence in the Philippines that was led by its patriot leader, Emilio Aguinaldo, between 1899 and 1902. Dissatisfaction with U.S. rule also arose in Puerto Rico, which experienced occasional protests and a violent uprising of Nationalists in the years between 1899 and 1954. Puerto Rican women, such as the Nationalist Lolita Lebrón, a participant in the shootings in the U.S. House of Representatives in 1954, played an active role in these protests.

Nevertheless, the eventual outcome of this process, in addition to the establishment of a firm imperialist control over the islands, was increased migration to the United States and Hawaii, which also became a U.S. possession in 1898 and received an influx of Puerto Rican migrants between 1900 and 1901. After the signing of the Treaty of Paris, and with increased intensity in the decades that followed, waves of Cubans, Puerto Ricans, Filipinos, and Guamanians came to the U.S. mainland and changed the demographic makeup of the country, a process that continues.

See also Cuban-Spanish-American War; Ten Years' War

SOURCES: "Focus/En foco 1898–1998, Part I." 1998. *CENTRO: Journal of Centro de Estudios Puertorriqueños* (Hunter College, CUNY) 10:1–2; "Focus/En foco 1898–1998, Part II." 1999. *CENTRO: Journal of Centro de Estudios Puertorriqueños* (Hunter College, CUNY) 11:1; Jones, Jacqueline, Peter Wood, Thomas Borstelmann, Elaine Tyler May, and Vicki L. Ruiz. 2003. *Created Equal: A Social and Political History of the United States.* New York: Longman; Library of Congress. "The Spanish American War." www.loc.gov/rr/hispanic/1898 (accessed June 25, 2005); Scarano, Francisco A. 1993. *Puerto Rico: Cinco Siglos de Historia.* New York: McGraw-Hill.

Gabriel Haslip-Viera

TREVIÑO-SAUCEDA, MILY (1958–)

Mily Treviño-Sauceda, founder and executive director of Líderes Campesinas (Organization of Farmworker Women Leaders), was born in Washington State to Francisca Sosa-Barba and Leopoldo Treviño-Guerrera, both migrant farmworkers. She was one of ten children. When Mily was seven, the family moved to Idaho, where her father found steady work on a ranch, enabling Mily and her siblings to attend school. The children also worked in the fields before and after school in order to contribute to the family's modest income. They returned to Mexico and, when Mily was fifteen, the family moved to California, where they continued laboring in the fields.

Treviño began to work with the United Farm Workers (UFW) in 1975. Both her father and brother had joined the union, and her father was working as a union staff member. Treviño persuaded him to let her join as well, and at sixteen she became a volunteer organizer. She also worked with Catholic youth groups and was chosen to attend a youth leadership conference. The conference inspired her to continue her work, sharpened her leadership skills, and convinced her to return to school.

Treviño was intelligent, charismatic, and well liked, and her talents as a natural organizer came to the attention of California Rural Legal Assistance (CRLA), which offered her a job as a community organizer in the Coachella Valley. Treviño had married fellow UFW organizer Humberto Luna-Sauceda and continued to organize even after she became pregnant. Her husband encouraged her to leave fieldwork, take the job with CRLA, and continue the community organizing she loved. "He was supportive of my organizing, but he also encouraged me to enhance my skills working outside the fields. He knew I was very smart and he always reminded me I could do more." During her ten-year association with CRLA she established contacts across the state. Her husband's untimely death in 1985 changed her life. She became committed to organizing, returning to school, and especially caring for her small son, Humberto.

As a CRLA organizer, she worked with Mexican farmworkers in the agricultural towns and labor camps of the Coachella Valley. In 1988 Mara Elena López-Treviño, a graduate student at California State University, Long Beach, enlisted Mily Treviño's help in conducting a survey among farmworker women. Farmworker women conducted the survey and in the process shared with other women the problems they faced as farmworkers and women: sexual discrimination, harassment, domestic violence, pesticide poisoning, poor housing, and low wages. In response to the women's desire to organize and change these conditions, Treviño formed Mujeres Mexicanas.

In 1991 Treviño returned to school full-time, studying at Mount San Antonio College. In 1992, while still a full-time student, she formed Líderes Campesinas, an organization of, for, and led by Mexican farmworker women. It was the first grassroots organization to develop leadership from among farmworker women and create a structure that they could use to advocate for themselves. She began organizing local Líderes branches across California, driving 1,000 miles each weekend to meet with women. Her son Beto learned about organizing in the fields, but he also learned "about working with women and respecting women," a feeling reciprocated by his "many aunts" in Líderes, who called him "el hijo de la comunidad" (the community's son).

In ten years the organization has developed twenty-four chapters in California and has worked with similar groups within the United States and internationally. Treviño and a few Líderes staffers have attended the International Women's Conferences, an experience that strengthened their understanding of their commonalities with rural women around the world. In 2005 Mily Saucedo-Treviño and Lideres Campesinas received an award from the Leadership in a Changing World program, co-sponsored by the Ford Foundation. This program recognizes extraordinarly leaders or leadership teams across the United States who are changing lives and transforming communities—often against great odds.

Treviño continued as the full-time Líderes organizer, a full-time student, and the soccer coach for her son's team. Upon graduating with honors from Mount San Antonio, she attended California State University at Fullerton, studying Chicano studies and women's

studies. In 1999 she began work on her master's degree. She plans to step down from the directorship by 2006 so other women can take over the position and manage the organization. Treviño hopes to establish an institute for farmworker women that will encourage them to continue their education and, for those with the desire, work for higher degrees. Treviño plans to turn her thesis on Líderes Campesinas into a book and also plans to write children's books "so children, specially girls, can learn how to be leaders and the role models they have with women from their community."

See also Líderes Campesinas; United Farm Workers of America (UFW)

SOURCES: López, Pablo. 1993. "Campesinas Project Seeded." *Los Angeles Times*, March 28, B5; Pulaski, Alex. 1993. "Female Farmworkers Take Care of Business." *Los Angeles Times*, February 28, B1; Ruiz, Vicki L. *From out of the Shadows: Mexican Women in Twentieth-Century America*. New York: Oxford University Press; Street, Richard Steven. 1992. *Organizing for Our Lives: New Voices from Rural Communities*. Portland, OR: Newsage Press and California Rural Legal Assistance.

Devra A. Weber

TUFIÑO, NITZA (1949–   )

The daughter of the well-known Puerto Rican artist Rafael Tufiño and a Mexican dancer, Luz María Aguirre, Nitza Tufiño was born in Mexico City and taken to Puerto Rico when she was a year old. During her adolescence her parents divorced, and she spent the next few years commuting between her mother's house in Manhattan and her father's in San Juan, Puerto Rico. Surrounded by artists at her father's home and encouraged by her mother to develop her artistic talents, she spent most of her high-school years taking courses in ceramics, graphics, and painting. When she graduated from high school in Puerto Rico in 1966, her mother sent her to study fine arts at San Carlos Academy at the Universidad Autónoma of Mexico. There she met the great Mexican muralist Alfaro Siqueiros and was exposed to the importance of murals as public art.

With a B.F.A. from Mexico, she settled in Manhattan in 1970 and began to work as an artist. In 1973 she created her first ceramic mural for the façade of el Museo del Barrio, a community-based museum that she had helped found. The theme of the mural was from her memories of the vegetation of Loiza Aldea, a coastal village east of San Juan, best known for its surviving African traditions. Some of Tufiño's earliest works were also inspired by the petroglyph designs of Puerto Rico's Taino Indians.

During the 1970s she also served as a consultant on Puerto Rican and Caribbean art at the Brooklyn Museum and the Metropolitan Museum of Art. In the early 1980s she returned to school, obtaining an M.S. in urban affairs (1982) from Hunter College, City University of New York, with the support of a fellowship from the U.S. Department of Housing and Urban Development (HUD). Shortly thereafter she was commissioned to create a mural for the Third Street Music School in the Lower East Side of Manhattan. Inspired by the history of the Taíno Indians of Puerto Rico, she called her work *Sinfonía Taína* (Taino Symphony). Her next ceramic mural, *Neo-Boriquén*, installed in the subway station at 103rd Street and Lexington Avenue, depicted a tropical landscape, reminiscent of the Caribbean, with Taino spirits overseeing the lush, flowering trees and plants. The mural was commissioned by the New York City Metropolitan Transit Authority as part of an Art Underground project.

The same agency commissioned her to train a group of high-school dropouts in mural making as a way to help them obtain their high-school diplomas. The collective ceramic mural, titled *Community Life,* is a permanent feature of the subway station at Eighty-sixth Street and Lexington Avenue. Another of her ceramic murals was commissioned by the New York City Health and Hospital Corporation and is part of the Pediatric Ward of the City's Metropolitan Hospital at Ninety-seventh Street and First Avenue.

In more recent years Tufiño has taught dozens of students in New Jersey and Connecticut. One of her most recent student projects is *The Wall of Peace,* a ceramic mural displayed in the lobby of the Thomas Jefferson School in South Orange, New Jersey. The mural, a collective work she did with fourth-grade students at Jefferson, was funded by the Essex County School District. Her latest and largest ceramic mural is *Patience*, a work eighty-two feet long by nine feet wide, commissioned by the Hospital for Special Care at New Britain, Connecticut. The mural's theme is the ever-changing facets of life, depicted by the changing seasons. It was created as part of a two-year training program that included eighteen art students from Central Connecticut University at New Britain. Appointed as a visiting artist at Central Connecticut University (1997–1998), Tufiño established a program in public art and taught drawing and design.

Tufiño's commitment to public art led el Taller Boricua, at 111th Street and Madison Avenue, to recognize her in 1970 as its first woman artist. She continues to work with el Taller by teaching art to the community's children. Tufiño has also served on numerous boards, including the Board of Trustees of el Museo del Barrio, where she coordinated workshops for children for many years on Puerto Rico's arts and culture. She has collaborated with the Cayman Gallery in Soho and with Loisaida's Economic Development Program, aimed at improving the lives of young people in the Lower East Side.

Tufiño has received recognition and awards for her work, including the Donald G. Sullivan Award, Hunter College, Department of Urban Affairs and Planning (1997), the Mid-Atlantic National Endowment for the Arts Regional Award from the Mid-Atlantic Arts Foundation (1992), the New York Foundation for the Arts Artist's Fellowship (1984, 1987), the Puerto Rican Legal Defense and Education Fund Award for Outstanding Contributions to the Arts (1992), and the New York City Council Excellence in Arts Award, given by the Office of Andrew Stein (1991), among others. Tufiño resides in South Orange, New Jersey, with her husband Shimpei Taniguchi and their son Ken. She also has an older daughter, Rachel Breitman, from an earlier marriage who lives in Manhattan.

See also Artists

SOURCES: "Exhibition Catalog for *Art Underground.* 1990. New York: El Museo del Barrio; Tufiño, Nitza. 2001. Oral history interview by Olga Jiménez de Wagenheim, June 16.

Olga Jiménez de Wagenheim

U

ULIBARRÍ SÁNCHEZ, LOUISE (1893–1983)

Louise Ulibarrí Sánchez, recognized as the first Latina school principal in the Albuquerque public school system, was also a woman who refused to follow the social parameters set for women at the beginning of the twentieth century. Ulibarrí was born on June 21, 1893, in Las Vegas, New Mexico, to Marillita Dominique and José Ulibarrí. Marillita and José met when he rode shotgun for Wells Fargo stagecoaches. Marillita gave birth to seven surviving children, of whom Louise was the fourth.

Louise Ulibarrí was an excellent student. Bright and inquisitive, she graduated from eighth grade and then attended New Mexico Western Normal School, which in those days enabled her to teach. Excited about her career, she became a teacher in a one-room schoolhouse at age fourteen in Anton Chico, New Mexico, in 1907. At that time her pupils ranged in age from six to twenty-two years. During the winter one of her jobs was to start a fire in the wood stove to warm the classroom for the children.

In 1912 Ulibarrí married Juan Bautista Sánchez, a cattle rancher, and moved to Duran, New Mexico. She gave birth to five children in her home. The eldest, Frank, went to live with her parents. The youngest, Alfred, died at age two. Despite her domestic obligations, she never stopped teaching and taught in Duran for fifteen years.

She divorced Juan Bautista Sánchez in 1927 because she believed that he was having extramarital affairs. Her devoutly Roman Catholic family was not in agreement with her decision. Her parents told her that she was a heretic; her brothers and sister expressed dismay; her uncles and aunts shunned her; and her grandparents told her that no one had ever done such a terrible thing.

After her divorce Ulibarrí attended Western New Mexico University in Silver City, New Mexico, to work on her high-school education during the summer while she was still teaching. There, in 1929, she opened a

Louise Ulibarrí Sánchez, standing in the door on the left, and her first class in Anton Chico, New Mexico, 1907. Courtesy of Evelia Cobos Yusuf.

restaurant where she met Donaciano Nevarez, a coal miner.

After the death of Nevarez's wife, he frequented Ulibarrí's restaurant, where he found solace, comfort, and good food, since she was a fabulous cook. They began a relationship, fell in love, and were married in the same year. They lived together blissfully until he died of emphysema in 1939. Her family continued to criticize her personal decisions and told her that she would be excommunicated from the church. Because of her second marriage, she was no longer welcomed in their homes.

Shunned by her family and widowed at age forty-six, Ulibarrí came to seek her livelihood in Albuquerque, New Mexico. She arrived in Albuquerque in a wagon with her three children and $10.00 in her pocket. Upon arrival in Albuquerque she went to the Albuquerque Federal Credit Union and convinced the president to give her a loan, which enabled her to establish herself in Albuquerque.

Ulibarrí reconciled with her family during the depression. Still teaching, she was the only one employed among her relatives, and she clothed, fed, and gave shelter to nineteen members of her family. Her youngest sister Eleanor said, "They would have died had it not been for Louise."

Realizing that her career depended on furthering her education, she attended Albuquerque High School at night while teaching during the day in the elementary schools. In 1940 she enrolled as a freshman at the University of New Mexico (UNM). At that time her daughter Rita had already obtained her master's degree from UNM in 1936. Two of her other children were also enrolled in the same university, and she encouraged them to finish their education. Ernesto graduated from business school in 1940, and Patricio graduated first in his class from law school in 1954. Although she educated herself through high school and college, she never stopped teaching, nor did she neglect her duties as a mother.

Not satisfied with a bachelor's degree, in 1944 Ulibarrí drove from Albuquerque, New Mexico, in a Model T Ford to Columbia University in New York, which she attended for two summers to pursue a master's degree. In 1948 she attended the University of Wisconsin at Madison and graduated with a master's degree.

Upon receiving her master's degree she was hired as the principal of Mountain View Elementary School in 1948. In 1950 she was the first principal of a new elementary school and helped organize the curriculum. It was customary at that time to name a school after the founding principal. However, Ulibarrí preferred to name the school La Luz in order to reflect her philosophy of education.

She married Jim Giddings, a distant cousin, in 1950. They were married for only a few years. Jim Giddings became mentally ill, and when he began exhibiting bizarre symptoms, Ulibarrí was forced to institutionalize him. Divorced for the second time, she threw herself into her work, which was to develop the Nambé School Project, a project study on the educational system for underprivileged children that was funded by the Kellogg Corporation. This project, created by Ulibarrí and three other members, was a forerunner to the Federal Title I, a program to help lower-income children designated as educationally deprived.

Ulibarrí had an amazing repertory of stories and songs, both in Spanish and in English, with which she entertained children. She was a true Pied Piper as she enchanted and charmed children down the path of enlightenment. Her advice to the new teachers was to "love the little children, be kind to them and give them guidance." She was a fun-loving and outgoing person. She loved to laugh and sing and believed in gentle persuasion. She disciplined children by talking to them and convincing them to change their ways.

Ulibarrí retired from La Luz Elementary School in 1964 after more than fifty-three years of continuous teaching. In 1969 she remarried her first husband, Juan Bautista Sánchez, after having been divorced from him for forty-two years. They remained married until she died in her sleep on February 6, 1983.

SOURCES: 2001. Oral history interview by Evelia Cobos Yusef. September 10; Cobos Chénier, Helene. 2001. Oral history interview. September 16; Sánchez, Ernesto. 2001. Oral history interview. September 13; Ulibarrí, Joe R. 2001. Oral history interview by Evelina Cobos. September 10.

Evelia Cobos Yusuf and Carlos A. Cruz

UNITED CANNERY, AGRICULTURAL, PACKING, AND ALLIED WORKERS OF AMERICA (UCAPAWA/FTA) (1937–1950)

Founded in 1937, the United Cannery, Agricultural, Packing, and Allied Workers of America (UCAPAWA) in its prime became the seventh-largest union affiliated with the Congress of Industrial Organizations (CIO). UCAPAWA actively recruited workers of color and was the first union to do so on a national basis. Indeed, within its first year UCAPAWA represented African American sharecroppers in the South, Filipino lettuce packers in California, and Mexican pecan shellers in Texas. Several Latinas held leadership positions from the outset, including Monica Tafoya, a Colorado beet worker, Angie González, a Florida cigar roller, and Manuela Sager Solís, a Texas labor organizer. Luisa Moreno, a veteran labor leader, joined UCAPAWA in

1938 and three years later served as a national vice president.

The union attracted attention quickly. At the second annual meeting in 1939, Eleanor Roosevelt wired the following message: "I hope you continue to improve the conditions and bring a better life to the members of your union." The *San Francisco News* noted the union's popularity among farmworkers in California, especially Mexican migrants. Mobilizing a multiracial rank and file (including Mexicans, African Americans, Filipinos, and Euro-Americans), the union staged several strikes in the state's San Joaquin Valley. In October 1939 more than 1,000 workers walked off their jobs in the Madera cotton strike. Organized by UCAPAWA, the workers demanded a living wage. As one journalist wrote, "Men, women, and little children with nowhere to sleep, nothing to eat are hunted, shot and beaten because they asked for a wage they could live on." The next month UCAPAWA negotiated a contract with the Mineral King Farm Association that was perhaps the first farmworker contract in California. However, Mineral King was an atypical grower cooperative because its members, all Dust Bowl migrants, were part of a New Deal experimental farming project.

Because of considerable harassment by the Associated Farmers and local law enforcement and because of the financial drain on national union coffers, UCAPAWA left the fields in order to focus on workers more stably employed in canneries and packinghouses; its most notable successes included Campbell's Soup in New Jersey and the California Sanitary Canning Company in Los Angeles. Led by Luisa Moreno, cannery workers across southern California considerably improved their wages, working conditions, and benefits. Not afraid to break the CIO's no-strike pledge during World War II, Moreno organized a successful walkout at Val Vita in Fullerton, the largest cannery in California. In addition to union recognition and improved wages, management agreed to provide on-plant day care for its workers.

Women constituted half of UCAPAWA's national membership, and across the country they exercised considerable leadership. For example, Mexican women in their California locals held 46 percent of the executive board positions and were 43 percent of the shop stewards. On a day-to-day basis women provided the backbone of the union. During a Colorado beet-worker strike in 1942, Eleanor Cassados directed the relief committee. "No strikers went hungry," *UCAPAWA News* reported, "and we have Eleanor to thank for that." During an era when few unions addressed the concerns of women, this CIO affiliate paved the way. By 1946, 66 percent of its contracts nationwide contained equal pay for equal work clauses, and 75 percent provided for leaves of absence without loss of seniority.

To reflect its growth in organizing tobacco workers and cigar rollers, especially in the South, UCAPAWA became the Food, Tobacco, Agricultural, and Allied Workers of America (FTA) in 1944. In addition to local leadership, people of color were well represented at the national level. For example, in 1946, out of the nine executive board positions, six were held by people of color (three African Americans and three Latinos).

UCAPAWA Local No. 3 negotiating committee, including Luisa Moreno (far left in plaid coat) and Carmen Bernal Escobar (third from left with hands around her child Albert), 1943. Courtesy of Carmen Bernal Escobar.

African American tobacco workers in North Carolina, Italian and Polish women cannery workers in the Midwest, their Mexican and Jewish counterparts in southern California, and Japanese, Filipino, Chinese, and Alaska Native food-processing workers in the Pacific Northwest were all under the union's big tent. As part of the UCAPAWA pledge, members swore "never to discriminate against a fellow worker because of creed, color, nationality, religious or political belief."

From its earliest days UCAPAWA/FTA came under a cloud of suspicion by conservative politicians and pundits because many of the union's organizers had current or past affiliation with the Communist Party, including its founding president. During the cold war red-baiting of the union escalated, and it was expelled from the CIO in 1950 on grounds of Communist domination. However, as a grassroots union, UCAPAWA/FTA's commitment to rank-and-file leadership and to inclusion, recruiting members across race, nationality, and gender, remains its greatest legacy.

See also Labor Unions

SOURCES: Ruiz, Vicki L. 1987. *Cannery Women, Cannery Lives: Mexican Women, Unionization, and the California Food Processing Industry, 1930–1950*. Albuquerque: University of New Mexico Press; Vargas, Zaragosa. 2004. *Labor Rights Are Civil Rights: Mexican American Workers in Twentieth-Century America*. Princeton, NJ: Princeton University Press; Weber, Devra. 1994. *Dark Sweat, White Gold: California Farm Workers, Cotton, and the New Deal*. Berkeley: University of California Press.

Vicki L. Ruiz

UNITED FARM WORKERS OF AMERICA (UFW) (1962–   )

The United Farm Workers of America (UFW) was the most significant and long-lasting effort to unionize agricultural labor in the United States during the twentieth century. Ideologically linked to the civil rights movement, it began as a grassroots struggle in Delano, California, in 1962 and was originally called the National Farm Workers Association (NFWA). The founders included the charismatic César Chávez, his supportive wife, Helen Fabela Chávez, their passionate colleague, Dolores Huerta, and various like-minded sympathizers. The group fought to ameliorate the appalling conditions endured by agricultural laborers: poverty-level wages, substandard housing, dismal working conditions, lack of benefits, poor job security, exploitation by unscrupulous labor contractors, and racism on the part of employers and their allies. Farm laborers suffered from high rates of disease, elevated infant mortality rates, short life expectancy, and low educational attainment. In the words of one campesino (farmworker), the union was "the best thing that ever happened to the farm workers."

The founders had gained valuable skills and experience as a result of their association with the Community Service Organization (CSO), a Mexican American self-help group that had emerged out of the heightened civic and civil rights consciousness that arose in southwestern barrios in the aftermath of World War II. When the more urban-oriented CSO declined to take up the farmworker issue, Chávez and Huerta left the group to concentrate on the problems of agricultural laborers. The spark that ignited the unionization effort proved to be a strike sponsored by a group of Filipino workers that the NFWA voted to join in 1965. Unsuccessful in its initial attempts to gain union recognition from unyielding and well-financed agribusiness, the fledgling organization turned to a consumer boycott. Striking farmworker families packed up their meager belongings and headed to boycott offices that were springing up all over the country, often traveling in family groups. The experience transformed field workers, many of whom participated in the civic and political life of the nation for the first time. "The union has to win," declared one farmworker woman. "We're making this sacrifice so they [growers] will pay so we can educate our children." The public speaking and picketing of farmworker families struck a nerve with middle-class consumers. The boycott attracted widespread support from coalitions of students, organized labor, religious organizations of all denominations, women's groups, environmentalists, and ethnic activists. At the same time La Causa, as the union's struggle was sometimes called, exerted a galvanizing impact on the Mexican American community, an important symbol of La Raza.

The intersection of so many reformist constituencies placed extraordinary pressure on agribusiness and led to the historic grape contracts in 1970. The union had little time to savor this momentous victory before it confronted an organizing campaign in the lettuce fields of northern California. This conflict turned violent with the entry of the Teamsters into the fray and the negotiating of "sweetheart" contracts with the industry. These less exacting work arrangements encouraged other companies to oppose vehemently the UFW and to balk at negotiating contracts up for renewal. The turmoil in the fields and renewed boycotts of the period prompted the California state government to broker a settlement between growers and the United Farm Workers. Under the auspices of Governor Jerry Brown, the Agricultural Labor Relations Act was passed in 1975. The union turned its energies to conducting field elections. Although the UFW was successful in winning the majority of contests, growers, through appeals in the courts, held up the certification

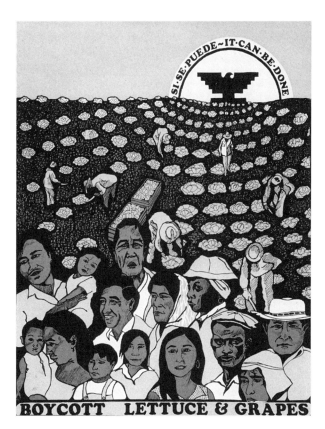

United Farm Workers, "Boycott Lettuce & Grapes," circa 1978. Courtesy of the Prints and Photographs Division, Library of Congress (Digital ID: cph 3g02420).

of the union as the collective bargaining agent for their employees.

Frustrated by the legal process and undergoing internal dissension about the direction of the union, many long-term staff and supporters left. The fortunes of the UFW declined further with the election in 1982 of Republican governor George Deukmejian, a strong supporter of agribusiness. The antiunion posture of the Reagan presidency also contributed to the union's difficulties. Despite the setbacks, the union had succeeded in raising the standard of living of union members, negotiated better wages, improved working conditions, created health and pension programs, raised awareness of sexual harassment, and increased concern over pesticides.

The greatest challenge for the UFW came with the unexpected death of César Chávez in 1993. His funeral brought an outpouring of grief and support from individuals from all walks of life who had been touched by La Causa, but also raised questions about the continued existence of the union without its powerful leader. Dolores Huerta and other colleagues vowed to carry on his work. Chávez was succeeded by his son-in-law, Arturo Rodríguez, a college-educated Chicano who had met and married Linda "Lu" Chávez while working

on the boycott in Detroit, Michigan. Far from disappearing, the union rededicated itself to organizing workers and concluded contracts with strawberry growers in California. Despite such gains, the union faces numerous obstacles, including the continued immigration of desperate and powerless workers from Mexico and Central America willing to work for low pay under horrendous conditions.

Although the UFW has not maintained the membership levels of the 1970s, it continues to be the largest and most visible agricultural union in California. In addition, it has spun off smaller-scale organizations in a number of other states, including Arizona, Texas, Florida, Washington, Ohio, and Michigan. With funding from the U.S. Department of Agriculture, the United Farm Workers has built low-income senior housing complexes with the aim of providing decent, affordable housing for elderly farmworkers. For example, Desert Garden Apartments in Indio, California, is a full-service assisted-living facility with hot meals, transportation, and health care. The UFW bettered the conditions of a marginalized and impoverished group of workers, politicized a generation of Mexicans and Mexican Americans, and became an important symbol of cultural pride. Appropriating the phrase "Sí, se puede" (it can be done), the UFW instilled courage and confidence. César Chávez remains the most recognizable Latino leader. The best-known facet of the Chicano movement of the 1960s, the union and its legacy lives on.

See also Labor Unions

SOURCES: Alvarez, Fred. 2002. "After a Life in the Fields, Farm Workers Looking for a Place to Call Their Own." *Los Angeles Times*, July 8, A1, A16; Ferriss, Susan, and Ricardo Sandoval. 1997. *The Fight in the Fields: César Chávez and the Farmworkers Movement*. New York: Harcourt Brace; Majka, Linda C., and Theo J. Majka. 1982. *Farm Workers, Agribusiness, and the State*. Philadelphia: Temple University Press; Rose, Margaret. 1990. "From the Fields to the Picket Line: Huelga Women and the Boycott, 1965–1975." *Labor History* 31, no. 3 (Summer): 271–293; _____. 2002. "César Chávez and Dolores Huerta: Partners in 'La Causa.'" In *César Chávez*, ed. Richard Etulain. Boston: Bedford/St. Martin's Press.

Margaret Eleanor Rose

Women in the United Farm Workers (UFW) (1962–)

"We want union contracts and I'm willing to stay here until they're signed," vowed thirty-two-year-old Enedina Hernández, a UFW picketer. Her sentiments represent the sense of empowerment she and other women experienced as a result of their association with the union. Perhaps misled by the popular and scholarly treatments of the farmworker movement that focused largely on the charismatic César Chávez, historians have missed the important role women have played in the vanguard and behind the scenes.

Since the development of large-scale agriculture in the late nineteenth century in the Southwest, Chicanas and Mexicanas have worked in the "factories in the fields" and contributed to the family income as daughters and wives. Like their husbands and sons, they endured low pay, poor working conditions, substandard housing, nonexistent benefits, lack of job security, exploitation by contractors, and prejudice on the part of employers; they also faced sexual harassment. Furthermore, lacking adequate resources for child care, women were often forced to take their children with them to the fields. The double day took its toll because women rose early in the morning to prepare breakfasts and lunches for their husbands and children and then, upon returning home after a long day in the fields, cooked the evening meal and tended to household chores. They had strong motivations to support any efforts to improve their difficult lives.

Perhaps the two most significant women in the early stage of the union's history are Helen Chávez, spouse of César Chávez, and Dolores Huerta. Their examples influenced other women in the United Farm Workers. Helen Chávez played a largely behind-the-scenes but critical role. She shared a firm conviction with her husband regarding the urgent need to help farmworkers. "After all," she recalled, "we were both farm workers, and my parents and his parents and our whole families. I thought a lot of people felt the way we did." Not only did she avidly support the goal of organizing, but her work in the fields allowed Chávez to devote his time to the union. "While César was organizing, I was picking grapes or doing whatever field work was available. When the grape harvest was pretty heavy," as she remembered the early difficult years before the 1965 grape strike, "sometimes I'd work ten hours a day, five days a week for eighty-five cents an hour." At times she would take the older children with her to work during the summers and weekends. After work she had to cook, clean, and care for their eight children. When the union became more established, she was persuaded, over her initial reluctance, to work in the union's credit union, first as a bookkeeper and later as manager. Work and domestic responsibilities did not prevent her from joining picket lines and even facing arrest. However, she was only comfortable participating with her family. She actively shunned an independent role and refused to speak before groups. Because of her quiet legacy, her lifelong commitment to the union has gone unrecognized.

Dolores Huerta, the first vice president of the union, exerted a more visible presence in its history. She was a teacher in Stockton, California, in the 1950s, but her life took another direction when she joined the Community Service Organization (CSO), a Mexican American civic group that emerged after World War II. It was through the CSO that she met and began to work with César Chávez, who soon became the national director while she served as its lobbyist. Although they both gained valuable skills and experience, they became disenchanted when the urban-oriented CSO declined to organize farmworkers. Chávez resigned, soon followed by Huerta, to focus on creating the National Farm Workers Association (NFWA). Both recognized the financial and emotional sacrifices they would confront.

In her thirties with seven children and an estranged second husband, whom she later divorced, Huerta shouldered considerable economic and familial burdens. Struggling to make ends meet, she survived on irregular payments from her ex-husbands, odd jobs, assistance from family members, and occasional anonymous donations of food and clothing. These hardships did not deter her ambition to achieve meaningful changes for farmworkers. From her base in Stockton she spent hours publicizing the new organization, setting up meetings, calling on workers at their homes, and visiting migrant camps to get workers to join the union. Collecting dues proved difficult, and after deducting expenses, Chávez and Huerta shared the slim proceeds for living expenses. "César was very fair about that," she asserted. "He would always divide it down the middle." After repeated requests from Chávez, Huerta relocated her family to Delano to concentrate on the NFWA's efforts in the central San Joaquin Valley. Not long after her move the fledgling organization faced its first real test when the union voted unanimously to honor a strike called by Filipino grape workers in 1965.

Huerta became an inspirational leader on the picket lines, as well as a strategist behind the scenes. In a relatively short time the union won a few contracts with the more vulnerable wine grape producers as the result of negotiations led by the tenacious Huerta. Against the more intransigent table grape growers, the union devised a consumer boycott strategy to bring the industry to terms. Huerta added "boycott director" to her list of responsibilities. A fiery speaker, she became very effective in publicizing La Causa and in raising significant sums to support the union.

She also provided an important model for other campesinas to join the union's nationwide boycott. Striking farmworker families heeded the call to help staff the boycott offices that sprang up across the country. Historians have been slow to recognize what Huerta realized: "Families are the most important part of the UFW because a family can stick it out in a strange place, on $5 a week per person, the wage [in the early 1970s] everyone in the union is paid (plus expenses)." María Luisa and Hijinio Rangel transplanted their family to Detroit, Michigan; Juanita and Merced Váldez moved their family to Cincinnati, Ohio; Herminia and Conrado Rodríguez packed up their family and personal belongings to work on the boycott in Washington, D.C. These are just a few examples of the women who disrupted their lives to bring justice to the fields.

Work on the boycott was often a life-changing experience for families who had lived and worked in rural areas. Becoming active participants in the boycott propelled Mexicanas and Chicanas into the national spotlight. Many learned or improved their English, mastered office skills, broadened their perspectives, and gained confidence. Through experience on urban picket lines they asserted themselves in new public ways. Boycott experience also transformed the personal lives of participants by altering the dynamic between husbands and wives. Women and men worked together and developed more open relations and equal partnerships. Mexicanas and Chicanas recognized new opportunities for personal growth and raised their expectations for themselves and their children.

The presence of farmworker women also gave the boycott an additional dynamic in appealing to middle-class consumers, particularly female shoppers, who became aware of the exploitation in the fields through the vivid firsthand accounts of women and children. "I grew up in the fields," revealed one farmworker woman. "In Fresno, some workers still live in tents, with no toilets and kerosene stoves to cook on, the same as when I was a child." Often moved by such testimony, middle-class housewives volunteered their time to the local union operations. Boycott directors were quick to seize upon an aroused female constituency. "Volunteers needed for the LADIES DELEGATION," proclaimed a boycott newsletter. "Bring the kids and the babysitter. They should be involved in changing history too."

Chicanas and Mexicanas participated not only as family members, but also as autonomous women. Encouraged by the example of Dolores Huerta, they emerged as boycott directors. Important examples of this more independent activism included Jessica Govea in Montreal, Canada, María Saludado in Indianapolis, and Hope López in Philadelphia. These activists were distinct from women who participated as part of a family unit. They were second-generation Mexican Americans with more education, having graduated from high school and, in some cases, having attending college. Often these women were single, lived in nonmarital relationships, and were divorced or widowed. Because of their education and relative mobility, they were in great demand by union officials confronted with

chronic personnel shortages. Directing a boycott center was a challenging task: contacts had to be made, picket lines organized, newsletters produced, speeches given, endorsements collected, funds solicited, and volunteers recruited. "It has been difficult to come from the 'farm' to the big city," remarked Jessica Govea, a director in her early twenties from Bakersfield, California, "but we are making tremendous headway in the boycott in Montreal now." It was through the sacrifices of striking farmworker women and boycott leaders like Jessica Govea that the union could pressure growers to sign the historic grape contracts in Delano in 1970.

Before the ink was dry on the agreements, a strike erupted in the lettuce fields of northern California. Huerta, Govea, and other women became involved in organizing campaigns in the Salinas Valley. Faced with little progress, union staff and workers called for the boycott of lettuce, and later Gallo wines and table grapes, as agribusiness launched an all-out offensive to defeat the United Farm Workers. Alarmed by the violence in the fields, eventually the California state legislature, working with Governor Jerry Brown, passed the Agricultural Labor Relations Act (ALRA) in 1975 to check the acrimonious relations between growers and the union.

After passage of the ALRA the union turned its resources to organizing field elections throughout California. While it won a substantial number of contests, it soon became apparent that agribusiness would pursue a tactic of obstruction and delay by appealing unfavorable outcomes through the legal system. At the companies where the union was successful, it was necessary to train workers to negotiate and administer contracts. Although this area of union work was considered men's work, Chicanas and Mexicanas exercised influence as they served on negotiating and ranch committees (equivalent to a union local). These bodies participated in the negotiation process with their employers, and once the contract was accepted, they supervised the administration of the agreement at their individual companies, handling issues such as seniority, dismissals, layoff procedures, and local grievances. Even with the strong model of Dolores Huerta to encourage them, women faced opposition to their presence around the bargaining table. "There were no women on the first ranch committee," recalled Jessie de la Cruz, who eventually served on the committee at her company. De la Cruz and others like her, such as Mary Magaña, a rose worker, Carolina Guerrero, a grape laborer, Cleo Gómez, a walnut and fruit picker, and Juana Arroyo, a celery and tomato employee, faced resistance and skepticism from husbands, fathers, sons, colleagues, and employers. Initially lacking self-confidence, women seemed reluctant to speak forcefully. Gradually hostility toward women eased as their enforcement of the contracts gave laborers more control over the workplace, improved wages and benefits, and secured better working conditions. Moreover, the UFW expanded female autonomy and eroded barriers between male- and female-defined endeavors.

Although service on ranch committees was a more nontraditional area of participation for women, managing campesino or service centers became a more acceptable pursuit for Chicanas and Mexicanas. Scholars and journalists have overlooked the administrative and social welfare apparatus of the union because it lacked the allure of the boycott or the drama of the picket line or ranch committee. From its earliest days the union provided social services for its members. The campesino center directors and staff contributed a direct and vital link between the union and farmworkers. Women such as Helen Chávez followed a more conventional pattern of activism, combining family, work, and unionism. Unlike Chicanas and Mexicanas who served on ranch committees, they encountered little or no opposition from their families and husbands.

Campesino centers seek to improve the quality of life for farmworkers and their families through education, action, and service programs, methods women have traditionally employed to achieve social change. Directors such as Minnie Ybarra in San Ysidro, Monica Alfaro in Santa Maria, and Sandra Rodríguez in Hollister inform farmworkers of their basic rights to various economic, social, and health benefits, available from both the UFW and government agencies. Center staff members also advise workers on union medical and pension programs and devote substantial time to discussing eligibility for such programs as unemployment insurance, state disability insurance, workers' compensation, food stamps, and Medi-Cal Center directors and personnel further assist union members with immigration questions, translation assistance, housing, and aid during natural disasters. Traditional gender ideologies that viewed women as the heart of their homes eased their entry into campesino centers to direct the provision of shelter, clothing, food, and education for striking workers and union members. Because this type of activity does not draw headlines, the contributions of these women have remained unacknowledged.

Women have always been involved in the farmworker movement. During the 1970s the UFW began to encourage the participation of Chicanas and Mexicanas. Stories on women with headlines like "A Woman's Place Is . . . on the Picket Line" (which appeared in the union's newsletter, *El Malcriado*) symbolized the change in attitude. Union officials also recognized the appeal of farmworker women to middle-class Americans, especially the female consumer. Later in the decade another woman, Jessica Govea, served on the nine-member UFW executive board. Women, however, remain clustered in the traditionally female areas of administration and behind-the-scenes support.

Women gave their loyalty to the farmworker movement, but they also gained validation. "On the one hand, it was tough," remembered Jessica Govea, "on the other, it was an incredibly liberating and wonderful experience." This quest brought about change for impoverished workers and raised hopes. "If we win this fight," noted Josephine Hernández, "then we can give our children what they need."

SOURCES: Baer, Barbara L., and Glenna Matthews. 1974. " 'You Find A Way': The Women of the Boycott." *Nation* (February 23): 232–238; Majka, Linda C., and Theo J. Majka. 1982. *Farm Workers, Agribusiness, and the State.* Philadelphia: Temple University Press; Rose, Margaret. 1990. "From the Fields to the Picket Line: Huelga Women and the Boycott, 1965–1975." *Labor History* 31, no. 3 (Summer): 271–293; _____. 1995. " 'Woman Power Will Stop Those Grapes': Chicana Organizers and Middle-Class Female Supporters in the Farm Workers' Grape Boycott in Philadelphia, 1969–1970." *Journal of Women's History* 7, no. 4 (Winter): 6–36; Ruiz, Vicki L. 1998. *From out of the Shadows: Mexican Women in Twentieth-Century America.* New York: Oxford University Press.

Margaret Eleanor Rose

U.S.-MEXICAN WAR (1846–1848)

On February 2, 1848, beside Mexico's most sacred site, la Basilica de la Virgen de Guadalupe, representatives of the newly constituted Mexican government met with U.S. representatives to sign the Treaty of Guadalupe Hidalgo, ending what Mexicans remember as the "war of northern aggression." As a result, almost 530,000 square miles of the land Mexico had inherited from Spain, including the coveted bays of San Diego and San Francisco, became what is now known as the western United States. The treaty crushed any hopes that Mexico had harbored of regaining approximately 350,000 square miles of territory claimed by the Republic of Texas, which the United States had annexed in 1845. With the signing of this treaty, the United States became a transcontinental nation, and more than 96,000 Mexican citizens from New Mexico to California became American citizens.

In the 1830s and early 1840s conflict between the two nations for these lands was inevitable, but war was not. Examined from three vantage points, however, the internal struggles of both countries and the weakness of the borderlands did create a complicated scenario in which to negotiate. First, when Mexico became a republic in 1824, the country faced crippling problems. Its finances and infrastructure were fractured after an eleven-year fight for independence and a brief, unsuccessful attempt at becoming an empire. Leaders struggled to create the Constitution of 1824 and put into operation a government that reflected a unified vision of how their country would be structured, what the states' relationship to the national government would be, and how the country would survive financially. Several power groups confounded these attempts, particularly the military generals, the hierarchy of the Catholic Church, and international creditors.

Second, while political forces struggled in the capital, citizens in the northern territories, from the Gulf coast to the Pacific coast, looked elsewhere for support. They took advantage of the end of Spain's mercantile system and the opening of seaports and overland commerce to develop relationships with British, American, French, and South American merchants. In the 1830s and early 1840s, when women from important Mexican families, like María de las Angustias de la Guerra, married foreigners, commercial bonds with these merchants became even stronger, while the families' political bonds with Mexico City weakened as centralists exerted their power. In an attempt to weaken the states' power, the central government ordered a reduction in the state militias and expanded the national army. Citizens in California and New Mexico battled against the new centralist-appointed governors—and with each other—over this issue. Tejanos not only revolted over it, in 1836 they declared themselves a republic.

Third, the United States faced its own internal discord, financial stress, and international threats, especially from Britain. Memories of the Battle of New Orleans and the British attack on Washington were still vivid. U.S. leaders continued to feel threatened by the economic and military power of Great Britain. Although the United States had achieved independence from Britain, sections of the border with Canada remained undefined. American leaders knew that they were competing with the British not only for control of the Northwest Territories, where hundreds of Americans were beginning to settle, but also for two harbors important to international trade in the Pacific. Both claimed Puget Sound, and both coveted Mexico's San Francisco Bay.

As 1844 drew to a close, while Mexico prepared to welcome a leader who offered internal reconciliation, voters in the United States elected a leader ready to risk war with both Britain and Mexico. In the fall James K. Polk campaigned for president with a focus on three geographic targets. He wanted to win the Oregon Ter-

ritories from Britain. He wanted to see Texas join the Union, knowing that Mexico had still not given up hope of regaining its former state. He also wanted to acquire California.

In Mexico the fall of 1844 offered new hope for the federalists. They were able to force out the centralists and their leader, General Antonio López de Santa Anna, and elect a wiser leader and political moderate, General José Joaquín Herrera, whose primary goal was to return the Republic to its original Constitution of 1824. Herrera took office in January 1845, two months before Polk.

On March 1, 1845, three days before Polk became president, Congress voted to offer statehood to Texas. Soon after Polk's inauguration, in protest over the congressional vote, Juan Nepomuceno Almonte, Mexico's minister to Washington, broke off diplomatic relations and returned home. On July 4 a majority of Texans voted for statehood, despite attempts by Britain and Mexico to persuade them to reject it. One of Polk's three campaign goals, the annexation of Texas, was accomplished. Expecting a military response from Mexico, Polk ordered the navy to move into the Gulf of Mexico and General Zachary Taylor to move his troops from Louisiana to Texas, where they camped at Corpus Christi, on the mouth of the Nueces River. Mexico viewed the Nueces as the southern boundary of Texas. The United States claimed that the southern boundary was the Rio Grande. Whoever entered this disputed territory invited trouble. Then Polk sent his emissary John Slidell to Mexico City with an offer to buy California, New Mexico, and land on the U.S. side of the Rio Grande line.

President Herrera knew the implications of Polk's actions. He ordered a study of the military's preparedness to do battle, which found it wanting. A realist, he would rather lose part of Mexico's territory than engage in a disastrous war and so agreed to meet with Polk's emissary in November. Herrera's political enemies, however, accused him of treason, so he and Slidell never met. The call of treason was loudest from an ambitious general, Mariano Paredes y Arrillaga, who threatened to use military force against him, so Herrera resigned rather than have the Constitution of 1824 overthrown. Paredes won a dubious election, assumed the presidency in January 1846, and led the country toward war.

Polk continued to pursue his strategy of graduated pressure, also willing to risk a war. In January he ordered General Zachary Taylor to march his troops across the disputed territory to the Rio Grande. On April 25, soon after Major General Mariano Arista arrived in Matamoros to take command, Mexican troops fought a U.S. scouting party. Eleven American soldiers were killed. As far as the generals were concerned, war had begun. On May 8 and 9 the armies fought two major battles, Palo Alto and Resaca de la Palma, near Matamoros. The fighting ended with the retreat of the Mexican army. Instead of receiving reinforcements, however, they learned that antagonism against Paredes for disregarding the Constitution of 1824 was so deep that the city of Guadalajara had revolted. Rather than send much-needed troops to help fight against the U.S. Army, Paredes ordered them to lay siege to Guadalajara. Even though Polk had not received news of the battles on May 8 and 9, he had begun to develop his case for war on the basis of the failure of Slidell's mission and news of the skirmish on April 25. On May 11 Polk presented his message to Congress asking for a declaration of war. On May 13 the U.S. Congress complied with Polk's wishes and authorized $10 million and 50,000 twelve-month volunteers.

While Polk and his cabinet began implementing their war plans, they received welcome news that they no longer had to worry about a war with Britain. U.S. and British negotiators had agreed on the terms of a treaty to settle the Oregon boundaries. Polk had achieved the second of his campaign goals.

In June 1846 Polk ordered Colonel Stephen W. Kearny to lead the Army of the West from Fort Leavenworth to New Mexico. This army included a battalion of Mormons, who joined as a way to migrate west with their families. Although there was a threat of battle in New Mexico, Kearny's troops entered Santa Fe peacefully and claimed it for the United States.

Women's experiences in the war varied greatly. Susan Magoffin, wife of a successful merchant involved in commerce on the Santa Fe Trail, wrote in her diary about her entry into Santa Fe and how she and Mexican women of the privileged class met and cautiously became acquainted. In Santa Fe, as well as other sites where soldiers were stationed, women took advantage of business opportunities the war created. Historian Deena González described how one Santa Fe woman, María Gertrudis Barceló, ran a popular gambling saloon that catered to U.S. soldiers. Near Matamoros and then in Saltillo, Sarah Bowman, known as the Great Western, operated an inn and restaurant for soldiers. Samuel Chamberlain was one patron who described her forceful character in his book *My Confession*. Most Mexican women in occupied cities and towns tried to continue daily life and stay out of danger.

Once the army settled in Santa Fe, Kearny sent Colonel Alexander Doniphan south to Chihuahua with his First Missouri Mounted Volunteers while he proceeded to San Diego, California. Outside San Diego Californios routed Kearny and his troops at San Pas-

cual, but they joined with the U.S. Navy and Marines to win the battles of San Gabriel and La Mesa and force the Californios to surrender in January 1847. Polk had achieved the third of his campaign goals but would need a treaty with Mexico to make it official. The rest of the war was fought to get that treaty.

In northeastern Mexico, after the battles of Palo Alto and Resaca de la Palma, General Zachary Taylor moved his Army of the North toward its target, the city of Monterrey, Nuevo León. On September 20–24 the Mexican and U.S. armies fought in the streets and on hillsides surrounding the city. Monterrey residents—men and women—aided the Mexican soldiers, but all were forced to surrender. Later one woman's heroism was commemorated in the song "The Maid of Monterrey." Taylor's troops then marched to Saltillo, where in November 1846 leaders allowed them to occupy the city rather than have it become a battleground. U.S. soldiers began to write in letters and journals about their admiration of the beautiful Mexican women they met.

Meanwhile, the former Mexican president, Antonio López de Santa Anna, who had surrendered Texas in 1836, had been allowed to pass through the U.S. naval blockade and return to Mexico from his exile in Cuba on the promise of helping Polk buy California. Instead, Santa Anna became provisional president and rallied an army that he then led north to Saltillo. Many of the 20,000 troops were conscripts, rural people pressed into service who traveled with their wives rather than leave them unprotected at home. These women cooked for and nursed the soldiers. All suffered from shortages of food and water and the bitterly cold weather.

On February 22–23 Santa Anna engaged Taylor's army on the plains of Buena Vista. Taylor feared, and some historians believe, that if Santa Anna had not withdrawn during the night of February 23, the Mexican army might have won this strategic battle. One theory is that Santa Anna withdrew because he had news of an insurrection in Mexico City and raced back to settle it. Supporters and opponents of his controversial vice president, Valentín Gómez Farías, had started a poorly timed battle in the streets of Mexico City, known as the "polka revolt" (named for a favorite dance of the period), sapping much-needed resources from the defense of the country and particularly the port city of Veracruz.

General Winfield Scott's Army of the Center had already begun to land in Veracruz. On March 17 Scott insisted on the surrender of the city, but when that did not happen, he bombarded the port for eight days until its leaders did submit. The news reached Santa Anna, who was back in control of the government. He reorganized his army in time to confront Scott's troops on the road to Jalapa. At Cerro Gordo, on April 19–20, Santa Anna met defeat and barely escaped capture.

From April until August Winfield Scott and Nicholas Trist, the U.S. treaty negotiator, attempted to arrange a truce with Mexican leaders, but when that failed, Scott led his troops into the Valley of Mexico. On August 19–20, south of Mexico City, a rolling battle from Padierna to Churubusco ended with a stalemate. Scott and Santa Anna agreed to an armistice to give Nicholas Trist and Mexican negotiators a chance to end the war. When it became clear that they could not agree, Scott ordered his troops forward. The battle of Molino del Rey on September 8 was followed by the battle of Chapultepec on September 12, which spilled over to the gates of the city and by the next day into the city itself. Santa Anna withdrew his troops in the early morning of September 14. Later that morning city leaders surrendered, and the occupation of the capital began.

From September to December 1847 Mexican leaders in the temporary capital of Querétaro reconstituted the government, held elections, and named a team of negotiators. In January, as formal negotiations began in Mexico, the U.S. Congress was dealing with the repercussions of winning the war. Some even called for conquering "all of Mexico." The issues between slave and nonslave states became heated, exacerbated by the Wilmot Proviso, which prohibited slavery in any territory acquired from Mexico. While the lands won by the United States as a result of the war would enable the country to become a transnational power, one of the costs was that they would fuel tensions that led to the Civil War.

The Treaty of Guadalupe Hidalgo was signed in Mexico on February 2, ratified by the U.S. Congress on March 10, and returned to Mexico to be ratified by the newly elected Mexican Congress on May 25. Terms included that Mexico would receive $15 million and cede its northern borderlands to the United States. Polk had finally achieved his goals, the biggest of which was California, where news of the January discovery of large deposits of gold did what the Mexican government had tried to do: it attracted thousands of settlers.

See also Treaty of Guadalupe Hidalgo

SOURCES: Bauer, K. Jack. 1992. *The Mexican War, 1846–1848.* Lincoln: University of Nebraska Press; Cashion, Peggy M. 1990. "Women and the Mexican War, 1846–1848." M.A. thesis, University of Texas at Arlington; Francaviglia, Richard V., and Douglas W. Richmond, eds. 2000. *Dueling Eagles: Reinterpreting the U.S.-Mexican War, 1846–1848.* Arlington: Center for Greater Southwestern Studies, University of Texas at Arlington; Padilla, Genaro M. 1993. *My History, Not Yours: The Formation of Mexican American Autobiography.* Madison: University of Wisconsin Press; Pletcher, David M. 1973. *The Diplomacy of Annexation: Texas, Oregon, and the Mexican War.* Columbia: University of Missouri Press; Weber, David J. 1982. *The Mexican Frontier, 1821–1846: The American Southwest Under Mexico.* Albuquerque: University of New Mexico Press.

Andrea Boardman

URQUIDES, MARÍA LUISA LEGARRA (1908–1994)

Often called "the mother of bilingual education," María L. Urquides dedicated her life to improving education for Mexican American children. Urquides was born in 1908 in Tucson, Arizona, to two prominent families. Her father, Hilario Urquides, was a businessman and civic leader. In 1894 he helped found the Alianza Hispano-Americana, the largest Mexican American mutual-aid society. Her mother, Mariana Legarra, belonged to a longtime Tucson family. María Urquides spent much of her life working with organizations that addressed social issues. Involved with the Catholic Church throughout her life, she once said that she was a member of three minorities: she was a woman, a Mexican, and a Catholic.

In high school Urquides's teachers encouraged her to become an elementary-school teacher, and she attended Tempe State Teachers College, earning a two-year teaching certificate in 1928. Since it was unusual for a Mexican American woman to leave home for college during the 1920s, she defied her family's expectations. She remembered, "My older brother pitched a fit and my mother cried. But I went." She was the first person in her family to go to college. Her father had no formal schooling, and her mother went to school only through third grade. At the Tempe State Teachers College she financed her education by cleaning the bathrooms in her dormitory and singing Mexican songs at a local restaurant. During the summers Urquides continued her education at the University of Arizona, eventually earning a B.A. in 1946 and an M.A. in 1956.

Urquides began her forty-six-year teaching career at Davis Elementary School, then the largest school in Tucson, with a student body of 750 students, mostly Mexican American. At Davis Elementary she witnessed the learning difficulties and loss of self-esteem experienced by Spanish-speaking children who were forcibly immersed in English. She then began to formulate her ideas about teaching Mexican American children, ideas that would coalesce into bilingual education. Beginning her career at a time when children were not allowed to speak Spanish at school, she recalled teaching some of her students some songs in Spanish, only to have her supervisor insist that she translate them into English. Later in life she often remembered the educational policies, stating, "If I ever go to hell, it will be because of the kids I punished for speaking Spanish."

In 1948, after twenty years working with working-class Mexican American children, Urquides was transferred to Sam Hughes Elementary School, a predominantly Anglo school in an affluent area of Tucson. Noting the different resources available to the two groups of children, she wondered, "Why couldn't these children be brought together as part of the whole system?" In the mid-1950s Urquides joined the faculty at the newly built Pueblo High School, and it was there that she and her colleagues began to develop what would become one of the first bilingual education programs, creating Spanish classes for the Spanish-speaking students.

In 1966 Urquides and fellow educators Hank Oyama and Adalberto Guerrero coauthored *The Silent Minority,* a report that documented their survey of thirty-five school districts in five southwestern states. The report eventually went to Congress and initiated debates over the education of Mexican American children. The same year Texas senator Ralph W. Yarborough attended a bilingual education conference in Tucson that Urquides organized. Yarborough left the conference committed to supporting bilingual education. In 1967 he introduced the bill that would fund bilingual education under the Elementary and Secondary Education Act, and a year later the U.S. Congress passed the Bilingual Education Act.

During her long career Urquides received more than sixty honors and was named to influential state and national commissions. In 1950 President Harry Truman appointed her to the White House Conference on Children and Youth. She was reappointed to the commission by President Dwight Eisenhower in 1960 and by President Richard Nixon in 1970. In the early 1960s President John F. Kennedy appointed her to the Arizona State Advisory Committee to the Civil Rights Commission, and in 1967 President Lyndon Baines Johnson appointed her to the National Advisory Committee to the Commissioners of Education on Mexican American Education. Urquides continued to work in the school system until her retirement in 1974. In 1983 the University of Arizona awarded her an honorary doctor of law degree.

Although Urquides said that she had no regrets over her years in the classroom, she did express disappointment over bilingual education. "Bilingual education is not what I hoped it would be—because we didn't teach the monolingual child, the Anglo child, to speak Spanish." She died at the age of eighty-six in 1994.

See also Bilingual Education

SOURCES: González, Elizabeth Quiroz. 1986. "The Education and Public Career of María Urquides: A Case Study of a

Mexican American Community Leader." Ed.D. thesis, University of Arizona; Sheridan, Thomas E. 1992. *Los Tucsonenses: The Mexican Community in Tucson, 1854–1941.* Tucson: University of Arizona Press.

Yolanda Chávez Leyva

URREA, TERESA (1872–1906)

Teresa Urrea was a local *curandera,* international healer, border exile, and fledgling labor activist. Her fame as a *curandera,* or Mexican folk healer, straddled two nations. Illuminated by her followers as a folk saint, la Santa de Cabora, she drew the ire of the Catholic Church. Her insistent criticism of President Porfirio Díaz's land policies cast her as a revolutionary. Consequently, the Mexican government carefully scrutinized her. Exiled in 1892, she became a media sensation in the United States. During the closing years of her life she allied with Mexican labor activists in Los Angeles before returning to Clifton, Arizona.

Born in Ocoroni, Sinaloa, on October 15, 1872, Teresa Urrea was reared by her mother, Cayetana Chávez, a Tehuecan domestic servant. Her father, Tomás Urrea, was a moderately successful dairy farmer. The *casa chica* (the home provided for a mistress and her children) relationship between elite men, like Urrea, and poor women, including indigenous women, like Chávez, appeared common during the nineteenth century. Teresa Urrea was reared in the modest surroundings of the servants' quarters, but her life changed drastically in 1888.

She arrived at her father's Cabora estate as she approached her sixteenth birthday. In the months immediately following she developed important relationships with her stepmother, Gabriela Cantúa, and the local *curandera,* Huila. Huila treated patients with herbals and massages, and Urrea became her apprentice through the fall of 1889. On October 28, 1889, Urrea lapsed into the first of a series of trancelike comas that lasted two weeks. After regaining consciousness, she displayed bizarre behavior; she frequently experienced seizures and catatonic states and began exuding a heavy perfumed odor. Moreover, in exchange for renewed health, Urrea promised the Virgin Mary that she would be devoted to "healing humanity."

By December 1889 she had amassed a considerable local, regional, and national following. Her adherents dubbed her la Santa de Cabora, an unrecognized folk saint, which provoked skepticism from the Catholic Church. She frequently proselytized about equality and love, but her denunciation of Catholic sacraments and her renegade style of sacramental dispensation drew the most criticism.

Legendary healer Teresa Urrea. Courtesy of the William Curry Holden Papers, the Southwest Collection, Texas Tech University.

Mexico underwent monumental changes at the end of the nineteenth century. With a shift to modernization, large-scale foreign investments marked the Mexican landscape, while Porfirian policies eroded *ejido* communal landholding, resulting in the displacement of millions of indigenous and mestizo *ejido* farmers. In the wake of these changes Teresa Urrea emerged as a beacon of hope for the disenfranchised.

Recognizing her ubiquitous following, and possibly challenged by it, the central government moved to undercut her support. After surviving three years of watchful government surveillance, Teresa Urrea was exiled to the United States. Even after she left Mexico, controversy surrounded her. Relocating initially to Nogales, Arizona, the Urrea family was counseled to move inland away from volatile borderland strife. Shortly thereafter she moved to Solomonville, Arizona.

Throughout the 1890s political conflict followed her. An anti-Díaz tract was published from Solomonville, and the Mexican government speculated about Urrea's involvement in an opposition faction. She responded by moving to El Paso to continue healing. However, a series of border rebellions flung her back into the limelight. Mexican rebels, attempting to take over the Nogales customhouse in August 1896, evoked her name as la Santa de Cabora. Sensing turmoil, Urrea retreated to the insulated mining community in Clifton, Arizona.

During the closing years of her life she began to exert her own autonomy. She briefly married miner Lupe Rodríquez in June 1900, but a medical healing tour in 1900 represented her personal independence. In August, at the behest of local Clifton businessmen, she traveled to San Jose, California, to cure an ill boy. This marked the beginning of a three-year healing tour with stops at several major metropolitan areas. Unlike Urrea's earlier days, she earned a considerable income from touring, but by all accounts she felt uneasy and terribly isolated. In early 1901 she wrote to a Clifton friend, Juana Van Order, imploring her to send her bilingual son John to serve as an interpreter. By spring their working relationship blossomed into an intimate relationship, and Urrea bore a daughter, Laura Van Order, in February 1902.

While living in East Los Angeles, she drew comfort from the growing Sonoran community. Drawn to Los Angeles by Henry Huntington's Pacific Electric Railway, Sonorans labored under poor living conditions and racially stratified wages. From her Brooklyn Avenue cottage Urrea continued healing, but she also began protesting dire labor conditions. Her reputation quickly spread both as a healer and as a labor activist who frequently encouraged railroad laborers to join the fledgling Mexican *mutualista* whose members had gone out on strike. Mirroring past years, the laborers glorified her as the symbolic la Santa de Cabora. Yet after several months battling with Pacific Electric, Urrea retreated to Clifton.

Never losing her devotion to the poor, oppressed, and infirm, Teresa Urrea continued her healing activities. In June 1904 she bore a second daughter, Magdalena Van Order. By late 1905 her health had deteriorated markedly. She died of tuberculosis on January 12, 1906.

See also Folk Healing Traditions; Religion

SOURCES: Domecq, Brianda. 1994. "Teresa Urrea: La Santa de Cabora." In *Tomóchic: La revolución adelantada*, ed. Jesús Vargas Valdez, 2:13–30. Ciudad Juárez: Universidad Autónoma de Ciudad Juárez; Perales, Marian. 2005. "Teresa Urrea: *Curandera* and Folk Saint." *Latina Legacies: Identity, Biography, and Community*, ed. Vicki L. Ruiz and Virginia Sánchez Korrol. New York: Oxford University Press; Vanderwood, Paul. 1998. *The Power of God against the Guns of Government: Religious Upheaval in Mexico at the Turn of the Nineteenth Century*. Stanford, CA: Stanford University Press.

Marian Perales

V

VALDEZ, PATSSI (1950?–)

Patssi Valdez was born in Los Angeles. She was educated through the experiences of the Los Angeles blowouts of 1968, the Chicano moratorium of 1970, the performance art collective Asco (1974–1987), and the Otis Parsons School of Art and Design (1981–1985). Her artistic career began at Garfield High School in East Los Angeles, where she met Harry Gamboa and Willie Herron. Through their collaborations at school and in the community they eventually developed Asco (Spanish for nausea), a performance art group whose aesthetic choices and directions emerged from urban realities of police brutality, poverty, gang warfare, Hollywood glamour, barrio counterculture, a sense of humor, and increasing distance from Chicano nationalism and *movimiento* art. The artists of Asco did not intend to establish themselves as authentic Chicano or folk artists. Instead, they worked to displace and rupture the image of the so-called real Chicano.

Through Asco Valdez worked in performance and installation art, photo-collage and photography, "no-movies," and costume design. In 1981 she enrolled at Otis Parsons in Los Angeles and New York City, which provided her with a vocabulary and larger historical context for her work. "Even though going to school was not considered the thing to do by the artistic community at the time, I wanted to educate myself . . . learn the vocabulary and more technical

Chicana artist Patssi Valdez. Photograph by Vern Evans. Courtesy of Patricia Correia Gallery.

aspects of my chosen profession." In 1985 she received her bachelor's degree in fine arts and full-page coverage in Andy Warhol's *Interview* magazine. In 1988 she began to seriously pursue painting as a medium, and her first solo exhibition at the Pico House in Los Angeles was a success: she sold all but one of her paintings. As a mixed-media artist, she continues to develop a style that is both familiar and disturbing. Beyond her work as a visual artist, Valdez established a career in theater and films as an art director and set designer.

Valdez has been the recipient of several prestigious awards, including the National Endowment for the Arts U.S./Mexico Artist-in-Residence (1994), the Durfee Foundation Artist Fellowship (1999), and the Brody Arts Fellowship in Visual Arts (1988). Her work has gathered wide recognition in France, Germany, and the United States and is included in the collections of the Smithsonian American Art Museum, Laguna Art Museum, Tucson Museum of Art, the Mexican Fine Arts Center Museum in Chicago, and the Mexican Museum in San Francisco. Valdez is widely recognized for her domestic spaces—both installations and paintings—and her images of women, including self-portraits and portraits by Harry Gamboa and representations of celestial and earthly women.

The inspiration for strong women came from her mother and sister, and her images of virgins, madonnas, queens, and goddesses articulate a social commentary on gender stereotypes and a reorientation of spiritual and female icons. Unconventional motifs all point to her rejection of assimilation rhetoric and Chicano cultural nationalism, both of which confine women to domestic and service labor, demand obedience to patriarchial rule, or silence challenges to gender politics. Although her reconfiguration of glamour and sexuality can produce ambivalence in the spectator, Valdez's art of the female body and spirit is a visual demonstration of dignity and power through grace and self-representation. Her works speak to a Chicana public about spiritual authority, intolerance for abuse, healing, and women-centered power.

See also Artists

SOURCES: Lewis, Louise. 1998. "Interview with Patssi Valdez." *Patssi Valdez: Private Landscapes, 1988–1998* (exhibition brochure). Northridge Art Gallery, California State University, Northridge; Pasqual Erkanat, Judy. 1995. "Burning Colors: Dynamic Interpretations Dominate LA Artist's Exhibit." *El Observador*, August 1, 16–22; Romo, Tere. 1999. "Patssi Valdez: A Precarious Comfort." In *Patssi Valdez: A Precarious Comfort* (exhibition catalog), ed. Elizabeth Ptak, 9–31. San Francisco: Mexican Museum; Wiggins, Susan. 1992. "Patssi Valdez." *Artweek*, March 26, 15.

Karen Mary Dávalos

VALLEJO, EPIFANIA DE GUADALUPE (1835–1905)

Pioneer photographer Epifania de Guadalupe Vallejo, also known as Epifania Gertrudis "Fanny" Vallejo, was the daughter of early Californios Mariano Guadalupe Vallejo and Francisca Benicia Carrillo of Sonoma, California. Born on August 4, 1835, Epifania was the third of sixteen children born to Mariano and Francisca in the period before the American occupation and conquest of Alta California that began in 1846 and ended with the signing of the Treaty of Guadalupe Hidalgo in February 1848. Though her life was full of grand achievements and interactions with some of the most notable people of her time, Epifania's role as a pioneer photographer in 1840s Mexican-era California stands as a pivotal moment in the history of art and science in North America.

As the daughter of the founders of Sonoma, Epifania Vallejo was heir to a rich Californio cultural tradition replete with the many social trappings and cultural graces of that day. She was tutored and mentored in the classical arts from a young age and was surrounded by the academic and scholarly atmosphere that her father and mother built into their rancho headquarters and home at Lachryma Montis (Mountain Tear), named for the artesian spring located at that site on the edge of the town of Sonoma. Situated as it was on one of the largest Mexican ranchos of early California, with holdings of some 175,000 acres, Lachryma Montis was groomed into the premier cultural center of the region. With more than 12,000 volumes in Mariano's personal library, the Vallejos were well educated and highly cultured. Accordingly, young Epifania played the piano and spent a good deal of her time as an amateur artist and painter. In addition, she had access to a personal music teacher and to the very best in tutors and classical works. The benefits of her family's access to early Californio traditions ultimately translated into what soon became the basis for some of Epifania's many cultural and artistic pursuits, not the least of which was her early experimentation with the daguerreotype process and her assembly of the earliest known photographic images ever produced in early California and the West.

The daguerreotype process, initially documented in California and the West through images produced by Epifania de Guadalupe Vallejo, was first made commercially available through the introduction of the Giroux daguerreotype camera in 1839. The Giroux daguerreotype camera, invented by early French photographer Louis-Jacques-Mandé Daguerre, required twenty- to thirty-minute exposure times for individual stills and the photochemical processing of copper plates, and was thus a relatively new, cumbersome, complex, and experimental process that was only beginning to become popular in the period after the 1840s. At this time Vallejo obtained access to a daguerreotype camera and began producing images while still only between the ages of twelve and fourteen. Despite her youth, Vallejo family photographic collections and early documents provide clear indications that Vallejo had in fact mastered the art of photography and the daguerreotype process in the period before 1849, and years before the formal American occupation and settlement of Alta California. One of her images found its way into the mounting of a finger ring with photo locket worn by General Mariano Vallejo himself. That ring ultimately came into the possession of Vallejo family descendant Martha McGettigan, whose quest for Vallejo's story inspired the research underlying this narrative. The image in question portrays Vallejo's mother, Francisca Benicia Carrillo Vallejo. Thus the earliest known photographic image on record for the period before the American occupation is that of a Californio woman of the Mexican or ranchero era of early California history.

On April 3, 1851, Epifania Vallejo married Captain John Blackman Frisbie, who was stationed at the town of Sonoma under Mariano Vallejo. At that time she was only fifteen years of age to his twenty-six years of age, but that was the beginning of a long and prosperous relationship with the American entrepreneur. Soon after their marriage the couple moved to San Francisco, where they boarded with California businessman and politician Thomas Larkin in 1854. Subsequently they relocated to the town of Vallejo. In March 1861 Vallejo attended President Abraham Lincoln's inaugural ball. According to Linda Lorda, a descendant of the Carrillo and Vallejo families who now lives in Sebastopol, California, Vallejo and her husband moved to Mexico in 1877–1878. Their residence was located at Calle Luis Moya or Hacienda Careaga, and it is likely that the move to Mexico was necessitated by John Frisbie's mismanagement of Vallejo family holdings. In Mexico Vallejo and her husband prospered, and some measure of their prosperity is made evident by the fact that the president and first lady of Mexico ultimately became godparents to Vallejo's family of twelve children. On February 14, 1905, Epifania de Guadalupe Vallejo succumbed to pneumonia and died in Cuautla, Mexico. She is buried in the French Cemetery in Mexico City. Her husband, John Frisbie, died in the family home on Calle Ancha in Mexico City on May 15, 1909. Vallejo's cherished piano was subsequently purchased and returned to the Vallejo home at Lachryma Montis, where it now stands in the museum along with other Vallejo family treasures.

Epifania Vallejo's work stands as a historical benchmark for the introduction of photography to California

and the American West and heralds the acknowledgment of Latina roles in the earliest contributions to that body of art, science, and technology made manifest north of the Rio Grande before the advent of the Americans. Clearly, Epifania de Guadalupe Vallejo's contributions to the art and science of early photography and phototechnical processes in California and the West will necessitate a fundamental reappraisal of the history of art, science, and technology in the Americas.

See also Spanish Borderlands

SOURCES: Empáran, Madie Brown. 1968. *The Vallejos of California*. San Francisco: Gleeson Library Associates, University of San Francisco; McGettigan, Martha A. 2000. "Epifania de Guadalupe Vallejo: California's 1st Woman Daguerreotypist." *The Seventeenth Conference of the California Mission Studies Association*. Mission San Gabriel Arcángel, San Gabriel, CA, February 19; Mendoza, Rubén G. 2000. "Villains Honored and Heroes Unsung: California State University Historian on the Vallejos of California." *Hispanic Outlook in Higher Education* 10, no. 23 (August 11): 35–37; Rosenus, Alan. 1995. *General M. G. Vallejo and the Advent of the Americans: A Biography*. Albuquerque: University of New Mexico Press.

Rubén G. Mendoza

VALLEJO DE LEESE, MARÍA PAULA ROSALÍA (1811–1889)

Born on January 25, 1811, in Monterey, California, Rosalía Vallejo was the tenth of thirteen children born to Ignacio Vicente Vallejo and his wife María Antoñia Lugo. Vicente Vallejo arrived in California in 1774 as a member of the Fernando Moncada expedition, and the Lugos were original settlers of San Luis Obispo, where María Antoñia was born in 1776. In time both families rose to prominence in northern and southern California. As a member of one of the richest, most politically influential, and largest landholding families in northern California, Rosalía Vallejo grew up in relative prosperity and comfort, exemplifying the life experiences of the female ranchero elite, or the *gente de razón* class, of early-nineteenth-century California. Both her father and her brothers, especially Mariano and Salvador, were influential politicians and community leaders who extended the family's social honor and prestige throughout California. The Vallejos, both male and female, were known for their wealth and influence, personal intelligence, talents, and strong personalities.

In the 1840s William Heath Davis described Rosalía Vallejo as "a tall, handsome, beautifully formed woman, full of vivacity and remarkably intelligent," but prone to sarcasm and "quite expert" with firearms. Of the eight Vallejo sisters, none was more independent and high spirited than Rosalía, traits she demonstrated throughout her adult life, particularly in when and whom she chose to marry. Her brother, Mariano Guadalupe, as head of the household, favored the courtship of Timothy Murphy, an Irish trader involved in the Lima trade, whom he placed as administrator to the Mission San Rafael. Refusing to obey her brother's wishes, the twenty-six-year-old Vallejo took advantage of Mariano's absence and secretly married Jacob Primer Leese, an American trader born in Ohio, on April 13, 1837, in the Mission San Francisco. Mariano never fully forgave Rosalía for her actions, and it remained a sore point throughout their lives. Little is known of Murphy, but Leese's business correspondence indicates that he was a literate, but hardly an educated, man. For any other woman this action would have been highly irregular; however, Vallejo was by all accounts a determined, strong-minded person. Luckily for her, she and her husband were not estranged from the Vallejo clan, and the couple eventually purchased land and raised a family.

During the Mexican-American War Vallejo again showed her personal courage and stubbornness. When four Americans attempted to rob her family's storehouse, she physically blocked the entrance, and only after the men threatened her at gunpoint did she reluctantly step aside. In another incident, after American forces had captured Sonoma and set up camp near the Vallejos' rancho, Captain John C. Frémont requested that Rosalía Vallejo personally bring a seventeen-year-old Indian servant girl to the officers' barracks, obviously to be used for sexual pleasure. Vallejo defiantly wrote back that she would not do so, regardless of the consequences, and since Frémont was unwilling to press the point, she won the round. To Vallejo, this incident provided evidence of the depraved and opportunistic motivations of the American conquerors. Later Frémont exacted revenge when he forced her to write a letter to Captain Padilla beseeching him to return to San Jose and not attack Sonoma. Vallejo regretted writing the letter, but, as she explained, she was pregnant at the time, and when Frémont threatened to burn down the buildings with the women inside, she was forced to comply in order to protect her unborn child and her fellow countrywomen.

In 1876 Vallejo was interviewed and asked to comment on the Mexican-American War and to give her opinion of the American conquest. Her response was short and to the point: "Those hated men inspired me with such a large dose of hate against their race that though twenty-eight years have elapsed since that time, I have not forgotten the insults heaped upon me and not being desirous of coming in contact with them I have abstained from learning their language." One of the reasons why she refused to have continued contact with Americans was Jacob Leese's abandonment of his family in 1865. In 1864 Leese was given a massive land grant in Baja California as part of a colonization enterprise. The enterprise was a tremendous failure and financially bankrupted Leese, who chose to leave California without his family. By 1876 Vallejo and her children were being supported by her brother Mariano on his Lachryma Montis estate.

Rosalía Vallejo died on July 31, 1889, and was buried at Mission San Carlos de Monterey, the same place where she was baptized in 1811, but the transformations during her lifetime spoke volumes about tremendous changes for the *gente de razón* class, women included. Born a Californio elite, Rosalía Vallejo died a reluctant American, a true testament to her resisting Californio identity.

See also Spanish Borderlands

SOURCES: Davis, William Heath. 1929. *Seventy-five Years in California, 1831–1906.* San Francisco: John Howell; Rosenus, Alan. 1995. *General M. G. Vallejo and the Advent of the Americans: A Biography.* Albuquerque: University of New Mexico Press; Vallejo de Leese, Rosalía. "History of the Bear Flag Party." Bancroft Library, University of California, Berkeley.

María Raquel Casas

VANGUARDIA PUERTORRIQUEÑA (1935–1950s)

The Vanguardia Puertorriqueña (including its Women's Auxiliary) established in 1935, functioned as Lodge No. 4797 of the International Workers' Order (IWO). The Vanguardia was one of ten IWO lodges in the New York area and formed part of the Sociedad Fraternal Cervantes, the national umbrella organization for the Spanish-speaking lodges of the IWO. In 1938 there were nearly 1,400 Spanish- and Portuguese-speaking members in the IWO. Another Puerto Rican lodge in New York was the Mutualista Puertorriqueña, IWO Lodge No. 4792.

Founded in 1930, and originally chartered in New York State, the International Workers' Order was a progressive multinational fraternal benefits organization that provided its members life insurance and sickness, disability, and death benefits. Open to men and women regardless of nationality, race, color, creed, or political affiliation, the IWO also sponsored educational, recreational, cultural, and social programs and activities for its members and their families. These programs included choral groups, drama clubs, music bands, sports teams, and summer youth camps. In addition, the IWO encouraged its members to establish trade union organizations, promote adequate social and security legislation, discharge the duties of a citizen of the United States of America, and support progressive political causes. These included the fight against fascism, support for the Republicans during the Spanish

Vanguardia Puertorriqueña, Mother's Day celebration. Courtesy of the Jesús Colón Collection. Centro Archives, Centro de Estudios Puertorriqueños, Hunter College, CUNY.

civil war, and the struggle for Puerto Rican independence.

Among others, the IWO had Jewish, English, Russian, Ukrainian, Hungarian, Italian, and Polish lodges and in 1938 claimed more than 135,000 members. The Vanguardia Puertorriqueña, numbering some 200 members and centered in the Puerto Rican working-class community in the Brooklyn Navy Yard district of that borough in New York City, participated in all IWO programs and activities. In addition, on a local level, it sponsored English-language classes, conferences, lecture series, dances, beauty pageants, recreational excursions, and special celebrations for Mother's Day, Columbus Day, Thanksgiving, and Christmas. Its most outstanding leaders were Puerto Rican community activist and writer Jesús Colón, his wife, Concha, and brother, Joaquín Colón.

See also Puerto Rican Radical Politics in New York

SOURCES: Acosta-Belén, Edna, and Virginia Sánchez Korrol, eds. 1993. *Jesús Colón: The Way It Was and Other Writings.* Houston: Arte Público Press; Colón, Jesús. Jesús Colón Archival Collection, Centro de Estudios Puertorriqueños Library and Archives, Hunter College, CUNY; Iglesias, César Andréu, ed. 1984. *Memoirs of Bernardo Vega: A Contribution to the History of the Puerto Rican Community in New York.* New York: Monthly Review Press.

Carlos Sanabria

VARELA, BEATRIZ (1927–   )

Retired Spanish professor Beatriz Varela is considered an authority on Spanish linguistics, especially the language as it is spoken in Cuba and other parts of the

Americas. She has published four books: *Mejora tu español* (coauthored with Marta de la Portilla, 1979), a textbook for students of the Spanish language; *Lo chino en el habla cubana* (1980), an examination of Chinese influences in Cuban Spanish; *El español cubano-americano* (1992), a noted examination of Spanish as it is spoken not only in Cuba but also by Cubans in exile; and *José Varela Zequeira (1854–1939): Su obra científico-literaria* (1997), a biography of her grandfather, famed Cuban poet and doctor José Varela Zequeira, a work that was based on her University of Havana thesis.

Graduating from the University of Havana and the Universidad Católica de Santo Tomás de Villanueva in 1950, this daughter of María Antonia Dumás y Alcocer and Dr. Roberto Varela Zequeira taught grammar and linguistics at her alma mater, Ruston Academy in Havana. Her brief marriage to Dr. Jorge Cuéllar produced one son, Jorge. Suffering the pain of exile in 1960, Beatriz Varela settled in New Orleans, where she taught at Cabrini High School while completing graduate studies at Tulane University. She obtained a master's degree in 1964 and her doctorate in 1965. From 1964 until her retirement Varela was a professor of Spanish at the University of New Orleans. She has published numerous articles on the folklore and linguistics of Cuba and has been actively involved in various organizations. She was elected to the Academia Norteamericana de la Lengua Española in 1993.

Upon her retirement from the University of New Orleans, Beatriz Varela moved to Miami. She has since presented at conferences in Costa Rica, New York, and the Czech Republic. Her current area of research is Spanish as it is spoken in Central America, with particular emphasis on Costa Rica. With her keen inquisitiveness and scholarly distinction, Beatriz Varela continues to contribute to the understanding of the unique shades, as well as the common roots, of Spanish as it is spoken in the Americas and the influences of other languages and cultures on the language.

See also Education

SOURCES: Varela, Beatriz. 1980. *Lo chino en el habla cubana.* Miami: Ediciones Universal; _____. 1992. *El español cubano-americano.* New York: Senda Nueva de Ediciones; _____. 1997. *José Varela Zequeira (1854–1939): Su obra científico-literaria.* Miami: Ediciones Universal.

María R. Estorino

VARELA, MARÍA (1940–)

María Varela has been organizing in rural communities of color since 1962. Born of a Mexican immigrant father and an Irish American mother, she graduated from Alverno College in Milwaukee in 1961 with a degree in secondary education. Long active in the Young Christian Students (YCS), a progressive Catholic social justice organization, Varela joined the national staff after graduation. In 1962 she was recruited by the Student Nonviolent Coordinating Committee (SNCC) and moved to Selma, Alabama, to work for voting rights. She became the first Latina photographer to document the organization's work in the Deep South. In addition, Varela was jailed twice and learned firsthand the risks associated with organizing. These experiences, however, only served to solidify her commitment to social change. "The movement raised a lot of questions about democracy and left them unanswered. I needed to find those answers."

In 1967 land-grant leader Reies López Tijerina invited Varela to work with la Alianza Federal de Mercedes (Federal Land Grant Alliance) in Albuquerque. Although Varela had also been recruited to organize farmworkers in California, her experience in the South reaffirmed her belief in the importance of land. "I learned from Black farmers, who were aggressive in defending farm and community, that landlessness was worse than political disenfranchisement. Owning land is key to taking control of community, economy, and culture. For land-based cultures to lose their land was to ensure [their] extinction."

Varela left La Alianza in 1968 to work with heirs of the Tierra Amarilla Land Grant and helped establish La Cooperativa Agricola. La Cooperativa was a community-based organization that promoted self-help projects in agriculture, legal affairs, and health. Varela served as the director of the primary health clinic, La Clinica, from 1975 to 1979, helping to develop northern New Mexico's first rural birthing center.

She resigned in 1980 to have a daughter, Sabina, with Lorenzo Zúñiga, a local plumber she had married in 1977. During this time Varela won a National Rural Fellowship, which funded her M.A. from the University of Massachusetts in community and regional planning (1982). Her master's work included researching ways of preserving agriculture in the traditional villages of northern New Mexico.

Although many local Hispanos still owned ancestral land, much of the area had been appropriated by the federal government in 1905 for the creation of the Carson and Santa Fe national forests. The loss of land, low livestock prices, an inability to compete for grazing allotments, government neglect, and out-migration, particularly of young people, led to a century of poverty. Varela and her neighbors Gumercindo Salazar and Antonio Manzanares began to search for alternatives. They sought to show how rural communities could modernize their economies in ways that would not destroy the environment or pastoral lifestyle. Their first step was to gain higher prices for their lamb by participating in an existing lamb cooperative's teleauction. The group then reinstated traditional pastoral practices, including cooperative grazing and breeding to revitalize the nearly extinct Churro breed. Incorporating as Ganados del Valle, a nonprofit corporation, in 1984, Varela and her neighbors then created several businesses, which marketed weavings, wool products, organic lamb, crafts, and products from recycled tires. Considered to be a national and international model of sustainable rural economic development, Ganados and related enterprises together constitute the largest private employment source in northern Rio Arriba County.

Varela's work with Ganados and other nonprofits was recognized in 1990 when she received a

Chicano movement leader and community visionary María Varela. Photograph by Lorenzo Zúñiga Jr. Courtesy of María Varela.

MacArthur Foundation Fellowship, also known as a "genius award." One of the first Latinas to win a MacArthur, Varela was especially pleased that the award recognized community organizing. "I was stunned that they chose a community organizer, because community work is not often recognized." Varela left Ganados in 1997 to teach, write, and expand her business, the Rural Resources Group, which assists traditional rural cultures. She, Manzanares, and Salazar serve as advisors for life on the Ganados board of directors. Varela taught at the University of New Mexico for nearly a decade and in 1997–1998 was appointed to an endowed chair at the Hulbert Center for Southwest Studies at Colorado College, where she currently teaches. An acclaimed organizer and photographer whose work has been exhibited at the Smithsonian, she has coauthored *Rural Environmental Planning for Sustainable Communities* and has contributed to *Across the Great Divide: Explorations in Collaborative Conservation in the American West.*

See also Ganados del Valle

SOURCES: Chu, Dan, and Leslie Linthicum. 1991. "MacArthur Grant Winner Maria Varela Shepherds a Rural New Mexico Community towards Economic Rebirth." *People,* January 14, 115–117; Hazelhurst, John. 2000. "Chronicling the Dream: Photos Depict Dignity in Civil Rights Struggle." *Colorado Springs Independent,* February 27, 2–8; Jackson, Donald Dale. 1991. "Around Los Ojos, Sheep and Land Are Fighting Words." *Smithsonian* 22:37–47; Pulido, Laura. 1996. *Environmentalism and Economic Justice: Two Chicano Struggles in the Southwest.* Tucson: University of Arizona Press.

Laura Pulido

VÁSQUEZ, ANNA (1918–)

Anna Torres was born in Mexico but was raised in Indiana. She was the only Hispanic female from her neighborhood to join the World War II effort. She served as a Wac during the war, working as a trainer with the Third Air Force, which was based in Florida. She was sent to Florida to train Allied pilots in the 201st Squadron Mexicano to fight in the South Pacific. "They held her here (Florida) because they were training all those Allied pilots," her husband, Roberto Vásquez recalled. "They didn't want to let her go."

Roberto Vásquez was born in Laredo, Texas, on August 1, 1923. From the beginning Vásquez was made to feel at ease with his culture. Located on the Texas-Mexico border about 160 miles south of San Antonio, Laredo was unique. In the 1930s the sheriff and most of the local police department, as well as the mayor and a number of teachers, were all Hispanic. Vásquez said that after the war he experienced racial inequalities he had not encountered in southern Texas and during the war. "We came out of the service, and they used to seat us in a separate colored section in the theaters," he said. "Here we were out of the war with a bunch of medals, and we had to sit on the side. So we got involved in politics and changed a lot of things."

Roberto Vásquez met his wife, Anna Torres, in East Chicago, Indiana, where they live today. They had three sons, David, Arturo, and Richard. The Vásquezes began their activist involvement in 1948 when they joined the League of United Latin American Citizens (LULAC), one of the largest and oldest Hispanic organizations in the United States. For Roberto and Anna Vásquez, LULAC embodied a philosophy that they believed in, one in which the will of a people can overcome inequalities of discrimination and injustice and people can enjoy their rights as U.S. citizens.

Roberto and Anna Vásquez organized a men's and ladies' council in East Chicago. Roberto Vásquez was a pioneer president of LULAC, first in East Chicago; later he became second national vice president. Anna Vásquez was first state president in the Midwest. Together they attended thirty-nine consecutive LULAC national conventions all over the United States.

Awards and plaques cover the walls of their home as symbols of all their hard work. Through war, discrimination, and sickness, the Vásquezes have remained partners and set a legacy for themselves and others in East Chicago and beyond. Anna Vásquez is unable to speak and is mostly confined to her bed be-

Roberto and Anna Vásquez at a 1960 LULAC dance in East Chicago, Indiana. Courtesy of the U.S. Latino and Latina World War II Oral History Project, University of Texas, Austin.

cause of a series of strokes in recent years. "She can't speak very well," Roberto Vásquez remarks, "but she can think better than I can."

See also League of United Latin American Citizens (LULAC); Military Service

SOURCES: Jenschke, Callie. 2003. "Post-war Racism Inspired Pair to Fight Discrimination." *Narratives: Stories of U.S. Latinos and Latinas and World War II* (U.S. Latino and Latina WWII Oral History Project, University of Texas at Austin), 4, no. 1 (Spring): 69. Vásquez, Anna and Roberto Vásquez. Interviewed by Bill Luna, East Chicago, IN.

Callie Jenschke

VÁSQUEZ, ENRIQUETA LONGEAUX Y (1930–)

Born in the agricultural town of Cheraw, Colorado, Enriqueta Vásquez became a well-known Chicano movement columnist whose writings captured her lifelong dedication to the advancement of social justice in the face of racial, class, and gender inequality. Appearing from 1968 to 1972 in New Mexico's *El Grito del Norte*, a leading Chicano movement publication, the column "Despierten Hermanos!" (Awaken, Brothers and Sisters!) aimed to inspire the Mexican American population to political action. A powerful critic of U.S. foreign policy, the institutional Catholic Church, and consumer society, Vásquez was also an unrelenting advocate of women's equality, the dignity of the poor, and the richness of Mexican American culture. The column reflected her politicization and radicalization as a working-class single parent and mestiza living in the United States.

Vásquez's early years were spent working in the fields and local canning factories with her Mexican immigrant parents and her twelve siblings, five of whom died in childhood. After high-school graduation she moved to Denver with the hope of improving her standard of living but instead encountered blatant job discrimination and personal upheaval. Despite her excellent secretarial skills, Vásquez was initially denied front-desk jobs because she was dark skinned. In 1950 Vásquez married a man who proved to be physically abusive. Their divorce left her nearly destitute with two children to raise.

In 1965 Vásquez joined the local chapter of the American GI Forum, a civil rights organization founded by Mexican American World War II veterans. Through the American GI Forum Vásquez became one of the local directors of a War on Poverty employment agency, Proyecto SER (Service, Employment, and Redevelopment Project; "ser" means "to be" in Spanish). She also met Rodolfo "Corky" Gonzales, a fellow Forum member and emerging Chicano movement leader. In 1966 Gonzales founded the Crusade for Justice, a Chicano organization that vigorously criticized police brutality and educational inequality. Vásquez became a dedicated Crusade member. In 1967 she married Bill Longeaux, an artist, political activist, and friend of Gonzales. The following year the Longeaux-Vásquez family moved from Denver to northern New Mexico to become caretakers of a ranch that served as an educational and cultural center for Crusade youth. In New Mexico Vásquez also joined a circle of activists who were organized around the fiery activism of la Alianza Federal de Mercedes (Federal Land Grant Alliance) whose members sought the return of lands granted to their ancestors by the Spanish and Mexican governments. Vásquez became part of a cooperative effort that launched *El Grito del Norte*, a publication that covered the local land-grant movement, as well as national and international events.

Embracing a similarly broad sweep, Vásquez's columns ranged from celebrating Mexican folk culture as a source of personal and community regeneration to praising socialist Cuba, which she visited in 1969, as a model of revolutionary liberation and freedom. She was also among the first Chicanas to attempt to reconcile feminism and cultural nationalism. Although some men—and women—within the Chicano movement labeled feminism divisive and culturally inauthentic, Vásquez argued in 1969 in one of her most celebrated pieces, "The Women of La Raza," that "total liberation" for Mexican Americans meant liberation for both sexes and the entire family. Yet because "the family must come up together," she asserted, "there is little room for a woman's liberation movement alone."

In another well-known column, 1971's "Soy Chicana primero," Vásquez again stated that her first loyalty lay with the Chicano movement versus the "white women's liberation movement." Still, she had little patience with any implied subordination. A staunch critic of the conflict in Vietnam, Vásquez instead proposed that Chicanas emulate the women fighters in Vietnam who, she claimed with slight exaggeration, carried "a gun in one hand" and a suckling child in the other. Vásquez frequently suggested that the urban struggles of Mexican American women made them prime candidates for politicization and collective action. In her estimation women and women's issues were central to the Chicano movement. During the 1970s Vásquez developed her interest in Native American culture and spirituality by participating in sweat lodges, sacred dances, and other ceremonies as an elder. She continues to live and write in northern New Mexico, where she has recently completed a sweeping history of Raza women.

See also Chicano Movement; Feminism

SOURCE: Espinoza, Dionne, Elaine. 1996. "Pedagogies of Nationalism and Gender: Cultural Resistance in Selected Representational Practices of Chicana/o Movement Activists, 1967–1972." Ph.D. diss., Cornell University.

Lorena Oropeza and Dionne Espinoza

VELÁZQUEZ, LORETA JANETA (1842–?)

Madame Loreta Janeta Velázquez has been described as a patriot, a cross-dresser, a heroine, or a hoax, but her true story continues to elude historians. Nonetheless, it is known that in 1876 Loreta Janeta Velázquez published an astonishing and controversial Civil War memoir titled *The Woman in Battle: A Narrative of the Exploits, Adventures, and Travels of Madame Loreta Janeta Velázquez, Otherwise Known as Lieutenant Harry T. Buford, Confederate States Army.* This was no ordinary war story, for Velázquez claimed to have so passionately supported the Confederate cause that she disguised herself as Lieutenant Harry T. Buford and fought at the battles of First Bull Run, Fort Donelson, and Shiloh. Velázquez's book depicts her dangerous work as a spy, a transporter of dispatches, a secret-service agent, and a blockade runner. Also described are her adventures in Washington, D.C., her career as a bounty hunter and substitute broker in New York, travels to Europe and South America, mining escapades in the American West, residence among the Mormons, love affairs, courtships, and four marriages.

Velázquez was born on June 26, 1842, in Havana, Cuba, the daughter of a *hacendado,* formerly a native of Cartagena, Spain. An educated man, he had acquired great wealth in the sugar, tobacco, and coffee trades. Velázquez confessed that her girlhood was spent "haunted with the idea of being a man." She maintained that she wished for the privileges and status granted to men and denied to women and often compared herself to Spanish conquistadores, Joan of Arc, and Deborah of the Hebrews. She further admitted to an "impulsive and imaginative disposition," often prone to idealize every episode of her life. "I could not even write a social letter to my father to inform him of the state of my health, or my educational progress, without putting in it some romantic project which I had on hand. This propensity of mine evidently annoyed him greatly, for he frequently reprimanded me with much severity."

Velázquez was sent to New Orleans at a young age to live with her mother's sister and complete her education. Cuban families of means often sent their sons and daughters abroad for education. While sons, like Velázquez's brother Josea, studied in Spain or France, daughters often went to Catholic girls' schools in the United States to learn English and domestic arts. However, Velázquez was far from the typical antebellum adolescent. In addition to dressing up as a man—"It was frequently my habit, after all in the house had retired to bed at night, to dress myself in my cousin's clothes and to promenade before the mirror, practicing the gait of a man, and admiring the figure I made in masculine raiment"—she was unusually independent. At age fourteen she ran away from her school in New Orleans to marry a young American Army officer named William, breaking an engagement to a Spaniard that had been previously arranged by her family.

By the time Velázquez was eighteen, she and William had had—and lost—three children, two of them to fever. It was also around that time that William's state (Arkansas) seceded from the Union and he resigned his commission to join the Confederate army. Velázquez states that her grief over the loss of her children "probably had a great influence in reviving my old notions about military glory, and of exciting anew my desires to win fame on the battle-field." In this regard Velázquez was not alone. Women attempted to sign up for battle in both the Union and Confederate armies. Some 200 women are said to have fought in the Civil War, and they could join the army because physical examinations were superficial. The general assumption was that anyone dressed in pants as a man must be a man. Unable to persuade William to let her fight for the Confederacy, Velázquez simply waited for him to leave, adopted the name Lieutenant Harry T. Buford, was measured for several uniforms, and proceeded to Arkansas to raise a battalion for the Southern cause.

Thus began her military adventures, which are described in *The Woman in Battle*. The end of the story finds Velázquez traveling through the American West, where she stopped long enough to have a baby in Salt Lake City and to meet Brigham Young. In Nevada she claimed to have married for the fourth time; the gentleman is unnamed. Then she was off again "with my little baby boy in my arms, starting a long journey through Colorado, New Mexico and Texas, hoping perhaps but scarcely expecting to find the opportunities which I failed to find." Velázquez's story ends at that point. Her final plea was that the public would buy her book so that she could support her child.

It should be noted that the historical validity of *The Woman in Battle* has never been determined. Historians, as well as Velázquez's contemporaries, point out that *The Woman in Battle* is not entirely verifiable based on information that can be confirmed. Other than citing the right generals in the right battles, Velázquez wrote in vague generalities. Many of the people cited in her book have only a first or a last name, including three of her four husbands. Velázquez also stretches her credibility by claiming to have done too much. The

Civil War soldier and writer Loreta Janeta Velázquez. Courtesy of Documenting the American South Collection. Wilson Annex, University of North Carolina at Chapel Hill Libraries.

author herself mentions that "the loss of my notes has compelled me to rely entirely upon my memory, and my memory is apt to be very treacherous." She goes on to say that she "has been compelled to write hurriedly, as the necessities I have been under of earning my daily bread being such as could not be disregarded, even for the purpose of winning the laurels of authorship."

Nonetheless, the arguments cited by Velázquez's main critic, a former Confederate general, Jubal Early, are based on equally flimsy evidence. He claimed that Velázquez was not of Spanish origin because she did not have an accent, and that she was probably a Yankee. Above all, he criticized her lifestyle, unladylike deportment, and aggressive nature. Yet there are enough references to validate Velázquez's claims. An 1863 record of the Confederate secretary of war has a request for an officer's commission from an H. T. Buford; wartime pay stubs from the U.S. government list an Alice Williams, one of Velázquez's aliases; and a newspaper article in New Orleans reports that Velázquez served as an agent for a company attempting to establish a colony of ex-Confederate patriots in Venezuela. While the definitive truth of Velázquez's claims may never be known, she remains one of the hundreds of Latinos and Latinas residing in Southern states or His-panic Caribbean countries who were drawn to the American Civil War because of ideological interests, and the only Latina to have written a memoir about her experiences.

See also Military Service

SOURCES: Docker, Amy. 2005. "The Adventures of Loreta Janeta Velázquez: Civil War Spy and Story Teller." In *Latina Legacies: Identity, Biography, and Community*, ed. Vicki L. Ruiz and Virginia Sánchez Korrol. New York: Oxford University Press; Velázquez, Loreta Janeta. 1876. *The Woman in Battle: A Narrative of the Exploits, Adventures, and Travels of Madame Loreta Janeta Velasquez, Otherwise Known as Lieutenant Harry T. Buford, Confederate States Army.* Ed. C. J. Worthington. Richmond, VA: Dustin, Gilman and Co. Electronic edition of the Academic Affairs Library, University of North Carolina at Chapel Hill, 1999.

Pamela J. Marshall

VELÁZQUEZ, NYDIA M. (1953–)

Nydia M. Velázquez is the first Puerto Rican woman elected to the U.S. House of Representatives. She won her seat to the 103rd Congress on November 3, 1992, representing the Twelfth Congressional District of New York. A heavily Democratic, largely Latino district consisting of poor, working-class neighborhoods, it spans three of New York City's boroughs. These communities include Corona in the Bronx, East Chinatown in Manhattan, and Williamsburg, Bushwick, Sunset Park, and Cypress Hills/East New York in Brooklyn.

Velázquez was born on March 28, 1953, in the sugarcane town of Yabucoa, Puerto Rico. According to her official congressional biography, "I grew up in a rural area surrounded by mountains. I was always asking myself what was on the other side of those mountains." She started school early, skipped a few grades, and was the first member of her family to earn a college degree. In 1974 she graduated magna cum laude from the University of Puerto Rico in Río Piedras with a degree in political science. She then earned her master's at New York University in 1976. In 1981 she joined the faculty at Hunter College as an adjunct professor of Puerto Rican studies. She and her twin sister were among nine children raised by Doña Carmen Luisa Velázquez and Don Benito Velázquez. Benito Velázquez was a butcher, a sugarcane cutter, and a local politician in their hometown.

In 1983 Nydia Velázquez entered New York City politics as the special assistant to U.S. representative Edolphus Towns, a Brooklyn Democrat. One year later she became the first Latina appointed to serve on the New York City Council. In 1986 she served as the director of the Department of Puerto Rican Community Affairs in the United States, where she initiated a very successful empowerment program titled Atrevete

Velázquez, Nydia M.

(Dare to Go for It!). It consisted of a massive voter registration drive that ultimately registered more than 200,000 new voters.

Her bid for Congress coincided with a surge in the national efforts to increase the voice and participation of minorities in America's political agenda. The Twelfth Congressional District was formed by redistricting after the 1990 census. Although Velázquez garnered a fraction of the $3.2-million war chest raised by her opponent, Stephen Solarz, she gained a key endorsement from former New York City mayor David Dinkins. In 1992, after running a hard, grassroots campaign and shored up by her family, friends, and community network, Nydia Velázquez became the first Puerto Rican woman elected to the U.S. House of Representatives. She describes herself as "progressive, concentrating on the problems that would affect the lives of the working class and the poor."

Congresswoman Velázquez sits on the House Banking and Financial Services Committee and on the Small Business Committee. Her assignments include the Housing and Community Opportunities and General Oversight and Investigations subcommittees. She is the ranking member on the Small Business Committee, which includes the Regulation and Paperwork Reduction Subcommittee. At the vanguard of hate crimes legislation, she also sponsored the Family Violence Prevention Act, which provides violence prevention services to underserved populations regardless of race, culture, or language. Velázquez cosponsored the English Plus Act with Congressman José Serrano (D-NY) and Congresswoman Ileana Ros-Lehtinen (R-FL), which encourages the teaching of foreign languages in addition to English. She assisted in the coordination of a historic summit between national Latina health care professionals and First Lady Hillary Rodham Clinton to discuss health care issues in the Latino community. Outspoken against NAFTA, the elimination of bilingual education, the denial of federal benefits for legal immigrants, amending laws against lending discrimination, reduction of funds for fair housing, and welfare reform that fails to provide jobs and job training with adequate health care benefits and child-care options, she always focuses her concerns on the disenfranchised.

In the 109th Congress, 1st Session, Velázquez continues to serve on the Small Business Committee where she is the ranking member. She serves on the House Financial Services Committee, and she is a member of the Capital Markets, Financial Institutions, and Consumer Credit Subcommittee. She also serves on the Subcommittee for Consumer Credit, Housing, and Community Opportunity.

At the district level Velázquez sponsored a service of free tax-filing assistance for her local residents. She

Congresswoman Nydia M. Velázquez. Courtesy of Kate Davis and the Office of Congresswoman Nydia M. Velázquez.

brought together Housing and Urban Development personnel, real-estate consultants, and local lenders for forums to discuss increased home ownership in her district. She has worked for increased policing in the areas of her district where there were high crime statistics. Working with HUD, Velázquez pointed out the need for federal dollars for fair housing and economic development in her district. She is an uncompromising fighter for equal rights for the underrepresented and a staunch proponent of economic opportunity for the working-class poor.

In 2001 the United States Hispanic Chamber of Commerce honored Congresswoman Velázquez and California lieutenant governor Cruz Bustamante for their tireless efforts on behalf of Latino small business. Bustamante received the Chairman's Award, and Velázquez was honored with the President's Award. Velázquez has held federal departments accountable for their record of accomplishment regarding minority federal procurements and has been quoted as saying, "We need to take responsibility in life and try to be somebody that everybody can be proud of."

See also Latinas in the U.S. Congress; Politics, Electoral

SOURCES: Newman, María. 1992. "From Puerto Rico to Congress, a Determined Path; A Cane Cutter's Daughter, Nydia M. Velázquez Is Now a Force in New York Politics." *New York Times*, September 37, 33; Tardiff, Joseph C., and L. Mpho Mabunda, eds. 1996. *Dictionary of Hispanic Biography.* New York: Gale Research; U.S. House of Representatives. "Congresswoman Nydia Velázquez." www.house.gov/velazquez/ (accessed July 12, 2005).

Linda C. Delgado

VÉLEZ, LUPE (1908–1944)

Born María Guadalupe de Villalobos in San Luis Potosí, Mexico, in 1908, film star Lupe Vélez was one of four children. Her father, Jacob Villalobos, served as a military officer. Her mother, Josefina Vélez, was a former opera singer. Vélez studied for a time at a girls' Catholic school in San Antonio, Texas, but the Mexican Revolution forced her to return and help support her family. She first worked in a department store before finding the opportunity to dance and sing on the Mexican stage.

An American talent agent persuaded her to travel to Hollywood, where there was a part waiting for her. But when she arrived, the director thought that she was too young for the part, and instead Vélez found work as an extra. In 1928 Vélez got a break when Douglas Fairbanks Sr. chose her to co-star with him in *The Gaucho*. RKO then offered her a five-year contract. Her aggressive personality and sexuality meshed with her ethnicity, and producers gave her exotic and half-caste parts in such films as *Wolf Song* (1929), *East Is West* (1930), *Cuban Love Song* (1931), and *Broken Wing* (1932).

From the beginning Hollywood studios and film magazines portrayed Vélez as a "sex kitten," "hot tamale," and "Mexican spitfire." Proclaiming, "I am not wild. I am just Lupe," Vélez developed a public reputation as the "Hot Baby" of Hollywood, an image that was promoted both on and off the screen.

While filming *Wolf Song*, Vélez met Gary Cooper, and they began a two-year relationship. With the debut of *Cuban Love Song* (1931), Vélez's relationship with Cooper ended, but while promoting the film in New York, she met Johnny Weissmuller, who had just finished his own film *Tarzan the Ape Man* (1932). MGM viewed Weissmuller as its newest star and encouraged the romance between him and Vélez. The couple began their tumultuous marriage on October 8, 1933, separated several times, and then finally divorced in 1939.

In 1939, under contract to RKO Studios, Vélez introduced the Mexican Spitfire series with *Girl from Mexico* (1939). Vélez played Carmelita, a singer hired by an American ad executive, Dennis Woods, played by actor Donald Woods. Dennis falls for her, much to the dismay of his aunt. In the second film of the series, *Mexican Spitfire* (1939), Carmelita marries Dennis, reversing the Hollywood stereotype of the Latin woman who loses the Anglo man to an Anglo woman. Yet through all eight films other stereotypes abound, including Carmelita's lack of breeding and social unacceptability, her refusal to put her show-business career aside, her lack of desire to have children, and her failure to promote Dennis's career. Throughout the series, including *Mexican Spitfire Out West* (1940), *Mexican Spitfire's Baby* (1941), *Mexican Spitfire at Sea* (1942), *Mexican Spitfire Sees a Ghost* (1942), *Mexican Spitfire's Elephant* (1942), and *Mexican Spitfire's Blessed Event* (1943), misunderstandings abounded. With the end of the Spitfire series, Vélez returned to Mexico in 1944 and made the film *Nana*. While she waited for a Hollywood release of the film, Vélez made plans to star in a new play in New York. Instead, Vélez, single and pregnant, committed suicide in December 1944 at her Beverly Hills home.

Vélez's stardom manifested images that focused upon her sexuality and aggressive personality, an image that appeared consciously negotiated. From the moment Vélez was introduced to Hollywood audiences, her sexuality was attributed to her ethnicity. Her image and behavior transgressed accepted Anglo boundaries. Yet Hollywood, the studios, and movie magazines, such as *Photoplay*, promoted this image. Some critics have argued that Vélez internalized her image as a "Mexican spitfire," but others believe that there is ample evidence to support the theory that Vélez knew and understood the difference between real life and acting.

See also Media Stereotypes; Movie Stars

SOURCES: López, Ana M. 1991. "Are All Latins from Manhattan? Hollywood, Ethnography, and Cultural Colonialism." In *Unspeakable Images: Ethnicity and the American Cinema*, ed. Lester D. Friedman. Urbana: University of Illinois Press; Pinto, Alfonso. 1977. "Lupe Velez, 1909–1944." In *Films in Review* 28 (November): 513–524; Ramírez, Gabriel. 1986. *Lupe Vélez: La mexicana que escupía fuego*. Mexico: Cinéteca Nacional; Rodríquez-Estrada, Alicia I. 1997. "Dolores Del Río and Lupe Vélez: Images on and off the Screen, 1925–1944." In *Writing the Range: Race, Class, and Culture in the Women's West*, ed. Elizabeth Jameson and Susan Armitage. Norman: University of Oklahoma Press.

Alicia I. Rodríquez-Estrada

VÉLEZ DE VANDO, EMELÍ (1917–1999)

Emelí Vélez de Vando was one of the pioneers of the *colonia puertorriqueña* in New York. Not long after her arrival in the early 1930s from Puerto Rico, she immersed herself in the cultural and political activities of the Puerto Rican community and supported early efforts to build organizations. Vélez took part in theatrical productions and acted in some of the first Puerto Rican plays to be presented in New York. However, she is mostly recognized for her extraordinary dedication to the cause of Puerto Rican independence, her organizational skills, and her talent for public speaking. Upon her return to Puerto Rico in the late 1940s, she joined the Partido Independentista Puertorriqueño and in 1960 was the party's candidate for mayor of San Juan. Vélez remained active in the independence movement until the end of her life, tireless in her efforts to transform Puerto Rico into a republic.

Emelí Vélez Soto was born in the Canas barrio of Ponce on January 2, 1917, and was one of the nine children of José Dolores Vélez and Beatriz Soto Medina. She moved frequently, which made it hard for her to get a formal education. Her early schooling took place in her hometown school. She then lived with her sister Genoveva in Santurce, where she completed the eighth grade. Later Vélez moved to the home of her older sister Otilia in Arecibo and was briefly employed by the Puerto Rican Reconstruction Administration.

At the age of seventeen, faced with economic hardships, Emelí Vélez decided to leave Puerto Rico in search of better opportunities. In 1934 she traveled on the SS *San Jacinto* to New York, where she intended to live with her brother José. In New York she moved in with her sister Adela in Brooklyn instead. Vélez's first job in the city was at the Pilsen Brothers Curtain Factory, located on Twenty-third Street and Madison Avenue in Manhattan, where she earned ten dollars per week.

On March 21, 1937, unarmed members of the Nationalist Party in Puerto Rico were fired upon by the insular police as they attempted to carry out a peaceful march. Twenty people were killed and more than 100 were wounded in what came to be known as the Ponce massacre. When the news reached New York, Emelí Vélez was deeply saddened and worried about her younger brother Fernando, who was a member of the Nationalist Party and believed to be among the marchers. As it turned out, he was unharmed, but she was suddenly made conscious of Puerto Rico's political reality and shortly thereafter joined la Junta Nacionalista de Nueva York, an organization linked to the Nationalist Party of Puerto Rico. From then on she became committed to the struggle for Puerto Rican independence and devoted a good deal of her time to the activities organized by the Nationalists. As she ventured out, she gained a reputation as a good public speaker and *declamadora* and was called upon to be the master of ceremony for events, often opening for the main speakers. The young Vélez honed her skills amid a group of freedom fighters and leaders from Puerto Rico and Latin America who worked together in New York.

Emelí Vélez's enthusiasm for her newfound cause created tensions within her family in Manhattan, and they presented her with an ultimatum. In order to stay with them, she would have to give up her political work. She chose her political activities and the adventure of being on her own. With just small change in her pocket, Vélez decided to go out on her own. Although she was still quite young, she became part of a circle of women experienced in political organizing who formed a women's group called el Comité Femenino del Partido Nacionalista (Women's Committee of the Nationalist Party).

Some of the women who became Vélez's friends and mentors were closely connected to the Nationalist Party leadership. Among them was Lolín Quintana, a goddaughter of Nationalist Party president Pedro Albizu Campos, who took Vélez in; Rosa Collazo, the wife of nationalist militant Oscar Collazo; Consuelo Lee, the wife of renowned poet and revolutionary leader Juan Antonio Corretjer; Juanita Arocho, a community activist and organizer; Laura Meneses, the wife of Pedro Albizu Campos; and Julia de Burgos, considered one of the greatest poets of Puerto Rico and Latin America. Apart from these extraordinary women, some of the men she met who influenced her political thinking were the Cuban journalist and scholar Juan Marinello, the fiery Puerto Rican Nationalist leaders Pedro Albizu Campos and Juan Antonio Corretjer, and Gilberto Concepción de Gracia, who was to become a founder and president of the Partido Independentista Puertorriqueño.

It was through the activities of the Junta Nacionalista that she met her husband, Erasmo Vando. He was an activist, an actor, and a playwright who became captivated with her beauty and invited her to join his acting troupe. Vando was in fact the first to present Puerto Rican theater in New York. The productions, which included some of his own plays and those of writers like Gonzalo O'Neill, were usually fund-raisers for political events. Emelí Vélez became one of Vando's favorite actresses and soon his wife. They were married on June 11, 1942, and from then on pursued their numerous political and artistic interests together. For example, they helped create la Asociación de Escritores y Periodistas (Association of Writers and Journalists) and the Asociación pro Independencia de Puerto Rico en la Ciudad de Nueva York (the Proindependence Association for Puerto Rico in New York City). Together they also participated in the political campaigns of Vito Marcantonio in East Harlem.

In 1944 Vélez de Vando left New York with her two young children, Bertha Borinquen and Gabriel, to visit her ailing parents in Puerto Rico. In 1945 Erasmo Vando joined her there. She returned briefly to New York for medical reasons, but was back in Puerto Rico by 1948. In 1949 she had her third child, Emelí Luz. Vélez was briefly employed as a host for a radio program on station WPRP in Ponce, but she resumed her

Emelí Vélez de Vando during a political campaign. Courtesy of the Emelí Vélez de Vando Papers. Centro Archives, Centro de Estudios Puertorriqueños, Hunter College, CUNY.

political work and, with her husband, participated in the founding of the Partido Independentista Puertorriqueño (PIP). Distinguishing herself as a leader of the PIP for more than twelve years, she became the party's candidate for mayor of San Juan in 1960.

Years later, disenchanted with the PIP, Vélez helped found the Movimiento pro Independencia (MPI), where she served as the secretary of Acción Femenina, the organization's women's division. She also coordinated public events for the MPI and organized major activities such as the celebration of Pedro Albizu Campos's seventy-fifth birthday and demonstrations against the Vietnam War. The MPI became the Partido Socialista Puertorriqueño in 1971, and Emelí and Erasmo Vando remained active members. Their home in Santurce, Puerto Rico, served as a central meeting place for many of the party's members, including its leader, Juan Mari Brás. Additionally, Emelí Vélez de Vando represented her political organizations and the case for Puerto Rico's independence in international forums such as the United Nations Decolonization Committee. In the 1970s she organized tours to the Soviet Union and Cuba. She died in Puerto Rico on November 10, 1999.

SOURCE: Vélez de Vando, Emelí. 1919–1999. Papers. Centro de Estudios Puertorriqueños Library and Archives, Hunter College, CUNY.

Ismael García, Nélida Pérez, and Pedro Juan Hernández

VÉLEZ-MITCHELL, ANITA (1916–   )

Poet, writer, and performer Ana (Anita) Vilia Vélez was born in Vieques, Puerto Rico, on February 21, 1916, and named after her maternal aunt, Ana Rieckehoff de Benitez. Her mother, Lucila Rieckehoff Medina de Vélez (1880–1967), became a widow shortly before Anita was born. Her husband, Francisco "Paco" Vélez, took his life after the hurricane of 1915 wiped out his coffee crop in Añasco. When Anita was four years old, her mother married Rafael Malpica Hoard. They sent Anita to live with Lucila's sister and brother-in-law, Isaura and August Bonnet, in Vieques. Anita remained in Vieques until her mother and stepfather, who had migrated to New York City, sent for her in 1929, at the height of the depression.

Vélez went from a privileged, idyllic existence in Vieques to tenement living in New York's El Barrio—though her mother insisted: "We are not poor; we just don't have any money." But poverty had its charms: Vélez felt free for the first time in her life, because she was allowed to play in Central Park, sleep on the fire escape, and attend school with other children. In Vieques she had been tutored at home, where she became an avid reader of the classics in her family's library, memorizing and performing the poems of famous Latin American writers by the time she was ten. She was also fluent in Spanish, French, and English, skills that kept her from being held back two years, as was the custom for Spanish-speaking children entering the city's public schools. As the oldest child living at home, however, Vélez was called on to contribute to the family income. At fifteen she got a job after school as an usherette in a movie theater, where she learned dance routines, acting, and songs by watching Hollywood musicals.

At seventeen Vélez married the thirty-five-year-old Puerto Rican writer and political activist Erasmo Vando (1898–1988). They had a daughter, Gloria, but the marriage did not last. A few years later Vélez was chosen by a talent scout to appear in *Mexican Hayride*. From there she toured for a season as an aerialist with Ringling Brothers Circus, where she could draw a salary large enough to support the family. Her beauty and talent enabled her to land roles in Broadway shows and television commercials: she portrayed the "Dole Pineapple Girl," danced the mambo for Coca-Cola, squeezed Charmin with Mr. Whipple, sashayed with Cantinflas for the Hilton hotels, and sang with the Xavier Cugat orchestra.

In 1950, with the help of legendary producer George Abbott, Vélez formed the Anita Vélez Dancers. Herbert Ross choreographed the dances, and Tito Puente wrote "Mambo Macoco" for her. They opened the famed Caribe Hilton in San Juan, played the Hilton hotels throughout the United States, the Caribbean, and Canada, and in 1951 reopened the Palace Theatre in New York City. The company received raves everywhere. One reviewer in Montreal wrote, "Ms. Velez has more curves than the Laurentian Mountains."

Vélez performed on *The Ed Sullivan Show* and in Carnegie Hall and appeared in nightclubs as a solo act and with various dance partners. In the mid-1950s she was signed by Columbia Concerts to tour as a classical Spanish dancer with Marina Svetlova, prima ballerina of the Metropolitan Opera, and to perform "A Night of García Lorca" with Antonio Valero. In 1955 Vélez married Pearse Mitchell (1916–1983), an advertising executive. They had a child, Jane, and remained married until his death. Her dance career culminated in 1963 when she starred as Anita in *West Side Story*, returning

in 1972 to coach the dancers in its Lincoln Center revival.

Throughout her life Vélez wrote stories, poems, essays, and plays. In 1981 the Institute of Puerto Rican Culture named her Poet of the Year. In 1986 she won Puerto Rico's coveted Julia de Burgos Poetry Prize for her bilingual, autobiographical book-length poem *Primavida: Calendario de amor* (1986). The book's title, *Primavida*, a word she coined, describes the rite of passage from childhood to adulthood. *Primavida* also won the Association of Puerto Rican Writers and Poets Award and the University Press Award. Other awards followed: the Prince of Asturias Award for Belles Lettres, the Partners in Education Award, Center of Ibero-American Poets and Writers awards in four separate genres (short story, poetry, essay, and drama), the Isaac Perez Award (1994), and others. In 1999 she received a grant from the Thanks Be to Grandmother Winifred Foundation to complete a PBS documentary on the poetry of Julia de Burgos, "Child of the Waters," which was broadcast the following year. She was named Poet of the Year by the Institute of Puerto Rico in New York and Woman of the Year, 2000 by the National Conference of Puerto Rican Women in the USA. Her bilingual poetry, short stories, essays, and translations (from and to Spanish, French, and English) have appeared in many literary magazines and anthologies.

Vélez's plays have been presented throughout New York City, including La Casa de la Herencia, the Spanish Repertory Theatre, and La MaMa Theatre, from which she received an INKY Award for playwriting. She

The Anita Vélez Dancers, circa 1954. Anita Vélez stands in the center. Photograph by James Kreigsmann, New York. Courtesy of Anita Vélez-Mitchell.

directed *Salsa of the Hispanic Woman* for Lincoln Center's Out of Doors Festival and received the 1996 Director's Award from the Latino Newspapers Association for *Butterflies Are Free.* She remains active in the theater as a playwright, director, and actor.

Anita Vélez: Dancing through Life, a documentary that follows her early career in theater, won four awards at the New York and Los Angeles Film Festivals in 2000. The film was produced and directed by her daughter, Jane Vélez-Mitchell. In 2002 Vélez costarred in the film *Voice of an Angel,* which won Best U.S.A. Short Film Award from the Silver Image and Los Angeles film festivals. Vélez has also composed and translated many songs for theater and films. In 1999 she performed her songs at Lincoln Center in a tribute given to her by the Panamerican Symphony Orchestra.

For many years Vélez has worked as a journalist with various Spanish newspapers. Among the luminaries she has interviewed are Alexander Solzhenitsyn and Pablo Neruda, both winners of the Nobel Prize in Literature (1970 and 1971, respectively), and two of her acting teachers, Marcel Marceau and José Ferrer. She also worked with inner-city schoolchildren, conducting poetry residencies for the Board of Education and Poets in the Schools Program and teaching drama to children at the Museum of Natural History. In 1989, representing the Hispanic community, she accompanied Mayor Ed Koch in the mayoral exchange between New York City and its sister city, Madrid, Spain. In 2001, 2002, 2003, and 2004 she addressed the United Nations General Assembly as part of the Special Committee on Decolonization, urging the United States to halt military maneuvers on Vieques and, subsequently, to decontaminate the island. "Wherever one goes one represents one's culture and one's humanity, no matter what one's race or age."

See also Literature; Theater

SOURCES: Fernández, Roberta, ed. 1994. *In Other Words: Literature by Latinas of the United States.* Houston: Arte Público Press; *Helicon Nine Reader.* 1990. Kansas City, MO: Helicon Nine Editions; Stanton, Daniel E., and Edward F. Stanton, eds. 2003. *Contemporary Hispanic Quotations.* Westport, CT: Greenwood Press; Vélez-Mitchell, Anita. 1986. *Primavida: Calendario de amor.* San Juan, Puerto Rico: Mairena Press; Vélez-Mitchell, Jane, director and producer. 2000. *Anita Vélez: Dancing through Life.* Documentary. San Francisco, CA: Eastwind Enterprises.

Gloria Vando

VICIOSO SÁNCHEZ, SHEREZADA "CHIQUI" (1948–   )

Sherezada (Chiqui) Vicioso Sánchez is a poet, playwright, essayist, and cultural activist. She was born in Santo Domingo, the daughter of Juan Antonio Vicioso

Contín and María Luisa Sánchez. After the death of her father, Chiqui Vicioso moved with her mother and three siblings to New York City, where she completed her studies. She holds a B.A. in sociology and history from Brooklyn College (CUNY) and an M.Ed. from Teachers College, Columbia University. She also studied administration of cultural projects at the Getulio Vargas Foundation in Rio de Janeiro, Brazil.

In 1980 Chiqui Vicioso returned home to the Dominican Republic after having lived in New York City for eighteen years. In her homeland Vicioso found the encouragement and support needed to publish her first collection of poetry, *Viaje desde el agua* (1981). This first book is a collection of poems written mostly while living in the United States and during her many travels abroad. To Vicioso in her early collection and in much of what she has written since, the world is indeed small—so small, in fact, that everyday survival in New York City goes hand in hand with the struggles of the African people or of a Dominican youth drifting, seeking to find direction.

In the Dominican Republic Vicioso assumed a number of important positions, including director of education for Pro-Familia (1981–1985) and consultant on women and children's programs for the United Nations, in particular UNICEF. She writes a weekly column in the *Listín Diario,* a daily newspaper comparable to the *New York Times,* and has been a contributor to *La Noticia* (another daily) and the editor of the literary page "Cantidad Hechizada" for *El Nuevo Diario* (another daily).

At the beginning of the 1980s Vicioso founded the Circle of Dominican Women Poets. In 1988 the Dominican Writers Association awarded Vicioso the Golden Caonabo prize, and in 1992 the National Women's Bureau awarded her a gold medal as the most accomplished woman of the year. She has published four collections of poetry, *Viaje desde el agua* (1981), *Un extraño ulular traía el viento* (1983), *Internamiento* (1991), and *Wish-ky Sour* (1996), a poetic biography of Julia de Burgos, and a collection of feminist essays. She has edited a collection of Salomé Ureña's poems and has become one of the leading scholars on the subject.

She travels often to the United States to share her experiences as a transnational Dominican, educated in the United States. Vicioso is also the author of a script for *Desvelo,* for ballet and theater. Since 1996 she has published and staged several plays, including the award-winning *Wish-ky Sour* (National Theater Award, 1996) and *Salomé U: Cartas a una ausencia* (Cassandra Award, 2000). In 2000 *Perrerías* was staged in Spain and Cuba. Her poems and essays have been translated into several languages and have been included in numerous anthologies published at the national and international levels in the Dominican Republic and abroad.

See also Literature

SOURCES: Cocco De Filippis, Daisy. 2000. *Para que no se olviden: The Lives of Women in Dominican History.* New York: Alcance; Gutiérrez, Franklyn. 2004. *Diccionario de la literatura dominicana.* Santo Domingo: Editorial Búho.

Daisy Cocco De Filippis

VIDAL, IRMA (1921–1997)

Dr. Irma Vidal was a Latina pioneer in medicine who specialized in hematology and oncology. She was born in Cuba in 1921, the youngest of eight children in a comfortable, middle-class family involved in the tobacco industry. Her family had ties to the late-nineteenth-century independence movement among cigar workers in Tampa, Florida, and other cities in the United States. At the beginning of the Cuban-Spanish-American war (1895–1898) her father, Ramón Vidal, joined the army on the side of the insurgency and earned the rank of colonel. After the establishment of the independent republic in 1902, Colonel Vidal was appointed a senator of the new Cuban government.

Dedicated to both the family business in Pinar del Río and political activities, Senator Ramón Vidal spent most of his time away from home in Havana, leaving his wife, María Julia Vidal, to raise the family on her own. A strong woman devoted to her children, María Julia encouraged all of them to further their education. As a result, her son and seven daughters all became professionals.

Inspired by her mother's convictions, young Irma Vidal defied traditional standards for the women of her times and enrolled in the School of Medicine at the University of Havana in 1938. During that period there were very few women attending medical school in Cuba. Vidal had to be strong enough to survive gender discrimination from her male colleagues and professors who believed that medicine was a field for men. While attending school, Vidal worked as a volunteer in the Hematology Department of Nuestra Señora de las Mercedes Hospital. In 1944 she proved herself by graduating from the School of Medicine with honors. That same year Vidal applied for a position in the Hematology Department at the Municipal de la Infancia Hospital. Despite her education and experience, she was not considered a possible candidate because she was a woman.

The discrimination Vidal faced in her country did not discourage her. Her desire for improvements overcame rejections and served to motivate her to apply for an internship and residency training program in the United States. A year later she was accepted by a hospital in Boston and moved to Massachusetts.

Far from her family, Vidal not only had to adapt to the drastic changes in weather and a new language, but faced yet another type of discrimination, that of being a single white woman. The Boston hospital served a predominantly black community of a Boston suburb. Vidal was told by hospital officials that the color of her skin was creating tension among black patients and with her colleagues. After completing the internship, Vidal was forced to look for another place to continue her training.

Determined in her pursuit of a medical career, Vidal applied for training positions at several hospitals in New York City. In 1946, at the age of twenty-five, she was accepted at Lenox Hill Hospital and was finally given the opportunity to complete her training. But accomplishing academic and career goals had an unanticipated consequence: Vidal fell in love with New York City and decided to stay. For the next ten years she dedicated herself to providing health care in her newfound home. Unfortunately, her mother's fragile health forced her to return to Cuba. In Cuba Vidal was offered the opportunity to head the Department of Hematology

Dr. Irma Vidal, standing in front, during the visit of her sisters from Cuba, Caridad Vidal (sitting) and Yolanda Vidal (third from left), New York, circa 1948. Courtesy of Jorge Sastre Vidal.

at the Municipal de la Infancia Hospital, ironically, the same hospital that had denied her a position in the past. In addition to her responsibilities at the hospital, Vidal established a private practice specializing in hematology.

In the late 1950s she met a New York–born former colleague from the School of Medicine in Havana and shortly thereafter married him. The couple had three sons. They established their home close to the Vidal family estates, where Vidal performed professional and familial duties. In 1959, when Fidel Castro took power, the couple supported his ideas of social equality. However, the majority of her family and most middle-class families turned against the government and fled the country. Vidal and her husband continued to support the revolution. They were among the few physicians who decided to stay in Cuba. Despite her American education, Vidal renounced her private practice and devoted herself to improving health care for the Cuban people while also caring for her mother and raising her family.

From 1960 until her retirement in 1991, *la doctora* Vidal, as people called her, headed hematology departments at many hospitals in Havana, including the Calixto García Hospital, where she was on the staff during the last fifteen years of her life. Throughout this period she also served as chairperson and professor of the Hematology Department of the School of Medicine in Havana. Vidal became a well-respected figure in her field, recognized as a scientist and educator who taught a whole new generation of Cuba's doctors.

In the early 1990s she lost one son, and the other two moved to the United States. Vidal remained in Cuba with her husband, granddaughter, and two older sisters. When she was diagnosed with terminal cancer in 1996, her last dream was to be reunited with her sons at their family home in Havana. However, because of Cuban government restrictions, the family was not granted a humanitarian visa. In 1997 Vidal died in Havana, Cuba.

See also Medicine; Scientists

SOURCES: Sastre Sisto, Luis, husband of Dr. Irma Vidal. 2004. Oral interview by Jorge Sastre. New York, August 3; Sastre Vidal, Jorge, son of Dr. Irma Vidal. 2004. Oral interview by Carlos A. Cruz. New York, June 20; Vidal, Irma. 2004. Papers. Family collection. New York.

Jorge Sastre Vidal and Carlos A. Cruz

VIDAURRI, RITA (1924–   )

Rita Vidaurri was born to María de Jesus Castillo and Juan Vidaurri in San Antonio, Texas, where she was raised. Rita began singing at the age of eleven, even though she was strongly discouraged by her father from becoming a singer. However, her mother, whom she lost at the age of seventeen, did support her interest in singing, which was very significant for Rita since it was very rare at that time for Mexicanas or Mexican American women to be public performers. In 1938, at the age of fourteen, she recorded her first 78 rpm single, "Alma Angelina," for Bluebird Records at Tomás Acuña Studios with her sister Queta. Since Rita's father owned and operated various cantinas in San Antonio, he was somewhat familiar with the business of hiring persons to sing and in fact often hosted singers from Mexico to perform in his establishment. Some of these same singers from Mexico, as well as local radio personalities, persuaded Rita's father to take her to Monterrey, Mexico, in 1944 to try and establish her talents in music. Although she was only nineteen years old, she found assistance from the legendary comedian Mario Moreno, "Cantinflas," who taught her how to obtain permits for jobs.

Among the first places Vidaurri performed was one of the finest nightclubs in Monterrey, El Parthenon, where Lalo "Piporro" González was then master of ceremonies. There she decided to sing "El heredero," "Por un amor," and "Guadalajara." Vidaurri left quite an impression on her audience, and her career was effectively launched, taking her to perform around Mexico and throughout Latin America. Although most of her fame was in cities throughout Colombia, Panama, Mexico, and Cuba, she did record and perform frequently throughout Texas. She was a regular on José Davila's radio program *La Hora Anahuac*, the most popular radio show of the time, and she performed regularly at the Teatro Nacional in downtown San Antonio.

Vidaurri referred to herself as "an international *Tejana*" because she was one of the few Tejanas to sing for the famous Mexico City radio station XEW, the station she listened to as a child in order to memorize the popular Mexican rancheras and boleros of the time. In Mexico City it was common for her to share the stage with notables such as Tito and Pepe Guízar y sus Corporales, Lucho Gatica, Gloria Martínez, and comedian Tin Tan. Famous venues where Vidaurri performed included the Follies, Club Ritz, El Maxim, El Waikiki, and Rio Rosa. She eventually toured with Pedro Vargas and even had the opportunity to be flown to Havana, Cuba, where she performed in the same lineup with Celia Cruz and Olga Guillot for three shows during one year.

During her heyday in the 1940s and 1950s Vidaurri also recorded more than forty singles for José Morante's Norteño International Records, along with several other recordings for local Tejano record labels. She has earned several nicknames along the way, including la Belleza Morena de Tejas and Rita la Ranchera. She even became an entrepreneur in the early 1960s, opening several music nightspots, including Lo Dudo Nightclub and Rita's Club: El Rincón de los Artistas, where artists such as Freddy Fender (Baldemar Huerta) occasionally stopped in to perform. By the mid-1960s Vidaurri decided to spend more time raising her two sons and her daughter. Yet she has remained active over the decades singing and performing throughout San Antonio at private gatherings and community events.

In 1995 she was honored along with Lydia Mendoza, Chelo Silva, and other early Tejana pioneers with a photo exhibit in the Texas Capitol rotunda in Austin, Texas. Her oral history is included in the Texas Music Museum. In 1999 Vidaurri produced and recorded a self-initiated compact disc, *Canciones del recuerdo*, which was sold through independent record stores and local cafés in San Antonio. Along with Eva Garza, Chelo Silva, and other early Tejana singing pioneers, Rita Vidaurri's greatest contribution to Texas-Mexican music remains her musical ambassadorship to Mexico and Latin America.

SOURCES: Esperanza Peace and Justice Center (San Antonio, TX). 2004. *La Calandria*. www.esperanzacenter.org/yearly2004/Folder/rita.htm (accessed July 19, 2005); "Rita Vidaurri." 2004. Texas Public Radio KSTX 89.1 San Antonio. Texas Matters. Program archive: SHOW #233, December 3; Vargas, Deborah Rose Ramos. 2003. "Las tracaleras: Texas-Mexican Women, Music, and Place." Ph.D. diss., University of California, Santa Cruz.

Deborah Vargas

VILLARREAL, ANDREA AND TERESA (18??–19??)

In the early twentieth century, sisters Andrea and Teresa Villareal were known as social activists who advocated women's and workers' rights. Andrea Villareal joined efforts with Mother Jones. The two made public speeches demanding the release of Mexican revolutionaries imprisoned in San Antonio. Teresa Villareal was also involved in social justice causes. She established a socialist newspaper titled *El Obrero* (The Worker). In 1910 Andrea and Teresa founded *La Mujer Moderna* (The Modern Woman). *La Mujer Moderna* was based in San Antonio and held the emancipation of women as its central focus. Alongside their journalistic endeavors, Andrea and Teresa were also active in Regeneración, a San Antonio women's group. The group, under the leadership of Teresa Villareal, felt that women's liberation should be a critical goal and outcome of the Mexican Revolution. The Villareal sisters participated in a variety of functions in organizing

Mexican women. They assisted in fund-raising and organizing activities of the feminist organizations Leona Vicario and the Liberal Union of Mexican Women.

Their interest in women's role and influence in the Mexican Revolution led to their involvement in, and support of, the Partido Liberal de Mexico (PLM). Since the male leadership of the PLM was continuously politically threatened, the Villareal sisters and other feminists played key roles in maintaining revolutionary causes and messages. One observer recalled how women like Andrea and Teresa Villareal took on responsibilities that men feared because of the heightened threats of the revolution: "Women in Texas were particularly active . . . had to continue the work men were now too intimidated to do."

See also Journalism and Print Media

SOURCES: Acosta, Teresa Palomo, and Ruthe Winegarten. 2003. *Las Tejanas: 300 Years of History*. Austin: University of Texas Press; Gómez-Quiñones, Juan. 1973. *Sembradores: Ricardo Flores Magón y el Partido Liberal Mexicano*, Los Angeles: Aztlan Ruiz, Vicki L. 1998. *From out of the Shadows: Mexican Women in Twentieth-Century America*. New York: Oxford University Press.

Margie Brown-Coronel

VIRAMONTES, HELENA MARÍA (1954–)

Novelist Helena María Viramontes was born in California. Her parents raised nine children in East Los Angeles, a community that offered refuge to Mexicans who had crossed the border into California. Her childhood experiences as a daughter of migrant workers who labored in the fields form the base of her creative process.

Viramontes attended Immaculate Heart College and received a baccalaureate degree in 1975. She began to write in college while majoring in English literature and won prizes for her short stories "Requiem for the Poor," "The Broken Web," and "Birthday." In 1981 she was able to assure a writing career when she entered a master of fine arts in creative writing program at the University of California at Irvine. During her years as a graduate student Viramontes was also a wife, a full-time mother of two children, and an active intellectual in a community with a large number of Latinos.

Major influences in Viramontes's literature include the work of César Chávez and the United Farm Workers, as well as her childhood in East Los Angeles. Literary influences include authors such as Gabriel García Márquez, Toni Morrison, Sandra Cisneros, and Ana Castillo. Like many Chicano writers, Viramontes writes about the personal life of individuals and their families. In her literary representations she deals with issues related to the struggles of Chicana women in their households and beyond.

Viramontes's childhood experiences with friends and family have also influenced her writing. Her parents met while picking cotton in the fields and suffered as underpaid migrant workers. Viramontes has admitted that both parents influenced her in different ways: "If my mother showed all that is good in being female, my father showed all that is bad in being male." Nonetheless, Viramontes dedicated her novel *Under the Feet of Jesus* to both parents and to César Chávez.

Two of Viramontes's best-known short stories are "The Moths" and "The Jumping Bean," both of which show different aspects of Latino life. "The Moths" (1985) is a story of family relationships, caregiving, and dying. A Latina narrator tells about providing care to her dying grandmother at the age of fourteen. Manuel de Jesús Hernández-Gutiérrez has pointed out the author's representation of feminist concerns in this story. María Herrera-Sobek describes "The Jumping Bean" as an excellent portrayal of a hardworking Latino father struggling to survive. The writer's first book, *The Moths and Other Stories*, was published in 1985. This collection also includes the short story "Growing," in which the writer again presents a feminist perspective and an interest in sexual discrimination against young women.

In 1989 Viramontes won a fellowship from the National Endowment for the Arts to collaborate in a workshop with Colombian Nobel Prize winner Gabriel García Márquez at the Sundance Institute. She also wrote a screenplay based on her second book of short stories, *Paris Rats in E.L.A.*, which was produced by the American Film Institute. In addition, she adapted the short story "Candystripers" for the screen. She received her masters of fine arts in creative writing from the University of California, Irvine, in 1994.

Since 1993, Viramontes has taught creative writing at Cornell University, where she is associate professor of English. In 1995 she was the first Latina to receive the John Dos Passos Prize; previous recipients of the prize have included Graham Greene and Tom Wolfe. Martha E. Cook, professor of English at Longwood College and chair of the Dos Passos Prize committee, stated that Viramontes "brings a new perspective to understanding our American culture and heritage by giving a voice to those whom many readers have not heard." A dedicated, approachable writer who truly mentors students, she is married with children. Her husband, Eloy Rodríquez, holds an endowed chair in environmental studies at Cornell. In the words of Eric Rosario, a Cornell student affairs officer, "Helena is a successful Chicana who is passionately and profoundly proud of her heritage," and he notes with appreciation, "her message that our heritage is not a liability but an asset we should nurture." In 2005 she was recognized for her literary works with an honorary doctorate from St. Mary's College of Notre Dame.

See also Literature

SOURCES: *Cornell (University) Chronicle* (online edition). Geddes, Darryl. 1996. "Author Counsels Chicano students at CU Summer College, August 8. www.news.cornell.edu/Chronicle/96/8.8.96/Viramontes-counsel.html (accessed July 24, 2005); Davidson, Cathy N., Linda Wagner-Masrtin, and Elizabeth Ammons, eds. 1993. *Oxford Companion to Women's Writing in the United States.* New York: Oxford University Press; Hernández-Gutiérrez, Manuel de Jesús, and David William Foster, eds. 1997. *Literatura Chicana, 1965–1995: An Anthology in Spanish, English, and Caló.* New York: Garland Publishing; Telgen, Diane, and James Kamp, eds. 1993. *Notable Hispanic American Women.* Detroit: Gale Research; Viramontes, Helena. 2005. "Curriculum Vitae." www.arts.cornell.edu/english/cv/viramontes.short.html (accessed July 24, 2005).

María E. Villamil

VIRGEN DE GUADALUPE

Mythology, oral tradition, and literary texts date the Guadalupe event to 1531 when the Virgen de Guadalupe appeared in central Mexico to a Christianized Mexica man, Juan Diego or Cuauhtlatóhuac (He Who Speaks like an Eagle). Surrounded by cosmic symbols and dressed in the colors of Mexica deities, she appeared four times and told Juan Diego to advise the Catholic bishop, Juan de Zumárraga, to build a temple on the site of her appearance, the ancient worshiping grounds of the Nahua mother goddess, Tonantzin. In order to prove her existence, she miraculously imprinted her image on the *tilma* (a course cloak of maguey fiber) of Cuauhtlatóhuac. She also gifted him with many roses, rare and seasonal flowers, to further prove the sacredness of her presence in New Spain. Flowers and the soothing sound of her voice signified *flor y canto,* the Nahua tradition of communicating with the deities through flower, song, and poetry. Her message of unconditional maternal love and protection to all that honored her gave the conquered indigenous peoples renewed hope for their survival amid the violence and genocide of the Spanish conquest. The divine woman appeared a fifth time, to the uncle of Juan Diego, whom she cured of smallpox.

The bishop commissioned a small chapel at Tepeyac dedicated to Guadalupe, and by 1556 Mexicas and Spaniards could be found worshiping her there and experiencing miraculous healings. The first written text of the apparitions appeared in 1648, authored in Spanish by Father Miguel Sánchez. One year later Father Luis Laso de la Vega translated the tale into Nahuatl. This later text, titled *Huei tlamahuicoltica*, agrees closely with Sánchez's version, but has a more flowing dialogue between the characters. The account of the apparitions appears in a section titled *Nican mopohua* (Here Is Recounted), which states that the uncle of Juan Diego identified the woman as Tlecuauhtlacupeuh (She Who Comes Flying from the Light like an Eagle of Fire). The Spaniards christened her Nuestra Señora Santa María de Guadalupe, after the image of the Virgin Mary from Guadalupe, Extremadura, the hometown of Hernán Cortés.

In 1746 Guadalupe became the patroness and national symbol of Mexico, and in 1754 the papacy designated December 12 as her holy day. In the war for independence from Spain (1810–1821) Father Miguel Hidalgo y Costilla chose her image to rally criollos, mestizos, and indigenous peoples. After the Mexican-American War (1846–1848), the treaty that ceded Mexico's northern territories to the United States received her name, the Treaty of Guadalupe Hidalgo. During the Mexican Revolution (1910–1920) the banner of Guadalupe rode alongside the peasant fighters under Emiliano Zapata and Pancho Villa, and Mexicano immigrants seeking refuge and work in the United States sought her assistance and mercy.

Under the leadership of César Chávez beginning in the 1960s, she appeared as a labor rights advocate for farmworkers, and more recently as an immigrant rights proponent and defender of land rights for indigenous peoples in southern Mexico. Guadalupe continues to represent struggles for justice and has won countless devotees across many cultures. Pope John Paul II named her patroness of the Americas in the early 1990s and commissioned a replica of her image to tour parts of the United States in 1999. Many Latino/a Catholic theologians understand her to be the feminine face of God and Mother of the mestizo people. Her original image remains enshrined at her basilica in Mexico City, defying all attempts to prove its historical origins. Scholars admit that little about the Guadalupe event can be proved or disproved.

As a multivalent symbol, Guadalupe stands not only for divine protection and revolutionary struggle, but also for female chastity, passivity, and self-sacrifice. In response, Chicana artists began (re)imaging Guadalupe in the mid-1970s to reflect their emerging feminist politics. In 1976 Ester Hernández offered the first revisionist work. Her portrayal of Guadalupe as a karate master defending the rights of Chicanos inspired other artists to reassess the cultural myths and archetypes that shaped what it meant to be a woman. Yolanda López's *Guadalupe Triptych* in 1978 portrays her as a runner, a seamstress, and an elder who challenges viewers to see all women as sacred. Alma López's *Our Lady* (2001) suggests the sacredness and power of female sexuality. In creating new role models, Chicana artists imbue Guadalupe with traits and qualities reflecting their own lives. These artists and their feminist revisionist images of the primary female icon of Mexican Catholic culture have not been well received by conservative Latino/a Catholics.

Creative writers have also reworked the Guadalupe event to reflect their contemporary multidimensional lives. Gloria Anzaldúa, Ana Castillo, and Sandra Cisneros are among the many Chicana/o writers who have challenged readers to ponder the multiple ways

Mexican Americans celebrating the patron saint la Virgen de Guadalupe, New York, 1958. Courtesy of the Justo A. Martí Photograph Collection. Centro Archives, Centro de Estudios Puertorriqueños, Hunter College, CUNY.

in which the indigenous mother goddess through Guadalupe remains active in our troubled world. Images of the divine mother continue to take on new meanings for the descendants of mestizo peoples in the Americas.

See also Religion

SOURCES: Anzaldúa, Gloria. 1987. *Borderlands/La frontera: The New Mestiza.* San Francisco: Spinsters/Aunt Lute; Castillo, Ana, ed. 1996. *Goddess of the Americas: Writings on the Virgen of Guadalupe.* New York: Riverhead Books; Elizondo, Virgilio. 1997. *Guadalupe: Mother of the New Creation.* Maryknoll, NY: Orbis Press; Rodríguez, Jeanette. 1994. *Our Lady of Guadalupe: Faith and Empowerment among Mexican-American Women.* Austin: University of Texas Press; Sousa, Lisa, Stafford Poole, and James Lockhart, eds. 1998. *The Story of Guadalupe: Luis Laso de la Vega's* Huei tlamahuicoltica *of 1649.* Stanford, CA: Stanford University Press.

Lara Medina

Virgen de la Caridad. Illustrated by and courtesy of Carlos A. Cruz.

VIRGEN DE LA CARIDAD DEL COBRE

The representation of the Virgin Mary as Our Lady of Charity of El Cobre is the patroness of the Cuban people. Her basilica is located in copper mines sixteen kilometers west of the city of Santiago, on the southeastern coast of Cuba. Her origins date back to the early seventeenth century, possibly between 1604 and 1606. In 1687 a notarized account of the virgin's appearance became the first written testimonial of her growing importance. Variations of this story were elaborated in the eighteenth and nineteenth centuries as religious and political reinterpretations of this Marian tradition.

In the 1687 version three men first sighted the image in the middle of the Bay of Nipe on their way to a small cay in the bay named Cayo Francés. Two were assumed to be Indians and brothers, Juan and Rodrigo de Hoyos. The third was a young slave boy named Juan Moreno, who gave the 1687 account. They collected salt in the bay for a flourishing cattle ranch on the mainland, named Hato de Bajaragua. On one of their trips they sighted "something white" on the water. On coming closer they discovered that it was an icon of the Virgin with a small baby Jesus in her arms. The image was riding on a small piece of wood with a sign saying, "I am the Virgin of Charity." Her clothes were dry, which the men interpreted as being a miraculous fact.

The administrator of the ranch built a small sanctuary for the image. According to popular folklore, she mysteriously disappeared several times from this location, which was interpreted as a message to be relocated to another site. That final place was the town of El Cobre, a copper-mining community mostly formed

by slaves owned by the king. By the end of the seventeenth century there was a small church dedicated to this virgin and a well-rooted worship by the slave community. In time this image became the patroness protector of the slaves and freedmen working the mines and attracted many pilgrims of all races on account of her miracles. The patronage of rich and poor led to the construction of a large sanctuary cared for by several chaplains, and by the end of the eighteenth century it was the most important shrine in Cuba. The first available history of the virgin and its worship was published in 1829. Throughout the nineteenth century her popularity increased, and she became the object of devotion of all Cubans.

The rebels in the Cuban-American war against Spain (1895–1898), known as *mambises*, held her as their special protector. On August 12, 1898, a mass of thanks for the end of the war was celebrated in her sanctuary. The veterans of this war requested that the Vatican declare the Virgen de la Caridad del Cobre the national patron. Benedict XV issued a papal decree on May 10, 1916, elevating her to that position. In 1977 Pope Paul VI consecrated the sanctuary as a basilica, and during his visit to Cuba in 1998, John Paul II crowned the image as the "queen" of Cuba.

As a result of the Cuban Revolution, the image is

also worshiped in Miami by Cuban exiles—largely pre-1980 immigrants—for whom the Virgin has become a national symbol for the community. A shrine to the virgin in Biscayne was dedicated in 1973. It was consecrated in 1994 by the archbishop of Miami. In Afro-Cuban folklore religion this image is associated with Oshun, the queen of rivers and springs, goddess of fertility and love, and one that must be consulted by all those becoming priests in that type of worship. This parallel syncretic worship was probably introduced in the nineteenth century by newly arrived slaves who practiced Yoruba religions of West Africa.

See also Religion

SOURCES: Arrom, Juan J. 1971. "La Virgen del Cobre: Historia, leyenda y símbolo sincrético." In *Certidumbre de América: Estudios de letras, folklore y cultura*, 184–214. Madrid: Editorial Gredos; Corbea Calzado, Julio. 1996. "La Virgen de la Caridad del Cobre: Construcción simbólica y cultura popular." *Del Caribe* 21:4–11; Díaz, María Elena. 2000. *The Virgin, the King, and the Royal Slaves of El Cobre: Negotiating Freedom in Colonial Cuba, 1670–1780*. Stanford, CA: Stanford University Press; Paz y Ascanio, Alejandro. 1829. *Historia de la aparición milagrosa de Nuestra señora de la Caridad del Cobre*. Santiago de Cuba: Imprenta de la Viuda e Hijos de Espinal; Portuondo Zúñiga, Olga. 1995. *La Virgen de la Caridad: Símbolo de cubanía*. Santiago de Cuba: Editorial Oriente; Tweed, Thomas A. 1997. *Our Lady of the Exile: Diasporic Religion at a Cuban Catholic Shrine in Miami*. New York: Oxford University Press.

Asunción Lavrin

VOTING RIGHTS ACT

The Voting Rights Act (VRA) has served as a tool to empower people of color who have been historically blocked from voting. For instance, before the VRA African Americans and Mexican Americans had to pay poll taxes or pass literacy or English tests in order to vote. Furthermore, they were physically intimidated, threatened, and harmed when they sought to register to vote, to cast their ballots, or otherwise to participate in the political process.

In 1965 Congress enacted two primary sections of the VRA. Section 2 prohibited all voting and election practices that discriminated on the basis of race or color. This included abuses of the redistricting process. The U.S. Constitution requires that a census be con-

ducted every ten years, and state and local governments use these data to redraw local districts to reflect shifts in population. Historically, incumbent elected officials have often gerrymandered political districts to favor European American candidates. The VRA did not guarantee that people of color would control districts, but it was intended to ensure that white block voting or political gerrymandering would not defeat their choices. If patterns of gerrymandering emerged, complaints could be brought to the Justice Department to halt these practices.

In many states, however, Section 2 was not enough. New discriminatory practices began almost as soon as old discriminatory practices were struck down. Congress enacted Section 5 to require the U.S. Justice Department to review, or "preclear," the election practices of certain states before implementation to prevent discriminatory practices.

In 1975 the VRA was amended to protect Latinos, Asian and Pacific Islanders, Native Americans, and Alaskan Natives and Aleuts who do not speak English. In communities where large numbers of the population are not proficient in English, if more than 5 percent of these people are of voting age, then ballots and other voting materials must be made available in the appropriate languages.

In 1982 the VRA was again amended to prohibit voting and election practices that had a discriminatory effect, as well as a discriminatory intent. For instance, the courts could now examine historic practices and patterns of discrimination, including the extent of polarized voting, district size, and the candidate slating process. More important, the courts could consider discrimination in education, unemployment, and even health in determining the extent of VRA violations. The Voting Rights Act has been an important piece of civil rights legislation that seeks to level the political playing field.

SOURCES: De la Garza, Rodolfo O., and Louis DeSipio. 1999. "Save the Baby, Change the Bathwater, and Scrub the Tub: Latino Electoral Participation after Seventeen Years of Voting Rights Act Coverage." *Texas Law Review* 71, no. 7 (June): 1479–1539; DeSipio, Louis. 1999. *Counting on the Latino Vote: Latinos as a New Electorate*. Charlottesville: University Press of Virginia.

Lisa Magaña

W

WATSONVILLE STRIKE

In September 1985, 1,600 workers, mostly Mexican and Mexican American women, went on strike at the Richard Shaw Frozen Food Company and the Watsonville Canning and Frozen Food Company in Watsonville, California. In response to drastic cuts in wages and benefits, the women took on one of the largest frozen food manufacturers in the nation. Watsonville and the fertile Salinas Valley were commonly known as the frozen food capital of the world. The Watsonville Canning and Frozen Food Company alone produced half the country's supply of frozen vegetables and employed 5,000 workers. Of the entire Watsonville frozen food workforce, nine out of ten workers were Latino, and the majority of activists were Latina women.

Once thriving, successful companies, the Shaw and Watsonville companies responded to foreign competition by lowering workers' wages dramatically, by 40 percent, terminating benefits, and increasing the pace of work. Work in the canneries required a great deal of stamina and strength. Because of increased demand on production, many women were forced to stand extra long hours and face deteriorating working conditions. Fedelia Carrisoza was reprimanded several times for challenging cannery management. On one occasion she defended her need to use the restroom. During breaks the three to four stalls were not enough for the eighty-four women working a line. Carrisoza, pregnant at the time, responded to management's complaints of her frequent use of the restroom by demanding, "Show me a law that says I cannot go to the bathroom!" Increased injuries and poor working conditions were among the many hardships workers faced from the canneries' attempts to produce more profits.

In response to these conditions, workers attempted to call upon the assistance of local Teamsters Union Local 912. This particular union had organized workers in the region during World War II and was led mostly by white men who shared the interests of the corporate owners. The union did little to improve the workers' contract or to understand their demands for an improved contract.

In addition to the dramatic cuts in wages and the termination of benefits, workers also went on strike to protest lack of leadership and support required of the Teamsters Union. Teamsters Union leaders often collaborated with company leaders and encouraged workers to settle. Strikers organized committees to lead and organize the strike. One committee, the Teamsters for Democratic Union, focused on operating within the existing union (the Teamsters) while demanding improved working wages, as well as decent and equal representation within the union. The other committee, the Strikers' Committee, strategized and instituted more militant tactics. Gloria Betancourt and Chavela Moreno were among the leaders of the Strikers' Committee who continuously fought for the workers as part of the negotiating committees.

Latina workers were instrumental in the organizing of the Watsonville strike. As one source explained, the important lesson learned from the Watsonville Strikes was that there is no separation between the private and public worlds. The women who went on strike used mostly female networks to encourage support for the strike. Women worked the picket line and distributed food to striking workers. Women also used family networks and friends to provide food and resources to striking families. For the Latinas involved in the strike, there was no distinction between home and work life. They struck for their dignity, family, and rights.

The strike lasted eighteen months and garnered support from all over the state. Picket lines, rallies, and marches served as instruments to inform and motivate the community. In some instances peaceful gatherings of strikers turned violent. The Watsonville court denied the strikers the right to assemble and deployed the Watsonville police to break up group gatherings at the picket lines. Students from the University of California at Santa Cruz often supported strikers and "volunteered" to be the ones arrested. Support for the strike came from prominent individuals such as César Chávez, Dolores Huerta, and Jesse Jackson. One form of protest that gained considerable attention was the procession of hunger strikers who marched on their knees to Watsonville's St. Patrick's Church. Anita Contreras helped lead the procession and stated, "As long as God is in Heaven, I will never give up." The Strike Committee also organized a boycott of Wells Fargo Bank, the financial lender to the canneries.

The strike ended with a reinstatement of benefits but no increase in salary. Many strikers saw this as a compromise but not as a victory. Women agreed to the terms of the new contract in order to go back to work and provide for their families. The strike held valuable lessons about political activism when it is organized among women. In recognizing their potential, some women chose not to return to the canneries, others sought opportunities elsewhere, and others, like Gloria Betancourt, pursued leadership roles in the fight for Latina workers' rights.

SOURCES: Castillo, Ana. 1995. *Massacre of the Dreamers: Essays on Xicanisma*. New York: Plume; Flores, William V., and Rina Benmayor, eds. 1997. *Latino Cultural Citizenship: Claiming Identity, Space, and Rights*. Boston: Beacon; Ruiz, Vicki L. 1987. *Cannery Women, Cannery Lives: Mexican Women, Unionization, and the California Food Processing Industry, 1930–1950*. Albuquerque: University of New Mexico Press; Silver, Jon, director and writer, and Migrant Media Productions, producer. 1989. *Watsonville on Strike: A Documentary*. [Videocassette]; Zavella, Patricia. 1987. *Women's Work and Chicano Families: Cannery Workers of the Santa Clara Valley*. Ithaca, NY: Cornell University Press.

Margie Brown-Coronel

WELCH, RAQUEL (1940–)

Born in Chicago on September 5, 1940, Jo Raquel Tejada burst into stardom in 1966 with two science fiction classics, *Fantastic Voyage* and *One Million Years B.C.* In 1969 *Time* magazine featured her clad in a prehistoric deerskin garb on the year's November issue and lauded her as "Today's Sex Symbol." Downplaying her Latina background until she was well established in her career, Jo Raquel Tejada became known to the world as Raquel Welch. Years later she recalled that her rise as an internationally known sex symbol and comedic movie starlet developed under nearly complete ethnic invisibility, a choice mostly encouraged by movie studios and marketing managers who purposefully deemphasized Welch's ethnicity. As a condition to popularity and access to multiple roles, her Hispanic background was deliberately ignored. Welch commented during an interview that pressures to forget her Latina roots started at home. Her father, Armand C. Tejada, a Bolivian-born aerospace engineer, relocated his family to California, where he raised Raquel under an assimilationist ethos, stressed the speaking of English in the home, and chose to live in non-Latino neighborhoods in order to Americanize his family.

As a little girl, Welch frequented the movies to avoid her parents' fights and became an avid cinema fan, later identifying the ballet classic *The Red Shoes* as both escape and inspiration. As a teenager, she took dance classes and participated in and won several California beauty pageants, including Miss Contour, Miss La Jolla, Miss Photogenic Teen, and Miss San Diego. At the age of eighteen she enrolled in San Diego State University. She married a year later and gave birth to her daughter Tahnee in 1960. "You just couldn't be too different," she remarked about her journey into movie stardom, arguing that early on in her career she agreed to temporarily dye her hair blonde and to change her last name from Tejada to Welch, but insisted on remaining Raquel.

Raquel Welch reached the heights of popularity during the mid-1960s and early 1970s. A thriving 1963 publicity tour in Europe with her second husband Patrick Curtis propelled her career into a major international phenomenon. However, the year 1964 found Welch struggling as a divorced single mother of two children. Still, the striving actress persevered and landed the role of "billboard girl" on the television variety show *Hollywood Palace*, where Welch's stunning appeal gained her notoriety that led to various television appearances in shows such as *The Virginian* and *Bewitched*.

Beginning as a sex symbol and later performing multiple roles as a comedienne, Welch debuted in movies with a small role as a college student in the 1964 *Roustabout*, starring Elvis Presley. She played a bordello girl in *A House Is Not a Home* (1964), which starred Shelley Winters. Other films to her credit include *A Swinging Summer* (1965), *100 Rifles* (1969), *The Last of Sheila* (1973), *The Three Musketeers* (1973), *Stunt Woman* (1981), and *Naked Gun 33½: The Final Insult* (1994). She also appeared in noteworthy television productions, including *A Right to Die* (1987), in which she played a victim of Lou Gehrig's disease, *Trouble in Paradise* and *Scandal in a Small Town*, both in 1988, and *Tainted Blood* in 1993.

Welch costarred opposite numerous leading men, including Richard Burton, Burt Reynolds, Dudley Moore, James Stewart, Frank Sinatra, Dean Martin, Vittorio De Sica, Jean Paul Belmondo, and Bill Cosby, and became a favorite star of film and television directors such as Richard Lester, Herbert Ross, Peter Yates, and James Ivory. A contract darling of Twentieth Century Fox, the scene-stealer Raquel Welch was carefully crafted for stardom roles in films that capitalized on her sex appeal and magnetic screen presence. Reflecting upon her career choices at the age of sixty-one, Welch argued: "You can be a legitimate sex symbol up until the age of thirty-five and then after that you just can't take that too seriously. As I was coming up to forty, I was looking for breadcrumbs along the road of sex-symbolism. I couldn't find any that were very positive."

Grateful for the many opportunities that accrued from her fame as a sex symbol, Welch also confessed feeling limited by the narrow acting opportunities granted to her by her sexualized identity on screen. Yet, Welch has to her credit more than sixty-two films. In 1981, she surprised critics with her successful Broadway debut as the headliner in the hit musical *Woman of the Year*. Reawakening to her Latina identity during the 1980s, Raquel Welch has made important contributions to promoting a Latino presence in television. With a busy acting career into the twenty-first century, she had a leading role in *An American Family*, the first PBS dramatic series with a Latino theme.

In a *New York Times* interview published on October 7, 1987, she remarked that the time had arrived in her career to "let go of everything I had ever used before in a part. . . . It was a big relief, and there was a great freedom in knowing for myself what a range of things I could look forward to personally, as well as for myself as an actress." Raquel Welch continues to reinvent herself. She is the author of a best-selling fitness book stressing the virtues of yoga and nutrition and has created her own line of wigs and beauty products.

See also Movie Stars

SOURCES: Hadley-Garcia, George. 1990. *Hispanic Hollywood: The Latins in Motion Pictures*. New York: Carol Publishing Group; Keller, Gary D. 1997. *A Biographical Handbook of Hispanics in United States Film*. Tempe, AZ: Bilingual Press; Reyes, Luis, and Peter Rubie. 2000. *Hispanics in Hollywood: A Celebration of 100 Years in Film and Television*. Hollywood, CA: Lone Eagle Publishing Company; Rodríguez, Clara. 2004. *Heroes, Lovers, and Others: The Story of Latinos in Hollywood*. Washington, DC: Smithsonian Books.

Soledad Vidal

WEST SIDE STORY

West Side Story opened on Broadway in 1957. Because the stage version was such a smashing success, a film version was made in 1961. Chita Rivera played the role of Anita in the play, and Rita Moreno played this role in the film version. There were few other Latinos in the film or the play. Because of its huge success as a movie, more than any other drama, it has influenced the images of Latinas and Latinos. The question is how. On the one hand, there are those who view *West Side Story* as reflecting the ageless Romeo and Juliet love story. On the other hand, there are those who contend that this cold-war era film conveyed a more subtle message that ethnic differences were a threat to the

Anita Vélez as Anita in *West Side Story*, 1963. Courtesy of the Erasmo Vando Papers. Centro Archives, Centro de Estudios Puertorriqueños, Hunter College, CUNY.

national, territorial, racial, and linguistic identity of the United States. In addition, they maintain that Latina women were stereotypically portrayed as either madonnas or harlots.

Regardless of one's perspective, it cannot be denied that, as the first major film and play about Latinos in the Northeast, it has had a major impact on how Latinas/os, and more specifically Puerto Ricans, have been viewed. In many ways it paralleled the impact that *Giant*, a film of the same era and magnitude, had on the perception of Chicanos or Mexican Americans. There are few films that have equaled the impact of both these epics.

Puerto Ricans in New York were clearly the focus of this drama. However, when Arthur Laurents originally wrote the play in 1949, it was about a Jewish girl and an Italian Catholic boy. When the scriptwriters turned their attention to the play's production, the original Jewish-Catholic conflict was seen as dated. At the time stories of juvenile delinquency and gang activity filled the news; in particular, Leonard Bernstein was inspired by the idea of Chicano gangs fighting so-called ethnic Americans. The possibility of making the play about Chicanos was contemplated, but it was decided that it would be easier to set it in New York. Puerto Ricans, perhaps because they were concentrated in New York and had arrived in large numbers during the 1950s, ended up "fitting the bill."

Not only was *West Side Story* the first major film about Latinos in the Northeast, it was also a megafilm in its own right. It not only was the top-grossing film of 1961, but also received ten Academy Awards, including best picture, best supporting actress, director, cinematography, art direction/set decoration, sound, score, editing, costumes, and supporting actor and an honorary award for choreography, given to Jerome Robbins. It was also for this film that an Oscar was awarded for the first time to a Latina, Rita Moreno for best supporting actress. In addition to these awards, the film received other prestigious awards, which included Golden Globe awards for Best Film (in Musical/Comedy) and Best Supporting Actor and Actress and the Directors Guild of America award for Best Director. Indeed, no other film had ever garnered this many awards, and only one has matched this record since (*Titanic*).

West Side Story was an extremely popular film during its time, and the musical has had, and continues to have, immense appeal as a drama production for repertory companies, schools, and colleges. Indeed, many consider *West Side Story* to be an American classic. Moreover, many of the songs, written by Leonard Bernstein and Steven Sondheim, have joined the pantheon of American all-time classics—for example, "Maria," "I Feel Pretty," "Tonight," "Something's Coming," and "Somewhere." Other songs, such as "One Hand, One Heart," "America," "Gee, Officer Krupke!" "The Rumble," "Dance at the Gym," "A Boy like That/I Have a Love," and "Cool," have become some of the best-known American songs today, recognizable even when played without their lyrics.

However, despite the film's popularity, Latino writers have raised a number of criticisms of it. Alberto Sandoval Sánchez maintains that it reflected a view of Latinos, in this case Puerto Ricans, as coming from another world and invading the United States. He contends that although on one level it is simply a love story, on a deeper level it is the beginning of an explicit discourse of discrimination and prejudice toward immigrant Latinos. This discourse projects a series of binary oppositions about class, race, and ethnicity. For example, the very title implies the contrast between the "then" working-class West Side and the upscale East Side of New York. The names of the gangs reflect a negative binary in which the Puerto Ricans/Latinos are threateningly named the Sharks, while the earlier white, Anglo-heritage residents of the area are referred to as the Jets to connote modernism and technological prowess. In addition, the film focuses on "stories," as the title indicates, and ignores "histories." Thus the troublesome political and economic history between the United States and Puerto Rico is ignored, particularly its relationship to the migration of Puerto Ricans to New York. Similarly overlooked is the long history of Puerto Ricans on the West Side and in New York, which dates to the nineteenth century. Last, the long and rich immigrant history of the West Side is not part of the film. Essentially, Sandoval Sánchez views the film as providing an early and important medium within which the confrontation of Anglos/whites with foreign or immigrant Latino "others" is depicted and continues to subsequently be understood.

Others argue that the film established definitively the image of Puerto Ricans, and more generally Latinos, as urban ghetto dwellers and juvenile delinquents who were social misfits or personally inadequate victims. Moreover, it perpetuates the stereotype of Puerto Rican males as knife-carrying gang members who could only solve their problems through violence. These same images find their counterparts in the "social problem" films, which featured Chicanos on the West Coast. With regard to Latinas, *West Side Story* personified and established in the public mind a dualist image of Puerto Rican women as either the innocent, passive, virginal Madonna, as played by Natalie Wood as María, or as the hot-blooded, fiery, sexy spitfire or whore, as played by Rita Moreno as Anita.

See also Cinema Images, Contemporary; Media Stereotypes

SOURCES: Pérez, Richie. 1997. "From Assimilation to Annihilation: Puerto Rican Images in U.S. Films." In *Latin Looks: Images of Latinas and Latinos in the U.S. Media*, ed. C. Rodríguez, 142–163. Boulder, CO: Westview Press; Sandoval Sánchez, Alberto. 1997. "*West Side Story*: A Puerto Rican Reading of America." In *Latin Looks: Images of Latinas and Latinos in the U.S. Media*, ed. C. Rodríguez, 164–179. Boulder, CO: Westview Press; _____. 1999. *José, Can You See? Latinos on and off Broadway*. Madison: University of Wisconsin Press.

Clara E. Rodríguez

WILCOX, MARY ROSE GARRIDO (1949–   )

Mary Rose Garrido Wilcox, a fourth-generation member of a pioneer Mexican American family, was born in Superior, Arizona. She was the first Latina to be elected to the Phoenix City Council and the Maricopa County Board of Supervisors. She is one of the most recognized Latina leaders in the state.

Raised in a union family in an Arizona mining community, Mary Rose Wilcox saw firsthand the ability of common folk to achieve power through organizing. She applied these lessons to her own endeavors throughout her life. As a nineteen-year-old student at Arizona State University in the 1960s, she became part of the core group that organized the Mexican American Student Organization (MASO). Within a short time MASO effectively pressured the university's administration for accountability regarding the educational needs of Mexican Americans in the Valley of the Sun (Maricopa County). Like that of many other students, Wilcox's concern for social justice evolved from university reform to helping the larger community gain civil rights and economic empowerment.

In a 1972 attempt to recall an Arizona governor considered insensitive to the needs of Chicanos, Wilcox gained valuable political insights. Although the removal efforts were unsuccessful, the experience helped her and other Mexican Americans gain a foothold in the arena of Arizona politics. Her political training continued as she worked to elect Valley Chicanos to school boards, the state legislature, and the Maricopa County Board of Supervisors and in Raúl Castro's successful campaign to become the first Mexican American governor of Arizona in 1974. By 1978 Senator Dennis DeConcini hired Wilcox as a community liaison, a position that provided Mexican Americans access to the senator's office in Washington, D.C.

Confident that she could serve the people directly, in the 1980s Wilcox concentrated on her own political ambitions. With the help of her husband, Earl Wilcox, a former state legislator and justice of the peace, she was elected to the Phoenix City Council in 1983 and served until 1993, when she won a seat on the Maricopa County Board of Supervisors. In 2000 and 2004 she was reelected for third and fourth four-year terms.

As a city council member and county supervisor, Mary Rose was instrumental in revitalizing downtown Phoenix. The building of America West Arena and Bank One Ballpark, projects that put Phoenix at the forefront as a national sports center, were goals to which she committed much of her energy. Such projects as the "fight back movement," which combats neighborhood crime by involving local residents, and the City of Phoenix Kool Kids program, a summer swimming program for inner-city children, exist largely through her efforts.

Mary Rose and Earl Wilcox spawned numerous community projects as volunteers, especially those focusing on youth in the Phoenix inner city, where Earl grew up. With the help of other community activists, the couple runs Late Night Basketball, a signature program that provides recreation and positive activity for Phoenix's young people. In addition, Mary Rose has served on numerous boards and commissions, such as the Phoenix Economic Growth Corporation, the Phoenix Symphony, the Genesis Program, Friendly House, and the Downtown Phoenix Partnership. In 1983 she was a founding member of the Arizona Hispanic Women's Corporation and served as executive director in 1988–1989. Besides involvement in local activities, her participation with the national Hispanic community is extensive. She has served in such organizations as the Mexican American Legal Defense and Educational Fund (MALDEF), the National Council of La Raza (NCLR), and the National Association of Latino Elected and Appointed Officials (NALEO).

Mary Rose Wilcox has received numerous honors for her community and political work. She and her husband reside in downtown Phoenix, own *New El Sol*, a weekly newspaper serving the Hispanic community, and operate the restaurant El Portal Mexicano. Earl and Mary Rose Wilcox have a daughter and five grandsons.

See also Politics, Electoral

SOURCES: Luckingham, Bradford. 1994. *Minorities in Phoenix: A Profile of Mexican American, Chinese American, and African American Communities, 1860–1992.* Tucson: University of Arizona Press; Luey, Beth, and Noel J. Stowe, eds. 1987. *Arizona at Seventy-five: The Next Twenty-five Years.* Tempe: Arizona State University Public History Program and the Arizona Historical Society; Navarro, Armando. 2000. *La Raza Unida Party: A Chicano Challenge to the U.S. Two-Party Dictatorship.* Philadelphia: Temple University Press; Rosales, F. Arturo. 1996. *Chicano! The History of the Mexican American Civil Rights Movement.* Houston: Arte Público Press.

F. Arturo Rosales

WOLF, ESTHER VALLADOLID (1940–)

Born in El Paso, Texas, Esther Valladolid Wolf attended Catholic schools along with her three sisters. Her father, Rosendo Alfero Valladolid, immigrated to the United States from Mexico, where he had been a leader in an underground movement that helped secure the passage of Catholic priests and nuns from Mexico to the United States when they were escaping persecution during the Mexican Revolution. Her mother, Guadalupe Pérez Valladolid, volunteered for many local church-related and social organizations. Her family believed in the value of education, and Esther began her career in community service in grade school, where she volunteered as an interpreter, translating for the nuns in her school and recent immigrants from Mexico.

After completing high school, she attended the National Conservatory of Music in Mexico City and the University of Texas at El Paso. She graduated from the University of Kansas with undergraduate and graduate degrees in social work, as well as a postgraduate certificate in gerontology. She was awarded a Kellogg Fellowship to the John F. Kennedy School of Government Executive Program at Harvard University. In 1964 she married James Wolf and has two children, Paul and Judith.

Following the spirit of the feminist movement of the 1960s, Esther Wolf learned firsthand that the personal is political. After her mother was diagnosed with cancer and needed help with Medicare forms and bills, Wolf found her cause. Since then her primary mission has been helping older Americans, especially Latinos, who need assistance with health care, insurance, and hospital information. Her energy and enthusiasm for life are obvious in her long list of achievements. In the early 1980s she was the director of social services for el Centro de Services para Hispanos in Kansas City, Kansas. She has been the executive director of the Richard Cabot Clinic in Kansas City, Missouri, a primary-care clinic that provides medical services for Kansas City residents. She took a run-down, one-story, poorly equipped health center with a leaky roof and turned it into a modern, cheerful facility with the latest equipment for low-income Latino families. "Before I knew it, I was considered a Hispanic leader . . . because of the passion I felt for working in the community," she observed when she recounted the early years of her career.

From 1987 to 1991 she served as secretary of aging for the state of Kansas. In addition, she has been a clinical instructor and project director at the University of Missouri, Kansas City, in the Institute of Human Development and the Graduate School of Social Work. She continues as a consultant for Wolf and Associates, specializing in issues concerning gerontology and cultural diversity. One of her more recent projects has been working with Nelson-Atkins Museum of Art at Kansas City, Missouri, to promote art education for senior citizens who want to increase their creativity.

"I act as if what I do makes a difference," Wolf remarked with typical passion about her life's work, and she has indeed made a difference. In 1987 she was featured in *Newsweek* as an American hero. She received the Public Service Achievement Award the following year, one of seven given nationally by Common Cause. She has received the National Mexican-American Women's Community Service Award, the Women of Color Service Award, the YMCA Hearts of Gold Health Award, the Greater Kansas City Hispanics Chamber of Commerce Humanitarian Award, and the Missouri Commission on the Status of Women Service Award, among many others. She serves on the board of directors for the National Hispanic Leadership Institute, the National Association of Hispanic Elderly, the American Red Cross, the Kansas Humanities Board, the Heart of America United Way Executive Association, and the Posada del Sol Senior Housing Center. She has also been involved in several international projects, working with the United Nations Commission on the Status of Women, and as a consultant to the Mexican government.

In addition to her work with senior citizens, Esther Wolf serves as a mentor to young Latinas. She is actively involved with the League of United Latin American Citizens (LULAC), the oldest Hispanic civil rights organization, and conducts workshops in the Kansas City, Missouri, and Kansas City, Kansas, public schools to promote leadership qualities in middle- and high-school students. Her warmth and compassion make her a frequent recipient of evening telephone calls from young women who have attended her workshops and who seek her advice.

Esther Wolf continues to give back to U.S. society, even though she was forced to sit in the back of the bus when she was young, just because she was Latino. She has often observed, "You can't stay angry forever." In fact, it is her love of life that makes her vitality infectious. She breathes energy into every project she touches. She has reached out to thousands of Latinos with her passionate belief that one person has the power to change the way that ordinary people live their lives.

See also League of United Latin American Citizens (LULAC)

SOURCE: *Newsweek.* 1987. "A Celebration of Heroes." July 6, 78.

Mary Ann Wynkoop

WORLD WAR II (1941–1945)

World War II was a pivotal point for the United States and was no less so for U.S. Latinas, who contributed to the war effort as both civilians and military enlistees. On the home front Latinas participated in rationing efforts, recycling drives, and letter-writing campaigns and took jobs in defense-related industries. Untold thousands married young soldiers right before they left for overseas tours of duty. Still others found themselves performing work from which they had been restricted before the war because of their gender or their race/ethnicity or both.

For American women in general, and especially for married women, who had often been discouraged from working outside the home after marriage, the war created unprecedented employment opportunities. In 1940 most of the 11.5 million working American women were single, but by 1944 nearly a third of female defense workers had been housewives previously. A typical week's salary in war-industry work was $35 to $40. For many Latinas, however, participation in the workforce had come out of necessity during the Great Depression of the 1930s; World War II represented an opportunity to earn higher wages.

The United States began war readiness before the bombing of Pearl Harbor on December 7, 1941, when it began to produce equipment and armament for its allies even before the passage of the Lend-Lease Act on March 11, 1941. A by-product of that acceleration in production, in conjunction with the beginning of a draft program, was a substantial lowering of the unemployment rate—to 14.6 percent at the end of 1940, the lowest unemployment rate in a decade. During the war years the country enjoyed full employment, and Latinas received higher wages working in many industries.

After the attack on Pearl Harbor, the entire country became fully mobilized for war. The workforce participation of women was essential, because young men served in the military. Some 16 million American men, including an estimated 500,000 Mexican Americans and some 65,000 Puerto Ricans, were pressed into duty. There were also Cuban Americans and Spanish Americans, including those from Ybor City, in what is now Tampa, Florida. As those men left for battlefields and other war-related work, women were called upon to fill the men's jobs in industry and in other workplaces. From 1940 to 1944 the number of women working rose dramatically, from 12 million to 18.2 million.

By the end of the war with the atomic bombing of the Japanese cities of Hiroshima on August 6, 1945, and Nagasaki three days later, the United States had built nearly 300,000 airplanes, 5,777 merchant ships, 635,000 jeeps, 2.4 million trucks, and 1,556 naval vessels. The nation's factories had also built 6.5 million rifles and made 40 billion bullets. Latinas were among those involved in that production. For Latina women, those high-salaried jobs represented unprecedented independence and prosperity.

To understand Latinas of the World War II generation, it is essential to understand the forces that shaped them. Key among those forces was the prevailing discrimination in the United States against Spanish speakers in many parts of the country before and during the war. Another important factor was the Great Depression, which rendered between 11 million and 13 million Americans unemployed. Some estimates place the rates of unemployed and underemployed (involuntary part-time) Americans as high as 50 percent. Latinas of the World War II generation repeatedly assert that families "made do" by cultivating vegetable gardens and, in some cases, accepting government relief. Some Latino families refused any government help out of pride. It was common for entire families to hire out, in pecan shelling in San Antonio, Texas, for instance, or by working as migrant laborers in the cotton fields of Texas or the sugar-beet industry in the Midwest.

The depression also stemmed migration from Puerto Rico because jobs dried up on the mainland. One authority puts the return migration (back to Puerto Rico from the mainland) of the 1930s at 10,000 people, or about 20 percent of the Puerto Rican population in the United States. In Puerto Rico, however, circum-

stances were just as bleak, because sugar and tobacco cultivation took a nosedive, which led to high unemployment and food shortages. One writer characterizes the period as "the Desperate '30s." Women often did "piecework," the edging or embroidery on handkerchiefs, or sewing collars. It was a system that paid the work-at-home women a pittance—they might earn thirteen cents for a dozen handkerchiefs—but that was better than no income whatsoever. In addition, the women could also do the work while keeping up with their children and housework.

The poverty suffered as a consequence of the depression was only one challenge. In many areas Latinos, most notably Mexican Americans, also grappled with discrimination that relegated them to segregated schools and other social institutions. In some communities in the Southwest there were no provisions for Mexican American children beyond fourth grade. Latinos in the Midwest also suffered; those who worked as migrant workers lived in substandard housing and were generally treated harshly by the dominant society.

For Mexican Americans, the Great Depression also led to the deportation or repatriation of 400,000 to 500,000 Mexicans. About 200,000 Mexican immigrants, as well as Mexican Americans, went to Mexico voluntarily between 1929 and 1931. Government institutions and a few companies also began repatriating Mexicans in 1931 and 1932. In some instances men, women, and children were loaded onto trains. In other cases church groups, the Red Cross, and Mexican American societies began programs to take people back across the border.

Latinas interviewed as part of the U.S. Latinos and Latinas and World War II Oral History Project also recall the generosity of their own parents during the Great Depression. Theresa Herrera Casarez (1926–), a young girl in the hardest years of the depression, said that her mother often gave food to people who came knocking on their Austin door. "My mother never, never sent anyone away without giving them the little bit that we had," said Casarez. "She was always sewing things and mending . . . [in case] anyone came by the house that needed clothing."

It was common for Latinas to quit school to help their families. One such woman, Henrietta López Rivas (1924–), left school in the eighth grade when she and her family traveled to the Midwest to work in the *betabel*, or sugar-beet fields—an arrangement favored by the sugar-beet producers, who were able to maximize the labor of the entire family. When she returned to San Antonio, she worked cleaning houses and barns for $1.50 a week. At the outbreak of war López took a job with the civil service, translating for non-English-

Rita Rodríguez, a real-life "Rosie the Riveter." Photograph by Howard R. Hollem, October 1942. Courtesy of the Library of Congress, America from the Great Depression to World War II: Photographs from the FSA-OWI, 1935–1945. (Digital ID: fsac la34937).

speaking residents instructions on the security measures in place. In that job she began making $90 a month. Thus her ability to speak Spanish, seen as a liability to be discouraged in school, became a job skill that earned her more than she had dreamed possible.

Other Latinas worked in defense plants, bringing home a salary they could never have hoped for before the war. The high-paying jobs gave some women an entrée into the working world, as well as a measure of independence they had never known before. For one thing, many young Latinas began frequenting USO clubs or other similar clubs for Latino servicemen. The young Latinas sported the style of the day, curled hair, dresses with fitted bodices, and dark lipstick. The music they listened to was of two worlds, that of the dominant culture—Glenn Miller, Benny Goodman, and Tommy Dorsey, to name a few of the most celebrated—but also Spanish-language music, which varied from region to region and ethnic group to ethnic group.

For the first time it seemed that the Hispanic system of chaperonage took a back seat to patriotism. As Sherna Berger Gluck observed in *Rosie the Riveter Revisited*, servicemen were "respected and trusted and social activities with them were permissible. The resulting social climate often led to increased independence for young women."

In some cases young women were swept away by the romance of the war years and married young servicemen they had only recently met, or boyfriends who were on the verge of leaving for battle. Elizabeth Ruiz García (1924–), of Austin, was introduced by a friend to a young soldier from western Texas named Willie García. After three months of dating, García proposed

to her just before leaving for the battlefield in North Africa and Sicily. Although she preferred to wait until he returned, she finally agreed to the proposal. The two were married hurriedly, but properly: she wore a new white wedding dress, the ceremony was at her parish church, and her mother put together a large family party, with live music and food. The young groom departed the following morning. The two remained married for the rest of their lives.

One Latina who worked in the defense industry was Josephine Ledesma (1917–), the mother of a young boy when the war broke out. Ledesma worked as an airplane mechanic during the war years, traveling to Randolph Air Force Base, near San Antonio, about seventy miles south of San Antonio. She learned to be a mechanic by doing. "In Bergstrom Field (Austin, Texas) our duty was 'to keep them flying.' We were taking care of all transit aircraft that came that needed repairs," she said.

She was stationed in Bergstrom Air Field and then Big Spring, both in Texas. Besides Ledesma two other women, both Anglos, served in Bergstrom Air Field, and several more in Big Spring, all working in the sheet-metal department. At Big Spring Ledesma was the only woman working in the hangar.

Other Latina women worked in other areas. Puerto Rican women in New York, for instance, worked as censors for the U.S. Postal Service, using their Spanish-language skills to check civilian mail between the mainland and Spanish-speaking countries, as well as Puerto Rico. In the Midwest Mexican American women worked in defense-related industries, performing the myriad tasks required in order to build airplanes and other equipment and munitions. A few worked at the steel mills and in the railroad industry.

If it is true that an army travels on its stomach, then it follows that the nation's food producers had to struggle mightily to feed the 16 million Americans in military service in World War II. Labor unions enjoyed a measure of leverage as canneries and packing houses won federal contracts to feed servicemen abroad and at home, as well as to help feed U.S. allies. Historian Vicki L. Ruiz notes that the cannery industry in southern California found itself appeasing the labor unions, and their employees in general, with better working conditions and higher wages as the defense-related industries became viable employment alternatives.

Women, comprised three-quarters of the canning employees in California, included hundreds of Latinas in the 1940s, and some Latinas served in leadership roles within their locals. On a national level, the demands of the federal government during World War II on food producers enabled the United Cannery, Agricultural, Packing, and Allied Workers of America (UCA-PAWA-CIO) to secure substantial wage increases and

A highly decorated army nurse, Carmen Contreras Bozak, in New York City, 1945. Courtesy of the U.S. Latino and Latina World War II Oral History Project, University of Texas, Austin.

other benefits, so by the end of the war, nationally nearly 90 percent of the cannery contracts included a minimum-wage stipulation of 65 cents an hour, and two-thirds of those contracts required equal pay for equal work. Within the context of labor organizing, the cannery workers' union, like hundreds of other U.S. organizations, participated in blood drives, war bond sales, and baking for area USO clubs.

Some Latinas served in the military, usually as nurses, and were usually stationed at installations back home. A few, including Rafaela Muñiz Esquivel (1920–), of San Antonio, Texas, were sent overseas. Muñiz was one of five Mexican Americans to graduate from Robert B. Green Memorial Hospital School of Nursing in May 1942; the remaining four of them joined the military. Muñiz joined the Army Nurse Corps on October 1, 1942 (the Army Nurse Corps became a part of the Regular Army of the United States by an act of Congress in April 1947) and become a second lieutenant in the Reserve. After working at Fort Sill, Oklahoma, Second Lieutenant Rafaela Muñiz was shipped out in late 1944, assigned to the 242nd General Hospital at Sissonne, France. She was later assigned to the 101st Evacuation Hospital in Luxembourg. "[We were] always on the go," Muñiz recalled in 2001. "Most of the time we were dressed. We didn't have time. There was no way that we could really get undressed [to sleep]." From Luxembourg Rafaela Muñiz was later sent to a makeshift hospital in a German town near Coblenz, about five miles away from George Patton's Third Army. In 2001 she recalled hearing bombs exploding in the distance, and flashes of light could be seen at night. Here the nurses were dressed in combat clothing at all

times. In recognition of her exemplary service, Nurse Muñiz was promoted to first lieutenant in France in May 1945.

After the war Rafaela Muñiz returned to home and civilian life and married Efrain (Frank) Esquivel, who served as a radio operator in the air force in the South Pacific during the war. Esquivel later retired from professional nursing and has been a caregiver to various family members since then. The World War II generation of Latinas has repeatedly followed the pattern of working as reliable and compassionate caregivers for their families.

Throughout the country the war effort also encompassed the many small tasks that made life a bit more bearable for the overseas serviceman. One example, an organized letter-writing campaign by women for lonesome overseas soldiers, was the effort of the Spanish-American Mothers and Wives Association. This organization, 300 strong, began in 1944. Women worked baking cookies, selling war bonds, raising money through raffles, and writing a four-page newsletter, *Chatter*, which carried tidbits about Mexican American servicemen and women and local milestones, such as births, deaths, and weddings. Relatives bought *Chatter* for a nickel to send to their loved ones on assignment overseas. The dues in this organization were fifty cents a month.

A recurring theme for the Latina mothers who took jobs outside their homes during World War II was the lack of day care or after-school programs for their children. The federal government sought to alleviate the problem by establishing day-care centers for women in defense jobs, but care was available for only around 135,000 of the 4.5 million children under the age of fourteen. Josephine Ledesma, working as a mechanic at Kelly Air Force Base in San Antonio, left her young boy with her mother and mother-in-law in Austin and saw her child when she could on weekends.

In one survey, taken in 1944, half the women workers said that they wanted to keep working after the war. But many were given pink slips to make employment available for returning GIs. For example, only 14 percent of the women who had worked in the aircraft industry in Los Angeles during the war years retained their jobs in June 1946. Ledesma was one who reluctantly returned to her routine after the war. "Oh, I loved it. I thought I was just doing a real big thing," she said. "After the war there was not anything like that. You had to put your mind to work at something else."

World War II ushered in momentous changes for U.S. Latinas by providing jobs, independence, and outlets for civic participation. Latinas rose to the occasion and in many instances embraced the newfound opportunities, carefully negotiating the new independence with respect to the old ways of deferring to the husband, father, or brother. As the men returned stateside, it is a matter of debate how much lasting change had taken place for Latinas. Anecdotal evidence suggests that in some cases there was no turning back: some Latinas were less tolerant of bad marriages, and divorce became an attractive option. Most Latinas resumed their prewar domestic roles, and many deferred to the male head of household. However, it is certainly true that this generation of Latinas enjoyed an unprecedented measure of freedom and self-reliance and perhaps filled their own daughters' imaginations with dreams of exciting new possibilities.

See also Military Service

SOURCES: Acosta-Belén, Edna. 1986. "Puerto Rican Women in Culture, History, and Society." In *The Puerto Rican Woman: Perspectives on Culture, History, and Society*, ed. Edna Acosta-Belén. New York: Praeger; Campbell, Julie A. 1990. "Madres y esposas: Tucson's Spanish-Speaking Mothers and Wives Association." *Arizona History* 31, no. 2 (Summer): 161–182; Colman, Penny. 1998. "On Writing Rosie the Riveter: Women Working on the Home Front in World War II." *Social Science Record* 35, no. 1 (Spring): 15–19; García, Juan. 1996. *Mexicans in the Midwest, 1900–1932.* Tucson: University of Arizona Press; Gluck, Sherna Berger. 1987. *Rosie the Riveter Revisited: Women, the War, and Social Change.* New York: Twayne; Griswold del Castillo, Richard, and Arnoldo De Leon. 1997. *North to Aztlán: A History of Mexican Americans in the United States.* New York: Twayne; Kennedy, David M. 1999. *Freedom from Fear: The American People in Depression and War, 1929–1945.* New York: Oxford University Press; Ruiz, Vicki L. 1987. *Cannery Women, Cannery Lives: Mexican Women, Unionization, and the California Food Processing Industry, 1930–1950.* Albuquerque: University of New Mexico Press; Sánchez Korrol, Virginia. 1994. *From Colonia to Community: The History of Puerto Ricans in New York City.* 2nd ed. Berkeley: University of California Press.

Maggie Rivas-Rodríguez

YBARRA, EVA (1945–)

Eva Ybarra was born on March 2, 1945, and was raised in San Antonio, Texas. Ybarra has been playing the accordion for more than thirty-five years around southern Texas and the Southwest. She is the undisputed "queen of the accordion" in *conjunto* music, "la reina de la acordeón." Along with Chabela Ortiz and Brown Express of San Jose, California, and the lesser-known Lupita Rodela of San Antonio, Ybarra is among only a few women in the history of traditional *conjunto* music to lead her own *conjunto* band. Moreover, Ybarra writes most of her songs, thereby creating some of the few *conjunto* tunes written by a woman. Ybarra was given her first accordion by her father Pedro at the age of four, and by the time she was six, she was playing in local restaurants, cantinas, and dance halls. Ybarra was raised in a family of musicians, including her mother, who was a singer and songwriter. She often practiced with her older brother Pedro Jr., also an accordionist, who along with their father encouraged Ybarra to pursue the instrument, despite the fact that there existed no woman accordionists as role models within the conventional male stronghold in *conjunto* music.

Ybarra considers the radio her greatest teacher, because she listened for hours at a time to accordionists such as Narciso Martínez and Tony de la Rosa. Ybarra comments that she has known from the beginning that adopting the accordion as her own instrument would require more determination and effort than that required of men in this field of music. "What I dislike the most is when people try to compliment me by saying 'you play really good for a woman' [. . .] that's like saying I don't play as good as the men because we all know that I'm the only woman playing." Ybarra's playing style is unique, often described as "making the accordion cry with emotion," and she has established inroads for other woman accordionists in contemporary *conjunto* music. As a master accordionist, Ybarra has been commissioned to teach accordion classes for the Guadalupe Cultural Arts Xicano Music education program in San Antonio, Texas, for several years. She has also served in a music apprentice project sponsored by Texas Folklife Resources in Austin, Texas, teaching young women the instrument. Ybarra has released two CDs, *A mi San Antonio* (1994) and *Romance inolvidable* (1996), both on Rounder Records. In January 1999 Ybarra joined las Madrugadores, Tish Hinojosa, Rosie Pérez, Shelly Lares, and Clemencia Zapata, to form las Super Tejanas, the first all-star Tejana music performance ensemble in the history of Texas music. Las Super Tejanas performed to a sellout crowd in Austin, Texas. Ybarra also participated in the Latino Music Oral History project of the Smithsonian Institution, National Museum of American History. She was one of the first five Tejano music artists selected to be part of this historic project to capture the life histories of significant Latina/o music artists in the United States. Ybarra continues to make her home in San Antonio, where, among other sites, she can be found performing live at the annual Tejano Conjunto Music Festival.

SOURCES: RootsWorld (world music website). "La reina de acordeón". Silja J. A. Talvi talks with accordion queen Eva Ybarra. www.rootsworld.com/rw/feature/ybarra.html (accessed July 24, 2005); Vargas, Deborah Rose Ramos. 2003. "Las tracaleras: Texas-Mexican Women, Music, and Place." Ph.D. diss., University of California, Santa Cruz.

Deborah Vargas

YOUNG LORDS (1968–1972)

With the cry "All Power to the People," the Young Lords advocated independence for Puerto Rico, a socialist society, and grassroots community services controlled by, and meeting the needs of, the people. In 1968 Puerto Rican youth in Chicago, many of them former gang members, started the Young Lords Organization. A year later Puerto Rican students in New York City affiliated and formed a second chapter. When these two chapters split, the New York group became the Young Lords Party. Chapters emerged in Newark, New Jersey, Philadelphia, Pennsylvania,

Bridgeport, Connecticut, and briefly in Hayward, California. Puerto Rican women were active in the New York Young Lords from the beginning, fomenting a "revolution within a revolution" and demanding that the Young Lords confront "male chauvinism" within the party and society.

The Young Lords' four major offensives addressed the challenges that Puerto Ricans faced in New York, and often women's needs. During the 1969 Garbage Offensive, the Lords cleaned up the streets for several consecutive Sundays. They piled the trash in the streets, forcing the city to remove it. When a church refused space for the Lords to provide children with a free hot breakfast before school, they started the Peoples Church Offensive. They took over and occupied the church for eleven days, running their breakfast program, free clothing drives, "a liberation school," a day-care center, and health programs, as well as providing entertainment via poetry readings, music, or movies. For their third offensive, the Young Lords and the Health Revolutionary Unity Movement, a group of hospital workers, took over Lincoln Hospital in the South Bronx. They ran lead poisoning and tuberculosis detection programs and operated a day-care center. Earlier health initiatives had included door-to-door testing of children for lead poisoning and "liberating" the city's tuberculosis X-ray truck, which was underused. The fourth offensive's central issues were prison conditions and reported "suicides" among Puerto Rican and African American inmates. When Young Lord Julio Roldán was found hung in his cell, the Lords occupied the church at the end of his funeral procession. The Lords also addressed police brutality, drug addiction, education, the war in Vietnam, and independence for Puerto Rico, organizing a march of 10,000 people to the United Nations in 1970 to demand the liberation of Puerto Rico.

Writing in 1971, Young Lord Denise Oliver linked these initiatives with the need for women's participation. Noting that "when the Party got started, there were very few sisters," she explained, "We saw that we really weren't gonna be able to do any kind of constructive organizing in the community without sisters actively involved in the Party, because most of the people that we're organizing are women with children, through the free-breakfast program and through the free-clothing drive and health care programs." Women questioned their roles in the party. "We didn't have a chance to contribute politically. . . . We were relegated to doing office work, typing, taking care of whatever kids were around, being sex objects." They formed a women's caucus to foster their own political development and then pushed for a men's caucus. Richie Pérez explained, "We have been having a weekly male cau-

cus to discuss the oppression of our sisters not only in the Party, but in our community in general, because we recognize *machismo* as one of the biggest problems in making our revolution." The Lords identified women's oppression as stemming from "capitalism that affects all people of the Third World" and "capitalism that affects women in terms of jobs," as well as "the oppression that we receive from our own men." They revised their Thirteen Point Program from calling for "revolutionary machismo" to asserting, "We want equality for women. Down with machismo and male chauvinism." In 1969 Denise Oliver became the first woman on the Central Committee, and a year later, she was joined by Gloria Fontánez.

Young Lords challenged the gender constructions they had grown up with. Iris Morales described her family as "a very strict, patriarchal type of family" and explained that her father maintained "his role as an authority figure," and her mother was "just one step above the children—she doesn't question anything that the father does." Morales saw a change: "There used to be only four choices for the Puerto Rican woman—housewife, prostitute, or drug addict, and then, when the society needed more labor for its sweatshops, she would become a worker. Now there's a new choice open to her that threatens the existence of the family and the state itself: The Revolution." Pablo "Yoruba" Guzmán added, "See, there is a biological division in sex, right—however, this society has created a false division based on a thing called gender. Gender is a false idea, because gender is merely traits that have been attributed through the years to a man or a woman." The gay liberation movement offered an alternative. "We're saying that to be totally real, it would be healthy for a man, if he wanted to cry, to go ahead and cry. It would also be healthy for a woman to pick up the gun, to use the gun. . . . That's how you round people out. The Gay Liberation struggle has shown us how to complete ourselves, so we've been able to accept this and understand this." Challenges remained. "We found out it's a lot quicker for people to accept the fact that sisters should be in the front of the struggle, than saying that we're gonna have gay people in the Party."

Although short lived, the Young Lords mounted a critique of Puerto Rico's status, of the conditions confronting Puerto Ricans in the United States, and of gender constructions. When the Young Lords opened a chapter in Puerto Rico in 1971 to promote independence, divisions emerged within the group over whether to focus on independence or on issues in the United States. Repression from outside the group increased as well. By 1972 the remaining Young Lords became the Puerto Rican Revolutionary Workers Organization.

SOURCES: Laó, Agustín. 1994–1995. "Resources of Hope: Imagining the Young Lords and the Politics of Memory." *Centro Bulletin* 7 (Winter/Spring): 34–49; Morales, Iris, director. 1996. *Palante, Siempre Palante! The Young Lords*. Latino Education Network Service Inc. New York: Third World Newsreel; Torres, Andrés, and José E. Velázquez, eds. 1998. *The Puerto Rican Movement: Voices from the Diaspora*. Philadelphia: Temple University Press; Young Lords Party and Michael Abramson. 1971. *Palante: Young Lords Party*. New York: McGraw-Hill.

Carmen Teresa Whalen

Z

ZAMORA, BERNICE B. ORTIZ (1938–)

Bernice Ortiz Zamora is one of the preeminent poets to emerge from the Chicano movement of the 1960s and 1970s. She has affirmed the importance of Chicano oral tradition and communal heritage to her writing, which reveals the keen eye of both social critic and mystic. She has wielded her pen to address the politics of language and race, sexual double standards, and the complex legacies of colonization and community. As a poet whose writing operates on multiple levels, she delights in the various dimensions of meaning possible in mixing Spanish and English.

Many of Zamora's poems reflect her family's deep roots in southern Colorado: six generations of farmers on her father's side and countless generations of Tewa and Acoma descent on her mother's side. Like her parents, she was born in Aguilar, a village at the foot of the East Spanish Peak. In 1945 her family moved to Pueblo. Her father worked as a coal miner and then a car painter; when he became disabled, her mother took a job in an optical shop.

Zamora, the oldest of five children and a precocious reader from the age of three, attended Catholic schools through the eighth grade. In high school she began to develop her artistic talent and to explore philosophy. After graduating she worked in a bank.

It was in college that she developed her passion for writing. She entered Southern Colorado University in 1968 and majored in English and French. Inspired by Emily Dickinson and Japanese poetry, she began to write poems in English, Spanish, and Caló, experimenting with a range of techniques and styles. By this time she had married and become the mother of two daughters, Rhonda and Katarina. In 1972 she completed an M.A. degree at Colorado State University in Fort Collins, writing a thesis on the poetry of Wallace Stevens and Francis Ponge. In the same year her award-winning first short story, "Flexion," was published in *Caracol*.

Involvement in the Chicano movement was a heady defining period in her life. In 1974 her marriage ended, and she moved to California with her daughters to pur-

sue a Ph.D. at Stanford University. While juggling family duties, literary studies, and teaching jobs, she became active in the movement, which she credited with accomplishing "a great deal in diminishing the degree of isolation we felt before we became visible to each other. . . . It was . . . the catalyst to cultural cohesiveness." Zamora became part of a lively community, joining Trabajadores Culturales of San Jose and other groups. She and literati such as Alurista, Ron Arias, and Cecilia and José Antonio Burciaga gathered monthly to share their work.

Because a vibrant part of this movement focused on community empowerment, Zamora and other poets served as "cultural workers," doing readings at bookstores, churches, parks, and college campuses from coast to coast. Through their poetry they countered racial stereotypes, proudly reclaimed ethnic heritage, and challenged social injustice and inequity. Zamora boldly critiqued sexism not only in the larger society but also in the ethnic community and the movement. Her poems often addressed the experiences and concerns of women, as in "Notes from a Chicana 'Coed' " who wakes up "alone each morning and ask[s], / 'Can I feed my children today?' " Like many Chicana activists, Zamora called attention to survival issues rarely broached by European American feminists of the era.

Zamora was one of the first Chicana poets to publish a volume of verse: *Restless Serpents*, a back-to-back book featuring her work and that of José Antonio Burciaga, appeared in 1976. In this landmark work, deftly mixing Spanish and English, her scope encompassed identity, religion, gender relations, language, politics, and love. As literary scholar Juan Bruce-Novoa said, "*Restless Serpents* is a must for any serious student of Chicano literature." Of her title poem, Zamora has remarked, "For me [it] was a metaphor of that act . . . the writing of poetry." In 1994 *Restless Serpents* reappeared in a stand-alone edition, retitled *Releasing Serpents* and augmented by thirty new poems.

Concerned by the need of Chicano youth for texts reflecting their experiences and culture, Zamora helped nurture the growth of ethnic literature. In 1979 she moved to New Mexico to work on the journal *De*

Bernice Zamora painting with watercolors. Photograph by and courtesy of Valerie J. Matsumoto.

Colores. She coedited early anthologies of Chicano literature from the Flor y Canto Festivals in Albuquerque and Tempe, Arizona. She continued to work as an editor while finishing her Ph.D. dissertation on cultural archetypes in Chicano poetry, filed in 1986. Through subsequent literary scholarship she has illuminated the roles of Chicanos and Native Americans in the *corrido* and the position of Chicanas in American literature.

Zamora is a distinguished, innovative teacher, as well as a poet and scholar. During her nine years as an assistant professor at Santa Clara University in California, her classes on Chicano and Native American literature routinely overflowed with eager students. In 1997 she returned to Colorado and has continued to teach creative writing, composition, literature, and third-world feminisms at Colorado State University in Pueblo (formerly the University of Southern Colorado).

Though she has not focused on publication, Zamora has continued to write steadily and is a member of las Compañeras, a bilingual Chicana poetry group in Pueblo. Her work includes a vast stockpile of poems and two completed manuscripts, one on the poetic effect of modernism on Native American women and Chicana writers, the other a novel/memoir that weaves her parents' history together with the politics of land and memory in Colorado. Her writing both traces patterns of meaning in the past and offers a vision for the future. As one stanza of her 2001 poem "Sublime Strength Reclamations" suggests:

> Do no harm for you can dance,
> Make music, sing away slavery, and
> Piece impatience to bead arrangements.
> In your heart's barometer, create atoms.

She invokes the power of words, averring that "lyrics alone can soothe the restless serpents," and she reminds readers of their own power: "You can charm the snakes."

See also Feminism; Literature

SOURCES: Binder, Wolfgang, ed. 1985. "Bernice Zamora." In *Partial Autobiographies: Interviews with Twenty Chicano Poets*, 221–229. Erlangen: Palm and Enke; Desai, Parul. 1985. "Interview with Bernice Zamora, a Chicana Poet." *Imagine: International Chicano Poetry Journal* 2, no. 1 (Summer): 26–39; Zamora, Bernice. 1994. *Releasing Serpents*. Tempe, AZ: Bilingual Press/Editorial Bilingüe; ———. 2001. "Sublime Strength Reclamations." Manuscript; Zamora, Bernice, and José Armas, eds. 1980. *Chicano Literary Criticism, Chicano Short Stories, Barrio Oral History, Chicano Poetry Anthology*. Albuquerque: Pajarito Publications; Zamora, Bernice, José Armas, and Michael Reed, eds. 1980. *Flor y Canto IV and V: An Anthology of Chicano Literature*. Albuquerque: Pajarito Publications.

Valerie Matsumoto

ZÁRATE, ROSA MARTA (1942–)

Born in Guadalajara, Jalisco, Mexico, in 1942, Rosa Marta Zárate immigrated to the United States in 1966 as a member of the Sisters of the Blessed Sacrament. Her family's involvement in church activities and charitable works influenced her decision to become a women religious or sister at the age of eighteen. "I wanted to be doing what the seminarians were doing, studying theology and organizing activities for students. I didn't want to have a boyfriend. . . . I wanted to serve, that is why I entered the convent."

Zárate and her religious community journeyed to the United States to establish a convent and school in San Ysidro, California. They quickly experienced exploitation and discrimination. "We were teaching the children for less pay than the Irish sisters before us and the priest was always ridiculing us." Meeting with an organization of Chicana sisters, Las Hermanas, in 1971 exposed Zárate to the challenges of social change. Initially she believed, "Las Hermanas was too radical. Little by little I began to see they had something to say . . . then I saw

Rosa Marta Zárate singing protest songs at the UCLA student hunger strike in 1992. Photograph by and courtesy of Lara Medina.

them as very free, *mujeres muy libres.*" Involvement with Las Hermanas led Zárate to become the first Mexicana in Latino ministry for the Diocese of San Diego in 1973 at a time when the U.S. Roman Catholic Church had only begun to acknowledge the distinct culture of Mexican American Catholics. Her own religious community disapproved of her position and prohibited her from sharing her work with the other sisters. Zárate's exposure to Latin American liberation theology influenced her organization of youth choirs, ministries for the laity, and *comunidades eclesiales de base* (grassroots or small church communities).

Her reputation as a community organizer took her to the San Bernardino Diocese in 1978, where she took the position of coordinator of the Department of Evangelization and Catechesis for Hispanics (DECH). She worked closely with Father Patricio Guillen, who supported her ideology. Her teachings on liberation theology eventually proved too radical for her superiors and some of her peers. Bishop Phillip Straling of San Bernardino branded her a Communist and ultimately forced her to leave her position as coordinator. Father Guillen was reassigned, and DECH was placed under new leadership. Receiving no support from her religious community, Zárate filed a $1.5-million lawsuit against the diocese alleging sexual discrimination, fraud, and breach of contract.

Losing her suit in 1994 has not discouraged Zárate from working with impoverished Chicano/Mexicano communities. She continues to organize small base communities through *calpulli,* a network of cooperatives in San Bernardino County emphasizing economic self-empowerment and cultural knowledge. Zárate and Guillen work closely with a team of laity in successfully applying the tenets of liberation theology in southern California. The inspiration for their efforts comes not only from liberation theology but also from knowledge about the economic systems of their Mesoamerican ancestors. The cooperative system, or *calpulli,* stresses that social and economic change is possible through collective action.

In addition to her strong leadership abilities, Zárate is an internationally recognized composer and singer of *la nueva canción* music echoing themes of justice and self-determination of oppressed peoples. Zárate travels frequently to Chiapas, Mexico, to assist textile cooperatives operated by indigenous women and to participate in the Zapatista struggle as a civil rights observer. Her revolutionary vision of the role of the church in society has not faded.

See also Las Hermanas; Nuns, Contemporary

SOURCES: Cadena, Gilbert R., and Lara Medina. 1998. "Liberation Theology and Social Change: Chicanas and Chicanos in the Catholic Church." In *Chicanas and Chicanos in Contemporary Society,* ed. Roberto M. DeAnda. Needham Heights, MA: Allyn and Bacon; Medina, Lara. 2004. *Las Hermanas: Chicana/Latina Religious-Political Activism in the U.S. Catholic Church.* Philadelphia: Temple University Press; Ruiz, Vicki L. 1998. *From out of the Shadows: Mexican Women in Twentieth-Century America.* New York: Oxford University Press.

Lara Medina

ZÚÑIGA, ALEJANDRA ROJAS (1923–)

Born in Gonzalez, Texas, on May 17, 1923, Alejandra Rojas Zúñiga was one of eleven children who helped her father, Boreteo Rojas, and mother, Zarita Ruiz, work in the fields of cotton and sugarcane. The fields were a major part of the Rojases' family life because their produce yielded money for the family to survive. Strong family ties and a work ethic made the difficulties of the depression and World War II a learning experience, according to Alejandra Rojas Zúñiga. "It was rough for us attending school in Texas because discrimination was bad there. I remember trying to get along with all the kids in the classroom, but they looked at us like we didn't belong there."

Gradually Rojas Zúñiga's older brothers left Gonzalez to work in San Antonio. The family eventually followed, and Rojas Zúñiga attended Burbank High School. The family traveled between San Antonio and Michigan, always looking for opportunities to work. They traveled to Michigan every year and eventually settled there in 1942.

"At the time when World War II started in 1941, our family got word that there was an attack on Pearl Harbor," Rojas Zúñiga recalled. Not long after that her brothers were drafted. She believes that the reason all of her brothers served in the U.S. Army is that the government was targeting Hispanics to go into the military.

After her brothers were drafted, Rojas Zúñiga looked for work in Greenville, Michigan, to support the family. Working in a plant, she saved enough money to attend the School of Cosmetology in Saginaw, where she eventually opened her own beauty shop after finishing beauty school in 1948.

Rojas Zúñiga married Tom Zúñiga and started a family in 1947. They settled in Saginaw, where the couple raised five children and managed to run the beauty shop while the children went to school. Through the support of her family, especially her brothers, Rojas Zúñiga became a member of the American GI Forum, the nation's largest group to support Ameri-

Alejandra Zúñiga. Courtesy of the U.S. Latino and Latina World War II Oral History Project, University of Texas, Austin.

can military veterans of Hispanic descent. The organization continues to advocate for Hispanics and is actively involved in issues concerning the Hispanic community.

The American GI Forum of the United States was founded on March 26, 1948, in Corpus Christi, Texas, by Dr. Héctor Pérez-García, a veteran of the Army Medical Corps during World War II. His goal was to provide good health care for veterans who needed it and were refused because they were of Mexican ancestry. The organization links Hispanic veterans together for the same cause in 500 chapters throughout thirty states.

Rojas Zúñiga became involved with the women's chapter in such issues as employment, housing, civil rights, women's programs, and youth activities. "I learned a lot from my own people joining this organization, because it is a national organization. Going to conventions, I learned and got acquainted with other people that make it into the higher world." "In Texas, there was so much discrimination," she said. "The returning veterans, like my brothers, were finding it hard to get help. The founder made it possible by organizing the American GI Forum nationwide. So with that, the organization started having chapters in different states." "One year I attended (a national convention), and I came back here to Saginaw and told the women's chapter that I was so tired of listening to the comments and people telling us we have problems with dropout rates. We started our program, Adopt-A-School, for the American GI Forum in 1974. I was also serving on the Women in Community Service National Board, which recruits boys and girls for the job corps centers in regions," Rojas Zúñiga remembered. "We've come a long way, and all of that is due to the knowledge that I have learned with my husband and brothers being in the military and Dr. García's efforts to educate children for the benefit of our Hispanics."

She is thankful that her parents gave their children the understanding and knowledge a big family needs, and she is proud of her children, who have decent jobs and did not have to struggle as her family did. "My mom passed down a tradition where she wanted all of us to work together and produce for one another," Rojas Zúñiga said. "It's a learning experience, and I feel good I am trying to do something."

See also World War II

SOURCES: Babb, Stephanie. 2003. "Veterans Group Has Been Educational Experience." *Narratives: Stories of U.S. Latinos and Latinas and World War II,* (U.S. Latino and Latina WWII Oral History Project, University of Texas at Austin) 4, no. 1 (Spring): 86; Zúñiga, Alejandra Rojas. 2002. Interviewed by Raul García Jr., Saginaw, MI, October 19.

Stephanie Babb

List of Biographical Entries

Art

Alvarez, Cecilia Concepción
Baca, Judith Francesca
Barraza, Santa Contreras
Hernández, Ester
Lomas Garza, Carmen
López, Yolanda
López Córdova, Gloria
Martínez, Agueda Salazar
Mendieta, Ana
Mesa-Bains, Amalia
Montemayor, Alice Dickerson
Romero Cash, Marie
Tufiño, Nitza
Valdez, Patssi

Athletics

Casals, Rosemary
Fernández, Beatrice "Gigi"
Fernández, Mary Joe
Gallegos, Carmen Cornejo
Lobo, Rebecca Rose
López, Nancy Marie

Aviation and Aerospace

De Acosta, Aida
Ochoa, Ellen
Pauwels Pfeiffer, Linda Lorena
Rodríguez McLean, Verneda

Business

Avila, María Elena
Barceló, María Gertrudis ("La Tules")
Barnard, Juana Josefina Cavasos
Briones, María Juana
Burciaga, Mirna Ramos
Calvillo, Ana María del Carmen
Ceja, Amelia Moran
De León, Patricia de la Garza

DiMartino, Rita
Gutiérrez, Luz Bazán
Hernández, Victoria
Herrera, Carolina
Lozano, Mónica Cecilia
McBride, Teresa N.
Muñoz, María del Carmen
Olivarez, Graciela
Otero-Smart, Ingrid
Reid, Victoria Comicrabit
Rodríguez, Hermelinda Morales
Rodríguez, Sofía
Sada, María G. "Chata"
Saralegui, Cristina
Toraño-Pantín, María Elena

Education

Agostini del Río, Amelia
Babín, María Teresa
Bencomo, Julieta Saucedo
Bernal, Martha
Caballero, Diana
Crawford, Mercedes Margarita Martínez
De Avila, Dolores C.
Del Castillo, Adelaida Rebecca
Esquivel, Yolanda Almaraz
Figueroa Mercado, Loida
Gómez-Potter, Socorro
González, Laura
González, Matiana
Henríquez Ureña, Camila
Herrera, María Cristina
Maldonado, Amelia Margarita
Meléndez, Sara
Mora, Magdalena
Navarro, M. Susana
Nieto, Sonia
Ontiveros, Manuela
Ortega, Carlota Ayala
Otero-Warren, Adelina
Pantoja, Antonia
Peñaranda, Ana Marcial

List of Biographical Entries

Quesada, Alicia Otilia
Quesada, Dora Ocampo
Ramírez, Emilia Schunior
Sánchez, María E.
Sosa-Riddell, Adaljiza
Ulibarrí Sánchez, Louise
Urquides, María Luisa Legarra
Varela, Beatriz

Film and Theater

Braga, Sonia
Colón, Miriam
Del Río, Dolores
Escalona, Beatríz ("La Chata Noloesca")
Fornés, María Irene
Hayworth, Rita
Jurado, Katy
Miranda, Carmen
Montez, María (María Africa Gracia Vidal)
Moreno, Rita (Rosa Dolores Alverio)
Prida, Dolores
Reid, Marita
Rivera, Chita
San Juan, Olga
Tovar, Lupita
Vélez, Lupe
Vélez-Mitchell, Anita
Welch, Raquel

Grassroots Community Activism and Civil Rights

Acosta Vice, Celia M.
Alatorre, Soledad "Chole"
Alvarez, Delia
Antonetty, Evelina López
Apodaca, Felicitas
Arocho, Juanita
Bernasconi, Socorro Hernández
Betanzos, Amalia V.
Blake, María DeCastro
Burciaga, Mirna Ramos
Caballero, Diana
Calderón, Rose Marie
Canales, Nohelia de los Angeles
Canino, María Josefa
Cardona, Alice
Castillo, Guadalupe
Castro, Rosie
Castro, Victoria M. "Vickie"
Cepeda-Leonardo, Margarita
Colón, Rufa Concepción Fernández "Concha"
Cotera, Martha
De Avila, Dolores C.

Del Castillo, Adelaida Rebecca
Espinosa-Mora, Deborah
Esquivel, Yolanda Almaraz
Fierro, Josefina
Flores, Francisca
Fontañez, Jovita
Gallegos, Carmen Cornejo
Garcíaz, María
Gómez Carbonell, María
Gómez-Potter, Socorro
Hernández, María Latigo
Hernández, Olivia
Herrada, Elena
Huerta, Cecilia Olivarez
Jiménez, María de los Angeles
López, María I.
López, Rosie
Lozano, Emma
Martínez, Demetria
Martínez, Elizabeth Sutherland "Betita"
Martínez, Frances Aldama
Martínez Santaella, Inocencia
Medina, Esther
Mercado, Victoria "Vicky"
Montes-Donnelly, Elba Iris
Mora, Magdalena
Morales, Iris
Nieto Gómez, Anna
Palacio-Grottola, Sonia
Pantoja, Antonia
Payán, Ilka Tanya
Reyes, Guadalupe
Robles Díaz, Inés
Rodríguez, Patricia
Sánchez, María Clemencia
Santiago, Petra
Saucedo, María del Jesús
Talamante, Olga
Torres, Alva
Torres, Lourdes
Treviño-Sauceda, Mily
Varela, María
Vásquez, Enriqueta Longeaux y
Vélez de Vando, Emelí
Zárate, Rosa Marta

Journalism

Alvarez, Aida
Alvarez, Linda
Arías, Anna María
Armiño, Franca de
Betances Jaeger, Clotilde
Carbonell, Anna
Casanova de Villaverde, Emilia

Idar Juárez, Jovita
Lozano, Alicia Guadalupe Elizondo
Lozano, Mónica Cecilia
Martínez, Demetria
Martínez, Elizabeth Sutherland "Betita"
Olivera, Mercedes
Quintero, Luisa
Saralegui, Cristina
Silva de Cintrón, Josefina "Pepiña"
Villarreal, Andrea and Teresa

Labor Activism

Betanzos, Amalia V.
Capetillo, Luisa
Chávez, Helen
Chávez-Thompson, Linda
De la Cruz, Jessie López
Durazo, María Elena
Escobar, Carmen Bernal
Govea, Jessica
Guillen Herrera, Rosalinda
Huerta, Dolores
Lucas, María Elena
Marshall, Guadalupe
Mercado, Victoria "Vicky"
Moreno, Luisa
Parsons, Lucia González
Patiño Río, Dolores
Ramírez, Sara Estela
Rodríguez, Patricia
Schechter, Esperanza Acosta Mendoza "Hope"
Tenayuca, Emma
Torres, Ida Inés
Treviño-Sauceda, Mily

Law

Callejo, Adelfa Botello
Echaveste, María
Hernández, Antonia
López, María I.
Madrid, Patricia A.
Martínez, Vilma S.
Morales-Horowitz, Nilda M.
Perales, Nina
Rodríguez, "Isabel" Hernández
Sánchez Garfunkel, Aura Luz

League of United Latin American Citizens

Acosta, Lucy
García, Eva Carrillo de
Gonzáles, Elvira Rodríguez de
Machuca, Ester
Méndez, Consuelo Herrera

Montemayor, Alice Dickerson
Ontiveros, Manuela
Orozco, Aurora Estrada
Sloss-Vento, Adela
Vásquez, Anna
Wolf, Esther Valladolid

Libraries

Belpré, Pura
López, Lillian
Miller, Esther
Núñez, Ana Rosa
Ruiz, Irene Hernández

Literature

Alfau Galván de Solalinde, Jesusa
Allende, Isabel
Alvarez, Julia
Anzaldúa, Gloria
Babín, María Teresa
Belpré, Pura
Betanzos, Amalia V.
Borrero Pierra, Juana
Cabeza de Baca, Fabiola
Cabrera, Lydia
Castillo, Ana
Cervantes, Lorna Dee
Chávez, Denise
Cisneros, Sandra
De Acosta, Mercedes
De Aragón, Uva
De Burgos, Julia
De la Cruz, Sor Juana Inés
De la Garza, Beatríz
Del Prado, Pura
Escajeda, Josefina
Espaillat, Rhina P.
Esteves, Sandra María
García, Cristina
García-Aguilera, Carolina
González Mireles, Jovita
Guerra, Fermina
Henríquez Ureña, Camila
Jaramillo, Cleofas Martínez
Martí de Cid, Dolores
Martínez, Demetria
Meléndez, Concha
Mistral, Gabriela (Lucila Godoy Alcayaga)
Mohr, Nicholasa
Mora, Patricia "Pat"
Moraga, Cherríe
Norte, Marisela
Núñez, Ana Rosa

List of Biographical Entries

Obejas, Achy
Ortiz Cofer, Judith
O'Shea, María Elena
Peña de Bordas, (Ana) Virginia de
Ramírez, Sara Estela
Ramírez de Arellano, Diana
Rivera, Roxana
Rodríguez Cabral, María Cristina
Rodríguez de Tió, Lola
Ruiz de Burton, María Amparo
Sánchez Garfunkel, Aura Luz
Sepúlveda, Emma
Trambley, Estela Portillo
Vicioso Sánchez, Sherezada "Chiqui"
Viramontes, Helena María
Zamora, Bernice B. Ortiz

Medicine and Science

Aragón, Jesusita
Novello, Antonia Coello
Ochoa, Ellen
Rodríguez-Trias, Helen
Vidal, Irma

Military Service

Bozak, Carmen Contreras
Novello, Antonia Coello
Phillips, Carmen Romero
Quesada, Dora Ocampo
Rodríguez McLean, Verneda
Vásquez, Anna
Velázquez, Loreta Janeta

Music and Dance

Alonzo, Ventura
Arroyo, Martina
Baez, Joan Chandos
Boyar, Monica
Canales, Laura
Carr, Vikki
"Charo" (María Rosario Pilar Martínez Molina Baeza)
Cruz, Celia
De Arteaga, Genoveva
Dueto Carmen y Laura
Estefan, Gloria
Fernández, Rosita
García, Providencia "Provi"
Guerrero, Rosa
Hamlin, Rosalie Méndez
Hernández, Victoria
Hinojosa, Tish
"La Lupe" (Guadalupe Victoria Yoli Raymond)

Lares, Michelle Yvette "Shelly"
León, Tania
Mendoza, Lydia
Miranda, Carmen
Moreno, Rita (Rosa Dolores Alverio)
Morillo, Irma
Olivarez, Graciela
Pérez, Graciela
Quintanilla Pérez, Selena
Ramírez, Tina
Rico, Angelina Moreno
Rivera, Chita
Rivera, Graciela
Silva, Chelo
Torres, Patsy (Patricia Donita)
Vélez-Mitchell, Anita
Vidaurri, Rita
Ybarra, Eva

Philanthropy

Avila, María Elena
Callejo, Adelfa Botello
Gutiérrez, Luz Bazán
Lobo, Rebecca Rose
Lozano, Alicia Guadalupe Elizondo
Meléndez, Sara
Munguía, Carolina Malpica de
Olivarez, Graciela
Quesada, Alicia Otilia
Quesada, Dora Ocampo

Politics

Alvarez, Aida
Arroyo, Carmen E.
Baca Barragán, Polly
Cabrera, Angelina "Angie"
Casal, Lourdes
Chacón, Soledad Chávez
Chávez, Linda
Collazo, Rosa Cortéz
Cotera, Martha
Davis, Grace Montañez
DiMartino, Rita
Echaveste, María
Figueroa Mercado, Loida
Flores, Diana
Grau, María Leopoldina "Pola"
Gutiérrez, Luz Bazán
Hernández, María Latigo
Kimbell, Sylvia Rodríguez
Lebrón, Dolores "Lolita"
Lee Tapia, Consuelo
Madrid, Patricia A.

Martínez, Anita N.
Mederos y Cabañas de González, Elena Inés
Méndez, Olga A.
Mendoza, María Estella Altamirano
Mojica-Hammer, Ruth
Molina, Gloria
Morales-Horowitz, Nilda M.
O'Donnell, Sylvia Colorado
Ortiz y Pino de Kleven, María Concepción "Concha"
Otero-Warren, Adelina
Pedroso, Paulina
Rangel, Irma
Rincón de Gautier, Felisa
Rivera, Aurelia "Yeya"
Rodríguez de Tió, Lola
Rodríguez Remeneski, Shirley
Ros-Lehtinen, Ileana
Roybal-Allard, Lucille
Sánchez, Loretta
Solis, Hilda L.
Souchet, Clementina
Toraño-Pantín, María Elena
Velázquez, Nydia M.
Wilcox, Mary Rose Garrido

Public Health and Social Work

Abarca, Apolonia "Polly" Muñoz
Del Valle, Carmen
Delgado, Jane L.
Olivares, Olga Ballesteros
Rodríguez-Trias, Helen
San Antonio, Ana Gloria
Sánchez Cruz, Rebecca
Smith, Plácida Elvira García
Wolf, Esther Valladolid

Religion

Arguello, María de la Concepción (Sister María Dominica)
De la Cruz, Sor Juana Inés
Ferré Aguayo, Sor Isolina
Figueroa, Belén
Florez, Encarnación Villarreal Escobedo
García Cortese, Aimee
Guzmán, Madre María Dominga
León, Ruth Esther Soto ("La Hermana León")
Lorenzana, Apolinaria
Nuestra Señora de la Divina Providencia
Pérez, Eulalia
Rivera Martínez, Domitila
Rosado Rousseau, Leoncia ("Mamá Léo")
"Sister Carmelita" (Carmela Zapata Bonilla Marrero)
Soto Feliciano, Carmen Lillian "Lily"
Tarango, Yolanda

Urrea, Teresa
Virgen de Guadalupe
Virgen de la Caridad del Cobre
Zárate, Rosa Marta

Spanish Borderlands and Colonies, 1521–1900

Arballo, María Feliciana
Arguello, María de la Concepción (Sister María Dominica)
Avila, Modesta
Barceló, María Gertrudis ("La Tules")
Barnard, Juana Josefina Cavasos
Borrero Pierra, Juana
Briones, María Juana
Callis de Fages, Eulalia Francesca y Josepha
Calvillo, Ana María del Carmen
Carrillo de Fitch, Josefa
Casanova de Villaverde, Emilia
Cossio y Cisneros, Evangelina
Cuero, Delfina
De la Cruz, Sor Juana Inés
De León, Patricia de la Garza
Jaramillo, Cleofas Martínez
La Llorona
La Malinche (Malinalli Tenepal)
Lorenzana, Apolinaria
Martínez Santaella, Inocencia
Mugarrieta, Elvira Virginia (Babe Bean; Jack Bee Garland)
Nuestra Señora de la Divina Providencia
Parsons, Lucia González
Pérez, Eulalia
Pinedo, Encarnación
Reid, Victoria Comicrabit
Rodríguez, Josefa "Chepita"
Rodríguez de Tió, Lola
Ruiz, Bernarda
Ruiz de Burton, María Amparo
Swilling, Trinidad Escalante
Toypurina
Urrea, Teresa
Vallejo, Epifania de Guadalupe
Vallejo de Leese, María Paula Rosalía
Velázquez, Loreta Janeta
Virgen de Guadalupe
Virgen de la Caridad del Cobre

World War II

Abarca, Apolonia "Polly" Muñoz
Albelo, Carmen
Barrera, Plácida Peña
Bozak, Carmen Contreras
Chabram, Angie González
Córdova, Lina

List of Biographical Entries

Dimas, Beatrice Escadero
Esquivel, Gregoria
Guerrero, Victoria Partida
Kissinger, Beatrice Amado
Ledesma, Josephine
Moraga, Gloria Flores
Nerio, Trinidad

Ontiveros, Manuela
Phillips, Carmen Romero
Quesada, Dora Ocampo
Rodríguez McLean, Verneda
Sena, Elvira
Vásquez, Anna
Zúñiga, Alejandra Rojas

List of Organizations

Antonio Maceo Brigade
Aprenda y Superese
Asociación Nacional México-Americana (ANMA)
ASPIRA
Cannery and Agricultural Workers Industrial Union
    (CAWIU)
Cántico de la Mujer Latina
Casita Maria, New York
Centro de Acción Social Autónomo (CASA)
Centro Hispano Católico
Centro Mater
Chicana Caucus/National Women's Political Caucus
Chicana Rights Project
Chicanos Por La Causa (CPLC)
Círculo Cultural Isabel la Católica
Clínica de la Beneficencia Mexicana
Comisión Femenil Mexicana Nacional (CFMN)
Communist Party
Communities Organized for Public Service (COPS)
Community Service Organization (CSO)
Congreso del Pueblo
Cuban and Puerto Rican Revolutionary Party
Cuban Women's Club
Dominican American National Roundtable (DANR)
El Congreso de Pueblos de Hablan Española
El Movimiento Estudiantil Chicano de Aztlán (MEChA)
El Rescate
Friendly House, Phoenix
Fuerza Unida
Ganados del Valle
Head Start
Hijas de Cuauhtémoc
Hispanic Mother-Daugher Program (HMDP)
Houchen Settlement, El Paso
Hull-House, Chicago
International Ladies Garment Workers' Union (ILGWU)
La Mujer Obrera

La Raza Unida Party
Labor Unions
Las Hermanas
League of United Latin American Citizens (LULAC)
Líderes Campesinas
Mexican American Legal Defense and Educational Fund
    (MALDEF)
Mexican American Women's National Association
    (MANA)
Mexican Mothers' Club, University of Chicago Settlement
    House
Mothers of East Los Angeles (MELA)
Mujeres in Action, Sunset Park, Brooklyn
Mujeres Latinas en Acción (MLEA)
Mujeres por la Raza
National Association for Chicana and Chicano Studies
    (NACCS)
National Association of Puerto Rican/Hispanic Social
    Workers (NAPRHSW)
National Chicana Conference
National Conference of Puerto Rican Women (NACOPRW)
National Council of La Raza (NCLR)
National Hispanic Feminist Conference
National Puerto Rican Forum
New Economics for Women (NEW)
New York City Mission Society (NYCMS)
Pilsen Neighbors Community Council
Puerto Rican Association for Community Affairs (PRACA)
Southwest Voter Registration Education Project (SVREP)
Substitute Auxiliary Teachers (SATs)
Tabaqueros' Unions
Tempe Normal School
United Cannery, Agricultural, Packing, and Allied Workers
    of America (UCAPAWA/FTA)
United Farm Workers of America (UFW)
Vanguardia Puertorriqueña
Young Lords

Selected Readings in Latina History

Acosta, Teresa Paloma, and Ruthe Winegarten. *Las Tejanas: 300 Years of History*. Austin: University of Texas Press, 2003.

Acosta-Belén, Edna, Margarita Benítez, José E. Cruz, Yvonne González-Rodríguez, Clara E. Rodríguez, Carlos E. Santiago, Azara Santiago-Rivera, and Barbara Sjostrom. *"Adíos Borinquen querida": The Puerto Rican Diaspora, Its History and Contributions*. Albany, NY: Center for Latino, Latin American, and Caribbean Studies, SUNY, 2000.

Alvarez, Julia. *Something to Declare*. New York: Plume, 1998.

Anzaldúa, Gloria. *Interviews = Entrevistas*. Ed. Ana Louise Keating. New York: Routledge, 2000.

Aparicio, Frances. *Listening to Salsa: Gender, Latin Popular Music, and Puerto Rican Cultures*. Hanover, NH: University Press of New England, 1998.

Aquino, María Pilar, Daisy L. Machado, and Jeanette Rodríguez, eds. *A Reader in Latina Feminist Theology*. Austin: University of Texas Press, 2002.

Blocker, Jane. *Where Is Ana Mendieta? Identity, Performativity, and Exile*. Durham, NC: Duke University Press, 1999.

Bouvier, Virginia M. *Women and the Conquest of California, 1542–1840: Codes of Silence*. Tucson: University of Arizona Press, 2001.

Brooks, James F. *Captives and Cousins: Slavery, Kinship, and Community in the Southwest Borderlands*. Chapel Hill: University of North Carolina Press, 2002.

Cantú, Norma, and Olga Najéra-Ramírez, eds. *Chicana Traditions: Continuity and Change*. Urbana: University of Illinois Press, 2002.

Casas, María Raquel. *"Married to a Daughter of the Land": Interethnic Marriages in California, 1820–1880*. Reno: University of Nevada Press, 2006.

Castañeda, Antonia I. "The Political Economy of Nineteenth-Century Stereotypes of Californianas." In *Between Borders: Essays on Mexican/Chicana History*, ed. Adelaida Del Castillo, 213–238. Encino, CA: Floricanto Press, 1990.

Castillo, Ana. *Massacre of the Dreamers: Essays on Xicanisma*. New York: Plume, 1995.

Chávez, Marisela R. " 'We Lived and Breathed and Worked the Movement': The Contradictions and Rewards of Chicana/Mexicana Activism in el Centro de Acción Social Autónomo-Hermandad General de Trabajadores (CASA-HGT), Los Angeles, 1975–1978." In *Las obreras: Chicana Politics of Work and Family*, ed. Vicki L. Ruiz, 83–105. Los Angeles: UCLA Chicano Studies Research Center Publications, 2000.

Chávez-García, Miroslava. "Guadalupe Trujillo: Race, Culture, and Justice in Mexican Los Angeles." In *The Human Tradition in California*, ed. Clark Davis and David Igler, 31–46. Wilmington, DE: Scholarly Resources, 2002.

———. *Negotiating Conquest: Gender and Power in California, 1770s to 1880s*. Tucson: University of Arizona Press, 2004.

Cocco De Filippis, Daisy, ed. *Documents of Dissidence: Selected Writings by Dominican Women*. New York: CUNY Dominican Studies Institute, 2000.

Cotera, María Eugenia. "Engendering a 'Dialectics of Our America': Jovita González's Pluralist Dialogue as Feminist Testimonio." In *Las obreras: Chicana Politics of Work and Family*, ed. Vicki L. Ruiz, 237–256. Los Angeles: UCLA Chicano Studies Research Center Publications, 2000.

Dávila, Arlene. *Barrio Dreams: Puerto Ricans, Latinos, and the Neoliberal City*. Berkeley: University of California Press, 2004.

de la Torre, Adela, and Beatríz Pesquera, eds. *Building With Our Hands: New Directions in Chicana Studies*. Berkeley: University of California Press, 1993.

Deutsch, Sarah. *No Separate Refuge: Culture, Class, and Gender on an Anglo-Hispanic Frontier in the American Southwest, 1880–1940*. New York: Oxford University Press, 1987.

Doran, Terry, Janet Satterfield, and Chris Stade, eds. *A Road Well Traveled: Three Generations of Cuban American Women*. Fort Wayne, IN: Latin American Educational Center, 1988.

Flores, María Eva. "St. Joseph's Parish, Ft. Stockton, Texas, 1875–1945: The Forging of Identity and Community." *U.S. Catholic Historian* 21 (Winter 2003): 13–31.

Flores, William, and Rina Benmayor, eds. *Latino Cultural Citizenship*. Boston: Beacon Press, 1997.

Fregoso, Rosa Linda. *MeXicana Encounters: The Making of Social Identities on the Borderlands*. Berkeley: University of California Press, 2003.

García, María Cristina. "Adapting to Exile: Cuban Women in the United States, 1959–1973." *Latino Studies Journal* 2, no. 2 (May 1991): 17–33.

———. *Havana USA: Cuban Exiles and Cuban Americans in South Florida, 1959–1994*. Berkeley: University of California Press, 1996.

García, Matt. *A World of Its Own: Race, Labor, and Citrus in the Making of Greater Los Angeles, 1900–1970*. Chapel Hill: University of North Carolina Press, 2001.

Gil-Montero, Martha. *Brazilian Bombshell: The Biography of Carmen Miranda*. New York: Donald I. Fine, 1989.

Goldman, Anne E. " 'I Think Our Romance Is Spoiled,' or, Crossing Genres: California History in Helen Hunt Jackson's *Ramona* and María Amparo Ruiz de Burton's *The Squatter and the Don*." In *Over the Edge: Remapping the American*

West, ed. Valerie J. Matsumoto and Blake Allmendinger, 65–84. Berkeley: University of California Press, 1999.

González, Deena J. *Refusing the Favor: The Spanish-Mexican Women of Santa Fe, 1820–1880.* New York: Oxford University Press, 1999.

González, Jovita. "Jovita González: Early Life and Education." In *Dew on the Thorn*, ed. José E. Limón. Houston: Arte Público Press, 1997.

Gordon, Linda. *The Great Arizona Orphan Abduction.* Cambridge, MA: Harvard University Press, 1999.

Gutiérrez, Ramón. "Community, Patriarchy, and Individualism: The Politics of Chicano History." *American Quarterly* 45 (1993): 44–72.

———. *When Jesus Came, the Corn Mothers Went Away: Marriage, Sexuality, and Power in New Mexico, 1500–1846.* Stanford, CA: Stanford University Press, 1991.

Haas, Lisbeth. *Conquests and Historical Identities in California, 1769–1936.* Berkeley: University of California Press, 1995.

Hart, Dianne. *Undocumented in L.A.: An Immigrant's Story.* Wilmington, DE: Scholarly Resources, 1997.

Henkes, Robert. *Latin American Women Artists of the United States: The Works of 33 Twentieth-Century Women.* Jefferson, NC: McFarland, 1999.

Hewitt, Nancy A. *Southern Discomfort: Women's Activism in Tampa, Florida, 1880s–1920s.* Urbana: University of Illinois Press, 2001.

Hondagneu-Sotelo, Pierrette. *Doméstica: Immigrant Workers Cleaning and Caring in the Shadows of Affluence.* Berkeley: University of California Press, 2001.

———, ed. *Gender and U.S. Immigration: Contemporary Trends.* Berkeley: University of California Press, 2004.

Jensen, Joan M. "Disenfranchisement Is a Disgrace: Women and Politics in New Mexico, 1900–1940." *New Mexico Historical Review* 56 (January 1981): 5–36.

Katz, Robert. *Naked by the Window: The Fatal Marriage of Carl Andre and Ana Mendieta.* New York: Atlantic Monthly Press, 1990.

Latina Feminist Group. *Telling to Live: Latina Feminist Testimonios.* Durham, NC: Duke University Press, 2001.

Leonard, Elizabeth D. *All the Daring of the Soldier: Women of the Civil War Armies.* New York: W. W. Norton, 1999.

Leyva, Yolanda Chávez. "Breaking the Silence: Putting Latina Lesbian History at the Center." In *New Lesbian Studies*, ed. Bonnie Zimmerman and Toni McNaron, 145–152. New York: Feminist Press, 1996.

Lucas, María Elena. *Forged under the Sun/Forjado bajo el sol: The Life of María Elena Lucas.* Ed. Fran Leeper Buss. Ann Arbor: University of Michigan Press, 1993.

Martin, Patricia Preciado, ed. *Beloved Land: An Oral History of Mexican Americans in Southern Arizona.* Tucson: University of Arizona Press, 2004.

———, *Songs My Mother Sang to Me: An Oral History of Mexican American Women.* Tucson: University of Arizona Press, 1992.

Matos Rodríguez, Felix V., and Linda C. Delgado, eds. *Puerto Rican Women's History: New Perspectives.* Armonk, NY: M. E. Sharpe, 1998.

Medina, Lara. *Las Hermanas: Chicana/Latina Religious-Political Activism in the U.S. Catholic Church.* Philadelphia: Temple University Press, 2004.

Menjívar, Cecilia. *Fragmented Ties: Salvadoran Immigrant Networks in America.* Berkeley: University of California Press, 2000.

Mirabel, Nancy Raquel. "*Ser de aquí*: Beyond the Cuban Exile Model." *Latino Studies* 1, no. 3 (November 2003): 366–382.

Montoya, María. *Lost in Translation: The Maxwell Land Grant and the Conflict over Land in the American West, 1840–1900.* Berkeley: University of California Press, 2000.

Mora, Pat. *Nepantla: Essays from the Land in the Middle.* Albuquerque: University of New Mexico Press, 1993.

Moraga, Cherríe, and Gloria Anzaldúa, eds. *This Bridge Called My Back: Writings by Radical Women of Color.* Watertown, MA: Persephone Press, 1981.

Moreno, Luisa. "Caravans of Sorrow: Noncitizen Americans of the Southwest." In *Between Two Worlds: Mexican Immigration in the United States*, ed. David G. Gutiérrez, 119–123. Wilmington, DE: Scholarly Resources, 1996.

Muñiz, Vicki. *Resisting Gentrification and Displacement: Voices of Puerto Rican Women of the Barrio.* New York: Garland, 1998.

Ochoa, María. *Creative Collectives: Chicana Painters Working in Community.* Albuquerque: University of New Mexico Press, 2003.

Orozco, Cynthia E. "Alice Dickerson Montemayor: Feminism and Mexican American Politics in the 1930s." In *Writing the Range: Race, Class, and Culture in the Women's West*, ed. Elizabeth Jameson and Susan Armitage, 435–456. Norman: University of Oklahoma Press, 1997.

Ortiz Cofer, Judith. *Woman in Front of the Sun: On Becoming a Writer.* Athens: University of Georgia Press, 2000.

Pantoja, Antonia. *Memoir of a Visionary.* Houston: Arte Público Press, 2002.

Pedraza, Silvia. "Beyond Black and White: Latinos and Social Science Research on Immigration, Race and Ethnicity in America." *Social Science History* 24 (Winter 2000): 697–826.

———. *Political and Economic Migrants to America: Cubans and Mexicans.* Austin: University of Texas Press, 1985.

Pérez, Emma. *The Decolonial Imaginary: Writing Chicanas into History.* Bloomington: Indiana University Press, 1999.

Pérez, Gina. *The Near Northwest Side Story: Migration, Displacement, and Puerto Rican Families.* Berkeley: University of California Press, 2004.

Pessar, Patricia. "Sweatshop Workers and Domestic Ideologies: Dominican Women in the New York Apparel Industry." *International Journal of Urban Regional Research* 18, no. 1 (March 1994): 127–142.

Pitti, Gina Marie. "The *Sociedades Guadalupanas* in the San Francisco Archdiocese, 1942–1962." *U.S. Catholic Historian* 21 (Winter 2003): 83–98.

Ponce, Mary Helen. *Hoyt Street: An Autobiography.* Albuquerque: University of New Mexico Press, 1993.

Prieto, Yolanda. "Cuban Women in New Jersey: Gender Relations and Change." In *Seeking Common Ground: Multidisciplinary Studies of Immigrant Women in the United States*, ed. Donna R. Gabaccia, 185–210. Westport, CT: Greenwood Press, 1992.

Rebolledo, Tey Diana, and Eliana S. Rivero, eds. *Infinite Divisions: An Anthology of Chicana Literature.* Tucson: University of Arizona Press, 1993.

Rodríguez, Clara. *Heroes, Lovers, and Others: The Story of Lati-*

nos in Hollywood. Washington, DC: Smithsonian Books, 2004.

————, ed. *Latin Looks: Images of Latinas and Latinos in the U.S. Media.* Boulder, CO: Westview Press, 1997.

Rodríquez-Estrada, Alicia. "Dolores Del Río and Lupe Vélez: Images on and off the Screen, 1925–1944." In *Writing the Range: Race, Class, and Culture in the Women's West,* ed. Elizabeth Jameson and Susan Armitage, 475–492. Norman: University of Oklahoma Press, 1997.

Rose, Margaret. "César Chávez and Dolores Huerta: Partners in 'La Causa.'" In *César Chávez,* ed. Richard Etulain. Boston: Bedford Press, 2002.

————. "From the Fields to the Picket Line: Huelga Women and the Boycott, 1965–1975." *Labor History* 31, no. 3 (Summer 1990): 271–293.

Ruiz, Vicki L. *Cannery Women, Cannery Lives: Mexican Women, Unionization, and the California Food Processing Industry, 1930–1950.* Albuquerque: University of New Mexico Press, 1987.

————. *From out of the Shadows: Mexican Women in Twentieth-Century America.* New York: Oxford University Press, 1998.

————, ed. *Las obreras: Chicana Politics of Work and Family.* Los Angeles: UCLA Chicano Studies Research Center Publications, 2000.

Ruiz, Vicki L., and Virginia Sánchez Korrol, eds. *Latina Legacies: Identity, Biography, and Community.* New York: Oxford University Press, 2005.

Ruiz, Vicki L., and Susan Tiano, eds. *Women on the U.S.-Mexico Border: Responses to Change.* Winchester, MA: Allen and Unwin, 1987; rpt. Westview Press, 1991.

Ruiz de Burton, María Amparo. [C. Loyal, pseud]. *The Squatter and the Don: A Novel Descriptive of Contemporary Occurrences in California.* San Francisco: Samuel Carson and Co., 1885. Rpt. with an introduction and notes by Rosaura Sánchez and Beatrice Pita. Houston: Arte Público Press, 1992; 2nd ed., 1997.

————. *Who Would Have Thought It?* Philadelphia: J. B. Lippincott, 1872. Rpt. with an introduction and notes by Rosaura Sánchez and Beatrice Pita. Houston: Arte Público Press, 1995.

Salas, Elizabeth. "Ethnicity, Gender, and Divorce: Issues in the 1922 Campaign by Adelina Otero Warren for the U.S. House of Representatives." *New Mexico Historical Review* 70 (October 1995): 367–382.

Sánchez, George J. *Becoming Mexican American: Ethnicity, Culture, and Identity in Chicano Los Angeles, 1900–1945.* New York: Oxford University Press, 1993.

Sánchez, Rosaura. *Telling Identities.* Minneapolis: University of Minnesota Press, 1995.

Sánchez González, Lisa. *Boricua Literature: A Literary History of the Puerto Rican Diaspora.* New York: New York University Press, 2001.

Sánchez Korrol, Virginia. *From Colonia to Community: The History of Puerto Ricans in New York City.* 2nd ed. Berkeley: University of California Press, 1994.

————. *Teaching U.S. Puerto Rican History.* Washington, DC: American Historical Association, 1999.

Sánchez Walsh, Arlene. *Latino Pentecostal Identity.* New York: Columbia University Press, 2003.

Torres, Lourdes, and Immaculada Pertusa, eds. *Tortilleras: Hispanic and U.S. Latina Lesbian Expression.* Philadelphia: Temple University Press, 2003.

Tywoniak, Frances Esquibel, and Mario T. García. *Migrant Daughter: Coming of Age as a Mexican American Woman.* Berkeley: University of California Press, 2000.

Valle, Isabel. *Fields of Toil: A Migrant Family's Journey.* Pullman: Washington State University Press, 1994.

Veciana-Suarez, Ana. *Birthday Parties in Heaven: Thoughts on Love, Life, Grief, and Other Matters of the Heart.* New York: Plume, 2000.

Velázquez, Loreta Janeta. *The Woman in Battle: The Civil War Narrative of Loreta Janeta Velázquez, Cuban Woman and Confederate Soldier.* With an introduction by Jesse Alemán. Madison: University of Wisconsin Press, 2003.

Villarreal, Mary Ann. "The Synapses of Struggle: Martha Cotera and Tejana Activism." In *Las obreras: Chicana Politics of Work and Family,* ed. Vicki L. Ruiz, 273–295. Los Angeles: UCLA Chicano Studies Research Center Publications, 2000.

Weber, Devra. "Historical Perspectives on Mexican Transnationalism." *Social Justice* 26, no. 3 (Fall 1999): 39–58.

————. "*Raiz Fuerte*: Oral History and Mexicana Farmworkers." *Oral History Review* 17, no. 2 (1989): 47–62.

Whaley, Charlotte. *Nina Otero-Warren of Santa Fe.* Albuquerque: University of New Press, 1994.

Whelan, Carmen Teresa. *From Puerto Rico to Philadelphia: Puerto Rican Workers and Postwar Economies.* Philadelphia: Temple University Press, 2001.

Yarbro-Bejarano, Yvonne. *The Wounded Heart: Writing on Cherríe Moraga.* Austin: University of Texas Press, 2001.

Yohn, Susan. *A Contest of Faiths: Missionary Women and Pluralism in the American Southwest.* Ithaca, NY: Cornell University Press, 1995.

Zamora, Emilio, Cynthia Orozco, and Rodolfo Rocha, eds. *Mexican Americans in Texas History: Selected Essays.* Austin: Texas State Historical Association, 2001.

Zavella, Patricia. *Women's Work and Chicano Families.* Ithaca, NY: Cornell University Press, 1987.

Notes on Contributors

Edna Acosta-Belén is Distinguished Service Professor of Latin American and Caribbean Studies and Women's Studies at the State University of New York at Albany and director of the Center for Latino, Latin American, and Caribbean Studies (CELAC). Her publications include *"Adíos Borinquen querida": The Puerto Rican Diaspora, Its History and Contributions* (with Margarita Benítez, José E. Cruz, Yvonne González-Rodríguez, Clara E. Rodríguez, Carlos E. Santiago, Azara Santiago-Rivera, and Barbara Sjostrom, 2000) and *Women in the Latin American Development Process* (with Christine E. Bose, 1995).

José M. Alamillo is an assistant professor of Comparative American Cultures at Washington State University. He researches the intersections of labor, leisure, sport, and politics among Mexican Americans in twentieth-century California. Recent publications include "Mexican American Baseball: Masculinity, Racial Struggle, and Labor Politics in Southern California, 1930–1950," in *Sports Matters: Race, Recreation, and Culture*, ed. John Bloom and Michael Willard (2002). He is the author of *Bitter Lemons, Sweet Lemonade: Mexican Labor and Leisure in a California Town* (forthcoming).

Jonathan Alexander was a student in a class dedicated to the U.S. Latinos and Latinas in World War II Oral History Project at the University of Texas, Austin.

Benny Andrés Jr. teaches history at Imperial Valley College. His essay "La Plaza Vieja (Old Town Albuquerque): The Transformation of a Hispano Village, 1880s–1950s" is in *The Contested Homeland: A Chicano History of New Mexico* (2000). His dissertation, "Power and Control in Imperial Valley, California: Nature, Agribusiness, Labor and Race Relations, 1900–1940," was completed in 2003.

Frances R. Aparicio is a professor and director of the Latin American and Latino Studies program at the University of Illinois, Chicago Circle. Among her many publications are *Listening to Salsa: Gender, Latin Popular Music, and Puerto Rican Cultures* (1998) and *Latino Voices* (1994).

Linda Apodaca studies Chicana historiography and feminism, the history of the Los Angeles Community Service

Organization, and the 1960s counterculture movement. She holds a Ph.D. in comparative cultures from the University of California, Irvine.

Bettina Aptheker is a professor of Women's Studies at the University of California, Santa Cruz. She is the author of several books, including *The Morning Breaks: The Trial of Angela Davis* (1976, 1999), *Woman's Legacy: Essays on Race, Sex, and Class in American History* (1982), and *Tapestries of Life: Women's Work, Women's Consciousness, and the Meaning of Daily Existence* (1989).

Gabriela F. Arredondo is an assistant professor of Latin American and Latina/o Studies at the University of California, Santa Cruz. She wrote "Navigating Ethno-racial Currents: Mexicans in Chicago 1919–1939, *Journal of Urban History* (2004) and co-edited *Chicana Feminisms: A Critical Reader* (with Aida Hurtado, Norma Klahn, Olga Najera-Ramírez, and Patricia Zavella, 2003). She is the author of *Mexican Chicago: Race, Identity, and Nation, 1919–1939* (forthcoming).

Bruce Ashcroft is an air force historian, Headquarters Air Education and Training Command (AETC) History Office, Randolph AFB, Texas. He has been active in air force education and training heritage and developed a World Wide Web site and a CD-ROM describing AETC and air force history. He authored *The Territorial History of Socorro, New Mexico* (1988), and *In Remembrance: The Centennial History of Trinity Presbyterian Church* (1991).

Carole Autori is a doctoral student in history at the University of California, Irvine. As an undergraduate at UC Irvine, she was a Chancellor's scholar and the 2003 Shirley Hine scholar in history. She is a former television and documentary film producer.

Stephanie Babb was a student in a class dedicated to the U.S. Latinos and Latinas in World War II Oral History Project at the University of Texas, Austin.

Bettie Baca is a consultant with the firm Alex Rodríquez and Associates. She was a senior member of the Clinton

Notes on Contributors

administration from 1994 to 2001, serving first as assistant director of the Minority Business Development Agency and later as executive secretary of the U.S. Department of Commerce under the late secretary Ronald H. Brown.

David Badillo is a historian who conducts research on Latinos/as in the United States, published a monograph on Latinos in Michigan (2003), and has recently completed a book on Latinos and urban Catholicism. He has taught at Lehman College, CUNY, the University of Notre Dame, Brooklyn College, CUNY, the University of Illinois at Chicago, the University of California at Santa Cruz, and Wayne State University.

Francisco Balderrama is a professor of Chicano Studies and history at California State University, Los Angeles. He coauthored *Decade of Betrayal: Mexican Repatriation in the 1930s* (1995), and published *In Defense of La Raza, The Los Angeles Mexican Consulate, and the Mexican Community, 1929 to 1936* (1982).

Victor Becerra holds an M.A. and C.Phil. in urban planning from the University of California, Los Angeles. He directs the Community Outreach Partnership Center (COPC) at the School of Social Ecology, University of California, Irvine, and engages in applied research initiatives, service learning, and outreach activities to foster community development.

Julia Bencomo Lobaco is an award-winning Mexican American journalist and was editor of *VISTA* magazine. During her tenure at *VISTA* she was named one of the 100 most influential Spanish-language journalists in the United States (2001) by the Hispanic Media 100. She is also an independent consultant and writer/editor.

Maylei Blackwell is an assistant professor in the César Chávez Center for Interdisciplinary Instruction in Chicano Studies at the University of California, Los Angeles. Her research interests include globalization, oral history, and transnational cultures in the Americas. She is writing a book on early Chicana feminism.

Carlos Kevin Blanton is an assistant professor of history at Texas A&M University. In addition to articles on Mexican American education in the *Pacific Historical Review* and *Social Science Quarterly*, his monograph *The Strange Career of Bilingual Education in Texas, 1836–1981* was published in 2004.

Andrea Boardman is executive director of the William P. Clements Center for Southwest Studies, Southern Methodist University. She was the writer and producer of "U.S.-Mexican War, 1846–1848" for PBS and KERA-TV and designed the exhibition *Destination Mexico: A Foreign Land a Step Away—U.S. Tourism to Mexico, 1880s–1950s* at the DeGoyler Library, Southern Methodist University.

Ramón Bosque-Pérez is a researcher at the Center for Puerto Rican Studies, Hunter College, CUNY. With José Javier Colón-Morera he coauthored *Las carpetas: Persecución política y derechos civiles en Puerto Rico* (1997). He is the co-editor of *Puerto Rico under Colonial Rule: Political Persecution and the Quest for Human Rights* (with Colón-Morera, 2005).

Margie Brown-Coronel is a Ph.D. candidate in history at the University of California, Irvine. Becoming a Latina historian has been her dream since her undergraduate days at the University of California, Berkeley. She is most interested in late-nineteenth-century Californianas and early-twentieth-century Mexican immigration.

Enrique M. Buelna is a Ph.D. candidate in history at the University of California, Irvine. His research interests include labor, working-class social movements, race and ethnic relations, and environmental justice. He has a tenure-track position in history at Cabrillo College in Santa Cruz, California.

Emily Burgess was a student in a class dedicated to the U.S. Latinos and Latinas in World War II Oral History Project at the University of Texas, Austin.

Melanie E. L. Bush teaches at Brooklyn College and is the associate editor of the American Sociological Association Section on Racial and Ethnic Minorities newsletter, *RE-Marks*. She holds a Ph.D. in anthropology from the City University of New York and researches racism and intergroup relations. She is the author of *Breaking the Code of Good Intentions: Everyday Forms of Whiteness* (2004).

Susanne Cabañas, a poet and writer, completed *For a Whole World*, a compilation of four *poemarios, America Poems, In Mourning, The Rose and the Ghetto,* and *Love Poems,* published in a limited edition. She has a tenure-track position in history at Cabrillo College in Santa Cruz, California. She is working on *Songs of My Childhood,* a collection of autobiographical free prose.

Dagmaris Cabezas, a writer and journalist, has worked for Columbia University's Health Sciences Division and the City University of New York (CUNY) and was the first Hispanic vice president at a CUNY senior college. She participated in the Antonio Maceo Brigade, the first group of Cubans to be invited to visit Cuba after the 1959 revolution.

José Z. Calderón is the holder of the Michi and Walter Weglyn Endowed Chair for Multicultural Studies, Cal Poly, Pomona. He has published numerous articles based on his experiences and observations, including "Lessons from an Activist Intellectual: Participatory Research, Teaching, and

Learning for Social Change" in *Latin American Perspectives* and "Organizing Immigrant Workers: Action Research and Strategies in the Pomona Day Labor Center."

Roberto R. Calderón is an associate professor of history at the University of North Texas. His research interests include social and labor history. He published *Mexican Coal Mining Labor in Texas and Coahuila, 1880–1930* (2000), and is completing a book, *Mexican Politics in Texas: Laredo, 1845–1911*.

Yolanda Calderón-Wallace teaches the history of Mexicans in the United States at Los Medanos Community College in northern California. She holds an M.A.T. in history from the University of California, Davis, and is co-owner of Human Behavior Associates, Inc.

Albert M. Camarillo is the Miriam and Peter Haas Centennial Professor in Public Service at Stanford University. Among his many publications are *Chicanos in a Changing Society: From Mexican Pueblos to American Barrios* (1979) and *Chicanos in California: A History of Mexican Americans* (1984). His most recent book is *Not White, Not Black: Mexicans and Racial/Ethnic Borderlands in American Cities* (forthcoming).

Elaine Carey is an assistant professor of Latin American and gender history at St. John's University in New York. She researches student movements, human rights movements, and gender and sexuality in Latin America. From 1997 to 2002 she taught at the University of Detroit and directed the James Guadalupe Carney Latin American Solidarity Archive (CLASA).

Eve Carr is a prospect research analyst with the Zoological Society of San Diego. She was formerly a staff historian at the Cape Fear Museum in North Carolina. She holds a Ph.D. in history from Arizona State University.

Hector Carrasquillo is the Murray Koppelman Professor of Puerto Rican and Latino Studies at Brooklyn College. He holds a Ph.D. in sociology from Syracuse University and a degree in divinity from Union Theological Seminary, New York. He teaches courses on Puerto Rican and Latino culture and education.

María Raquel Casas is an associate professor of history at the University of Nevada, Las Vegas, where she teaches undergraduate and graduate courses on Chicano/a history and general American history. Her scholarly interests include colonialism, gender history, and the Spanish borderlands. She is the author of *Married to a Daughter of the Land: Interethnic Marriages in California, 1820–1880* (2006).

Carolina Castillo Crimm is an associate professor of history at Sam Houston State University. Among her publications are *Cabin Fever* (2001), *Turn-of-the-Century Photographs from San Diego, Texas* (2003), and *De León: A Tejano Family History* (2004).

Philip C. Castruita teaches Chicano Studies at California State University, Fullerton, and is a doctoral student in history and cultural studies at Claremont Graduate University.

Angie Chabram-Dernersesian is a professor of Chicana/o Studies at the University of California, Davis. Her research interests and numerous publications are in the emergent area of Chicana/o cultural studies, transnationalism, critical literacy, and multiculturalism.

Dorian Chandler studies at Brooklyn College and volunteers at WBAI 99.5 Pacifica Radio, where she and other volunteers have a weekly talk radio program, *Student Voices for Peace*, on issues affecting young people.

Alicia Chávez is a doctoral candidate in history at Stanford University. She resides in southern California, where she is completing a dissertation about Mexican American union laborers in Los Angeles in the 1970s and 1980s. She recently published "Dolores Huerta and the United Farm Workers," in *Latina Legacies: Identity, Biography, and Community* (2005).

Marisela R. Chávez is an assistant professor of Chicano/Latino Studies at California State University, Dominguez Hills. She wrote " We Live and Breathed and Worked the Movement: The Contradictions and Rewards of Chicana/Mexicana Activism in el Centro de Acción Social Autónomo-Hermandad General de Trabajadores (CASA–HGT), Los Angeles, 1975–1978." In *Las obreras: Chicana Politics of Work and Family*, ed. Vicki L. Ruiz, 83–105. Los Angeles: UCLA Chicano Studies Research Center Publications, 2000.

Miroslava Chávez-García is an assistant professor in Chicana/o Studies at the University of California, Davis. Her publications focus on Mexican and Native women, patriarchy, and nineteenth-century law in California. She is the author of *Negotiating Conquest: Gender and Power in California, 1770s to 1880s* (2004).

Evelia Cobos Yusuf is a retired educator who lives in Rio Rancho, New Mexico. She holds a B.F.A. from the University of New Mexico. In 1981 she established Milpitas Piano Instruction in California.

Daisy Cocco De Filippis is Provost and Vice President for Academic Affairs at Eugenio María de Hostos Community College, CUNY. Among her many publications are *Docu-*

Notes on Contributors

ments of Dissidence: Selected Writings by Dominican Women (2000) and *From Desolation to Compromise: The Poetry of Aida Cartagena Portalatín* (1988).

Julie Cohen teaches at Santa Monica City College and is a doctoral candidate in history at the University of California, Irvine. Her areas of interest include twentieth-century California, the western United States, and gender studies.

Marcelle Maese Cohen is a doctoral student in English literature at the University of California, Berkeley. Her research interests include critical race theory, postcolonial and ethnic studies, and labor history.

Elizabeth Conde-Frazier is an assistant professor of Religious Studies at the Claremont School of Theology and received the Hispanic Theological Initiative's Dissertation Series Award for her work on Hispanic Bible institutes. Ordained with the American Baptist Churches, she formerly directed Hispanic and Latin American Ministries at the Andover Newton Theological School in Massachusetts.

Alicia M. Cortez is a counselor in the Office for International Student Programs at De Anza College in Cupertino, California. She received recognition for the Chicana/Latina History Project.

María Eugenia Cotera is an assistant professor in American culture and Women's Studies at the University of Michigan, Ann Arbor. Her publications include "Engendering a 'Dialectics of Our America': Jovita González Pluralist Dialogue as Feminist Testimonio" in *Las obreras: The Politics of Work and Family* (2000).

Natasha Mercedes Crawford is a nonprofit housing attorney in Phoenix, Arizona. She earned a B.A. in government from the University of Texas, Austin, and a J.D. from Boalt Hall, the University of California, Berkeley. She was admitted to the Arizona bar in 1997.

Mercedes Cros Sandoval is a professor emerita of anthropology at Miami-Dade College and an adjunct professor in the Department of Psychiatry of the School of Medicine of the University of Miami. She is the author of various publications, including *Mariel and Cuban National Identity* (1986).

Bárbara C. Cruz is a professor of Social Science Education at the University of South Florida. She conducts research on the representation of Hispanics in school curricula and textbooks, diversity issues in education, and the teaching of Latin America and the Caribbean. Her publications include young adult biographies of Frida Kahlo and Rubén Blades and *Multiethnic Teens and Cultural Identity* (2001).

Carlos A. Cruz is managing editor of *Latinas in the United States: A Historical Encyclopedia.* He holds a master's in graphic and computer arts, was an art editor and critic for the Spanish-language press, and curated several exhibitions on Latin American artists. He wrote *Herencia Clásica* (1990) and "Ana Mendieta" in *Latina Legacies* (2005).

María D. Cuevas, a doctoral candidate in sociology at Washington State University, is an adjunct faculty member at Washington State-Tri-Cities. In 2006 she will be affiliated with Yakima Community College. She is interested in documenting Chicana activism in Washington.

Karen Mary Dávalos is an assistant professor of Chicana/o studies at Loyola Marymount University. Her publications include *Exhibiting Mestizaje: Mexican (American) Museums in the Diaspora* (2001) and *The Chicano Studies Reader: An Anthology of Aztlán Scholarship, 1970–2000* (2001).

Adela de la Torre is a professor and director of Chicana/o Studies at the University of California, Davis. Her research and publications focus on health care and finance issues affecting the Latino community. She is the co-author of *Mexican Americans and Health: Sana¡ Sana¡* (with Antonio L. Estrada, 2001) and co-edited *Building with Our Hands: New Directions in Chicana Studies* (with Beatríz Pesquera, 1993).

Maritza de la Trinidad is a doctoral candidate in history at the University of Arizona and authored "The Segregation of Mexican Americans in Tucson Public Schools: Chicanos in Arizona, Southwest Have Long History of Fighting Discrimination" in *Arizona Report* (Spring 2000) and, with Adela de la Torre, "The Chicano Movement: Intersection of a Social Movement and Institutional Reform" in *Poverty and Social Welfare in the United States: An Encyclopedia*, edited by Gwendolyn Mink and Alice O'Connor (2003).

Arnoldo De León is C. J. "Red" Davidson Professor of history at Angelo State University, Texas. His significant publications include *The Tejano Community, 1836–1900* (1982, 1997), *They Called Them Greasers: Anglo Attitudes toward Mexicans in Texas, 1821–1900* (1983), and *Ethnicity in the Sunbelt: Mexican Americans in Houston* (2001). His most recent work is *Racial Frontiers: Africans, Chinese, and Mexicans in Western America, 1848–1890* (2002).

Linda C. Delgado conducts research on nineteenth- and twentieth-century U.S. immigration history, race, class, and ethnicity in Latino and gender studies. Her publications include *Puerto Rican Women's History: New Perspectives* with Félix Matos Rodríguez (1998) and five biographies in *Making It in America: A Sourcebook on Eminent Ethnic Americans,* edited by Elliott Barkan (2001).

Christa Desimone was a student in a class dedicated to the U.S. Latinos and Latinas in World War II Oral History Project at the University of Texas, Austin.

José A. Díaz is head reference and humanities bibliographer at Eugenio María de Hostos Community College of the City University of New York (CUNY). His most recent accomplishments include cotranslating into Spanish the new CUNY Information Competency Tutorial and cowriting a book chapter, "Language and Literary Research in a Bilingual Environment."

Eileen Diaz McConnell is an assistant professor of sociology at the University of Illinois, Urbana-Champaign. Her recent project, "Variation and Transition in the Hispanic Experience in the United States," documented demographic changes in the Latino population between 1990 and 2000 and evaluated the quality of Hispanic data in U.S. Census Bureau data sources.

Ana María Díaz-Stevens is a professor of Church and Society at Union Theological Seminary, New York. Her publications include *An Enduring Flame: Studies on Latino Popular Religiosity* (1994), coedited with Anthony M. Stevens-Arroyo, and *Recognizing the Latino Resurgence in U.S. Religion: The Emmaus Paradigm*, coauthored also with Anthony M. Stevens-Arroyo (1998).

Edward J. Escobar is an associate professor of Chicana and Chicano Studies and history at Arizona State University. His most recent book is *Race, Police, and the Making of a Political Identity* (1999). He teaches about race and the American criminal justice system and Mexican American history and coedited *Forging a Community: The Latino Experience in Northwest Indiana, 1919–1975* with James B. Lane (1987).

Elizabeth Escobedo is an assistant professor of history at the University of Texas, San Antonio. Her dissertation focuses on Mexican Americans in Los Angeles during World War II. She consulted on "Zoot Suit Riots" (2001), a PBS documentary in which she offered commentary on the roles of Mexican American women in the Sleepy Lagoon case of 1942.

Virginia Espino is a doctoral candidate in history at Arizona State University. She is a recipient of a Ford Foundation Fellowship and a Woodrow Wilson grant for women's studies and the author of "Women Sterilized As They Give Birth: Forced Sterilization and Chicana Resistance," in *Las obreras: Chicana Politics of Work and Family* (2000).

Dionne Espinoza is an assistant professor of Chicano Studies at California State University, Los Angeles. Holding a Ph.D. in English from Cornell University, her work focuses on youth culture, feminisms of color, and literary theory. She is completing a manuscript titled *Revolutionary Sisters: Chicana Activism and the Cultural Politics of Chicano Power*.

Martha Espinoza authored entries in *Women Building Chicago, 1790–1990: A Biographical Dictionary*, edited by Rima Lunin Schultz and Adele Hast, and a feature piece for *Hispanic Magazine*, "A Passion for History: A Conversation with Rudolfo Anaya" (1999), and contributed to *500 Years of Chicano History in Pictures*, edited by Elizabeth Martínez.

María R. Estorino is the project director and archivist of the Cuban Heritage Digital Collection, a digital preservation and access project of the University of Miami's Cuban Heritage Collection. She holds graduate degrees in history and library science from Northeastern University and Simmons College, respectively.

Elisa Linda Facio is an associate professor of Ethnic Studies at the University of Colorado, Boulder. Her publications include *Understanding Older Chicanas: Sociological and Policy Perspectives* (1996). She has also published several articles on Chicana feminism. She researches globalization, gender violence, and aging.

Lilia Fernández holds a postdoctoral fellowship in Latina/Latino Studies at the University of Illinois, Urbana-Champaign. Receiving a Ph.D. in Ethnic Studies from the University of California, San Diego, she focuses on the history of migration and community formation among Mexicans and Puerto Ricans in Chicago. Beginning July 2006, she will be an assistant professor of history at Ohio State University.

Nancy Page Fernández is a professor and director of the Interdisciplinary General Education Program at California State Polytechnic University, Pomona. She researches home dressmaking and the industrialization of women's clothing fashion and has published articles on paper pattern technology, household dressmaking, and the sewing machine.

Margarite Fernández-Olmos is a professor of Spanish at Brooklyn College, CUNY, and writes extensively on contemporary Caribbean and Latin American literatures. Among her recent publications are *U.S. Latino Literature: A Critical Guide for Students and Teachers* (2000), coedited with Harold Augenbraum, and *Healing Cultures: Art and Religion as Curative Practices in the Caribbean and Its Diaspora* (2001), coedited with Lizabeth Paravisini-Gebert.

Yvette G. Flores-Ortiz is a professor of Chicano Studies at the University of California, Davis. Her current studies examine intimate partner violence among Mexicans on both sides of the border. Her publications bridge clinical psychology and Chicano/Latino studies, where she focuses on gender, ethnicity, and sexuality. She is also a licensed research psychologist.

Estelle B. Freedman is the Edgar E. Robinson Professor of history at Stanford University. Among her many publications are *Their Sisters' Keepers: Women's Prison Reform in America, 1830–1930* (1981), *Maternal Justice: Miriam Van Waters and the Female Reform Tradition* (1996), and *No Turning Back: The History of Feminism and the Future of Women* (2002). Her articles have appeared in numerous scholarly journals.

Rosa Linda Fregoso is a professor and chair of Latin American and Latino Studies, University of California, Santa Cruz. Her publications include *MeXicana Encounters: The Making of Social Identities on the Borderlands* (2003), *Lourdes Portillo: The Devil Never Sleeps and Other Films* (2001), *Miradas de mujer* (with Norma Iglesias, 1998), and *The Bronze Screen: Chicana and Chicano Film Culture* (1993).

Lori Gallegos-Hupka received a J.D. from Loyola Law School, Los Angeles. A family law attorney, she lives in Huntington Beach, California.

Alma M. García is a professor of sociology and Women's Studies at Santa Clara University. She has published *The Mexican Americans* (2002), *Chicana Feminist Thought: The Basic Historical Writings* (1997), and several articles in *Gender and Society, Latin American Research Review*, and *Journal of American Ethnic History*.

Georgina García pursues graduate studies at Hunter College, CUNY. An honors graduate of Brooklyn College, CUNY, she is interested in combining her experiences in the performing arts with advanced studies in the social sciences on Latin Americans and Latinos in the United States.

Ismael García engages in archival research at the Center for Puerto Rican Studies Library and Archives, Hunter College, CUNY.

María Cristina García is an associate professor of history at Cornell University and director of the Latino Studies Program. She conducts research on comparative immigration and ethnic history and authored *Havana USA: Cuban Exiles and Cuban Americans in South Florida, 1959–1994* (1996).

Matt García is an associate professor of American civilization at Brown University, author of *A World of Its Own: Race, Labor, and Citrus in the Making of Greater Los Angeles, 1900–1970* (2001), and coeditor with Angharad Valdivia

and Marie Leger of *Geographies of Latinidad: Mapping the Future of Latina Studies for the 21st Century* (forthcoming).

Lisa García Bedolla is an assistant professor of Chicano/Latino Studies and political science at the University of California, Irvine. Her area of specialty is Latino political incorporation and representation in the United States. She is the author of *Fluid Borders: Latino Power, Identity, and Politics in Los Angeles* (2005).

Antonia García-Orozco was a dissertation fellow in the Department of Chicano Studies at the University of California, Santa Barbara. She teaches courses in the field at California State University, Northridge. In 2005 she completed her doctorate in Cultural Studies at Claremont Graduate University.

Anelisa Garfunkel holds a degree in journalism from Boston University School of Communication and a certificate in filmmaking from Rockport College. A videographer in the Federated States of Micronesia, she produced a number of educational videos for the region of Micronesia and is completing a documentary on surviving a spinal cord injury.

Raquel C. Garza was a student in a class dedicated to the U.S. Latinos and Latinas in World War II Oral History Project at the University of Texas, Austin.

Dorcas R. Gilmore teaches English and computer skills for the Presidential Anti-poverty Plan in Neyba, Bahoruco, Dominican Republic. She graduated magna cum laude from the Honors Degree Program at Rollins College with a major in psychology and double minors in Women's Studies and African/African-American Studies.

Marylou Gómez holds degrees from the University of Washington and the University of Chicago. She studies American ethnic groups, Spanish literature, and U.S. history and plans to complete a doctoral degree.

Deena J. González is a professor and chair of the Department of Chicana/o Studies at Loyola Marymount University, Los Angeles. She has published extensively on nineteenth-century New Mexico and authored *Refusing the Favor: The Spanish-Mexican Women of Santa Fe, 1820–1880* (1999). She is coeditor of *The Encyclopedia of Latinos and Latinas in the United States* (2005).

Gabriela González is an assistant professor of history at the University of Texas, San Antonio. Her dissertation, titled "Two Flags Entwined: Transborder Activists and the Politics of Race, Ethnicity, Class, and Gender in South Texas, 1900–1950," focuses on gendered transborder or *fronterizo* politics and the struggle for civil rights in Texas.

María de Jesús González is an assistant professor of art and art history at the University of Central Florida. She has published articles on modern Mexican art and collecting practices in Mexico. She currently researches Mexican photography and contemporary Puerto Rican women artists.

Monica González was an undergraduate at St. Mary's College.

Luis G. Gordillo was a student in a research class dedicated to the *Latinas in the United States: A Historical Encyclopedia* project at Brooklyn College, City University of New York.

Linda Gordon is a professor of history at New York University. Her book *The Great Arizona Orphan Abduction* won the Bancroft Prize for best U.S. history book and the Beveridge Prize for best book on the history of the Americas. The author of several award-winning books in U.S. women's history, she is working on a book about photographer Dorothea Lange and the New Deal.

Rachel Greene was a student in a research class dedicated to the *Latinas in the United States: A Historical Encyclopedia* project at Brooklyn College, City University of New York.

Richard Griswold del Castillo is a professor of Mexican American Studies at San Diego State University. Among his significant publications are *North to Aztlán: Mexican Americans in United States History* (with Arnoldo De Leon, 1992), *César Chávez: A Triumph of Spirit* (with Richard García, 1995), and *The Treaty of Guadalupe Hidalgo: A Legacy of Conflict* (1990).

Guadalupe Gutiérrez holds a degree in clinical psychology from the University of Michigan, Ann Arbor. Her clinical work focuses on adult and juvenile justice, with special training in forensics and competency. She researches ethnopsychology, specifically cross-cultural assessment, and the role of race and gender in the juvenile justice system.

Ramón A. Gutiérrez is a professor of history and Ethnic Studies at the University of California, San Diego, and author of *When Jesus Came, the Corn Mothers Went Away: Marriage, Sexuality, and Power in New Mexico, 1500–1846* (1991). The winner of eleven major academic book awards, including the Frederick Jackson Turner Prize, he is completing *Community, Patriarchy, and Individualism: A Cultural History of the Chicano Movement, 1965–1990* and *Crucifixion, Slavery, and Death: Genizaro Politics and Identity in New Mexico, 1700–1990.*

Laura Gutiérrez-Witt was director of the internationally prestigious Nettie Lee Benson Latin American Collection at the University of Texas, Austin. She currently serves as executive secretary of the Seminar on the Acquisition of Latin American Library Materials (SALALM) and is a freelance writer and researcher.

Michelle Habell-Pallán is an assistant professor of American Ethnic Studies at the University of Washington. She coedited *Latino/a Popular Culture: Cultural Politics into the 21st Century* (with Mary Romero, 2002).

Linda B. Hall is a professor of history at the University of New Mexico. Among her many publications are *Oil, Banks, and Politics: The United States and Postrevolutionary Mexico, 1917–1924* (1995), *Tangled Destinies: Latin America and the United States* (1999), and *Mary, Mother and Warrior: The Virgin in Spain and the Americas* (2004).

Gabriel Haslip-Viera is an associate professor and director of the Latin American and Latino Studies program at City College, CUNY. He authored *Crime and Punishment in Late Colonial Mexico City, 1692–1810* (1999) and edited *Taino Revival: Critical Perspectives on Puerto Rican Identity and Cultural Politics* (2001).

Pedro Juan Hernández is senior archivist at the Centro de Estudios Puertorriqueños, Hunter College, CUNY. He was head archivist and director of the Archives of the Puerto Rican Migration to the United States, 1898–1948, and coauthored *Pioneros: Puerto Ricans in New York City, 1892–1948.*

Nancy A. Hewitt is a professor of history and Women's and Gender Studies at Rutgers University, New Brunswick. She has authored two books, *Women's Activism and Social Change: Rochester, New York, 1822–1872* (1984) and *Southern Discomfort: Women's Activism in Tampa, Florida, 1880s–1920s* (2001), and edited *A Companion to American Women's History* (2002). She is also coeditor of *Visible Women: New Essays on Women's Activism* (with Suzanne Lebsock, 1993).

Karen V. Holliday conducts research on Latina health issues at the University of California, Los Angeles, where she held a postdoctoral fellowship. She explores the role of Latinas in the healing process and the impact of gender distinction on Latina/o health outcomes. She was a Peace Corps Health Sector volunteer in the Dominican Republic and holds a Ph.D. in anthropology from the University of California, Irvine.

Rachel Howell was a student in a class dedicated to the U.S. Latinos and Latinas in World War II Oral History Project at the University of Texas, Austin.

Albert L. Hurtado holds the Travis Chair in Modern American History at the University of Oklahoma. Among his publications are *Intimate Frontiers: Sex, Gender, and Cul-*

Notes on Contributors

ture in Old California (1999), *Indian Survival on the California Frontier* (1988, 1989, 1998), "Romancing the West in the Twentieth Century: The Politics of History in a Contested Region," *Western Historical Quarterly* 32 (Winter 2001): 417–435, and "When Strangers Met: Sex and Gender on Three Frontiers," *Frontiers: A Journal of Women Studies* 17, no. 3 (1996): 52–75.

Jorge Iber is an associate professor of history at Texas Tech University. His publications include *Hispanics in the Mormon Zion, 1912–1999* (2000), "El diablo nos esta llevando: Utah Hispanics and the Great Depression," *Utah Historical Quarterly* (1998), and articles in *Southwestern Historical Quarterly, Journal of the West, Perspectives in Mexican American Studies,* and *West Texas Historical Association Yearbook.*

Ada María Isasi-Díaz is a professor, founder, and codirector of the Hispanic Institute of Theology at Drew University. Among her many publications are *Hispanic Women: Prophetic Voice in the Church,* with Yolanda Tarango (1988), *Inheriting Our Mothers' Gardens,* coeditor and contributor (1988), *Mujerista Theology: A Theology for the Twenty-first Century* (1996), and *Hispanic/Latino Theology: Challenge and Promise,* coeditor and contributor (1996).

Margaret D. Jacobs is an associate professor of history at the University of Nebraska, Lincoln. Her publications include *Engendered Encounters: Feminism and Pueblo Cultures, 1879–1934* (1999). She is currently writing "White Mother to a Dark Race: White Women and the Removal of Indigenous Children in the United States and Australia, 1880–1940."

Callie Jenschke was a student in a class dedicated to the U.S. Latinos and Latinas in World War II Oral History Project at the University of Texas, Austin.

Olga Jiménez de Wagenheim directs the Hispanic Research and Information Center (HRIC) at Newark Public Library. Among her many publications are *Puerto Rico: An Interpretive History from Pre-Columbian Times to 1900* (1998), *Puerto Rico's Revolt for Independence: El Grito de Lares* (1984), and *The Puerto Ricans: A Documentary History* (1973), with Kal Wagenheim. She holds a Ph.D. in history from Rutgers University.

Nicolás Kanellos is the Brown Foundation Professor of Hispanic Literature at the University of Houston and founding publisher of the literary journal the *Americas Review* and the publishing house Arte Público Press. He is the director of Recovering the U.S. Hispanic Literary Heritage, a national research program.

Katie Kennon was a student in a class dedicated to the U.S. Latinos and Latinas in World War II Oral History Project at the University of Texas, Austin.

Asunción Lavrin is a professor of history at Arizona State University. Among her many significant publications are *Latin American Women: Historical Perspectives* (1978), *Sexuality and Marriage in Colonial Latin America* (1989), and *Women, Feminism, and Social Change in Argentina, Chile, and Uruguay, 1890–1940* (1995). She is completing book projects on nuns and on masculinity and the religious orders in colonial Mexico.

Luis Daniel León is a visiting assistant professor in Ethnic Studies and Religious Studies at the University of California, Berkeley. He authored *La Llorona's Children: Religion, Life, and Death in the U.S.-Mexican Borderlands* (2004) and researches transnationalism, ethnicity, race, culture, and queer theory.

Yolanda Chávez Leyva is an assistant professor of history at the University of Texas, El Paso. She is completing a scholarly monograph on children's immigration experiences and has authored several articles on border lives and identities.

Amy Lind teaches in the Studies of Women and Gender Program at the University of Virginia. She authored *Gendered Paradoxes: Women's Movements, State Restructuring, and Global Development in Ecuador* (2005).

Iris López is an associate professor of sociology at the City College of New York and directs the program in Latin American and Hispanic Caribbean Studies. Her publications and research interests focus on Puerto Rican and Latina sterilization. She is currently working on a manuscript on the development of the Hawaiian Puerto Rican community.

Tomás López-Pumarejo is an assistant professor of economics at Brooklyn College. He teaches multicultural marketing and business and conducts research on the Latin American television industry and marketing of historic, revitalized urban sites.

Alessandra Lorini is a professor of history at the University of Florence, Italy. Her publications include *Rituals of Race: American Public Culture and the Search for Racial Democracy* (1999) and *Ai confini della libertà: Saggi di storia americana* (2001).

Olga Loya is a professional storyteller who grew up in East Los Angeles, California, and specializes in dramatic thematic theatrical performance. A nationally recognized Latina performer, she uses a mix of Spanish and English stories in a one-woman show for adults and children.

Lisa Magaña is an associate professor of Chicano and Chicana Studies at Arizona State University. She researches and writes about immigration and Latino public policy.

Her publications include *Straddling the Border: Immigration Policy and the INS* (2003).

Pamela J. Marshall holds an M.S. in management from the University of Maryland. She studied history at the University of Massachusetts, Amherst, and served in the U.S. Army Reserve and the Maryland Army National Guard. She trains examiners for the National Association of Securities Dealers.

Elena Martínez is a folklorist at City Lore: The New York Center for Urban Folk Culture. The primary fieldworker for the South Bronx Latin Music Project, she interviews musicians, arranges photo and archival research, and produces public programs. She coproduced the exhibition A Float for All Seasons: New York City's Ethnic Parades at the Museum of the City of New York.

Virginia Martínez directs the International Center for Health Leadership Development at the University of Illinois at Chicago. An attorney, she has spent most of her career working in nonprofit organizations. An advocate for women and children, she was executive director of Mujeres Latinas en Acción from 1992 until 1997.

Irene Mata is a doctoral candidate in literature at the University of California, San Diego. Her research interests include women and labor, Chicana/o literature, and U.S. ethnic literature.

Félix V. Matos Rodríguez is an associate professor of Africana and Puerto Rican/Latino Studies at Hunter College, CUNY, and the CUNY Graduate Center and directs the Center of Puerto Rican Studies at Hunter College. His publications include *Women in San Juan, Puerto Rico, 1820–1868* (2001), *Boricuas in Gotham* (2004), and *Puerto Rican Women's History* (1998).

Valerie Matsumoto is an associate professor of history at the University of California, Los Angeles. She conducts research on Asian American, women's, and oral history. Her publications include *Over the Edge: Remapping the American West* (coedited with Blake Allmendinger, 1999), and *Farming the Home Place: A Japanese American Community in California, 1919–1982* (1993).

Wendy McBurney-Coombs is a professor of Spanish at Clark Atlanta University in Georgia. She taught school in her native Trinidad and Tobago, completed advanced education in the United States, and currently researches Afro-Hispanic literature and cultural studies from a multicultural and interdisciplinary perspective.

Lara Medina is an associate professor of Chicano Studies at California State University, Northridge. Her recent publications include *Las Hermanas: Chicana/Latina Religious-*

Political Activism in the U.S. Catholic Church (2004) and "Día de los muertos: Public Ritual, Community Renewal, and Popular Religion in Los Angeles" (with Gilbert Cadena) in *Horizons of the Sacred: Mexican Traditions in U.S. Catholicism* (2002).

Lisa Meléndez is an associate professor of Library Services at Suffolk County Community College. She coordinates the library instruction program, teaches library research methods, and advises the Ammerman Campus's Latino student club. She has also served on a local advisory board to the New York State Documentary Heritage Program on Latinos in New York State.

Rubén G. Mendoza is a professor in the Social and Behavioral Sciences Center, California State University, Monterey Bay, and directs the Institute for Archaeological Science, Technology, and Visualization. He has published extensively on Mesoamerican archaeology and in reference books, including *Herencia Mexicana: The Mexican Americans of Kern County, 1870–1955* (1986).

Sylvia Mendoza was a student in a class dedicated to the U.S. Latinos and Latinas in World War II Oral History Project at the University of Texas, Austin.

Cecilia Menjívar is an associate professor in the Department of Sociology at Arizona State University. Her research interests include immigration, family dynamics, and religious communities among Central Americans in the United States. She is the author of *Fragmented Ties: Salvadoran Immigrant Networks in America* (2000).

Edward Mercado is the director of the Division of Diversity Planning and Management (DPM) in the New York State Department of Civil Service and former commissioner of the New York State Division of Human Rights. He writes about ethnic and social issues.

Ronald L. Mize is an assistant professor of Latino Studies and sociology at Cornell University. He conducts research on the historical origins of racial and class oppression in the lives of U.S. Mexicans and published "Crossing the Border for Health Care: Access and Primary Care Characteristics for Young Children of Latino Farm Workers along the U.S.-Mexico border" in *Ambulatory Pediatrics* (2003).

Allison Mokry was a student in a class dedicated to the U.S. Latinos and Latinas in World War II Oral History Project at the University of Texas, Austin.

Douglas Monroy is a professor of history at the Colorado College and author of *Thrown among Strangers: The Making of Mexican Culture in Frontier California* (1990), winner of the James Rawley Prize of the Organization of American

Historians, and *Rebirth: Mexican Los Angeles from the Great Migration to the Great Depression* (1999).

Anthony Mora is an assistant professor of history at Texas A&M University and currently studies the historical construction of race, gender, and sexuality. His next project explores the relationship between African Americans and Mexican Americans in the early-twentieth-century Midwest.

Milga Morales is Dean of Student Life at Brooklyn College, CUNY. Her academic interests center on English-language acquisition among Hispanics, multicultural education, and the education of Puerto Ricans in the United States. She has developed curricula for educating elementary and non-English-speaking students.

Jackie Morfesis is an instructor in the Department of Fine Arts at Rutgers, the State University of New Jersey. She researches art history and women's studies and is a recipient of a Rotary International Ambassadorial Scholarship to Greece and an Andrew W. Mellon Program grant in art history.

Vicky Muñiz is an associate professor of social geography in the School of General Studies at the University of Puerto Rico, cofounder of Mujeres in Action in Brooklyn, and the author of *Resisting Gentrification and Displacement: Voices of Puerto Rican Women of the Barrio* (1998). She examines gender issues, immigrant groups, and return migration in Puerto Rico.

Laura K. Muñoz, a Ph.D. candidate in history at Arizona State University, held a Ford Foundation Predoctoral Fellowship and is an AERA/Spencer Predissertation fellow. She is completing a dissertation on Mexican American education in Arizona during the era of segregation and published a lesson plan based on her research in *OAH Magazine of History* 15, no. 2 (Winter 2001).

Lorena Muñoz, a Ph.D. candidate in geography at the University of Southern California, is writing a dissertation, "Informal Landscapes: Gender, Place, and Culture: A Study of Latino Street Vending Practices in Los Angeles."

Frances Negrón-Muntaner is an assistant professor of English and Comparative Literature at Columbia University. An award-winning filmmaker, writer, and scholar, she includes among her publications *Puerto Rican Jam: Rethinking Nationalisim and Colonialism, Boricua Pop: Puerto Ricans and the Latinization of American Culture,* and *None of the Above: Puerto Rican Culture and Politics.*

Carrie Nelson was a student in a class dedicated to the U.S. Latinos and Latinas in World War II Oral History Project at the University of Texas, Austin.

Victoria Núñez is a doctoral candidate in American Studies at the University of Massachusetts, Amherst. Her research focuses on cultural texts generated during the post–World War II migration of Puerto Ricans and Dominicans to the northeastern United States.

Tey Marianna Nunn received a Ph.D. from the University of New Mexico and is curator of contemporary Hispano and Latino collections at the Museum of International Folk Art in Santa Fe, New Mexico. She has curated acclaimed exhibitions, including Sin nombre: Hispana and Hispano Artists of the New Deal Era, Cyber arte: Tradition meets Technology, and Flor y canto: Reflections from Nuevo México.

Holly Ocasio Rizzo teaches journalism at California State University, Fullerton, and has been recognized for her writing by the Society of Professional Journalists, Associated Press Managing Editors, and other journalism organizations. Her work has appeared in the *Miami Herald, New York Daily News, Chicago Tribune, Dallas Morning News, Los Angeles Times, Hispanic,* and *Hispanic Business.*

María Ochoa is a lecturer in Women's Studies at San Jose State University and focuses on women of color in the United States, Chicana/o visual culture, and feminist oral history methodologies. She authored *Creative Collectives: Chicana Painters Working in Community* (2003) and is writing about Rita Hayworth for an anthology, *From Bananas to Buttocks: Latina Bodies in Popular Culture.* She holds a Ph.D. in the History of Consciousness from the University of California, Santa Cruz.

Annette Oliveira was the first director of fund-raising and public relations for the Puerto Rican Legal Defense and Education Fund in New York City. For two years she was the media and publications director for the Mexican American Legal Defense and Educational Fund. She wrote *Diez anos,* a ten-year history of MALDEF and of its roots in Mexican American history.

Lorena Oropeza is an associate professor of history at the University of California, Davis. She focuses on Chicano/Chicana history and American foreign relations. Her publication include *Raza Sí! Guerra No! Chicano Protest and Patriotism during the Viet Nam War Era* (2005).

Cynthia E. Orozco teaches history and humanities at Eastern New Mexico University in Ruidoso and holds a Ph.D. from the University of California, Los Angeles. She is the author of *No Mexicans, Women, or Dogs Allowed: The Rise of the Mexican American Civil Rights Movement* (forthcoming) and coedited *Mexican Americans in Texas History* (with Emilio Zamora and Rodolfo Rocha, 2000). She wrote eighty entries for the *New Handbook of Texas.*

Victoria Ortiz is Assistant Dean for Student Services at Boalt Hall, School of Law, University of California, Berkeley. She holds a J.D. from the City University of New York and is currently finishing a book on the court cases brought by Sojourner Truth.

Lydia R. Otero is an assistant professor in the Mexican American Studies and Research Center at the University of Arizona. A public historian, she conducts research on the politics of saving Mexican American historical sites and wrote "Refusing to Be Undocumented: Mexican Americans in Tucson during the Depression Years" in *Visions in the Dust: Arizona through New Deal Photography* (2004).

Jeff Paul is the Multicultural Center librarian at San Jose State University. He has served as the director of SJSU's Chicano Library Resource Center since its inception in 1979 and is an adjunct professor in the School of Library and Information Science at SJSU.

Marian Perales is a doctoral candidate in history at the Claremont Graduate University. She is completing a dissertation on the life and times of Teresa Urrea. She recently published "Teresa Urrea: *Curandera* and Folk Saint" in *Latina Legacies: Identity, Biography, and Community* (2005).

Monica Perales is an assistant professor in the Department of History at the University of Houston. The winner of the Galarza Prize at Stanford University, she conducts research in Chicana/o labor and social history, race and migration in the twentieth century, and the history of the U.S./Mexico border region.

Nélida Pérez holds an M.L.S. from the School of Library Service at Columbia University and an M.A. in history and archives management from New York University. She is director and archivist at the Center for Puerto Rican Studies Library and Archives at Hunter College, CUNY.

María Pérez y González is an associate professor and chair of the Department of Puerto Rican and Latino Studies at Brooklyn College, CUNY. She authored *Puerto Ricans in the United States* (2000) and conducts research on the role of women in the Pentecostal Church.

Andrés Pérez y Mena is an adjunct associate professor of Puerto Rican and Latino Studies at Brooklyn College, CUNY. Among his publications are *Speaking with the Dead: Development of Afro-Latin Religion among Puerto Ricans in the United States* (1991) and *Enigmatic Powers: Syncretism with African and Indigenous Peoples' Religions among Latinos* (with A. Stevens-Arroyo, 1995).

Marifeli Pérez-Stable is currently vice president for democratic governance at the Inter-American Dialogue in Washington, D.C. Among her most significant publications is *The Cuban Revolution: Origins, Course, and Legacy.* (1998). She is a professor of sociology and anthropology at Florida International University.

Susan L. Pickman taught history for more than twenty years at the State University of New York at Stony Brook and the University of Central Florida in Orlando. She received a Ph.D. in History from SUNY, Stony Brook, and holds a CFE from the Association of Certified Fraud Examiners. She is a sworn law enforcement officer.

Kinchen C. Pier III is the manager of Trust Oil and Gas Legal and Compliance at the Bank of America in Dallas, Texas. He holds a J.D. from South Texas College of Law and is a master's candidate in history at the University of North Texas.

Beatrice Pita teaches in the Spanish Section of the Department of Literature at the University of California at San Diego. With Rosaura Sánchez, she has edited and written the introduction to María Amparo Ruiz de Burton's two novels, *The Squatter and the Don* (1992) and *Who Would Have Thought It?* (1995), and also *Conflicts of Interest: The Letters of María Amparo Ruiz de Burton* (2001).

Merrihelen Ponce, also known as Mary Helen Ponce, has written *Taking Control* (1987), *The Wedding* (1980), and *Hoyt Street: An Autobiography* (1993). Her forthcoming works include a play based on her book *The Wedding*, the novel *Raising Albuquerque*, and an essay collection. She holds a Ph.D. in American Studies from the University of New Mexico.

Yolanda Prieto is a professor of sociology at Ramapo College of New Jersey. She researches Cuban migration to the United States, with particular attention to the role of women. She is writing a book-length manuscript on the origins, development, and transformation of the Cuban community in Union City, New Jersey.

Laura Pulido is an associate professor of geography and the Program in American Studies and Ethnicity at the University of Southern California. She is the author of *Environmentalism and Economic Justice: Two Chicano Struggles in the Southwest* (1996) and *Black, Brown, Yellow, and Left: Radical Activism in Los Angeles, 1968–78* (2006).

Naomi H. Quiñonez is a poet, scholar, and educator whose publications include *Hummingbird Dream/Sueño de colibri* and *The Smoking Mirror*. She coedited *Decolonial Voices: Chicana and Chicano Cultural Studies in the 21st Century*. She holds a Ph.D. in History from Claremont Graduate School.

Notes on Contributors

Jorivette Quintana majored in business and Latino Studies at Brooklyn College, CUNY, and has worked in many of Manhattan's most prestigious spas. She is a freelance writer, has mentored high-school students and foster children, and plans to join the Peace Corps in Latin America.

Mario Ramírez is a project archivist at the Centro de Estudios Puertorriqueños at Hunter College, CUNY. He holds an M.A. in rhetoric from the University of California, Berkeley, an M.S. in Library and Information Science, and a Certificate in Archives and Records Management from the Palmer School of Library Information Science at Long Island University.

Annette L. Reed is an associate professor and director of the Native American Studies program at California State University, Sacramento. Her research interests and publications focus on comparative ethnic studies and Tolowa (Deeni/Huss) tribal history, precontact to 1934.

Bárbara O. Reyes, a Ford Foundation postdoctoral fellow, is an assistant professor of history at the University of New Mexico. She teaches Chicano history, gender, race and ethnicity, and borderlands and immigration histories and is completing a manuscript, "Private Women, Public Lives: Gender and the 19th Century California Missions."

Jeannette Reyes was assistant to the managing editor of *Latinas in the United States: A Historical Encyclopedia.* A Ford Colloquium Honors graduate from Brooklyn College, CUNY, she plans to pursue advanced studies on Latino/Latin American history.

Jean Reynolds is public history coordinator for the city of Chandler, Arizona. She works on projects that document the stories of local minority and working-class communities. Her publications include *The History of the Grant Park Neighborhood, 1880–1950* (1999), *African American Historic Property Survey* (2004), and *Victory Acres/Escalante Neighborhoods: Historias de la comunidad* (2004).

Nora E. Rios McMillan is a professor of history at San Antonio College in San Antonio, Texas. Her most recent publications include " 'Siendo mi derecho . . . ': The Hispanic Woman's Legal Identity in the Spanish Southwest," *South Texas Studies* (1999), published also in the *Journal of South Texas* (2000), and "The Repatriation of Mexicans during the Great Depression," *Journal of South Texas* (1998).

Maggie Rivas-Rodríguez is an associate professor of journalism at the University of Texas, Austin. A founding member of the National Association of Hispanic Journalists, she founded and directs the U.S. Latino and Latina World War II Oral History Project, a multifaceted effort that includes a conference, an edited volume of academic manuscripts, a documentary film with educational materials, and a general-interest book, *Mexican Americans and World War II* (2005).

Monica Rivera was a student in a class dedicated to the U.S. Latinos and Latinas in World War II Oral History Project at the University of Texas, Austin.

Sally Robles is an assistant professor of psychology at Brooklyn College, CUNY.

Clara E. Rodríguez is a professor of sociology at Fordham University's College at Lincoln Center. She is the author or coauthor of numerous books, including *Heroes, Lovers, and Others: The Story of Latinos in Hollywood* (2004), *Changing Race: Latinos, the Census, and the History of Ethnicity in the United States* (2000), and *Latin Looks: Images of Latinas and Latinos in the U.S. Media* (1997).

Alicia I. Rodríquez-Estrada is a tenured instructor of history and chair of the Behavioral and Social Sciences Department at Los Angeles Trade-Technical College. She researches popular culture and media and is a Ph.D. candidate in American history at Claremont Graduate University. She is the author of "Dolores del Río and Lupe Vélez: Images on and off the Screen, 1925–1944" in *Writing the Range: Race, Class, and Culture in the Women's West* (1997).

Maythee Rojas is an assistant professor of Women's Studies at California State University, Long Beach. A literary critic and historian, she focuses on gender and sexuality in the work of Chicana/o and Latina/o writers.

F. Arturo Rosales is a professor of history at Arizona State University and the author of *¡Chicano! A History of the Mexican American Civil Rights Movement* (1996), *"¡Pobre Raza!": Violence, Justice, and Mobilization among México Lindo Immigrants, 1900–1936* (1999), and *Testimonio: A Documentary History of the Mexican American Struggle for Civil Rights* (2000).

Steven Rosales is a doctoral candidate in history at the University of California, Irvine. He is completing a dissertation, "Soldados Razos: Chicano Politics, Identity, and Masculinity in the U.S. Military, 1940–1975."

Ana E. Rosas is a doctoral candidate in history at the University of Southern California. The recipient of a Ford Foundation Dissertation Fellowship, she is completing a dissertation titled " 'Familias Flexibles (Flexible Families): Bracero Families' Lives across Cultures, Communities, and Countries, 1942–1964."

Margaret Eleanor Rose directs the California History–Social Science Project at the Interdisciplinary Humanities

Center, University of California, Santa Barbara. Her recent publications are "César Chávez and Dolores Huerta: Partners in 'La Causa' " in *César Chávez: A Brief Biography with Documents*, edited by Richard Etulain (2002), and " 'My Own Life's Worth': Dolores Huerta and the United Farm Workers' Union" in *The Human Tradition in American Labor History*, edited by Eric Arnesen (2004). She holds a Ph.D. in history from the University of California, Los Angeles.

Raquel Rubio-Goldsmith holds degrees in law and philosophy from the National Autonomous University of Mexico. She teaches in the Mexican American Studies and Research Center at the University of Arizona, where she specializes in research on Mexican American women's history, human rights, and immigration issues.

Daniel Ruiz is an M.F.A. student in Critical Studies at the California Institute for the Arts. He graduated from the University of California, Irvine, with a major in English in 2005.

Vicki L. Ruiz is a professor of history and Chicano/Latino Studies at the University of California, Irvine. Among her most significant publications are *Cannery Women, Cannery Lives* (1987), *From out of the Shadows: Mexican Women in Twentieth-Century America* (1998), and *Latina Legacies: Identity, Biography, and Community* with Virginia Sánchez Korrol, 2005.

Elizabeth Salas is an associate professor of American Ethnic Studies at the University of Washington, Seattle. She is the author of *Soldaderas in the Mexican Military: Myth and History* (1990) and has published articles on New Mexico Hispana and Washington State Chicana politicians.

Carlos Sanabria teaches courses in Latin American, Hispanic Caribbean, and Puerto Rican history at Hostos Community College, City University of New York. His published articles include "Patriotism and Class Conflict in the Puerto Rican Community in New York during the 1920s," *Latino Studies Journal* (1991). He holds a Ph.D. in History from the City University of New York.

Reinaldo Sánchez is a professor in the Department of Modern Languages at Florida International University and directs its Spanish graduate program.

Rosaura Sánchez is a professor in the Department of Literature at the University of California, San Diego. She is the author of *Chicano Discourse* (1994) and *Telling Identities* (1995) and coeditor with Beatrice Pita of *Conflicts of Interest: The Letters of María Amparo Ruiz de Burton* (2001). She coedited the republication of Ruiz de Burton's novels *The Squatter and the Don* and *Who Would Have Thought It? He Walked In and Sat Down*, a bilingual collection of her short stories, appeared in 2000.

Virginia Sánchez Korrol is a professor in the Department of Puerto Rican and Latino Studies at Brooklyn College, CUNY. Among her most significant publications are *From Colonia to Community: The History of Puerto Ricans in New York* (1994) and *Latina Legacies: Identity, Biography, and Community* with Vicki L. Ruiz, 2005. She holds a Ph.D. in history from the State University of New York, Stony Brook.

Arlene Sánchez Walsh is an associate professor of religion at the Haggard School of Theology, Azusa Pacific University. She is the author of *Latino Pentecostal Identity: Evangelical Faith, Self, and Society* (2003) and several articles on Latino Pentecostal history.

Diane Sandoval is a biomedical information specialist in New York who has many interests, including family history. She holds a B.A. and an M.A. from the University of California at Berkeley.

Gabriela Sandoval is an assistant professor in the Department of Sociology at the University of California, Santa Cruz. She conducts research on the effects of racial, ethnic, class, and gender identities on political practices.

Janine Santiago is an assistant professor of Spanish at the State University of New York at Brockport. She teaches courses in bilingual and multicultural studies. She wrote the manual *Tolerance, Community Action, and Cultural Understanding: A Guide to Assist Latina Victims of Violence.*

Jorge Sastre Vidal is an attending physician and course instructor in the Department of Family Practice at Lutheran Medical Center in Brooklyn, New York. He holds an M.D. degree from the University of Havana School of Medicine, Havana, Cuba.

Katherine Sayre was a student in a class dedicated to the U.S. Latinos and Latinas in World War II Oral History Project at the University of Texas, Austin.

Bettina E. Schmidt is an assistant professor of anthropology at Philipps-University Marburg (Germany) and a visiting professor at Oxford University, England. Her recent publications include *Anthropology of Violence and Conflict* (with Ingo W. Schröder 2001) and "Mambos, Mothers and Madrinas in New York City: Religion as a Means of Empowerment for Women from the Caribbean," *Wadabagei: A Journal of the Caribbean and its Diaspora* (2002).

Antoinette López Sedillo is Associate Dean for Clinical Affairs and a professor at the University of New Mexico School of Law. Among her many publications is the six-volume anthology *Latinos in the United States*. Her poetry and creative writings appear in numerous journals, and she is the current president of the Clinical Legal Education Association.

Notes on Contributors

Christine Marie Sierra is an associate professor in Political Science at the University of New Mexico. She coedited *Chicana Voices: Intersections of Class, Race, and Gender* (1993) and *Chicana Critical Issues* (1993).

Lori Slaughenhoupt was a student in a class dedicated to the U.S. Latinos and Latinas in World War II Oral History Project at the University of Texas, Austin.

Celest Smith is a transplanted New Yorker who lives in California.

Lauren Smith was a student in a class dedicated to the U.S. Latinos and Latinas in World War II Oral History Project at the University of Texas, Austin.

Irene Sosa is an independent film and video maker and an assistant professor in the Department of Television and Radio at Brooklyn College, CUNY. She holds degrees from Universidad Central de Venezuela and New York University. She produced *Sexual Exiles* (2002) and *Woman as Protagonist: The Art of Nancy Spero* (1993).

Kathleen Staudt is a professor of political science and director of the Center for Civic Engagement at the University of Texas at El Paso. Among her many publications are *Fronteras no mas: Toward Social Justice at the U.S.-Mexico Border* (with Irasema Coronado, 2002) and *Policy, Politics and Gender: Women Gaining Ground* (1998).

Darcie Stevens was a student in a class dedicated to the U.S. Latinos and Latinas in World War II Oral History Project at the University of Texas, Austin.

K. Lynn Stoner is an associate professor of history at Arizona State University. She is the author of *From the House to the Streets: The Cuban Woman's Movement for Legal Reform, 1898–1940* (1991) and has produced two major bibliographic works on Latin American women: *Latinas of the Americas: A Source Book* (1989) and *Cuban and Cuban-American Women: An Annotated Bibliography* (2000).

Margaret Strobel is a professor of history and Women's Studies at the University of Illinois, Chicago. Her publications include *European Women and the Second British Empire* (1991), *Three Swahili Women: Life Histories from Mombasa, Kenya* (1989), and *Muslim Women in Monbasa, 1890–1975* (1979).

Ben Tatar, a graduate of the University of Pittsburgh and the American Theatre Wing School of Drama in New York City, appeared in the films *The Battle of the Bulge*, *The Wind and the Lion*, *The Long Duel*, and *The Christmas Kid*. His memoir, *The Dream Never Dies*, relates his experiences as personal assistant to Jackie Gleason and "confidential secretary" to actress Ava Gardner.

Sam Thompson is an attorney and spokeswoman for Patricia Madrid, attorney general of the state of New Mexico.

Maura I. Toro-Morn is an associate professor of sociology at Illinois State University and the author of numerous articles focusing on the gender and class dimensions of Puerto Rican migration to the United States. She coedited *Migration and Immigration: A Global View* (with Marixsa Alicea, 2004).

Benjamin Torres is an associate professor of Spanish at Western Michigan University. He was born in Havana, Cuba, and was raised in Puerto Rico.

Rebecca Torres-Wilkner is a literary agent and publicist for Latina/o writers. She is located in Fort Lauderdale, Florida.

Amanda Traphagan was a student in a class dedicated to the U.S. Latinos and Latinas in World War II Oral History Project at the University of Texas, Austin.

Nicole Trujillo-Pagán teaches courses in the social sciences in the Department of Puerto Rican and Latino Studies at Brooklyn College, CUNY. She researches the intersection of politics and health policies in Puerto Rico, Guam, and the Philippines and among Latinos in the United States. She holds a Ph.D. in Political Science from the University of Michigan.

Rita E. Urquijo-Ruiz is an assistant professor of Modern Languages and Literatures at Trinity University in San Antonio, Texas. Her research interests include Mexican and Chicana/o literature, theater, music, language, and film in the twentieth century.

Omar Valerio-Jiménez is an assistant professor of history at California State University, Long Beach. He teaches U.S. urban history, borderlands, Chicana/o studies, and immigration. He is the author of *River of Hope: Identity and Nation along the Rio Grande Valley, 1749–1890* (forthcoming).

Gloria Vando edited *The Helicon Nine Reader* and coedited *Spud Songs: An Anthology of Potato Poems to Benefit Hunger Relief* (with Robert Stewart, 1999). Her work was adapted for productions at the Women's Work Festival, Lincoln Center for the Performing Arts, the New Federal Theatre, and the Latino Playwrights Theatre in New York. She published *Shadows and Supposes* (2002).

Deborah Vargas is an assistant professor of Chicano/Latino Studies at the University of California, Irvine. She is completing a manuscript, *Las Tracaleras: Texas-Mexican Women, Music, and Place.*

María Vega has worked at *El Diario–La Prensa* in New York City for more than a decade. She has written about housing policy, nonprofit institutions, and local politics, among other subjects. She currently writes for the "Folklore, Arts, and Culture" section of the newspaper.

Soledad Vidal is a Ph.D. candidate in history at the University of California, Irvine. A Eugene Cota-Robles fellow, she is interested in immigrant histories, community studies, and oral history projects.

Joseph M. Viera is an associate professor of American literature at Nazareth College. He is writing *Understanding Oscar Hijuelos*, a book-length study of the Pulitzer Prize–winning Cuban American novelist.

María E. Villamil is an assistant professor of Spanish at the University of Nebraska at Omaha. She conducts research on Chicano testimonials and the Mexican and Colombian narrative in the second half of the twentieth century and has published numerous articles on these subjects.

Mary Ann Villarreal is an assistant professor of history and Ethnic Studies at the University of Utah. She is the author of "Synapses of Struggle: Martha Cotera and Tejana Activism" in *Las obreras: Chicana Politics of Work and Family.* She is completing a manuscript, *Con ganas y amor: Tejanas and Family Owned Businesses, 1935–1955.*

Angela Walker was a student in a class dedicated to the U.S. Latinos and Latinas in World War II Oral History Project at the University of Texas, Austin.

Devra A. Weber is a professor of history at the University of California, Riverside. She is the author of *Dark Sweat, White Gold: California Farmworkers, Cotton, and the New Deal* (1994) and coedited *Manuel Gamio, el inmigrante Mexicano: La historia de su vida; Entrevistas completas, 1926–1927* (2002).

Carmen Teresa Whalen is an associate professor of history at Williams College. She researches labor history and women in the garment industry and is the author of *From Puerto Rico to Philadelphia: Puerto Rican Workers and Postwar Economies* (2001).

Norma Williams was a professor of sociology at the University of Texas at Arlington. She was the author of *The Mexican American Family: Tradition and Change* (1990) and editor of a special issue of *Journal of Family Issues* (1995) on cultural diversity. She was the first Mexican American to be elected president of the Southwestern Sociological Association. After a valiant battle against cancer, she died in the fall of 2004.

Mary Ann Wynkoop is the director of the American Studies Program at the University of Missouri, Kansas City.

Julia Young is a journalist. She was managing editor for the bimonthly *Latina Style* magazine and is the author of "Our Hidden History" in *Latina Style* (2003).

Index

Page numbers in **bold** indicate the main listing for each entry. Page numbers in *italics* refer to photographs.

Abarca, Apolonia "Polly" Muñoz, **29–30**, *29*

Abella, Rosa, 529

Abortion rights: and Graciela Olivarez, 537; and Helen Rodríguez-Trias, 642

Acción Cívica Hispana: and Inés and Emilio Robles, 632

Acevedo, María: and Voter Registration Education Project (SVREP), 696

Acosta, María Ofelia, 209, 210

Acosta Bañuelos, Romana, 374

Acosta, Guadalupe: and *Madrigal v. Quilligan*, 416

Acosta, Lucy, **30–31**

Acosta Vice, Celia M., **31–32**, *32*, *47*

Actors' Studio: and Miriam Colón, 165

Acuña y Rosetti, Elisa: and Mexican Revolution, 463, 608; *Vesper* and *La Guillotina* newspapers founder of, 463, 465

Adam Díaz Early Childhood Development Center: and Friendly House, 272

Addams, Jane: founded Hull-House, 333, 334, 335; Children's Book Award, 481; High School, 666

Adelante con Nuestra Vision: First National Latina Lesbian Leadership and Self-Empowerment Conference, 338

Administrative Conference of the United States: and Linda Chávez, 148

Adopt-A School: American GI Forum program, 821

(AFL-CIO) American Federation of Labor (AFL) and Congress of Industrial Organizations (CIO): Socorro Hernández Bernasconi worked for the, 87; Linda Chávez-Thompson first Latina executive vice president of, 150; and María Elena Durazo, 220; Jessica Govea New Jersey state director for the, 295; and Dolores Huerta, 332; and Labor Unions, 371; Alicia Sandoval public relations director of, 371; and Dora Ocampo Quesada, 598

African Caribbean Poetry Theater: Sandra María Esteves executive artistic director of the, 244

Aging, **33–34**; and Family, 245–49; Esther Valladolid Wolf served for the state of Kansas as secretary of, 810

Agosín, Marjorie, 680

Agostini del Río, Amelia, 7, **35**; and Education, 222

Agricultural Labor Relations Act (ALRA) and the United Farm Workers of America (UFW), 333, 772; and Women in the United Farm Workers (UFW), 775

Agripino, Antolina, 184

Agüero Sisters, 279

Aguila, Lourdes, 183

Aguilar, Laura, 64, 65

Aguilera, Victoria, 678

Aguirre, Mirta, 316

Aid to Families with Dependent Children (AFDC), 21: and Aprenda y Superese, 54

Al Frente de Lucha: Rose Marie Calderón developed, 107

Alaníz, Yolanda, 26

Alarcón, Norma, 395

Alarm: Lucia González and Albert Parsons coedited the newspaper, 559

Alatorre, Soledad "Chole," **35–36**; and Centro de Acción Social Autónomo (CASA), 137; and Labor Unions, 370; and Emma Lozano, 411; and Sterilization, 723

Alavez, Francisca, 473, 718

Alba, Jessica, 501

Albelo, Carmen, **36–37**, *37*

Albita: and Celia Cruz, 181; and Salsa, 654, 655

Albizu Campos, Pedro: and Juanita Arocho, 60; and Lolita Lebrón, 380; and Consuelo Lee Tapia, 383; and Helen Rodríguez-Trias, 641; and Sister Carmelita, 683; and Lourdes Torres, 758; and Emilí Vélez de Vando, 794, 795; and Laura Meneses, 794; and Movimiento pro Independencia (MPI), 795

Alfaro Siqueiros, David, 264, 767

Alfaro, Olympia, 670

Alfau Galván de Solalinde, Jesusa, **37–38**

Alfonso Schomburg, Arturo: and Puerto Rican section of Cuban Revolutionary Party, 181

Ali, Tatyana (Marisol), 501

Alianza Hispano-Americana, 450; and the Americanization project, 271; and Luisa M. González, 719

Alianza Nacional Femenista: and María Gómez Carbonell, 288; and Elena Inés Mederos y Cabañas de González, 434

Alinsky, Saul, 169

Allende Gossens, Salvador, 26, 38

Allende, Isabel, **38**; and Literature, 395

Alma Latina journal: and Clotilde Betances Jaeger, 87; and Diana Ramírez de Arellano, 610

Alomar, Edith, 645

Alonso, María Conchita, 160

Alonzo, Ventura, **38–39**; and Teodoro Estrada mural of, *39*

Altar for Dolores del Río, 453

Altars, **40–41**, *40*; and Marie Romero Cash, 644

Alvarado, Linda, 6

Index

Alvarez, Aida, **41–42**

Alvarez, Cecilia Concepción, 28, **42–43**

Alvarez, Delia, **43–44**

Alvarez, Ina, 506

Alvarez, Julia, 13, 279, **44**; and Camila Henríquez Ureña, 316; and Literature, 395

Alvarez, Linda, **44–45**

Alvarez, Lissette: and Operation Pedro Pan, 541

Alvarez Muñoz, Celia, 66

Alvarez v. Lemon Grove School District, **45–46**

Alvin Ailey American Dance Theater: and Tania León, 386

Amador, Alicia: and Mujeres Latinas en Acción (MLEA) , 506

Amador, María Ignacia: and San Gabriel Mission, 705

Amalgamated Clothing Workers (ACW), 249: and Jessica Govea, 295; and International Ladies Garment Workers' Union (ILGWU), 350

América Latina: and Emilia Casanova de Villaverde, 353

American Bar Association: and Adelfa Botello Callejo, 111, 112; and Legal Issues, 384; and Vilma S. Martínez, 432

American Book Award from Before Columbus Foundation: and Ana Castillo, 128; and Lorna Dee Cervantes, 141; and Denise Chávez, 144; and Sandra Cisneros, 162; and Nicholasa Mohr, 481; and Cherríe Moraga, 489

American Civil Rights Union: and Linda Chávez, 147

American College of Obstetricians and Gynecologists (ACOG): and Sterilization, 723

American Committee for Devastated France: and Aida de Acosta, 189

American Federation of Labor (AFL): and Bracero Program, 98; and El Paso Laundry Strike, 228–29; and the anti-immigrant policy, 228; and Congress of Industrial Organizations (CIO), 410; and Luisa Moreno, 493. *See also* AFL-CIO

American Federation of Teachers (AFT): and Linda Chávez, 147; and Yolanda Almaraz Esquivel, 242; and Dora Ocampo Quesada, 598

American Friends Service Committee: and María de los Angeles Jiménez, 352; and Olga Talamante, 734

American GI Forum: and Chicano Movement, 152; and *Mendoza v. Tucson School District No. 1,* 450; and Enriqueta Longeaux Vásquez, 789; and Alejandra Rojas Zúñiga, 821

American Legion Ladies Auxiliary: and Ester Machuca, 415

American Library Association (ALA): and Lillian López, 401

American Red Cross: and Apolonia "Polly" Muñoz Abarca, 29; and Grace Montañez Davis, 188; and Anita N. Martínez, 427; and Pachucas, 554; and Carmen Romero Phillips, 574, 575; and Esther Valladolid Wolf, 810

Americanization Programs, **46–48**, *47, 48*; and Bilingual Education, 89; and Chicano Movement, 152, 153, 154; and Education, 222; and Friendly House, Phoenix, 271, 272; and Houchen Settlement, 329; and Journalism and Print Media, 355; and Literature, 393; and The Mexican Mother's Club, 460; and Mexican Schools, 467; and Mining Communities, 478; and Placida Elvira García Smith, 689

Amnesty International, 22: and Joan Chandos Baez, 77

Ana Gabriel: and Vikki Carr, 121; and Intermarriage, Contemporary, 342

Ana María Díaz-Stevens, 617

Anderson, Karen, 574

Andrade v. Los Angeles County: and Sterilization, 724

Anti-defamation League of B'nai B'rith: and Harvey Schechter, 675; Gloria Estefan, 243

Antiwar Protests, 153, 227, 373, 510, 738, 752, 795: and Delia Alvarez, 43; and Joan Chandos Baez, 77; and Movimiento Estudantil de Chicano de Aztlán (MEChA) , 289; and Elizabeth Sutherland "Betita" Martinez, 429; Magdalena Mora participated in movements, 487; and Patricia Rodríguez, 636; and Young Lord's, 816

Anti-Violence Project of the Los Angeles Gay and Lesbians Center, 116

Antonetty, Evelina López, **48–49**, *49, 401*; and Alice Cardona, 121; and Lillian López, 401

Antonio Maceo Brigade (BAM), **49–50**; and Lourdes Casal, 124

Anza, Juan Bautista de, 700, 706: and María Feliciana Arballo, 55

Anzaldúa, Gloria, 6, **51–52**, 802; and Cántico de la Mujer Latina, 118; and Feminism, 254; and La Malinche, 366; and Lesbians, 387; and Literature, 394, 395; and Cherríe Moraga, 489; and Religion, 621; and Sexuality, 681; and Playwrights, 748

Apodaca, Felicitas Córdova, **52–53**, *53*

Apodaca, Jerry, 537

Apolinaris, Reverend Yamina: and American Baptist Churches of Puerto Rico, 620

Aprenda y Superese, 21, **54**

Aquilino, Casimira, 184

Aquino, Pilar María, 621

Aragón, Jesusita, **54–55**

Araiza García, Alma, 142

Arancibia, Josefina, 169, 465

Arballo, María Feliciana, 1, **55–56**; and Intermarriage, Historical, 346

Arce, Rose, 740

Archuleta Sierra, Victoria, 26

Archuleta-Sagel, Teresa, 426

Arciniega, Lupe, 373

Arco Iris/RainbowHouse: and Mujeres Latinas en Acción (MLEA), 506

Arcos, Pilar, 613

Areíto magazine: and Lourdes Casal, 124; and Latinas in the editorial roles of the, 23; and Antonio Maceo Brigade, 50

Arguello María de la Concepción (Sister María Dominica), **56–57**, *57*

Arías, Anna María, **57–58**, *58*

Ariel Awards: and Dolores Del Río, 201; and Katy Jurado, 358

Arizona Hispanic Community Forum: and Rosie López, 404

Arizona Orphan Abduction, **58–59**

Arizona *Republic*, 328, 670, 689, 730

Arizona State University (ASU): and Julieta Saucedo Bencomo, 85; and Martha Bernal, 86; and Socorro Hernández Bernasconi received the Martin Luther King Jr. Servant Leadership Award from, 87; and Mexican American Student Organization (MASO), 155; and Hispanic-Mother-Daughter Program (HMDP), 328; and Phelps Dodge Strike, 574; and The Ocampo Family, 597; and Tempe Normal School (TNS), 740

Arizona's Border Ecology Project, New Mexico, 235

Armed Commandos of Liberation (CAL), 590

Armed Forces of National Liberation (FALN), 590

Armed Independentist Revolutionary Movement (MIRA), 590

Armiño, Franca de, **59–60**; and Journalism and Print Media, 355

Army Air Corps Nurses: and Colonel Nilda Carrulas Cedero Fuentes, 474; and Lieutenant María García Roach, 474; and Clelia Perdomo Sánchez, 474; and Dora Ocampo Quesada, 597; and Rafaela Muñiz Esquivel, 813

Arnaz, Desi, 94, 738

Arno, Max, 309

Arnold, Cindy: and El Puente Community Development Corporation (CDC), 366

Arocho, Juanita, **60–61**, *61*; and Emilí Vélez de Vando, 794

Arriaga, Rosa, 746

Arroyo, Carmen E., **61–62**

Arroyo, Felicia, 632

Arroyo, Martina, **62–63**

Artists, **63–66**; and Cecilia Concepción Alvarez, 42–43; and Judith Francesca Baca, 74–75; and Santa Contreras Barraza, 80–81; and Ester Hernández, 318–319; and Carmen Lomas Garza, 397; and Yolanda López, 404–405; and Gloria López Córdova, 406; and Agueda Salazar Martínez, 426; and Ana Mendieta, 447–448; and Amalia Mesa-Bains, 452–53; and Marie Romero Cash, 643–644; and Nitza Tufiño, 767–768; and Patssi Valdez, 782–783

Asamblea de Iglesias Cristianas Pentecostal: and New York City Mission Society (NYCMS), 522

Asamblea de Iglesias Cristianas, 566–567

Asencio, Carmen, 11

Asociación de Trabajadoras Domésticas, 299

Asociación de Trabajadores Fronterizos (ATF): and La Mujer Obrera (LMO), 366

Asociación de Vendedores Ambulantes (AVA), 726

Asociación Ministerial de Mujeres Cristianas: and Leoncia Rosado Rousseau, 645

Asociación Nacional México-Americana (ANMA), **67–68**; and Communist Party, 168–169; and Francisca Flores, 264

Asociación Protectora de Madres, 319

Asociación Puertorriqueña de Mujeres Sufragistas: and Josefina "Pepiña" Silva de Cintrón, 682

ASPIRA, 10, **68**; and Yolanda Sánchez, 11; Antonia Pantoja founded, 11, 557–558; and *ASPIRA v. New York Board of Education*, 69; and Bilingual Education, 89; and María DeCastro Blake, 93; and Angelina (Angie) Cabrera, 105; and María Josefa Canino, 116; and Alice Cardona, 121; and Education, 224; and María Isolina Ferré Aguayo, 258; and Luisa Quintero, 356, 601; and Sara Meléndez, 443; and National Puerto Rican Forum, 516; and Lourdes Torres, 758

ASPIRA Consent Decree, 68, 69, 89, 224

ASPIRA v. New York Board of Education, **69**; and ASPIRA, 68

Asociación para la Educación Teológica Hispana (AETH), 390

Association for Improving the Conditions of the Poor (AICP). *See* Community Service Society

Association of Hispanic Arts (AHA): and Anna Carbonell, 120, and Ilka Tanya Payán, 562; and Dolores Prida, 582

Association of Minority Entrepreneurs (WAME): and Luz Bazán Gutiérrez, 305–306

Ateneo Puertorriqueño: and María Teresa Babín, 74; and Julia de Burgos, 194; and Diana Ramírez de Arellano, 610; and Lola Rodríguez de Tió, 638

Aurora, 354, 465, 608

Austin Commission for Women: and Eva Carrillo de García, 280; and Asamblea de Iglesias Cristianas Pentecostal, 522

Austin Latina/o Lesbian Gay Organization (ALLGO), 388

AVANCE and LEAP: and National Puerto Rican Forum, 517

Avila, Chelo, 368

Avila, María Elena, **69–70**, *70*, *231*

Avila, Modesta, **70–71**, *71*

Ayala, Isabel: and *Méndez v. Westminster*, 446

Azlor, María Ignacia, 530

Aztlán, **71–73**, *72*; and Chicano Movement, 151–154; and El Movimiento Estudiantil Chicano de Aztlán (MEChA), 227–228

Azusa Street: and Pentecostal Church, 565–556, 617

Babe Bean, Jack Bee Garland. *See* Mugarrieta, Elvira Virginia

Babín, María Teresa, **74**

Baca, Judith Francesca, 6, **74–75**; and Artists, 64; Pachucas, 555

Baca Barragán, Polly, **75–76**; and Cecilia Olivarez Huerta, 331

Baca Zinn, Maxine, 245

Baca, José, 143

Backiel, Linda: and Puerto Rican Women Political Prisoners, 590

Badillo, Herman: and Carmen E. Arroyo, 61; and Luisa Quintero column "Marginalia," 602; and Aurelia "Yeya" Rivera, 626; and Shirley Rodríguez Remeneski, 641; and Rebecca Sánchez Cruz, 667

Baez, Joan Chandos, **76–78**, *77*; and Tish Hinojosa, 327

Baldorioty de Castro, Román, 638

Balenciaga, Cristobal, 325

Balmaseda, Liz, 23: and Journalism and Print Media, 356

Baptist Society: and Eva Torres Frey, 617

Barajas, Teresa, 621

Baraldini, Silvia, 590

Barbosa de Rosario, Pilar, 7, 222

Barbosa, Irma Lerma, 64

Barcelata, Lorenzo, 280

Barceló, María Gertrudis ("La Tules"), 3, **78–79**, *78*; and Women in New Mexico, 712, 713; and Women's Wills, 720; and U.S.-Mexican War, 778

Barker, Walter: and Evangelina Cossio y Cisneros, 176, 177

Barnard, Juana Josefina Cavasos, **79–80**; and Intermarriage, Historical, 347

Baró, Juanita: and Santería, 670

Barragan, Guadalupe, 321

Barraza, Santa Contreras, **80–81**; and Religion, 621; and Artists, 66

Barrera, Plácida Peña, **81–83**, *82*

Barroso, Ari, 280

Basic Occupational Language Training (BOLT): and National Puerto Rican Forum, 516

Basso, Theresa, 373

Batista, Fulgencio, 242, 296, 435, 754

Bay of Pigs invasion, 296, 542, 580

Beame, Abraham: and Amalia V. Betanzos, 88; and Luisa Quintero, 602; and Patricia Rodríguez, 636

Beauchamp Ciparick, Judge Carmen, 11

Becerra Seguín, Josefa, 717

Belén Figueroa Foundation, 261

Index

Belén Jesuit High School: and Centro Hispano Católico, 139

Bello, Andrés, 441

Bello, José: and Dominican American National Roundtable (DANR), 218

Belpré, Pura, **83–84**, *84*

Beltrán, Alma, 738

Beltrán, Haydee: and Puerto Rican Women Political Prisoners, 590

Beltrán, Lola, 175

Benavides, Estela: and *Madrigal v. Quilligan*, 417

Bencomo, Julieta Saucedo, **84–85**, *85*

Beneficencia Mexicana: and Alicia Guadalupe Elizondo Lozano and Ignacio Lozano, 162, 163, 411

Benítez Rodríguez-Aviles, Julia, 474

Benito Júarez High School: and Pilsen Neighbors Community Council, 576, 622; and María del Jesús Saucedo, 673

Benito Júarez Society: and Hull-House, 334

Berio, Aida, 513

Bernal, Martha, **85–86**

Bernasconi, Socorro Hernández, **86–87**

Bernstein, Leonard: and Martina Arroyo, 62; Tania León studied with, 386; and *West Side Story*, 807, 808

Berríos, Luz M., 590

Berry, Richard, 308

Betances Jaeger, Clotilde, **87–88**

Betancourt de Mora, Ana, 742

Betancourt, Emma, 181

Betancourt, Gloria: and Watsonville Strike, 805, 806

Betanzos, Amalia V., **88**

Between Borders, 200

Bilingual Education, 32, 301, 636, **88–89**, *89*, *90*; and Ana Marcial Peñaranda, 9, 564; and Evelina López Antonetty, 49; and ASPIRA Consent Decree, 68; and Julieta Saucedo Bencom, 85; and Comisión Femenil Mexicana Nacional (CFMN), 167; and Jessie López de la Cruz, 195; and the Hispanic Professional Women's League, 203; and the Supreme Court case *Lau v. Nichols*, 242; and Socorro Gómez-Potter, 290; and Matiana González, 292; and Olivia Hernández, 320; and Cecilia Olivarez Huerta, 331; and Lillian López, 401; and Rosie López, 404; and Amelia Margarita Maldonado, 419, 420; and Amalia Mesa-Bains, 452; and Sonia Nieto, 523; María Concepción "Concha" Ortiz y Pino de Kleven, early promoter of the, 547; and Adelina Otero Warren, 550; and Antonia Pantoja, 558; and Tempe Elementary School District No. 3 (TESD), 598; and Shirley Rodríguez Remeneski, 641; and María Clemencia Sánchez, 664; and María E. Sánchez helped create, 665; and Hilda L. Solis, 691; and Student Movements, 727–728; and Substitute Auxiliary Teachers (SATs), 729; and María Luisa Legarra Urquides, 779, 780

Bilingual Education Act, 89

Billboard magazine, 144, 243

Billy Graham Evangelistic Team in Latin America: and Aimee García Cortese, 282

Birdwell, Yolanda, 367

Black and Latino Coalition against Police Brutality: and Diana Caballero, 104

Black Legend, **90–91**; and *Encomienda*, 708–709

Black Panthers Party: and Sandra María Esteves, 243; and Fred Hampton leader of the Chicago's, 491

Blair House: and Oscar Collazo, 163; and Puerto Rican Women Political Prisoners, 588

Blake, María DeCastro, 11, **91–93**, *92*

Blanca, Canales, 588

Blessed Trinity Mother Missionary Cenacle in Philadelphia, Pennsylvania: and "Sister Carmelita" (Carmela Zapata Bonilla Marrero), 684

Bolton, Herbert E., 699

Bonilla, Pura, 730

Border Environment Cooperation Commission, 235

Border Industrialization Program (BIP), 420, 233

Borderlands/La frontera: The New Mestiza, 52, 395

Borgnine, Ernest, 358

Boricua College: and Celia M. Acosta Vice, 32; and Sor Isolina Ferré Aguayo, 258; and Antonia Pantoja, 558

Borrero Pierra, Juana, **93–94**, *93*

Boston University Law School, 402

Botiller et al. v. Domínguez: and Treaty of Guadalupe Hidalgo, 764

Botiller, Brigido, 763

Bouvier, Virginia Marie, 704

Boyar, Monica, **94–95**, *94*

Bozak, Carmen Contreras, **95–96**, *96*, *473*, *813*

Bracero Program, 26, **96–99**, 420; and Environment and the Border, 233; and United Farm Workers (UFW), 333; and Migration and Labor, 469, 470; and Adela Sloss-Vento, 687

Braga, Sonia, **99**; and Cinema Images, Contemporary, 160; and Movie Stars, 501; and Television, 738, 739

Brando, Marlon, 165

Brandon, George, 267, 269

Brás, Juan Mari, 795

Bright, John, 259

Briones, Brigida: and María de la Concepción Arguello, 57

Briones, María Juana, 2, 3, **99–100**

Bronx Community College: and Student Movement, 727

Brooklyn College, 11, 31, 49, 668, 797; and Miriam Colón received Presidential Medal from, 165; and Loida Figueroa Mercado, 262; and Tania León, 386; and Sara Meléndez, 442; and Mujeres in Action, Sunset Park, 503; and Sonia Nieto, 524; and María E. Sánchez headed the Department of Puerto Rican Studies at, 665; and Student Movements, 727–728; Margarita Mir de Cid established a bilingual and bicultural program at, 665

Brooks, Homer, 659, 168: and Emma Tenayuca, 744

Brown v. Board of Education, 446, 468, 573: and Education, 222; and League of United Latin American Citizens (LULAC), 379; and *Méndez v. Westminster*, 445, 446

Brown, Jerry: and the United Farm Workers of America (UFW), 772; and Women in the United Farm Workers (UFW), 775

Broyles-González, Yolanda, 752

Bruce, Babbitt, 85: and Phelps Dodge strike, 574

Buenas Amigas, 388

Buenaventura, Fabiana, 184

Buford, Lieutenant Harry T. *See* Loreta Janeta Velázquez

Buñuel, Luis, 358

Burciaga, Mirna Ramos, 6, **100–102**, *101*

Burton, Richard, 806

Burton, Henry Stanton, 3, 650

Bush, George H.: and Catalina Vásquez Villalpando, 375; Antonia Coello Novello was nominated surgeon general by, 527; and Ileana Ros-Lehtinen, 645; and María Elena Toraño-Pantín, 755

Bush, George W., 148, 577, 580, 611: and Latina U.S. Treasurers, 375; and Aurora Estrada Orozco, 544

Buzz magazine, 525

Caballé, María, 746

Caballero, Diana, **103–104**, *103*

Caballero, Laura: and Líderes Campesinas, 391

Cabeza de Baca, Fabiola, **104–105**; and Literature, 393

Cabrera, Angelina (Angie), **105–106**, *106*

Cabrera, Lydia, **106–107**, *107*, 670

Cabrera, Marta, 620

Calderón, Rose Marie, **107–108**, *108*

California Institute of Technology: and France Anne Córdova, 677

California Labor School: and Francisca Flores, 67

California Missions, **108–110**, *109*

California Rural Legal Assistance (CRLA): and Mily Treviño-Sauceda, 390, 766

California Sanitary Canning Company Strike, 4, **110–111**, *111*, 238, 299, 771; and Carmen Bernal Escobar, 237–238

California State University, Los Angeles: and Linda Alvarez graduated from, 45; and Felicitas Apodaca, 53; Judith Francesca Baca was faculty at, 75; and Hijas de Cuauhtémoc, 327; and Lucille Roybal-Allard, 376; and the first Chicano studies program, 727

California State Assembly: and Grace Flores Napolitano, 377; Hilda L. Solis served in the, 378; and Lucille Roybal-Allard, 646

California State Legislature: and Gloria Molina, 483

California State Senate: and Hilda L. Solis, 378, 578, 961

California State University, Long Beach (CSULB): *Hijas de Cuauhtémoc* published at, 326, 727; and Anna Nieto Gómez, 524, 525; and Roxana Rivera graduated from, 629; and Mily Treviño-Sauceda, 767

California State University, Monterey Bay, 453

California State University, Northridge (CSUN): and Judith Francesca Baca, 75; and Anna Nieto Gómez, 525; and Esperanza Acosta Mendoza Schechter ("Hope"), 675

California State University, San Bernardino (CSUSB), 241, 289

California State University, San Jose, 141

Calixto García Hospital in Havana: and Irma Vidal, 799

Callava, Leticia, 183

Callejo, Adelfa Botello, **111–112**

Callis de Fages, Eulalia Francesca y Josepha, **112–113**

Calvillo, Ana María del Carmen, 3, **113–114**

Camacho Souza, Blasé: and Puerto Ricans in Hawaii, 592, *592*, 593

Camarillo, Lydia: and the Democratic National Convention Committee, 696

Canales, Alma, 506: and La Raza Unida Party (LRUP), 367, 368

Canales, Laura, **114–115**; and Selena Quintanilla Pérez, 600; and Patsy Torres, 759

Canales, Nohelia de los Angeles, **115–116**

Cancel Miranda, Rafael, 381, 588

Candelario, Fermina, 184

Canino, María Josefa, 11, **116–117**

Cannery and Agricultural Workers Industrial Union (CAWIU), 4, **117–118**; and El Monte Berry strike, 226–227; and Carmen Bernal Escobar, 237, 238; and Labor Unions, 368; and San Joaquin Valley Cotton strike, 660, 661

Canonization: and Madre María Dominga, 307

Cántico de la Mujer Latina, **118**

Cantú Pérez-Guillermety, Lieutenant Colonel Lupita, 474

Cantú, Norma V.: and Chicana Rights Project, 151

Cantú, Norma, 395

Capetillo, Luisa, 8, **119**, 585; and Cigar Workers, 158; and Feminism, 253, 254; and Journalism and Print Media, 354; and Literature, 394; and Luisa Moreno, 493; and Puerto Rican Women Political Prisoners, 587; and Federación Libre de Trabajadores (FLT), 732, 733

Carbajal de Valenzuela, Romanita, 565

Carbonell, Anna, **119–120**

Carcaño, Reverend Minerva: and United Methodist Church, 620

Cardona, Alice, **120–121**; and Antonia Pantoja, 10, 11; and the Hispanic Young Adult Association (HYAA), 584

Carmona, Dolores, 422

Carnegie Hall: and Martina Arroyo, 62, 63, and Celia Cruz performed at the, 181; and Genoveva de Arteaga celebrated fifty years as a music artist at the, 192; and "La Lupe" (Guadalupe Victoria Yoli Raymond), 363; and Irma Morillo, 496; and Anita Vélez-Mitchell, 796

Carr, Eve, 330

Carr, Vikki, **121–122**

Carranza, Venustiano, 337, 354, 461, 462, 463

Carrasco, Barbara, 64

Carrera, María Teresa: and Operation Pedro Pan, 542

Carrillo de Fitch, Josefa, **122–123**

Carrión, Lizette, 501

Carrisoza, Fedelia: and Watsonville Strike, 805

Carta Editorial: and Francisca Flores, 264

Carter, Jimmy: and Antonio Maceo Brigade, 50; and the Nationalist Party, 164; and Cuban Political prisoner, 296; and María Leopoldina "Pola" Grau, 296; and Hilda L. Solis, 378, 692; and Dolores "Lolita" Lebrón, 381; and Elena Inés Mederos y Cabañas de González, 435; and Ruth Mojica-Hammer, 482; Gloria Molina deputy for presidential personnel of, 483; Graciela Olivarez the highest-ranking Hispanic female during the administration of, 537; and Puerto Rican Women Political Prisoners, 588; and María Elena Toraño-Pantín, 755

Casa Aztlán, 673

Casa Borinquen, 60

Casa de Recogidas, 176

Casa Esperanza, 270

Casa Loma: and New Economics for Women (NEW), 521

Casa Puerto Rico: and Patricia Rodríguez and Antonia Denis, 636

Casa Ramona Community Center in San Bernardino: and War on Poverty program, 289

Casa Victoria: and Comisión Femenil Mexicana Nacional (CFMN), 167

Casal, Lourdes, **123–124**; and Antonio Maceo Brigade, 50

Casals Istomin, Marta, 12, 225

Casals, Rosemary, **124–125**

Casañas Masón, Rosa, 112

Index

Casano, Gertrudis, 181

Casanova de Villaverde, Emilia, 8, **125–126**, *126*; and the struggles for the Cuban independence, 182, 184; and Journalism and Print Media, 353

Casarez Vásquez, Enedina, 41

Casas, María Raquel, 577, 700

Cash, Rosanne, 327

Casiano-Colón, Aida: and Scientists, 677–678

Casilda Amador Thoreson, 748

Casita María, New York, **126–128**, *127*; and Gloria Estefan, 243; and Sister Carmelita, 683

Cassados, Eleanor: and United Cannery, Agricultural, Packing, and Allied Workers of America (UCAPAWA/FTA), 771

Cassaude de León, Carmen, 746

Castañeda, Antonia, 700, 709

Castañeda, Emilia, 209, 210, 211

Castañeda, Irene, 26

Castañeda, Sister Margarita, 619

Castellanos, Isabel, 670

Castillo de González, Aurelia, 7

Castillo, Ana, 65, **128–129**, 800, 802; and Chicano Movement, 154; and Literature, 395

Castillo, Guadalupe, **129–130**, *130*

Castillo, Soledad, 746

Castro, Fidel, 22, 200, 279, 646, 754, 799; and Antonio Maceo Brigade, 50; and María Leopoldina "Pola" Grau, 296; and Elena Inés Mederos y Cabañas de González, 435, 436

Castro, Juanita, 541

Castro, Rosie, **130**, 368; and Feminism, 254

Castro, Sadie: and El Monte Berry Strike, 227

Castro, Sergeant Mary, 474

Castro, Victoria M. "Vickie," **131–132**, *132*; and Education, 225

Catalina, Vásquez Villalpando: and Latina U.S. Treasurers, 374

Catholic Daughters of America, 415

Catholic Service Bureau: and Operation Pedro Pan, 542

Catholic University in Ponce, 258, 628

Catholic University in Washington, D.C., 326

Cedero Fuentes, Nilda Carrulas, 474

Cedillos, María, 137

Ceja, Amelia Moran, 6, 7, **132–134**, *134*

Center for Emerging Female Leadership (CEFL): and Latino Pastoral Action Center (LPAC), 523; and Religion, 620

Center for Law and Justice: and *Madrigal v. Quilligan*, 417, 418; Center for Policy Studies, 235

Central American Free Trade Agreement (CAFTA), 218

Central American refugees: and Guadalupe Castillo, 129

Central American Immigrant Women, **134–137**; and Immigration of Latinas to the United States, 337–341; and Migration and Labor, 468–473

Central Michigan University, 545

Centro de Acción Social Autónomo (CASA), **137–138**; and Soledad "Chole" Alatorre, 36, 411; and Adelaida Rebecca del Castillo, 199, 200; and María Elena Durazo, 219; and Feminism, 254; and Emma Lozano, 411; and Magdalena Mora, 487; and "Isabel" Hernández Rodríguez member of, 633, 634; and Sterilization, 724

Centro de Derechos Humanos del Movimiento Demócrata Cristiano, 22

Centro Hispano Católico, **139**

Centro Mater, **139**

Centro sin Fronteras: and Emma Lozano founded, 411, 412

Cepeda-Leonardo, Margarita, **140**; and Dominican American National Roundtable (DANR), 218

Ceprano, Dorita, 746

Cerda, Maria, 18

Cervantes, Lorna Dee, **140–142**; and Literature, 394

Cervantes, Maggie, 521

Cervántez, Yreina, 64

Chabram, Angie González, **142–143**, *142*

Chacón, Soledad Chávez, **143–144**, *144*

Chambers, Claude: and *Alvarez v. Lemon Grove School District*, 46

Chapa, Evey, 368: and Chicana Caucus, 150; and Mujeres por la Raza, 506

"Charo" (María Rosario Pilar Martínez Molina Baeza), **144**; and Movie Stars, 501

Chávez Marta, 64

Chávez, Elsa: and Farah Strike, 249, 250

Chávez, César, 5, 149, 802; and Helen Chávez, 146; and Chicano Movement, 153; and Community Service Organization (CSO), 172; and *Corridos*, 175; and Jessie López de la Cruz, 195; and *El Diario*, 239; and Yolanda Almaraz Esquivel, 242; and Farah Strike, 249; and Farmworkers, 252; and Jessica Govea, 294; and Rosalinda Guillen Herrera, 304; and Dolores Huerta, 332; and Labor Unions, 370; and Rosie López, 404; and María Elena Lucas worked with, 414; and Amalia Mesa-Bains, 452; and María del Jesús Saucedo, 673; and Teatro Campesino, 752; and United Farm Workers of America (UFW), 772, 773; and Women in the United Farm Workers (UFW), 774; and Helena María Viramontes influenced by, 800, 801

Chávez, Denise, **144–145**, *145*; and Literature, 395; and Playwrights, 750

Chávez, Ernesto, 138, 507, 633

Chávez, Helen, **146–147**, 370; and Labor Unions, 370; and Teatro Campesino, 752; and United Farm Workers of America (UFW), 772, 774, 776

Chávez, Linda, **147–148**

Chávez, Marisela, *138*, 411, 412

Chávez, Ravine, Los Angeles, California, **148–149**

Chávez-García, Miroslava, 2, 703

Chavez-Thompson, Linda, **149–150**; and Labor Unions, 371

Chicago Tribune, 533

Chicago Working Women's Union: and Lucia González Parsons, 559

Chicana Caucus/National Women's Political Caucus (NWPC), **150–151**

Chicana Rights Project, 151: and Mexican American Legal Defense and Educational Fund (MALDEF), 458

Chicana Service Action Center (CSAC): and Comisión Femenil Mexicana Nacional (CFMN), 167; and Francisca Flores, 265

Chicano Coordinating Council on Higher Education (CCHE), 73, 153

Chicano Movement, 6, 128, **151–154**, 452; and Delia Alvarez, 43; and Guadalupe Castillo, 129; and Victoria M. "Vickie"Castro, 131; and Centro de Acción Social Autónomo (CASA), 138, 139, 487; and Lorna Dee Cer-

vantes, 141; and Chicana Caucus/National Women's Political Caucus (NWPC), 150; and Chicanos Por La Causa (CPLC), 156; and Comisión Femenil Mexicana Nacional (CFMN), 167–168; and Communities Organized for Public Service (COPS), 170; and Adelaida Rebecca Del Castillo joined the, 199; and María Elena Durazo, 219; and El Movimiento Estudantil Chicano de Aztlán (MEChA), 227; and Feminism, 253; and María Garcíaz, 284; and Chicano moratorium, 289, 782; and Ester Hernández, 318; and *Hijas de Cuauhtémoc*, 326; and Intermarriage, Contemporary, 344; and Las Hermanas, 373; and League of United Latin American Citizens (LULAC), 379; and Lesbians, 387; and Cherríe Moraga, 388, 489; and *Madrigal v. Quilligan*, 416–419; and Gloria Molina, 483; and Magdalena Mora, 487; and National Chicana Conference, 512; and National Council of La Raza (NCLR) founded during, 514; and Anna Nieto Gómez, 525; and "Isabel" Hernández Rodríguez, 633, 664; and María del Jesús Saucedo, 673; and And Adela Sloss-Vento, 687; and *Soldaderas*, 691; and Playwrights, 749; and Patssi Valdez, 782; and Enriqueta Longeaux Vásquez, 789; and Bernice Ortiz Zamora, 818
Chicanos Por La Causa (CPLC), **155–156**
Chirino, Willy: and Operation Pedro Pan, 541, 542
Chorens, Olguita, 496
Chumacero, Olivia: and Teatro Campesino, 749, 753
Church of God: and María Rivera Atkinson, 567, 568
Cigar Makers' International Union (CMIU), 158, 732, 733
Cigar Workers, 8, 20, **156–159**, *157*; and Luisa Capetillo, 119; and Cuban and Puerto Rican Revolutionary Party, 181; and Luisa Moreno, 493; and *Tabaqueros'* Unions, 732
Cinema Images, Contemporary, **159–161**; and Media Stereotypes, 436–438; and Movie Stars, 497–502
Círculo Cultural Isabel la Católica, **161**; and Carolina Malpica de Munguía, 508
Cisneros, Sandra, 6, **161–162**, 629, 800, 802; and Literature, 395; and Demetria Martínez, 428
City College of the City University of New York: and Diana Caballero, 103, 104; and Diana Ramírez de Arellano taught at the, 610; and Helen Rodríguez-Trias, 642; and Iris Morales cofounded Puerto Ricans in Student Activities (PRISA) at the, 727
City of Providence Minority Business and Women Development Enterprise: and Margarita Cepeda-Leonardo, 140
City University of New York (CUNY) , 212, 442, 562: and María Josefa Canino, 116; and Lourdes Casal, 123; and Iris Morales, 491; and Graciela Rivera, 628
Civil Rights Act of 1964, 69, 89; and Vilma S. Martínez, 432
Claramunt, Teresa, 733
Clemson University, 255
Clínica de la Beneficencia Mexicana, **162–163**; and Círculo Cultural Isabel la Católica, 161; and Great Depression, 297; and Alicia Guadalupe Elizondo Lozano, 411
Clínica Monseñor Romero: and El Rescate, 229
Clinton, Bill: and Aida Alvarez, 41, 42; and Polly Baca Barragán, 76; and Communities Organized for Public Service (COPS), 169; and María Echaveste, 221, 222; and Sor Isolina Ferré Aguayo, 259; and Ellen Ochoa, 534; and Puerto Rican Political Prisioners, 590; and Vieques, 642; and Loretta Sánchez, 663; and Diana García-Prichard, 678; and María Elena Toraño-Pantín, 755

Clinton, Hillary Rodham: and health care issues, 792
Club Hermanas de Ríus Rivera: Inocencia Martínez Santaella founded the, 433; and Lola Rodríguez de Tió, 433, 638; and Aurora Fonts, 433
Club Mercedes de Varona, 433
Club Obrero Español, 163
Clubes femeninos. See Cuban Independence Women's Clubs
CNN: and Anna María Arías, 57, 58; and Television, 740
Coalition for Humane Immigrant Rights in Los Angeles (CHIRLA), 217
Coalition of Hispanic American Women (CHAW), 24
Coalition of Labor Union Women, 758
Coalition on Violence against Women and Families on the Border, 421
Cocco De Filippis, Daisy, 38, 316
Colegio Nacional de Bibliotecarios en el Exilio, 21
Collazo, Candita, 587
Collazo, Esmeralda: and el Movimiento del Dios Vivo founder, 618
Collazo, Oscar, 163, 164, 587–588, 794
Collazo, Rosa Cortéz, **163–164**, *164*, *589*; and Puerto Rican Women Political Prisoners, 588, 589; and Emelí Vélez de Vando, 794
Collins, María Antonietta, 740
Colmenares, Margarita: and Scientists, 678
Colombian civil war, 357
Colón, Carmelita, 25
Colón, Jesús: and Evelina López Antonetty, 49; and Rufa Concepción Fernández "Concha" Colón, 166; and Puerto Rican Radical Politics in New York, 586; and the Vanguardia Puertorriqueña, 785
Colón, Marcus, 165
Colón, Miriam, **164–166**, *165*; and *Lone Star*, 398; and Theater, 747, 750; and Puerto Rican Traveling Theater (PRTT), 751, 752
Colón, Rufa Concepción Fernández "Concha," **166–167**, *166*
Colón, Shirley, 593
Colón, Willie, 652, 654
Colonial Law, **700–703**. *See also* Spanish Borderlands
Colorado House of Representatives and Senate: and Polly Baca Barragán, 76
Colorado State University in Fort Collins, 818
Colorado State University in Pueblo, 240, 819
Colorado State University, 75, 818
Columbia University, 35, 37, 728, 770; and María Teresa Babín, 74; and María DeCastro Blake, 92; and Diana Caballero, 103; and María Josefa Canino, 116; and Pilar Barbosa de Rosario, 222; and Loida Figueroa Mercado, 262; and Lillian López, 401; and Vilma S. Martínez, 432; and Concha Meléndez, 441; and Olga A. Méndez, 444; and Antonia Pantoja, 558; and Nina Perales, 569; and Diana Ramírez de Arellano, 610; and Helen Rodríguez-Trias, 642; and Student Movement, 727; and Sherezada "Chiqui" Vicioso Sánchez, 797
Comadrazgo, 1, **703**. *See also* Spanish Borderlands
Comisión Femenil Mexicana Nacional (CFMN), **167–168;** and Grace Montañez Davis, 188; and Feminism, 254; and Francisca Flores, 264; and *Madrigal v. Quilligan*, 417, 418, 419; and Gloria Molina, 417, 483; and New Economics for Women (NEW), 521

Index

Commission for Environmental Cooperation, 235

Committee against Fort Apache: and Diana Caballero formed the, 103, 104, and Lourdes Torres, 758

Committee for a Fair Education, 444

Committee for Abortion Rights and against Sterilization Abuse (CARASA), 642

Committee to Denounce Cruelties to Cuban Political Prisoners, 22

Committee to Free Los Tres (CTFLT): and Centro de Acción Social Autónomo (CASA), 137; and "Isabel" Hernández Rodríguez, 633

Communist Party, U.S.A., **168–169**; and the Cannery and Agricultural Workers Industrial Union (CAWIU), 117; and Centro de Acción Social Autónomo (CASA), 138; and El Congreso de Pueblos de Hablan Española, 226; and Dorothy Healy, 238; and Josefina Fierro, 259, 260; and Consuelo Lee Tapia, 383; and Guadalupe Marshall, 425; and Luisa Moreno, 493; and Puerto Rican Radical Politics in New York, 585–586; and United Cannery, Agricultural, Packing, and Allied Workers of America (UCAPAWA/FTA), 772; and Emma Tenayuca, 744

Community Anti-drug Coalitions of America (CADCA), 642

Community Committee for Alternatives in Education (CCAE), 241, 289

Communities Organized for Public Service (COPS), **169–170**

Community Service Organization (CSO), 5, **170–172**; and Felicitas Córdova Apodaca, 53; and Grace Montañez Davis, 187; and Jessica Govea was an officer of, 294; and Dolores Huerta, 332; and Esperanza Acosta Mendoza Schechter ("Hope"), 369, 674; and Labor Unions, 370; and Women in the United Farm Workers (UFW), 774

Compañeras: Latina Lesbians, an Anthology: and Juanita Ramos, 388

Compean, Mario: and La Raza Unida Party, 367

Concepción de Gracia, Gilberto, 60, 794

Concerned Citizens of Sunset Park Head Start Center: and Mujeres in Action, 503

Concilio de Iglesias Cristianas Damasco: and Leoncia Rosado Rousseau, 567, 618, 620, 644

Conesa, María, 746

Confederación de Uniones de Campesinos y Obreros del Estado de California (CUCOM): and El Monte Berry Strike, 226

Conference on Women in Copenhagen (United Nations), 167, 265

Congreso del Pueblo, **172–173**

Congreso Evangélico Hispanoamericano del Norte de América, 616

Congress of Industrial Organizations (CIO): and Guadalupe (Lupe) Marshall, 425; and Alicia Otilia Quesada, 596; and San Antonio Pecan Sheller's Strike, 659; and United Cannery, Agricultural, Packing, and Allied Workers of America (UCAPAWA/FTA), 770, 771, 772. *See also* AFL-CIO

Congressional Caucus on Women's Issues, 375, 377

Congressional Hispanic Caucus: and Rita DiMartino, 212; and Latinas in the U.S. Congress, 375–378; and Lucille Roybal-Allard, 646; and Antonia Coello Novello, 528; and Ellen Ochoa, 534

Congressional Human Rights Caucus, 377

Connecticut House of Representatives: and María Clemencia Sánchez, 663

Constitution of 1917, 642

Consumer Credit, Housing, and Community Opportunity, 377, 792

Contreras, Carmen, 169

Contreras, Miguel: and María Elena Durazo, 220; and Labor Unions, 368–372

Cooper, Gary, 358 , 793

Coral Way School in Dade County, Florida, 89

Córdova, France, 7, 225, 677

Córdova, Lina, **173–174**, *174*

Córdova, Major Cathleen, 474

Cornell University, 295, 758, 801

Corona, Bert, 36, 137, 226, 411, 431

Coronado, Linda: and Mujeres Latinas en Acción (MLEA), 506

Coronado's expedition, 1, 700, 704, 710

Corpi, Lucha, 283: and Literature, 394, 395

Corretjer, Juan Antonio: and Julia de Burgos, 194; and Consuelo Lee Tapia, 382; and Emelí Vélez de Vando, 794

Corridos, **175–176**; and Literature, 395; and *Lone Star*, 398; and María Elena Lucas, 414; and Mexican Revolution, 462; and María del Jesús Saucedo, 673; and *Soldaderas*, 691

Corrine: and Salsa, 654, 655

Cortés, Hernán, 690, 704: and La Malinche, 364; and *Encomiendas*, 708

Cortez, Beatrice, 170

Cortéz, Carmen, 388

Cortéz, Gregorio, 175, 464

Cortina, Juan, 464

Coser y cantar: and Dolores Prida, 394, 582, 750

Cossio y Cisneros, Evangelina, **176–177**, *177*; and the Cuban-Spanish-American War, 184

Costa, María, 501

Cotera, Martha, 6, **177–178**, 320; and Chicana Caucus, 150, 367; and La Raza Unida Party, 367, 368; and Mujeres por la Raza, 506

Council of Brooklyn Organizations, 31, 32, 635

Council on Foreign Relations: and Linda Chávez, 148; and Rita DiMartino, 212; and Vilma S. Martínez, 432; and María Elena Toraño-Pantín, 756

Court of Private Land Claims in New Mexico: and Treaty of Guadalupe Hidalgo, 763

Covarrubias, Consuelo, 619

Cranston, Alan, 188

Crawford, Mercedes Margarita Martínez, **178–179**, *179*

Cristal, Linda, 160, 738

Cristero Civil War: and *Corridos*, 175

Cros Sandoval, Mercedes, 670

Cross-dressing: and Luisa Capetillo, 119; and Mercedes de Acosta, 189; and Elvira Virginia Mugarrieta, 502; and Loreta Janeta Velázquez, 790–791

Crossroads Tabernacle in the Bronx: and Aimee García Cortese, 282, 618

Crusade for Justice, 789

Cruz Takash, Paula, 578

Cruz, Celia, **179–181**, *180*, 799; and Cuban Women's Club, 183; and "La Lupe," 363; and Irma Morillo, 496; and Selena Quintanilla Pérez, 601; and Salsa, 653, 654, 655

Cruz, Irma Violeta, 620

Cruz, Migdalia, 750

Cruz, Penelope, 436–438, 497

Cruzada de Jovenes Cristianos de la Iglesia Cristiana de Damasco, 567, 618, 644

Cruzada Educativa Cubana (CEC), 288

Cruzada Femenina Cubana, 22

Cuadra, María, 512

Cuarón, Ralph, 67

Cuauhtémoc Club and the Aztecas: and Hull-House, 334

Cuban Adjustment Act, 580

Cuban American National Council, 212

Cuban American National Foundation's (CANF), 183

Cuban American organization Of Human Rights, 434

Cuban and Puerto Rican Revolutionary Party (PRC), **181–182**, 288, 471; and José Martí, 19, 157, 433; and Cigar Workers, 157; and Cuban Independence Women's Club, 182; Inocencia Martínez Santaella, 433; and Leopoldo Mederos, 434; and Paulina Pedroso, 563; and Ten Years' War, 742

Cuban Children's Program, 541

Cuban Democracy Act of 1992, 646

Cuban Independence Women's Club, 19, **182**, 433; and Cigar Workers, 156–159; and Cuban and Puerto Rican Revolutionary Party (PRC) 181–182; and *Tabaqueros'* Unions, 732–733

Cuban Liberty and Democratic Solidarity Act of 1996, 646

The Cuban Minority in the United States, 123

Cuban political prisoner, 296

Cuban Refugee Center in Miami, 21

Cuban Refugee Program (CRP), 20, 472; and Aprenda y Superese, 54

Cuban Revolution, 18, 19, 436, 582; and Lourdes Casal, 123, 124; and Immigration of Latinas to the United States, 340; and Elizabeth Sutherland Martínez "Betita," 429; and Migration and Labor, 472; and Estela Portillo Trambley, 394; and Enriqueta Longeaux Vásquez, 789

Cuban Teacher Training Program, 21

Cuban Women's Club, 23, **183–184**, *183*

Cuban-Spanish-American War, 19, 20, **184–185**, *185*, 368, 473, 585; and José Martí, 93; and Evangelina Cossio y Cisneros, 176; and Inocencia Martínez Santaella, 433; and Rafaela Mederos, 434; and Migration and Labor, 470; and Paulina Pedroso, 563; and Ten Years' War, 742–743; and Treaty of Paris, 766; and Virgen de la Caridad del Cobre, 803

Cuero, Delfina, **185–186**

Cueto, María, 590

Cuevas, Evelyn, 503

Cuevas, Nydia: and Puerto Rican Women Political Prisoners, 590

Cugat, Xavier, 95, 144, 322, 609, 796

Cuomo, Mario: and Carmen E. Arroyo, 62; and Angelina "Angie" Cabrera, 106; and María Josefa Canino, 116; and Nilda M. Morales-Horowitz, 492; and Shirley Rodríguez Remeneski, 641

Curbelo, María Ana, 717

Curtis, Jesse W.: and *Madrigal v. Quilligan* suit, 418

Dallas Baptist University (DBU), 263

Dallas Morning News, 538, 539, 652

Danau, Rita, 7

Darío, Rubén: and Juana Borrero Pierra, 93; and Uva de Aragón, 190; and Concha Meléndez wrote about, 441, 442; and Lola Rodríguez de Tió collaborated with, 638

Davalos Ortega, Katherine: and Latina U.S. Treasurers, 374

Davis, Angela, 451

Davis, Grace Montañez, **187–188**, *188*; and Asociación Nacional México-Americana (ANMA), 169

Dawson, Rosario, 344, 501

De Acosta, Aida, **188–189**

De Acosta, Mercedes, **189–190**

De Aragón, Uva, **190–191**, *190*

De Arcos, Elena, 183

De Arteaga, Genoveva, **191–192**, *192*

De Avila, Dolores C., **192–193**

De Burgos, Julia, 6, 60, **193–194**, *193*, 794, 796, 797; and Journalism and Print Media, 355, 356; and Literature, 394

De Cardenás, Isidra, 465

De Castro, Dr. Marta, 183

De Erausco, Catalina, 704

De Fernández de Gamboa, Juana, 465

De Figueroa, Inocencia M., 181

De Figueroa, María Dolores, 7

De Gallo, Natividad R., 181

De García, María, 346

De Golconda, Ligia, 746

De Hostos, Eugenio María, 262, 315, 316, 638

De Jesús García, María, 27

De Jesús, Santa Teresa, 316

De la Cruz, Jessie López, **194–195**, 775

De la Cruz, Sor Juana Inés, 6, **196–197**, 316, 530, 762; and Amalia Mesa-Bains, 452; and Religions, 615; Pat Mora wrote a book about, 488

De la Encarnación, Leonor: and *Encomenda*, 708

De la Garza, Beatríz, **197–198**, *198*

De la Guerra y Noriega, Doña Anita, 346

De las Angustias de la Guerra, María, 777

De las Casas, Bartolomé, 90, 708

De León, Patricia de la Garza, **198–199**, 718

De los Santos, Nancy, 739

De Moncaleano, Blanca, 354

De Narváez, Panfilo, 704

De Oñate, Juan, 704, 710

De Quesada, Angela R., 181

De Rivero, Adelaide, 181

De Soto, Rosana, 160

De Varona, Mercedes, 19, 182

De Zavala, Adina Emilia, 393, 719

Dealofeu, Bonifacia, 743

Del Castillo, Adelaida Rebecca, 6, **199–200**

Del Prado, Pura, **200–201**, *200*

Del Río, Dolores, **201–202**, 340, 495; and Cinema Images, Contemporary, 159; and Media Stereotypes, 436; and Movie Stars, 498

Del Toro, Gloria, 11

Del Valle, Carmen, **202–203**, *202*

Del Valle, Clara María, 184

Del Villard, Sylvia, 496

Delgado, Adela S., 209

Delgado, Jane L., **203–204**

Delgado, Leonor, 717

Delgado Votaw, Carmen: and National Conference of Puerto Rican Women (NACOPRW), 513

Delta University, 540

Index

Democratic Club: and Jovita Idar Juárez, 337

Democratic National Committee (DNC): and Anna María Arías worked for, 58; and Polly Baca Barragán, 76; and Linda Chávez-Thompson, 150; and María Echaveste, 222; and Gloria Molina, 483

Democratic National Convention: and Angelina (Angie) Cabrera, 106; and James Hinkle, 143; and Jessie López de la Cruz, 195; and Lydia Camarillo, 696

Democratic Party, 356, 683: and Celia M. Acosta Vice worked with, 31, 32; and Carmen E. Arroyo, 61, 62; and Angelina (Angie) Cabrera, 105, 106; and Soledad Chávez Chacón, 143; and Grace Montañez Davis, 187, 188; and Francisca Flores, 265; and Jovita Fontañez, 270; and Carmen Cornejo Gallegos, 274; and Great Depression and Mexican American Women, 299; and Rosalinda Guillen worked with, 304; and Sylvia Rodríguez Kimbell, 359; and Labor Unions, 369; and Latinas in the U.S. Congress, 375–378; and Rosie López, 404; and Frances Aldama Martínez, 431; and Gloria Molina, 483; María Concepción "Concha" Ortiz y Pino de Kleven, 546; and María Elena O'Shea, 548; and Alicia Otilia Quesada, 597; and Dora Ocampo Quesada, 598; Felisa Rincón de Gautier active member of the, 625; Loretta Sánchez switched to the, 663; and Esperanza Acosta Mendoza Schechter ("Hope"), 674; and Emma Sepúlveda, 680; and Tempe Normal School (TNS), 741; and María Elena Toraño-Pantín, 754

Demography, **204–209**

Dena, María, 26

Denis, Antonia: and Latinas in the Northeast, 8, 9, *13*; and Patricia Rodríguez, 636

Department of Evangelization and Catechesis for Hispanics (DECH), 820

Department of Health Services (DHS), 584

Department of Homeland Security: and Lucille Roybal-Allard, 376

Department of Puerto Rican Community Affairs in the United States: and Nydia M. Velázquez, 376, 791

DePaul University in Chicago, 129

Deportations During the Great Depression, 4, 5, 16, **209–211**, *210*, 623; and *Alvarez v. Lemon Grove School District*, 46; and the Sleepy Lagoon murder case, 171; and Placida Elvira García Smith and Friendly House, 272, 689; and Mexican American Women, 297; and Journalism and Print Media, 355; and Migration and Labor, 469; and World War II, 811

Diana García-Prichard: and Scientists, 678

Diario Las Americas newspaper, 288

Díaz Miranda, Mercy: and Cuban Women's Club, 183

Díaz, Cameron, 501

Díaz, Marcelina, 632

Díaz, Marie: and Hull-House, 335

Díaz, Matilde, 180

Díaz, Porfirio, 265, 326, 465, 469, 608, 680, 780: and Mexican Revolution, 460–464

Díaz, Sylvia: and National Association of Puerto Rican/Hispanic Social Workers (NAPRHSW), 512

Diego, Juan: and Virgen de Guadalupe, 801, 802

Dietrich, Marlene: and Mercedes de Acosta, 189

DiMartino, Rita, **211–212**, *212*

Dimas, Beatrice Escadero, **212–213**, *213*

Dinos, Carmen, 665

Diocese of San Diego: and Rosa Marta Zárate, 820

Directorio Estudiantil Revolucionario, 123

Directorio Estudiantil Universitario: and María Leopoldina "Pola"Grau, 295

Dobie, J. Frank: and the collection of folktales *Puro Mexicano* and *Straight Texas*, 236; and Jovita González Mireles, 293; and Fermina Guerra, 300; and María Elena O'Shea, 548

Domestic Violence, 24, **214–216**, 428; and Guadalupe's Refugio de Colores, 87; and Central American Immigrant Women, 134–137; and Chicano Movement, 154; and Juan Diego Community Center (JDCC), 321, 322; and Legal Issues, 383–384; and Líderes Campesinas, 390–392; and María Elena Lucas, 413; and Iris Morales, 491; and Mujeres in Action, Sunset Park, 503; and Mujeres Latinas en Acción (MLEA), 505, 506; and New Economics for Women (NEW), 522; and María Concepción "Concha" Ortiz y Pino de Kleven, 546; and María Clemencia Sánchez, 663; and Clementina Souchet, 695; and Enriqueta Longeaux Vásquez, 789

Domestic Workers, **216–217**, 470; and Central American Immigrant Women, 134–137

Domínguez, Dominga, 763

Domínguez, Laura: and *Madrigal v. Quilligan*, 417

Domínguez, Margarita, 346

Domínguez, María del Carmen: directed La Mujer Obrera (LMO), 366

Dominican American National Roundtable (DANR), **217–218**, 254; and Margarita Cepeda-Leonardo, 140

Dominican American Voter Registration Project, 218

Dominican Women's Caucus, 562

Doña Ines, 704

Dopico, Elvira: and Cuban Women's Club charter officer, 183

Dr. White Community Center in Brooklyn: and Sor Isolina Ferré Aguayo, 258

Du Molins, Carmen María, 746

Dueto Carmen y Laura, **218–219**, 600

Duke, Yolanda, 653, 654, 655

Duncan, Isadora: and Mercedes de Acosta, 189

Durán Méndez, Margarita: and Community Service Organization (CSO), 171, 172

Durán, Blanca: and *Madrigal v. Quilligan*, 417

Durán, María: and the Committee to Save Chávez Ravine for the People, 149

Durazo, María Elena, 6, **219–220**; and Labor Unions, 370, 371

Dylan, Bob: and Joan Chandos Baez, 77; and Tish Hinojosa, 327

Early Settlement Life in the Borderlands, **704–708**. *See also* Spanish Borderlands

East Brooklyn Mental Health Project: and Inés Robles Díaz, 632

East Los Angeles Blowouts: and Victoria M. "Vickie" Castro, 131; and Chicano Movement, 151–154; and Patssi Valdez, 782

Eastern Academy, 645

Eastern New Mexico State University, 374

Echaveste, María, **221–222**

Echeverría Mulligan, Rose: and Intermarriage, Contemporary, 344

Eckles, Isabel: and Democratic Party, 143

Education, **222–225**, *223*, *224*, *225*; and Amelia Agostini del Río, 35; and Cecilia Concepción Alvarez, 42; and Linda Alvarez, 45; and María Teresa Babín, 74; and Julieta Saucedo Bencomo, 84–85; and Martha Bernal, 85–86; and Diana Caballero, 103–104; and Centro de Acción Social Autónomo (CASA), 137; and Community Service Organization (CSO), 171; and Mercedes Margarita Martínez Crawford, 178–179; and Dolores C. De Avila, 192–193; and Adelaida Rebecca Del Castillo, 199–200; and Carmen Del Valle, 202; and Yolanda Almaraz Esquivel, 241–242; and Loida Figueroa Mercado, 261–263; and Socorro Gómez-Potter, 289–290; and Camila Henríquez Ureña, 315–317; and Sylvia Rodríguez Kimbell, 359; and the case *Plyler v. Doe*, 432; and *Méndez v. Westminster*, 444–447; and Esther Miller, 475; and Gabriela Mistral, 480; and Susana M. Navarro, 519; and New York City Mission Society (NYCMS), 522; and Sonia Nieto, 523–524; and Carlota Ayala Ortega, 545; and Adelina Otero Warren, 550; and Antonia Pantoja, 557–558; and Diana Ramírez de Arellano, 610; and María G. "Chata" Sada, 652; and María E. Sánchez, 664–666; and Aura Luz Sánchez Garfunkel, 668; and Louise Ulibarrí Sánchez, 769–770; and Young Lords, 816

EEOC v. Tortillera "La Mejor," 383

Eighteenth Street Development Corporation: and Pilsen Neighbors Community Council, 576; and Mujeres Latinas en Acción (MLEA), 506

Eisenhower, Dwight, 500: and Adela Sloss-Vento, 687; and María Luisa Legarra Urquides, 780

El Ballet Hispánico: and Tina Ramírez, 609, 747

El Barrio, 127, 172, 586: Evelina López Antonetty lived in, 48; and María Josefa Canino, 116; and Jesús and Concha Colón, 166; Jovita Fontañez grew up in, 270; Almacenes Hernández located in, 323; and Lillian López, 401; and Nicholasa Mohr, 480; and Young Lords, 491; Aurelia Rivera settled in, 626; Anita Vélez-Mitchell lived in, 795

El Centro de la Raza, 26

El cocinero español, 576

El Comité de Orgullo Homosexual Latinoamericano in New York City, 387

El Comité Femenino del Partido Nacionalista, 794

El Congreso de Pueblos de Hablan Española, 5, **226**, 253; and Communist Party, 168–169; and Josefina Fierro, 259; and Great Depression and Mexican American Women, 300; Luisa Moreno principal organizer of, 492

El Demócrata, 355

El Diario de Nueva York, 192, 355

El Diario/La Prensa, 281, *357*, 670: and Journalism and Print Media, 355, 357; Luisa Quintero wrote the "Marginalia" column for, 356, 601, 602; and Rossana Rosado, 356; Ilka Tanya Payán columnist for, 562

El Diario, 239

El Grito del Norte, 429, 789

El Habanero, 288

El Heraldo Christiano, 337

El Imparcial de Texas, 355

El lector: and Luisa Capetillo, 119; and Cigar Workers, 157; and Labor Unions, 368–372; and Tabaquero's Unions, 732–733

El Malcriado newspaper: and United Farm Workers of America (UFW), 333, 776

El Mesquite, 547, 548

El Misisipí, 392

El Monte Berry Strike, **226–227**, and the Cannery and Agricultural Workers Industrial Union (CAWIU), 117–118

El Movimiento Estudiantil Chicano de Aztlán (MEChA), **227–228**, 241; and Yolanda Alaníz, 27; and Aztlán, 73; Guadalupe Castillo founder of, 129; and Adelaida Rebecca Del Castillo, 199; and Socorro Gómez-Potter, 289; and *Hijas de Cuauhtémoc*, 327; and Elizabeth Sutherland Martinez "Betita," 430; and Magdalena Mora, 487; and Anna Nieto Gómez, 525; and Student Movements, 727; Olga Talamante active member of, 733

El Movimiento Mujeres pro Derechos Humanos, 22

El Mundo newspaper: and Clotilde Betances Jaeger, 87; and Genoveva de Arteaga, 191; and Diana Ramírez de Arellano, 610

El Museo del Barrio, 32, 767

El Obrero: and Andrea and Teresa Villarreal, 354, 393, 465, 800

El Paso Inter-religious Sponsoring Organization (EPISO), 192, 193

El Paso Laundry Strike, **228–229**

El plan espiritual de Aztlán, 73

El Progreso, 336, 337

El pueblo Chicano con el pueblo centroamericano, 64

El Puente Community Development Corporation (CDC): and La Mujer Obrera (LMO), 366

El Rescate, **229**; and Central American Immigrant Women, 134–137

El Show de Cristina, 601, 672, 740

El Teatro Chicano, 199

El Valor Corporation: and Guadalupe Reyes, 576, 622

Eleanor Roosevelt Job Orientation in Neighborhoods Center (JOIN), 32

Elizonda, Evangeline: and Mexican American Women's National Association (MANA), 459

Elizondo, Matilde: and Clínica de la Beneficencia Mexicana, 163

Emilia Castañeda v. the State of California, County of Los Angeles, and Los Angeles Chamber of Commerce: and Deportations During the Great Depression, 211

Emiliano Zapata National Liberation Army (EZLN), 691, 820

Emmy Awards: Aida Alvarez nominated for, 41; Linda Alvarez won eight, 45; and Sonia Braga, 99; Rita Moreno won two, 160, 494, 500, 739; and Cristina Saralegui, 672; and Emma Sepúlveda, 680; and Linda Cristal, 738; and María Hinojosa, 740

Empire Zinc Mining strike, 160, 369: and Phelps Dodge Strike, 574; and *Salt of the Earth*, 656–657

Emporia State University, 649

Encomienda, **708–709**; and Black Legend, 90–91; and *Mestizaje*, 455; and Slavery, 684, 685. *See also* Spanish Borderlands

Encuentro Femenil, 199, 327, 525

Index

English as a second language (ESL), 89, 90, 517, 729: and Mercedes Margarita Martínez Crawford, 178; and Carmen Gallegos, 274; and Amalia Mesa-Bains, 452; and New York Women's Foundation, 504; and Basic Occupational LanguageTraining (BOLT), 516; and Carolina Malpica de Munguía, 508

English First, 89

English Plus Act, 792

Entre Ellas: health and community services program for lesbians in Texas, 388

Entrepreneurs, **229–232**, *230*

Environment and the Border, **232–236**; and Bracero Program, 96–99; and Migration and Labor, 468–473

Equal Rights Amendment (ERA), 167, 513

Escajeda, Josefina, **236**

Escalante, Beatriz, 26

Escalona, Beatríz ("La Chata Noloesca"), **236–237**, *237*, *747*; and Theater, 747; and Playwrights, 749

Escobar, Carmen Bernal, 4, **237–238**, *771*; and California Sanitary Canning Company Strike, 110–111; and United Cannery, Agricultural, Packing, and Allied Workers of America (UCAPAWA/FTA), 770–772

Espaillat, Rhina P., **238–239**

Esparza, Laura, 750

Esparza, Ofelia, 41

Esperanza Peace and Justice Center in San Antonio, Texas, 388

Esperanza School for disabled children: and Guadalupe Reyes, 622

Espinosa-Mora, Deborah, **239–240**

Esquivel, Gregoria, **240–241**

Esquivel, Yolanda Almaraz, **241–242**, *242*; and *Alvarez v. Lemon Grove School District*, 45–46; and ASPIRA, 68; and Socorro Gómez-Potter, 289

Essays on la Mujer, 199

Estefan, Gloria, 240, **242–243**

Esteves, Sandra María, **243–244**; and Literature, 394

Estrada Palma, Tomás, 742

Estrada, Carmen A., 151

Eugenio María de Hostos Community College, 12, 62, 116, 225, 628, 759; and Nilda M. Morales-Horowitz, 492; and Lourdes Torres, 758

Evelina's Heart/El corazón de Evelina, 49

Evolución, 337

Fábregas, Virginia, 746, *749*: and Playwrights, 748

Faccio, Carmen, 202

Falcón García, Ana María: and Iglesias de Dios Pentecostal, 618

Familias Unidas, 543

Family Violence Prevention Act, 792

Family Violence Prevention Fund: and Líderes Campesinas, 391

Family, **245–249**, *246*, *247*, *248*; and Aging, 33–34

Fantasía Boricua: Estampas de mi tierra, 74

Farah Strike, **249–250**; and Chicana Caucus, 150; and Feminism, 253; and La Mujer Obrera, 266

Faras, Concepción, 741

Farmworkers, 5, 16, **250–253**, *251*; and Latinas in the Pacific Northwest, 25, 27; and Bracero Program, 96–99; and Do-

lores Huerta, 332–33; and Labor Unions, 370; and Líderes Campesinas, 390–392; and Migration and Labor, 468–473; and Teatro Campesino, 752–753; and United Farm Workers of America (UFW), 772–773; and Women in the United Farm Workers (UFW), 773–776

Federación Cubana de Tabaqueros, 732

Federación Libre de Trabajadores (FLT), 8: and Franca de Armiño, 59; and Luisa Capetillo, 119; and the Cigar Workers, 158; and Labor Unions, 369; and the voting rights for women, 732

Federal Bureau of Investigation (FBI): and Gonzales, Rodolfo "Corky," 153; and Josefina Fierro, 260; and "Letter from Chapultepec," 388–389; and Young Lords, 491; and COINTELPRO, 589; and Centro de Acción Social Autónomo (CASA), 633; and Clementina Souchet, 695

Federal Correctional Institution for Women: and Rosa Cortéz Collazo, 164; and Dolores "Lolita," Lebrón, 381

Federation of Architects, Engineers, Chemists, and Technicians: and Ida Inés Torres, 757

Feminism, **253–255**, 802; and Gloria Anzaldúa, 51–52; and Clotilde Betances Jaeger wrote about, 88; and Luisa Capetillo, 119; and Rosie Castro, 130; and Centro de Acción Social Autónomo (CASA), 137–138; and Chicano Movement, 151–154; and Comisión Femenil Mexicana Nacional (CFMN), 167–168; and Sor Juana Inés de la Cruz, 196; and El Congreso de Pueblos de Hablan Española, 226; and Farah Strike, 249–250; and Josefina Fierro, 259–260; and Francisca Flores, 264–65; and Camila Henríquez Ureña, 315–317; and María Latigo Hernández, 319–320; and La Raza Unida Party (LRUP), 367–368; and Las Hermanas, 373–374; and *Madrigal v. Quilligan*, 416–419; and Ana Mendieta, 447–448; and Magdalena Mora, 487–88; and Luisa Moreno, 492–494; and Mujerista Theology, 507–508; and National Chicana Conference, 512, 513; and National Hispanic Feminist Conference, 515; and New Economics for Women (NEW), 521–522; and Anna Nieto Gómez, 525; and Adelina Otero Warren, 549–551; and Antonia Pantoja, 557–558; and Phelps Dodge Strike, 574; and *Salt of the Earth*, 656–657; and *Soldaderas*, 690–691; and Adaljiza Sosa-Riddell, 692–694; and United Cannery, Agricultural, Packing, and Allied Workers of America (UCAPAWA/FTA), 770–772; Enriqueta Longeaux Vásquez wrote about, 789; and Andrea and Teresa Villarreal, 800

Feo, Hilda: and Operation Pedro Pan, 541

Fernández, Beatrice "Gigi," **255**; and Mary Joe Fernández, 256

Fernández, Christina, 64

Fernández, Dolores, 12: and Hostos Community College, 225

Fernández, Evelina, 160, 750

Fernández, María Elena, 750

Fernández, Mary Joe, **255–256**; and Beatrice Fernández "Gigi,"255

Fernández, Nelly, 746

Fernández, Roberta, 395

Fernández, Rosita, **256–257**, *257*

Fernández, Ruth, 496, 652

Fernández-Kelly, Patricia, 420

Ferré Aguayo, Sor Isolina, **257–259**, *258*

Fierro, Josefina, **259–260**, *259*; and El Congreso de Pueblos de Hablan Española, 5, 169, 253, 300; and The Sleepy Lagoon Case, 67; and Luisa Moreno, 226; and Feminism, 253

Fiesta del Sol: and Pilsen Neighbors Community, 576, 622

Fiesta Noche del Rio: and Rosita Fernández, 256, 257

Figueroa, Belén **260–261**, *260*

Figueroa Mercado, Loida, **261–263**, *262*

Figueroa, María, 416

Figueroa, Rebecca, 417

Finkler, Kaja, 269

Fireworks Silueta series, 447

First Conference of Puerto Rican Studies, 665

Flores de Baker, Josefa, 719

Flores Magón, Ricardo, 259

Flores, Belén: and San Joaquin Valley Cotton strike, 661

Flores, Diana, **263–264**, *263*

Flores, Francisca, **264–265**; and Asociación Nacional México-Americana (ANMA), 67; and the Comision Femenil Mexicana National, 167; and Feminism, 254

Flóres, María: and the Los Angeles Garment Workers' Strike, 408, 409

Flores, María Carolina, 373

Florez, Encarnación Villareal Escobedo, **265–266**

Florida Atlantic University, 545

Florida International University, 376, 356, 645

Folk Healing Traditions, **266–270**, *267*, *268*; and Pentecostal Church, 568; and Religion, 615–622; and Santería, 669–670; and Spiritism, 720–721; and Spiritism in New York City, 721–723

Fontáñez, Gloria, 816

Fontañez, Jovita, **270**; and the Hartford School Board, 11

Fontes, Montserrat, 395

Food, Tobacco, Agricultural and Allied Workers of America (FTA): and Luisa Moreno, 494

Ford Foundation: and Guadalupe Castillo, 129; and Chicanos Por La Causa, 155; and "No Sweat " campaign, 221; and Mexican American Legal Defense and Educational Fund (MALDEF), 431, 457; and Sara Meléndez, 442; and Council of La Raza, 514; and Puerto Rican Research and Resources Center, 558; and Mily Treviño-Sauceda and Lideres Campesinas, 767

Ford, Gerald: and Anita N. Martínez, 427; and María Concepción (Concha) Ortiz y Pino de Kleven, 547

Fordham University, 105, 258

Fornés, María Irene, **270–271**; and Playwrights, 750

Fourth United Nations Conference for Women in Beijing, China, 482, 569

Fraga, Teresa, 576

Frances De Pauw School in Los Angeles: and Americanization Programs, 46

Franco, Rose, 474

Freedom, 559

Frente Indígena Oaxaqueño Binacional (FIOB): and Líderes Campesinas, 391

Frida, 160

Friendly House, Phoenix, **271–272**; and Americanization Program, 46; and Placida Elvira García Smith, 689, 690; and Mary Rose Garrido Wilcox, 809

From Colonia to Community: The History of Puerto Ricans in New York City, 371

From out of the Shadows, 247, 414

Frontani, Hilda: and Mujeres Latinas en Acción (MLEA), 505

Fuerza Unida, **272–273**

Gabriela Mistral Award, 38

Gadsden Treaty in 1853, 764

Gaitán, María Elena, 750

Galán, Nelly: and Television, 739, 740

Galeria de la Raza, 452

Galileo and the *Mars Observer*, 677

Galina, Laurita, 25

Galindo, Martivón, 64

Gallardo, Sister Gloria, 373

Gallegos, Carmen Cornejo, *14*, **274**

Galloway, María, 67

Galván Velázquez, Eugenia, 37

Galván, Dolores: and San Joaquin Valley Cotton strike, 661

Gamboa, María, 673

Ganados del Valle, **274–275**; and María Varela, 787

Gamboa, Diane, 64

Gandhi, Mahatma, 153, 333

Gang Retirement and Continued Education/Employment (GRACE), 509

Gangs, 131, **276–278**, 282, 334; and Judith Baca projects, 75; and Casita Maria Programs, 127, 683; and Socorro Gómez-Potter, 290; and United Neighborhood Organization (UNO), 320–321; and Juan Diego Community Center (JDCC), 321, 322; and Hull-House, 333- 336; and Young Lords, 491, 815; and Mujeres Latinas en Acción, 505–506; and Gang Retirement and Continued Education/Employment, 509; and Pachucas, 552, 553; and Pentecostal Church programs, 568; and Rape, 612; and the Teen Challenge program, 618, 645; and Lower East Side Neighborhood Association, 671; and Iglesia Luterana La Trinidad, 694; and *West Side Story*, 807–808

Garbo, Greta, 190, 498: and Mercedes de Acosta, 189

García, Alma: and National Association for Chicana and Chicano Studies (NACCS), 511

García, Cristina, **278–280**, *279*; and Literature, 395

García, Elsa, 759

García, Eva Carrillo De, **280**

García, Evelyn, 503

García, Francisca, 25

García, Juliet V.: and University of Texas at Brownsville, 225

García, Lorraine, 64

García, Margaret, 63

García, Millie: and Berkeley College in New York City, 225

García, Providencia "Provi," **280–282**, *281*

García Cortese, Aimee, **282**, *523*; and Penetecostal Church, 568; and Religion, 618

García Márquez, Gabriel, 279, 800

García Roach, Lieutenant María, 474

García-Aguilera, Carolina, **283–284**, *283*

Garcíaz, María, **284–285**

Garfias Woo, Yolanda, 452

Garment Industry, **285–286**, *285*; and Doña María del Valle, 202; and International Ladies Garment Workers' Union (ILGWU), 348–350; and Migration and Labor, 470

Garza, Belda, 459

Garza, María Luisa: and Literature, 355, 393

Garza-Falcon, Leticia, 548

Index

Gaspar de Alba, Alicia, 395

Gay and Lesbians Latinos Unidos (GLLU), 388

Gay Latino Alliance in San Francisco, 387

Gay, Lesbians, and Bisexual Affairs, 86

The Genuine New Mexico Tasty Recipes, 352, 393

George Balanchine's School of American Ballet in New York City, 500, 626, 627

Georgetown University, D.C.: and E. E. Chávez, 145; and Carolina García-Aguilera, 283; and Sara Meléndez, 443; and Antonia Coello Novello, 527

Georgia Institute of Technology, 678

Giant, **286–287**; and *West Side Story*, 807

Glendale Adventist Hospital in Glendale: and Sterilization, 724

Gody, Vera, 209

Golden Globe Awards: and Sonia Braga, 99; and Raquel Welch, 160; and Katy Jurado, 358; Rita Moreno won a, 494, 500, 808

Goldman, Emma, 119

Gómez Carbonell, María, **288–289**, *288*

Gómez, Elizabeth, 645

Gómez, Elsa, 12: and Kean College in New Jersey, 225

Gómez, Magdalena, 368

Gómez, Marga, 750

Gómez-Potter, Socorro, **289–290**, *290*; and Yolanda Almaraz Esquivel, 241, 242

Gonzáles, Elvira Rodríguez De, **290**

Gonzáles, Isabel: and Asociación Nacional México-Americana (ANMA), 67, 169

Gonzáles, Mary, 576

Gonzales, Rodolfo "Corky": and Lorna Dee Cervantes, 141; National Chicano Youth Liberation Conference in Denver organizer, 73, 153; and Chicano Movement, 153, 154; and Deborah Espinosa-Mora, 239; and Enriqueta Vásquez Longeaux, 789

Gonzáles, Sophie: and International Ladies Garment Workers' Union (ILGWU), 745

Gonzáles, Sylvia: and National Hispanic Feminist Conference, 515, 516

González, Berta, 26

Gonzalez, Deena J., 707, 712, 778

González, Elma: and Scientists, 677

González, Laura, **290–292**, *291*

González, Luisa M., 719

González, Matiana, **292**

González, Michelle, 621

González, Myrtle, 159, 498

González, Patricia, 696

González, Rebecca, 422

González Mireles, Jovita, 5, **292–294**, *293*, 548; and League of United Latin American Citizens (LULAC), 378; and Literature, 393

The Good Life: New Mexico Traditions and Food, 105

Good Neighbor Policy: and Carmen Miranda, 478; and María Montez (María Africa Gracia Vidal), 486; and Movie Stars, 498

Govea, Jessica, **294–295**; and Women in the United Farm Workers (UFW), 775, 776

Graduate Association for Bilingual Education, 665

Gráfico, 87, 355

Grajales, Mariana, 19, 354

Grammy Awards: and Vikki Carr, 121; and Rita Moreno, 160, 494, 500, and Gloria Estefan, 243; and Reverend Aimee García Cortese, 282; and Graciela Pérez, 572; and Selena Quintanilla Pérez, 600

Gran Logia Masónica Gran Oriente, 261

Granda, Chabuca, 652

Grau, María Leopoldina "Pola," **295–297**, *296*; and Operation Pedro Pan organizer, 183, 541

Great Depression and Mexican American Women, 20, 30, **297–300**, *298*, 334; and deportation and repatriation campaigns, 16; and protest against segregation in education, 46; and Clínica de la Beneficencia Mexicana, 162; and Comisión Femenil Mexicana Nacional (CFMN), 168; and Journalism and Print Media, 355; and Labor Unions, 368; and Migration and Labor, 469; and *Tabaqueros'* Unions, 733; and World War II, 810, 811

Great Society programs: and Voting Rights Act, 579; and Esperanza Acosta Mendoza Schechter ("Hope"), 674; and María Luisa Legarra Urquides, 779

The Great Wall of Los Angeles, 75, 149

Greater Boston Legal Services, 402, 668

Grijalva de Orozco, Teresa, 1

Grupo Anacaona, 652

Guadalupe Cultural Arts Xicano Music, 815

Guadalupe Organization: and Socorro Hernández Bernasconi, 87; and Alicia Otilia Quesada, 596, 597; and Dora Ocampo Quesada, 598

Guanche, Carmelina, 183

Guardiola, Gloria, 367

Guerra, Fermina, **300**

Guerrero, Rosa, **300–302**, *301*; and Las Hermanas, 373

Guerrero, Victoria Partida, **302–303**, *302*

Guevara, Ernesto (Ché), 164

Guggenheim Fellowship, 271, 279

Guillen Herrera, Rosalinda, **303–305**, *304*; and United Farm Workers (UFW), 27

Guillermoprieto, Alma: and Journalism and Print Media, 356, 357

Guillot Olga, 183, 496, 799

Gustavo, Soledad, 733

Gutiérrez de Mendoza, Juana Belén: and Journalism and Print Media, 354; and Mexican Revolution, 463, 608; and Mexican Revolution, Border Women in, 465

Gutiérrez Gillians, Alicia, 474

Gutiérrez, José Angel: and La Raza Unida Party (LRUP), 153, 305–306, 367

Gutiérrez, Juana B., 497

Gutiérrez, Luz Bazán, **305–306**, 368

Gutiérrez, Marina, 66

Gutiérrez, Ramón, 700, 704, 711

Gutiérrez-Kenney, Phyllis, 27

Guzmán, Madre María Dominga, **306–307**, *306*

Hamlin, Rosalie Méndez, **308–309**, *309*

Hardy-Fanta, Carol, 577, 578

Harjo, Joy, 162

Harvard Business School, 211

Harvard University: and Spanish-speaking teachers programs, 7, 221, 375, 809; and Polly Baca Barragán, 75; and

María Josefa Canino graduated from, 116; and Margarita Cepeda-Leonardo, 140; and Rosario Marín, 375; and Sara Meléndez, 442; and Aura Luz Sánchez Garfunkel, 668; and Esperanza Acosta Mendoza Schechter ("Hope"), 674; and Lydia Villa-Komaroff, 677; and Evelyn M. Rodríguez, 678

Hawaii Pacific University, 57

Hawaiian Sugar Plantation Association (HSPA): and Puerto Ricans in Hawaii, 591

Hayek, Salma: and Cinema Images, Contemporary, 160; and Intermarriage, Contemporary, 344; and Movie Stars, 498, 501

Hayworth, Rita (Margarita Cansino), **309–310**, *310*, 494, 760; and Cinema Images, Contemporary, 160; and Movie Stars, 499, 500

Head Start, **310–311**, 360, 503, 632, 636, 734; and Casita María, New York, 127; and Grace Montañez Davis, 187; and Sor Isolina Ferré Aguayo, 258; and Graciela Olivarez, 537; and Tina Ramírez, 609; and Guadalupe Reyes, 622; and Loretta Sánchez, 662; and Esperanza Acosta Mendoza Schechter ("Hope"), 674; and Aura Luz Sánchez Garfunkel, 668; Enriqueta Longeaux Vásquez worked for, 789

Health Care, 158, 170, 252, 254, 269, 522, 816: and Apolonia "Polly" Muñoz Abarca, 30; and Polly Baca Barragán, 76; and Rose Marie Calderón, 108; and Rufa Concepción Fernández ("Concha"), 166; and Jessie López de la Cruz, 194; and Jane L. Delgado, 203–204; and Head Start, 310–11; and Health: Current Issues and Trends, 311–315; and Juan Diego Community Center (JDCC), 321, 322; and Houchen Settlement, El Paso, 329, 330; and Hull-House, Chicago, 333- 336; and Lucille Roybal-Allard, 376; and Líderes Campesinas, 390–391; and *Madrigal v. Quilligan*, 416–419; and Olga A. Méndez, 444, 445; and Rebecca Sánchez Cruz, 666, 667; and Esther Valladolid Wolf, 809

Health: Current Issues and Trends, **311–315**, *314*

Health Disparities National Advisory Committee, 642

Heart of Aztlán, 73

Henríquez Ureña, Camila, 7, **315–317**; and Julia Alvarez, 44; and Education, 223; and Feminism, 253

Here Lies the Heart, 190

Heredia de Serra, Gertrudes, 8

Heredia, Dolores, 169

Hermanas de la Revolución Mexicana: and Francisca Flores, 264

Hermosillo, Consuelo: and *Madrigal v. Quilligan*, 417

Hernández, Concepción: and Villalongín Dramatic Company, 753, 754

Hernández et al. v. Cockrell et al., 151

Hernández Tovar, Ines, 368

Hernández, Antonia, **317**, 724; and *Madrigal v. Quilligan*, 417, 419; and Mexican American Legal Defense and Educational Fund (MALDEF), 458

Hernández, Carmen and Laura. *See* Dueto Carmen y Laura

Hernández, Colonel Dora, 475

Hernández, Ester, **318–319**, *318*; and Artists, 64; and Virgen de Guadalupe, 802

Hernández, Georgina: and *Madrigal v. Quilligan*, 417

Hernández, María Latigo, **319–320**; and Círculo Cultural Isabel la Católica, 161; and Feminism, 253

Hernández, Melvina, 724

Hernández, Nancy, 723

Hernández, Olivia, **320–322**

Hernández, Victoria, 9, **322–323**, *323*

Herrada, Elena, **323–324**

Herrera Casarez, Theresa: and World War II, 811

Herrera, Carolina, **324–325**

Herrera, Luisa: and Federación Libre de Trabajadores (FLT), 732, 733

Herrera, María Cristina, **325–326**

Herrera, Petra, 691

Herrera-Sobek, María, 395, 801: and *Corridos*, 175

Hidalgo Society: and María Estella Altamirano Mendoza, 449

Hidalgo, Hilda, 11

High Noon, 160, 358, 500

Hijas de Borinquen, 8

Hijas de Cuauhtémoc, **326–327**; and Student Movements, 525, 727

Hijas del Pueblo in New Orleans: and Ten Years' War, 19, 471

Hinojosa de Ballí, Rosa María, 717

Hinojosa, Antonia, 300

Hinojosa, Tish, **327–328**; and Joan Chandos Baez, 78; and Television, 740; and Eva Ybarra, 815; and Las Super Tejanas, 815

Hisbrok Cole, Orelia, 507

Hispanic Business magazine, 434, 549, 755: and Anna Carbonell, 120; and Entrepreneurs, 231, 232

Hispanic Chamber of Commerce: and Anna María Arías, 58; and Polly Baca Barragán, 76; and María del Carmen Muñoz, 510; and Hilda L. Solis, 692; and María Elena Toraño-Pantín, 756; and Nydia M. Velázquez, 792

Hispanic chapter of the United Federation of Teachers, 665, 730

Hispanic Engineer National Achievement Award, 534

Hispanic magazine, 600: and Anna María Arías edited the, 58

Hispanic Mother-Daughter Program (HMDP), **328–329**; and Rosie López, 404

Hispanic National Bar Association, 111, 416, 611

Hispanic Theological Initiative: Zaida Maldonado-Pérez director of, 621

Hispanic Women:Prophetic Voice in the Church, 374, 507, 621, 735

Hispanic Women's Center (HACER), 121

Hispanic Women's Network (HWN), 28

Hispanic Young Adult Association (HYAA): and Antonia Pantoja, 558, 584

History of Puerto Rico from the Beginning to 1892, 262

History Speaks Project: Visions and Voices of Kansas City's Past, 649

Hofstra University, 103, 475, 492

Hollywood: and Cinema Images, Contemporary, 159–161; Celia Cruz worked in, 180; and Mercedes de Acosta, 189; and Dolores Del Río, 201, 202; and Josefina Fierro, 259; and Rita Hayworth, 309, 310; and Katy Jurado, 358; and *Lone Star*, 397; and Media Stereotypes, 437; and Carmen Miranda, 479; and María Montez, 485, 486, 487; and *Salt of the Earth*, 656–657; and *West Side Story*, 807

Hospital Workers Union, 635

Hospital, Carolina, 395

Hotel Employees and Restaurant Employees Union (HERE), 6: and María Elena Durazo, 219, 220, 370, 371

Index

Houchen Settlement, El Paso, **329–331**, *330*; and American-ization Programs, 46, 47,

House Appropriations Committee and Lucille Roybal-Allard, 376, 646

House Armed Services Committee: and Loretta Sánchez, 377

House Banking and Financial Services Committee, 377, 792

House Committee on Un-American Activities (HUAC): and Josefina Fierro, 260; and Francisca Flores, 264; and *Salt of the Earth* distribution was blocked by, 656

House International Relations Committee, 646: and Latinas in the U.S. Congress, 375–378

House Judiciary Committee, 377

The House of the Spirits, 38

The House on Mango Street, 161, 162, 395, 629

How the García Girls Lost Their Accents, 13, 44, 395

Huber, Lidia, 616

Huerta, Cecilia Olivarez, **331–332**

Huerta, Dolores, 5, **332–333**, *332*, 370; and Yolanda López art, 64, 405; and Community Service Organization (CSO), 171, 172; and Jessie López de la Cruz, 195; and Jessica Govea, 294, 295; and Teatro Campesino, 752; and The United Farm Workers of America (UFW), 772, 773; and Women in the United Farm Workers (UFW), 774, 775; and the Watsonville strike, 805

Huertas, Gloria, 9

Hull-House, Chicago, **333–335**, 425, 624; and Americaniza-tion Program, 46, 47

Of Human Rights, 22, 436

Humanitas International, 77

Hunter College, 62, 582, 657, 666: and Evelina López An-tonetty, 49; Library and Archives of the Center for Puerto Rican Studies at, 61; María Teresa Babín taught at, 74; Center for Puerto Rican Studies at, 116; and Nydia M. Velázquez, 377, 791; and Lillian López, 401; and Esther Miller, 475; and Antonia Pantoja, 558; and Student Move-ments, 727–728; and Nitza Tufiño, 767, 768

Huntington Park Vendors Association (HPVA), 726

Hurtado, Aida, 395

Hurtado, María, 416

I, Carmelita Tropicana: Performing between Cultures, 750

Idaho State University, 26

Idar Juárez, Jovita, **336–337**, *336*, *461*; and Education, 222; and El Paso Laundry Srike, 228; and Journalism and Print Media, 354; and Literature, 393; and Sara Estela Ramírez, 608

Idar, Jovita Vivero, 336

Ideal Records, 218, 219

Iglesias que trabajan por la communion Cristiana: and Ruth Esther Soto León, 385

Iglesias, Sister María, 620

Immigrants with HIV Project of the Gay Men's Health Crisis, 562

Immigration and Naturalization Act, 18, 67

Immigration and Naturalization Service (INS), 391, 744: and Felicitas Córdova Apodaca, 52; and Asociación Nacional México-Americana (ANMA), 67; Bracero Program agree-ment, 96; and Centro de Acción Social Autónomo (CASA), 138 and Domestic Violence, 214–216; and Matiana González, 292; and Violence against Women Act, 384; and

Juan Diego Community Center (JDCC), 321; and Immigra-tion Reform and Control Act (IRCA), 341–342; and *Salt of the Earth*, 656

Immigration of Latinas to the United States, **337–341**, *338*, *339*, *340*; and Americanization Programs, 46; and Central American Immigrant Women, 134–137; and Farmworkers, 250–253; and Josefina Fierro, 259; and Mexican Revolu-tion, 463, 464, 469

Immigration Reform and Control Act (IRCA), **341–342**; Immi-gration of Latinas to the United States, 338, 341; and Rosario Vásquez, 172

In the Time of the Butterflies, 44, 395

Independent Juvenile Baseball League, 671

Independent Progressive Party: and Josefina Fierro, 260

Indiana University, 538, 678: and Martina Arroyo, 62; and Martha Bernal, 85, 86; and María Cristina Rodríguez Cabral, 637

Industrial Areas Foundation (IAF): and Saul Alinsky, 169; Community Service Orgnization (CSO) supported by, 172; and Dolores De Avila, 192; and Elba Iris Montes-Donnelly, 485

Industrial Workers of the World (IWW), 465: and Communist Party, 168

Influencias de las ideas modernas, 119, 354, 394

Inquilinos Boricuas en Acción (IBA), 270

Institute for Paraprofessional Farmworker Women: and Líderes Campesinas, 391

Institute of Cuban Studies (ICS): Lourdes Casal cofounded, 123, 124; and María Cristina Herrera, 326; and the Cuban government, 326

Intermarriage, Contemporary, **342–344**; and Alice Dickerson Montemayor, 483; and *Pérez v. Sharp*, 573; and Puerto Ri-cans in Hawaii, 591; and Estela Portillo Trambley family, 762

Intermarriage, Historical, **344–347**; and María Amparo Ruiz de Burton, 3, 650; and Josefa Carrillo de Fitch, 122–123; and *Giant*, 286–287; and Cardinal Jiménez de Cisneros, 454; and *Mestizaje*, 453–457; and Victoria Comicrabit Reid, 614, 615; and Bernarda Ruiz, 647; and Spanish Border-lands, 697–700; and Early Settlement Life in the Border-lands, 704–708; and Women in California, 709–710; and Women in New Mexico, 710–714; and Women in Texas, 716–719

Internal Security Act, 67

International Arts Relations (INTAR): and Santa Contreras Barraza, 81; and María Irene Fornés, 271; and Amalia Mesa-Bains, 452; and Dolores Prida, 582; and Playwrights, 750; and The Puerto Rican Traveling Theater, 752

International Cigarmakers Union (ICU), 20: and Puerto Rican Radical Politics in New York, 585; Dolores Patiño Río joined the, 560

International Labor Defense (ILD), 559

International Ladies Garment Workers' Union (ILGWU), **348–350**, *348*, *349*, 757; and Margarita Durán Méndez, 172; and Community Service Organization (CSO), 172; Elena Durazo worked for, 219, 370; and Garment Industry, 285–286; and Great Depression and Mexican American Women, 299; and Labor Unions, 368–372; and *The History of Puerto Ricans in New York City* book, 371; and Los Ange-les Garment Workers' Strike, 408–410; and Lucia González

Parsons, 559; and Esperanza Acosta Mendoza Schechter ("Hope"), 674; Emma Tenayuca founded the San Antonio local of, 744; and Tex-Son Strike, 745–746

International Mine, Mill, and Smelter Workers: and Communist Party, 169; and El Paso Laundry Strike, 228; and Labor Unions, 269; and Mining Communities. 478; and *Salt of the Earth*, 656

International Retail/Wholesale Department Store Union (RWDSU), 757

International Society of Women Airline Pilots, 561

International Women's Year, 167, 435, 485, 513

International Workers' Organization (IWO): and Puerto Rican Radical Politics in New York, 585; and Vanguardia Puertorriqueña, 785, 786

Intimate partner violence (IPV), 214

Introducción a la cultura hispánica, 74

Isales, Carmen, 17

Isasi-Díaz, Ada María, 118, 507, 735: and Las Hermanas, 373, 374; and Religion, 621

Jackson, Reverend Jesse, 304, 590: and the Watsonville strike, 805

Jaime, Rosa: and Tempe Normal School (TNS), 741

Jaramillo, Annabelle, 27

Jaramillo, Cleofas Martínez, **351–352**, *351*, *393*; and Literature, 393

Jasso, Mary, 169

Jiménez Underwood, Consuelo, *65*: and Artists, 66

Jiménez y Muro, Dolores: and Mexican Revolution, 463, 608

Jiménez, María de los Angeles, **352–353**

Jiménez, María Elena: and Bracero Program, 97

John Dos Passos Prize, 801

John F. Kennedy Center: and Rosa Guerrero performed at the, 301; and Tania León, 386; Cherríe Moraga, 489; and Marisela Norte performed at the, 526; and Chita Rivera was honored by the, 627; and The Puerto Rican Traveling Theater (PRTT), 752

John F. Kennedy Library Foundation, 578, 692

John F. Kennedy School of Government's Programs at Harvard University, 140; and María Echaveste, 221; and Rosario Marín graduated from, 375; and Esther Valladolid, 809

John Hay Whitney Foundation, 271

John Wesley Hospital in South Central Los Angeles: and Sterilization, 724

Johns Hopkins University: and Aida de Acosta, 189; and Sor Isolina Ferré Aguayo, 258; and Cristina García, 279; and Antonia Coello Novello, 527; and Marian Lucy Rivas, 678

Johnson, Lyndon B.: and Polly Baca Barragán, 76; Joan Baez performed for, 77; and Grace Montañez Davis, 187; Rosita Fernández performed for, 257; and María Concepción (Concha) Ortiz y Pino de Kleven, 547; and the Cuban Adjustment Act, 580

The Jones Act, 564, 684

Journal of Latino/Hispanic Theology, 390

Journalism and Print Media, **353–357**; and Anna María Arías, 58; and Franca de Armiño, 59–60; and Juanita Arocho, 60; and Luisa Capetillo, 119; and Emilia Casanova de Villaverde, 125–126; and Jovita Idar Juárez, 336–337; and Mercedes Olivera, 539; and Adelina Otero Warren,

549–551; and Lucia Eldine González Parsons, 558–559; and Sara Estela Ramírez, 608; and Lola Rodríguez de Tió, 637–639; and Silva de Cintrón, Josefina "Pepiña," 682–683; and Denise Oller, 740; and Emma Tenayuca, 743–745; and Andrea and Teresa Villarreal, 800

Jované de Zayas, Elvira: and Operation Pedro Pan, 541

Jóven Cuba, 23, 50

Juan Bobo and the Queen's Necklace: A Puerto Rican Folk Tale, 83

Juan Diego Community Center (JDCC): and Olivia Hernández, 321, 322

Juana: and Padua Hills Theater, 748

Juárez, Debora, 27

Juilliard School of Music, 628

Junior LULAC: and Houchen Settlement, 330; and Alice Dickerson Montemayor, 378, 484

Junta Patriótica de Damas de Nueva York: and Ten Years' War, 19, 471

Jurado, Katy, **358**; and Cinema Images, Contemporary, 160; and Dolores Del Río, 201; and Movie Stars, 500, 501

Juventud y Comunidad Alerta: and Sor Isolina Ferré Aguayo, 258

K. Starr, Brenda: and Salsa, 654, 655

Kahlo, Frida, 319, 452, 481, 644, 64

Kanellos, Nicolás, 141, 281

Kathy Vargas, 64

Kennedy, John F., 238, 578, 765: and Polly Baca Barragán, 76; and Olga Ballesteros Olivares, 535; and María Concepción (Concha) Ortiz y Pino de Kleven, 547; and Cuban exiles, 580; and María Luisa Legarra Urquides, 780

Kennedy, Robert F.: and Polly Baca Barragán, 76; and Angelina "Angie" Cabrera, 105; Gloria Molina campaigned for, 483; and Antonia Pantoja, 558; and Luisa Quintero, 602

Kennedy, Ted, 431

Kimbell, Sylvia Rodríguez, **359–360**, *359*

Kingsolver, Barbara, 574

Kiss of the Spider Woman, 99, 160, 500, 627

Kissinger, Beatrice Amado, **360–361**, *361*, *439*, *575*

Knights of Labor, 19

Koch, Edward: and Amalia V. Betanzos, 88; and Aimee García Cortese, 282; and Shirley Rodríguez Remeneski, 641; and Petra Santiago, 672; and Anita Vélez-Mitchell, 797

La Asamblea Apostólica: and Pentecostal Church, 566

La Asociación Cívica Lareña, 60

La Asociación de Cultura Hispánica Puertorriqueña: and Genoveva de Arteaga, 192

La Asociación pro Independencia de Puerto Rico en la Ciudad de Nueva York, 794

La Causa, 152, 228, 772, 773: and Helen Chávez, 147; and Jessica Govea, 294, 295; and United Farm Workers of America (UFW), 772–773; and Dolores Huerta, 774

La Cooperativa Agricola, 787

La Correspondencia de Puerto Rico, 191

La Crónica: and Jovita Idar Juárez, 336, 337; and Journalism and Print Media, 354; and Sara Estela Ramírez, 354, 608; and Literature, 393

La Democracia, 87

Index

La Epoca, 355

La Federación de Sociedades Mexicanas y Latinas Americanas, 389

La Frontera Divina/The Divine Frontier, 146

La Guardia, Fiorello, 586: and Aida de Acosta, 189; and Olga A. Méndez, 445

La Hermana León. *See* León, Ruth Esther Soto

La humanidad del futuro, 119

La India: and Celia Cruz served, 180; and "La Lupe," 364; and Salsa, 653, 654, 655

La Junta Nacionalista de Nueva York, 794

La Liga de Costureras: and Luisa Moreno, 493

La Liga Puertorriqueña e Hispana, 83

La Llorona, **362–363**

"La Lupe" (Guadalupe Victoria Yoli Raymond), **363–364**; and Salsa, 653, 654, 655

La Malinche (Malinalli Tenepal) *42*, **364–366**, *365*; and *Corridos*, 176; and La Llorona, 362; and *Soldaderas*, 690

La Mujer en el Siglo XX, 682

La mujer magazine: and Luisa Capetillo, 119

La Mujer Moderna journal: and Andrea and Teresa Villarreal, 253, 354, 393, 465, 800

La Mujer Obrera (LMO), **366–367**, *367*

La Nueva Democracia, 616

La Opinión, 356, 357: and Alicia Guadalupe Elizondo Lozano and Ignacio Lozano, 355, 410; and Monica Lozano , 411, 412, 413; and Pachucas, 553

La Paz Agreement: and Environment and the Border, 234

La Placita Committee: and Alva Torres, 756

La Prensa newspaper: and Alicia Guadalupe Elizondo Lozano and Ignacio Lozano, 162, 355, 410, 411, 412; and Jovita Idar Juárez, 337

La Prensa: and Journalism and Print Media, 355, 356, *357*; and Luisa Quintero, 601

La Raza Medical Student Association, 439

La Raza Unida Party (LRUP), 6, 253, **367–368**; and Guadalupe Castillo, 129; Rosie Castro organizer of, 130; and National Women's Political Caucus (NWPC), 150, 151, 506; and Chicano Movement, 153; and Martha Cotera, 178; and Deborah Espinosa-Mora, 239; and Magdalena Mora, 254; and Luz Bazán Gutiérrez, 305–306; and María Latigo Hernández, 319, 320; and María de los Angeles Jiménez, 352; and Frances Aldama Martínez, 431; and Ruth Mojica-Hammer, 482; and Texas Women's Political Caucus (TWPC), 506; and Mujeres por la Raza, 506, 507; and Aurora Estrada Orozco, 544; and Politics, Party, 579; and Student Movements, 728

La Razón Mestiza/Union Wage: and the National Hispanic Feminist Conference, 516

La Resistencia: and Puerto Rican Radical Politics in New York, 20, 585

La respuesta, 196, 197

La Revista de Laredo, 354

La Salle Vega, Felicita, 620, 645

La Sociedad Folklorica, 352

La Tules. See María Gertrudis Barceló

La Vanguardia newspaper, 280

La Voz de America, 353

La Voz de la Mujer, 465

La Voz newspaper, 744

Labarca, Amanda, 616

Labor Unions, 238, 239, **368–372**, *370*; and Soledad "Chole" Alatorre, 35–36; and Community Service Organization (CSO), 170–172; and María Elena Durazo, 219–220; and Los Angeles County Federation of Labor, 221; and International Ladies Garment Workers' Union (ILGWU), 348–350; and Luisa Moreno, 492–494; and Sara Estela Ramírez, 608; and *Salt of the Earth*, 656–657; and Esperanza Acosta Mendoza Schechter ("Hope"), 674–675; and United Cannery, Agricultural, Packing, and Allied Workers of America (UCAPAWA/FTA), 770–772; and United Farm Workers of America (UFW), 772–773; and Emma Tenayuca, 743–745

Ladies Home Journal, 204

Ladies of the Sacred Heart, 617

Ladies Professional Golf Association (LPGA) Championship, 403

Landeros, Elena, 746

Laredo's Sociedad Josefa Ortiz de Domínguez, 719

Lares, Michelle Yvette "Shelly," **372**; and Patsy Torres, 760; and Las Super Tejanas, 815

Las Coronelas, 421

Las Discípulas de Martí: and Cuban Independence Women's Club, 181

Las Generalas, 421

Las Guadalupanas, 543, 617

Las Hermanas Cantú, 600

Las Hermanas Dominícas de Nuestra Señora del Rosario de Fátima: and Madre María Dominga, 307, 531

Las Hermanas Gongora, 600

Las Hermanas, **373–374**; and Rosa Guerrero, 300–302; and Demetria Martínez, 428; and Mujerista Theology, 507–508; and Nuns, Contemporary, 531–532; and Religion, 620; and Teresa Barajas, 621; and Yolanda Tarango, 734–735; and Rosa Marta Zárate, 819–820

Las Novedades, 37

Las Pachucas, Razor Blade 'do, 555

Las Siete Partidas: and Colonial Law, 700

Las tres Marías, 555

Latin American Action Project, 664

Latin American Bible Institute (LABI), 567

Latin Women's Group of Brooklyn College: and Mujeres in Action, 503

Latina Rights Initiative (LRI), 569

Latina Style magazine, 57

Latina U.S. Treasurers, **374–375**

Latinas in Ministry Program, 523

Latinas in the Midwest, 14–18, *15, 16, 17*

Latinas in the Northeast, 7–14, *9, 10, 11, 12, 13*

Latinas in the Pacific Northwest, 24–28, *28*

Latinas in the Southeast, 18–24, *21, 23*

Latinas in the Southwest, 1–7, *2, 4, 5*

Latinas in the U.S. Congress, **375–378**, 578; and Ileana Ros-Lehtinen, 645–646; and Lucille Roybal-Allard, 646–647; and Loretta Sánchez, 662–663; and Hilda L. Solis, 691–692; and Nydia M. Velázquez, 791–793

Latino Institute, 18: and Mujeres Latinas en Acción (MLEA), 506

Latinoamerica: and Ester Hernández, 318; and Yolanda López, 64

Lau v. Nichols case, 69, 89, 224, 242

Laundry Workers' Union: and El Paso Mexicana laundry workers, 228, 229

Leadership Conference of Women Religious (LCWR), 373–374

League of Nations: and Gabriela Mistral, 480

League of United Latin American Citizens (LULAC), 4, 5, **378–380**, *379*; and Guadalupe Castillo, 130; and Círculo Cultural Isabel la Católica, 161; and Community Service Organization (CSO), 172; and Deportations During the Great Depression, 211; and Education, 222; Eva Carrillo de García founding member of, 280, 687; and Jovita González Mireles, 292–294; and Great Depression and Mexican American Women, 299, 300; and Ester Machuca, 415; and Alice Dickerson Montemayor, 483, 484; Houchen Settlement sponsored, 330; and Martínez, Anita N., 427; Méndez, Consuelo Herrera leader of the, 443; and *Méndez v. Westminster*, 444–447; and *Mendoza v. Tucson School District No. 1*, 450; and Manuela Ontiveros, 540; and Aurora Estrada Orozco, 543; and María Concepción Ortiz y Pino de Kleven, 547; and Nina Perales, 570; and *Pérez v. Sharp*, 573; and Politics, Party, 580; and Adela Sloss-Vento, 687; and Emma Tenayuca, 744; and the San Antonio Pecan Shellers' Strike, 744; and Anna Vásquez, 788; and Esther Valladolid Wolf, 810

Lebrón, Dolores "Lolita," 64, **380–381**, *380*, 766, 695; and Juanita Arocho, 60; and Rosa Cortéz Collazo, 164; and Puerto Rico Women Political Prisioners, 588, 590, 591

Ledesma, Josephine, **381–382**, *382*; and World War II, 812, 813

Lee Tapia, Consuelo, **382–383**, 794; and Journalism and Print Media, 356

Leeper Buss, Fran, 54, 414

Legal Issues, **384**; and Central American Immigrant Women, 134–137; and Domestic Violence, 214–216; and Immigration of Latinas to the United States, 337–341; and Mexican American Legal Defense and Educational Fund (MALDEF), 457–458; and Migration and Labor, 468–473

Legalization Amnesty program, 757

Legion of Mary: and María Clemencia Sánchez, 664

Lehman College in New York City, 74, 628, 727

The Lemon Grove Incident, 46

León, Ruth Esther Soto ("La Hermana León"), **384–385**

León, Tania, **385–386**, *386*

Lesbianas Latinas Americanas in Los Angeles, 387

Lesbianas Unidas (LU), 388

Lesbians of Color (LOC), 388

Lesbians, **386–388**; and Gloria Anzaldúa, 51–52; and Chicano Movement, 151–154; and Mercedes de Acosta, 189; and Cherríe Moraga, 488–489; and "Las dos," 550

Letter: and Asociación Nacional México-Americana (ANMA), 67

"Letter from Chapultepec," **388–389**

Levi Strauss and Company: and La Fuerza Unida, 273

Levins Morales, Aurora, 13

Liberal Union of Mexican Women, 800

Liberation Theology, **389–390**; and Las Hermanas, 373–374; and Mujerista Theology, 507–508; and Rosa Marta Zárate, 820

Liberato, 559

Líderes Campesinas, **390–392**; and Mily Treviño-Sauceda, 766–767

Life magazine, 309

Liga de las Hijas de Cuba, 8, 126, 182, 184

Liga Feminil Mexicana, 393

Liga Puertorriquena e Hispana: and Rufa Concepción Fernández ("Concha") Colón, 166

Liga Socialista: and Consuelo Lee Tapia, 383

Lila Wallace–Reader's Digest Community Folklife Program: and Denise Chávez, 146; and Cecilia Olivarez Huerta, 332

Lila Wallace-Readers' Digest Fund, 271

Lilly Endowment: and New York City Mission Society (NYCMS), 522

Limited English proficiency (LEP), 88, 89

Limón, Graciela, 395

Lincoln, Abraham: and María Amparo Ruiz de Burton, 650, Epifania de Guadalupe Vallejo Vallejo, 784

Lincoln, Lady Mary Todd, 650

Lindsay, John: and Amalia V. Betanzos, 88; and María Josefa Canino worked for, 116; and the War on Poverty, 258; and Patricia Rodríguez, 636

Lightner, Consuelo, 27

Literature, 353, **392–396**; and Isabel Allende, 38; and Julia Alvarez, 44; and Gloria Anzaldúa, 51–52; and Fabiola Cabeza de Baca, 104–105; and Luisa Capetillo, 119; and Ana Castillo, 128–129; and Lorna Dee Cervantes, 140–142; and Denise Chávez, 144–145; and Sandra Cisneros, 161–162; and Julia De Burgos, 193–194; and Sandra María Esteves, 243–244; and Cristina García, 278–280; and Jovita González Mireles, 292–294; and Jovita Idar Juárez, 336–337; and Cleofas Martínez Jaramillo, 351–352; Dolores Martí de Cid was specialist on, 425; and Patricia (Pat) Mora, 488; and Cherríe Moraga, 488–489; and Judith Ortiz Cofer, 545–546; and Adelina Otero Warren, 549–551; and Achy Obejas, 533; and Dolores Prida, 582–583; and Sara Estela Ramírez, 608; and Diana Ramírez de Arellano, 610; and Lola Rodríguez de Tió, 637–639; and Andrea and Teresa Villarreal, 800

Livingston College in New Jersey: and Student Movements, 727

Lo Nuestro Latin Music Awards: and Gloria Estefan, 243

Lobo, Rebecca Rose, **396–397**, *396*

Local Mexican Mission, 630

Lolita Lebrón, 64

Lomas Garza, Carmen, 6, 80, 367, **397**; and Artists, 64; and Pachucas, 555

Lone Star, 165, **397–401**; and Cinema Images, Contemporary, 160; and Miriam Colón, 165

Long Island Coalition for English Plus (LICEP), 556

Long Island University, 103, 211, 442

Loperena, María, 503

López, Alma: and Virgen de la Guadalupe, 802; and Artists, 63

López, Enedina, 289

López, Jennifer: and Cinema Images, Contemporary, 160; and Movie Stars, 497–502

López, Josefina, 750

López, Lillian, **401–402**, *401*; and Evelina López Antonetty, 49

López, Lisa, 759

López, María I., **402**

López, Nancy Marie, **403**, *403*

Index

López, Rosa: and Pentecostal Church, 566

López, Rosie, **403–404**; and Chicanos Por La Causa (CPLC) founder, 155; and Hispanic-Mother-Daughter Program (HMDP), 328

López, Yolanda, **404–405**, *405*; and Artists, 64; and Virgen de la Guadalupe, 802

López Córdova, Gloria, **406–407**, *406*

López de Santa Anna, Antonio, 778

López Prentice, Margarita, 27

López Tijerina, Reies, 153, 274, 787

López-Treviño, María Elena, 767: and Líderes Campesinas, 390

Loraiza, Josefa, 3

Lorenzana, Apolinaria, 2, **407–408**; and Early Settlement Life in the Borderlands, 707; and Women in California, 709

Loreto Academy, 104

Loroña, Eliza, 741

Los Amigos Club, 431

Los Angeles Catholic Interracial Council (LACIC): and *Pérez v. Sharp* suit, 573

Los Angeles City Council: and Gloria Molina, 483

Los Angeles County-USC Medical Center (County Hospital): and *Madrigal v. Quilligan*, 317, 416

Los Angeles Garment Workers Strike, 4, **408–410**, *410*

Los Angeles Regional Family Planing Council: and Sterilization, 724

Los Angeles Times, 134, 148, 724: and Sandra Cisneros, 162; Jane L. Delgado writes a column for the, 204; and Achy Obejas, 533

Los County Federation of Labor, 220

Los Four: and Artists, 64

Los Libres Pensadores de Martí y Maceo, 563

Losoya Taylor, Paula, 719

Loving in the War Years/Lo que nunca paso por sus labios, 394, 489: and Lesbians, 386–388

Loya, Gloria, 621

Loyola University in Los Angeles, 162, 258, 727

Lozano, Alicia Guadalupe Elizondo, 162, **410–411**; and Clínica de la Beneficencia Mexicana, 162, 163

Lozano, Emma, **411–412**

Lozano, Ignacio, 410, 412: and Clínica de la Beneficencia Mexicana, 162, 163; and Journalism and Print Media, 355

Lozano, Mónica Cecilia, *357*, **412–413**, *412*; and Journalism and Print Media, 356; and National Council of La Raza (NCLR), 515

Lucas, María Elena, **413–414**, *414*

Lucero, Linda, 64

Lucia di Lammermoor: and Graciela Rivera, 62, 627

Luera, Juanita, 368

Lugo María. Antoñia, 784

Lugo, Isabel, 566

Lugo, María Ygnacia, 647

Luis López de Quesada, 365

LULAC News: and Ester Machuca, 415; and Alice Dickerson Montemayor, 415, 484

Luna Mount, Julia, 67

Luna Rodríguez, Celia, 67

Luna, Carmen, 521

Luna, Florencia: and Asociación Nacional México-Americana (ANMA), 169

Luna, Sister Anita de: and the Conference of Women Religious, 621

Lupe & Sirena in Love, 63

Lusgardia Ernandes, Anttonía, 2

Luther King, Martin Jr., 87: and Joan Chandos Baez, 77; and Julieta Bencomo, 85; and César Chávez, 153; and United Farm Workers (UFW), 333; and Student Movements, 728

Luz J. Martínez-Miranda, 678

Luz Rodríguez, Ida, 590

MacArthur Foundation Fellowship, 357, 788

MACHA Theatre Company: and Odalys Nanin, 190

Machado, Daisy, 621

Machado, Gerardo, 296, 571, 435

Machuca, Ester, **415**

Madrid, Patricia A., **415–416**

Madrigal v. Quilligan, **416–419**; and Comisión Femenil Mexicana Nacional (CFMN), 167; and Feminism, 254; and Gloria Molina, 483; and Sexuality, 681; and Sterilization, 724

Madrigal, Dolores: and *Madrigal v. Quilligan*, 416

Magaña, Delia, 236

Magón, Ricardo Flores: and Partido Liberal Mexicano (PLM), 465

Malcolm X, 152, 728

Maldonado Koenig, Nilda: and Substitute Auxiliary Teachers (SATs), 730

Maldonado, Amelia Margarita, **419–420**; and Education, 223

Maldonado, Laura, 730

Mamá Léo. *See* Leoncia Rosado Rousseau

Mangual, María, 505

Manrique, Vicereine María Luisa: and Sor Juana Inés de la Cruz, 196

Maquiladoras, **420–421**; and International Ladies Garment Workers' Union (ILGWU), 348–350; and Migration and Labor, 470

Maravilla Housing Project of East Los Angeles: and Adelaida Rebecca Del Castillo, 199; and Antonia Hernández, 371; and Gloria Molina, 483

Marcantonio, Vito: and Juanita Arocho worked with, 60; and Puerto Rican Radical politics in New York, 586; and Emilí Vélez de Vando, 794

Marga Gómez Is Pretty, Witty, and Gay and *Half Cuban/Half Lesbian*, 750

María Paula Rosalía Vallejo de Leese, 784

María Pérez, Carmen, 588

Mariachi, **421–422**

Mariachi Estrella de Topeka, **422–423**; and Mariachi, 421

Marianismo and *Machismo*, **423–424**

Marie, Constance, 160

Marín, Mari: and Friendly House, 272

Marín, Rosario: and Latina U.S. Treasurers, 374

Maris, Mona, 499

Mariscal, Celia D., 27

Marquez, Brixeida, 620

Márquez, Evelina, 138

Márquez-Magaña Leticia: and Scientists, 677

Marshall, Guadalupe, **424–425**; and The Mexican Mother's Club at the University of Chicago Settlement House, 459

Martell, Esperanza, 727

Martell-Otero, Loida, 621

Martí de Cid, Dolores, **425**

Martí, José, 157, 190, 433, 441, 471, 637: and Jesusa Alfau Galván de Solalinde, 37; and Juana Borrero Pierra, 93; and Carolina Rodríguez, 158; and Paulina Pedroso, 563; Partido Revolucionario Cubano (PRC) founder, 181; and Cuban-Spanish-American War, 184–185; and María Gómez Carbonell, 288; Lola Rodríguez de Tió collaborated with, 638

Martínez, Agueda Salazar, **426**

Martínez, Altagracia, 732

Martínez, Anita N., **426–428**, *427*

Martínez, Carmela, 741

Martínez, Carmen, 210, 211

Martínez, Demetria, 6, **428–429**, *428*; and Las Hermanas, 373

Martínez, Elizabeth Sutherland "Betita," **429–430**, *430*

Martínez, Frances Aldama, **430–431**, *431*

Martínez, Julia, 7

Martínez, Laura, 324

Martínez, Margarita, 620

Martínez, María "Maruca," 505

Martínez, María del Carmen, 746

Martínez, María Elena: and La Raza Unida Party (LRUP), 368, 507

Martínez, Vilma S., **431–433**, *432*; and the Chicana Rights Project, 151; and Mexican American Legal Defense and Educational Fund (MALDEF), 458; and Graciela Olivarez, 538

Martínez Bernat, Rubi: founded Cántico de la Mujer Latina, 118

Martínez Santaella, Inocencia, **433**

Martínez, Teresa, 210, 211

Martínez-Cañas, María, 63

Mas Gráfica, 264

Massachusetts's District Attorney's Office: and María I. López, 402

Matillas, Carmen, 181

Maya Murray, Yxta, 395

McBride, Teresa N., **433–434**

McCarran-Walter Immigration Act, 674

McCarthyism, 187, 190, 264: and Asociación Nacional México-Americana (ANMA), 67; and Demetria Martínez, 428

McCormick, Paul: and *Méndez v. Westminster*, 222, 445, 446

McKinley, William: and Evangelina Cossio y Cisneros, 176; and Mercedes De Acosta, 189

Medallion of Merit for Leadership in Public Education: and Julieta Saucedo Bencomo, 85

Mederos y Cabañas de González, Elena Inés, 22, **434–436**, *436*

Media Stereotypes, **436–438**, *437, 438*; and Cinema Images, Contemporary, 159–161; and Movie Stars, 497–502

Medicine, **438–440**, *440*; and Antonia Coello Novello, 12; and Helen Rodríguez-Trías, 641–643; and Irma Vidal, 798–799

Medina, Esther, **440–441**

Meléndez, Concha, **441–442**; and Journalism and Print Media, 355

Meléndez, Ivonne, 590

Meléndez, Lisette: and Salsa, 654, 655

Meléndez, Sara, **442–443**, *442*

Mena, María Cristina, 354, 393

Méndez, Ana: and Early Settlement Life in the Borderlands, 704

Méndez, Angélica, 746

Méndez, Consuelo Herrera, **443–444**

Méndez, Felícitas: and *Méndez v. Westminster*, 222, 446

Méndez, Herminia, 26

Méndez, Olga A., **444–445**, *445*

Méndez v. Westminster, 5, **445–447**, 573; and Education, 222; and League of United Latin American Citizens (LULAC), 379; and Mexican Schools, 468

Mendieta, Ana, *66*, **447–448**, *447*; and Artists, 65; and Feminism, 254

Mendoza, Francisca J., 465

Mendoza, Judy, 505

Mendoza, Lydia, 175, **448**, 749, 800; and Ester Hernández, 319; and Selena Quintanilla Pérez, 600

Mendoza, María Estella Altamirano, **448–450**, *449*

Mendoza, Mona, 27

Mendoza v. Tucson School District No. 1, **450–451**

Mercado, Victoria "Vicky," **451–452**

Merchan, Ana, 181, 742

Mesa-Bains, Amalia, 6, **452–453**, *453*; and Altars, 41; and Artists, 66

Mestizaje, 1, 361, **453–457**, 579, 630, 697, 781, 802; and Altars, 40; and María Feliciana Arballo, 55; and Artists, 63–66; and Aztlán, 73; and *Giant*, 287; and Intermarriage, Historical, 345; and Liberation Theology, 390; and *Lone Star*, 400; and Encarnación Pinedo, 576; and Race and Color Consciousness, 603–607; and *Comadrazgo*, 703; and Early Settlement Life in the Borderlands, 704–708; and Women in California, 709–710; and Women in New Mexico, 710–714; and Women in Texas, 716–719

Methodist Church, 280, 282, 290, 337, 508: and Americanization Programs, 46; and Houchen Settlement, 329; and Pentecostal Church, 568; and Religion, 620

Mexia, Ynés: and Scientists, 676–677

Mexican American Bar Association: and Vilma S. Martínez, 432; Irma Rangel, 611; and "Isabel" Hernández Rodríguez, 633, 634

Mexican American Business and Professional Women's Association, 735

Mexican American Community Services Agency (MACSA), 441

Mexican American Legal Defense and Educational Fund (MALDEF), **457–458**; and Adelfa Botello Callejo, 111; and Chicana Rights Project, 151; and Vilma Martínez, 151, 431, 432, 538; and Deportations During the Great Depression, 211; and Antonia Hernández, 317, 384; and Gloria Molina, 317; and Proposition 187, 317; and Legal Issues, 384; and Patricia A. Madrid, 416; and *Mendoza v. Tucson Schools District No. 1*, 450; and Graciela Olivarez, 538; and Nina Perales, 569, 570; and Political Party, 580; and Irma Rangel, 611; and Mary Rose Garrido Wilcox, 809

Mexican American Medical Association, 439

Mexican American Political Association (MAPA): and Grace Montañez Davis founding member of the, 187; and Francisca Flores, 264; and Frances Aldama Martínez, 431

Index

Mexican American Student Organization (MASO): and Chicanos Por La Causa (CPLC), 155; and Rosie López, 404; and Mary Rose Garrido Wilcox organized the, 808

Mexican American Traditions in Nebraska project, 332, 536

Mexican American War. *See* U.S.–Mexican War

Mexican American Women's National Association (MANA), 27, **458–459**; and Anna María Arías, 58; and Jane L. Delgado, 204; and Irene Hernández Ruiz, 649

Mexican American Youth Organization (MAYO): and Santa Contreras Barraza, 80; and Luz Bazán Gutiérrez, 305–306; and María de los Angeles Jiménez, 352; and La Raza Unida Party, 367; and Magdalena Mora, 487

Mexican Civic Committee, 623

Mexican Mother's Club, University of Chicago Settlement House, **459–460**; and Americanization Programs, 46–48; and Guadalupe Marshall, 424–425

Mexican Revolution, 148, 233, 336, 394, 452, **460–464**, *462, 463,* 473, 660, 687, 793; and Ventura Alonzo, 38; and Felicitas Apodaca, 52; and Angie González Chabram, 142; and Communist Party of the United States (CPUSA), 168; *corridos'* golden age, 175°d Leonor Villegas de Magnón, 337, 354; and Andrea and Teresa Villarreal, 392, 800; and Migration and Labor, 469; and Carlota Ayala Ortega family, 544; and Sara Estela Ramírez, 608; and Angelina Moreno Rico, 623; and *Soldaderas,* 691; and Theatre, 746; and Villalongín Dramatic Company, 753; and Virgen de Guadalupe, 802

Mexican Revolution, Border Women in, **464–466**, *466;* and Teresa Urrea, 3, 465, 568, 616, 780–781; and Sara Estela Ramírez, 6, 222, 368. *See also* Mexican Revolution

Mexican Schools, **466–468**, *467, 468;* and Americanization Programs, 47; and Education, 222; and Jovita Idar, 354; and Consuelo Herrera Méndez, 443; and *Mendoza v. Tucson School District No. 1,* 450; and Petra Ochoa, 741

Mexican Teachers Organization (MTO), 674

Mexican Women in the United States: Struggles Past and Present, 200

Mi libro de Cuba, 638

Mi opinión sobre las libertades, derechos, y deberes de la mujer, 119, 354

Miami Beach Hispanic Community Center: and Margarita Cepeda-Leonardo, 140

Miami chapter of the American Civil Liberties Union: and María Cristina Herrera, 326

Miami Herald newspaper, 23, 200, 356, 541

Miami-Dade Community College, 326, 376, 561: and The Floridana award, 183

Michel, Louise, 733

Michelin, Beatríz, 159, 498

Michigan Department of Education: and Carlota Ayala Ortega, 545

Middlebury College: and Amelia Agostini del Río, 35; and Julia Alvarez, 44; and Camila Henríquez Ureña, 223, 315; and Gabriela Mistral, 480

Migration and Labor, **468–473**, *470, 471;* and Bracero Program, 96–99; and Central American Immigrant Women, 134–137; and Farmworkers, 250–53; and Immigration of Latinas to the United States, 337–341

Migrant Bilingual Program, Indiana: and Gloria Anzaldúa, 51

Migrant Daycare Centers of Washington, 27

Migration Division Office in the Department of Labor and Human Resources of Puerto Rico: and Nydia M. Velázquez, 376

Military Citizenship Act, 692

Military Service **473–475**, *474;* and Carmen Contreras Bozak, 95–96; and Antonia Coello Novello, 526–528; and Carmen Romero Phillips, 574–575; and Dora Ocampo Quesada, 597–598; and Verneda Rodríguez McLean, 639–640; and Loreta Janeta Velázquez, 790–791

Miller, Esther, **475–476**

Miller Raut, Anna "Ann" Manuela, 741

Mills, Juana, 589

Mining Communities, 5, **476–478**, *477;* and Environment and the Border, 233; and Farmworkers, 250, 251; and Mexican Revolution, Border Women in, 464–466; and Migration and Labor, 469; and Phelps Dodge Strike, 573–574; and *Salt of the Earth,* 656–657; and Smeltertown, 687–689

Mir de Cid, Margarita, 665

Miranda, Carmen, 99, **478–479**; and Cinema Images, Contemporary, 159; and Media Stereotypes, 436; and Movie Stars, 499, 501; and Olga San Juan, 662

Mireles, Irma, 368

Mission Coalition: and Elba Iris Montes-Donnelly, 485

Missionary Servants of the Most Blessed Trinity, 257, 531

Mistral, Gabriela (Lucila Godoy Alcayaga), **479–480**; and *Revista de Artes y Letras,* 9; and Lydia Cabrera, 107; and Journalism and Print Media, 355; and Religion, 616

The Mixquiahuala Letters, 128, 395

Moctezuma, Isabel, 708

MODA award for Top Hispanic Designer, 325

Mohr, Nicholasa, 13, **480–481**; and Literature, 394

Mojica-Hammer, Ruth, **481–482**, *482*

Molina, Gloria, **482–483**; Grace Montañez Davis campaigned for, 188; and Mexican American Legal Defense and Educational Fund (MALDEF), 317, 458; Comisión Femenil Mexicana Nacional (CFMN), 417; and *Madrigal v. Quilligan,* 417, 418; and Mothers of East Los Angeles (MELA), 497

Monárrez Fragoso, Julia, 420

Montalbo, Gregoria, 180: and Tex-Son Strike, 745–746

Montemayor, Alice Dickerson, **483–484**; and League of United Latin American Citizens (LULAC), 5, 300, 378; and Ester Machuca, 415; and Adela Sloss-Vento, 687

Montes-Donnelly, Elba Iris; **484–485**

Montez, María (María Africa Gracia Vidal), **485–487**; and Cinema Images, Contemporary, 160; and Movie Stars, 499

Montiel, Sarita, 160

Montoya, Delilah, 64, *65*

Montoya, Teresa, 746

Montoya, Virginia, 169

Moon over Parador, 99, 144, 160

Mora, Magdalena, 6, 200, **487–488**; and Feminism, 254

Mora, Patricia "Pat," 6, **488**; and Literature, 395; Intermarriage, Contemporary, 344

Moraga, Cherríe, 6, 50, **488–489**; and Ana Castillo, 129; and Feminism, 254; and Lesbians, 387; and Literature, 394; and Pachucas, 621; and Playwrights, 749, 750

Moraga, Gloria Flores, **489–491**, *490*

Morales, Iris, **491–492**; and Student Movements, 727; and Young Lords, 816

Morales, Rebecca, 521

872

Morales-Horowitz, Nilda M., **492**

Mordaza law, 588

Morejón, Nancy, 190

Moreno Wykoff, Gloria, 521

Moreno, Chavela, 805

Moreno, Dorinda, 516, 749

Moreno, Luisa, 5, 6, 9, 171, **492–494**, *493*, *771*; and California Sanitary Canning Company, 110; and Communist Party, 169; and Congreso de Pueblos de Hablan Española, 226, 300; and Feminism, 253; and Josefina Fierro, 259; and United Cannery, Agricultural, Packing, and Allied Workers of America (UCAPAWA/FTA), 299, 770, 771; and Labor Unions, 369, 371

Moreno, Rita (Rosa Dolores Alverio), *160*, **494–496**, *495*, 662; and Cinema Image, Contemporary, 160; and Movie Stars, 500; and Television, 739; and *West Side Story*, 807, 808

Morillo, Irma, **496–497**, *496*

Mother Francisca Josefa de la Concepción del Castillo, 530

Mothers of East Los Angeles (MELA), **497**; and Communities Organized for Public Service (COPS), 169

Mountain View Elementary School: and Louise Ulibarrí Sánchez, 769

Movie Stars, **497–502**; and Sonia Braga, 99; and Cinema Images, Contemporary, 159–161; and Media Stereotypes, 436–438; and Carmen Miranda, 478–79; and Montez María, 485–487; and Rita Moreno, 494–496; and Olga San Juan, 662; and Raquel Welch, 806–807

Movimiento Estudiantil de Teatro y Arte (META), 629

Movimiento Femenino Anticomunista de Cuba, 22

Mugarrieta, Elvira Virginia (Babe Bean, Jack Bee Garland), **502–503**, *502*

Mujeres Activas en Letras y Cambio Social (MALCS), 254, 693

Mujeres del Longo: and *Hijas de Cuauhtémoc* newspaper, 326

Mujeres in Action, Sunset Park, Brooklyn, **503–504**, *504*

Mujeres Latinas en Acción (MLEA), 18, **505–506**, 673

Mujeres Mexicanas, 390, 767

Mujeres por la Raza, **506–507**; and National Chicana Conference, 512

Mujeres Unidas de Idaho in Boise, 27

Mujerista Theology, **507–508**; and Las Hermanas, 374; and Religion, 621

Munguía, Carolina Malpica de, **508–509**; and Círculo Cultural Isabel la Católica, 161

Muñiz Esquivel, Rafaela, *312*: and World War II, 813

Muñiz, Ramsey, 320, 367, 368

Muñiz, Vicky: and Mujeres in Action, 503

Muñoz Lee, Munita, 17

Muñoz Marín, Luis, 17, 105, 624

Muñoz, Cecilia: and National Council of La Raza (NCLR), 515

Muñoz, María del Carmen, **509**

Muñoz, Maria Elena, 421

Murgía, Janet: and National Council of La Raza (NCLR), 515

Murillo, Hilda, 496

Museum of International Folk Art, 406, 426, 644

Musquiz, Virginia, 368

Napolitano, Grace Flores: and Latinas in the U.S. Congress, 375, 377, 338

Nat King Cole, 121, 281

Nation magazine, 429

National Advisory Council on Bilingual Education, 89

National Alliance for Hispanic Health, 204

National Association for Chicana and Chicano Studies (NACCS), 6, **510–511**; and Elizabeth Sutherland Martínez "Betita," 430; and Aurora Estrada Orozco, 544; and Adaljiza Sosa-Riddell, 693

National Association for Puerto Rican Civil Rights, 88

National Association for the Advancement of Colored People (NAACP), 4: and Celia M. Acosta Vice, 32; and Bracero Program, 98; and Community Service Organization (CSO), 172; and *Méndez v. Westminster*, 222, 445, 446; and Vilma S. Martínez, 432; and Iris Morales, 491; and *Pérez v. Sharp*, 573

National Association of Ethnic Studies (NAES), 629

National Association of Hispanic Journalists (NAHJ), 45, 120, 739

National Association of Hispanic Elderly, 810

National Association of Latino Elected Officials (NALEO), 578, 580: and Rita DiMartino, 212; and Mary Rose Garrido Wilcox, 809

National Association of Minority Business Women, 106, 120

National Association of Pastoral Musicians, 118

National Association of Puerto Rican/Hispanic Social Workers (NAPRHSW), **511–512**; and Sonia Palacio-Grottola, 556

National Association of Spanish Broadcasters (NASB), 755

National Catholic Reporter, 428

National Chicana Conference, 327, **512–513**; and Feminism, 254

National Chicano Youth Liberation Conference held in Denver, 73, 153, 254

National Conference of Puerto Rican Women (NACOPRW), **513–514**; and Anna Carbonell, 120; and Alice Cardona, 121; and Sonia Palacio-Grottola, 557

National Congress for Puerto Rican Rights: and Diana Caballero, 103, 104; and María Josefa Canino, 116; and Lourdes Torres, 758, 759

National Council of La Raza (NCLR), **514–515**; and Mónica Cecilia Lozano, 413; and Politics, Party, 580; and Mary Rose Garrido Wilcox, 809

National Education Association: and Rosa Guerrero, 302; and Alicia Sandoval, 371; and Consuelo Herrera Méndez, 443; and Emilia Schunior Ramírez, 608; María L. Urquides leader of the, 741

National Endowment for the Arts: and María Irene Fornés, 271; and Ester Hernández, 319; and Carmen Lomas Garza, 397; and Lydia Mendoza, 448; and Achy Obejas, 533; and Marie Romero Cash, 643; and Nitza Tufiño, 768; and Patssi Valdez, 783; and Helena María Viramontes, 801

National Endowment for the Humanities, 538, 547

National Farm Workers Association (NFWA), 146, 294: and De la Cruz Jessie López, 195; Dolores Huerta cofounded the, 332; and Women in the United Farm Workers (UFW), 774. *See also* United Farm Workers of America (UFW)

National Hispana Leadership Institute, 434

National Hispanic Feminist Conference, **515–516**; and Mexican American Women's National Association (MANA), 459; and Comisión Femenil of Los Angeles, 459

Index

National Hispanic Heritage Award: and Judith Francesca Baca, 75; and Centro Mater, 139; and Gloria Estefan, 243; and Nicholasa Mohr, 481; and Ellen Ochoa, 534; and Tina Ramírez, 609

National Hispanic Leadership Institute, 755, 810

National Hispanic Medical Association (NHMA), 440

National Institute of Child Health and Human Development, 527

National Labor Relations Board (NLRB), 333; and Luisa Moreno, 494

National Museum of American History at the Smithsonian: and Celia Cruz, 180; and Ganados del Valle, 275; Ester Hernández work included in the, 319; and Carmen Lomas Garza, 397; and Gloria López Córdova, 406; and Ageda Salazar Martínez, 426; and Amalia Mesa-Bains, 453; and Patssi Valdez work included in the, 783; and María Varela, 788; and Eva Ybarra, 815

National Organization for Women (NOW) , 515, 537, 578, 758

National Puerto Rican Day Parade, *173*: and María Clemencia Sánchez, 11; and Celia M. Acosta Vice, 31, 32; Luisa Quintero founder of, 601°d Patricia Rodríguez, 635

National Puerto Rican Forum, **516–517**, *517*; and Angelina (Angie) Cabrera, 105; and Sor Isolina Ferré Aguayo, 258; and Sara Meléndez, 443; Antonia Pantoja created the, 558; and Dolores Prida, 582; and Luisa Quintero, 601

National Recovery Administration (NRA), 299, 409, 410

National Women's Political Caucus (NWPC): and Chicana Caucus, 150; and Rosa Guerrero, 302; and La Raza Unida Party, 367; and Ruth Mojica-Hammer, 482; and Mujeres por la Raza, 507; and Politics, Electoral, 578

Nationalist Party, 695, 794: and Rosa Cortéz Collazo, 163, 164, 588; and Julia de Burgos, 194; and Dolores Lebrón "Lolita," 380; and Juan Antonio Corretjer, 382; and Puerto Rican Women Political Prisioners, 587, 588, 589

Naturalization, **517–518**, *518. See also* Immigration and Naturalization Service (INS)

Navarrete, Lisa, 515

Navarro, Susana M., **519–520**, *519*

Nazario, Dolores, 730

Nebraska Mexican American Commission, 332, 536

Needle Trades Workers Industrial Union: and Los Angeles Garment Workers' Strike, 409

Negrón, Edna, 11

Neri, Margarita, 463

Nerio, Trinidad, **520–521**, *520*

Neruda, Pablo, 441, 442, 480, 797

Nevel Guerreo, Xochitl, 64

New Deal programs: and Hull-House, 334

New Economics for Women (NEW), 253, **521–522**

New Mexico Agricultural Extension Service (NMAES), 104

New Mexico Highlands University, 104, 679

New Mexico House of Representatives: and Soledad Chávez Chacón, 143–144; and María Concepción "Concha" Ortiz y Pino de Kleven, 546

New Mexico State University, 466, 699, 713: and Fabiola Cabeza de Baca, 104; and Denise Chávez, 145; and Katherine Davalos Ortega, 374

New School for Social Research, 123, 481, 558

New York City Central Labor Council, 369, 757

New York City Mission Society (NYCMS), **522–523**; and

Aimee Garcia Cortese, 282; and Religion, 615–622; and Leoncia Rosado Rousseau ("Mamá Léo"), 644–645

New York Public Library (NYPL): and Pura Belpré, 83; and María DeCastro Blake, 93; and Lillian López, 401; and Esther Miller, 475; and New York City Mission Society (NYCMS), 522

New York State Assembly: and Carmen E. Arroyo, 61; and Sonia Palacio-Grottola, 557; and Puerto Rican Radical politics in New York, 586

New York State Department of Health's AIDS Institute: and Helen Rodríguez-Trias, 642

New York Times, 12, 50, 62, 279, 403, 406, 545, 562, 601, 797, 807: and Julia Alvarez, 44; and Sandra Cisneros, 162; and Nicholasa Mohr, 481; and Achy Obejas, 533

New York University: and Amalia V. Betanzos, 88; and Anna Carbonell, 120; and Alice Cardona graduated from, 121; and Jane L. Delgado, 203; and Nydia M. Velázquez, 377, 791; and Iris Morales, 492; and Sonia Nieto, 523; and Mercedes Olivera, 538

New Yorker, 357

Newark Methodist Maternity Hospital, 329, 320

Newsday newspaper, 121

Newsweek, 810, 325: and Pachucas, 553

Nicaraguan Adjustment and Central American Relief Act (NACARA), 229

Niebla, Elvia, 677

Nieto, Sonia, **523–524**, *524*; and Education, 223; and María E. Sánchez, 665

Nieto Gómez, Anna, 6, **524–525**; and *Las Hijas de Cuauhtémoc*, 327

Nieves, Josephine, 10, 584

Nilda, 13, 394, 480, 481

Nixon, Richard M., 149:and Delia Alvarez, 43; and Romana Acosta Bañuelos, 374; and Anita N. Martínez, 427; and María Luisa Legarra Urquides, 780

Nobel Prize in Literature, 480, 797, 801: and Gabriela Mistral, 479

Norat, Sara, 202

Noriega, Carlota, 421

Norte, Marisela, **525–526**; and Literature, 395

North American Free Trade Agreement (NAFTA), 240, 366, 420: and urban and environmental problems, 233, 234, 235; and La Fuerza Unida, 273

Northeastern University, 270, 668

Northwestern University, 85, 128, 280

Novello, Antonia Coello, 12, **526–528**, *527*

Nuestra Señora de la Divina Providencia, **528–529**

Nuestro magazine, 516, 582

Nueva Generación magazine, 23, 123, 124

Núñez, Ana Rosa, **529–530**, *529*

Nuns, Colonial, **530–531**; and Sor Juana Inés De la Cruz, 6, 196–197, 316, 762; and María de la Concepción Arguello, 56, 57

Nuns, Contemporary, **531–532**; Sister Mary Imelda, 127; Sister Consuelo Tovar, 170; Sister Thomas Marie, 257; and Sor Isolina Ferré Aguayo, 257–259; and Madre María Dominga Guzmán, 306–307; and Las Hermanas, 373–374; and Mujerista Theology, 507–508; and Religion 615–622; and Sister Carmelita, 683; and Yolanda Tarango, 734–735

Nursing, 48, 59, 158, 176, 184, 392, 462, 466, 522, 583, 690,

778; and, Apolonia "Polly" Muñoz Abarca, 29, 30; and Jesusita Aragón, 54, 55; and Plácida Peña Barrera, 82; and Carmen Contreras Bozak, 95–96; and Rosa Cortéz Collazo, 163; and Community Service Organization (CSO), 171; and Gregoria Esquivel, 240; and Ruth Figueroa, 261; and Eva Carrillo de García, 280; and Hull-House, Chicago, 333–336; and Cruz Blanca/White Cross, 337, 354; and Beatrice Amado Kissinger, 360; and Apolinaria Lorenzana, 407, 707; and *Madrigal v. Quilligan*, 416, 417, 419; and Military Service, 473–475; and Elvira Virginia Mugarrieta, 502; and Eulalia Pérez, 570, 571; and Carmen Romero Phillips, 574; and Dora Ocampo Quesada, 597; and Patricia Rodríguez, 635; San Joaquin Valley Cotton Strike, 660, 661; and Elvira Sena, 679; and María Ignacia Amador, 706; and Rafaela Muñiz, 813

Obejas, Achy, **533**
Obreras de la Independencia, 742, 743
O'Brian, Soledad, 740
Ocampo, Adriana: and Scientists, 677
Ochoa, Ellen, 321, **534**
Ochoa, Petra, 741
O'Donnell, Sylvia Colorado, **535**, *535*
Odyssey House program, 618
O'Farrill, Julieta, 183
Ojeda, Juanita, 588
O'Leary, Ana: and and Phelps Dodge Strike, 574
Old Spain and the Southwest, 393, 550
Olga Talamante Defense Committee (OTDC), 734
Olivares, Olga Ballesteros, **535–536**
Olivarez, Graciela, **537–538**, *537*; and Mexican American Legal Defense and Educational Fund (MALDEF), 458
Oliver, Denisse, 816
Olivera, Mercedes, **538–540**, *538*
Oller, Denisse: and Television, 740, *740*
Olvera Stoltzer, Beatríz: and New Economics for Women (NEW), 521
Olverding, Liliana, 27
Olympic Games, 255, 256, 396
One Million Years B.C.,160, 501, 806
One Stop Immigration: and Grace Montañez Davis, 188
One-Eyed Jacks, 165, 358
Ontiveros, Lupe, 160
Ontiveros, Manuela, **540–541**, *540*
Operation Bootstrap, 105, 202, 471
Operation Gatekeeper, 235
Operation Pedro Pan, **541–543**, *542*; and María Leopoldina "Pola" Grau, 295–297
Operation Wetback: and Migration and Labor, 98, 469
Orange Tomboys, 274
Orden de la Estrella de Oriente, 60, 658
Order of the Trinitarian Sisters, 683
Oriondo, Sylvia: and Madres y Mujeres Anti-Represión (MAR), 184
Orozco, Aurora Estrada, **543–544**
Orozco, Cynthia, 297
Orozco, Helena, 416
Orozco, Monica and Lucy: and Hispanic Mother-Daughter Program (HMDP), 328
Orsini, Lillian, 202

Ortega, Carlota Ayala, **544–545**, *545*
Ortega, Margarita, 466
Ortega, Sister Gregoria, 373
Ortiz Cofer, Judith, 13, **545–546**, *546*; and Literature, 395
Ortiz y Pino de Kleven, María Concepción "Concha," **546–547**, *547*
Ortiz, Chabela, 815
Ortíz, Nancy, 592
Ortiz, Reverend Blanca, 620
Oscars (Academy Award): and Katy Jurado, 201; and Rita Moreno, 494, 500, 739, 807, 808; Rosie Pérez, 501
O'Shea, María Elena, **547–548**
Osorio, Lady Ana de: and Scientists, 676
Otero, Carmen, 27
Otero-Smart, Ingrid, **548–549**, *549*
Otero Warren, Adelina, **549–551**, *550*; and Education, 222; and Feminismo, 253; and Journalism and Print Media, 355; and Literature, 393
Our Lady of Conception, 530, 531
Our Lady of Fátima: and Madre María Dominga, 306
Our Lady of the Lake University, 130, 179, 649, 745

Pachucas, **552–555**, *554*; and Feminism, 253–255; and Sexuality, 681
Pact of Zanjón, 182, 742
Padilla de Armas, Encarnación, 620
Padilla, Nancy, 27
Padilla, Elena, 17
PADRES: and Las Hermanas, 374
Padua Hills Theater, 748
Pagán, Dylcia, 590
Palabras juntan revolución, 124
Palacio-Grottola, Sonia, **555–557**, *556*
Palacios, Mónica, 750
Palomo Acosta, Teresa, 544
Pan American College. *See* University of Texas, Pan American
Pan American Round Table, 411, 607, 608
Paniagua, Juana Ana María: and Women in St. Augustine, 715
Pantoja, Antonia, 9, 10, 11, *68*, **557–558**, *557*; and ASPIRA, 68, 121; and Education, 223; and Feminism, 253; and The Puerto Rican Association for Community Affairs (PRACA), 584; and The Puerto Rican Forum, 516
Pardo, Mary, 577
Paredes, Américo, 300
Parent Teacher Associations (PTA): and Lucy Acosta, 31; and Martha Cotera, 117; and Carmen Cornejo Gallegos, 274; and Elvira Rodríguez de Gonzáles, 290; and Frances Aldama Martínez, 430; Consuelo Herrera Méndez founded, 443; and Elba Iris Montes-Donnelly, 485; and Mothers of East Los Angeles (MELA), 497; and Carolina Malpica de Munguía, 508; and Aurora Estrada Orozco, 543
Parra, Violeta, 652
Parra, Yolanda, 753
Parsons, Lucia González, 171, **558–559**; and Journalism and Print Media, 355
Partido Independentista Puertorriqueño (PIP), 60, 602, 795
Partido Liberal Mexicano (PLM): and Communist Party, 168; and Josefina Arancibia, 169; and Ricardo Flores Magón, 259; and *Las Hijas de Cuauhtémoc*, 327; and Journalism and Print Media, 354; and Labor Unions, 368; and Mexican

Index

Revolution, Border Women in, 465; and Sara Estela Ramírez, 608; and Andrea and Teresa Villarreal, 800

Partido Revolucionario Cubano (PRC). *See* Cuban and Puerto Rican Revolutionary Party

Paternal authority: and Colonial Law, 700

Patiño Río, Dolores, 159, **559–561**, *560*

Patria, 182, 433

Paul, Alice, 550

Pauwels Pfeiffer, Linda Lorena, **561–562**, *562*

Payán, Ilka Tanya, **562**

PBS: and *Alvarez v. Lemon Grove School*, 46; and *Vikki Carr: Memories, Memorias* program, 121, 122; and María Echaveste, 222; and Jessica Govea, 295; and Victoria Aguilera, 678; and Olga Talamante, 734, and Raquel Welsh, 807

Peace and Freedom Party, 429

Pearl Harbor: and Plácida Peña Barrera, 82; and El Monte berry strike, 227; and Beatrice Amado Kissinger, 360; and Gloria Flores Moraga, 489; and Irene Hernández Ruiz life, 649; and World War II, 810, 811; and Alejandra Rojas Zúñiga, 821

Pedroso, Paulina, **563**; and Cigar Workers, 157; and Cuban and Puerto Rican Revolutionary Party, 181

Pelaez, Aida, 26

Peña de Bordas, (Ana) Virginia de, 8, **563–564**

Peña, Elizabeth: and Cinema Images, Contemporary, 160; and Movie Stars, 501; and Television, 739

Peña, Yvonne, 512

Peñaranda, Ana Marcial, 9, **564–565**; and Education, 224

Pentecostal Church, 261, 364, **565–569**, *566*; and Leoncia Rosado Rousseau ("Mamá Léo"), 11, 644–645; and María Elena Avila, 69; and Central American Immigrant Women, 137; and Aimee García Cortese, 282; and Ruth Esther Soto León, 385; and New York City Mission Society (NYCMS), 522, 523; and Religion, 617, 618

People magazine, 396, 601

People v. de la Guerra: and Treaty of Guadalupe Hidalgo, 764

People's College of Law, 219, 562, 633

Perales, Nina, *458*, **569–570**, *569*

Perdomo Sánchez, Clelia, 474

Perdomo-Ayala, Lynda, 512

Perez and Martina: A Porto Rican Folk Tale, 83

Pérez Cassiano, María Gertrudis: and Women in Texas, 717

Pérez López, Beatriz: and Operation Pedro Pan, 541

Pérez, Andrea, 344, 573

Pérez, Carmen María, 589

Pérez, Emma, 465

Pérez, Eulalia, 2, **570–571**; and Apolinaria Lorenzana, 407; and Victoria Comicrabit Reid, 614; and Women in California, 709

Perez, Gina, 17

Pérez, Graciela, **571–573**, *572*

Pérez, Mignón, 183

Pérez, Rosie, 160, 501, 739

Pérez, Ruby Nelda, 750

Pérez, Sandra, 696

Pérez, Sonia, 515

Pérez v. Sharp, **573**; and Intermarriage, Contemporary, 344

Pérez-Brown, María, 739

Pérez-Hogan, Carmen, 11

Pérez-Stable, Marifeli, 50

Pescador, Maria: and Cigar Makers' International Union (CMIU), 733

Pesotta, Rose, 408, 409

Pesquera, Beatriz, 247

Phelps Dodge Strike, **573–574**

Phillips, Carmen Romero, **574–575**, *575*

Phoenix Americanization Committee (PAC): and Friendly House, Phoenix, 271

Pia Martínez, Paula, 64

Picasso, Pablo, 264

Pico, Ysidora, 347

Pilsen Neighbors Community Council, **575–576**, 622

Pineda de Hernández, Antonia, 753

Piñeda, Adela: and Bracero Program, 97

Pineda, Ana María, 621

Pineda, Cecile, 395

Pinedo, Encarnación, **576–577**

Plan de San Diego, 464

Plan de Santa Barbara: and Chicano Movement, 151–154, and Anna Nieto Gómez, 525

Plan of Agua Prieta, 463

Plan of Ayala, 461, and Dolores Jiménez y Muro, 463

Playwrights, 748–751; and Denise Chávez, 144–145; and Miriam Colón, 164–66; and María Irene Fornés, 270–721; and Cherríe Moraga, 488–89; and Dolores Prida, 582–83; and Puerto Rican Traveling Theater (PRTT), 751–52; and Teatro Campesino, 752–53; and Estela Portillo Trambley, 762

Plyler v. Doe, 457: and Vilma S. Martínez, 432

Poema en veinte surcos, 194, 394

Politics, Electoral, **577–579**, 671; and Mujeres por la Raza, 507

Politics, Party, **579–580**, *580*; and La Raza Unida Party (LRUP), 367–368; and League of United Latin American Citizens (LULAC), 378–380; and Mexican American Legal Defense and Educational Fund (MALDEF), 457–458; and National Council of La Raza (NCLR), 514–515. *See* Democratic Party. *See also* Republican Party

Pomares, Anita, 499

Ponce Massacre, 163, 380, 794

Ponce, Mary Helen, 395

Pope Benedict XIV: and Nuetra Señora de la Divina Providencia, 528–529

Pope Benedict XV: and Virgen de la Caridad del Cobre, 803

Pope Paul VI: and Nuetra Señora de la Divina Providencia, 528–529; and Virgen de la Caridad del Cobre, 803

Popular Democratic Party, 624, 625, 683

Popular Religiosity, **581–582**; and Altars, 410–411; and Folk Healing Traditions 266–270; and Religion, 615–622; and Santería, 669–670; and Spiritism, 720–721; and Spiritism in New York City, 721–723

PoroAfro, 270

Posada del Sol Senior Housing Center, 810

Power, María, 730

Premio Casa de las Américas, 124, 637

Presidential Citizen's Medal, 642

Presidential Medal of Freedom, 259, 557

Prida, Dolores, **582–583**, *582*; and Literature, 394; and Playwrights, 750

Prieto, Isabel, 743

Prieto, Luz María: and Mujeres Latinas en Acción (MLEA), 505

Primer Congreso de Mujeres Trabajadoras (socialist labor movement), 60

Princeton University, 428

Proposition 187 and 209, **583–584**, and Nohelia de los Angeles Canales, 115; and Health: Current Issues and Trends, 313; and Mexican American Legal Defense and Educational Fund (MALDEF), 317; and Vilma S. Martínez, 432

Public Law 78, 98

Public School 25 in the South Bronx, 9, 224, 564

Pueblos Hispanos journal: and Clotilde Betances Jaeger wrote for, 87; and Julia de Burgos, 194, 356; and Consuelo Lee Tapia founded, 356, 383

Puente, Tito: and Celia Cruz, 180; and Victoria Hernández, 322; and "La Lupe," 363, 364; and Irma Morillo, 496; and Graciela Pérez, 571; and Salsa, 653, 654; and Anita Vélez-Mitchell, 796

Puerto Rican Association for Community Affairs (PRACA), 10, 11, **584–585**; and María Josefa Canino, 116; and Antonia Pantoja founded the, 558

Puerto Rican Day Parade: and Congreso del Pueblo, 173, *173*

Puerto Rican Educators Association (PREA), 665, 729, 730

Puerto Rican Family Insitute, 106, 204

Puerto Rican Legal Defense and Education Fund (PRLDEF): and ASPIRA, 68; and *ASPIRA vs. Board of Education*, 69; and Bilingual Education, 89; and María Josefa Canino, 116; and Anna Carbonell, 120; and Legal Issues, 384; and Iris Morales, 492; and Nina Perales, 569; and Politics, Party, 580; Nitza Tufiño received a recognition from the, 768

Puerto Rican Political Prisoners Committee, 382

Puerto Rican Radical Politics in New York, **585–587**, *586, 587*; and Cigar Workers, 156–159; and Communist Party, 168–169; and Labor Unions, 368–372; Tabaquero's Unions, 732–733

Puerto Rican Socialist Party, 138, 261, 670

Puerto Rican Student Union, 727, 728

Puerto Rican Traveling Theater (PRTT), 751–752, *751*; and Miriam Colón founded the, 165; and Theater, 747; and Playwrights, 750

Puerto Rican Women Political Prisoners, **587–591**, *589*; and Luisa Capetillo, 119; and Rosa Cortéz Collazo, 163–164; and Dolores "Lolita" Lebrón, 380–381; and Puerto Rican Radical Politics in New York, 585–587

Puerto Ricans in Hawaii, **591–595**, *593*

Pujol, Aida, 496

Pulido Sánchez, Pat: and Medicine, 439

Pulitzer Prize, 23, 271, 356, 533

Queens College, 258, 758, 759: and Student Movements, 727

Quesada, Alicia Otilia, **596–597**

Quesada, Dora Ocampo, **597–598**, *597*

Quesada, Francisca Ocampo, *1*, 597

Quinceañera, 375, **598–600**, *599*; and Eva Castellañoz, 26

Quinn, Anthony, 201

Quintanilla Pérez, Selena, 114, **600–601**, 760; and Salsa, 654

Quintanilla, Stella, 388

Quinteras de Meras, María, 462

Quintero, Luisa, **601–602**, *602*, 670; and Journalism and Print Media, 356

Quiroga, Camila, 746

Quiroga, Mercedes, 616

Quisqueya en Acción, 140

Race and Color Consciousness, **603–607**; and *Mestizaje*, 453–457

Rainbow Coalition, 304

Ramírez, Elizabeth, 754

Ramírez, Emilia Schunior, **607–608**

Ramírez, Juanita, 25

Ramírez, Julie, 618

Ramírez, María, 11

Ramírez, Sara Estela, 6, **608**; and Education, 222; and Labor Unions, 368; and Journalism and print media, 354; and Literature, 392; and Mexican Revolution, Border Women in, 465

Ramírez, Tina, **609**; and Theater, 747

Ramírez de Arellano, Diana, *394*, **609–611**, *610*

Ramírez-Jara, Hilda: Padua Hills Theater, 748

Ramona, 615

Ramonita, García, 632

Ramos, Juanita, 388

Rancho Jamul, 3, 650

Rangel, Irma, **611**; and Theater, 746, 747

Rape, 55, 99, 296, 495, 526, **611–613**, 701, and Spanish settlement, 25, 697; and Black Legend, 91; and Colonial slavery, 345, 604; and Mexican Revolution, 466, 660; and Maravilla Housing Project cases of, 483

Reagan, Ronald: and Bilingual education, 199; appointed Rita DiMartino to the UNICEF, 212; and Katherine Davalos Ortega, 374; and Olga Ballesteros Olivares, 536; and Political Party, 580; and Proposition 187 and 209, 583; and United Farm Workers of America (UFW), 773

The Rebel, 354, 392

Rebolledo, Tey Diana, 395

Recipes from the Heart of Hawaii's Puerto Ricans, 592

Regeneración magazine, 264, 354

Regiment Victoria, 463

Reid, Marita, **613–614**, *614*, 609; and Theater, 746, 747

Reid, Victoria Comicrabit, 1, 2, **614–615**

Religion, **615–622**, *617, 618, 619, 620*; and Santería, 41, 363, 669–670, 722; and Pentecostal Church, 261, 364, 565–568; and Folk Healing Traditions 266–270; and Las Hermanas, 373–374; and Popular Religiosity, 581–582

Rentería, Teresa, 138

Repatriation Project, 324

Republican Party: and Rita DiMartino, 211; and Katherine Davalos Ortega, 374; and Ileana Ros-Lehtinen, 376, 646; and Olga A. Méndez, 445; and María Estella Altamirano Mendoza, 449; and "Concha" Ortiz y Pino de Kleven, 546; and Adelina Otero Warren, 550

Revista Chicano-Riqueña, 394

Revista de Artes y Letras, 9: and Clotilde Betances Jaeger, 87; and Journalism and Print Media, 355; and Josefina Silva de Cintrón "Pepiña," 682

Revueltas, Rosaura, 160, 437, 656

Reyes, Guadalupe, **622–623**; and Pilsen Neighbors Community Council, 576

Index

Reyes, Lucha, 421

Rhode Island University, 140, 218

Rico, Angelina Moreno, **623–624**, *624*

Rincón de Gautier, Felisa, 9, 31, **624–625**, *625*

The Rink, 500, 627

Rios, Elena, 439

Ríos, Marita, 746

Ríos, Reverand Elizabeth: and Center for Emerging Female Leadership (CEFL), 620

Risk, Georgina Torres: and *Madrigal v. Quilligan* suit, 417, 418

Rivas Cacho, Lupe , 236

Rivas, Marian Lucy, 678

Rivera, Aurelia "Yeya," **625–626**, *626*

Rivera, Carmen, 752

Rivera, Chita, **626–627**; and Movie Stars, 500; and Television, 739; and *West Side Story*, 807

Rivera, Edith M., 616

Rivera, Graciela, 62, 496, **627–628**, *628*

Rivera, Jovita: and *Madrigal v. Quilligan*, 416; and Sterilization, 724

Rivera, Lourdes and Nidia, 503

Rivera, Roxana, **629–630**, *629*

Rivera Atkinson, María, 567

Rivera de Alvarez, Josefina, 87

Rivera Diego, 264, 335, 452, 481, 492, 644

Rivera Martínez, Domitila, **630–631**

Rivera Salgado, Elsa, 496

Robles Díaz, Inés, **631–632**, *631*

Robles, Belén, 380

Robles, Darlene, 578

Robles, Margarita, 616

Rock and Roll Hall of Fame, 308, 655

Rockefeller Foundation, 271, 293

Rodela, Lupita, 815

Rodríguez, Hermelinda Morales, **632–633**

Rodríguez, "Isabel" Hernández, 137, 138, **633–634**

Rodríguez, Arturo, 773

Rodríguez, Carmen, 730

Rodríguez, Carolina, 181, 743

Rodríguez, Cecilia, 366

Rodríguez, Celia, 64

Rodríguez, Diane, 749: and Teatro Campesino, 753

Rodríguez, Evelyn M.: and Scientists, 678

Rodríguez, Genoveva, 9

Rodríguez, Jeanette, 621

Rodríguez, Josefa "Chepita," **634**

Rodríguez, Lisa, 501

Rodríguez, Margarita, 26

Rodríguez, María: and New Economics for Women (NEW), 521

Rodríguez, Michelle, 501

Rodríguez, Patricia, 11, **635–636**, *635*

Rodríguez, Sofía, **636–637**

Rodríguez, Teresa, 23

Rodríguez Cabral, María Cristina, **637**

Rodríguez de Tió, Lola, 8, **637–639**, *638*; and Cuban-Spanish-AmericanWar, 184; and Journalism and Print Media, 353, 354, 356; and Literature, 394; and Inocencia Martínez Santaella, 433

Rodríguez McLean, Verneda, **639–640**, *639*

Rodríguez Plá, Carmen: and Santería, 670

Rodríguez Remeneski, Shirley, 121, **640–641**

Rodríguez-Trias, Helen, 12, *440*, **641–643**, *643*; and Medicine, 439

Roe v. Wade, 537

Rolling Stone magazine, 144

Roman Catholic Church in Mexico: and Mexican Revolution, 462

Romero Cash, Marie, **643–644**, *643*

Romero, Elaine, 26

Romero, Rosario, 25

Romero, Simmie: and Comisión Femenil Mexicana Nacional (CFMN), 167

Romo v. Laird, 468

Ronstadt, Linda, *1*, 175

Roosevelt, Eleanor, 640, 31: and United Cannery, Agricultural, Packing, and Allied Workers of America (UCAPAWA/FTA), 771

Roosevelt, Franklin Delano, 82, 579, 586, 659: Monica Boyar performed in benefit shows for, 95; and Soledad Chávez Chacón, 143; and Mexican American voters, 299; and María Latigo Hernández, 320; and *Pueblos Hispanos*, 356

Roosevelt, Theodore, 189

Rosado Rousseau, Leoncia ("Mamá Léo"), 11, *523*, **644–645**; and Pentecostal Church, 567; and Religion, 618, 620

Rosado, Isabel, 588

Rosado, Olimpia, 183

Rosado, Rossana: and *El Diario/La Prensa*, 356, *357*

Rosa-Rey, María, 202

Rosario, Ana, 503

Rose García, Camille, 66

Ros-Lehtinen, Ileana, 23, **645–646**, *646*, 792; and Latinas in the U.S. Congress, 375, 376

Ross, Fred, 172: and Dolores Huerta, 332, 370; and César Chávez149,

Roybal, Edward R., 646: and Chávez, Ravine, Los Angeles, 149; and Community Service Organization (CSO), 171; and Grace Montañez Davis, 187; and Latinas in the U.S. Congress, 376; and Esperanza Acosta Mendoza Schechter ("Hope"), 674

Roybal, Lucille, 646: and Community Service Organization (CSO), 171

Roybal-Allard, Lucille, **646–647**, *647*; and Latinas in the U.S. Congress, 375, 376

Ruiz, Bernarda, **647–648**, *648*

Ruiz, Irene Hernández, **649–650**

Ruiz, Dorotea: and Las Obreras de la Independencia, 181

Ruiz, Erminia, *6*: and Latinas in the Southwest, 3

Ruiz, Vicki L., 168, 220, 245, 298, 371, 465, 550, 577, 656, 697, 700, 812

Ruiz, Virginia X.: and Asociación Nacional México-Americana (ANMA), 67, 169

Ruiz de Burton, María Amparo, 3, **650–651**; and Literature, 392

Ruiz García, Elizabeth, 812

Rutgers University, 11: and María DeCastro Blake, 92; and Nohelia de los Angeles Canales, 115; Lourdes Casal taught at, 123, and Miriam Colón, 165; and Student Movements at, 227; and Jessica Govea, 295; and Diana Ramírez de Arellano, 610; and Rebecca Sánchez Cruz, 666; and Elma González, 677

Sada, María G. "Chata," **652**

Sager Solís, Manuela, 169, 299, 770

Saginaw Valley State University, 540, 545

Salas, Elizabeth, 466

Salas, Julie, 503

Salazar, Carmen, 474

Salazar, Gumercindo: and Ganados del Valle, 275, 787

Salazar, Maria Elvira, 23

Salcido, Sister Alicia, 619

Saldívar-Hull, Sonia, 293

Salinas, María Elena, 740

Salsa, **652–655**, *563*; and Cruz, Celia, 179–181; and "La Lupe" (Guadalupe Victoria Yoli Raymond), 363–364

Salt Lake City Neighborhood Housing Services (SLNHS), 284

Salt of the Earth, 5, 253, **656–657**, *656*, *657*; and Cinema Images, Contemporary, 160; and Feminism, 253; and Francisca Flores, 264; and Labor Union, 369; and Media Stereotypes, 436; and Phelps Dodge Strike, 574

Salvatierra v. Del Rio Independent School District, 687

Salvation Army, 163, 184, 188

San Antonio de Bexar, 113, 199, 717

San Antonio, Ana Gloria, **657–658**, *657*

San Antonio Pecan Shellers' Strike, 4, **658–659**, *658*; and María Latigo Hernández, 320; and Luisa Moreno, 493; and Emma Tenayuca, 743–745

San Diego Mission, 709

San Diego State University: and Alvarez, Cecilia Concepción, 42; and Chicano Movement, 154; and Adelaida Rebecca Del Castillo, 199; and Yolanda López, 405; and Raquel Welch, 806

San Fernando Vendors Association (SFVA), 726

San Francisco settlement, 709

San Francisco State University: and Carmen Lomas Garza, 397; and Victoria Mercado "Vicky," 451; and Amalia Mesa-Bains, 452; and Elba Iris Montes-Donnelly, 485; and Cherríe Moraga, 488; and Leticia Márquez-Magaña, 677

San Gabriel del Yunque, 710

San Gabriel Mission, 56, 122, 407, 701, 706, 709: and Eulalia Pérez, 570, and Victoria Comicrabit Reid, 614; and Toypurina, 761

San Joaquin Valley Cotton Strike, 4, **659–661**, *660*; and Cannery and Agricultural Workers Industrial Union (CAWIU), 117; and Labor Unions, 368; and United Cannery, Agricultural, Packing, and Allied Workers of America (UCA-PAWA/FTA), 771

San Juan Capistrano: and Modesta Avila, 70

San Juan, Olga, *500*, **662**, *662*; and Movie Stars, 499

Sánchez, Loretta, **662–663**; Latinas in the U.S. Congress, 375, 377

Sánchez, María Clemencia, 11, **663–664**

Sánchez, María E., 11, **664–666**, *665*; and Substitute Auxiliary Teachers (SATs), 730

Sánchez Cruz, Rebecca, **666–667**, *667*

Sánchez Garfunkel, Aura Luz, **667–669**, *668*

Sánchez Korrol, Virginia, 322

Sánchez sisters, 473

Sánchez, Elisa: and Mexican American Women's National Association (MANA), 459

Sánchez, George I., 607

Sánchez, Linda, 663: and Latinas in the U.S. Congress, 375, 377

Sánchez, Major Aida Nancy, 474

Sánchez, Rosaura, 395

Sánchez, Yolanda, 11: and Hispanic Young Adult Association (HYAA), 584, 585

Sánchez-Scott, Milcha, 750

Sandoval, Chela, 395, 516

Sandoval, Lala, 343

Sandoval, Matilde, 343

Santa Fe County: and Adelina Otero Warren, 550

Santería, 41, *267*, 363, *618*, **669–670**, 722; and Lydia Cabrera, 106–107; and Folk Healing Traditions, 266–270; and Ana Mendieta art, 447; and Religion, 615, 622

Santiago Baeza, Elisa, *8*, 667: and Latinas in the Northeast, 9

Santiago Santiago, Isaura, 12: and Hostos Community College, 225

Santiago, Esmeralda, 13, 118: and Literature, 394

Santiago, Helena, 654, 655

Santiago, Petra, *343*, **670–672**, *671*

Santigosa, Paquita, 746

Sarabia, Elena, 505

Saralegui, Cristina, 23, **672–673**; and Television, 739, 740

Sarraga, Belén, 733

Saucedo, María del Jesús, **673–674**

Schechter, Esperanza Acosta Mendoza "Hope," **674–675**, *675*; and Labor Union, 369, 370

Schlafly, Phyllis, 141

Scientists, 7, **675–679**

Search for Education, Elevation, and Knowledge (SEEK), 728

Sedillo, Sister Sylvia: and Women's Spiritual Center in Santa Fe, 619

Segura Bustamante, Inés, 183

Segura, Denise, 247

Selena Live, 600

Selena, 160, 600

Selena. *See* Quintanilla Pérez, Selena

Sena, Elvira, **679–680**, *679*

Sepúlveda, Emma, **680–681**, *679*

Seraphina, María, 346

Serdán, Carmen, 463

Serra, Junípero, 700: and California Missions, 108; and Intermarriage, Historical, 345, 346

Serrano Sewell, Sandra, 521

Serrano, Irma, 175

Serrano, Nina, 394

Service Employees International Union (SEIU), 324

Seventh-Day Adventist Church: and Eva Carrillo de García, 280

Sexuality, **681**; and Chicana Rights Project, 151; and Chicano Movement, 151–154; and Comisión Femenil Mexicana Nacional (CFMN), 167–168; and Feminism, 253–255; and Lesbians, 386–388; and Pachucas, 552–555; and Sterilization, 723–725

The Sexuality of Latinas, 129

Siete cartas de Gabriela Mistral a Lydia Cabrera, 107

Sigler, Jaime, 160

Silent Dancing: A Partial Remembrance of a Puerto Rican Childhood, 13, 395, 545

Silva, Chelo, 600, **682**, 800

Silva de Cintrón, Josefina "Pepiña," 9, **682–683**; and Journalism and Print Media, 355–356

Index

Sin Fronteras: and Centro de Acción Social Autónomo (CASA), 137, 138; Adelaida Rebecca del Castillo wrote for, 199; and Magdalena Mora, 487; Isabel Hernández Rodríguez editor of, 633

Singerman, Paulina, 746

"Sister Carmelita" (Carmela Zapata Bonilla Marrero), *128*, **683–684**, *684*

Sister Mary Imelda: and Casita Maria, 127

Slavery, **684–686**; and Black Legend, 91; and Emilia Casanova de Villaverde, 125–126; and Intermarriage, Historical, 345; and La Malinche, 366; and Paulina Pedroso, 563; and Race and Color Consciousness, 603–607; and Lola Rodríguez de Tió, 638; and *Comadrazgo,* 705; and Women in St. Augustine, 714–716; and Women in Texas, 718; and The Treaty of Guadalupe Hidalgo 764; and U.S.-Mexican War, 779

Sleepy Lagoon Case, 171: and Francisca Flores, 67; and Grace Montañez Davis, 187; and Josefina Fierro, 260; and Luisa Moreno, 493; and Pachucas, 553

Sloss-Vento, Adela, **686–687**; and Alice Dickerson Montemayor, 484

Small Business Administration (SBA), 41, 105, 755

Smeltertown, El Paso, **687–689**

Smith Act, 67, 588

Smith, Placida Elvira García, **689–690**; and Friendly House, 272

Sobrino, Laura, 422

Socarrás Varona, Angela, 7

Social and Public Art Resource Center (SPARC), 555: and Judith Francesca Baca, 75

Socialist Labor Movement, 59, 585

Sociedad Beneficencia in Corpus Christi, 719

Sociedad de Socorros la Caridad, 563

Society of Hispanic Professional Engineers, 678

Society of Legal Services, 663

Society of Military Widows: and Carmen Contreras Bozak, 96

Society of Puerto Rican Auxiliary Teachers (SPRAT), 665, 729

Sol Ross University, 145

Soldaderas, 660, **690–691**; and *Corridos*, 175, 176; and Mexican Revolution, 462; and Mexican Revolution, Border Women in, 466; and The Padua Hills Theater, 748

Solis, Hilda L., **691–692**, *691*; and Latinas in the U.S. Congress, 375–378; and Politics, Electoral, 578

Solis, Jesusita, 209

Sonora Matancera: and Celia Cruz, 180; and Irma Morillo, 496; and Salsa, 654

Sontag, Susan, 271

The Squatter and the Don, 3, 392, 650

Sor Juana and Other Plays, 750, 762

Sor María Agueda de San Ignacio, 530

Sosa, Mercedes, 652

Sosa-Riddell, Adaljiza, 344; **692–694**, *693*; and Feminism, 254; Intermarriage, Contemporary, 344

Sotelo, Maria, 741

Soto de Vásquez, Carmen, 749

Soto Feliciano, Carmen Lillian "Lily," **694–695**, *694*

Soto, Elizabeth, 330

Soto, Lourdes, 321

Sotomayor, Sonia, 11

Souchet, Clementina, **695–696**

South Bronx Community Corporation, 62

South Bronx congregation of Thessalonica Christian Church, 282

South Bronx Development Organization, 641

South End Neighborhood Action Program (SNAP), 270

Southeast Community College (SCC), 178

Southern California Association of Governments, 449

Southern Methodist University (SMU), 111, 112, 280

Southern New York Baptist Women's Association: and Eva Torres Frey, 617

Southwest Network for Economic and Environmental Justice (SNEEJ), 235

Southwest Toxics Campaign, 497

Southwest Voter Registration Education Project (SVREP), **696–697**; and Rosie López, 404; and Vilma S. Martínez, 432; and Consuelo Herrera Méndez, 443; and Aurora Estrada Orozco, 544

Spanish Affairs Committee, 49

Spanish American Republican Club, 211

Spanish Assemblies of God, 568

Spanish Borderlands, **697–720**, *698*, *699*, *700*; and Intermarriage, Historical, 344–347; and Colonial Law, 700–703; and *Comadrazgo,* 705; and Early Settlement Life in the Borderlands, 704–708; and *Encomienda*, 708–709; and Women in California, 709–710; and Women in New Mexico, 710–714; and Women in St. Augustine, 714–716; and Women in Texas, 718; and Women's Wills, 719–720

Spanish Civil War, 35, 60, 159, 786: and Congreso de Pueblos de Hablan Española, 169; and Francisca Flores, 264; and Dolores Patiño Río raised funds for, 561; and Marita Reid, 613, 614

Spanish Colonial Arts Society, 406, 643, 644

Spanish-American war. *See* Cuban-Spanish-American War

Spanish-Speaking Parent-Teacher Association (PTAs). *See* Parent Teacher Associations (PTA)

Special agricultural workers (SAWs), 341

Spiritism, **720–721**, *720*, *721*; and Lydia Cabrera,106–107; and Folk Healing Traditions, 266–270; and Religion, 615–622; and Aurelia "Yeya" Rivera, 625; and Santería, 669–670; and Spiritism in New York City, 721–723

Spiritism in New York City, **721–723**, *722*. *See* Spiritism

St. John's University, 523, 758

St. Joseph's Hospital School of Nursing, 597

St. Joseph's Roman Catholic Church, 683

St. Mary's College, 219, 292, 801

St. Mary's Hospital School of Nursing in Tucson, 360

St. Mary's University School of Law in San Antonio, 611

St. Patrick's Catholic Church: and Ester Machuca, 415

Stanford University: and María Echaveste, 221; Yolanda López taught at the, 405; and Ellen Ochoa, 534; and Susana M. Navarro, 519; and Bernice B. Ortiz Zamora, 818

State University of New York at Buffalo, 202 203

State University of New York, Stony Brook, 204, 444, 512, 556, 666

Steel Workers Organizing Committee (SWOC): and Guadalupe Marshall, 425; and Community Service Organization (CSO), 172

Stephen F. Austin University, 192

Sterilization, 6, 12, **723–725**; and Chicana Rights Project, 151; and Chicano Movement, 151–154; and Comisión Femenil Mexicana Nacional (CFMN), 167–168; and Feminism, 253–255; and *Madrigal v. Quilligan*, 416–419; and Mexican American Legal Defense and Educational Fund (MALDEF), 457–458; and Helen Rodríguez-Trias, 641–643; and Sexuality, 681

Stowe, Madeline, 501

Street Vending, **725–726**, *725*

Student Movements, 665, **727–728**, *728*; and Chicano Movement, 151–154; and Comisión Femenil Mexicana Nacional (CFMN), 167–168; and El Movimiento Estudiantil Chicano de Aztlán (MEChA), 227–228; and *Hijas de Cuauhtémoc* newspaper, 326; and La Raza Unida Party (LRUP), 367–368; and Iris Morales, 491

Student Nonviolent Coordinating Committee (SNCC), 429, 491, 787

Student Union for Bilingual Education, 665

Substitute Auxiliary Teachers (SATs), **728–730**, *729*; and Education, 222–225; and Ana Marcial Peñaranda, 564–565; and María E. Sánchez, 664, 665

Surgeon general of the United States: and Antonia Coello Novello, 526

Swilling, Trinidad Escalante, **730–731**

Tabaquero's Unions, **732–733**; and Luisa Capetillo, 119; and Cigar Workers, 156–159; and Labor Unions, 368–372; and Luisa Moreno, 493; and Puerto Rican Radical Politics in New York, 585–587

Tabares, Ofelia, 183

Taco Shop Poets, 311

Tafoya, María Josefa, 25

Talamante, Olga, **733–734**

Tanguma, Ninfa, 26

Tapia, Victoria: and Sterilization, 723

Tarango, Yolanda, **734–735**; and Las Hermanas, 373, 374; and *Mujerista* Theology, 507; and Religion, 619, 621

Taylor, Quintard, 697

Teacher Corps, 452

Teamsters for Democratic Union: and Watsonville Strike, 805

Teatro Campesino, 394, 752–753; and Playwrights, 749

Teatro Nacional de Aztlán (TENAZ), 749

Teatro Raíces, 749

Tejada, Tia, 501

Tejano Conjunto Music Festival, 815

Tejano Music Awards: and Laura Canales, 114; and Michelle Yvette "Shelly" Lares, 372; and Selena Quintanilla Pérez, 600; and Patsy Torres, 759

Tejano Music Hall of Fame, 219, 448

Telemundo, 23, 739

Telenovelas, **735–736**

Television Academy Hall of Fame: and Chita Rivera, 627

Television, 23, 38, 63, 144, 160, 209, 237, **736–740**, *737*; and Aida Alvarez, 41; and Linda Alvarez, 44, 45; and Sonia Braga, 99; and Diana Caballero, 103; and Laura Canales, 114; and Anna Carbonell, 119, 120; and Vikki Carr, 122; and Miriam Colón, 165; and Jane L Delgado, 203–204; and Katy Jurado, 358; and Rita Moreno, 494–496; and Mercedes Olivera, 539; and Chita Rivera, 627; and Cristina Saralegui, 672–673; and Raquel Welch, 806–807

Tellez, Jessie, 574

Tempe Normal School (TNS), **740–742**, *741*; and Education, 222

Temporary Protected Status, 229

Temporary resident alien (TRA), 341

Ten Years' War, 93, 288, **742–743**, *743*; and Latinas in the Southeast, 19; and Emilia Casanova de Villaverde, 125–126; and Cigar Workers, 156, 158; and Cuban and Puerto Rican Revolutionary Party, 181; and Cuban Independence Women's Club, 182; and Cuban-Spanish-American War, 184–185; and Journalism and Print Media, 354; Paulina Pedroso participated in the, 563

Tenayuca, Emma, 6, 171, **743–745**; and Communist Party, 168, 300; and San Antonio Pecan Sheller's Strike, 299, 659; and Labor Unions, 368, 369; and Luisa Moreno, 493

Tennis Hall of Fame: and Rosemary Casals, 125

Texas A&M University, Kingsville, *293* (Texas A&I University, Kingsville): and Plácida Peña Barrera, 82; and Santa Contreras Barraza, 81; and Laura Canales, 115; and Mercedes Margarita Martínez Crawford, 179; and Fermina Guerra, 300; and Luz Bazán Gutiérrez, 305–306; and Carmen Lomas Garza, 397; and Mercedes Olivera, 539; and Irma Rangel, 611

Texas Association of Chicanos in Higher Education (TACHE), 263, 292

Texas Folklore Society, 293, 300

Texas House of Representatives, 611

Texas Revolution of 1836, 464, 473, 634

Texas Tech University, 87, 649

Texas Women's Political Caucus (TWPC), 150, 507

Tex-Son Strike, **745–746**, *745*; and International Ladies Garment Workers' Union (ILGWU), 348–50

Theater, **746–754**; and Miriam Colón, 164–66; and Beatríz Escalona ("La Chata Noloesca"), 236–237; Dolores Martí de Cid was specialist on, 425; and Marita Reid, 613–614; and Tina Ramírez, 609; and Padua Hills Theater, 748; and Puerto Rican Traveling Theater (PRTT), 751–752; and Playwrights, 748–751; and Teatro Campesino, 752–753; and Villalongín Dramatic Company, 753–754

Theatre-in-the-Red, 145

Thessalonica Christian Church, 568

This Bridge Called My Back: Writings by Radical Women of Color, 51, 254, 387, 394, 489, 749

Thomas, Alicia: and Operation Pedro Pan, 541

Ticotín, Rachel, 160

Tierra Wools, 275

Time magazine, 279, 501, 806

Toña la Negra, 180, 652

Tony Awards: and Rita Moreno, 160, 494, *495*, 500; and Chita Rivera, 500, 627

Top 10 Percent Law, 611

Toraño-Pantín, María Elena, **754–756**, *755*

Torres Frey, Eva, 616, 617

Torres Maes, María, 474

Torres, Alejandrina, 590

Torres, Alva, **756–757**, *756*

Torres, Ida Inés, **757–758**, *757*

Torres, Jesusita, 227, 226

Torres, Liz, 160

Torres, Lourdes, **758–759**, *759*

Torres, Lureida, 590

Index

Torres, Nery, 670

Torres, Patsy (Patricia Donita), 600, **759–760**

Torres, Raquel, 499

Torres, Reverend Olga, 620

Torresola, Carmen Dolores (Lolita), 588, 589

Tovar, Lupita, **760–761**; and Cinema Images, Contemporary, 159

Tovar, Sister Consuelo, 170, 620

Toypurina, **761–762**

Trade Union Unity League (TUUL), 117

Trambley, Estela Portillo, **762**; and Literature, 394; and Playwrights, 750

Treaty of Cahuenga: and Bernarda Ruiz, 648

Treaty of Guadalupe Hidalgo, 3, 59, **762–765**, *765*, 783, 802; and Environment and the Border, 232; and María Amparo Ruiz de Burton, 392, 650; and Migration and Labor, 469; and Religion, 615; and Sara Estela Ramírez, 608; and Bernarda Ruiz, 648; and Women in New Mexico, 712; and Women's Wills, 720; and U.S.-Mexican War, 776–779

Treaty of Paris, 19, 715; **766**; and Cuban-Spanish-American War, 184–185

Treaty of Santa Ysabel, 185

Tree of Life, 64, 447

Trevino Hart, Elva, 248

Treviño-Sauceda, Mily, **766–767**; and Líderes Campesinas, 390–391

Tristani, Gloria, 578

Tropicana, Carmelita, 653, 750

Trujillo, Carla, 388

Trujillo, Catalina, 25

Trujillo, Emilia, 236

Trujillo, Lorenzo, 426

Trujillo, Rafael Leónidas, 44, 486; Dominican against, 12, 95

Trujillo-McDonnell, Lieutenant Mary Agnes, 474

Truman, Harry, 163, 780

Tufiño, Nitza, **767–768**

Tulane University, 786

Tulle, Mary, 505

Twilight Treasures, 568

Ulibarrí Sánchez, Louise, **769–770**, *769*

Ulibarri, Tina, 275

Unemployed Councils: and Emma Tenayuca, 744

Unión Cívica Mexicana, 540

Unión Estudiantil Pedro Albizu Campos, 758

Union for Puerto Rican Students (UPRS), 673

United Auto Workers (UAW), 36, 324

United Bronx Parents (UBP), 49, 120, *225*

United Cannery, Agricultural, Packing, and Allied Workers of America (UCAPAWA/FTA), 4, **770–772**; and California Sanitary Canning Company strike, 110, 111; and Communist Party, 169; and Carmen Bernal Escobar, 238; Dorothy Healy organizer for the, 238; and Feminism, 253; and Great Depression and Mexican American Women, 299, 300; and Labor Unions, 368, 369; and Luisa Moreno, 492, 493; and San Antonio Pecan Sheller's Strike, 659; and San Joaquin Valley Cotton Strike, 659–661; and World War II, 812

United Catering, Restaurant, Bar, and Hotel Workers, 324

United Farm Workers of America (UFW), **772–776**, *773*; and Latinas in the Southwest, 5; and Latinas in the Pacific Northwest, 27; and Soledad "Chole" Alatorre, 36; and Gloria Anzaldúa, 51; and Socorro Hernández Bernasconi, 87; and Nohelia de los Angeles Canales, 115; and Helen Chávez, 146, 147; and The Chicana Caucus/National Women's Political Caucus, 150; and Chicano Movement, 153; and Community Service Organization (CSO), 172; *corridos* described the struggles of the, 175; and Jessie López de la Cruz, 195; and Movimiento Estudiantil Chicano de Aztlán (MEChA), 227; and Deborah Espinosa-Mora, 239; and Farah Strike, 249; and Farmworkers, 250–253; and Carmen Cornejo Gallegos, 274; and Socorro Gómez-Potter, 289; and Jessica Govea, 294, 295, 775, 776; and Rosalinda Guillen Herrera, 304; Dolores Huerta co-founded, 332; and Labor Unions, 369; María Elena López-Treviño supporter of the, 390; and María Elena Lucas, 413, 414; and Victoria Mercado "Vicky," 451; and Amalia Mesa-Bains, 452; and Magdalena Mora, 487; and Mytyl Glomboske, 494; and The National Association for Chicana and Chicano Studies (NACCS), 510; María del Jesús Saucedo, 673; and Olga Talamante, 733; and Teatro Campesino, 752; Mily Treviño-Sauceda worked with the, 766; and Women in the United Farm Workers (UFW), 773–776; and Helena María Viramontes, 800

United Mexican American Students (UMAS): and Victoria M. "Vickie" Castro, 131; and Adelaida Rebecca Del Castillo, 199; and Deborah Espinosa-Mora, 239; and Gloria Molina, 483; and Anna Nieto Gómez, 525; and "Isabel" Hernández Rodríguez, 633; and Student Movements, 727

United Mine Workers, 478

United Nations, 153, 482, 601, 816: Food and Agriculture Organization (FAO), 38; and Linda Alvarez, 45; and Human Rights Commission, 148; and International Women's Year, 167; and We the People: Community Awards, 170; and International Children's Emergency Fund (UNICEF), 212, 527, 797; and Gloria Estefan, 243; and World Conference on Racism in Durban, 429; and Elena Inés Mederos y Cabañas de González, 435; and Nicholasa Mohr, 480; and Decolonization Committee, 795; and Commission on the Status of Women, 810

United Neighborhood Organization (UNO), 321

United Puerto Rican Association of Hawaii (UPRAH), 592

U.S. Commission on Civil Rights, 148, 519, 598

U.S. Community Services Administration in Washington, 375, 755

U.S.-Cuba dialogue: and María Cristina Herrera, 326

U.S.-Cuba policy: and Antonio Maceo Brigade, 49, 50; and Ileana Ros-Lehtinen, 376, 646; and Politics, Party, 579–580; and María Elena Toraño-Pantín, 755

U.S. Department of Health and Human Services (DHHS): and Anna Carbonell, 120; and Jane L. Delgado worked for, 203; and Head Start Project, 310; and Proposition 187, 584; and Placida Elvira García Smith, 689; and Lourdes Torres, 759

U.S. Department of Housing and Urban Development (HUD), 172, 755, 768, 792

U.S. Department of Labor, 167, 221, 485, 517

U.S. English, 89

U.S.-Mexican War, 3, 25, 228, 606, **776–779**; and Barceló, María Gertrudis ("La Tules"), 78–79; and *Corridos*, 175;

Jovita González Mireles book about, 293; and Intermarriage, Historical, 347; and Mexican Schools, 467; and Migration and Labor, 469, 470; and Military Service, 473–475; and Encarnación Pinedo, 576, 577; and Bernarda Ruiz, 648; and María Amparo Ruiz de Burton, 650; and Women in New Mexico, 711, 712; and Women in Texas, 718; and Treaty of Guadalupe Hidalgo, 762–765; and María Paula Rosalía Vallejo de Leese, 785

U.S. Peace Corps, 170, 427, 668, 674

U.S. Supreme Court: and Arizona orphan abduction, 59; and *Lau v. Nichols*, 89, 224, 242; and María Juana Briones land dispute, 100; legalized the use of animal sacrifices in Santería, 268, 670; and *Méndez v. Westminster*, 446; and *Plyler v. Doe*, 457; and *Loving v. Virginia*, 573; and *Botiller et al. v. Domínguez* case, 763

United States Tennis Association (USTA), 255, 256

United Way, 150, 184, 272, 376, 810

United Women in Ministry, 568

Universidad Autónoma de Mexico, 548, 767

Universidad Boricua/Boricua College: and Antonia Pantoja, 558

Universidad Católica de Puerto Rico, 258, 307

University of Arizona: and the Movimiento Estudiantil Chicano de Aztlán, 129; and Guadalupe Castillo, 129, 130; Yolanda López taught at the, 405; *Mendoza v. Tucson School District No. 1*, 415; and Amelia Margarita Maldonado, 419, 420; and María Luisa Legarra Urquides, 779, 780

University of Bridgeport: and Sara Meléndez, 442

University of California at Berkeley: and Rita DiMartino, 211; and María Echaveste, 221; and Ester Hernández, 318; Yolanda López taught at the, 405; and Amalia Mesa-Bains, 452; and Cherríe Moraga, 489; and Sylvia Colorado O'Donnell, 535; and Mercedes Olivera, 538; and Placida Elvira García Smith, 689; María Elena Zavala earned a doctorate from, 677; and Leticia Márquez-Magaña, 677; and Adaljiza Sosa-Riddell, 693

University of California, Davis, 680, 693

University of California, Irvine, 75, 800

University of California, Los Angeles (UCLA): and *Aztlán* journal, 73; and Adelaida Rebecca Del Castillo graduated from, 200; and Cristina García, 279; and Antonia Hernández, 317; and Magdalena Mora, 487; Cherríe Moraga taught at the, 489

University of California, Riverside, 677, 693

University of California, San Diego, 46, 113, 405

University of California, Santa Barbara (UCSB), 153, 291, 292

University of California, Santa Cruz (UCSC): and Gloria Anzaldúa, 52; and Victoria M. Castro, 131; and Lorna Dee Cervantes, 141; Yolanda López taught at, 405; and Olga Talamante, 733; and the Watsonville Strikes, 805

University of Chicago, 17, 128, 459, 460

University of Colorado, 147, 239

University of Havana: and Julia Martínez, 7; and Lourdes Casal, 123; and Pura Del Prado, 200; and María Gómez Carbonell, 288; and Camila Henríquez Ureña, 315, 316; and (Guadalupe Victoria Yoli Raymond) "La Lupe," 363; and Dolores Martí de Cid the, 425; and Elena Inés Mederos y Cabañas de González, 434, 435; and Ana Rosa Núñez, 529; and Argelia Velez-Rodríguez, 678; and Beatriz Varela, 786; and Irma Vidal, 798, 799

University of Houston, 145, 352

University of Illinois at Chicago, 575: and Hull-House, 334

University of Iowa, 162, 447

University of Kansas (KU), 425, 649, 809

University of Madrid, Spain, 35, 262, 610

University of Massachusetts at Boston, 270, 428

University of Miami: and Uva de Aragón, 191; and Gloria Estefan, 242; and María Cristina Herrera, 326; and Ileana Ros-Lehtinen, 376; and Ana Rosa Núñez, 529; Judith Ortiz Cofer taught at the, 548; and Cristina Saralegui, 672

University of Minnesota: and Camila Henríquez Ureña, 223, 315

University of New Mexico: and Adelina Chacón, 143; and Denise Chávez, 145; and Patricia A. Madrid, 415; and Teresa N. McBride, 433, 434; and Patricia Mora, 488; and Graciela Olivarez, 538; and Maria Concepcion (Concha) Ortiz y Pino de Kleven, 547; and Louise Ulibarrí Sánchez,770; María Varela taught at the, 788

University of Puerto Rico (UPR): and Pilar Barbosa de Rosario, 7; and Amelia Agostini del Río, 35; and Pura Belpré, 83; and Leopoldo Santiago, 165; and Miriam Colón, 165; and Julia de Burgos, 193; and Concha Meléndez, 441; and Olga A. Méndez, 444; Gabriela Mistral taught at, 480; and Antonia Coello, 527; Ingrid Otero-Smart graduated from, 548; and Antonia Pantoja, 558; Olga Viscal student activist at the, 588; and Diana Ramírez de Arellano, 610; Lola Rodríguez de Tió received a tribute at the, 638; and Helen Rodríguez-Trias, 641; and Josefina "Pepiña" Silva de Cintrón, 682; and Carmen Lillian "Lily" Soto Feliciano, 694

University of Puerto Rico in Río Piedras: and Nydia M. Velázquez, 376, 791; and Inés Robles Díaz, 631; and Ana Gloria Cabañas San Antonio, 657; and Petra Santiago, 670; and María E. Sánchez, 665

University of Santa Clara, 441, 819

University of South Florida, 255, 283

University of Southern California, 171, 378, 692, 413

University of Texas at Austin: and Gloria Anzaldúa, 51; and Santa Contreras Barraza, 80; and Martha Cotera,178; and Beatriz De la Garza, 197; and Elva Trevino Hart, 248; and Eva Carrillo de García, 280; and Jovita González Mireles, 292; Lilia Casis professor at, 293; and Fermina Guerra, 300; and Vilma S. Martínez, 432; and Consuelo Herrera Méndez, 443; and Aurora Estrada Orozco, 543; and Emilia Schunior Ramírez, 607

University of Texas at El Paso: and Martha Cotera, 177; and Dolores C. De Avila, 192; and Josefina Escajeda, 236; and Elsa Chávez, 250; and Rosa Guerrero, 301, 302; and Patricia Mora, 488; and M. Susana Navarro, 519; and Estela Portillo Trambley, 762; and Esther Valladolid Wolf, 809

University of Texas, Pan American, 51, 607

Univision, 23, 739

Ureña de Henríquez, Salomé, 223, 315: and Julia Alvarez wrote a book about, 44, 316; and Sherezada (Chiqui) Vicioso Sánchez, 797

Uriburu, María Nicolasa, 707

Urquides, María Luisa Legarra, **779**–**780**; and Education, 222, 224; and Spanish American Democratic Club, 299; and Tempe Normal School (TNS), 741

Urrea, Teresa, 3, 568, 616, **780**–**781**; Mexican Revolution, Border Women in, 465

Urrutia, María, 321

Index

Valadez, Esther, 521
Valdez, María Rita, 2
Valdez, Patssi, 64, **782–783**, *782*
Valdez, Socorro, 749, 753
Valdez, Susie: and Pentecostal Church, 565, 568
Valentín, Carmen, 590
Valentín, Minerva, 503
Valenzuela, Romanita, 568
Vallejo, Epifania de Guadalupe, **783–784**
Vallejo de Leese, María Paula Rosalía, **784–785**
Vando, Gloria, 795
Vanguardia Puertorriqueña, **785–786**, *786*
Varela, Beatriz, **786–787**
Varela, María, **787–788**, *787*; and Ganados del Valle, 275
Vargas, Zaragoza, 15, 744
Vásquez, Anna, **788–789**, *788*
Vásquez, Enriqueta Longeaux, **789–790**; and Chicano Movement, 154
Vásquez, Patricia M.: and Chicana Rights Project in Texas, 151
Vassar College, 222: and Amelia Agostini del Río, 35; and Camila Henríquez Ureña, 315, 316; Gabriela Mistral taught at the, 480
Vela de Vidal, Petra, 347
Velásquez, Consuelo, 280
Velásquez, William C., 404, 696
Velázques, Jaci, 654
Velázquez, Loreta Janeta, 3, **790–791**, *791*; and Military Service, 473
Velázquez, Nydia M., 58, **791–793**, *792*; and Latinas in the U.S. Congress, 375, 376, 377; and Politics, Electoral, 578
Velázquez, Pauline, 512
Vélez, Lupe, 340, **793**; and Cinema Images, Contemporary, 159; and Media Stereotypes, 436; and Movie Stars, 498, 501
Vélez, Lauren, 501,739
Vélez de Vando, Emelí, 60, **793–795**, *795*
Vélez-Ibañez, Carlos G.: and *Madrigal v. Quilligan*, 418, 419
Vélez-Mitchell, Anita, **795–797**, *796, 807*
Vélez-Mitchell, Jane, 795
Velez-Rodríguez Argelia, 678
Veliz, Wendy, 27
Vellanoweth, Patricia, 138
The Vencedores en Cristo Church, 261
Venceremos Brigade, 451
Ventura School for Girls: and Pachucas, 553
Verena, Marisela: Operation Pedro Pan, 541
Vicioso Sánchez, Sherezada "Chiqui," 316, **797–798**
Victory Outreach, 567–58
Vidal, Irma, *676*, **798–799**, *798*
Vidal, Lisa, 501
Vidaurri, Rita, **799–800**
Vieques: and Dolores "Lolita" Lebrón, 381; and Mónica Cecilia Lozano, 412; and Puerto Rico Women Political Prisoners, 587, 590; and Anita Vélez-Mitchell, 797
Vieta, Dr. Lilia, 183
Vietnam war, 77, 80, 383, 475: Delia Alvarez fought against the, 43; and Antonio Maceo Brigade, 49, 50; Estela Portillo Trambley protested the U.S. involvement in, 394; and Shirley Rodríguez Remeneski, 641; Enriqueta Longeaux

Vásquez critic of, 789; and Movimiento pro Independencia (MPI), 795
Villa Parra, Olga, 620
Villa, Francisco "Pancho," 661, 802: and *Corridos*, 175; and Mexican Revolution, 460–464; and Mexican Revolution, Border Women in, 466
Village Voice, 61, 162, 271, 533
Villa-Komaroff, Lydia: and Scientists, 677
Villalongín Dramatic Company, 753–754
Villanueva, Hortensia, 27
Villarreal, Andrea and Teresa, **800**; and Literature, 392, 393; and Mexican Revolution, Border Women in, 465
Villarreal, Anita, 335
Villarreal, Edith, 750
Villegas de Magnón, Leonor, *461*: and Education, 222; and Jovita Idar Juárez, 336–337; and Journalism and Print Media, 354; and Literature, 392
Violence against Women Act, 383
Viramontes, Helena María, 395, **800–801**
Virgen de Guadalupe, *318*, 405, 599, 776, **801–803**, *802*; and *Corridos*, 176; and Religion, 616
Virgen de la Caridad del Cobre, **803–804**, *803*; and Irma Morillo, 496–497; and Religion, 617
Viscal, Olga, 588, 590
Viva Kennedy Campaign, 578, 579, 741
Voces, 693
Voting Rights Act, 579, **804**; and Adelfa Botello Callejo, 111; and Latino representation in the U.S. Congress, 375; and Mexican American Legal Defense and Educational Fund (MALDEF), 432, 457; and Shirley Rodríguez Remeneski, 641
Voting Rights,121, 434, 435, 624, 786
Voudou, 267
Voz Femenina magazine, 192

Warren, Earl, 446, 573
Washington Post, 357, 527
Watsonville Strike, **805–806**
Wayne State University (WSU), 324, 545
We Fed Them Cactus, 105, 393
Weber, Devra, 368
The Wedding, 395, 555
Welch, Raquel, 739, **806–807**; and Cinema Images, Contemporary, 160; and Movie Stars, 501
West Side Story, **807–808**; and Rita Moreno, 495; and Movie Stars, 500; and Chita Rivera, 627; and Ana Vélez-Mitchell, 796
Western Federation of Miners (WFM): and Mining Communities, 478
White Cross/Cruz Blanca, 337, 354
White House Conference on Children and Youth, 780
White House Interagency Immigration Working Group, 221
White Lea, Aurora Lucero, 392
Whitney Museum of American Art, 397, 453
Wilcox, Mary Rose Garrido, **808–809**
Williams, Norma, 245
Wilson, Woodrow, 337, 428, 629
Wolf, Esther Valladolid, **809–810**
The Woman in Battle: A Narrative of the Exploits, Adventures, and Travels of Madame Loreta Janeta Velázquez, Otherwise

Known as Lieutenant Harry T. Buford, Confederate States Army, 790
Women Airforce Service Pilots (WASP), 639, 640
Women in California, 709–710, *710*. *See also* Spanish Borderlands
Women in CommunityServices, 179, 821
Women in New Mexico, 710–714, *712*, *713*; and Treaty of Guadalupe Hidalgo, 762–765; and U.S.-Mexican War, 776–779. *See also* Spanish Borderlands
Women in St. Augustine, 19, 714–716; and Treaty of Paris, 766. *See also* Spanish Borderlands
Women in Teatro (WIT), 749
Women in Texas, 716–719. *See also* Spanish Borderlands
Women in the United Farm Workers (UFW), 773–776. *See* United Farm Workers (UFW)
Women's Air Corps (WAC), 26, 96, 474, 788
Women's Army Auxiliary Corps (WAAC), 95, 96, 474
Women's Hall of Fame: and Polly Baca Barragán, 76; and Carmen del Valle, 203; and Rosa Guerrero, 302; and Lydia Mendoza, 448; and Dora Ocampo Quesada, 598; and Irma Rangel, 611; and Placida Elvira García Smith, 690; and Patsy Torres, 760
Women's National Basketball Association, 396
Women's Trade Union League: and Hull-House, 334
Women's Wills, 719–720. *See also* Spanish Borderlands
Women's Work Is Never Done: El trabajo de las mujeres no termina nunca: Homenaje a Dolores Huerta, 405
Woods, Silviana, 749
World War I, 189, 285, 368, 464, 473, 522, 586, 591, 623: and Americanization Programs, 89; and Hull-House, 333, 334; and Puerto Rican migration, 470; and The Jones Act, 564
World War II, 5, 168, 171, 264, 489, 537, 585, **810–814**, *812*, *813*; and Latinas in the Midwest, 16, 17; and Julieta Saucedo Bencomo, 85; and Bracero Program, 96; and Fabiola Cabeza de Baca, 104; and Angelina (Angie) Cabrera, 105; and Adelfa Botello Callejo, 111; and Angie González Chabram, 142; and César Chávez, 146; and Gregoria Esquivel, 240; and María Gómez Carbonell, 288; Beatrice Amado Kissinger, 360; and Josephine Ledesma, 381; and Anita N. Martínez, 426; and Migration and Labor, 469; and Ruth Mojica-Hammer, 481; and María Montez, 486; and Movie Stars, 499, 500; and Guadalupe Ortega,

544; and Pachucas, 555; and Leoncia Rosado Rousseau, 567, 644; and Carmen Romero Phillips, 574; and Dora Ocampo Quesada, 597; and Sofia Rodríguez, 636; and Women Airforce Service Pilots (WASP), 639, 640; and Irene Hernández Ruiz served as a translator, 649; and United Cannery, Agricultural, Packing, and Allied Workers of America (UCAPAWA/FTA), 770–772; and Anna Vásquez, 788

Ximenes de Laquera, Maria, 714

Yáñez, Mirta, 316
Yarbro-Bejarano, Yvonne, 749
Yauco Amityville Dominicans: and Madre María Dominga Guzmán, 306, 307, 531
Ybarra, Eva, **815**
Ybarra, Sister María Jesús de, 620
Yeshiva University, 444, 642
Yo misma fui mi ruta, 194, 394
Yo y Frida, 319
Young Communist League (YCL), 49, 401: and Communist Party, 168
Young Lords, **815–817**; and Diana Caballero, 103; and Sandra María Esteves, 243; Iris Morales feminist voice within the, 491, 492, 727; and Helen Rodríguez-Trias, 642; and Lourdes Torres, 758

Zamarripa Mendoza, Leonor, 448, 749
Zamora, Bernice Ortiz, 394, **818–819**, *819*
Zapata, Carmen, 368: and Television 739; and Theater 747, *747*
Zapata, Clemencia, 815
Zapata, Emiliano, 323, 429, 802; and *Corridos*, 175; and Mexican Revolution, 460–464; and National Liberation Army (EZLN), 691
Zárate, Rosa Marta, **819–820**, *820*; and Las Hermanas, 373; and Religion, 619
Zavala, María Elena, 677
Zavella, Patricia, 245, 247, 371
Zúñiga, Alejandra Rojas, **820–821**, *821*
Zúñiga, Anastacia, 701
Zuñiga, Daphne, 501